DICTIONARY OF LABOUR BIOGRAPHY

VOLUME XI

DICTIONARY
OF
LABOUR BIOGRAPHY

Volume XI

Edited by

KEITH GILDART
Research Fellow, Department of Politics, University of York

DAVID HOWELL
Professor of Politics, University of York

and

NEVILLE KIRK
Professor of Labour and Social History, Manchester Metropolitan University

First published 2003 by
PALGRAVE MACMILLAN
Houndmills, Basingstoke, Hampshire RG21 6XS and
175 Fifth Avenue, New York, NY 10010
Companies and representatives throughout the world

PALGRAVE MACMILLAN is the global academic imprint of the Palgrave
Macmillan division of St. Martin's Press, LLC and of Palgrave Macmillan Ltd.
Macmillan® is a registered trademark in the United States, United Kingdom
and other countries. Palgrave is a registered trademark in the European
Union and other countries.

ISBN 0–333–96872–7

This book is printed on paper suitable for recycling and made from fully
managed and sustained forest sources.

A catalogue record for this book is available from the British Library.

Library of Congress Cataloging-in-Publication Data
A catalogue record for this book is available from the Library of Congress

10 9 8 7 6 5 4 3 2 1
12 11 10 09 08 07 06 05 04 03

Printed and bound in Great Britain by
Antony Rowe Ltd, Chippenham and Eastbourne

Contents

Acknowledgements

The research for this volume was funded by a generous grant from the Arts and Humanities Research Board (AHRB). This funding was indispensable. We are immensely grateful to all our contributors, not just for their entries but also for the tolerance with which they have responded to our suggestions.

This project has drawn on a wide range of library resources. Three institutions merit special attention: the Manchester Central Reference Library, the Modern Records Centre at the University of Warwick, and the Archive at the National Museum of Labour History, Manchester. In each case the richness of the holdings has been complemented by the helpfulness of the staff.

One concern of the editors is to highlight the diversity of national and ethnic identities within the labour movements of the British Isles. In this context we thank the Northern Ireland Record Office and the Linen Hall Library, both in Belfast, the National Library of Ireland in Dublin, and the Library of University College in Dublin; the National Library of Scotland in Edinburgh, and the Mitchell Library in Glasgow; the National Library of Wales in Aberystwyth, the Record Offices for Flintshire, Denbighshire and Glamorgan in Hawarden, Ruthin and Cardiff respectively, and the Newport Public Library.

Beyond the British Isles we thank the Russian State Archive for Socio-Political History and the Marx–Engels Institute, both in Moscow, the International Institute for Social History in Amsterdam, the Library of Columbia University in New York, and Yale University Library.

Amongst the many institutions that were indispensable to the project we are grateful to the Public Record Office in Kew, the British Library – including that most valuable repository of obscure facts, the Newspaper Library in Colindale – and the Working Class Movement Library in Salford. We also thank the TUC's Congress House, the Co-operative College in Loughborough, the Co-operative Library in Manchester, the Bishopsgate Institute Library in London, Chetham's Library in Manchester, the India Office Library, the Social Credit Secretariat, the National Union of Mineworkers in Wrexham, and Newark Advertiser office.

University libraries have provided essential help with primary materials and elusive secondary sources. We gratefully acknowledge the assistance of the Bodleian Library and Nuffield College in Oxford, the British Library of Political and Economic Science at the London School of Economics, the Brynmor Jones Library at the University of Hull, the John Rylands University Library at the University of Manchester and the Morrell Library at the University of York, together with the libraries at Ruskin College and the Universities of London, Cambridge, Nottingham, Staffordshire and Sussex.

Record Offices and public libraries provided vital information. The English Record Offices consulted included Derby, Whitehaven, Carlisle and Nottingham, together with the Leeds City Archive. Public libraries that provided information for this volume included the Salford Local Studies Library and the Boston, Doncaster, Newark and Spalding Libraries.

Essential details for all the entries have been obtained from the Family Records Centre in Finsbury, the General Register Office for Scotland in Edinburgh, and the Probate Office in Manchester.

The research inevitably raised many obscure questions, and Mark Curthoys of the *Oxford Dictionary of National Biography* offered much wise advice on where to look for answers. His support and that of our contributors has shown that despite all claims to the contrary, the ideal of a community of scholars is not anachronistic.

John Saville has been a model former editor, always encouraging and a source of wisdom. We owe him a great deal.

Notes to Readers

1. Place names are usually quoted according to contemporary usage in the period covered in each entry.
2. Where the amount of a will, estate or effects is quoted it is normally that given in *The Times*, in the records at Somerset House in London or at the Scottish Record Office in Edinburgh. For dates before 1860 the source is usually the Public Record Office.
3. Under the heading **Sources**, personal information relates to details obtained from relatives, friends or colleagues of the individual in question; biographical information refers to other sources.
4. The place of publication in the bibliographical sources is London unless otherwise stated.
5. The *See also* sections that follow some biographical entries include names marked with a dagger – these refer to biographies published in Volumes I–X of the *Dictionary of Labour Biography*; those with no marking are included in the present volume.
6. A consolidated list of the entries in Volumes I–XI can be found at the end of this volume, before the general index.

List of Contributors

Professor Owen Ashton — School of Humanities, Staffordshire University
Terence Bowman — *Mourne Observer*, Newcastle, County Down
Dr Amanda Capern — Department of History, University of Hull
Dr Stephen Catterall — University of Huddersfield
Dr Gisela Chan Man Fong — Rock Forest, Quebec, Canada
Dr Malcolm Chase — Department of Continuing Education, University of Leeds
Dr Gidon Cohen — Department of Politics, University of Northumbria
Dr Nina Fishman — School of Social Sciences, University of Westminster
Dr Andrew Flinn — School of Library, Archive, and Information Studies, University College London
Dr June Hannam — School of History, University of West England, Bristol
Ursula Masson — School of Humanities, University of Glamorgan
John McIlroy — Department of Sociology, University of Manchester
Dr Kevin Morgan — Department of Government, University of Manchester
Lowri Newman — School of Humanities, University of Glamorgan
Dr Emmet O'Connor — School of History, University of Ulster
Dr Paul Pickering — Australian National University, Canberra
Archie Potts — Gosforth, Newcastle-upon-Tyne
Dr Miles Taylor — University of Southamton
Richard Temple — Modern Records Centre, University of Warwick
Dr Andrew Thorpe — Department of History, University of Exeter
Dr Richard Whiting — Department of History, University of Leeds

List of Bibliographies and Special Notes

Bibliographies

The subject bibliographies attached to certain entries are the responsibility of the editors. The entries under which they will be found in Volumes I–VI are as follows:

British Labour Party		
1900–13	LANSBURY, George	II
1914–31	HENDERSON, Arthur	I
Chartism to 1840	LOVETT, William	VI
Christian Socialism, 1848–54	LUDLOW, John Malcolm Forbes	II
Cooperation		
Agricultural cooperation	PLUNKETT, Sir Horace Curzon	V
Cooperative education	HALL, Fred	I
Cooperative Party	ALEXANDER, Albert Victor	I
Cooperative production	JONES, Benjamin	I
Cooperative Union	HAYWARD, Fred	I
Cooperative wholesaling	REDFERN, Percy	I
Copartnership	GREENING, Edward Owen	I
International Cooperative Alliance	MAY, Henry John	I
Irish cooperation	GALLAGHER, Patrick	I
Retail cooperation		
Nineteenth century	HOLYOAKE, George Jacob	I
1900–45	BROWN, William Henry	I
1945–70	BONNER, Arnold	I
Scottish cooperation	MAXWELL, William	I
Guild socialism	SPARKES, Malcolm	II
Mining trade unionism		
1850–79	MACDONALD, Alexander	I
1880–99	PICKARD, Benjamin	I
1900–14	ASHTON, Thomas	I
1915–26	COOK, Arthur James	III
1927–44	LEE, Peter	II
Scottish mining trade unionism	SMILLIE, Robert	III
Welsh mining trade unionism	ABRAHAM, William (Mabon)	I
New model unionism	ALLAN, William	I
New unionism, 1889–93	TILLETT, Benjamin (Ben)	IV

Special Notes in Volume V

Parliamentary Recruiting Committee and Joint Labour Recruiting Committee in the First World War, *see* **BOWERMAN, Charles William**

1917 Club, *see* **HAMILTON, Mary Agnes**

Mosley Industrial Commission, *see* **STEADMAN, William (Will) Charles**

Special Notes in Volume VI

Woman's Industrial Independence (1848, reprinted), *see* **BARMBY, Catherine Isabella**

Boggart Hole Clough and Free Speech, *see* **BROCKLEHURST, Frederick**

Ca'canny, *see* **DAVIS, William John**

Special Notes in Volume VII

League Against Imperialism, 1927–37, *see* **Bridgeman, Reginald Francis Orlando**

Gateshead Progressive Players, 1920–80, *see* **DODDS, Ruth**

Meerut Trial, 1929–33, *see* **GOSSIP, Alexander (Alex)**

Execution of Francisco Ferrer and the Labour Movement, *see* **WARD, George Herbert Bridges**

Special Notes in Volume VIII

Guild of St Matthew, *see* **HANCOCK, Thomas**

Church Socialist League, *see* **MOLL, William Edmund**

Twentieth Century Press, *see* **QUELCH, Henry (Harry)**

British Labour Delegation to Russia, 1920, *see* **TURNER, Sir Ben**

Special Notes in Volume IX

Aid for Spain Movement in Britain, 1936–39, *see* **BROWN, Isabel**

British Trade Union Delegation to Russia, 1924, I, Official Report, II, The Zinoview Letter, *see* **GRENFELL, Harold**

British Joint Labour Delegation to Hungary, Inquiry into the White Terror, May 1920, *see* **JOWETT, Frederick William**

Special Notes in Volume X

Churches of Christ as a Labour Sect, *see* **TAYLOR, John Thomas**

Further Notes, *see* **HANNINGTON, Walter**

Further Notes, *see* **CONNELL, Jim**

Special Notes in Volume XI

Laski Libel Trial, *see* **HASTINGS, Patrick, Sir**

Labour Parliament, 1853–4, *see* **JONES, Ernest**

Independent Socialist Party, *see* **SANDHAM, Elijah**

Biographies

ANDREWS, Elizabeth (1882–1960)

LABOUR PARTY WOMEN'S ORGANISER FOR WALES

Elizabeth Andrews was born in Hirwaun near Aberdare in south Wales on 15 December 1882, the third child and eldest daughter of the 11, of whom nine reached adulthood, born to Samuel Smith, a coal miner, and his wife Charlotte, née Evans. The family moved from Hirwaun to Mardy in the Rhondda valley when Elizabeth was just two years old. Her father survived an underground explosion at Mardy pit in 1885; subsequently they returned to Hirwaun. Clearly a very bright child, Elizabeth, like many working-class girls of her generation, found that her services were urgently required at home as an assistant to her mother, and her formal education ended at the age of 13. Her labour was much needed in a household of three working miners and six schoolchildren, where babies arrived every two years: 'The washing, ironing, cooking and mending were endless'[Andrews (1951) 3]. In a way that is generally seen as more typical of working-class men, particularly in mining communities, than of women, the young girl took the opportunities offered by the new evening classes after her day of hard domestic work. However her hope of entering teaching, encouraged by her instructors, foundered on the family's poverty, and her waged working life began at the age of 17.

Opportunities for work for women and girls were limited in the coal-dominated economy of south Wales; there was hard outdoor labouring work in the brickyards or at the colliery screens, and there was always domestic service. Elizabeth took another traditional women's route: a dressmaking apprenticeship, which also provided an escape from home and the valleys for a short time (three years managing a workshop in Llanwrtyd Wells), which she appears to have welcomed. However when the chance arose both to improve her position and to move closer to home, she took it, taking a living-in post in Ystrad Rhondda. Clearly the burgeoning consumer culture of the south Wales valleys at the beginning of the twentieth century was profitable: she earned £40 a year for her 68-hour week.

Pamela Graves has described the characteristics of the pioneers of Labour women's organization in Britain:

> [T]hey had come from large working-class families. They had left school at fourteen or earlier and worked mostly as domestic servants or in the sewing trades. The majority were housewives and mothers. A significant percentage had been involved in the women's movement through a variety of pre-war organisations – the [Women's Labour] League, the Women's Cooperative Guild, the National Federation of Women Workers, or the Railway Women's Guild. [They] had shaped their political sensibilities around the needs and interests of women of their class [Graves (1998) 207].

In almost all respects Elizabeth Andrews was typical of this group, though with some crucial differences: she had no children, and it is doubtful whether one who had such a full working life can be described in any meaningful way as a housewife; and to the remaining elements, all of which describe her accurately, must be added the influence and place of religious faith in her life and her view of the world.

The major source for Andrews' life is her memoir of her work in the labour movement, *A Woman's Work is Never Done*, written in 1951 after her retirement from her post as The Labour Party's women's organiser for Wales. Such a text is rare in Welsh women's history, and that friends had urged her to write it is a mark of Andrews' rarity as a woman occupying a leading position in Welsh political life in the first half of the twentieth century; and one, moreover, who left behind a body of writing that included not just her memoir but also, perhaps even more significantly, the reports she wrote for *Labour Woman* and the monthly woman's page – edited and written from 1923–27 – of the South Wales Miners' Federation publication *The Colliery Workers' Magazine*. Her political activism was characterised by a determined and unrelenting drive for a better future for working-class people, and this is reflected in the way she structured

1

her life story. It was a story of steady progress and improvement for the working class in the care of the Labour Party; each chapter expresses this movement, ending on an upbeat note. 'That is the Socialist Way to Progress' are the final words in a very brief chapter on 'Women in the Labour Party', which ends with the election victory of 1945 and the creation of the welfare state [Andrews (1951) 15]. The subtitle of the work, 'Being the recollections of a childhood and upbringing amongst the South Wales miners and a lifetime of service to the Labour movement in Wales', and chapter headings such as 'I Was a Miner's Daughter' locate her firmly in a very specific Labourist tradition and culture, which her story exemplifies. The foreword by Jim Griffiths MP (Llanelli), a minister in the post-war Attlee government, emphasises the representative character of the narrative, as well as her service to the labour movement, and especially to 'the struggles of yesterday'.

The first chapter describes the family and community culture that produced Andrews: poverty, hard work, industrial accidents and deaths on the one hand, and a sense of a real, lived Christianity on the other. She describes listening in on her father's prayers, and refers to her mother's Sunday night bible stories and 'keen interest in religious work' [Andrews (1951) 2], something that Andrews emulated as she reached adulthood and returned to after her retirement from party work. Her first writings were on religious topics, first for a chapel group and then a letter to the press in support of the great religious revival of 1904–5. Andrews' belief in what she termed 'that great principle in Christianity – That we are our brother's keeper' [*Colliery Workers Magazine*, February 1925, 44] – appears to have been a real foundation of her life and work, both religious and political. Like so many of the home-grown socialists in Wales in the early part of the century, Andrews was a product not only of the harsh material reality of coalfield life, but also of the nonconformity that was 'a key element' in the political culture [Lewis (2000) 90].

The relationship between nonconformity and the developing labour movement in south Wales before the First World War was characterised by hostility from ministers and leading chapel members towards what they regarded as atheistical or 'godless' socialism. But as Andrews recalled, 'we said Socialism was the only way to put our Christian principles into practice in everyday life' [Andrews (1951) 20]. Even for those who rejected religious faith, the language of evangelism could become the language of socialism, as they 'launched out on this work with a deep conviction and missionary zeal, preaching this new gospel of Socialism and prepared to meet all opposition and difficulties' [Andrews (1951) 13]. A political meeting could turn into a prayer meeting, and a meeting of a religious group could be an opportunity for recruiting socialists [*Labour Woman*, December 1920, 192]. The role of religion in her life was recognised by her obituarists upon her death in January 1960. Writing in *Labour Woman* the editor, Mary Sutherland, suggested that religion had shaped Andrews' 'level-headed' approach to politics, and 'was perhaps the secret of her equanimity' [*Labour Woman*, March 1960, 32].

Andrews linked her political education, as well as the development of her character and religious faith, to her home and to the conditions of work and life for miners and their families. She claimed to remember the 1885 victory celebrations when Mabon (William Abraham) was first elected as MP for Rhondda, though she would have been just three years old at the time. It may be that she was remembering subsequent victory celebrations in Mabon's long career; as a newly enfranchised voter in 1918 she was one of his sponsors in his final election contest. Perhaps more to the point, she recalled her political education at her father's knee. As a girl she read the newspaper to her father, a radical who was literate in Welsh but not in English. She recalled reading the coverage of Keir Hardie's victorious 1900 election campaign in Merthyr and Aberdare, as well as receiving schooling in such landmarks of labour history as the Taff Vale strike. However her political activities appear to have developed, alongside her work for the church and Sunday school, when she was a young working woman in the Rhondda, away from the parental home, and especially through her relationship with Thomas Tyde Andrews, an insurance agent whom she married in 1910. Religion and politics were the twin motifs around which they built their life together. 'Our married life was a real partnership. We were interested in the same social and religious problems' [Andrews (1951) 7]. She was coming into active politics in a place and at a time when Liberalism and Lib-Labism were beginning to collapse, and the labour movement 'seized the political initiative, and retained it until it was in full command of local representative institutions' [Williams (1996) 84]. Andrews was to play an important part in that process.

In the 1920s Andrews was fond of writing about the 'three paths' to the emancipation of the working class: the trade union path, the cooperative movement path and the labour movement path [*Colliery Workers Magazine*, January 1925, 21]. The trade union path was less of an option for the majority of women in south Wales, and in her own political identity before the First World War the labour and cooperative paths were joined by the feminist path through the non-militant suffrage movement. Andrews remembered the Rhondda as being 'not very safe for Socialists or Suffragettes'. Her recollection of the routing of 'two prominent Suffragettes' who had come to address the Independent Labour Party (ILP) smacked of organised rowdyism by the local Young Liberals' League, perhaps in reaction to attacks by suffrage militants on the Liberal Government, and need not be taken as indicating general hostility to women's suffrage by Rhondda people. It is not clear how much Andrews was involved in suffrage activity separately from her labour movement work; the chapter of her autobiography entitled 'Votes for Women' was a very brief survey of the issue between 1792 (Mary Wollstonecraft) and 1928 (equal voting rights for men and women), with few personal or local insights. Writing in 1950 she recalled her case for equality:

> We were told when agitating for the Vote – often very patronisingly by men – that women's place was to fit the child for the world. We retorted that … it was also her place to fit the world for the child, and before we could do either, we must take an interest in politics [Andrews (1951) 11].

Support for women's rights, and for an equal place in the workplace and politics, seems to have been every bit as important to her sense of herself as her work for her class and community. Her autobiography describes the work – largely in the 'locust years' of the period between the wars – she devoted to the needs of working-class mothers, the focus of so much of Labour women's campaigning in this period. As suggested by her argument for women's place in the political public sphere, quoted above, Andrews had no problem with the primary identification of women in their political life with their maternal role and instincts; this was the dominant motif in her writings during the 1920s. Indeed she developed a view of socialist politics – local, national and international, for both women and men – as a politics that put the needs and development of 'the child' at the centre; it was no accident that one of the women she most admired in the Labour movement was Margaret Macmillan, the influential theorist of childhood and socialism. But Andrews supported the right for all women, married and single, to work, and saw her own work in the post-enfranchisement world as essentially emancipatory: 'I had to try and teach women not to be afraid of freedom' [Andrews (1951) 42]. In her columns in the 1920s she exhorted, 'Women! know your political power, treasure it, use it wisely' [*Colliery Workers' Magazine*, May 1925, 116]. In the 1920s she urged women's sections to demand an equal franchise, and in 1927 she welcomed the coming legislation to secure this objective: 'It will *raise our status as Voters*, and remove that insult to our womanhood that we got Votes because we were *married to men*, not because we were intelligent human beings and citizens' [*Colliery Workers' Magazine*, May 1927, 99, emphasis in original].

Andrews joined the cooperative movement after her marriage; almost a rite of passage into her new mode of life. She was an active promoter of the movement and in 1914 became secretary of the Women's Co-operative Guild (WCG) in Wales, at Ton Pentre. As a leading member of the WCG she threw herself into the campaigns to improve maternal and child welfare provision. Like so many women of her class and generation, Andrews' upbringing and family life had intimately acquainted her with the impact on women and their families of multiple births in the context of poverty. Following the publication in 1915 of the WCG's *Maternity: Letters from Working Wives*, she set out to shape opinion and put pressure on local authorities to use their powers. She came up against the attitude that it was not quite respectable to discuss maternal mortality and morbidity in public, but because of the sad facts that were part and parcel of the experience of working-class communities, she found the men in the movement to be sympathetic. This work continued throughout the interwar period through the WCG and the women's sections, with energetic campaigns to persuade local authorities to use their powers under the 1918 Child and Maternal Welfare Act. Their efforts were met with hostility and derision from a number of county medical officers of health, whose letters Andrews described as 'wild hysterical effusions' [Andrews (1951) 30–1]. After the Second World War, Andrews took satisfaction from the reduction in maternal and infant mortality and from the improved welfare provisions of the new welfare state.

Andrews was inducted into the ILP by her husband Tom (an ex-miner now working in insurance), who had been one of the small group of founders of the ILP in the Rhondda. The streams of their political life flowed through their home in the form of the socialist and suffragist pioneers to whom they gave hospitality. Andrews noted that few women were present at the ILP meetings she attended with Tom before their marriage, but she offered no explanation and the observation was not integrated into a critique of the way in which labour movement politics operated in the coalfield valleys before the First World War. However there were women who did make that critique: under the *nom de plume* 'Matron', a columnist in the *Rhondda Socialist* newspaper, analysing the structural exclusion of women from labour movement politics in the valleys, described ILP branches as being 'conducted with a total disregard to the existence of women in the district or to matters in which women are interested' [Williams (1998) 112], although there were signs of increased female membership at about the time Andrews became involved. Before 1918, Andrews was one of the few women who, while closely identifying herself with the available forms of women's activism, was able to break into male-dominated structures. In 1916 she was the first woman to be elected to the executive of the still rather inchoate Rhondda Labour Party (later the Rhondda Borough Labour Party, RBLP).

The war and the immediate post-war period brought new opportunities for public work to many women, including women in the labour movement. Andrews served on the War Pensions Committee and the Disablement Training Committees in the Rhondda. The creation of the Sankey Commission on the Mining Industry in 1919 offered the opportunity to bring to national attention the conditions in which mining families lived and worked. The inclusion of women as witnesses came at the suggestion of Marion Phillips, the Labour Party's new chief woman officer: Andrews addressed the commission on behalf of the South Wales Miners' Federation, along with a Mrs Brown from Scotland and a Mrs Hart from Wigan. The three women were described in the reports as 'miners' wives' and were subjected to rather patronising attention by the press. In making the case for pit-head baths and improved housing, Andrews described the miners' overcrowded homes and their wives' heavy domestic work, linking these to high maternal and infant mortality. She also drew the commission's attention to the damage caused to miners' wives by lifting and carrying water. Citing evidence given to her by a Rhondda midwife, she told the Commission that 'the majority of cases [she has had] of premature births and extreme female ailments are due to the physical strain of lifting heavy tubs and boilers' [*Labour Woman* (June 1919) 76]. Andrews' evidence thus threw light on the little-recognised effects of the conditions of mining on the health of women.

The campaign for pit-head baths gathered momentum after the war, with Andrews energetically spearheading efforts by Labour women's organisations. She organised visits of the women's sections and guilds to the baths built by the Ocean Coal Company at Treharris, and toured the coalfield with a slide lecture, breaking down prejudice with 'convincing facts', always her favourite approach to a problem, and bringing about, as she told the Sankey Commission, 'a revolution in ideas among the miners and their wives' [Andrews (1951) 18]. As Neil Evans and Dot Jones have shown, the movement passed out of women's hands in the

1920s when the argument had been won: the demand had become part of the programme of the miners' union and it was duly absorbed into the corporate politics of the industry [Evans and Jones (2000)]. However Andrews and other women revived the demand as an issue for women in the *Colliery Workers' Magazine* in 1924.

In 1919 Andrews was appointed to the Ministry of Health Welsh Consultative Council. The ministry had first appointed a council without women members, but after protests from women's organisations four women were given a place on the ten-member committee. On the council Andrews became a colleague of another outstanding figure in the Welsh Labour Party, Rose Davies of Aberdare. The two women submitted a joint memorandum to the ministry on maternity and child welfare provision. So 'bold and comprehensive in character' were the council's proposals in its reports to Whitehall, and so tight the rein on public finances, that its third and fourth reports were suppressed and the committee was wound up in 1926. In 1920 Andrews became Wales' first woman JP. She was to serve on the bench of magistrates in Ystrad until a year before her death 40 years later.

In 1919, at the age of 27, Andrews became one of the four women organisers working under Marion Phillips, the chief woman officer, in the reorganised party. One of her first jobs was to translate party literature into Welsh for women in north and mid Wales. Initially her remit went beyond Wales and she helped with election work in the south of England and Shropshire. Organisation work was revamped again in 1920, when Andrews was appointed as woman organiser for Wales, now one of seven regional women's organisers. Writing from the perspective of the 1950s, she made light of what must have often been difficult and tiring work. Armed with the organiser's equipment of 'a bundle of index cards with the addresses of Trade Union Secretaries, a report book and some leaflets' [Andrews (1951) 13], she travelled the country on the inadequate public transport system, often staying in dreary hotels.

Before the First World War the organisation of women in the labour movement in Wales had been patchy and weak, and by 1918 south Wales had just three branches of the Women's Labour League (WLL), located in the major port towns of Cardiff, Swansea and Newport. These provided the basis for the women's sections after the war, although the first women's section was organised by Andrews in Ton Pentre, Rhondda, in 1918. Development began with a women's conference in Pontypridd in 1918, with others to follow. From the conferences came the creation of advisory councils, with WLL members as the first officers, and the structuring of constituency women's sections, ward sections, central committees and federations. This did not happen all at once, and it culminated in the creation in the late 1930s of a joint advisory committee to organise summer schools, annual conferences and rallies. By 1933 more than 9000 women formed 45 per cent of the individual party membership in Wales, and by the time of Andrews' retirement in 1948 the number had increased to 12 814, although the percentage of women had fallen. In terms of women's sections, comprehensive figures do not appear to be available, but by the end of the first decade of organisation East Glamorgan, which included the Rhondda, had 95 sections. This achievement, considering the weakness of prewar organisation, was considerable; the tireless work undertaken by Andrews to the end of her career is reflected in the Welsh reports to *Labour Woman*.

Andrews was a product of the south Wales coalfield society, and her political commitment was bred from her dedication to her own community. She clearly found mid and north Wales more difficult territory, as it was for all Labour organisers in this period. Her sense of the foreignness of the country beyond the coalfield is strongly expressed in a chapter entitled 'The Walls of Jericho' in her autobiography. Religion – or at least, the dominant part still played by chapels in Welsh society – language and the strength of older political affiliations combined to make north Wales a special problem for organisation, added to which the women of the area were seen as particularly new to and shy of politics. Andrews tried to bridge the gap between the Welsh of north and south by using 'Bible' Welsh, which as Neil Evans and Dot Jones suggest may well have made her a less effective speaker and propagandist [Evans and Jones (2000)]. In the rural areas of Wales, the terrible toll taken by tuberculosis and the problems of housing and poverty that lay behind the disease were the focus of Labour women's activities in the 1930s. 'We were called "a lot of interfering women" for telling the Councils what they ought to do ... To-day we are seeing the reward of our efforts ... We still need "interfering women" to carry them on' [Andrews (1951) 22–3]. By the time Andrews retired, north Wales had two advisory councils to support and coordinate the work of the sections. Andrews saw the development of the councils as particularly important to the education of women, 'giving them a broader outlook and a wider vision of the needs of women and the work of the Party' [*Labour Woman* (February 1948) 29].

Much of Andrews' success as an organiser can be attributed to her determination 'to adopt new methods and new ideas continually' so that meetings would not become 'stereotyped and uninteresting' [*Labour Woman* (June 1933) 91]. She had, according to Mary Sutherland, 'the gifts of a true teacher and long before we heard much about visual aids, she showed great ingenuity in preparing charts and diagrams to illustrate subjects the women wanted to study; and she loved organising more spectacular events which gave scope to her flair for pageantry' [Obituary, *Labour Woman* (March 1960) 31]. The institution of day schools and week-long summer schools during the 1920s, with a system of bursaries to enable women to attend, was something that Andrews, working with the advisory councils, thought particularly important. She was very enthusiastic about 'Woman's Week', which became 'Woman's Month' in June 1927 – a recruitment campaign that combined propaganda with seaside outings or trips to the country. In 1927 the occasion was used to propagandise against the Trade Union Bill, characterised as 'the Blacklegs' Charter', with demonstrations in west Wales, Monmouthshire and East Glamorgan. Andrews' satisfaction with this demonstration of the strength of Labour women's organisation was clear. In the 1930s, in the face of a decline in recruitment to women's sections and in line with her belief that 'new times demands new methods', Andrews called for more varied programmes in the sections in order to broaden the appeal of the party. She was particularly keen to attract women who voted Labour but were not 100 per cent political. She suggested lectures that were 'not wholly political' but 'of real interest to housewives and mothers', and that section programmes should be expanded to include jam making, cake making and needlework nights. She had already, in the 1920s, inserted 'Home Hints' in the *Colliery Workers' Magazine* women's page, with tips for storing linen, removing peach stains and cleaning clocks. This mixture was linked to her pragmatism about recruiting and keeping members interested, but also reflected her belief 'that Socialism ... has to do with the whole of life, and in a real sense should teach us the art of living' [*Labour Woman* (June 1933) 91].

Andrews called the Labour Party women's sections the 'working women's university'. This catch phrase reflected her profound belief that education and organisation were the routes to power for her class. She presented this process as almost inevitable: 'Education in the things that matter will bring the vision, seeing the vision will give us renewed courage, courage will make us will, will will give us power, power will make us compel the establishment of the new Social Order' [*Colliery Workers' Magazine* (May 1924) 131]. She believed that women had a specific contribution to make to this process: their motherly 'instinct of preservation' and their need to 'fit the world to the child' would be a valuable weapon if introduced into mainstream politics. The clearest applications of this were in the movements for peace of the 1920s, in which the WCG was prominent, and the work of the League of Nations Union, which Andrews supported. She wrote that 'in the past it has been easier to get men to fight than to think. It is the work of women, mothers, and teachers, to create the right impression on the mind of the child' [*Colliery Workers Magazine* (October 1924)]. In 1927 she attended a League of Nations conference at the International Labour Office in Geneva. The 1930s provided more opportunities for fostering internationalism, with attendance at the International Socialist Congress in Vienna, and a visit with a party of Labour women to Sweden.

As far as party politics were concerned Andrews was no pacifist: she relished the fight against class enemies and delighted in the electoral victories that came regularly in south Wales in the 1920s. Organising women's sections for electoral work was an important part of her job. Her first experience of organising in the run-up to a by-election came in 1919 in Swansea East, where the Labour candidate, David Williams, was defeated by a Liberal, though only by a small margin and this was overturned in the 1922 general election. Andrews particularly enjoyed the campaign before the 1923 election, in Swansea again, when the target of women's demonstrations and propaganda was Swansea West MP Sir Alfred Mond, (Minister of Health) and his support for spending cuts on housing and milk for babies. Writing in 1950, Andrews savoured the defeat of Mond and the capture of the seat for Labour. In north Wales 'we had great times in By-elections even though we were storming Liberal strongholds'. She campaigned in Caernarfon Boroughs against Lloyd George in the 1924 election. He won, of course, 'but we had carried our message into the Liberal citadel' [Andrews (1951) 22].

Andrews worked under Marion Phillips, the chief woman officer of the party from 1918–32, and then under Mary Sutherland. Although Andrews described her work she rarely commented on her role, nor on Phillips or Sutherland and her working relationship with them. The position of women's organiser – or 'woman officer' – was an ambiguous one. While Andrews described her role, at least in her autobiography, as directed towards the interests of women and communities in Wales, both she and Phillips were party appointees, and the 1918 constitution made it clear that women officers' 'first loyalty was to the party leadership, which was overwhelmingly male'. As Graves has shown, Phillips 'consistently supported the party line, and worked hard to discourage "dissident" women' [Graves (1998) 186]. Presumably this 'discouragement' was passed down the line through the regional women's officers too. In the existing records it is difficult to detect this potential for conflict in Andrews' work, apart from the occasional declaration of independence in section minutes. The paucity of references to the national structures of the party that employed her is perhaps significant. Andrews ordered her autobiography into short chapters dealing with a series of campaigns directed at the good of the communities with which she identified: the pit-head baths campaigns, the campaign to beat TB by putting pressure on local authorities to improve housing, the implementation of the 1918 Child and Maternal Welfare Act, the introduction of nursery schools and pensions. This focus allowed her to avoid dealing with dissension in the party – for example, the crisis of 1931, features nowhere in her account. Missing too is any consideration of the controversial campaigns that highlighted different gender perceptions of Labour politics in the 1920s. While she did make a brief reference to the opposition of the trade unions to the 'endowment of motherhood' or family allowances, she glossed her account with 'but it was accepted in the end and the country today enjoys the result of these strenuous efforts of our pioneers' [Andrews (1951) 39]. During the 1920s, however, on the one occasion that Andrews wrote about the subject in her monthly column she warned that 'we need to be very guarded on this point', and linked family allowances to the subsistence allowance proposed by mine owners and to other attempts to drive a wedge between men and women of the working class in the context of the 1926 crisis [*Colliery Workers' Magazine* (April 1926) 91].

Birth control, the issue that was most revealing of the gulf between Labour women and men in the 1920s, also appears to have been a difficult topic for Andrews. In recent years historians analysing the powerlessness of women in the national party in the interwar years have seen this issue as central, and the role of Marion Phillips as being to ensure that 'the will of the vast majority of the women members' never broke through the male leadership line [Graves (1998) 186]. A chapter in Andrews' autobiography on mothers and babies highlighted the hideous statistics of maternal mortality in the coalfield areas, but made no mention of the campaigns by women in the party for the dissemination of birth control information through local clinics. She never addressed the topic in her monthly columns and even her reports on the annual conferences of Labour women omitted the issue. As editor of the women's page in the *Colliery Workers Magazine* she gave space in February 1927 to an article by the Workers' Birth Control Group, which in preparation for another vote on the question at the party conference appealed to the miners to support the women [*Colliery Workers' Magazine* (February 1927) 40]. While it was not until 1934 that a resolution on birth control appeared in the minutes of the East Glamorgan

Advisory Council (EGAC), of which Andrews was an *ex officio* member, there is evidence that a section of Labour women and men in Wales thought that birth control was a question for the party, as well as a matter of practical socialism. However the fate of the first hospital birth control clinic in Abertillery, which was opened by Labour campaigners but forced to close by the disapproval of the religious and the shyness of women, exemplified the difficulties, and would have aroused fears in the party about electoral consequences. It is arguable that in the mid 1920s solidarity between men and women of the working class might have seemed more important, from the perspective of the coalfields, than pursuing questions that might drive a wedge between them. Much of Andrews' work and writing during that time was dedicated to invoking class solidarity.

For women in Wales, and particularly those in south Wales, where the main strength of the party lay, life in the 1920s was dominated by the effects of the depression and industrial troubles. As wages fell and unemployment rose in the coal industry, the bitter and lengthy disputes of 1921 and 1926 defined the decade. In 1926 in particular, women from the mining districts came into their own. They were led by Andrews with her usual energy. Between 12 April and 13 May as last minute negotiations were followed by the General Strike, she addressed 20 meetings of over 10 000 women, rallying support for the miners and recruiting women into the party at the same time. She used her monthly column in the *Colliery Workers' Magazine* to make an impassioned appeal to women in the coalfield for 'unity, loyalty, and faith in our cause, and in each other'. Women in the coalfield were also being targeted by Flora Drummond's antisocialist and antistrike Women's Guild of Empire. Drummond held meetings in the coalfield and organised a London demonstration, absurdly led by herself on horseback, with 'workers' wives' walking behind. The wife of a south Wales miner addressed the demonstrators from the platform of the Albert Hall, earning a withering comment from Andrews, who urged mass meetings of miners' wives 'to counter [the guild's] mischievous activities' [Minutes, EGAC 6/3/26]. In a series of columns during the lockout, Andrews and other women explained the issues and vividly described 'the spirit of Comradeship and Fellowship ... kindness, love and sympathy' amongst the strikers and their communities.

Andrews played a leading role in the Women's Committee for the Relief of Miners' Wives and Children, established in the summer of 1926 under Marion Phillips. Women in local relief committees undertook the work of 'an industrial Red Cross' in their areas, providing a system of support aimed chiefly at ensuring that the children in coalfield communities did not suffer. Andrews' initiatives included arranging the temporary adoption of over 800 children by supporters outside the coalfield. Mother and baby schemes distributed food, milk, clothes, boots and blankets to those most in need, and a maternity allowance of ten shillings, rising to 30 shillings after the birth, was provided from relief funds.

Despite her absolute and unwavering support for the miners during the lockout, Andrews was disturbed by its outcome and its impact on mining families and communities. In a period when women were organising in large numbers against war, emphasising their special perspective as mothers, she described the dispute as 'Industrial War', which like the 1914–18 war had 'maimed' the combatants, and especially 'thousands of our young mothers and babies' [*Colliery Workers' Magazine* (January 1927) 20]. To prevent another such war she argued for 'a newer conception' of politics, a model for which was provided by the work of the women's committees during the lockout, which put the needs of children at the centre of their efforts. 'If we could only approach all our Economic, Social, National and International problems from this point of view, making the *welfare of the child the basis of human relationship in Human Society*, we would soon solve these problems' [*Colliery Workers' Magazine*, January 1927 p. 20, emphasis in original]. This was clearly something she felt with passion: above all it was the experience of the lockout, of the spirit of collectivity and of love at work in the community, particularly through the women's actions, that prefigured, for Andrews, a 'new era'. However in 1935 she was more than ready to urge women to throw themselves into another 'industrial war ... a war against Poverty. A just demand, so that miners get a square deal', and to call again for a 'hundred per cent loyalty' [*Rhondda Clarion* (October 1935) 3].

During the Second World War the structure of women's sections, advisory councils, committees and conferences allowed organisational work to proceed in its familiar pattern, as well as trying to reverse a decline in membership. However Andrews quickly turned to encouraging debate on Labour's peace aims through educational meetings and day schools. Post-war reconstruction, family allowances, housing and social security, as well as war-time nurseries and the organisation and welfare of women in factories – a new subject for south Wales – were important themes in the early 1940s. Encouraged by organisers such as Andrews, Labour women optimistically envisaged a different post-war world, one in which 'women in the New Britain', would enjoy economic freedom [Minutes, West Wales AC, April 1941]. As in 1914–18, Andrews combined her work for the party with work on war committees, representing Welsh Labour women on committees of the Ministries of Information, Food, Fuel and Power and the Board of Trade.

In addition to her role as women's organiser, with its local, regional and national dimensions, Andrews was also a long-standing and prominent member of the Labour Party in the Rhondda. She had become a member of the executive of the Rhondda Labour Party (RLP) in 1916, when the organisation was making an effort to improve its effectiveness in the valley. It is not clear how long she retained that position, and she perhaps relinquished it when she took up her paid role for the party. Her husband Tom remained as treasurer to the party into the 1930s, and was also a Labour councillor. She may have played a part in bringing about the inclusion of the Women's Co-operative Guild in the Mid-Rhondda Trades and Labour Council in 1919. Andrews and other women must have also had a hand in the decision of the Rhondda Burough Labour Party (RBLP) in 1919 to place a demand for mothers' pensions for widows with children in its district council election manifesto: this was a favourite demand of Labour and cooperative movement women, and a subject Andrews returned to many times in her writing in the 1920s. Andrews' relationship with the local party and its dominant section, the miners' lodges, was maintained through her *Colliery Workers' Magazine* columns in the 1920s, as well as in an article for the short-lived *Rhondda Clarion*, the RBLP paper, in the 1930s.

There are few notes of bitterness or dissension in Andrews' autobiography, and the sense that the working class was making steady progress in the arms of the Labour Party is pervasive. This was plausible, despite Labour's few and short periods in government, because the party virtually dominated local government in south Wales for much of the period of her memoir. However bitterness towards the Communist Party is discernible. From the end of the 1926 lockout and through the periods of 'class against class' and the united front, relations between the Labour and Communist Parties in the Rhondda deteriorated. In 1927 the RBLP was disaffiliated and reconstituted, with the now excluded Communists and others on the left forming, for a time, a majority RBLP (Disaffiliated). Andrews recalled the period in her memoir, and there are a number of references to personal attacks by the Communist Party on her and others [Andrews (1951) 1–2, 19].

The seriousness with which the party viewed the challenge from the Communist Party, and its possible appeal to women, is suggested by the number of times Andrews returned to the subject in her writing and during women's conferences in the 1930s and 1940s. In 1935, as local authorities struggled with the effects of the depression in south Wales, she used an article addressed to women to take a swipe at the Communists on the council: 'We must learn to know the difference between the big noise and steady work, between walking out and creating scenes in the Council Chambers and facing facts and difficulties of administration and obtaining the maximum out of every Act of Parliament for the common good' [*Rhondda Clarion* (October 1935) 3]. Two years later, at the annual conference of EGAC, Andrews appealed for loyalty in the women's sections, 'for the women not to be led away with the United Front', and reminded the delegates that the Socialist League was now outside the party [Minutes, Annual Conference, 1937]. During the Second World War the Communist-led People's Vigilance Committees and the 'Women's Parliament' beckoned to political women while Andrews held the line, again appealing for loyalty. The decline of communism in the Rhondda in the post-war period, which she attributed to improvements in the condition and welfare of the working class, gave her nothing but satisfaction.

The late 1940s brought major changes in Andrews' life. Her husband died in early 1946, and though she was soon back at work she became temporarily disabled when she broke her ankle-bones in a fall the following year. In autumn 1947 she attended her last advisory council meetings as organiser, receiving tributes from her colleagues. Given honorary membership of the councils, she attended less frequently in the years that followed. Over the years she had created a role for herself in the councils that would have been a difficult one for others to follow. She had spent a lot of time trying to build up the membership, pushing political education for women, and occasionally reminding members of the party line. As the key point of contact and coordination between individual sections, federations, advisory councils and the national party, she had been the lynchpin of the women's organisation in Wales. But in addition, and importantly, she had become a 'remembrancer' of women's place in Labour politics. Through her frequent reminders of the history of the party, invoking 'the early days' and especially women's involvement, by keeping party anniversaries, and especially by her generous naming and praising of other women who had worked for the cause, she had constructed a heritage for Labour women in south Wales. This was continued in her autobiography, which is punctuated with narratives of the achievements of other women – Mrs David Williams in Swansea, Rose Davies in Aberdare, Beatrice Green and others – during the 1926 lockout. So inspired were the Glamorgan women by her account of 25 years' work by the women's sections, that at their anniversary meeting in 1944 they decided to publish it as a booklet.

In 1949, after her retirement as organiser and the award of an OBE, Andrews contested the Ton Pentre ward for the Labour Party in the county council elections. It was expected to be a close-run thing, but in the event she was soundly beaten by the sitting councillor, an independent. The local newspaper questioned the wisdom of the party in putting up, for 'the exacting work of the County Council', a candidate past retirement age [*Rhondda Leader*, 9 April 1949 8]. However Andrews had ten energetic years of work in front of her as chairman of the Ystrad magistrates bench, and as a member of the Glamorgan Health Executive Council, the Pontypridd and Rhondda Hospital Management Committee and a Home Office committee for a local probation hostel run by the Salvation Army. She also remained active in her chapel, the Bethany Church and Mission in Gelli.

In March 1959 she attended her last advisory council meeting to pay tribute to 'our dear beloved Alderman Rose Davies', who had died. Almost exactly a year later the council stood in silent tribute to 'our beloved Elizabeth'. At the age of 77 she had died, as Mary Sutherland put it, 'in harness' after fracturing her femur in a fall as she entered a meeting of the Health Executive Council on 22 January. She was cremated in Pontypridd on 27 January, leaving an estate of £2146 2s 8d. Recalling the title of her autobiography, one of her colleagues said 'we can say her work is done, and she did it well' [*Rhondda Leader* (30 November 1960) 17].

Writings: *A Woman's Work is Never Done* (autobiography) (Rhondda, 1951); Wales Organiser's Monthly Reports, *Labour Woman*, April 1919–48; The Women's Page Monthly, *The Colliery Workers' Magazine*, 1923–27; 'The Section Programme', *Labour Woman*, June 1933; 'A Clarion Call – to the Rhondda Women', *Rhondda Clarion*, no. 2, October 1935; 'Labour Women in Wales', *Labour Woman*, November 1937; 'Bread and Peace', *Labour Woman*, August 1938; 'Wales and her Poverty, *Labour Woman*, July 1939; 'Curb Your Curiosity', *Labour Woman*, September 1940; compiled by Elizabeth Andrews, 'Coming of Age Souvenir East Glamorgan – West Wales – And Monmouthshire Labour Women's Advisory Councils Historical Survey and Chronicle of Events' (1940); 'Wales – Then and Now: 1919–1947, *Labour Woman*, February 1948.

Sources: (1) MS: Labour Party Records, National Library of Wales, Aberystwyth. **(2) Other:** Chris Williams, *Democratic Rhondda: Politics and Society 1885–1951* (Cardiff, 1996); Chris Williams, *Capitalism, Community and Conflict: The South Wales Coalfield 1898–1947* (Cardiff, 1998); Pamela Graves, 'An Experiment in Women-Centred Socialism: Labour Women in

Britain', in Helmut Gruber and Pamela Graves (eds), *Women and Socialism, Socialism and Women: Europe Between the Two World Wars* (Oxford, 1998); Neil Evans and Dot Jones, ' "To Help Forward the Great Work of Humanity": Women in the Labour Party in Wales', in Duncan Tanner, Chris Williams and Deian Hopkin (eds), *The Labour Party in Wales 1900–2000* (Cardiff, 2000), 215–40; Richard Lewis, 'Political Culture and Ideology 1900–1918', in Duncan Tanner, Chris Williams and Deian Hopkin (eds), *The Labour Party in Wales 1900–2000* (Cardiff, 2000).

URSULA MASSON
LOWRI NEWMAN

See also: Florence Rose DAVIES; Beatrice GREEN.

BOWMAN, Alexander (1854–1924)
FIRST WORKING-CLASS IRISHMAN TO STAND FOR WESTMINSTER

Alexander Bowman was born Patrick McKeown on 16 March 1854 in the townland of Derry, near Dromara in County Down. His mother Elizabeth (née Rogers 1823–c.1900) was first married to farm labourer John Bowman (1818–c.1851) of Derry townland, by whom she had two sons and a daughter. On 26 November 1853 she married again, her second husband being neighbouring farmer/weaver William McKeown. The second marriage produced two sons and two daughters, Alexander being the eldest, born four months after his parents' marriage.

The Great Famine had considerably affected rural areas of County Down. Life was difficult on the family's smallholding and the young boy was required to learn the art of weaving from his father to help make ends meet. However there was time to attend school and he had an early love for reading and writing. In later years his speeches would include occasional references to the classics, including Shakespeare, as well as quotations from the works of contemporary poets.

In January 1865 William McKeown died a slow and painful death from liver cancer at the age of 37, leaving his widow with the impossible task of maintaining the farm and looking after her surviving children. Elizabeth moved to the Tennent Street area of Belfast, some 20 miles away, where she and her young children resided with her sons from her first marriage: William Bowman, then aged 20, and James Bowman, 14. It was assumed by neighbours and friends that all the children were called Bowman and thus Alexander's true surname, McKeown, was lost.

In Ulster it would have been significant that Alexander's mother was a Presbyterian and his father a Roman Catholic. Although Alexander was baptised Patrick after his paternal grandfather, Patrick McKeown, he was raised in the Presbyterian faith and with a forename that was popular on his mother's side of the family. Details of this complicated family background remained largely hidden from his own family and certainly from his political opponents, to whom they would have been of immense value, and only came to light as the result of extensive research by his journalist great-grandson, Terence Bowman, in the mid 1990s. His last surviving child, Robert, died in 1970 and took with him any lingering memories he might have had of home, holidays and life away from politics and trade unionism in the late nineteenth century. Alexander Bowman himself left very little personal property, and no papers, records or diaries.

From the age of 10 Alexander Bowman worked part-time in a spinning mill in Agnes Street, Belfast, spending half the day in the machine room and the remainder in the adjoining school classroom. Despite the obvious restrictions this placed on his education, he read widely and studied the newspapers available in the factory's reading room. His interest in the welfare of his fellow workers manifested itself in 1874, when he was 20 and completing his apprenticeship as a flaxdresser. During a strike in the linen industry he led a delegation to the factory manager. He was dismissed for his efforts, but had little difficulty finding employment as a flaxdresser with William Ewart and Son at their Crumlin Road factory in Belfast. It was around this time that he met his future wife, Rosie Ritchie (1852–1947). A close relative of hers, Robert Ritchie, had been involved in setting up a short-lived trades council in Belfast in 1872, and was active in the 1874 linen dispute into which the young Alexander found himself drawn. Ritchie was an obvious candidate for the role of personal stimulus for the young flaxdresser.

Alexander and Rosie were married on 30 August 1880. William, the first of their six children, was born a year later. Despite the demands placed on a young husband with a limited income, Bowman was drawn ever more deeply into trade union activities. He joined the Flaxdressers' Trade and Benevolent Fund, which had been formed in 1872 and had a membership of some 1360 by the 1880s. Further strikes affected the Belfast linen industry during the winter of 1880, and in April 1881 the Belfast and North of Ireland Power Loom Tenters' Trade Union struck for a pay increase. The Tenters were a small union of key operatives, and as the dispute led to thousands being laid off, numerous union delegates, Bowman prominent among them, combined their efforts to persuade the factory owners to accept arbitration. These efforts failed, but the experience encouraged a renewed attempt to unite the trade bodies in the town (Belfast did not become a city until 1888), culminating on 29 October 1881 in the formation of the Belfast Trades Council.

Bowman was elected as its founding secretary, a post he would hold for five years. Not only was he invariably nominated as the main speaker for the various delegations that visited the Town Council and employer organisations, he was also the Belfast Trades Council's sole nominee to attend the British Trades Union Congress (TUC) in Manchester (1881) and Nottingham (1882). He was among Ireland's first trades council delegates to attend the TUC, where he also represented his own Flaxdressers' Union. Bowman was an active participant, for example speaking at Manchester in favour of the Payment of Wages in Public Houses Prevention Bill. He also attacked the judiciary in Ireland for being 'pre-eminently hostile to the working classes' [British TUC Report (1882)].

Thanks to a high public profile, due in no small measure to the favourable press he enjoyed in Belfast's pro-Liberal *Northern Whig* newspaper, Bowman was approached to stand for the North Belfast constituency in the November 1885 general election. The call was backed by a petition signed by 400–500 voters. A labour candidate seemed timely. The constituency redistribution that accompanied the Representation of the People Act (1884) had increased the number of Belfast MPs from two to four. Bowman was active in the Belfast Liberal Association, which had been encouraged by Gladstone to strengthen its working-class membership, and in Britain he might have contested as a 'Lib-Lab'. However in Belfast the Liberals were distrusted for their perceived appeasement of Irish nationalists. To save the Belfast Trades Council any embarrassment, Bowman distanced himself from the Liberals during the election, and the Liberals themselves were happy for him to stand as a 'working men's candidate' against the sitting Belfast Conservative MP, William Ewart, his former employer.

Bowman's decision to oppose a man standing first and foremost for the union with Great Britain led Ewart's supporters to argue that he was more than just a labour candidate taking on a rich employer. As far as they were concerned, he was also a hated Irish nationalist because he was enjoying support from the local Catholic community. Indeed Bowman's candidature was endorsed by Irish nationalist Charles Stewart Parnell, who hoped that in exchange for Catholic votes in North Belfast, working-class Protestants would back his party's candidate in the knife-edged West Belfast constituency.

Supporters were assaulted and subjected to verbal abuse at Bowman's election meetings, while his home in Berlin Street, off Belfast's Shankill Road, was targeted by a stone-throwing mob who forced the candidate and his family to flee to safety. Despite an unrelenting campaign of intimidation, Bowman's manifesto advocating the nationalisation of land and an end to the landlord system, plus free primary and technical education, unrestricted trade between nations, a reduction in working hours, improved welfare rights, temperance and votes for women, proved popular with many first-time voters. In a two-horse race (the Liberal Party having indicated its tacit support for Bowman by refraining from putting forward its own candidate), Ewart attracted 3915 votes to the 1330 cast for Bowman. While still a Liberal, 'the working men's candidate' had anticipated the impossibility of replicating the British 'Lib-Lab' option in Belfast, and shown that for local trade unionists the only alternative to the Conservative and Unionist Party was labour politics. North Belfast would become Belfast's most promising constituency for the Labour Party in the early twentieth century.

The return of Gladstone to 10 Downing Street in February 1886, with the backing of Parnell's Irish Nationalist MPs, prompted a new direction to Bowman's political career. Gladstone's Bill for the Better Government of Ireland – in other words, Home Rule – won the active support of Bowman, who favoured a Dublin parliament, answerable to Westminster. Although the Bill delivered a devastating blow to Ulster Liberals and was defeated by 343 votes to 313 on its second reading in the House of Commons on 8 June 1886, Bowman and a few steadfast Gladstonians regrouped into the Irish Protestant Home Rule Association, which they had founded almost three weeks earlier, on 21 May, in the Castle Restaurant in Belfast's Donegall Place.

Bowman's involvement in the relatively small and short-lived Protestant Home Rule Association provoked a stormy reaction by the Belfast Trades Council, which compelled him to resign as secretary on 12 June 1886. Although Bowman had been working as a commercial traveller for a Belfast clothier from the beginning of 1884, he had remained a delegate for the Flaxdressers' Union on the Council. In forcing Bowman's resignation, the Council made no comment on Home Rule – its rules forbade the discussion of 'politics' at meetings – but its unionist proclivities were no secret.

Bowman went on to serve the Irish Protestant Home Rule Association as its salaried secretary, immersing himself in the fight for self-determination for Ireland. He undertook speaking engagements in towns and villages throughout the north, earning the respect of Catholic nationalists but incurring the wrath of fellow Protestants. Yet Bowman totally opposed the use of violence to obtain land reforms and legislative freedom, and never faltered in his loyalty to Queen Victoria, viewing himself as a 'real unionist' who believed the best way to improve Ireland's social and moral well-being lay in rewriting the 1800 Act of Union to create an equal partnership between the two islands.

Faced with the unremitting bitterness of co-religionists and the reluctant realisation that, with a strong Conservative government under Lord Salisbury in office, a Dublin parliament remained many years off, Bowman decided in October 1888 to move with his wife and four young children to Scotland. Thanks to a generous farewell gift of 42 gold sovereigns from the Irish Protestant Home Rule Association, Bowman was able to settle his family in South Street and then Gordon Street in the rural suburb of Whiteinch, between Glasgow and Clydebank. He opened an office in Stockwell Place in the city centre as the agent for the Universal Automatic Machines Company. Within a short time he renewed his interest in politics. The Glasgow of the late 1880s was a centre for radical thinking and American land reformer Henry George – a leading exponent of the single tax policy for targeting wealthy but unproductive landowners – enjoyed considerable support, particularly from the city's large number of Highland migrants, many of whom were crofters who had lost their homes, and from the Irish population.

Bowman became a frequent speaker at the city's Henry George Institute, and at the beginning of February 1890 he was made its president. Among those he welcomed to its meetings were Keir Hardie, then secretary of the Ayrshire Miners' Union, and John Bruce Glasier, former secretary of the Socialist League's Glasgow branch. Both would play key roles in the Independent Labour Party. In July 1890 the various strands of the land restoration movement in Glasgow, namely the Bridgeton branch of the Scottish Land Restoration League, the Henry George Institute and the South Side Single Tax Association, formed an umbrella organisation, the Scottish Land Restoration Federation, with Bowman being elected as president of its 15-strong representative council. Six weeks later Henry George paid one of his occasional visits to Glasgow, where Bowman presided over a packed rally in the city hall.

Bowman was re-elected as president of the Federation in 1891, but by the spring of 1892 he had hit hard times, his all-consuming involvement in Glaswegian politics having cost him his job. The struggle to make ends meet proved too much and Bowman sent his family back to Ireland while he moved to London, where he found work as an agent for the Belfast-based Ulster Bacon Curing Company. There is strong evidence to suggest he took lodgings with his elder half-brother William, and that the latter was branch secretary of the Social Democratic Federation (SDF) in Clerkenwell. Alexander Bowman, expanding on the political interests he had cultivated during his years in Glasgow, rapidly established himself as a speaker at rallies organised by the SDF.

In early 1894 Bowman, having again brought his family over from Belfast, moved into a rented house at 29 Maude Terrace, Walthamstow, later moving to 57 Warner Road in the same London suburb. He joined the local branch of the SDF and became one of its most active members. That December he was one of 15 pioneering SDF candidates who sought election to Walthamstow District Council. While none was elected, Bowman's 209 votes in the James Street ward were the highest cast for any of the party's candidates. Hence in March 1895 he was selected to stand as an independent working man's candidate, with the support of the SDF, the United Workers' Organisation and the Christian Socialist League, to contest the High Street ward for a seat on Essex County Council. His opponent was local landowner Courtenay Warner, who was also Liberal MP for Somerset's northern division. Bowman suffered a second heavy electoral defeat, receiving 94 votes to the 449 cast for Warner in a low turnout.

Possibly prompted by his wife's sixth and final pregnancy, Bowman made it clear in an election speech in December 1894 that his time in Walthamstow was limited to a matter of months, prompting one to wonder, given his links with founder figures of the British Labour Party, what direction his life might have taken had he remained in England. However by the autumn of 1895 the eight-strong Bowman family was back in Belfast, and within a short time he reimmersed himself in the trade union movement. He became an unpaid spokesman for those members of the Municipal Employees' and Other Workers' Association who worked for the Belfast Corporation, and led a number of delegations to press for improved rights and wages for council workers. He was also made lecture secretary of the relatively short-lived Belfast branch of the Independent Labour Party.

He not only became acquainted with the workings of the Belfast Corporation but also gradually regained the respect he had enjoyed with the city's trade union movement prior to the Home Rule disagreement in 1886. By January 1897 he was again representing the Flaxdressers' Trade Union on Belfast Trades Council. That same year brought the introduction of new city boundaries, a redrawing of the municipal electoral districts and the creation of many first-time voters under new franchise rules, including women householders. At a time when the Corporation was facing serious public criticism over alleged inefficiency, corruption and failure to tackle serious health problems, including outbreaks of typhoid, the trades council saw an opportunity to seek a mandate from the people. It was decided to put forward candidates in seven of the 15 Belfast wards in the November 1897 triennial elections. Their manifesto included demands for corporation direct labour, fair wages for municipal workers and a fair wage clause for public contracts. Six of the candidates were successful, with five topping their respective polls, including Bowman in the Duncairn ward. They were the first labour councillors to be elected to any local authority in Ireland without the patronage of either the nationalist or unionist political parties.

With just six trades council members among the 60 councillors and alderman who served on the Belfast Corporation (33 were Conservatives), their impact was always more vocal than legislative. They defended the rights of corporation workers but rarely gained more than a few token crumbs from the business and wealth-dominated authority. For labour councillors such as Alexander Bowman there was more satisfaction to be derived from membership of the Belfast Trades Council and the Irish Trade Union Congress (ITUC). The ITUC had been created in 1894, largely in response to the widely held view among Irish delegates to the British TUC that matters relating to Ireland were receiving less consideration than they merited.

Bowman, representing both the Flaxdressers' Union and the Belfast Municipal Employees' and Other Workers' Association, attended four Irish Congresses – Belfast in 1898, Londonderry in 1899, Dublin in 1900 and Sligo in 1901. He was elected chairman of the ITUC's Parliamentary Committee in 1900. This body conducted the organisation's business and scrutinised relevant legislation going before Parliament in London. In that capacity he led a delegation of trade unionists to meet the Irish Chief Secretary, George Wyndham, at Dublin Castle on 23 January 1901, the day after the death of Queen Victoria. Three months later Bowman's trade union career peaked with his election as president of the ITUC. His presidential address, in which he called for the 'uniting of all sects, creeds and parties in the attempt to raise our common and beloved county to that material, moral and social position to which she is entitled', stressed his view that for labour to progress in Ireland it had to be non-sectarian. It stands among the most powerful delivered in the history of Congress [ITUC Report (1901)].

Bowman's year as president ended abruptly when he retired from labour and trade union politics during the summer of 1901. He had decided against seeking a second three-year term on the Belfast Corporation that January, largely due to the inability, and unwillingness, of the Trades Council to make good the wages he had forfeited to attend Corporation meetings between November 1897 and January 1901. Furthermore he had faced growing hostility from some of his colleagues, who claimed he had lost his socialist edge and sold out to the establishment. His views had been attacked at meetings of the Trades Council by one-time friends, and when on one occasion he had spoken up for a Conservative Councillor who had endeavoured to improve the city's sanitation, and thus create better living conditions for workers, Bowman had been mocked as 'the Apostle of Socialism'. It was an accusation he had firmly rejected, with matters coming to a head when he had been heckled during an election rally on behalf of a Belfast Liberal Unionist who had long been a strong supporter of the trade union movement. 'For the past twenty years', declared Bowman, 'I have stood up for the cause of the working man. I would have done much better if I had fought for myself, rather than the people – but I chose to fight their fight rather than my own' [*Belfast Newsletter*, 2 October 1900].

Penniless and finding it difficult to keep a roof over his family's head, it must have been the final straw to a man who had devoted a quarter of a century to the trade union movement but detected little gratitude in return. Aiming to provide a more secure future for his wife and children, Bowman rejoined the Belfast Corporation as a salaried member of staff. Living in the nine-roomed house that went with the job, he served for 21 years as the innovative superintendent of the municipal baths on the city's Falls Road.

Although his contract banned active involvement in politics, Bowman would surely have taken an interest in the 1920 Government of Ireland Act which created 'Home Rule' parliaments in Dublin and Belfast, and four years later in the election of Britain's first Labour government under another former acquaintance, Ramsay MacDonald. He also derived pride from the fact that one of his sons, Hugh, was honoured with an MBE from King George V for service with the Ministry of Munitions during the First World War. Another son, Robert, went on to become permanent secretary with Northern Ireland's Ministry of Labour and was awarded the CBE by King George VI in 1945, some 21 years after Bowman's death at the age of 70 on 3 November 1924, at the home of his son Hugh at 65 Rushfield Avenue, Belfast. Survived by his wife, daughter and four of his five sons, Bowman left an estate valued at £283. 3s. 5d. He was buried in the Victoria Cemetery, Carrickfergus, following a private service in Cooke Centenary Presbyterian Church, Belfast. His final resting place helped to keep concealed his intriguing family history. Bowman's only connection with the County Antrim town was that it had been the birthplace of his brother Hugh's in-laws. Hugh had buried a deceased daughter there in 1914 and Alexander followed suit when his son Charles died in 1923. Thus Carrickfergus became the Bowman family burying ground for future generations.

Alexander Bowman was a trailblazer in Victorian Belfast, and to a lesser extent in Glasgow and London. He set a pattern that became a model for others to follow. He would not have viewed himself as a pioneer and like so many other working-class leaders was undervalued in his day, and even now remains largely ignored by historians. With the benefit of hindsight he merits recognition as a pioneer of the Irish and British labour movements. In every case he encountered the complex obstacles faced by those concerned to develop the political representation of labour. In Glasgow and London these difficulties would eventually be overcome; but in Belfast it was a very different story. Bowman's career there was an early demonstration of the power of religious and national identities in one industrial city.

Writings: Alexander Bowman left no papers, diaries or other personal accounts of his life. Before his death in 1970 Robert, the last of his six children, gave a brief interview to the late John W. Boyle for his book *The Irish Labour Movement* (Washington, 1988). Otherwise all details about Bowman's life have been gleaned from his speeches, as recorded in contemporary newspapers and minute books, and from snippets of information passed on by family members.

Sources: (1) MSS: Belfast Trades Council, minute books for various years, also statements of accounts, Linen Hall Library, Belfast; Belfast Corporation, minutes of full council meetings and meetings of the Baths and Lodging House Committee 1897–1924, Belfast City Hall; British TUC, conference reports for 1882, 1883 and 1900, Congress House; Irish Protestant Home Rule Association, Dublin Executive minute book, National Library of Ireland, Dublin; Irish TUC, conference reports 1898–1904. **(2) Newspapers:** *Belfast Evening Star; Belfast (Evening) Telegraph; Belfast Morning News; Belfast Newsletter; Brixton Free Press; Brotherhood/Belfast Weekly Star; Freeman's Journal; Irish News; Irish Times; Justice; Labour Leader; Northern Whig; Sligo Champion; South London Press; The Times; Walthamstow Guardian; Walthamstow Reporter.* **(3) Theses:** David Bleakley, 'Trade Union beginnings in Belfast and district with special reference to the period 1881–1900, and to the work of the Belfast and District United Trades Council during that period', (MA thesis, Queen's University, Belfast, 1955); P. J. O. McCann, 'The Protestant Home Rule Movement, 1885–95' (MA thesis, University College Dublin, 1972); Emily Boyle, 'The Economic Development of the Irish Linen Industry, 1852–1913' (PhD thesis, Queen's University Belfast, 1979); Peter Collins, 'The Belfast Trades Council' (PhD thesis, University of Ulster, 1988). **(4) Other:** Jesse Dunsmore Clarkson, *Labour and Nationalism in Ireland* (New York, 1925); Henry Pelling, *The Origins of the Labour Party, 1880–1900* (1965); Ian Budge and Cornelius O'Leary, *Belfast Approach to Crisis: A Study of Belfast Politics, 1613–1970* (1973); Alan Carr, *The Early Belfast Labour Movement: Part 1 1885–1893* (1974); Ann McKee, *Belfast Trades Council: the first 100 years (1881–1981)* (Belfast, 1983); Sean Redmond, *The Irish Municipal Employees Trade Union, 1883–1983* (Dublin, 1983); Andrew Boyd, *Rise of the Irish Trade Unions* (1985); Henry Pelling, *A Short History of the Labour Party* (1985); James Loughlin, 'The Irish Protestant Home Rule Association and Nationalist Politics, 1886–93', *Irish Historical Studies*, 24, 95 (May 1985), 341–60; John W. Boyle, *The Irish Labour Movement* (Washington, 1988); Brian M. Walker, *Ulster Politics: The Formative Years 1868–86* (Belfast, 1989); Clive Behagg, *Labour and Reform: Working Class Movements, 1815–1914* (1991); Austen Morgan, *Labour and Partition: The Belfast Working Class 1905–1923* (1991); Emmet O'Connor, *A Labour History of Ireland 1824–1960* (Dublin, 1992); Liz Curtis, *The Cause of Ireland* (Belfast, 1994); Peter Collins (ed.), *Nationalism and Unionism: Conflict in Ireland 1885–1921* (Belfast, 1994); Eamon Phoenix (ed.), *A Century of Northern Life: The Irish News and 100 Years of Ulster History, 1890s to 1990s* (Ulster, 1995); Frank Wright, *Two Lands On One Soil: Ulster Politics Before Home Rule* (Dublin, 1996); Terence Bowman, *People's Champion: the Life of Alexander Bowman* (Ulster, 1997); Arthur Marsh, Victoria Ryan and John B. Smethurst, *Historical Directory of Trades Unions Vol. 4* (Aldershot, 1994).

TERENCE BOWMAN

BRIERLEY, Benjamin (1825–96)
CHARTIST, RADICAL, AUTHOR

Benjamin (Ben) Brierley, the fifth child in a family of six, was born on 26 June 1825 in The Rocks, a row of cottages on the Oldham Road in the weaving district of Failsworth, Lancashire. Ben's father James, formerly an army gunner and a veteran of Waterloo, was a handloom weaver from Middleton who married Esther Whitehead of Newton Heath before settling in Failsworth in 1819. The family's defencelessness against both poverty and disease in the declining trade of handloom weaving was underlined by the fact that only Ben and his brother Thomas survived infancy. Even that brother, who rose through the ranks to become a senior police officer in Oldham, was struck down by fever and died in early middle age. Ben, a sensitive and precocious child, inherited a love of reading and a good singing voice from his mother, who had been in the choir of All Saints' Church, Newton Heath. At the age of four he was sent to John Goodier's village school in Pole Lane, Failsworth, where he soon excelled – before his fifth birthday he took first prize for spelling; the test word was 'victual' and he won three marbles!

Ben's full-time schooling, however, was short-lived. The day before a school holiday granted to mark the coronation of William IV in 1830, his family moved to a cottage in Canal Street, Hollinwood, about three quarters of a mile away and situated on the towpath of the Manchester and Ashton canal. This new environment was still semirural and the young Brierley, when not required to supplement the family's declining income by hawking from door to door, was able to explore and enjoy the last vestiges of the surrounding countryside and its traditional way of life. This freedom to roam left an indelible impression and helped inform the content of much of his writing in adult life. At the tender age of six he was 'put to the bobbin wheel' at home, but his manual dexterity was in no way equal to his intellectual potential and his father gave up on him as a 'bad job'. He fared somewhat better when he was sent to work as a spinner in a neighbouring cotton factory, where he won promotion to the grade of middle piecer. At the age of 13, however, he was forced to leave because of failing health and returned home, where he worked either for his father or lugged coal from the local collieries for his neighbours.

Whilst employed in factory labour, Brierley's manager had spotted him poring over a copy of *Cleave's Gazette* during his break time and offered him the chance, which he had taken up, to read the *Pickwick Papers* provided he fetched each monthly part from the local shop. This thirst for literature had simultaneously been stimulated by his attendance, from the age of seven, at the Hollinwood Primitive Methodist Sunday School and later at a night school in Wrigley Head, Failsworth, kept by a cousin. In Sunday School he had read the Bible from beginning to end three times before his eighth birthday, and at night school his companions had marvelled at his rapid progress in learning to write. Brierley thus became a classic working-class autodidact.

In 1840, aged 15, Brierley returned to his old school in Pole Lane as a Sunday teacher. Within a year he was instrumental in forming a mutual improvement society, of which he was made secretary; this later became the Failsworth Mechanics' Institute. With the help of his uncle, Richard Taylor, Brierley and his band of fellow self-educators built up a library in the Pole Lane School, attended literary classes for reading and discussing Shakespeare, Burns, Keats and Byron, and organised their own stage productions. Encouraged by the reception given to their first play, Brierley wrote and performed in a tragedy called 'Marinello the Monk'. Soon the group was sufficiently self-confident to undertake *Othello*, in which Brierley was cast in the demanding role of Iago. Such versatility subsequently served him well when, as a household name in Lancashire, he performed either in connection with his public readings or acted on stage in his own farce, comedy or domestic drama.

Brierley's thirst for knowledge went hand in hand with his involvement in radical politics. His grandfather had been a notorious Jacobin supporter, while his father had been present at Peterloo in 1819 and had also played an active part in the radical agitation for political reform in 1832. Two years before this event, during William IV's coronation celebrations, Brierley had experienced at first hand the wrath of neighbours who were hostile to his family's radical views. An ox had been slaughtered and roasted in the centre of Failsworth, and a stew made from parts of the beast had been served out to whoever came along. Brierley's mother had sent him with a jug to partake, but when the hungry five year old had presented himself to the woman in charge of distribution, she had pushed him aside and refused to serve him on the ground that he had a Jacobinic grandparent. Brierley, hurt by this denial, imbibed the radical atmosphere in which he grew up.

Like his father, who became an avid follower of Feargus O' Connor, Brierley supported the Chartist movement. Helped by Samuel Collins – a veteran radical, weaver and aspiring poet – Brierley played an active role in the Failsworth branch of the National Charter Association. Among his weekly tasks were reading aloud the *Northern Star* to the weavers assembled at his canal-side home on Sunday mornings, and – entered into reluctantly by the family – assisting his father on Saturday afternoons to sharpen pikes for those in the branch who wanted to establish a republic. Both Brierley and his father threw themselves wholeheartedly into the industrial action of 1842, which brought about the stoppage of work by the simple strategy of removing the drain plugs from the boilers in nearby cotton mills. Brierley, narrowly avoided arrest because he appeared at the scene of plug-drawing heavily disguised.

Brierley's involvement in Chartist activities also attracted opprobrium from the local Anglican Church. A wave of clerical alarm was generated by Brierley's and his companions' use of the Pole Lane School for both political purposes and theatrical performances. By 1845 the Church party's influence, led by the local evangelical rector of St John's, had forced the school to close. Deprived of a meeting place, a defiant Brierley and friends temporarily removed to Hollinwood and opened another discussion class. Simultaneously they carefully planned and prepared in great secrecy 'to storm' the school in Failsworth, with the intention of reopening it on their terms. At dead of night, with Brierley leading the way, it was duly reoccupied by plying the night watchman with drink and carefully boring through the floor boards of the school to gain access to the lower schoolroom. Chartist activities were resumed, but it was some time before the Church authorities became aware of the re-establishment of the National Chartist Association branch. In desperation, they then tried to prosecute Brierley, the ringleader, for libelling Harry Walmsley – a local mill owner and Anglican supporter – in a skit that mocked his lack of authority in a Chartist stronghold such as Failsworth. Given the politically volatile situation at the time, Brierley was taken to court but again managed to escape retribution; an apology was made by his solicitor – without his knowledge – and the matter was grudgingly dropped.

Brierley's involvement in Chartism seems to have ended abruptly in 1845. However there is no doubt that it left an indelible impression on him, and later in adult life he was to draw on his teenage experiences in some of his sketches and tales. In the pamphlet *Old Radicals and Young Reformers. A Sketch for the Times* (1860) he complained about the vague and insipid support for radical political reform in the country. Three years later, drawing on his experiences of 1842, he wrote 'The Battle of Langley Height', which appeared in a volume on Lancashire life entitled *The Chronicles of Waverlow*.

The theme of this short story was the futility of agitation by physical force, but Brierley remained totally committed to winning battles against privilege and injustice by peaceful means. Between 1875 and 1881 he again became active in politics by representing the poor working-class area of St Michael's Ward on Manchester City Council. The success of his first attempt at standing for the council was attributed to the fact that he was perceived by voters as 'the educator of the people'. As a radical Liberal he gave fellow councillors within the mainstream Liberal fold an uncomfortable ride in the proceedings of the many committees and subcommittees on which he served. Brierley was a tough negotiator on such issues as the municipal provision of fresh drinking water, public baths and washhouses, parks, museums and libraries. As a member of the Free Libraries' Committee, in May 1876 he successfully led the campaign to overturn a decision by the full council to move the reference library to the attic of the new town hall and out of the reach of the public for whom it was intended. The whole episode was satirically conveyed by Brierley in his poem 'These Town Hall Stairs', a parody of Henry Longfellow's 'Excelsior'. In articulating such issues in favour of his own constituents' needs, he showed that the mid-century transition from Chartism to liberalism was fraught with difficulties.

Improving the living standards of his working-class electors was not Brierley's only concern. He retained an abiding antipathy towards clerical power and hypocrisy, which he sometimes vented on an out-of-touch Lord Bishop of Manchester, James Fraser, in the early 1880s. He was also sceptical about the economic benefits to working people derived from the expansion of the British Empire, ambivalent about the Prince of Wales' role at the time of the Queen's Jubilee celebrations of 1887, and not averse in his dialect writings or at public readings to ridicule middle-class pretentiousness and snobbery.

Between 1846 and 1856 Brierley found almost continuous employment in various silk warehouses in central Manchester. The social intercourse of the workplace in Manchester, the programme of reading undertaken in the radical and mutual improvement clubs, and the inspiration provided by the countryside on the journeys to and from work from Hollinwood combined to inspire a self-confident Brierley in his ambition to write verse and prose. In 1846 he contrived to make himself known to Elijah Ridings, who was popularly known as 'the Byron of the loom' in Manchester and where, in one of the city's oldest thoroughfares, Withy Grove, he kept a bookstall. Ridings became so impressed with the quality of his verse that he gave him a note of introduction to John Bolton Rogerson, a fellow author and editor of *Oddfellows' Magazine* in Dale Street. Rogerson liked what he saw and did not hesitate to print four short poems in the magazine between July 1846 and April 1847. These connections proved to be very important to Brierley's career. Both Ridings and Rogerson were members of a literary group that met at the Poets' Corner in the Sun Inn on Long Millgate. Other kindred spirits to whom Brierley was introduced at poetry meetings and readings in the 1850s included Charles Swain, Samuel Bamford, Edwin Waugh, Richard Rome Bealey and John Harland. All were, or became, members of the influential Lancashire Literary Association, founded in 1841 to protect and encourage literary interests both in and beyond the region. As poor authors they were also ably served by Abel and John Heywood, two brothers and ex-Chartists who ran a successful publishing empire from Deansgate and by 1875 had become extremely influential in the radical Liberal cause on Manchester City Council.

On 29 April 1855 Brierley was married in Manchester Cathedral to Esther Firth, a native of Bowlee Heights and a former silk worker in the warehouse in York Street where they had been simultaneously employed. They settled in the Collyhurst district of the burgeoning city of Manchester and had one child, Annie, in 1856; tragically she died from tuberculosis, aged 19, on 13 June 1875.

A crucial step in Brierley's rise 'to making his mark in the world of letters' began in September 1855 when his employers, Brotherton and Green in Fountain Street, gave a day's holiday to celebrate the fall of Sebastopol on 11 September. Brierley used the opportunity to take a summer's ramble in the countryside, walking from his home towards Waterhouses and the River Medlock on the east side of Manchester. This prompted him to write the short story *A Day Out*, which led to the name 'Daisy Nook' being given to the spot used by Brierley's friend, the artist Charles Potter, to illustrate the story. Published in Manchester, the story ran to several editions within the space of two years and attracted praise from many Lancashire newspapers. Brierley followed this up with some sketches, which were first published in the *Manchester Weekly Times* and then issued collectively as *Daisy Nook Sketches* under the Heywood imprint in 1862.

Despite considerable criticism of the sketches' quality by an influential publication – the *Athenaeum* – Brierley took the decision in 1861, when work in his branch of the silk trade was depressed, to capitalise on his new-found reputation and accept a post in a newspaper. For a year he was employed as sub–editor of the *Oldham Times*, but in 1862 he abandoned this and set out to make his mark in London. Here the gregarious Brierley, with a penchant for rum and milk, not only found work as an almanac writer but also quickly became associated with members of the Bohemian-inspired Savage Club. For their journal, *Colman's Magazine*, he was invited to write yet another Lancashire sketch, *The Layrocks of Langleyside*, which first appeared in serialised form in 1863. However the magazine folded after only three issues, at which point he abandoned his attempt to break into the London literary scene. He returned to Collyhurst and finished the story in the *Manchester Weekly Times*. The sketch, again well received, was published in book form in 1864. By that time Brierley had decided to become a professional writer. To help strengthen his new position, in 1863 he co-founded the influential Manchester Literary Club. Out of this association also emerged membership of two other clubs: the Manchester Titan Club, an amateur dramatic society in which every member had to assume the name of one of Shakespeare's characters (Brierley's was 'Bottom the Weaver'); and the Compton Amateur Dramatic Society, of which he eventually became president.

In February 1865, with the support of fellow writer R. R. Bealey, he was installed as a Freemason of the Merit Lodge, which met at the Masons' Arms, Bury New Road, Whitefield. He also signed a petition later in the year for the establishment of the Wilton Freemason's Lodge in Blackley, which he attended from time to time as an ordinary member. Recruited from the business quarter and professional groups the Manchester Freemasons, through their cultural activities and philanthropy, made a modest contribution to the city's attempt to create a sense of civic community. In 1886, when the Arthur Sullivan Lodge (named after the composer) was founded at Memorial Hall, Albert Square, Manchester, Brierley was invested as the first secretary. After two years he relinquished the post, but became senior warden at the lodge in October 1889. In appreciation both of this advancement and for the favourable reception afforded his writing by fellow Masons, Brierley dedicated his first major collection of verse, *Spring Blossoms and Autumn Leaves* (1893), to the Freemasons.

Between 1865 and 1870 Brierley's literary output was considerable. This was helped by the fact that he was invited to spend some time as a writer-in-residence at the Unitarian Parsonage at Stand in Pilkington whilst the minister and his family travelled across Europe. In the columns of Lancashire newspapers, in the Manchester Literary Club's journal, *Country Words* (1866–1867), and in book form he published many sketches based on aspects of everyday life in contemporary Lancashire. Using the local dialect, Brierley introduced his readers to a range of endearing village characters, including 'Fause Juddie', 'Jack O' Flunters', 'Owd Thurston' and the best known literary construct of all, 'Ab-o-'th'-Yate', the Walmsley Fowt (Bardsley Fold) philosopher. Such was the continuing popularity of these sketches that they were brought together and republished by Abel Heywood in 1886 as a nine-volume set, under the title *Tales and Sketches of Lancashire Life*. The village of Waterhouses on the River Medlock, in which cottages and tearooms were named after Brierley's characters and all kinds of associated memorabilia were offered for sale, remained a popular tourist attraction until the eve of the Second World War.

By 1869 Brierley was sufficiently well established to launch and edit his own *Ben Brierley's Journal*. This penny journal, which proved an outstanding success, remained in existence until December 1891 and made Brierley's name famous not only in Lancashire but also throughout the north of England. Dedicated to healthy and humorous reading, it became the medium for the development of the largely apolitical, fun-loving, working-class character 'Ab-o-'th'-Yate' (Abraham of the Gate). The stories about Ab's wide-ranging activities were eagerly read, thanks to Brierley's first-hand experiences as a weaver, store of knowledge about the rural past and shrewd appreciation of both the benefits and the limitations of the industrial present. What made the sketches bestsellers was their stoical characters, good humour, adept use of dialect and the presentation of both locations and incidents that readers could equate with people and places of their own acquaintance.

Brierley's fame also spread because of his skill on stage and in conducting public readings. One of his most successful stage productions was *The Lancashire Lad*, which was performed at the Theatre Royal in Manchester in September 1879. Brierley played the central role of the wily old weaver, 'Joe O' Dicks', and sang his best-known songs, including 'The Wayver of Welbrook'. He also obtained a paying market in penny readings in hotels and halls; sometimes he pitched the tone to suit a particular audience or change in taste. In the well-received *Goosegrove Penny Readings* of the 1870s, he blended recitations of literature on working-class humour with the singing of popular songs in a way that overlapped the culture of the new music hall.

By the early 1880s Brierley was making a reasonable living as an author. He and his wife moved from 12 St Oswald's Grove, Collyhurst, to a much larger house in the same street (number 94). They invested their hard-earned money in a building society and, in Esther's name, purchased shares in the Manchester Ship Canal Company. Although Brierley periodically suffered from depression as a result of the untimely death of his daughter, he kept himself busy by writing for his *Journal* and by his political work as a Manchester councillor. To recuperate from mental exhaustion, in the spring of 1880 he planned a six-week semiliterary tour of the United States and Canada. When news of this spread his Failsworth friends, quite spontaneously, decided to give him a financial send-off. Shortly before his departure in early April, upwards of five hundred Failsworth villagers assembled in their Co-operative Hall, where they presented him with an honorarium.

Upon his return Brierley resumed writing and entertaining. At times he appeared on the same literary platform as two other successful Lancashire dialect writers: Edwin Waugh (1817–1890) and Samuel Laycock (1826–1893). Unfortunately Brierley's health and composure were again shattered in 1884 by the collapse of the mutual building society in which he had invested most of the family's life savings. They were forced to move from St Oswald's Grove to a much smaller house – 'The Poplars' – at 17 Hall Street, Moston. Return to the poverty that Brierley had known in childhood, however, was avoided, partly because of Esther Brierley's shares in the Manchester Ship Canal Company and partly because admirers responded to his plight. A second and longer holiday in the United States was suggested, and to help him on his way a Ben Brierley Testimonial Fund was launched. Brierley did not get the bulk of the funds immediately, but sufficient was forthcoming to allow him to depart in mid May 1884 on a three-month tour. In March 1885 he was presented with a cheque for £650 by the Mayor of Manchester, Alderman Sir John Harwood, at the town hall in the company of civic dignitaries, fellow writers and close friends. Three months later the Clifton Hall Colliery disaster at nearby Pendlebury, in which 170 men lost their lives, prompted Brierley to write a moving poem as a tribute to the dead miners. This appeared in the *Manchester Guardian* and showed clearly that Brierley's loyalties still lay with the welfare of the class from which he had sprung. The poem was printed for public sale and the proceeds were given to the colliery relief fund.

In 1886 Brierley was elevated to the position of vice-president of the Manchester Literary Club. He also remained heavily involved in the activities of the city's Freemasonry circles. As a local celebrity he was called upon in 1889 to give speeches both at the newly opened Failsworth Liberal Club and at celebrations for the erection of the Failsworth Pole, a new village landmark. Brierley's public appearances, however, were severely curtailed in May 1890 when he was incapacitated by a stroke. Aware of his difficulties, local dignitaries tried in vain to secure the payment to him of the Civil List pension awarded to Waugh, who had died only a month earlier. By the end of the year, however, an all-party group of MPs had succeeded in persuading Lord Salisbury's Conservative government to grant him the same amount for a three-year period from the Royal Bounty Fund. When ill-health finally stopped Brierley from writing and appearing in public, his friends in municipal politics and the Freemasons organised yet another testimonial fund. In October 1892 he was presented with a cheque for £356, which protected him from poverty for his few remaining years.

Brierley died on Saturday 18 January 1896, aged 71. He was buried four days later next to his daughter in Harpurhey Cemetery before an immense gathering of the city's councillors, Freemasons, old Chartists, representatives of cultural groups from neighbouring towns and the working people of Failsworth. In his will Brierley left a personal estate amounting to £432 5s 3d. His wife was the sole benefactor; she died on 25 May 1914.

Even in his own lifetime Brierley was a legendary figure. He was lionised as the archetypal 'Lancashire Lad' because he articulated weavers' thoughts and ideas, hopes and aspirations. After his death the tributes were as generous as they were wide-ranging. A statue in Portland Stone – the city of Manchester's first for a literary figure and a working man, and paid for by public subscription – was unveiled in 1898 in Queen's Park, Harpurhey. In the same year a granite plaque was set in the brickwork of the terraced house in which he grew up in Failsworth. Three Masonic institutions were named after him between 1908 and 1936, and a public house in the suburb of Moston and a residential street in Failsworth still bear his name. There were other community memorials over time: to mark the centenary of his birth a concert was held in Brierley's old school in 1925; and to commemorate the centenary of his death a short, locally produced biography was completed in 1995.

Writings: The Local Studies Department of Manchester Central Library has an extensive collection of Brierley's published works. A much smaller collection can be found in the Working Class Movement Library in Salford. **(1) Books:** *Tales and Sketches of Lancashire Life*, 2 Vols (1863); virtually all of the sketches written and published by Brierley between 1857 and 1882, together with *Ab-o-'th'-Yate in Yankee-Land* (1885), are contained in *Tale and Sketches of Lancashire Life*, 9 Vols (1886); *Readings for the Winter Nights with Ben Brierley* (1882); *Pennorth's of Fun for Lancashire Firesides* (1883); *A Bundle of Fents from a Lancashire Loom: Comprising Pieces Humorous and Pathetic. Adapted for Reading at Working Men's Clubs* (1883); *Spring Blossoms and Autumn Leaves* (1893); *Lancashire Wit and Humour* (1893); *Humorous Rhymes* (1894); *Failsworth, My Native Village: with Incidents of the Struggles of Early Reformers* (1895); *Ab-o-'th'-Yate Sketches and Other Short Stories in Three Volumes*, edited by James Dronsfield (1896). **(2) Pamphlets:** *Old Radicals and Young Reformers. A Sketch for the Times* (1860); *Ab-o-'th'-Yate at the Oldham Election* (1877); *A Trip to Thirlmere and Borrowdale* (1878); *Some Phases of Municipal Life: An Address* (1879); *The Lessons of the Garden. An Oration delivered at the Oxford Hall, Ashton-under-Lyne, September 1884* (1891). **(3) Periodicals:** *Ben Brierley's Journal. Journal of Literature, Science, and Art- for the Promotion of Good-Will and Good Fellowship among Men* (1869–91). **(4) Other:** *The Cobbler's Stratagem* (1869); *The Lancashire Weaver Lad: A Domestic Drama in Three Acts* (1871, repr. 1879); Biographical notice of Collins in Samuel Collins, *The Wild Floweret* (1875); *Ab-o-'th'-Yate's Christmas Annual* (1876), various; *Ben Brierley's Seaside Annual* (1878); *Ab Gooing to Cyprus* (1878); *Ab-o-'th'-Yate in Paddy's Land* (1881); *Ab-o-'th'-Yate's Dictionary: or Walmsley Fowt Skoolmaster* (1881); *Ab-o-'th'-Yate's Lancashire Folks' Almanack* (1885); *Ab-o-'th'-Yate and Buffalo Bill* (n.d., c.1887); *Ab-o-'th'-Yate's Lancashire Reciter* (1894).

Sources: (1) MS: Manchester Central Library, Local Studies Unit, Mc: m 524/13/2, p. 53, autographed letter (11 February 1867); F942.72 Hn7, vol. 5, pp. 95–6, letter to William Baron (1888); 427.76, six short stories, manuscript copy, pasted into a scrapbook, c.1890. **(2) Newspapers and Periodicals:** *Oddfellows' Magazine* (1846–7); *Manchester Spectator* (1849, 1857, 1863); *Athenaeum* (1863); *Saturday Review* (1863); *Colman's Magazine* (1863); *Manchester Weekly Times* (1863–4, 1868); *Country Words* (1866–7); *Momus*, 14 August 1879, biographical article; *Manchester Guardian* (1875–1900), particularly 4 May 1876, speech by Brierley against proposal to site the library in the attic of the town hall; 1 May 1883, letter regarding Bishop Fraser of Manchester; 18 March 1885, testimonial at town hall; 24 and 25 June 1885, the Clifton colliery disaster; 29 June 1886, consecration of the Arthur Sullivan Lodge of Freemasons; 28 October 1889, celebration of the new Failsworth Pole and quotes from Brierley's speech; 29 October 1892, presentation of Brierley's third testimonial; *Middleton Guardian* (1889–90); *Manchester Faces and Places* (1890–2) particularly vol. i, 1890, pp. 177–9, and vol. iii, 1892, pp. 109–11, and 165–7; *Manchester Evening Chronicle*, 23 November 1910, biographical article; *Manchester City News*, 2 May 1925, Ben Brierley's centenary; *Oldham Chronicle*, undated cutting in Manchester Central Library, Local Studies Unit (May 1925?) on centenary of Brierley's birth;

in connection with these celebrations see also Mc: M524/11/1/6, pp. 23–5, Scrapbook by William Baron: poem by Baron on 'Ben Brierley', specially written for the celebrations at Failsworth 27 June and read on the occasion; *Manchester Review*, 1948, 'The Lancashire Dialect', pp. 120–1; *Lancashire Life*, October 1972, biographical article, pp. 38–40; *Manchester Guardian*, 27 August 1977, Ben Brierley celebrations. **(3) Books:** John Harland and T.T. Wilkinson, *Ballads and Songs of Lancashire, Ancient and Modern* (1882); Charles Hardwick, *Pilgrimage through Collyhurst* (1883); William Axon, *The Annals of Manchester* (1886); William Andrews (ed.), *North Country Poets, Poems and Biographies of Natives or Residents of Northumberland, Westmorland, Durham, Lancashire and Yorkshire*, vol. 2. (1888); P. Wentworth, *History and Annals of Blackley and Neighbourhood* (1892); C. Roeder, *Memoir of Mosley* (1898); P. Percival, *Failsworth Folk and Failsworth Memories* (1901); Sim Schofield, *Short Stories about Failsworth* (1905); Samuel Hill (ed.), *Old Lancashire Songs and their Singers* (1906); John H. Swann, *Manchester Literary Club: some Notes on its History* (1908); May Yates, *A Lancashire Anthology* (1923); J. R. Swann, *Lancashire Authors: a Series of Biographical Sketches* (1924); Lucien Leclaire, *Le Roman Regionaliste Dans Les Iles Britanniques 1800–1950* (1954); R. M. Dorson, *The British Folklorists* (1968); Joan Pomfret, *Lancashire Evergreens. A Hundred Old Favourite Poems* (1969); Martha Vicinus, 'Literary Voices of an Industrial Town, Manchester 1810–70', pp. 739–61, in H. J. Dyos and M. Wolff (eds), *The Victorian City, Images and Reality*, vol. 2 (1973); Dennis Ball, *The Story of Failsworth* (1973); Martha Vicinus, *The Industrial Muse* (1974); D. Kynaston, *King Labour* (1976); Brian Hollingworth (ed.), *Songs of the People: Lancashire Dialect Poetry of the Industrial Revolution* (1977); Local History Library Staff, Manchester Central Library, *Men and Women of Manchester* (1978); Edwin Banks, *The Story of Ben Brierley and His Contemporaries* (1979) and *The Ben Brierley Companion* (1979); Patrick Joyce, *Work, Society and Politics: The Culture of the Factory in Later Victorian England* (1980); David Vincent, *Bread, Knowledge and Freedom. A Study of Nineteenth Century Working Class Autobiography* (1981); David Vincent, 'Reading in the Working Class Home', pp. 207–26 in J. K. Walton and J. Walvin (eds), *Leisure in Britain 1780–1939* (1983); John Burnett, David Vincent and David Mayall (eds), *Autobiography of the Working Class. An Annotated, Critical Bibliography*, (vol. 1, 1984); D. Thompson, *The Chartists* (1984); Margaret Beetham, 'Healthy Reading: The Periodical Press in Late Victorian Manchester', pp. 167–92 in A. J. Kidd and K.W. Roberts (eds), *City, Class and Culture: Studies of Cultural Production in Late Victorian Manchester* (1985); N. Kirk, *The Growth of Working Class Reformism in Mid-Victorian England* (1985); G. Messinger, *Manchester in the Victorian Age* (1985); Brian Maidment (ed.), *The Poorhouse Fugitives: Self-taught Poets and Poetry in Victorian Britain* (1987); Jonathan Rose, 'Working Class Poets and Poetry', pp. 877–8 in S. Mitchell (ed.), *Victorian Britain. An Encyclopaedia* (1988); Derek Brumhead and Terry Wyke, *A Walk round Manchester Statues* (1990); Patrick Joyce, 'The People's English: Language and Class in England, c.1840–1920', pp. 154–90 in Peter Burke and Roy Porter (eds), *Language, Self and Society: A Social History of Language* (1991); Andrew Davies and Steven Fielding (eds), *Workers' Worlds: Culture and Community in Manchester and Salford, 1880–1939* (1992); Paul A. Pickering, *Chartism and the Chartists in Manchester and Salford* (1995); David Huk, *Ben Brierley, 1825–1896* (1995); Martin Hewitt, *The Emergence of Stability in the Industrial City: Manchester, 1832–67* (1996); Owen Ashton and Stephen Roberts, *The Victorian Working Class Writer* (1999); Martin Hewitt and Robert Poole (eds), *The Diaries of Samuel Bamford* (2000). **(4) Articles:** Edmund Mercer, 'Brierley as a Writer of Fiction', *Manchester Quarterly*, XXVI (1900), pp. 454–6; Thomas Newbigging, 'A Reminiscence of Ben Brierley', *Manchester Quarterly*, XXII (1902), pp. 447–51; Walter Butterworth, 'Ben Brierley', *Papers of the Manchester Literary Club*, 52 (1926), 182–91; Clare Dunkerley, 'Ben Brierley (Ab-o-'th'-Yate) 1825–1896, Lancashire Dialect Author, Poet and Mason', *Transactions of the Manchester Association for Masonic Research*, 67 (1977), 19–45; David Vincent, 'Love and Death in the Nineteenth Century Working Class', *Social History*, 5:2 (1980), 223–47; Antony Taylor, '*Reynolds's Newspaper*, Opposition to Monarchy and the Radical Anti-Jubilee: Britain's Anti-Monarchist Tradition Reconsidered', *Historical Research: The Bulletin of the Institute of*

Historical Research, 68: 167 (1995), 318–37. (**5**) **Theses:** Sheila H. Lazarus, 'The Life and Times of Ben Brierley' (1964), typescript held by Manchester Central Library; Paul S. Salveson, 'Region, Class and Culture: Lancashire Dialect Literature 1746–1935' (PhD, thesis University of Salford, 1993). (**6**) **Obituaries:** *Manchester Courier*, 24 January 1896; *Manchester Guardian*, 20 January 1896; *Newcastle Weekly Chronicle*, 25 January 1896; *Papers of the Manchester Literary Club*, XXII (1896), 489–508, 'Memorial Notices: Ben Brierley'.

OWEN ASHTON

See also: †Abel HEYWOOD; †W. H. CHADWICK.

CHURCH, Archibald George (1886–1954)
LABOUR MP, TRADE UNION LEADER, SCIENTIST, BUSINESSMAN

Archibald George Church was born in the Mile End district of London on 7 September 1886, the son of Thomas William Church, a compositor, and his wife Ada Ellen, née Owen, a schoolmistress. Church was educated at the local county school and also at St. Thomas Charterhouse. He became a student at University College London (UCL) in 1906. Three years later he sat the intermediate examination in science and shortly afterwards entered the teaching profession. He married Gladys Hunter in 1912, and in the same year was awarded a BSc in physics by UCL. In 1914 he became president of the East London Teachers' Association. He joined the army shortly after the outbreak of the First World War and his active service began as a subaltern on the Western Front in 1915. He was transferred to the Royal Flying Corps in 1916 but returned to the Royal Artillery the following year and commanded the 238 Siege Battery until the Armistice. After hostilities had ceased on the Western Front he was dispatched to northern Russia and took charge of the centre column of the 237 Infantry Brigade. Church's military career was distinguished: in addition to attaining the rank of major, he was awarded both the Distinguished Service Order and the Military Cross.

   Church's leadership qualities were demonstrated by his military service and by his prewar prominence as a teachers' leader. Combined with his scientific background, these factors made him a leading candidate for the vacant position of general secretary of the National Union of Scientific Workers (NUSW) in 1919. In December that year he was duly appointed as successor to Eric Sinkinson. At that time the NUSW was a small union with fewer than a thousand members. Its aims were to advance the economic interests of scientific workers and to promote the cause of science in the public arena. Church was well equipped for the latter task: an able journalist, he edited the union's journal, *The Scientific Worker*, during his tenure as general secretary, and from 1920 he contributed unsigned leaders to *Nature* at the behest of his friend Sir Richard Gregory. In the years immediately after the First World War the NUSW's competitors were the Association of University Teachers (AUT) and the Institution of Professional Civil Servants. These unions were somewhat more successful than the NUSW in both recruiting and protecting their members' interests. In 1921, for example, the AUT stole a march on the NUSW by negotiating salary scales with the Treasury and the universities.

   Church's political career began in earnest in 1922 when he was chosen as Labour candidate for the Spelthorne constituency in Middlesex. It is doubtful whether Church's decision to join the Labour Party was motivated by strong radical or socialist convictions. Indeed W. H. G. Armytage claimed in his life of Sir Richard Gregory that Church was hustled into the Labour Party at the insistence of Hyman Levy, a left-wing member of the NUSW executive. Church did, however, believe that the Labour Party's success would prompt the release of greater resources for scientific research, and his consistent advocacy of science became the leitmotif of his political career. Church's decision to stand at Spelthorne caused controversy in the NUSW, although a majority of the union's Council, which met in May 1922, supported his candidature. At that stage Church was particularly active in organising the NUSW's campaign against the Geddes Committee's proposal for cuts in research expenditure at the Air Ministry. The original proposal would have resulted in the dismissal of 50 scientific workers, but the union's tactics, which included deputations to Parliament and a press campaign, were partially successful and only nine Air Ministry scientists were dismissed.

Church failed to win the Spelthorne seat at the 1922 general election, but he proved an able campaigner at the hustings and the Labour vote increased almost threefold.

Spelthorne, 1922: electorate 36 853, turnout 53.9 per cent

Sir P. E. Pilditch (Conservative)	11 604 (66.4 per cent)
A. G. Church (Labour)	5868 (33.6 per cent)
Majority	5736 (32.8 per cent)

As a result Church was nominated as the Labour candidate for East Leyton, where the party stood a much greater chance of success. However some activists in the NUSW felt that Church's party political activities were a distraction from his responsibilities as general secretary. By 1923 the union had recruited barely a fifth of its potential membership in terms of eligible scientific workers at universities and had had little success in attracting either industrial or government scientists into its ranks. Moreover members of the industrial section of the union were critical of Church when a propaganda leaflet to aid their recruitment failed to appear as promised in early 1923.

In December 1923 Church was elected as Labour MP for East Leyton:

Leyton East, 1923: electorate 29 166, turnout 69.1 per cent

A. G. Church (Labour)	7944 (39.5 per cent)
E. E. Alexander (Conservative)	6533 (32.4 per cent)
T. T. Broad (Liberal)	5669 (28.1 per cent)
Majority	1411 (7.1 per cent)

In the 1924 Labour Government he was appointed Parliamentary Private Secretary to Sidney Webb, President of the Board of Trade, and established himself as an assiduous and pragmatic MP. He quickly became an effective advocate on scientific issues. In February 1924, for instance, he used his speech on the Diseases of Animals Bill to deplore the absence of research into foot and mouth disease. The same year he championed the establishment of the Science Advisory Committee of the Labour Party and continued to campaign against the Geddes Committee's recommendation for cuts in research funding. At that time the NUSW Executive Committee was split between a left-wing faction, which wanted the NUSW to be an industrially based, political union, and a moderate group, which envisaged the NUSW campaigning as a non-partisan, professional body. Church's sympathies lay with the latter, but his frequent absences on parliamentary business in 1924 allowed the socialist faction to dominate the NUSW Executive.

His first period in the Commons included controversial interventions on imperial questions. On 18 June 1924 he spoke and voted in favour of specific proposals for imperial preference on tobacco, dried fruits, wines and sugar. The only other Labour MPs who took this position were Leslie Haden Guest, George Spencer and, on two of the categories, James Sexton. Church's case was that in a world where international cooperation was rare, the Empire offered 'a more fruitful field for social regeneration' [for his speech see *Hansard*, 18 June 1924, cols 2199–204, comment on 2201]. Subsequently Church, together with Haden Guest, Frank Hodges and the Engineers' MP, Robert Young, met leading members of the Empire Industries Association on 22 January 1926. The Labour quartet urged the association to place less emphasis on tariffs, and instead to work towards a cross-party programme aimed at reducing unemployment. This would involve development of the Empire. However the scheme proved abortive, partly because of opposition by the Conservative economist and tariff reformer W. A. S Hewins [Gupta (1975) 68–9].

During the lifetime of the 1924 Government, Church became heavily involved in Labour discussions on East African policy. The views of the party's Advisory Committee on Imperial Questions were influenced by reformers such as E. D. Morel, who championed the protection of Africans' land rights in the face of settlers' demands, and criticised the emphasis on development that typically reduced the African to the status of an abysmally paid wage labourer. The Secretary of State for the Colonies, J. H. Thomas, was not sympathetic to his own party's critics of imperial policy. Having appointed an East African Committee of 19, including a minority of critics, he then appointed an East African Commission of three, consisting of Church, W. G. A. Ormsby-Gore (a past and future Colonial Office minister) and a Liberal, Frederick Linfield. The larger East African Committee never visited Africa and its career was effectively terminated by the defeat of the Labour Government. In contrast the members of the East African Commission arrived in Cape Town on 1 September 1924, where they met the South African Premier Hertzog before travelling north. They spent most of their time in Kenya, Uganda and Tanganyika, but carried out limited surveys in Northern Rhodesia and Nyasaland. They arrived in England on 23 December.

Their report (Command 2387) was published in April 1925. Church claimed that most of the report had been written by Ormsby-Gore and himself. One Labour critic, Norman Leys, characterised the report as 'an official apologia'. Certainly within the Labour Party, Church's position was often viewed as pro-European settler especially in the Kenyan context. In other publications and in a memorandum to the party's Advisory Committee on Imperial Questions he emphasised the need for scientific development and railway construction, along with the need for more European settlers [see his 'Black and White in East Africa', *Labour Magazine*, March 1925, pp. 441–4, and his Memorandum to the Advisory Committee On Imperial Questions, 16B, May 1925, 'Report on East African Commission']. Inevitably he crossed swords with Labour critics of established imperial policies. One comment expressed a widely accepted conservative wisdom:

> The needs of the native are very easily satisfied. The small native cultivator needs only sufficient means to buy his wife or wives a few beads and a few yards of cloth, to pay his Government tax and to pay for liquor. Customarily, once he has broken the ground on his plot his women and children do the rest of the work until harvest time. In the intervening period he will often hire himself out to a European settler, and once he has earned enough money to satisfy his modest needs he will return home ['Black and White in East Africa', pp. 443–4].

Norman Leys responded to this in another memorandum to the Advisory Committee [no. 14, 'Notes for Speakers in the Forthcoming Debate on East African Policy'], in which he effectively accused Church of ignoring the widespread poverty amongst Africans. Typical wages were eight to ten shillings a month, which was an indication not of a preference for a simple life but of powerlessness – 'such wages are bitterly resented by those who receive them, unable as they are to make any effort to increase them without breaking the law' [Memorandum to the Advisory Committee on Imperial Questions, no. 14]. Leys likened Church's alleged lack of understanding and sensitivity to similar sentiments in Britain: 'One knows of people in this country who say workmen waste their money when paid more than enough for bare necessities' [ibid.] Church's involvement in the East Africa parliamentary enquiry led to him writing a book, *East Africa a New Dominion*, published in 1927. The moderate nature of his commitment to the Labour Party was emphasised by his admission in the book that capitalism, despite its imperfections, was 'the system which still obtains in all civilised countries'.

Although the Labour vote increased in East Leyton in the general election of 1924, Church lost his seat. The campaign was conducted in his absence as he was in the middle of his investigations for the East African Commission.

Leyton East, 1924: electorate 29 506, turnout 77.6 per cent

E. E. Alexander (Conservative)	10 649	(46.4 per cent)
A. G. Church (Labour)	9087	(34.7 per cent)
R. W. Puddicombe (Liberal)	3174	(13.9 per cent)
Majority	1562	(6.7 per cent)

Shortly afterwards, in December 1924, the left-wing faction of the NUSW was defeated by Church and his moderate allies at a Council meeting. As a result the union decided not to affiliate to the Trades Union Congress. It was clear from the NUSW's annual account for 1925 that the union's financial position had become perilous: Church's salary of £500 accounted for nearly half of the union's income. Church's decision to support the deregistration of the NUSW as a trade union in January 1926 was indicative of his moderation, but it was also motivated by pragmatism. By so doing, Church hoped that the NUSW would increase its recruitment amongst museum workers and scientists working in the navy and government laboratories. By September 1926, however, the NUSW was facing a crisis: the membership level had stagnated and, to make matters worse, over 500 of the union's 889 members had failed to pay their subscriptions. A few months previously the NUSW Executive Committee had censured Church for what it saw as his lackadaisical approach to the implementation of policies.

During 1926 Church made three visits to Germany at the instigation of his close friend, Heinrich Brüning. There he studied the Christian Trade Union Movement, of which Brüning was General Secretary. The following year he visited Germany again, this time for a lecture tour of the Ruhr. Brüning, a devout Catholic and centre party politician, became Reich Chancellor in March 1930 and held office, in the face of economic collapse and the increasing strength of the Nazi Party, until May 1932. His economic response to the great Depression was thoroughly orthodox. Although he and Hitler were mutually antipathetic, his resort to emergency powers demonstrated a willingness to consider authoritarian solutions to crises. The initiative further weakened the legitimacy of the beleaguered Weimar Republic. Church's friendship with Brüning was a curious one for a Labour politician as Brüning's government was a coalition of the centre-right and excluded that staple of Weimar administrations, the Social Democrats. A characterisation of Brüning as a 'pure technician' in politics suggests one reason for their affinity [Craig (1978) 538].

In a recruitment drive launched by Church and his colleagues in February 1927 it was claimed that the NUSW was a non-political body, and to emphasise this point the union changed its name to the Association of Scientific Workers (AScW) in May that year. The membership campaign met with some success, and by October 1927 the AScW had over 1600 members. However it soon became obvious that the membership drive had stalled. Very little propaganda was produced by the AScW to consolidate its membership gains, and despite prompting by the Industrial Section, Church failed to follow up and recruit potential members. Nor were the suggestions for new branches implemented, and although a subcommittee of the AScW recommended drastic changes in the organisation's structure, it remained unreformed. Furthermore Church faced renewed criticism at the AScW Council meeting in May 1928 for failing to follow through policy decisions. The Executive Committee, led by G. S. Baker, defended Church partly on the ground that he was a useful source of contacts for the AScW, and his pay rise, from £500 to £600 per annum, was confirmed. Nevertheless the AScW continued to lose ground to its competitors, not least the Institute of Professional Civil Servants. By 1929 the latter had recruited most of the scientists in the Civil Service and had more than doubled its total membership in four years.

In April 1929 Church founded *The Realist*, which he edited. *The Realist* was an innovative journal of scientific humanism – its contributors included J. B. S. Haldane, Julian Huxley and Sigmund Freud – but it folded a few months later when Lord Melchett, its main backer, lost heavily on the Stock Market. Church re-entered Parliament after the general election of May 1929, when he gained Wandsworth Central for Labour:

Wandsworth Central, 1929: electorate 39 258, turnout 69.5 per cent

A. G. Church (Labour)	11 404 (41.8 per cent)
Sir H. Jackson (Conservative)	11 104 (40.7 per cent)
A. W. Duthie (Liberal)	4784 (17.5 per cent)
Majority	300 (1.1 per cent)

Church was appointed as Parliamentary Private Secretary to the Secretary of State for War, Tom Shaw, and in August 1929 he travelled to Berlin. After discussions with Brüning, Hjalmar Schacht (president of the Reichsbank), and other prominent Germans, Church prepared a memorandum for Arthur Henderson and Philip Snowden on the Young Plan for reparations and the evacuation of the Rhineland.

By 1929 the AScW's financial position had worsened almost to the point of bankruptcy, and as a result it was forced to suspend publication of the *Scientific Worker*. At the annual meeting in February 1930, Church's critics rounded on him for neglecting the AScW's interests. In April 1930 an AScW committee concluded that the failed membership drive had exacerbated the association's financial problems. This prompted Church to offer his resignation, which the Executive refused to accept. In June, Church announced to the AScW Council that he had received a gift of £500, which he proposed to donate to the association. In return the Council appointed a membership officer to relieve Church of his day-to-day administrative duties. Church himself was retained on a much reduced salary to continue his parliamentary activities on behalf of the association. Church resigned as general secretary of the AScW in the spring of 1931 and became organising secretary of the British Science Guild, a body dedicated to promoting science and scientific methods.

Church's loyalty to the Labour government was called into question when he voted for an opposition amendment to the Expiring Laws Continuance Bill in December 1930 and resigned as a parliamentary private secretary. His specific concern was with the retention of the Dyestuffs Act. The government had decided against retention without, in Church's view, consulting scientific opinion, which was concerned about the prospect of repeal [*The Times*, 5 January 1931]. Shortly afterwards Church sounded out George Bowyer, the vice-chairman of the Wandsworth Conservative Association, about the possibility of transferring his allegiance [Bowyer to Church, 27 January 1931, Church Papers 9560]. Church defied the government whips again in March 1931 when he voted against the abolition of university constituencies. He insisted that he did not believe 'in the principle that one must merely count noses in order to determine representation' [*Hansard*, 16 March 1931, col. 1732]. His assertion in the debate that 'members of my party have had a curious affection [for Russia] since it lapsed into appalling tyranny' indicated the fragility of his adherence to some Labour Party sentiments [ibid., col. 1734]. In the same month Church appealed to Brüning to back a Social Democratic motion in the German parliament to remove the ban on the distribution of the film *All Quiet on the Western Front* in the Weimar Republic. The ban was subsequently lifted. When the Reich Chancellor visited London in June 1931, Church held a dinner for him at Claridges. Some of the other guests were far removed from Labour Party circles: Viscount Astor, Sir Robert Horne, Lord Weir and Count Bernstoff [*The Times*, 9 June 1931].

In June 1931 the Wandsworth Labour Party, exasperated by Church's parliamentary rebellions, announced that Church would not be asked to stand as Labour candidate for the constituency at the next general election [*The Times*, 27 June 1931]. Church continued to cause controversy by sponsoring a Private Member's Bill in July 1931 to legalise the sterilisation of mental defectives [*Hansard*, 21 July 1931, cols 1249–52]. The Bill failed to pass its first reading, a fact that Church later blamed on 'sentimentalists' in the Labour Party. In August 1931 he told an interviewer for the *Norwood News* that he believed that the Labour Party should not be dominated by the working class.

The Labour Party National Executive Committee met on 20 August 1931 amidst the economic and political crisis that would soon destroy the second Labour government. Prior to meeting senior ministers in conjunction with the Trades Union Congress General Council, the NEC conducted some routine business. One item was Church's relationship with the Wandsworth Central Divisional Party; the NEC agreed that the Wandsworth Party could select a new candidate. At odds with his constituency party and out of sympathy with the national Labour Party, it is not surprising that Church was one of the few Labour MPs to support Ramsay MacDonald after the formation of the National Government in August 1931. Unusually for a National Labour MP, the subsequent general election did not bring him success. He explored the possibility of standing for both Wandsworth and Leyton, but withdrew his canditure from both his old constituencies in rapid succession. In each case his chances were undermined by the unwillingness of the Conservative candidate to stand down in his favour. He stood instead for the London University seat, where the retiring MP, Sir Ernest Graham-Little had come forward as an independent supporter of the National Government. In his address Church claimed that while he could not give his allegiance to any party he would support MacDonald. As ever, he stressed that he wanted to advance the cause of science in Parliament. However he lost heavily to the incumbent [for Church's situation in October 1931, see letters in MacDonald Papers PRO 30/69 1176]:

London University, 1931: electorate 16 501, turnout 70.3 per cent

Sir E. G. G. Graham-Little (National Independent)	8461 (73.0 per cent)
A. G. Church (National)	3134 (27.0 per cent)
Majority	5327 (46.0 per cent)

In January 1932 Church travelled to the United States on behalf of Baird Television, whose board he had joined the previous year. Church returned to Britain in April 1932, but shortly afterwards Brüning urgently requested that he visit Berlin to discuss the reparations issue. Consequently Church travelled to Rome, Vienna, Warsaw and Prague in an attempt to rally support for a world economic conference. Amongst those he lobbied were Beneš and Masaryk in Prague and Pilsudski in Warsaw. Church was conscious that he was neglecting his responsibilities to the British Science Guild (BSG), and to make amends he donated £100 to the BSG and waived his salary for the first six months of the year. Nevertheless when the BSG Council met in July 1932 some members expressed their disappointment that Church was unable to report on any work that he had done for the Guild. In November 1932 Church was criticised by BSG Council members for using their names in interviews with the press. A few months later he resigned his position as organising secretary, citing as reasons the disagreements he had had with the BSG Council and his disappointment that he had been unable to increase the BSG's membership.

Church fought Bristol East as a National Labour candidate in the general election of 1935, declaring that he did not believe in the class struggle or in party politics. The campaign was rowdy, and violence flared at one meeting when Church claimed that anyone voting for his socialist opponent, Sir Stafford Cripps, was a traitor. Church later withdrew the remark but lost the election:

Bristol East, 1935: electorate 48 975, turnout 75.8 per cent

Hon. Sir R. S. Cripps (Labour)	22 009 (59.3 per cent)

A. G. Church (National Labour)   15 126 (40.7 per cent)

Majority   6 883 (18.6 per cent)

As a result of his contact with Brüning and other significant Germans, Church's views on Germany were eagerly sought by the press. In April 1936, for instance, he warned that the Nazis were unlikely to confine their aggressive intentions to Europe. When J. H. Thomas resigned his seat in Derby, Church was selected to fight the subsequent by-election as the National Labour candidate. The election was fought largely on the issue of the government's handling of foreign affairs, with Church supporting the government line that any intensification of the sanctions imposed against Italy for invading Abyssinia would be undesirable. His Labour opponent, Philip Noel-Baker, was a recognised specialist in international affairs and had the support of Lloyd George. During the Derby campaign Lord Allen of Hurtwood (formerly Clifford Allen), who had sided with MacDonald in 1931, asserted that 'the National Government is no longer fit to represent the nation' [*The Times*, 3 July 1936]. Church felt Noel-Baker would appeal more to Liberals, and that some Derby Conservatives, although not the Conservative MP, were luke-warm in their support for him [see his letters to Ramsay MacDonald on 29 June and 12 July, MacDonald Papers, 1182]. Church was unable to prevent Noel-Baker from wining the seat for Labour:

Derby, 9 July 1936: electorate 82 571, turnout 65.5 per cent

P. J. Noel-Baker (Labour)   28 419 (52.5 per cent)
A. G. Church (National Labour)   25 666 (47.5 per cent)

Majority   2753 (5.0 per cent)

Church remained the prospective National Labour candidate for Derby for a few years after the by-election. In January 1938 he presided over the first demonstration of television in the town. He remained a loyal supporter of the National Government, and of Chamberlain's policy of appeasement in particular. He continued to expound his unconventional and sometimes perspicacious views: in November 1939, for example, he supported the idea of a federal union of European states. Church was an occasional editor of the National Labour journal, *The Newsletter*, and in 1940 he was made treasurer of the National Labour Party. The following year he was appointed as assistant director of fighting-vehicle production at the Ministry of Supply, a post he held until 1945. He fought South Tottenham as an Independent National candidate in the general election of 1945, but finished bottom of the poll:

Tottenham, 1945: electorate 36 261, turnout 69.0 per cent

F. Messer (Labour)   18 335 (73.3 per cent)
A. L. Bateman (Conservative)   4480 (17.9 per cent)
A. G. Church (Independent National)   2193 (8.8 per cent)

Majority   13 855 (55.4 per cent)

Thereafter he concentrated on his business activities. He was chairman of the Raven Oil Company until 1951 and held a similar position with the Churwick Manufacturing Company.

Church's political career was colourful. Though elected twice as a Labour MP, he was never really a socialist and indeed felt more comfortable outside the conventional party system. His views were a quixotic mixture of the far-sighted and the eccentric, but he was a doughty and consistent champion of the cause of science. Unfortunately his parliamentary and publishing activities prevented him from concentrating on his work as general secretary of the AScW, and the latter's problems in the period 1925–30 can partly be attributed to this. He died in London on 23 August 1954 and was survived by his second wife, Katherine Mary Strange, whom he had married in 1945, and by a son and daughter from his first marriage. He left an estate valued at £9019 16s 8d.

Writings: 'The State and Research', *Scientific Worker*, 1:10 (December 1925), 184–5; 'Black and White in East Africa', *Labour Magazine*, February/March 1925; Memorandum to Labour Party Advisory Committee on Imperial Questions, May 1925, 16B Report of East Africa Commission; 'The Inter-relations of East African Territories', *Geographical Journal*, LXVII (May 1926), 215–31; 'Mr Ormsby-Gore's Service to Science', *Scientific Worker*, 5:1 (February 1929), 5–6; *East Africa, a New Dominion. A crucial experiment in tropical development and its significance to the British Empire* (1927); 'Science and the New Parliament – Parliamentary Science Committee', *Scientific Worker*, 5:4 (August 1929), 77–80, and *Scientific Worker*, 5:5 (October 1929), 92–3; *Proposals for the Extension of Old Age Pension and National Health Insurance*, with R. Davison, N. Moller, F. Stewart, J. Worthington (1938).

Sources: (1) **MSS:** Association of Scientific Workers archives (ref. MSS.79/AScW), MRC, University of Warwick; Archibald Church Papers (ref. add. 9560), Cambridge University Library; Ramsay MacDonald Papers, PRO. (2) **Other:** Two Memoranda to Labour Party by Norman Leys, 1925, nos 14 and 16; 'Association of Scientific Workers – ten years' work', *Scientific Worker*, 4:4 (August/September 1928), 83–8; *Scientific Worker*, 4:5 (October 1928), 113–7; B. Holman, 'The ASW – twenty years history', *Scientific Worker*, 11:3 (Autumn 1939), 68–73; W. H. G. Armytage, *Sir Richard Gregory, his life and work* (1957); P. S. Gupta, *Imperialism and the British Labour Movement 1914–1964* (New York, 1975); K. MacLeod, 'Politics, Professionalism and the Organisation of Scientists: the Association of Scientific Workers 1917–42' (unpublished PhD thesis, Sussex University, 1975); Gordon A. Craig, *Germany 1866–1945* (Oxford, 1978); R. and K. MacLeod, 'The Contradictions of Professionalism: scientists, trade unionism and the First World War', *Social Studies of Science*, 9 (1979), 1–32. (3) **Obituaries:** *The Times*, 24 August 1924; *Wandsworth Borough News*, 27 August 1954; *WWW 1951–60*.

RICHARD TEMPLE

COHEN, Rose (1894–1937)
COMMUNIST

Rose Cohen was born in Stepney, London, on 20 May 1894, the daughter of Morris Cohen, a Jewish tailor of Polish origin, and his wife Ada, née Desfatic. Little is known of Rose's family background, but it is likely that her father, who had formerly worked as a tailor's machinist, prospered at his trade. For summary biographical details we are heavily reliant on questionnaires filled out by Cohen in Russia at various times from 1923 onwards. In these she unambiguously describes her social origins as 'proletariat' and both her parents and herself as 'workers' [RGASPI 17/98/724, questionnaires of 14 October 1930 and 11 December 1935]. This could be taken as conclusive evidence of her background, were it not for the well-attested pressure to play down bourgeois antecedents in such documents, particularly after 1927, when Cohen moved permanently to Russia after marrying into the new Soviet elite. For this reason, the possibility that her circumstances were comfortable should not be dismissed. Furthermore Cohen had remained at secondary school until 1911 and then spent a year at commercial school, presumably supported by her family. She did not take up paid employment until she was 18, when she joined the rapidly expanding class of women clerical workers and soon afterwards secured employment with the London County Council's Education Department. She later dated her membership of the National Union of Clerks from 1914.

The other clue to her family circumstances dates from the war years, when Cohen, like many others, cut her political teeth at the Fabian (later Labour) Research Department (LRD). The LRD's tremendous activity depended largely on the voluntary or poorly paid efforts of a brilliant young cohort of middle-class activists, one of whose most persistent grumbles was about the alleged niggardliness of the LRD's founders, Sidney and Beatrice Webb. To the rebels of Cohen's generation the Webbs were simultaneously figures of fun, resentment and dependency, and their parsimony was celebrated in a satirical poem penned by two of the young activists, Margaret Postgate (later Cole) and Alan Kaye. The Sadie Heiser they refer to in the poem – the spelling varies according to the source – was another of the FRD's research workers, and the 'Statesman' is of course the *New Statesman*, another of the Webbs' creations, founded in 1913.

> In the Perfect Fabian State
> Sidney Webb,
> Do they pay the Standard Rate
> Webb, oh Webb?
> Where they read the Statesman's pages,
> And Miss Heiser's name is cursed
> For they dare not raise her wages,
> Lest the Petty Cash go burst;
> Does it matter if we rather
> Tend to underpay the Pleb,
> Since Miss Cohen has a father,
> Sidney Webb?
> [Postgate and Kaye (1917)]

Whatever her home circumstances, through her work at the LRD, Cohen became inseparable from this able, self-assured and sometimes conceited group of mainly university-educated socialists. In the early 1920s she even shared a London flat with Eva Reckitt and Olive Parsons, both of whom came from decidedly affluent backgrounds [Parsons (1991)]. Her father died at about the same time and she lost her mother later in the 1920s. She had two brothers and three sisters, one of whom, Nellie, married Hugo Rathbone, another LRD full-timer and close associate of R. Palme Dutt.

Cohen is said to have made her first contact with this rebel milieu when attending the Workers' Educational Association (WEA) classes of G. D. H. Cole, the young Oxford don who, in a series of writings, crystallised the philosophy of guild socialism, which provided these rebels with their cause. Possibly through her sister Nellie, who was Sylvia Pankhurst's secretary, she also came into contact with the Workers' Socialist Federation (WSF), and is pictured by Pankhurst contributing to the spring pageant held by the WSF in Bow Baths in 1916:

> The two pretty Cohens, one as slender as the lily she represented and the other, Nellie, my secretary, glowing as a ripe peach; fair, straight Violet Lansbury, garlanded with primroses, 'the Spirit of Spring'. Pale Lily Gatward was the 'Spirit of Liberty', and beside her Joan Beauchamp, a stern, stiff young 'Spirit of Peace', who afterwards became the editor of the *Conscientious Objectors' Tribunal*, and went to gaol for it [Pankhurst (1932) 274–5].

With the apparent exception of Gatward, all were later active in the British Communist Party. Lansbury like Cohen, also spent a decade in the Soviet Union, returning safely and apparently unmoved just a few months after Cohen's disappearance in the purges. The Cohens and Joan Beauchamp were also to become involved with the LRD, and it may have been through Cole's influence that Cohen gave up working for the LCC to take up the more uncertain prospect of employment at the department in 1916 or 1917. The LRD was initially located in the Fabian Society's offices in Tothill Street, Westminster, and until 1916 membership was confined to members of the parent body, away from which Cole and the rebels had stormed the previous year. However, in the summer of 1916, in what may be regarded as sage recognition of their interdependency and commonality of interest, the Webbs opened up the still 'Fabian' research department to members of all recognised labour and socialist bodies. Cohen, along with Cole, W. N. Ewer and Ellen Wilkinson, was one of the first to be admitted under the new dispensation, and all were members of the recently formed National Guilds League. The following month they were joined by J. T. Walton Newbold, Eva Reckitt, Daisy Lansbury (later Postgate) and Margaret Postgate [FRD executive minutes, 27 July and 21 September 1916]. With the exception of the Coles, all were to find their way into the infant Communist Party and to provide it with its most distinguished intellectual adherents.

Due largely to the several literary memorials of Margaret Cole, a romantic aura surrounds these rebel networks, which were based upon the LRD but also extended to the University Socialist Federation and the No Conscription Fellowship. In her memoirs, published in 1949, Cole described it (as apparently its initiates characterised it at the time) as the 'Movement': 'neither a party nor a defined and organised society, but rather a nucleus of "comrades", surrounded by a larger penumbra of "sympathisers"'.

The Movement proper contained, so far as I remember, nobody over thirty, and hardly any of its members had incomes of any size. As a result we had scarcely any personal ties ... in effect we lived as well as worked together with our eyes on the job, and almost oblivious to the events of the war – even of air-raids ... Being so dedicated, we were extraordinarily happy, so happy that we never realised it fully, but worked ourselves into states of tremendous agitation over minute differences in the philosophy of Guild Socialism ... None of these controversies, however, went really deep; what split 'the Movement' asunder was, alas, the aftermath of the Russian Revolution, which at first we had all hailed with such delight [Cole (1949) 61–2, 72–3].

It is an idyllic picture, written during the Cold War and rather deliberately pointing to the contrast with the more brutal and manipulative methods that arrived in Britain with the Communist Party. No doubt there is much to be said for such a view, but the lacunae in such mythologising should also be recorded. One is the omission of any reference to the LRD's assistant secretary, Alan Kaye: afterwards a forgotten figure but described by R. Page Arnot, the LRD's sometime secretary and historian, as the outstanding contributor to the LRD's wartime success [Arnot (1926) 16]. Nowhere in Cole's several accounts is it recorded that in May 1919 Kaye had committed suicide with Heiser in circumstances that had left both Margaret Cole and her husband wracked with guilt [Morgan (2003) vol. 2]. Evidently some things had gone 'really deep', but by the early 1970s Kaye's involvement with the LRD was not even being alluded to [Cole (1971)]. Cohen's tragic death in Stalin's purges was to give rise to a similar reticence.

It was through the LRD that Cohen made the first of the Russian contacts that were to lead to this awful reckoning. By 1918 she was full-time secretary to the LRD's women's section, and when in October that year the department officially became the Labour Research Department, operating under a new constitution from the offices of the newly established Labour Party, she was appointed as assistant secretary – succeeding, or perhaps supplanting, Kaye. Her salary – not quite as exiguous as the rebels suggested – was £182 [LRD-headed notepaper, *ca* 1918, Woolf papers I/L/10; LRD minutes, AGM, 12 October, 20 December 1918]. Remaining on the payroll until May 1923, Cohen was thus a dependent and a beneficiary of the arrangement by which Arcos (the All-Russian Co-operative Society, which was intimately linked to the Soviet Trade Delegation) stepped in with guaranteed contract work to safeguard the LRD's future after its links with the Labour Party were severed in 1921 [Morgan (2003) vol. 1]. That also proved the occasion for the LRD's founders to break their links with the department, for reasons which now seem rather persuasive. As Beatrice Webb noted in her diary on 7 October 1921, 'The FRD – a promising child of ours – ends in a lunatic asylum':

To take your livelihood from the Russian Government, when millions of Russians are starving, for services which are obviously unreal or, at any rate, irrelevant to famine, is rather a poor business ... The four paid officers of the LRD voted themselves into good salaries out of Russian funds ... and rejected the idea of a members' meeting ...

Although Arnot and G. D. H. Cole were chiefly responsible for the arrangement, Cohen was clearly one of the parties whose motives Beatrice interpreted so cynically. Certainly it was the Russians who were now best able to underwrite such forms of employment, and when two years later Cohen applied for unpaid leave of absence to take up employment in Russia she anticipated by a matter of weeks the formal announcement that the LRD's arrangement with Arcos was to be discontinued. Presumably already acting upon this information, in May 1923 she took up work in Moscow for the English section of the Comintern's press department [LRD minutes, 4 May 1923; Cohen questionnaire, 21 May 1923].

Details of the next period of her life are somewhat fragmentary. In May 1924 she was pictured in the *Workers' Weekly*, accompanying Tom Mann, Robert Dunstan and the CPGB's Moscow representative Bob Stewart to the agricultural village of Faustova, about 40 miles from Moscow. Dunstan was a visiting Labour candidate and on his return from Russia he announced his adhesion to the CPGB – it was presumably for his benefit that the visit had been arranged [*Workers' Weekly*, 6 June 1924]. Cohen herself returned to Britain before the end of the year. According to her party questionnaires, she was employed successively by the Soviet embassy and the Arcos Steamship Company. At least until he took up a readership at Oxford in the spring of 1925, she also worked for some months as part-time private secretary to G. D. H. Cole, a sign that the tightening Communist control over the LRD had not yet caused a severing of personal relations [Cole (1971) 203]. The following year Cohen went to Paris, where for several months she carried out undisclosed Comintern responsibilities before settling permanently in Moscow in the spring of 1927.

She went there as the wife or intended wife of Max Petrovsky, and it was Petrovsky who secured her release from party duties in Britain. Born in 1886, a Ukrainian Jew and former Bundist, in 1924 Petrovsky had been appointed as Comintern delegate to the CPGB under the pseudonym Bennett, and in the ensuing period he had established close relations with many of the party's leading figures. Cohen, as is well known, preferred his advances to those of the future CPGB general secretary, Harry Pollitt, who claimed to have been spurned by her 'fourteen times' [Morgan (1993) 126]. If we can trust the recollections of Ivy Litvinov, the British-born wife of Soviet Foreign Minister Maxim Litvinov, the relationship between Cohen and Petrovsky was not a physically close one, but Petrovsky offered more than just personal attraction and a shared commitment to Communism. A veteran of the Red Army, like all Bolsheviks he bore something of the glamour of the workers' state and for Cohen the marriage must have seemed like marrying into the Revolution itself. An enthusiast of Russian culture and the ballet even before 1917 [Reckitt (1941) 79, 148], once having lived there for a while and acquired the rudiments of the language, Cohen's life in Russia must have seemed a release from the pettier and more circumscribed world of the struggling British Communist Party. The very fact that she learned not only Russian but also French and a little German suggests an openness to the new world of the International that was not displayed by many British Communists.

In its early years the CPGB was strongly proletarian and heavily male-dominated, and there is a suggestion that the less restrictive world of the Moscow institutions held a particular attraction for a number of talented women party activists. From the LRD alone, Olive Budden and Jane Tabrisky, both university-educated, were among those who went to take up duties in Moscow in the course of the 1920s. Cohen herself, while being entrusted with more obviously 'political' responsibilities than most women Communists, had experienced at first hand the frustrations of the CPGB's rather orthodox attitude toward gender roles. In 1924 she had been proposed to replace the reportedly ineffectual Tom Bell as political secretary to the CPGB's Colonial Bureau. There is no suggestion that she lacked the required political skills, but on the urging of William Gallacher that 'a man' be chosen instead the appointment was blocked [Morgan (2003) vol. 1]. That was symptomatic. Generally speaking, the CPGB primarily regarded women cadres as a supply of technical workers, and though in 1927 the party initially resisted Cohen being sent at Petrovsky's behest to Moscow, the 'indispensable' work for which she alone was said to be qualified was merely that of assisting yet another Scottish male, J. R. Campbell, at the party's Parliamentary Department. By this time Cohen had served as secretary of the CPGB's 'Unattached Groups' Committee, as a member of its Colonial Committee and – presumably through her association with Pollitt – as secretary of the Central Industrial Committee. Nevertheless, in addition to her feelings for Petrovsky, it was understandable that for a woman of ambition and ability the more sexually egalitarian structures of the Comintern exercised their own pull.

For her first three years in Moscow, Cohen worked as a secretary and 'referent' – a sort of consultant – in the Comintern's Anglo-American Secretariat. In the straitened circumstances of the time this meant a relatively privileged existence, and doubly so through her marriage to Petrovsky, who on removal from Comintern work found employment with the Soviet Supreme Economic Council as a presidium member and chief of the Industrial Cadres' Department. Freda Utley, a close friend of Cohen until her own marriage to a non-party Russian brought her face-to-face with the harsher aspects of Soviet life, commented with some acerbity on this cosseted existence. 'Of course the English people have no conception of what life in Moscow is like; they are all provided with rooms & food etc', Utley wrote in August 1928.

Generally I find the English crowd here divided into cliques which makes one feel uncomfortable & afraid of butting in even when they seem to be very amiable and friendly. Rose Cohen I have taken rather an objection to – she is so very smooth & insincere and also so terribly conceited. She really implies herself to be *the* power in the Eng[lish] section of the Comintern' [Utley to Hutt, 29 August 1928].

One cannot know whether Cohen was among the London friends whom Utley accused of snubbing her husband because he was not a party member. But there is no doubt that she enjoyed the privileged existence that her former friend found so hypocritical [Utley (1949) 52 and *passim*].

According to Ivy Litvinov, Cohen even became 'quite a little celebrity'. After a period of study at the International Lenin School in 1930–31, she commenced work as head of the foreign department at the *Moscow Daily News*, a paper initially edited by Anne Louise Strong and serving as the voice – sometimes a quite critical one – of foreign specialists in the Soviet Union. Litvinov worked at the paper under Cohen, and in a brief memoir of the period describes how Cohen overdressed her son Alyosha in plus fours and cloth caps, and in all essential respects enjoyed the lifestyle of the emerging pseudo-bourgeoisie. 'Well, I think everybody has got a flat now, don't you', she would say if the question of overcrowding came up, and in 1934 she described a long summer vacation spent travelling through the Caucasus, visiting oil works and tea plantations as guests of honour (in a letter she referred to 'orgies' of food and drink), before spending three weeks 'recovering' in the Black Sea resort of Sochi. According to Litvinov, Cohen displayed exactly the same complacency when the arrests began. It is suggestive of her 'they don't take me' sort of attitude that she apparently returned from a visit to Britain of her own free will in 1936, the year the show trials began. Shortly afterwards she appears to have relinquished her British passport, despite the fact that the growing arbitrariness of the regime was becoming more apparent by the day [Litvinov (1983); Beckett (1995) 71]. Against this should be set the denial of the British authorities that her passport had ever been returned, as was customary in such cases, while the presence of her husband, and especially her son Alyosha, meant that she was now held fast to her adopted country by more than just career and political conviction. The absence of any real sense of insecurity nevertheless seems clear, and up to that point there was no hint of a sombre note in her letters home to her sister.

In one of the most brutal episodes in the relatively placid history of the CPGB, Cohen was arrested as an alleged British spy on 13 August 1937. Her case was heard three months later, on

28 November 1937, and she was shot the same day. No rational explanation of the charges can be attempted, but a number of possible contributory factors can be identified. One was her association with the *Moscow Daily News*, a focal point for foreign communists, which in the enveloping conservatism of the early 1930s had earned a considerable reputation for social heterodoxy. Utley referred caustically to attempts in Stalin's Moscow 'to recreate the London and New York radical Bohemian atmosphere of hard drinking and easy loving'. She particularly singled out Charles Ashleigh, a British-born former Wobbly working on the *News*, 'who was now a debauched, fat little man, who would lead in the singing of songs which might sometimes be funny but were usually just nasty'. Ashleigh – as Utley's somewhat stereotypical language suggests – was a homosexual, and in 1934 he was denounced by a housemate as a 'centre of demoralising vice' around whom there existed 'a group of foreigners – English and German – who were openly practising homosexuality'. After being reported to the Moscow Control Commission, Ashleigh was expelled from the country. According to the NKVD agent Julius Hecker, this episode largely precipitated Stalin's draconian decree against homosexuality the same year [Utley (1949) 119–20; Beatrice Webb Diaries, 22 August 1934]. There is no suggestion in these sources that Cohen was also inclined to 'bohemianism', however expressed, and the few descriptions we have of her even suggest respectability. But in a phantasmagoric world of guilt by association, especially in the case of foreigners, mere employment in such an institution might have provided a ground for suspicion.

More important were Cohen's connections with Petrovsky and Pollitt. The former had been arrested some five months before Cohen, and had been shot in September 1937. Nevertheless it was possibly her link with Pollitt that was more damaging. On receiving news of Petrovsky's arrest, Pollitt had responded to the Comintern's request for information about his activities with an unequivocal testimony in his favour, affirming his 'very warm personal friendship' with Petrovsky and his confidence in his unwavering loyalty to Stalin and the international Communist movement. The news of the arrest, he wrote, had come as 'one of the greatest shocks of my life' [RGASPI 495/74/34, Pollitt to 'Comrade Pitt' (Dimitrov), 12 April 1937]. Almost simultaneously Pollitt wrote Cohen a gossipy, diverting, pick-me-up sort of letter on party and personal affairs, wholly unexceptionable but ending obliquely: 'We all send our love. Don't lose heart' [RGASPI 495/14/265, ECCI Cadres Department report on CPGB leading personnel, 14 January 1939, citing Pollitt to Cohen, 10 April 1937]. The contents of that letter, which was unlikely to have reached Cohen, were carefully noted by the Comintern Cadres Department. As we now know, in the summer of Cohen's arrest materials were beginning to be collected for a proposed Comintern show trial in which Pollitt was initially to have figured among the chief accused. His support for and identification with an exposed 'traitor' was only one of the contributory factors, but it was hardly coincidental that Cohen's arrest occurred the very day that Pollitt arrived in Moscow to discuss the political situation in Britain. This would have been his first opportunity to meet with Cohen since the arrest of her husband. Was her arrest designed to prevent any discussion between them? Was it hoped that Cohen would provide incriminating information to use against Pollitt? Or was it indeed intended as a form of leverage against Pollitt himself, through the closest attachment he had in Moscow? Whatever the explanation, which only the NKVD records can reveal, while in Moscow Pollitt is said to have made strong representations about Cohen's case. This can hardly have assuaged the suspicions now being directed against himself, however his ultimate loyalty remained undoubted and intact, and on his return to Britain he apparently did nothing to publicise the case [Thorpe (2000) 237–41; Starkov (1994)].

Nevertheless, emanating from what was presumably a Communist source, news of the arrest soon began to percolate among the British left. In December 1937 Beatrice Webb noted it in her diary, along with the false but not – for those acquainted with Ashleigh's case – incredible rumour that Cohen was being allowed to leave the USSR [Beatrice Webb Diaries, 13 December 1937]. Nobody at that time, and apparently for several years afterwards, seems to have suspected that she had been shot [see for example Reckitt (1941)]. In April 1938 the Foreign

Office lodged a formal protest about the case and brief details were publicised in the national press [Thorpe (2000) 240; *Daily Herald*, 25 April 1938]. The *Daily Worker*'s response, which referred to Cohen only as a 'Soviet citizen' and disavowed both the right and the inclination to interfere in the case, has rightly been described by Barry McLoughlin as 'craven' [McLoughlin (2001) 222].

It was left to Maurice Reckitt, a former 'guildsman' who unlike his sister Eva had never been attracted by communism, to attempt to drum up a protest about her plight. The responses, as recorded in his memoirs, were distinctly discouraging, mirroring Emma Goldman's failure to gain support for an agitation on behalf of Russian political prisoners when she visited Britain in 1924–5 [Reckitt (1941); Wexler (1989) ch. 4]. 'A few offered the lame pretext that it would be better for Rose if every one kept silence', Reckitt recorded. 'Others added the barefaced assertion that Soviet justice could in any case be relied on ... Others, again, still more scandalously asserted that no individual's fate was of consequence if they came into contact with the interests of the Soviet Union' [Reckitt (1941) 150]. The 'lame pretext' could well have been offered by Pollitt, who was to express himself in similar terms regarding the post-war Slansky trial of Czech communist leaders, some of whom had been resident in Britain. Perhaps he drew his own inference that his support for Petrovsky had actually helped precipitate Cohen's arrest. The last and more 'scandalous' assertion sounds, by contrast, more like R. Palme Dutt (a former colleague of Cohen's at the LRD), who in 1937 had expressed strikingly similar sentiments to Harold Laski regarding the case of Freda Utley's husband [Morgan (1993) 175]. Worse than Dutt, we know that another communist, Pat Sloan, upheld the charges against Cohen, for in July 1938 Beatrice Webb recorded that he linked her, along with Freda Utley and her husband, with a group of 'hostile elements' at work against Stalin since the early 1930s [Beatrice Webb, diaries, 15 July 1938]. Sloan, an indefatigable Soviet publicist who had spent much of the 1930s teaching in Russia, was of a different generation from Cohen and probably had not known her personally. For the others, however, Reckitt's verdict seems unarguable. 'When it is remembered', he wrote, 'that those who took up these attitudes were not mere detached political observers, but persons who had been for years the very closest friends and admirers of the woman in this appalling predicament, the corrosive influence of Communist ideology upon rudimentary morals and natural affection alike is grievously illustrated' [Reckitt (1949) 150].

But if it is right to regard this affair as a lesson in the darker implications of 'communist ideology', what is less frequently remarked upon is how closely Cohen's life and death were interwoven with the history of a wider British left, unconstrained by such an ideology and yet in many cases not a whit more eloquent on Cohen's behalf. Reckitt approached not just Communists but also other public figures on the left, and over a period of many weeks he secured a derisory nine signatures for a 'studiously moderate' letter of protest to the *New Statesman*, redrafted several times to remove any possible suspicion of ulterior motives. Among the signatories were Cohen's old LRD associates Norman and Monica Ewer, the former now the foreign editor at the *Daily Herald*, plus Raymond and Daisy Postgate [*New Statesman*, 19 November 1938]. Among the absentees were the majority of Cohen's former associates, irrespective whether or not they had joined her in embracing Communism.

A number of eminent Labour figures may particularly be identified. One is George Lansbury, the erstwhile Labour Party leader, who had moved in the same East London Socialist circles and even performed the marionette show at the WSF pageant in 1916. Also Sidney and Beatrice Webb, at least, were reported to have made private enquiries about Cohen's case, but their general reservations about the Soviet 'disease of orthodoxy' did not apparently extend to the publicising of individual cases [RGASPI 495/198/733, Pollitt to CPSU Central Committee Secretariat, 18 July 1956]. More intimately linked with Cohen over a period of several years were Margaret and Douglas Cole. As Margaret Cole was the sister of and both had collaborated with Raymond Postgate, the Coles would certainly have known of the letter of protest, but evidently they declined to be associated with it. Even in later years Cohen's name, like Kaye's, was silently excised from Margaret Cole's standard accounts of guild socialism and the LRD. Though her husband is often remembered as a dissenting voice in an age of bleak polarities, on this occasion the flame did not even flicker. 'Nor am I one of those who, when everything in the new and struggling Socialist community does not go just as they would like, turn their backs on the struggle and proclaim that the Revolution is being betrayed', Cole wrote in Palme Dutt's *Labour Monthly* the month that Cohen was shot. 'Alas, men cannot make a new civilisation without growing pains, or liquidate an ancient tyranny without suffering' [*Labour Monthly*, November 1937, 671–2]. Very probably Cole had not yet even learned of Cohen's arrest. Even so, on behalf of all those who shared his sentiments – and therefore on behalf of Cohen herself – it serves as a sort of epitaph.

Rose Cohen was just one of a number of CPGB members who transferred their membership to the Soviet Communist Party during the 1920s. Many did so for limited periods and soon returned to Britain. Others may have settled permanently in the USSR, and it is easy to believe that in some of these cases the worst may have happened. Even so, Cohen's case was different: different in the sense of its specificity, its immediacy and the absolute disbelief in the charges, and different in what one hopes were sleepless nights of shared memories, requiring not just pushing to the back of one's mind but an active process of denial. To have succumbed to the compulsions of the Stalin era was bad enough. To fail to respond when the opportunity arrived for contrition was possibly even worse.

Following the Khrushchev admissions of 1956, Pollitt, having recently stepped down as CPGB secretary, took the opportunity to press the Soviet authorities for information about Cohen's case. Unable to grasp the implications of Khrushchev's revelations, he continued to deploy long-practised arguments about the dangers of adverse publicity, as if that would now matter to the Russians in the year of the secret speech. He even claimed that Cohen's family exercised a 'great influence in Jewish circles in Britain', though this does not appear to have been the case, and no sign of their alleged concerns has been discovered in the relevant issues of the *Jewish Chronicle* [Pollitt to CPSU Central Committee Secretariat, 18 July 1956].

As a result of Pollitt's intervention, the following month, on 8 August 1956, the charges against Cohen were rescinded by the Soviet Supreme Court. Two years later, on 3 March 1958, she was rehabilitated as a member of the Soviet Communist Party. Despite their apparent futility, these symbolic details mattered to British Communists. The CPGB's newspaper, the *Daily Worker*, was then edited by J. R. Campbell, the party's representative in Moscow in the latter part of the purges, who had privately developed strong reservations about aspects of Soviet rule [Macleod (1997)]. A small recantation would have posed no danger except to the party's reputation. A longer one might have done something to salvage it. But the paper does not appear to have reported either item.

Sources (1) MSS: Comintern Archives, Russian State Archive for Socio-Political History (RGASPI), Moscow; Labour Research Department Archives, London; Margaret Postgate and J. Alan Kaye, 'The apotheosis of socialism: an ode', 1917, Margaret Cole Papers, Nuffield College, Oxford; Sidney Webb, Russian Notebook (1932) and Beatrice Webb, Diaries, Passfield Papers, BLPES; Allen Hutt Papers, CPGB Archives, NMLH; Rose Cohen, letters to her sister Nellie Rathbone, 1034–7, held privately. **(2) Other:** CPGB Biographical Database, University of Manchester; R. Page Arnot, *History of the Labour Research Department* (1926); E. Sylvia Pankhurst, *The Home Front. A mirror to life in England during the World War* (1932); Maurice Reckitt, *As It Happened* (1941); Margaret Cole, *Growing Up Into Revolution*, (1949); Freda Utley, *Lost Illusion* (1949); Margaret Cole, *The Life of G. D. H. Cole* (1971); Margaret Cole, 'Guild Socialism and the Labour Research Department', in Asa Briggs and John Saville (eds), *Essays in Labour History 1886–1923* (1971); Ivy Litvinov, memoir of Rose Cohen in John Carswell, *The Exile. A life of Ivy Litvinov* (1983) 206–8; Alice Wexler, *Emma Goldman in Exile. From the Russian Revolution to the Spanish Civil War* (Boston, 1989); Olive Parsons, interview with Kevin Morgan, 9 October 1991; Kevin Morgan, *Harry Pollitt* (Manchester, 1993); B. Starkov, 'The trial that was not held', *Europe-Asia Studies*, 46 (1994), 1297–315; Francis

Beckett, *Enemy Within. The rise and fall of the British Communist Party* (1995); Alison Macleod, *The Death of Uncle Joe* (1997); Andrew Thorpe, *The British Communist Party and Moscow 1920–1943* (Manchester, 2000); Barry McLoughlin, 'Visitors and victims. British communists in Russia between the wars', in John McIlroy, Kevin Morgan and Alan Campbell (eds), *Party People, Communist Lives. Explorations in biography* (2001), 210–30; Kevin Morgan, *Bolshevism and the British Left*, 2 vols (2003).

Acknowledgements. This entry is based on research carried out as part of the CPGB Biographical Project funded by the ESRC (award R 000 23 8365). The translations of Russian documents are by Monty Johnstone and Francis King.

KEVIN MORGAN
GIDON COHEN

DAVIES, Florence Rose (1882–1958)
INDEPENDENT LABOUR PARTY ACTIVIST, LABOUR ALDERMAN

Rose Davies was born Florence Rose Rees in Aberdare, South Wales in 1882, one of seven children of William Henry Rees, a tin worker, and his wife Fanny. Six of those seven children, including Davies, became teachers. They took the recognised working-class route into the profession; at the age of 14 Davies became a monitor at the Aberdare Town National (Church of England) Infants School. This was followed by a four-year apprenticeship as a pupil teacher in the school, and appointment in December 1900 as assistant mistress. In May 1901 she signed a contract with the managers of the school that gave her a salary of £40 per annum. According to a testimonial written by her headmistress four years later, she was 'thoroughly hard-working and trustworthy … energetic, punctual, attentive to duty', with a 'bright yet firm way of controlling her class … very popular with both teachers and children' [Testimonial, Florence Rose Davies papers, Glamorgan Record Office, GRO].

None of the existing biographical articles or obituaries suggest that Davies' family was politically active (although a W. Rees was one of six members of the short-lived Cwmaman Independent Labour Party (ILP), formed in 1903), but she came into adulthood at a vital time in the political history of Aberdare and its surrounding colliery villages. Her obituarist in the *Aberdare Leader* in 1958 described her emergence into political life 'when Aberdare was feeling the first urgent stirrings of socialism and the scent of battle for feminine emancipation was much in the air' [*Aberdare Leader*, 13 December 1958]. She could not have been unaware, in 1898, of the bitter dispute in the coal industry that led to the creation of the South Wales Miners' Federation, which was to shape the politics of the region for much of the next century. In the year she became an assistant school mistress, at the age of 18, the constituency of Merthyr Tydfil Boroughs, of which Aberdare formed a part, had elected its first, and Wales's first, Independent Labour MP, James Keir Hardie, breaching the Liberal domination of the two-member constituency. The ILP was set to become an important force in local politics over the next few years.

However it seems that Davies' initial political awakening was as a feminist in the teaching profession. That teachers formed a significant occupational bloc in the ILP in south Wales has been noted by historians, and Aberdare provides perhaps one of the best examples of that. But teachers were a significant element of the suffrage movement too, not least in south Wales, which was home to women who were to become leading figures in the suffrage organisations and later in the National Union of Women Teachers (NUWT). If teachers occupied an ambiguous class position, for many women teachers the contradictions of their working lives, where equal training and responsibility for the nation's children were accompanied by gross inequalities in pay and professional opportunities, led straight to a feminist consciousness. The process of politicisation was described by the author of a profile of Davies in a way that historians of suffragist teachers would recognise:

> Until her marriage she was a certificated infant teacher, and it was during that time that she first became interested in politics. As a member of that profession she felt the need of placing men and women on an equal footing and giving the same pay for equal work, and it also brought her to recognise the need for women's suffrage [*Labour Woman*, October 1920, 157].

What opportunities were there for her to involve herself in the suffrage movement in Aberdare in this period? During the 1890s the town had an active Women's Liberal Association (WLA) which aligned itself firmly on the side of women's suffrage, but by 1901 it was in steep decline, losing its old members and failing to attract many young women of Davies' generation. There appears to have been no branch of the National Union of Women's Suffrage Societies (NUWSS) in the town, although there was one in Merthyr and in the neighbouring areas of Pontypridd and Rhondda. The WLA attempted to revive itself to campaign for the vote in 1907, and Davies may well have attended the public meetings associated with that attempt. In February 1906 the Aberdare Debating Society was the forum for a debate on women's suffrage, at which Miss Jenny Phillips BA, a teacher at the County (Secondary) School and one of Davies' comrades in the ILP, was the main speaker. Another ILP comrade, George Thomas, was the main opposer (the debate may have been a put-up job for the sake of airing the issue, especially as the arguments Thomas was reported to have employed were pretty threadbare). Two years later a branch of the Women's Freedom League (WFL) was established in the town, the active secretary of which was Jenny Phillips.

While direct evidence that Davies was a member of or active in suffrage societies is wanting, there is plenty of evidence that, for those who knew her, her feminist and suffragist identity was no less significant than her position as a socialist and a public woman. In her autograph book, which contains inscriptions dating from 1910–30, a significant number were written by known suffragists and/or express suffragist sentiments, including the undated one inside the front cover by a local socialist, David Evans, who expressed pro-militant sentiments and ended: 'All luck to the Gallant Fight for Women's Rights ... This is the sincere wish of one male wage slave. Sincerely yours in the Cause.' As well as the many Labour luminaries who added their names over the years, the book contains the signatures of Sylvia Pankhurst, Charlotte Despard (WFL president), Marguerite Sidley (WFL organiser), Nancy Richardson, and the secretary of the Cardiff WFL, Mary Keating Hill. In November 1910, the date of Sidley's signature and inscription, she addressed a large and enthusiastic public meeting in the town's Victoria Square, and this may also have been the occasion of the formation of the Aberdare WFL. Despard and Richardson both signed on 27 May 1912, when the ILP held its annual conference at Merthyr, when suffrage meetings were also held, and when the party passed a pro-suffrage resolution. All of this suggests that Davies may have been a member of, or at least sympathised with, the WFL specifically. The WFL was the political home of many women, including Despard and Margaret McMillan, who shared Davies' socialism and membership of the ILP. Her obituarist, clearly an old friend and admirer, recalled that she had 'embodied the militant spirit and courage of the feminist movement ... always courageous, enlightened, progressive and feminist, a tiny but eloquent, persuasive and sturdily militant figure pointing the way to the broader reaches of the future' [*Aberdare Leader*, 13 December 1958].

Davies took her feminism into the Labour movement in 1906, when she joined the ILP after attending one of Hardie's election meetings. The extent of her activism over the next two years is unclear. The Aberdare ILP was reorganised in 1905, and in 1906 opened the ILP Institute. The next year or two were extremely busy for the branch, with 133 public meetings in 1907, along with members' and executive meetings, the setting up of a socialist Sunday School, Ruskin classes and 52 meetings of the Children's choir (Davies may occasionally have helped to rehearse the children's choir in their socialist hymn-singing sessions), as well as Christmas parties with trees, and annual teas. The 1905 list of 21 officers (from chairman to caretaker) and 12 district secretaries appears to contain no women's names, apart from that of one of the three accompanists, and the 1906–7 list of subscriptions from each ward also appears not to include any women's names. However on 19 February 1908, 20 women were listed as forming a women's branch, with Jenny Phillips as chairman and Florence Rose Rees as its secretary, and from 1908 three women, including Davies, were listed as members of the branch executive, along with 12 men. In May she paid £1 17s 10d into the ILP coffers from subscriptions, a collection and the sale of badges, perhaps in the women's group. The receipt was signed by Edward Davies for the party. In July she took a £1 share in the Pioneer Printing and Publishing Company, which from 1911–29 was to publish the ILP organ, the *Merthyr Pioneer*. In 1908 Rose married Edward (Ted) Davies, a fellow teacher and a leading figure in the cooperative movement. At about that time Rose Davies became the first secretary of the Women's Co-operative Guild in Aberdare, a post she held until 1920, when pressure of work forced her to resign. By 1914 she was a member of the South Wales District Committee of the Guild.

Upon her marriage Davies gave up her teaching post. Though not universally applied, the marriage bar was widely implemented before the more notorious period of the 1920s. When one looks at the achievements of women such as Davies in the first half of the century, one is tempted to give thanks to this practice as it made women of great energy, talent and vision available for the unpaid work of civil and political life. Her abilities were quickly recognised locally. Not long after her marriage she was co-opted onto the Education Committee of the Aberdare Urban District Council. In 1914 she was one of the council's nominees for the board of governors of the local grammar schools, and was a governor of the South Wales and Monmouthshire Industrial (or Truant) School. By 1915 she was chair of the Education Committee, though still unelected, and was also co-opted onto the Maternal and Child Welfare Committee. Announcing her unique appointment as the chair of a local government committee, the *South Wales Daily News* described her as 'a socialist among socialists', and as playing 'a leading part in the propaganda activities of the ILP'. By then she had already marked out the area of work in local government that was to be her specialism and abiding interest: the provision of special schools for children who were deaf, dumb or blind, and later for 'mental defectives' (as the language of the day put it) and the physically disabled. In 1909, shortly after her co-option, she corresponded with Margaret McMillan – that great resource for socialists interested in the welfare and education of children, and whom Davies would have met when McMillan spoke at ILP meetings in the town – on medical inspections in schools and undernourished children. Very soon she became a mother herself: the first of her five children was born in 1910.

Along with her growing civic role, the years 1910–15 were marked by Davies' close friendship with Keir Hardie. The importance of this association is suggested by the number of letters from Hardie preserved by Davies, a mixture of political and personal material. Their collaboration appears to have begun before the general election of January 1910, when Hardie, apparently following up an earlier discussion, wrote to ask her advice on 'an Educational paragraph' for his election address [Rose Davies Papers, GRO, letter 6 December 1909]. During the campaign Davies was given the job of putting together a 'Women's Keir Hardie Election Committee' in the Aberdare division of the constituency. In a second letter on the subject, perhaps in response to a request for advice from Davies, Hardie wrote:

Get the women's committee formed and then take your marching orders from George Thomas. There will be canvassing to be done, literature to be distributed, buttons with portraits to be sold, rosettes and other favours to be made and sold (Green, white and Red are the colours). Will you yourself make one for me? When the committee is formed find out what each member can do best, and set her to work at that. That is the meaning of democracy. Try and get small committees formed in the different wards and villages. Apart from what they can do now, it will be good training for the future when they themselves are voters [Rose Davies Papers, GRO, undated letter].

The letter suggests that not only was Davies new to election organising, but that it was new to other Labour women in the constituency too. This was the first general election after the formation of the ILP women's group, and no branch of the Women's Labour League was formed in Aberdare until 1917. A branch was established in Merthyr in 1910, possibly in connection with the general election of that year, of which a Mrs Davies was secretary. The branch was defunct by 1912. During the 1910 election campaign Davies and her husband had Jim Hardie junior to stay with them. While still running second to the Liberal candidate, Hardie slightly increased his share of the vote despite a four-cornered contest. In his letter of thanks for their hospitality, Jim Hardie referred to their 'disappointment' at the result: it may be that with the departure of the senior Liberal member for another constituency, the local party had hoped to see Hardie do better. On 19 January 1910 Hardie himself inscribed in Davies' autograph book 'It was a gallant victory'. Over the next few years Davies and Keir Hardie corresponded frequently. The 'Dear Mrs. Davies' of early 1909 became the 'Dear Comrade' of January 1910, and then quickly gave way to 'Dear Rose'. She received postcards from Brussels, Chicago (which Hardie visited on his tour of the United States in 1912) and the Women's International Suffrage Alliance in Budapest in 1913, to which Hardie had been invited and from which he brought her a badge and some illustrated 'toy books for each of the bairns'.

Davies visited Hardie in London, sometimes along with other Aberdare comrades and sometimes alone, staying at the Bingham Hotel. Hardie's letters suggest that she visited the women's gallery in the House of Commons to hear questions and debates, and that they visited restaurants and the theatre together – including a Harry Lauder concert, and the Food Reform Restaurant in Furnival Street. Hardie flirted with Davies in his letters, anticipating their meetings and her 'sparkling eyes and cheery smile', and complimenting her 'bonny' and 'charming' appearance in group photographs, of which he sent her copies. He gave her encouragement and advice when she was faced with making speeches, and welcomed her personal tone and support when so much of his correspondence was political. Their friendship was undoubtedly one of Hardie's frequent warm attachments to young socialist women that Kenneth Morgan has noted, but he was also a friend of her husband, and he worried, and again offered sage advice and support when Ted had to go to Cardiff for an operation in 1913.

However, in the absence of parliamentary elections and as Davies' involvement in local government and education grew, there was a period in 1912 and 1913 when they corresponded less frequently and saw less of each other. Davies complained to Hardie's secretary, Margaret Symons, that he was neglecting her and her husband, and in turn Hardie claimed that she and Ned (as Hardie always called Ted) had neglected him, leaving others to tell him that they had moved house (from Abernant to 'the city of Aberdare') and that Ned was no longer secretary of the party, 'of which neither of you have ever given me an inkling'. Their correspondence and meetings seem to have picked up again in 1914, but there appears to be no surviving correspondence after the outbreak of war in August [Letters from Hardie, many undated, Rose Davies Papers, GRO].

The Labour movement was split by the war, in Merthyr and Aberdare as elsewhere. There is no evidence of the position Davies took at the time, or of whether she was present at the public meeting at which Hardie was howled down by the patriotic crowd and which ended in violent scuffles. Perhaps the lack of correspondence between them at this time is significant. When Hardie died in September 1915, Ted was one of the three members of the local ILP who travelled to Scotland for his funeral. In later years Davies proudly recalled their political and personal friendship: 'We had glorious meetings with Hardie, and fought many a great battle. It was good to be with him in those days' [*Labour Woman*, October 1920, 157].

If Davies had any doubts about the prosecution of the war she must have been fairly discreet about them, since for her, as for other able women, war brought the opportunity to take on further public responsibilities. She became the Glamorgan District representative of the Women's Branch of the Ministry of Agriculture and Fisheries, presumably dealing with women's work on the land. She also joined the Juvenile Welfare Advisory Committee of the Employment Exchange, and was its chair by 1920, as well as vice-president of the War Pensions Committee. One appointment that suggests she was not a vocal opponent of the war was her membership of the Military Tribunal, which would have heard pleas for exemption and conscientious objection, presumably including some by her local socialist comrades. Her work in the labour movement was not neglected: she was a member of the executive of the Aberdare Trades and Labour Council, and in 1918 was its first woman chair. It is unlikely that she was not involved in some way with the creation of the branch of the WLL in Aberdare in 1917.

It had been possible for women to be elected to district councils since 1894, and to county and borough councils since 1907. However local Labour parties proved no more eager than their Liberal predecessors to select women as candidates for council positions, and since they could call on the expertise of talented women such as Davies through co-option, why sacrifice an elected position that could be filled by a man? One of Hardie's letters suggests that Davies had been thinking about standing for election to the borough council in 1913. In April 1919 she stood unsuccessfully as the Labour candidate for the town ward in the district council elections. In April 1920 she was elected, second in the poll, to one of the two seats gained by Labour in the Gadlys ward in an election with a heavy turnout, particularly of women voters. As an elected member, she was able to pursue more effectively the causes she had espoused when co-opted, especially the provision of maternity homes, nursery schools and summer and winter play centres. She remained on the district council for three years.

In August 1920, on the recommendation of the Labour Women's Advisory Committee, she was made a JP. In 1925 she stood as candidate for the Aberaman ward in the county council elections. This time she had the party's only woman MP, Ellen Wilkinson, to speak for her from a platform that also included the Aberdare MP, George Hall, and the male Labour leadership of the district. Wilkinson said how pleased she was to have the opportunity 'of publicly acknowledging the great work which had been done for the Labour movement' by Rose Davies. She was elected in March, a Labour gain, in an election that saw the party regaining control of the county. Very shortly afterwards she was promoted to the Aldermanic bench, thus creating a vacancy on the country council. In the consequent by-election all the candidates were male. A month or two later Wilkinson brought Davies to the platform of the National Labour Women's Conference in Birmingham, introducing her as 'our one and only shingled Alderman': a report in the Labour press made more of Davies's fetching new hairstyle than of the substance of her speech, in seconding a motion on maternity and child welfare, on medical attendance at childbirth [cutting, writer unidentified, Rose Davies Papers, GRO].

From 1919–26 Davies and her colleague Elizabeth Andrews from the Rhondda, now the party's first women's organiser for Wales, were two of the four women members of the Board of Health Welsh Consultative Council, which – under the chairmanship of Sir Ewen McLean – had the task of reporting on health services in Wales and making recommendations for comprehensive health case provision. In late 1920 Andrews and Davies ensured that the proposals included the provision of home help for pregnant and nursing mothers, and were working on a report on the reorganisation of maternity benefit as a universal provision of mothers' pensions 'or some scheme of national endowment' [*Labour Woman*, October 1920, 157]. In 1926 the Minister for Health, Neville Chamberlain, pulled the plug on the Welsh Consultative Council as it had recommended reforms that the government was unwilling to fund. In 1928, as a Glamorgan county councillor on the Public Health Committee, Davies protested that the Ministry of Health (MoH) had failed to appoint Welsh representatives to the committees that dealt with the training of midwives and maternal welfare. She was supported by the MoH, and by a resolution by the Committee.

The post-war years brought women into the Labour Party under its new constitution, as individual members and as members of women's sections, the foundation for which was provided by the rather patchy organisation of the WLL. In addition to the WCG, Aberdare also had a branch of the Railway Women's Guild, and by the mid 1920s something that was confusingly called the 'Labour Women's Guild' – although this might simply have been a mistake by a newspaper reporter it nevertheless reflected the fact that these organisations had much of their leadership and membership in common. In the winter of 1920–21 Davies threw herself into the work of organising sections in the new constituency of Aberdare. Some time before 1925 she was made secretary of the East Glamorgan Labour Women's Advisory Council (AC). At the end of her term of office she spoke of the need for more political education to be provided for women, so that they could use their votes well and also do 'real work' during election campaigns [AC Minutes, 19 September 1925]. At the twice-yearly meetings of the AC in the 1920s and 1930s she paired with Elizabeth Andrews, with Andrews speaking as the women's organiser for Wales and Davies as the representative of the Standing Joint Committee of Industrial (later Working) Women's Organisations (SJC), of which she was now a member; they occasionally deputised for each other if one was unable to attend. The SJC, formed in 1916, brought together representatives of the women's sections, the WCG and the trade unions, and had an advisory role in relation to the Labour Party.

It was not always clear from the AC minutes just when Davies was passing down advice, instructions and suggestions from the SJC and when she was speaking for herself. Under the heading of reporting from the SJC in 1926, after explaining the function and composition of the committee she went on to stress 'the necessity for demanding equal suffrage for men and women', and – in the face of possible coalfield strikes – the importance of 'women standing by their menfolk in their resistance to lower wages and longer hours'. She spoke of working for peace, saying that 'women should demand with no uncertain voice that there should be "No More War"'. She also told the AC that unmarried mothers and their children needed the protection of Labour women, and that there should be an equal moral standard for men and women. Other topics were work schemes for the unemployed and national insurance payments by young workers [AC Minutes, 6 March 1926].

In the late 1920s and early 1930s, questions about maternal mortality, unemployment and benefits, the means test, and disarmament and peace recurred in her reports. She also spoke as a county councillor, and in the context of the demise of the Boards of Guardians she urged the sections to put forward more working women candidates for the county council so as 'to help forward the great work of humanity' [AC Minutes, 8 March 1930]. It appears to have been an uphill struggle to get the sections to take a real interest in the SJC, or to respond to the questionnaires the committee circulated in order to gather information on such subjects as maternal mortality and malnutrition as the economic slump deepened.

Davies did not retire from the SJC until the end of 1947, making her the longest serving member of the committee. Upon her retirement the committee recorded in its minutes their appreciation of her long years of service, and 'many members spoke with appreciation of the part you had taken in the discussions and decisions, and the great value to new members ... of the contribution to debates made by you and other members with long experience' [letter from Mary Sutherland, SJC secretary, 12 December 1947, Rose Davies Papers, GRO].

Davies took an active interest in the peace movements of the 1920s, and especially in women's movements in Wales. The Women's Co-operative Guild, in which she was still active, grew increasingly anti-war in the 1920s and 1930s. She was an admirer of the work and writings of the influential Christian pacifist George M. Ll. Davies, and in early 1923 invited him to address a meeting in her home, where he spoke about 'the Doctrine of Grace, the Grace of God – or Love and human fellowship'. In 1923 Davies was invited to speak at the Aberystwyth conference, initiated by the women's section of the Welsh School of Social Service, which launched a peace memorial from the women of Wales to the women of the United States. The memorial, intended as 'a national act of international significance', was aimed at persuading the United States to join the League of Nations in order 'to help bring sanity and peace to a distracted and war-weary world' [letter on 'Wales and World Peace', signed by Gwilym Davies, 2 May 1923].

On the back of the letter Davies made notes for a brief address, and this is one of the few surviving pieces of writing by her. Echoing the wording of the memorial on the 'opportunity and responsibility' of 'the women of this generation', she emphasised the duty of women 'to renew and sustain' not just physical life, but 'the "moral" and the "spiritual" also'. She quoted George Davies, interpreting his words as a message for women to 'bring the home spirit – and mothers know that this means not counting unto each one their offences but seeking for the good in each one – into our International Life'. The opportunity for women of her generation was an historic one:

> Woman has come into power just when all the world movements and questions concern her most vitally – and here is her opportunity – Looked at from the broad standpoint of humanity as a whole all the questions of the hour bear on woman's special function, the Care of Life ... all these problems need to be penetrated and solved by her highest ideals for the good of the individual and the whole ... the great call of today is for Love not Hate, Life not Death, and it is to that call that the True spirit of woman always answers [notes from speech, Rose Davies papers, GRO].

These sentiments are distinctively those of a woman of Davies' generation, heir to the nineteenth-century feminist vision of the special contribution of women to public and civic, and here international, life. The campaign was persuasive: almost 400 000 signatures were collected on the petition, representing, it was claimed, some 65 per cent of women over the age of 18 in Wales. It was presented, in an oak chest, in Washington the following year. Davies kept up her interest in international and peace issues into the early 1930s at least. In 1930 she was invited, on Marion Phillips' recommendation, by the League of Nations to observe its work in Geneva.

There had been a suggestion that Davies would be selected as a Labour candidate for the 1918 general election, but in the event she was not given the opportunity to stand for Parliament until 1929. Given the circumstances of her candidature, one has to question how seriously both she and the party wanted her to win a seat. She stood not in a constituency where her reputation and record would have stood her in good stead, where her commitment to the community could not be in doubt and where there was already a safe Labour seat, but in Honiton in Devon (near, as it happened, her mother's birthplace in Barnstaple). Furthermore Labour had never fought the seat before, there was a three-cornered fight, and the Liberal candidate, while fearing a split anti-Conservative vote, confidently predicted that Davies would lose her deposit. Her first public meeting was reported to have been well attended, but the press took little notice of her campaign and by nomination day it was being predicted that she would withdraw. Instead she was the first candidate to hand in her nomination papers. The nominations for the Liberal candidate revealed that several prominent Labour figures in the area had decided to give tactical electoral support to the Liberal in the hope of breaking the long-standing Tory hold on the seat. They almost managed it, and Davies gathered only 915 votes:

Honiton, Devon, 1929: electorate 41 723, turnout 84.3 per cent

Sir A. C. Morrison-Bell, Bt (Conservative)	17 911 (50.9 per cent)
J. G. H. Halse (Liberal)	16 353 (46.5 per cent)
Miss F. R. Davies (Labour)	915 (2.6 per cent)
Majority	1558 (4.4 per cent)

Davies gave an upbeat interpretation of the events: 'We have begun to sow the seed ... We shall reap the harvest at the next election' [*Express & Echo,* 1 June 1929]. Perhaps 'sowing the seed' had been the main point, and perhaps Davies did not truly have any parliamentary ambitions, but her fate was that of many a woman candidate in the history of the party, then and since. In her short time in the constituency she made some good friends who wrote an optimistic message in her autograph book: 'To the glorious 30 May 1929. In the Honiton Division we lit a torch, and into the hands of Rose Davies it was given to carry and out of the darkness shone forth Light' [Autograph Book, GRO].

The course of Davies' public life was now set. Her career, though involving numerous bodies and responsibilities, was all of a piece with her practical socialism, which sought power in the service of the communities she represented. She appears never to have said no to an invitation to join yet another committee. Throughout her long career she retained the interest in education, particularly special education, she had developed before the First World War in Aberdare. By 1925 she was a governor of the University College of Wales and of the South Wales and Monmouthshire University College. She was also a member of the governing body and council of the Welsh National Memorial Association, which campaigned and educated on the scourge of TB in Wales. In 1930 she accepted an invitation to join, as one of only two women, a Board of Control committee to investigate the costs and effectiveness of provisions for the mentally disabled. The following year she was invited by the Health Ministry to join a committee on garden cities and satellite towns, the only woman on the 12-member committee. She facilitated the setting up of one of the (now devalued) training centres for young women in domestic service of that period, resulting in the placement in work of more than 900 women. In the same period she was a member of a deputation from the county to Minister of Labour Oliver Stanley, making, according to the press, 'a deep impression by the moving and affecting case she made for hard-pressed South Wales' [*Aberdare Leader*, 20 December 1958].

In the 1934 birthday honours Davies was awarded an MBE, which was upgraded to a CBE 20 years later. In 1937 she was appointed to the Welsh Board of Health Insurance Committee. On the county council she chaired every committee in turn, and eventually became the first woman to chair the council as a whole. By the 1950s she was chair of the county council's Special Services Committee, and of the Special Services Committee of the Welsh Joint Education Committee. The post-war years saw the achievement of Davies' wish for a school for deaf and dumb children, and in the 1950s she was heavily involved in the founding of a school in Penarth for the physically disabled, for which she laid the foundation stone in the mid 1950s. The school opened a couple of months before she died.

In March 1951 Ted Davies died at the age of 71, and thereafter, according to observers, Rose Davies threw herself even more into her work. Later she suffered a seizure that almost killed her, but soon rose 'triumphantly from her sick bed' and returned to work.

She crammed an incredible amount of activity into a day. She would, generally on public transport, attend meetings in Cardiff, Bridgend and Aberdare in one day – always fresh and mentally vigorous. She would step off the train from Birmingham or Manchester and make her way hot-foot to gatherings in the town to rise and speak imperturbably as if she had come from the tea table at home. She would walk in smiling to meetings where no-one, knowing her crowded diary, expected to see her [*Aberdare Leader*, 13 December 1958].

Like her friend and colleague Elizabeth Andrews a year later, Davies collapsed on her way to a committee meeting at County Hall and died a month later, in December 1958, at the age of 76. She was accorded the nearest thing to a state funeral that the town and county could muster, with representatives of local government, the hospitals, the magistracy, the university and colleges, all the schools, including the special schools, and of course the trade unions and the Labour Party, making up the 400-strong congregation at the church. Amongst the mourners was Andrews, who was described in the funeral report simply as an 'old friend of pioneering days'. Senior girls from the grammar school stood to attention outside the school as Davies' cortege passed. In the exclusive Howell's Girls' School in Llandaff, of which Davies had for some time been the chair of governors, a new science laboratory was named after her, although the school no longer appears to be aware of this. At the annual conference of the East Glamorgan Advisory Committee in March 1959 the delegates stood in silence in memory of 'our dear beloved Alderman Rose Davies'. In addition 'Mrs. E. Andrews along with several other old members, who remembered the work Rose Davies had done for us in the early days, spoke with feeling and paid a last tribute to her wonderful life' [AC Minutes, 21 March 1959].

Sources: (1) MSS: Florence Rose Davies Papers, Aberdare Independent Labour Party Records, Glamorgan Record Office; East Glamorgan Labour Women's Advisory Council Minutes, 1925–6, National Library of Wales, Aberystwyth. **(2) Newspapers:** *Aberdare Leader*, 13 and 20 December 1958; *Labour Woman*, October 1920; *South Wales Daily News*, 1915; *South Wales Express and Echo*, 1 June 1929. Other: Kenneth O. Morgan, *Keir Hardie: Radical and Socialist* (1975).

URSULA MASSON

See also: Elizabeth ANDREWS; Beatrice GREEN.

DENMAN, Honourable Sir Richard Douglas (1876–1957)
LIBERAL, LABOUR AND NATIONAL LABOUR MP

Richard Douglas Denman was born on 24 August 1876, the son of Richard Denman and Helen Denman, née McMicking. Denman's father was the grandson of the 1st Baron Denman, the Whig politician and Lord Chief Justice; his elder brother Thomas became 3rd Baron in 1894 and served as Governor-General of Australia from 1911–14.

Denman was educated at Westminster School and Balliol College, Oxford. He was awarded the Stanhope Essay Prize in 1898, and the Chancellor's English Essay Prize in 1900. His Oxford friends included William Beveridge, R. H. Tawney and John Buchan. His friendship with Beveridge would be life long. On leaving university he took a flat in the Temple, and became an insurance broker at Lloyds. He shared his flat at different times with Buchan and Beveridge; and also with the talented and tragic Arthur Collings Carre, another Balliol contemporary and close associate of Beveridge. One evening early in 1902 Denman found Carre unconscious from an overdose of laudanum; he died soon afterwards. The inquest verdict was suicide during temporary insanity [for a discussion of Carre see Harris (1997) 10–12, 71–2]. John Buchan was sceptical about Denman's attachment to the Liberal Party. He wrote from Johannesburg, where he was a member of Milner's 'kindergarten,' to warn Denman of the party's obsolescence. 'Don't for heaven's sake become a Liberal Member of Parliament and ally yourself permanently with stereotypical policies and outworn creeds' [Buchan to Denman, 30 November 1902, quoted in Denman (1948) 121].

Yet as the Liberals recovered electorally and some began to rethink Liberal social and economic policies, Denman became increasingly identified with the more interventionist aspects of Liberalism. When the Liberal Government was formed in December 1905 he became personal secretary to the Postmaster-General, Sydney Buxton. Beveridge saw this as a chance for collectivist influence: 'the Post office is the one socialist experiment. Sydney Buxton's main interest is social reform and you'll get lots of that to do' [Beveridge to Denman, 18 December 1905, quoted in Harris (1997) 109].

More broadly Denman was attracted to the potential for informed and effective state action. 'It is highly refreshing to read about a state in which particular social results are achieved by the deliberate and wilful contrivance of the citizens' [Denman to Annette Beveridge, 29 August 1905, quoted in Harris (1997) 137). One influence was doubtlessly Edward Caird, the Master of Balliol, with his philosophy of 'practical idealism', but the general theme had several Edwardian exemplars – Progressive Liberalism, Fabianism and Conservative schemes for modernisation based on tariff reform.

The Liberal Government's increasing emphasis on redistributive taxation gave Denman an opening for a parliamentary career. The Liberal MP for Carlisle was unhappy about the land tax proposals in the 1909 People's Budget, and became the target of criticism of some in the Carlisle Liberal Association. The result was a vacancy, and Denman, perhaps with some support from the Liberal whips, became Carlisle's Liberal candidate.

In January 1910 he faced two opponents, a Conservative and a Social Democrat. Denman made a strong and largely successful bid for support by the Carlisle labour movement. In this he was helped by the town's recent history of labour politics. The local Trades Council had favoured the promotion of a Labour candidate. A Social Democrat proposal that the candidate must be a socialist had been defeated, in the Trades Council; the Social Democrats had then put forward their own nominee. Denman could appeal to trade union sense of solidarity that had been affronted by this Social Democrat initiative.

The essence of the trade union position was that men must work together if they were to produce a valuable result. If there had been an authorised Labour man here he should never have stood ... he would never have willingly voted against a genuine Labour man. He had had too much to do with them during the last four years to know how much they were in harmony [*Carlisle Evening Journal*, 18 January 1910.]

With the centrality of the constitutional question, this appeal was particularly powerful and Denman was a comfortable winner:

Carlisle, January 1910: electorate 7436, turnout 92.3 per cent

Hon. R. D. Denman (Liberal)	3270 (47.7 per cent)
V. J. Hussey-Walsh (Conservative)	2815 (41.0 per cent)
A. C. Barrington (Social Democrat)	777 (11.3 per cent)
Majority	455 (6.7 per cent)

The December 1910 contest was a straight fight between Denman and a Conservative candidate. Denman emphasised that a settlement of the constitutional question must be followed by economic and social measures, which would be 'the next step in the path of progress'. The problem of poverty must be addressed without 'any economics that might savour of class wars'. He believed in the essential reasonableness of the wealthy and disavowed deceptively simple panaceas. 'He could not dangle before them one simple word like Socialism or Tariff Reform that could cure their ills. These questions could only be dealt with by a long series of measures dealing with each disease at a time' [*Carlisle Evening Journal*, 5 December 1910]. Denman nevertheless appealed for socialist votes on the ground of democratic self-government. The absence of a Social Democrat candidate did not improve the Liberal position.

Carlisle, December 1910: electorate 7436, turnout 86.4 per cent

Hon. R. D. Denman (Liberal)	3243 (50.5 per cent)
I. W. Raymond (Conservative)	3179 (49.5 per cent)
Majority	64 (1.0 per cent)

Until August 1914 Denman demonstrated a strong concern with labour questions. Carlisle was an important railway centre, and the railway unions were preoccupied with the questions of low wages, onerous conditions, and – with the exception of the North Eastern Railway – union recognition. The conciliation scheme agreed by companies and the unions in November 1907 had disappointed many railway workers. The subsequent wage settlements had been deflated by the depression of 1908–9, there was considerable suspicion that the railway companies had sought to evade unpalatable elements of the arbitration awards by regrading, and the recognition question remained unresolved. One consequence of this discontent was the brief, partial and sometimes abrasive railway strike of August 1911. The Liberal Government responded by establishing a Royal Commission to review the conciliation scheme. Denman, who had expressed his sympathy for the railway workers' demands during his election contests (for example their call for an eight-hour day), responded to the 1911 strike, the hearings of the subsequent Royal Commission and the imminent Annual General Meeting of the Amalgamated Society of Railway Servants (ASRS), to be held in Carlisle, by considering a radical solution to the industry's difficulties:

> The Railway position is in a hopeless mess. The evidence before the Commission shows not only the bitter Anti-Unionist feeling of railway magnates, but also … the futility of expecting a permanent settlement from Conciliation Boards. The fundamental difficulty of Conciliation Boards for railway employees lies in the fact that the ordinary criterion upon which wages are based is lacking. There is no question of what expenditure the industry can economically stand, and the State cannot allow a fight between employers and workers which shall have time to show the bargaining strength of the two sides. Personally I am driven to the conclusion that the only solution of the difficulty is Nationalisation. The Amalgamated Society of Railway Servants are holding their annual conference in Carlisle in a few days, and I am proposing to suggest to them that they should start a campaign for Nationalisation, at the same time surrendering their right to strike- [Denman to Rowland Vernon (copy), 22 September 1911, Denman Papers, Box 12].

Denman elaborated on his ideas to two Liberal newspaper editors, J. A. Spender of the *Westminster Gazette* and C. P. Scott of the *Manchester Guardian*. He argued that the operation of the Post Office provided a model for a publicly owned railway system. Both editors sounded notes of caution – Spender on the prohibition of strikes, and Scott on the need to proceed slowly on nationalisation, a measure that he felt was 'only a question of time' [Scott to Denman, 1 October 1911, with other correspondence, Denman Papers Box 3]. The ASRS conference revealed to Denman that the temper of the railway workers rendered his proposal impracticable. He felt that the union leaders' control over their members could not be guaranteed in the future: 'despite occasional outbursts of wildness, the leaders kept things well in hand. Feeling, however, still runs high; and there is a real danger of further explosions this autumn' [Denman to J. A. Spender, 11 October 1911, Denman Papers, Box 3].

The immediate crisis was averted but discontent amongst the railway workers remained high. In October 1913 Denman became involved in the case of Sam Caudle, a senior Midland Railway driver based at Carlisle. In the wake of the Aisgill disaster, in which 16 people had died, Caudle had been found guilty of manslaughter and sentenced to two months' imprisonment. The case was a complex one that raised questions about the impact of a managerial strategy of economies – especially in respect of coal prices – on safety standards. Denman was sympathetic to Caudle, but was anxious to prevent unofficial stoppages, as were the leaders of the new amalgamated union, the National Union of Railwaymen. In a letter to the Home Secretary, Reginald McKenna, Denman stated that the Carlisle railwaymen were 'furious' about Caudle's sentence.

> I listened to a good deal of ugly talk after the sentence had been passed. Railwaymen … are not in too good a temper at present and the feeling that one of the most respected of their body has been imprisoned does not allay bitterness of feeling [Denman to Reginald McKenna, 21 October 1913, H.O. 144/1292 file 132928, PRO].

Cabinet ministers responded to the crisis by advising the King to grant Caudle a pardon.

Until 1914 the alliance between Progressive Liberalism and labour held firm in Carlisle. When the Liberal Government responded to the Osborne Judgment by tabling legislation that would permit trade unions to establish a political fund, Denman was amongst those Liberal backbenchers who were critical of the provision for contracting out, and instead favoured the Labour Party's position. His case was strongly majoritarian:

I do not see any need in our society to emphasise the rights of minorities. ... No adequate reason has yet been given why, if a political object is a lawful one in this kind of community, the decision of the majority shall not bind the whole membership. It is admitted that the fruits of the political object will come to the whole society [*Hansard*, 6 August 1912, col. 3654].

He also felt that binding all union members into the organisation's political activities would serve to protect representatives and safeguard against 'extremism' [ibid., col. 3657].

For Denman the pursuit of economic efficiency meant a significant increase in state intervention, not least to make the most effective use of trained workers:

You cannot possibly distinguish between unemployed and unemployable, unless you can first set up a great mass of machinery for the purpose. The Labour Exchange was, I should say, the outer shell of the whole fabric of that machinery for singling out the unemployed from the unemployable [*Hansard*, 10 February 1911, cols 655–6].

From 1910 Denman chaired the London Juvenile Advisory Committee. Such committees were one legacy of the introduction of labour exchanges [for this complex story see Harris (1997) 159–65]. Under Denman the committee actively sought to increase employment opportunities for disabled school leavers, promoted technical and further education, and waged a continuous war against sweated trades. In the summer of 1914 Denman seemed well established as a progressive Liberal. He favoured state intervention to reduce economic inefficiencies and to promote social justice; he was opposed to industrial militancy and political extremism but championed many Labour Party and trade union priorities. He had good reason to expect to be appointed to a junior government post [see Tanner (1991) 61].

On 2 August 1914 Denman received a telegram – from a group claiming to represent the Carlisle and Cumberland Liberals – urging that Britain remain neutral in the European crisis. The following day, when MPs met to hear Sir Edward Grey's assessment of the crisis, Denman was one of the few who openly opposed British involvement: 'To make Belgium the scene of a vast European War is not in the best interests of the country whose neutrality we wish to guarantee' [*Hansard*, 3 August 1914, col. 1877]. He amplified this position in a letter to the Carlisle press: 'That we should be plunged into war merely for the sake of assuring the triumph of Russia and the defeat of Germany is a stupid crime' [*Carlisle Journal*, 4 August 1914].

Once British involvement was certain, Denman was committed to an Allied victory. He spoke at recruiting meetings and volunteered for military service, but at that stage he was turned down as being too old. As he acknowledged many years later, the threat and then the outbreak of war proved personally profitable: 'I laid the foundation of a war-risk business that enabled my skilful underwriters to collect large sums for the State in Excess Profits Duty and enough for myself to buy Staffield' [Denman (1948) 21]. 'Staffield' referred to Staffield Hall in Kirkoswald, Cumberland, which was to be Denman's country house for the rest of his life. 'No business on which I have ever been engaged has proved to be so profitable' [ibid.]

Despite his endorsement of the need for British success in the war, for the next 16 months Denman's public image was that of an antiwar Liberal. He continued to criticise the policy that had led to British intervention, and he began to consider the type of post-war settlement that would prevent further hostilities. On 6 August 1914 he was present at a meeting of Liberals opposed to the government's foreign policy. Thereafter they met regularly. Inevitably links began to form between Liberal and Labour critics of the government, the Union of Democratic Control (UDC) provided one significant meeting place. Critics were bonded together as they shared the enthusiasms and risks of campaigning on unpopular views. Denman's involvement in the UDC was informed by a thorough insistence on what he characterised as traditional Liberal values.

we see clearly the gradual decline of old Liberal influences in foreign politics and the growth of the Liberal Imperialist forces we remember so well in the first years of the century. The school of Asquith, Grey and Haldane has waxed, that of Morley, Loreburn and Campbell-Bannerman has waned. Our whole drift of diplomacy with its secret obligations to France, and its corresponding menace to Germany would have been impossible under the Premiership of Campbell-Bannerman ... my own political training was in the Campbell-Bannerman school. To that school I shall, I hope, remain loyal for my life [Denman to 'My Dear Campbell' (copy), 29 July 1915, Denman Papers, Box 1].

Denman's UDC activities prompted a petition signed by members of Lloyds calling on him to resign. He stepped aside from his syndicate to prevent a boycott that would affect his partners, but he retained a significant interest in the share of another 'name' [Denman (1948) 25]. He was also the target of criticism within the Carlisle Liberal Association, and on 15 November 1915 its Council passed a vote of no-confidence in him and requested the Executive to find another candidate. Denman's response was that the council meeting had been unrepresentative and the decision 'desultory'. He characterised his position in terms far removed from the antiwar stereotype: 'support as far as possible to the Coalition Government with a view to the most efficient conduct of the war, and to the securing of a lasting peace' [Denman to Sir Robert Allison, president of Carlisle Liberal Association, 16 November 1915 (copy), Denman Papers, Box 2].

Whatever the complexities of Denman's position, the rebuff could have resulted in him going through a period of independent radicalism before joining the Labour Party, the path followed by C. P. Trevelyan and Arthur Ponsonby. Instead he joined the army – 'Peace Crank Becomes Artillery Officer' was the *Daily Express*'s comment on 1 December 1915. The following month in the Commons, Denman opposed the introduction of military conscription, and then left for France to serve with the 62nd Brigade of the Royal Field Artillery at Vermelles on the Somme, and at Arras.

In 1917 he left the army and returned to politics. The Liberal Party was divided, albeit often ambiguously, over its attitude towards Lloyd George's Coalition Government. Denman's initial response to his limited knowledge of the December 1916 crisis was opposition to the prospect of a Lloyd George government [Denman to Gulland (copy), 6 December 1916, Denman Papers, Box 2], but he subsequently became a strong supporter of the Coalition. He acted as parliamentary private secretary simultaneously to the Conservative Roland Prothero at the Board of Agriculture and to the Liberal H. A. L. Fisher at the Board of Education. His experiences revealed for him the value of cross-party cooperation: both ministers introduced significant pieces of legislation during 1917, neither of which 'could have been the fruit of a Party Government. My experience of them, in the stage of drafting as well as that of carrying through Parliament, showed me the immense value of Coalition and the co-operative method, as against the waste and futility of the Party dog-fight' [Denman (1948) 29–30].

His career as parliamentary private secretary to Prothero ended in the autumn of 1917 when he voted against a government proposal to fund royalties out of taxation for those prospecting for domestic petroleum reserves. He continued to serve as PPS for Fisher and claimed to have been offered the Coalition coupon for the 1918 election. However Carlisle already had a new Liberal candidate, who stood as a supporter of Lloyd George, and Denman, although a keen advocate of the Coalition's continuation, did not contest the election.

Denman's disillusionment with the post-war Coalition was rapid. He attacked the Versailles settlement, and then explained his broader concerns to the Coalition Liberal Frederick Guest. Even in wartime the 'Coalition Government had revealed extraordinary powers of progressive legislation', but 'coalition has come to mean the continued resistance of the more inert members of each Party to the required forward movement'. On the subject of coal, he felt that nationalisation was inevitable and that the government was deliberately delaying action on Mr Justice Sankey's recommendations. Nevertheless disenchantment with the Coalition did not lead Denman towards Labour, rather he reverted to traditional Liberalism. 'Way must be made for progressive leaders who are prepared to lead us along the old road toward the 20th century visions of peace, retrenchment and reform' [Denman to F. Guest, August 1919 (copy), Denman Papers, Box 4].

In the general elections of November 1922 and December 1923 Denman fought as a Liberal and in both cases experienced the problems often encountered by post-war Liberals in northern urban constituencies. In 1918 Liberals in Newcastle West had united behind a Coalition Minister, Edward Shortt, and when he stood down in 1922 some Coalition Liberals, along with Conservatives, backed a Lloyd George Liberal. While most Liberals supported Denman, their campaign lacked resources. Denman barely saved his deposit and had to find £500 to pay off his outstanding expenses. The seat was won for Labour by the Tyneside businessman David Adams:

Newcastle West, November 1922: electorate 32 964, turnout 80.5 per cent

D. Adams (Labour)	11 654 (43.9 per cent)
C. B. Rumage (Lloyd George Liberal)	11 499 (43.4 per cent)
Hon. R. D. Denman (Liberal)	3367 (12.7 per cent)
Majority	155 (0.5 per cent)

In his *post mortem* on the event Denman acknowledged that the increased prominence of the Labour Party posed a strategic problem for Liberals: 'The truth is ... that in a struggle between Labour and anti-Labour, the candidate who offered an alternative constructive policy going part of the way with Labour pleased neither side and was apt to be frozen out' – [Denman to J. Longstaff (copy), n.d., Denman Papers, Box 4].

Yet he remained optimistic and in the 1923 election contested Carlisle. The seat had been won by George Middleton for Labour in 1922. The Labour Member, an eminently respectable trade unionist, appealled to a similar constituency to that courted by Denman in 1910. Denman's response was to emphasise the contrast between liberalism and socialism. 'I oppose the Socialistic aim of the Labour Party believing that individual enterprise is a characteristic of the British race and deserves encouragement rather than repression' [1923 Carlisle election address, Denman Papers, Box 4]. In contrast Middleton could appeal to a sense of class, – 'he had the great advantage over his opponents of knowing the conditions of the lives of the people for whom he was fighting' [*Carlisle Journal*, 27 November 1923]. The result was:

Carlisle, December 1923: electorate 25 634, turnout 87.8 per cent

G. Middleton (Labour)	9120 (40.5 per cent)
Rt. Hon. W. Watson (Conservative)	8844 (39.3 per cent)
Hon. R. D. Denman (Liberal)	4541 (20.2 per cent)
Majority	276 (1.2 per cent)

The first Labour Government was the decisive moment in Denman's shift from Liberal to Labour. He felt that MacDonald's record as foreign secretary deserved support, and therefore the Liberals had been wrong to help defeat the Government. Moreover the backbone of the Labour Party was the kind of trade unionist who had supported him in Carlisle in 1910. His partisan language could be misleading; 'Though Liberals cannot talk the talk of the Socialists they have been able to work for the same concrete objects' [Letter to the *Manchester Guardian*, 12 November 1924]. Nevertheless Denman still hoped for some kind of Progressive understanding. If the Liberals were to be blamed for defeating the government in the Commons, Labour was equally culpable as it had stood candidates in hopeless seats where the consequence was to ensure a Conservative victory. Circumstances had made the Labour Party into Denman's preferred political instrument, but this did not entail a thorough partisanship.

Nevertheless Denman soon secured a Labour candidacy. On 8 October 1925 he was adopted by the Central Leeds Divisional Labour Party. At the selection conference he secured 49 votes well ahead of his two rivals, who obtained 15 and nine respectively [Central Leeds DLP Minutes, Leeds Archive, ALL 2102.63/1]. Central Leeds had never been a Labour seat. While the electorate contained a strong working-class element it also included members of the city centre business community, and some party members might have felt that Denman would appeal to them. His financial contribution to the local party was also significant – £200 a year for the agent's salary. His 1929 election address appealed to voters 'to be true to the old Progressive traditions of a Yorkshire manufacturing town'. Helped perhaps by the intervention of a Liberal, Denman duly became Central Leeds' first Labour MP:

Leeds Central, May 1929: electorate 56 417, turnout 68.9 per cent

Hon. R. D. Denman (Labour)	17 322	(44.6 per cent)
Sir C. H. Wilson (Conservative)	15 958	(41.0 per cent)
M. J. Landa (Liberal)	5607	(14.4 per cent)
Majority	1364	(3.6 per cent)

Within the Parliamentary Labour Party (PLP) Denman generally played the part of a loyalist who was prepared to be gently critical on specific points. In his first speech as a Labour MP he urged less caution on housing and education [*Hansard*, 5 July 1929, cols 458–62], and when the government's Unemployment Insurance Bill was under attack by many Labour backbenchers in late 1929, Denman was critical of both the Bill's content and the government's handling of the issue. He commiserated with an even more recent recruit from Liberalism, Sir William Jowitt, whom he saw as 'the one oasis of competence in Thursday's desert' [Denman to Jowitt, 9 December 1929 (copy), Denman Papers, Box 5]. Perhaps predictably he felt that the government's prospects depended on cooperation with the Liberals. On one symbolic issue he voted against the Labour government – the acceptability of Lord Hunsdon as a member of the Public Works Loans Board (PWLB). Hunsdon had been extremely hostile to the miners during the 1926 lockout; in a well-remembered comment he had compared them to the Germans in the 1914–18 war. When the question of Hunsdon's reappointment to the PWLB came up in July 1930 it was opposed by several Labour MPs – left-wingers, miners and habitual loyalists. In the end 64 Labour MPs, including Denman, opposed Hunsdon's reappointment.

In general Denman's relationship with his local party seems to have been amicable, although a controversy arose early in 1931 over his failure to vote for John Scurr's pro-Catholic amendment to the Education Bill. On this question, with its denominational passions, the Members of the Leeds Central Labour Party Executive were divided [Leeds Central DLP Executive, 11 February 1931, Leeds City Archive]. Otherwise Denman was able to endorse central elements of the party culture. For example in his column for the *Leeds Weekly Citizen* he praised 'the patient loyalty of the solid unobtrusive Trade Union MP ... the firm foundation on which the Government has been able to build ... the secure sanity of the heart of our movement' [*Leeds Weekly Citizen*, 10 April 1931].

However Denman's response to the economic and political crisis of August to September 1931 placed him permanently at odds with this ethos. His economic outlook was orthodox and his response to the May Report (on public expenditure) was positive, 'excellently done and exceedingly valuable as a warning to all progressives of whatever Party, of dangers ahead' [Notes, Denman Papers Box 5]. This assessment seemed free of any outrage about the proposed cuts in unemployment benefit and thus in the living standards of the poor. Sympathy with MacDonald did not mean a rapid and unambiguous shift to full support of the National Government. Denman's preference for cooperative responses to crisis indicated that he thought that Labour should be a constructive rather than a hostile opposition. He attended the PLP meeting on 28 August 1931 and expressed his views to Lord Chancellor Sankey:

I talked to a few of our men, Oldfield, Strauss and Malone, and found they held the view that while the Party should go into Opposition, its opposition should be discriminating and that we ought to maintain friendly contact with the P.M. ... I hope that when the House meets we shall have a slight influence in mitigating Party hostility [Denman to Sankey, 28 August 1931, Sankey Papers, MSS Eng. Hist. *c* 508].

None of those referred to by Denman broke with the party. The preference for limited opposition was probably shared by several MPs, not least some senior ex-ministers. However strong sentiments within the labour movement helped to undermine that prospect. Some politicians took a more combative line, in alliance with leading figures in the TUC. Even at the 28 August PLP meeting feeling towards the 'renegades' was hostile, and this emotion subsequently became more dominant. Many activists in the local parties were antipathetic to the new government, and showed little tolerance of Labour MPs who expressed more ambiguous views. By the end of August, Denman was under pressure from his Leeds activists. A concerned party member told him, 'My own view is that the Party rank and file is bitterly hostile, and in a very ugly mood throughout the country, and will be ruthless with MacD, Snowden, Thomas and others who will act with them' [S. Pearce to Denman, 31 August 1931, Denman Papers, Box 5]. Two days later Pearce came directly to the point 'The Party has decided against MacDonald, and both in the interests of Party and principles, I advise you to stand by us' [Pearce to Denman, 2 September 1931, loc. cit].

A parliamentary debate on 8 September 1931 ended with a vote of confidence in the new government. A small number of Labour MPs voted with the government, Denman and four others abstained. One of the latter, Josiah Wedgwood, was acting in a characteristically individualistic fashion; the others had discussed the tactic, including Norman Angell, who shared Denman's views: 'In the course of the evening, Dick Denman, Strauss and Miss Picton Turbeville came and said they were doubtful as to the wisdom of voting a lack of confidence. Denman left about ten o' clock. I said I would definitely abstain' [note dated 8 September 1931, quoted in Angell (1951) 258].

MacDonald attempted to persuade this group to support the Government, but only Denman took that further step. On 10 September he informed Labour's Chief Whip, Thomas Kennedy, of his feeling that vigorous opposition would only worsen the economic crisis: 'I am driven to prefer measurable wrongs and injustices that can later be remedied to the immeasurable injuries of chaos'. He affirmed that the severance would be temporary; he would never join another party [Denman to Thomas Kennedy, 10 September 1931, Denman Papers, Box 5].

The next evening, 11 September 1931, Denman attended a special meeting of the Leeds Central DLP following earlier discussions with the party officers. They had sensed his pro-MacDonald feelings, but he had not made a clear statement about his political future. Following his abstention in the Commons he had telegraphed the Leeds party about his decision to withdraw from opposition. His explanation at the party meeting acknowledged the power of recent Conservative propaganda on finance and economy. He felt that Snowden's April 1931 budget had not been sound, and that the crisis was imposing severe limits on possible political strategies:

> There was no alternative to a National Government. He wanted the Labour Party to get the crisis out of the way, and then deal with the problems. Their business was to form an effective criticism to [*sic*] the Government's proposals, in order to lessen its evil effects on the poorer classes of the community ... if the Government Majority had only been 40 there would have been an immediate run on the bank. The type of opposition which the Labour Party was putting up would lengthen the time of the present situation. People would be frightened to restore Labour to Power with no definite proposals to deal with the Situation. Generous emotions existing in the Labour Party are being turned in the wrong direction [Leeds Central DLP Special Meeting, 11 September 1931].

After questioning, the delegates, with one dissentient expressed their emphatic disagreement with Denman's support of the National Government and instructed the party executive to find another parliamentary candidate. Denman acknowledged that the party could have taken no other course; he pointed out that he had withdrawn from opposition but had not yet supported the National Government.

Subsequent events made this distinction untenable. Along with other supporters of MacDonald, Denman was expelled from the party by Labour's National Executive at its meeting on 28 September. The imminence of an election meant that Denman's position in Central Leeds required clarification. He wished to fight as a Labour supporter of MacDonald, but the local Conservatives already had a prospective candidate – Sir Edward Grigg. Denman met the Leeds Conservative officials on 9 October 1931.

> For neither side was it an agreeable meeting. They put up their excellent case firmly and per-suasively. I had obstinately to reject it and made it quite plain to them that in any event I should have to go to the poll. Meanwhile I think they had received information from London that agreement had been reached at Headquarters that seats of sitting supporters were not to be contested by others in the National team. When therefore they saw I was not to be moved, they accepted the position with surprising magnanimity and put their organisation freely at my disposal [Denman (1948) 13].

Even after his expulsion Denman hoped that his breach would be temporary; but the style, content and result of the election campaign destroyed this prospect. He shared a platform with Stanley Baldwin and commended the Conservatives for playing the national, not the party game. A lifelong Free Trader, he accepted the expediency of a tariff in the current crisis. Greeted by Labour supporters with cries of 'traitor', a response to heckling demonstrated his endorsement of the more hysterical element of the National Labour campaign. When a critic insisted he was 'trying to break the Labour Party', Denman retorted 'not to break them, but to prevent them breaking the country' [*Yorkshire Post*, 16 October 1931; other material from press cuttings book, 1931 Election, Denman Papers, Box 12]. The Central Leeds result was just one demonstration of the power of the national appeal:

Leeds Central, October 1931: electorate 56 082, turnout 66.2 per cent

Hon. R. D. Denman (National Labour)	26 496 (71.4 per cent)
M. Turner-Samuels (Labour)	10 633 (28.6 per cent)
Majority	15 863 (42.8 per cent)

Denman played an active role in the small National Labour parliamentary group in the 1931–35 parliament and remained committed to the possibility of progressive influence within the National majority. He told Ted Scott of the *Manchester Guardian* that there seemed little prospect of a strong party of the left: 'The Samuel Liberals are curiously isolated, and seem only to raise hostile animosities amongst those whose political instincts could make them allies. By perverse contrast, MacDonald Labour seems to get on excellently with young Tory progressives' [Denman to Ted Scott, copy, 14 March 1932, Denman Papers Box 5]. As for the Labour Party, he considered that its trade union link restricted its electoral appeal since the unions desired 'domination'. Furthermore there was an absence of the liberty of thought and action that had characterised the Liberal Party in its successful period had disappeared [see 'An Interlude or a Fresh Start?', paper by Denman at the Fabian Summer School 1932, Denman Papers, Box 5].

The search for an effective progressive politics achieved little through National Labour MPs; they were just a few individuals within a Conservative-dominated parliamentary majority and MacDonald seemed uninterested in the formulation of a distinctively National Labour position. As the 1931 crisis was followed by a geographically and occupationally uneven recovery, the idea of salvation through a cross-party government seemed less relevant. With the acrimonious shift of the Samuel Liberals to opposition, the government's cross-party identity seemed less plausible.

Denman's result in the November 1935 election in Central Leeds suggested that the distinctively National Labour element of 1931 had almost vanished:

Leeds Central, November 1935: electorate 51 182, turnout 61.4 per cent

Hon. R. D. Denman (National Labour)	17 747	(56.4 per cent)
F. W. Lindley (Labour)	13 701	(43.6 per cent)
Majority	4046	(12.8 per cent)

A Leeds Labour activist subsequently indicted Denman as a straightforward Conservative: 'You have become so attached to the Tory Party that you out Tory some of its most ardent representatives' [W. Withey to Denman, 12 March 1938, Denman Papers, Box 2]. Nevertheless he continued to argue that the National Labour government had considerable progressive achievements to its credit. In a letter to MacDonald he presented an evolutionary vision that harmonised with some of the latter's beliefs:

we are better occupied than in being indignant. We are all busy on a steady process of social improvement and social organisation that proceeds with a sureness which as yet shows no sign of coming to an end. That sort of work is better accomplished in an atmosphere of calm than in one of stress and everybody knows that the present type of Government does it better than any probable Labour Government [Denman to Ramsay MacDonald (copy), 14 July 1937, Denman Papers, Box 5].

Following the eclipse of Ramsay MacDonald, Denman was amongst those who sought to develop the National Labour organisation and formulate a distinctive politics. Other figures included 'Buck' de la Warr, Malcolm MacDonald, Kenneth Lindsay and Harold Nicholson. Their vision was of a centre party that would transcend divisive partisanship. The links with elements of Denman's earlier politics were clear.

The project failed. Resources were few and controversy over Chamberlain's foreign policy was producing new alignments. Denman, who was a supporter of appeasement, felt that Chamberlain's policy fitted in with the liberal precepts that had marked his own political career. He was unhappy about the British guarantee to Poland in March 1939: 'In Versailles days many of us thought the division of Germany by the Polish Corridor was an insanity which could not last. Are we now to undertake a European war to preserve it?' [Denman to H. J. Gundrip (copy), 29 March 1939, Denman Papers, Box 2].

In the Commons Denman was a loyal supporter of the Chamberlain government up to and including the critical censure vote on 8 May 1940. During the Churchill Coalition he intervened only infrequently in Commons debates and retired from Parliament with a baronetcy upon the 1945 dissolution. The closest Denman came to ministerial office was when he refused MacDonald's offer of the Assistant Postmaster Generalship in 1932. Outside parliament he was second Church commissioner and administered Queen Anne's Bounty between 1931 and 1943. Such concerns perhaps harmonised with Denman's style. A sympathetic journalist characterised him in the combative 1931 election: 'mild-mannered, a little precise, grey-haired, Mr Denman suggests at first sight a clergyman in mufti' [*Yorkshire Evening News*, 10 October 1931]. In retirement he published a book of reminiscences. He died on 22 December 1957.

Denman's first marriage took place on 11 February 1904 to Helen Christian Sutherland, daughter of Sir Thomas Sutherland, shipowner and Liberal, later Liberal Unionist MP for Greenock (1884–1900). They parted in 1909. Helen Denman later claimed that she had no longer been able to bear the spiritual suffocation of marriage [see Harris (1997) 116]. In 1914 Denman married May Spencer, daughter of James Spencer of Murrah Hall, Greystoke, Cumberland. They had three sons and two daughters. The eldest son, Charles, unsuccessfully contested Central Leeds as a National Labour candidate in the 1945 election.

Pre-1914 Liberalism provided Denman with a comfortable political home as an economic and social moderniser who endorsed appropriate state intervention and had a strong interest in labour questions. With the fracturing of Liberalism during and after the 1914–18 war he spent the remainder of his political career seeking an effective instrument for Progressive politics. His adherence to the Labour Party illustrates the attempt by MacDonald and others, after 1918, to construct a party of progress with broad social and ideological appeal. In turn his departure in 1931 reflected the problem of building a progressive identity for a party with strong trade union links and a robust sense of class. More broadly, Denman's career illuminates the complexities of Progressive Liberalism and the diverse paths by which such recruits came to Labour.

Writings: *On The Road to Peace An Essay* (February 1915); *An Address* by R. D. Denman, published for and on behalf of the Carlisle Branch of the Union of Democratic Control (Carlisle, 1915); *Political Sketches* (Carlisle, 1948); Articles in *The Newsletter* from 1932.

Sources: **(1) MSS:** Denman Papers, Bodleian Library Oxford; William Henry Beveridge Papers, British Library of Political Science; Annette and Henry Beveridge Papers, India Office Library; Ramsay MacDonald Papers, Public Record Office; Sankey Papers, Bodleian Library Oxford. **(2) Party Records:** Leeds City Divisional Labour Party Records, Leeds City Archive; Labour Party National Executive Committee Minutes, National Museum of Labour History Manchester. **(3) Newspapers:** *Carlisle Evening Journal*, 18 January 1910, 5 December 1910, 27 November 1923; *Manchester Guardian*, 12 November 1924; *Leeds Weekly Citizen*, 10 April 1931; *Yorkshire Evening News*, 10 October 1931. **(4) Other:** *Hansard*, 1910–45; Norman Angell, *After All* (1951); Reginald Bassett, *1931: Political Crisis* (1958); Nigel Nicholson (ed.), *Harold Nicholson: Diaries and Letters 1930–39* (1966); Maurice Cowling, *The Impact of Hitler: British Politics and British Policy 1933–1940* (Cambridge, 1975); Duncan Tanner, *Political Change and the Labour Party 1900–1918* (Cambridge, 1991); Jose Harris, *William Beveridge: A Biography*, 2nd edn (Oxford, 1997); David Howell, *MacDonald's Party - Labour Identities and Crisis 1922–1931* (Oxford, 2002).

DAVID HOWELL

EDWARDS, Huw Thomas (1892–1970)
TRADE UNIONIST, SOCIALIST, WELSH NATIONALIST

Huw Thomas Edwards, popularly known as Huw T., was born on 19 November 1892 in Pen-y-Ffridd, a cottage on top of Talyfan Mountain, Ro-Wen, in the Conwy Valley, Caernarfonshire. He was the youngest of the seven children of Huw Edwards, farmer and quarryman, and Elizabeth Edwards, née Williams. Edwards grew up steeped in the tradition of the struggle between workers and quarry owners that culminated in the great Penrhyn lockout of 1900–3. Workers were often exposed to the vagaries of the market and had to travel long distances to seek employment when the quarries temporarily closed. It was in this context of conflict and instability that Edwards spent his childhood. Edwards' father was seriously injured in a fall at a quarry and as a consequence the family suffered financially. Like many other children of quarrymen, he viewed employers as the enemy and the union as a means of support.

Edwards had little formal education and played truant whenever possible, although his mother was a keen advocate of the importance of reading and writing. In his autobiography, *Hewn From the Rock* (1967), he explicitly states that his formative influences were the relationship between capital and labour in the quarries and the culture of the chapel. Many settlements were almost company towns, with the local stores belonging to the quarry owners. High food prices forced workers to travel up to nine miles in search of cheaper suppliers. The early death of Edwards' mother was a traumatic experience for him, and his domestic life was further disrupted when his father married a policeman's daughter and the family fragmented.

At the age of 10, Edwards worked with his father at Greiglwyd quarry in Penmaenmawr during the school holidays. In 1907, at the age of 14, he began to work there full-time, but on the advice of his father, after three months he changed jobs and became a farm labourer [Edwards (1967) 31–5]. His last agricultural job was on a farm in Talybont near Bangor. Like other agricultural labourers of his generation, he saw the coalfields of the south as a shining beacon of opportunity. Edwards arrived in Tonypandy – a place that was soon to be the scene of intense industrial conflict – full of youthful optimism. He started work straight away at the Clydach Vale No. 2 Pit in the main heading. One of the principal sporting activities in the south Wales valleys at that time was boxing. Edwards became quite an accomplished fighter, paying for training sessions with a man named Blake, a black boxer with a good reputation. He gained extra money from bouts in boxing booths and travelled the local circuit. There he met other famous boxers, including Jim Driscoll, Fred Welsh and Tom Thomas (two other local boxers, Leslie Williams and Dai Bowen, perished on the *Titanic*) [Edwards (1967) 42].

The positive image of Tonypandy that had attracted Edwards was initially upheld. He made many friends, enjoyed secure employment and improved his boxing skills. However the calm of the community was increasingly challenged by growing industrial tension between miners and mine owners. As a young member of the South Wales Miners' Federation, he was soon involved in the Cambrian Combine strike. The conciliatory approach of William Abraham (Mabon) was threatened by the emerging radical section of the union, epitomised by Noah Ablett and A. J. Cook. This rank and file challenge was crystallised in a pamphlet entitled *The Miners' Next Step* (1912), which expressed a syndicalist approach to the deteriorating industrial relations in the local industry. Edwards later recalled a meeting in which Cook accused Mabon of having shares in the Cambrian Coal Company. Mabon gave a magisterial speech and turned the meeting against Cook and his critics [Edwards (1967) 42]. But even the diplomatic skills of Mabon could not prevent the growth of militancy. On a union march to Llwynpia during the Combine strike, Edwards received a head wound from a blow delivered by the London police. Towards the end of the dispute he joined the army, taking advantage of the opportunity it provided to develop his boxing career. However the army's rigid authority structure did not fit in with his developing view of society and he soon left and returned to south Wales. It was probably during his subsequent time in the coalfield that Edwards became a member of the Independent Labour Party (ILP).

For a while Edwards returned to Penmaenmawr, where he worked in a local quarry for three weeks. He then moved back to south Wales, first to Aberfan near Merthyr, then on to Cwm Cynon, where in 1913, 439 men lost their lives in the Senghenydd colliery disaster. Edwards rushed to the scene and joined the rescue party that went underground. Adding to his negative experience of quarry owners, coal capitalism instilled in him a keen sense of injustice, that he retained throughout his career as a trade unionist. He returned to Aberfan, where he formed a new circle of friends from the Bethania Chapel. Socialism and religion were to remain central to Edwards' conception of a Welsh identity and would lead him from Labour to Plaid Cymru then back to Labour in his search for a vehicle for Welsh working-class emancipation.

During the First World War, Edwards fought in France at Mons and Ypres. He was seriously injured and returned to Wales on 22 March 1918. He found work with a tree-felling firm at Cae Athro, near Caernarfon, rejoined the ILP, and became a member of the Workers' Union. He then moved back to Penmaenmawr, found work in a local quarry and joined the Quarrymen's Union. He was soon sacked because of an interunion dispute. The men were keen to join the Dockers' Union, whose persuasive representatives had paid a fruitful visit to Penmaenmawr. The dispute divided families and was only settled when TUC mediation forced the men back into the Quarrymen's Union. Edwards refused to rejoin and resisted attempts by the employer to force the issue – he was dismissed because of the intransigent position he adopted on what he felt was a question of principle [Edwards (1967) 55].

After a period of unemployment he found work in Llandulas. With regular employment sporadic, Edwards again travelled south to work in the mining industry while attempting to support his family back in the north. Work in the mines did not pay enough to sustain two homes, so he travelled north again and took employment at the Penmaenbach Quarry. Edwards had retained his links with the ILP and now worked hard to recruit members and set up village branches across north Wales. The Labour Party seriously thought about standing a candidate for the Caernarfon Boroughs, the seat held by Lloyd George. A. E. Zimmern, a professor at the University College Aberystwyth, was selected and fought the seat in 1924, gaining 3401 votes. After the election Edwards and others felt that a base had now been established in the north: in 1922 Robert Richards, another university academic, had successfully won Wrexham for Labour on a narrow majority. A year later a conference was organised to bring the parties in the north and south closer together. In the summer of 1925 party meetings were held on the banks of the River Conwy, attracting speakers such as George Lansbury and Stephen Walsh [North Wales Labour Council Minutes, 1923–30, Edwards Papers, C/1].

Edwards was also beginning to enhance his reputation in the trade union movement through his membership of the North Wales Quarrymen's Union (this union joined the Transport and General Workers' Union – TGWU – in 1922). In 1923 he was elected secretary of the Penmaenmawr branch of the TGWU. Throughout north Wales trade unionism was beginning to mature across a range of industries. For example the coal miners of Denbighshire and Flintshire had made great strides under the leadership of Edward Hughes and his son Hugh Hughes, and the John Summers Steel Works in Shotton was proving fertile ground, with the young Arthur Deakin (future leader of the TGWU) working to recruit members for the Dock, Wharf and Riverside Union (this became part of the TGWU in 1922). Earlier, in 1910, Ernest Bevin had led a recruitment drive for the union with mixed success. The workers at Courtaulds' rayon factory were organised, but after 1921 the membership fell and the TGWU remained a minority concern until its full recognition in 1934 [Edwards (1957) 52]. The increase in membership did not, however, signal domination by the Labour Party. An associate of Edwards in the TGWU in the early 1920s, John Hughes, was a staunch Conservative. Nonetheless he managed to put his party politics to one side and campaigned vigorously for the election of Edwards to the Penmaenmawr Rural District Council in 1929. Bill Quick, who was a branch secretary of the TGWU at Wrexham Gas Works, along with his uncle, was also an ardent Conservative [Edwards (1967) 65].

Throughout the 1920s Edwards kept up his work with the TGWU and the Labour Party while maintaining his rigorous regime of physical work in the quarry. He played a determined role in the general strike of 1926, organising relief funds for local miners, but was generally critical of the stance of the TGWU leadership:

Every single member of the unions knew that we had betrayed the miners and many of us throughout the country would much prefer to have been beaten to our knees by hunger than to be sent back to work as we were through the weakness of leadership ... It was to me that Bevin's telegram to Conway and Penmaenmawr calling off the strike was delivered. I had put it in Bartle's shop window for everybody to see but I was so disgusted with the whole proceedings that every time I passed the window I hung my head in shame [Edwards (1967) 66].

The TGWU in north Wales endorsed the critical views of the local miners' leader Hugh Hughes in a letter to Bevin, and also attacked Bevin for his part in engineering the return to work. In his reply Bevin poured scorn on Hughes and the reluctance of the MFGB to abide by the decisions of the TUC:

The miners claim to come in and have all, and then not accept the decision of the governing body ... they claim to go on their own when it suits them. This is an intolerable position ... The miners showed an absolute indifference to rest of the Trade Union Movement who supported them ... This union has nothing to be ashamed of and nothing to apologise for [Bevin to J. W. Williams, TGWU Area 13, 26 May 1926, Edwards Papers, A6/9].

The union movement in north Wales was divided throughout the lockout, with the coal miners of Flintshire returning to work some time before the end of the stoppage in December [Gildart (2001) 532–61]. Edwards felt that the aftermath of the lockout was a disaster for the labour movement, with wide-scale victimisation and the promotion of mediocre men to leadership positions in a number of unions. He lost his faith in the trade union leaders and for a time seriously questioned the respect he had accorded to labour figures such as Bevin.

Before the 1929 general election, Edwards turned down the first of many opportunities he was given to secure a seat in Parliament. Instead he became election agent to Tomos ap Rhys, who was fighting the Caernarfon Borough constituency. Rhys lost heavily to David Lloyd George and the Conservative J. B. Davies. Edwards became increasingly disillusioned with the divisions within the labour movement, especially regarding economic policy. He was clearly sympathetic to the position of the ILP, but was critical of the personality disputes within the party. In his autobiography he recalled a fight between Arthur Cook and Campbell Stephen. Stephen had accused Cook of disowning the contents of the Cook/Maxton manifesto, and the warring protagonists had had to be separated by James Maxton. Although politically on the left, Edwards remained sympathetic to the position taken by MacDonald in the crisis of 1931. Edwards' perception is important here in questioning some of the myths associated with the treachery of MacDonald. He felt that MacDonald's efforts in opposing the war and his endless travelling had left him physically unfit for the pressures of prime ministerial office [Edwards (1967) 77–81]. While acknowledging the betrayal, Edwards, along with others who had been influenced by MacDonald in the formative years of the party, retained a degree of affection for the discredited leader.

In 1931 Edwards was sacked from his job in the quarry for his trade union activities. During his period of unemployment he turned his hand to writing and completed two dramas. His passion for writing poetry, plays and radio scripts would stay with him throughout his time in the labour movement. Literature was an avenue in which Edwards could further express his sense of Welsh identity. Written in the Welsh language, his work evoked the idealisation of Welsh rural life, as well as the importance of the pulpit and the hearth in disseminating a particular culture that infused self-sacrifice with an acute sense of social transformation. Despite this, and unlike Saunders Lewis (the first president of Plaid Cymru) Edwards was aware of the potential that industrialisation offered for promoting collective action and wealth redistribution.

Edwards retained his enthusiasm for Labour politics and was the election agent in Flintshire for Frances Edwards, a 24-year-old teacher from Manchester who was heavily defeated by the National Liberal candidate, F. Llewellyn Jones, in 1931. Local government work also kept him busy, and in 1932, he became chairman of Penmaenmawr Council. The opportunity that led to Edwards becoming a figure of prominence throughout Wales came in the same year when Arthur Deakin left his union position in north Wales to pursue his rise to the top of the TGWU in London. Because Edwards had kept up his union membership during his period of unemployment he was eligible to apply for the vacant post of regional officer. He was clearly the outside candidate among the 23 applicants as he held no official position in the union. Nonetheless, after an intense interview by a panel that included Bevin he was informed that he would be offered the job. He then moved to Shotton in East Flintshire, working long hours for £5 per week [Bevin to Edwards, 19 August 1932, Edwards Papers, A1/3]. In his first year of office, W. H. Bennett, the head of Region 13 (covering north Wales and Merseyside) died. There was talk of Deakin returning to Shotton, but Edwards protested and threatened to resign, so Deakin remained in London. This was the first of many occasions on which Edwards and Deakin came into conflict as Deakin strove to maintain a thorough grip on north Wales as an element of his centralising ambitions.

The trade union movement in north Wales was still facing a membership crisis. In the coalfield, the 1926 lockout and the victimisation that followed undermined the strength of the Miners' Federation of Great Britain. (A company union had replaced the North Wales Miners Association at Point of Ayr Colliery and remained a constant irritation until the period of public ownership.) Moreover the 4000 workers at the large Courtaulds plants in Flintshire were unorganised, due largely to the anti-union stance of the employer. Within a month Edwards had completed a successful organising drive there and these workers became members of Region 13. Membership success was quickly realised in transport. The Crosville Bus Company was at that time buying up the smaller companies, recognising the TGWU and delivering new members by the month [Edwards (1967) 96]. Membership success also brought increased pressure on Edwards. He admitted later that he was not a natural leader of men and was uneasy about disciplining renegades. He felt that new, younger members were too eager to strike when immediate demands were not met. The influence of Deakin was also not lost on Edwards and he became increasingly suspicious of moves by the Communist Party to broaden its base within the movement, although he remained committed to an informal 'popular front' of progressive forces, an ideal that he would carry into the ranks of Plaid Cymru.

Averse to the factional politics that arose periodically within trade unions, Edwards concentrated on the less controversial initiatives available to a leader. Education became a central plank of his policies in Shotton. He ran courses for unemployed TGWU members and delivered lectures for the Workers' Educational Association at weekends. In 1936 he suffered a bout of nervous exhaustion, combined with a heart condition, and was hospitalised for a month. Bevin feared the worst after visiting Edwards and informed his wife that the family would be looked after until he made a full recovery. Bevin's personal intervention was not lost on Edwards and he retained his admiration for this giant of labour [Edwards (1957) 57]. The episode also illustrated Bevin's attachment to his union and his principal officers in the field.

Edwards was again offered the opportunity to pursue a parliamentary career through a candidacy in the 1935 election. After some serious thought on the matter, he took Bevin's advice and remained an official of the TGWU. This pattern was followed by a range of other union leaders who preferred to remain in the authoritative positions they had carved out in their own localities rather than disappear to the back benches of Westminster. Labour was again heavily defeated in Flintshire. The remaining beacon of socialist hope in north Wales was the Wrexham seat, where Robert Richards was elected with a majority of 5283.

In 1939 Edwards was elected to the Flintshire County Council, thus extending the influence of the union into local affairs. Throughout his tenure on the council he retained his interest in education, sitting on committees and becoming a Justice of the Peace (JP). In later years he admitted that he found it difficulty to administer the law as a JP, as he was often more sympathetic to the perpetrators of crime than to those who brought the prosecutions. This period also led him to question further the role of the Communist Party and its effect on the trade union movement. In preparation for the impending hostilities, new armaments factories were being constructed around the country, requiring a large influx of labour to particular localities. One such development was the plant at Marchwiel near Wrexham. Fourteen thousand men were drafted into the factory, with local unions reaping the benefit of increased membership and contributions. However members of the Communist Party gained prominence on particular committees and their militent strategies threatered construction and production. Local TGWU officials lost control of the situation – they were prevented from attending meetings, and allegations of sabotage became a regular occurrence. Edwards was pressed by the other unions to end the state of conflict at the plant and to disband the unofficial committee. There was no progress for a number of weeks, but Edwards eventually addressed the workforce. He informed the meeting that the committee would not be recognised by either the contractors or the unions. After some debate amongst the workforce it was agreed that the unofficial leadership should be disbanded. The Communists then left the area and industrial relations at the plant entered a period of calm [Edwards (1957) 61–4]. Although on the left of the Labour Party, Edwards was clearly opposed to the policies of what he viewed as the 'Stalin-directed' Communist Party and its disruptive tactics. His performance at Marchwiel led to the offer of senior positions with leading companies. These were rejected after much thought, as Edwards felt that his natural home was the labour movement.

During the war Region 13 of the TGWU prospered, new officials were appointed and new offices were opened in Bangor, Ellesmere Port, Dolgellau and Newtown. The first stirrings of Edwards' nationalist political sentiment began to take concrete form. The union was involved in the National Eisteddfod and Coleg Harlech. Edwards increasingly highlighted the economic problems facing Wales to the North Wales Committee of the Welsh Board for Industry, and prior to the election of the Labour Government in 1945 he boldly called for self-government of the principality. Nonetheless his sense of class and his belief in the transformative capacity of the state indicated a number of tensions in his thought. Unlike Aneurin Bevan and others who had no qualms about sacrificing Welsh national claims for socialist policies through Westminster, Edwards cut a more complicated figure concerning the national question. The division between Bevan and other Labour MPs on any form of devolution was clearly exposed on 17 October 1944 at the first 'Welsh Day' debate. Edwards was a follower of Bevan and corresponded with him on a range of issues throughout his period of office, but he was clearly opposed to Bevan's intransigence on the question of devolution.

Edwards' star continued to rise. He reluctantly accepted the MBE, but returned it to Churchill during the 1945 election campaign when the latter compared the Labour Party to Hitler's Gestapo. The election was to be crucial for Labour and the party began to streamline its organisational structure in the principality. A South Wales Regional Council of Labour had been formed in 1937, reflecting the importance of the south, particularly the coalfield. In the north, nine Constituency Labour Parties had been organised by the North Wales Labour Federation, with Edwards taking the position of secretary. Two seats were now reserved on the South Wales Council for representatives from the north, and from 1947 one Regional Council covered the whole of Wales.

Edwards was once again touted as a potential parliamentary candidate – this time for his home constituency of Flintshire. He again declined and threw his support behind Eirene White, who had the backing of Bevin and of Deakin at the TGWU headquarters. White was the outside candidate for the nomination, and it was the hard work of Edwards that ensured her defeat of the favoured miners' candidate at the selection meeting. White came within 1039 votes of taking Flintshire in 1945, reflecting the growing importance of Labour in this mixed industrial constituency. Edwards was elected first chairman of the Council of Wales in 1949. The Council seemed to be the answer to Edwards' search to combine his nationalist aspirations with his socialism, although it had limited powers and was seen as a lame duck by Herbert Morrison and others in the party. For the next ten years Edwards worked hard for a Welsh voice within Britain and was critical of the calls for a Welsh parliament by S. O. Davies (the MP for Merthyr) and others across the political spectrum. Plaid Cymru had stood eight candidates in the 1945 election, but most had lost their deposits. This was a telling lesson for Edwards as it highlighted the divisive capacity of political nationalism.

Edwards remained an admirer of Bevan and criticised the victimisation of those on the left in the unions and the Labour Party. 'I regarded Aneurin as the only possible leader of the Socialist Party' [Edwards to George Brown, 16 May 1962, Edwards Papers, A2/143]. In a letter to Bevin after the 1949 Labour conference he attacked the speech made by Sam Watson, the moderate leader of the Durham miners, and was critical of the treatment of Konni Zilliacus, who had been expelled for his alleged Soviet sympathies [Edwards to Bevin, 13 June 1949, Edwards Papers, A2/31]. In 1950 Edwards was asked by the local branch of the NUR to allow his name to go forward as prospective parliamentary candidate for Merioneth – he again declined. He also refused the offer of a knighthood in the birthday honours list, much to the disappointment of Attlee, the Labour Prime Minister [Attlee to Edwards, 15 May 1950, Edwards Papers, A/67].

The growing tensions within the labour movement, which had been greatly affected by the Cold War, created divisions within the TGWU, particularly between Edwards and Bevin's successor, Arthur Deakin. Edwards felt that Deakin was unprepared to let go of Region 13 as he was continuing to busy himself with the internal affairs of the union. He also felt that Deakin had consistently caused friction between Bevin and north Wales. The situation between Deakin and Edwards escalated when Edwards openly declared his support for Bevan in the internal party battles that followed the 1951 election. The final insult came when Deakin overruled the wish of Region 13 for funds to be provided for the publication of Edwards' history of the union, *It Was My Privilege*, which was eventually published in 1957 [Tom Jones to Edwards, 1 February 1955, Edwards Papers, A1/207]. In 1953 Edwards' disillusionment with the politics of the TGWU, coupled with ill health, prompted his early retirement. He also wanted to spend more time on the Welsh bodies of which he was a member. Along with his extensive work on a range of committees, Edwards was chosen as chairman of the Welsh Tourist Board in 1952.

His activities in specifically Welsh institutions and his dissatisfaction with Gaitskell's leadership caused Edwards to reassess his view of the Labour Party. His close friend Cyril O. Jones was having a similar crisis of confidence. Jones was a solicitor to the North Wales NUM and a pioneer of the socialist movement in north Wales. In a letter to Edwards in 1956 he expressed his disappointment with the party's abandonment of socialism and its aversion to Welsh devolution [Cyril O Jones to Edwards, 17 December 1956, Edwards Papers, A1/261]. In 1958 Edwards resigned his position as chairman of the Council of Wales, informing the Conservative Prime Minister, Harold Macmillan, that Wales would not have an adequate voice until the principality had a secretary of state and reforms already enjoyed by Scotland in terms of devolved decision making. Local Labour Party dignitaries voiced their concern about Edwards' criticism of the leadership, and James Idwal Jones (MP for Wrexham) called on Edwards to leave the party. However he retained significant support amongst rank and file members and was invited by the Ruthin Labour Party to become their nominee for the Denbigh parliamentary constituency; he again declined.

In August 1959, after much soul searching, Edwards left the party and resigned from Flintshire County Council. Throughout the year he had been conducting secret meetings with Plaid Cymru, but still maintained that he was a socialist. Some aspects of Plaid's policy were not to his liking, and he informed the party president, Gwynfor Evans, that what was needed for Wales was a movement not a party. Evans was sympathetic to Edwards' position and had earlier agreed that a platform for Wales was needed so that Edwards and others would not have to leave the Labour Party [Evans to Edwards, 29 July 1959, Edwards Papers, A1/539]. Edwards was obviously comfortable with Evans, a Nonconformist who advocated socialist policies. This was in stark contrast to Saunders Lewis, whom Evans had replaced. Lewis was a Catholic antisocialist who advocated deindustrialisation and the reconstruction of a rural idyll that was meant to represent a Welsh past untainted by Anglicisation. The class base of the nationalist party was also disconcerting for Edwards, who was uneasy with the leadership mix of middle-class intellectuals and literary romantics. He joined the party, but remained critical of what he saw as its narrow nationalism. A number of other socialists joined Plaid as a result of Edwards' statements and conversion to the nationalist cause [J. E. Jones, Plaid Cymru Organiser, to Edwards, 20 August 1959, Edwards Papers, A1/587]. His commitment to Plaid Cymru had been helped by the fact that he had served as an ambassador for the principality through his work with the Welsh Tourist Board, visiting Eastern Europe and other countries. In 1958 he had visited the United States, where he had met with John L. Lewis, president of the United Mineworkers of America and son of a south Wales miner. Securing Edwards was a considerable coup for Plaid Cymru, which felt that many more socialists and trade unionists would follow.

However it was clear to friends and opponents in the labour movement that Edwards was still a socialist and his shift to Plaid was widely viewed as a short-lived protest. He was close to Frank Cousins, the left-wing candidate who had replaced Jock Tiffin as head of the TGWU, and both men were dismissive of the direction of Labour policy. In a letter to Edwards, Cousins maintained that 'there is an apparent drift away from many of our basic socialist beliefs by some of those who are in the party now' [Cousins to Edwards, 6 November 1961, Edwards Papers, A1/675]. With the Labour Party making preparations for the 1964 general election, many felt that someone like Edwards was needed to rally the troops in north Wales. In May 1962 George Brown MP contacted Edwards to arrange a meeting to discuss future policies for Wales. Brown stated that 'we need a

Labour Government badly ... it would be marvellous if you were to come back and help us in a big way' [Brown to Edwards, 24 October 1963, Edwards Papers, A1/767]. In October he resigned from the Executive Committee of Plaid Cymru. He was opposed to the party fighting all the Welsh parliamentary seats and thought that it should dispense with its electoral policy altogether. A year later the new Labour leader, Harold Wilson, sent a similar letter to Edwards: 'I know you will always be a socialist – anyone who knew you as well as I did in my Board of Trade days could never be in any doubt' [Wilson to Edwards, 6 March 1963, Edwards Papers, A1/724].

The resurgence of the Labour Party before the 1964 general election clearly forced Edwards to rethink his political strategy. Throughout 1963 Edwards had been increasingly critical of the role of Plaid Cymru as a political party. He again called for the formation of a Welsh nationalist movement that would concentrate on retaining a Welsh culture, making the people proud to be Welsh and leaving politics to the politicians. In 1965 Edwards returned to the Labour Party, along with his friend Cyril O Jones and other socialists, after initially facing rejection by his local branch in Mold. He felt that under Wilson the party would again promote the socialist vision of its founders and develop a positive policy of devolution. Cliff Prothero, the Labour Party organiser for Wales, welcomed Edwards with an attack on the nationalists: 'your rightful place is inside the Labour Party and not spending your time in a political party which appears to be more anti-English than pro-Welsh' [Prothero to Edwards, 21 January 1965, Edwards Papers, A1/831]. In his autobiography Edwards himself claimed that his time in Plaid Cymru had been the worst four and half years of his life [Edwards (1967) 236].

Back in the Labour Party he retained his nationalism and campaigned vigorously for Welsh issues and devolution. His goals were partly realised when James Griffiths became the first Secretary of State for Wales in 1964. In a letter to Eirene White MP in 1968, he justified his conversion to Plaid Cymru: he felt that Gaitskell had been a disaster for the party and had failed to recognise that there was a distinctive Welsh problem. Nonetheless he increasingly poured scorn on the policies of the nationalists and intimated that 'a Conservative Government and all that that would entail for the workers may bring them to their senses' [Edwards to White, 25 March 1968, Edwards Papers, A2/162]. Ironically the nationalists went on to electoral success after Edwards' departure, most notably winning a seat in the Carmarthen by-election of 1966.

As well as holding positions on local government bodies, in later life Edwards pursued his love of literature by taking control of the Welsh language newspaper Y Faner. He was also a director of the publishing house Gwasg Gee of Denbigh, vice-president of the Honourable Society of Cymmrodorion and, for a time, president of the Welsh Language Society. His interest in Welsh culture was rewarded when he was made a director of Television Wales, a member of the National Broadcasting Council of the BBC and a member of the Council of the National Eisteddfod. His contribution to education was also rewarded when he received an honorary doctorate from the University of Wales. His wife Margaret Owen died at the family home, Crud -yr-Amel, Sychdyn, Mold on 1 June 1966. The marriage had produced two children, one son Gwyn for (1924–26) and a daughter Elizabeth Catherine (known all her life as Beti) (1920–79). Edwards continued to reside at this address with his daughter, her husband and their two daughters.

Edwards was a celebrated figure in Welsh industrial, political and cultural circles. Widely viewed as the unofficial prime minster of Wales, his passion for his country was matched by his commitment to socialism. This was recognised by the Labour Party and the trade union movement. In 1945, when the Attlee government established the Council of Wales, James Griffiths immediately put forward Edwards' name. In essence he was a cultural nationalist. He was proud of his roots and felt that Wales had a claim to nationhood – but this should never be at the expense of socialism. In the late 1950s he despaired at the inability of Plaid Cymru to pronounce itself a socialist party. He was also outraged at the policies it adopted on industrialisation and its attacks on Labour politicians such as James Griffiths and Bevan. Even more troubling for Edwards was his perception of the party's rural identity and apparent anti-Englishness. His support for Plaid Cymru came at a time when the Labour Party was racked by internal divisions and the Conservative Government was ignoring the feelings of the Welsh people by flooding the Tryweryn Valley in Merioneth to provide Liverpool with water. This was also a time of optimism for nationalists, with increased support for the preservation of the Welsh language and the indigenous culture.

Edwards soon rediscovered his belief in the central planning of the Labour Party to deliver economic change in Wales. In this respect he cut a similar figure to Bevan, but his overriding Welshness marked him out as a crucial character in the complex relationship between nationalism and socialism in British politics. No doubt he would have been a keen supporter of the 1974 and 1997 Labour governments' devolution policies.

Huw T. Edwards died on 9 November 1970 at Abergele hospital, and his remains were cremated at Pentrebychan Crematorium in Wrexham. He left an estate valued at £6258. A memorial stone was erected in Ro-wen, Conwy, to honour his memory.

Writings: *What I want For Wales* (1949); *They went to Llandrindod* (1951); *Tros y Tresi* (1956); *It Was My Privilege* (Denbigh, 1957); *Tros F'ysgwydd* (1959); *Ar y Cyd: Cerddi gan Huw T. Edwards, Mathonwy Hughes, Gwilym R. Jones Rhydwen Williams* (1962); *Troi' r Drol* (1963); *Hewn From the Rock* (Cardiff, 1967).

Sources: (1) MSS: Huw T. Edwards Papers, National Library of Wales, Aberystwyth; Tom Jones Papers, Flintshire Record Office, Hawarden; TGWU material, MRC, University of Warwick. **(2) Newspapers:** *Wrexham Leader; Birmingham Mail; Chester Chronicle; Flintshire County Herald; Mold, Deeside and Buckley Leader; Prestatyn Weekly; Rhyl and Prestatyn Gazette; The Flintshire Observer; Western Mail.* **(3) Other:** J. H. Howard, *Winding Lanes* (n.d.); Alan Butt Philip, *The Welsh Question: Nationalism in Welsh Politics 1945–70* (1975); John Osmond, *Creative Conflict: The Politics of Welsh Devolution* (1977); Cliff Prothero, *Recount* (Omskirk, 1982); John Osmond (ed.), *The National Question Again: Welsh Political Identity in the 1980s* (1985); Kenneth O. Morgan, *Rebirth of a Nation: Wales 1880–1980* (1987); David Pretty, *The Rural Revolt That Failed: Farm Workers' Trade Unions in Wales 1889–1950* (1989); R. Merfyn Jones, *The North Wales Quarrymen 1874–1922* (1991); Duncan Tanner, Chris Williams and Deian Hopkin (eds), *The Labour Party in Wales, 1900–2000* (Cardiff, 2000); Keith Gildart, 'Militancy, moderation, and the struggle against Company Unionism in the North Wales Coalfield, 1926–44', *The Welsh History Review*, 20:3 (2001) 532–64; Keith Gildart, *North Wales Miners: A Fragile Unity, 1945–1996* (Cardiff, 2001); personal information from Mrs Eleri Huws and Ms Sioned Williams, granddaughters and Kieth Jones, education officer, TGWU, Cardiff.

KEITH GILDART

See also: †Arthur DEAKIN; †Edward HUGHES; †Hugh HUGHES; Tom JONES.

GRAHAM, William (Willie) (1887–1932)
LABOUR MP AND CABINET MINISTER

William Graham was born on 29 July 1887 in Peebles, the eldest of the seven children of George Graham, a master builder, and his wife Jessie, née Newton. In 1892 George left the family building firm, Wilkie and Graham, and moved to Innerleithen, where he set up his own company. Willie was educated at home prior to starting school in the town, but after two years he and his brother were sent to the Tweed Green School in Peebles, which necessitated their living with their grandmother, a 'strong disciplinarian' who lived in a 'spotless' house [Graham (1948) 10]. As a child, Graham was hardworking and entrepreneurial: according to his brother he 'early developed business acumen' [ibid., 12]. But his father's own entrepreneurial skills appear to have been mediocre, for in 1899 his firm went bankrupt and he was forced to move the family to Edinburgh, where he took a post as a clerk of works. The family's income and status fell considerably as a result.

Although Willie won a bursary to Heriot's School in 1900 and a scholarship in 1902, it was clear that the family's financial straits ruled out any attempt at university entry. Accordingly Willie left school at the age of 15, and after taking a correspondence course he passed the examinations for a boy clerkship in the civil service with some ease. He was appointed to the War Office in London, where he lived with his grandmother, but when she moved back to Scotland he had no alternative but to follow her; in any case, he had rapidly become bored by the work. To compensate for this boredom he had taken courses in shorthand and bookkeeping at Pitman's College in London, and back in Edinburgh he took a job as a shorthand typist in a woollen warehouse. He filled his spare time by writing articles for newspapers, although none was published.

In the spring of 1904, however, largely thanks to his father's contacts he was appointed as a reporter on the Selkirk weekly paper, *The Southern Reporter*, which was the leading Liberal paper in the area. Working as a reporter meant that he became closely involved with politics for the first time. At first this merely meant reporting events in the council chamber. However by 1905 he was a member of a Church literary society, and that autumn led a discussion on the youth of Selkirk. He later presented a paper on 'Modern Socialism and its Future', and stood as a Labour candidate in a mock election. Meanwhile the Graham family had moved yet again, this time to Glasgow, and on his frequent visits there Graham attended Independent Labour Party (ILP) meetings. He joined the party in 1906 or 1907, and when a branch of the party was formed in Selkirk in 1908 he was elected secretary.

Graham's socialist activities brought him into conflict with his paper's Liberal proprietor, so he left to become the Selkirk reporter on the rival *Border Standard*. There he had great success and was paid commission on the increased circulation and advertising that he secured. This enabled him to set aside sufficient funds to consider taking a degree at the university in Edinburgh, to where his family soon removed. In April 1911 he left the *Standard* to undertake six months' private tuition prior to entering the university that autumn. His aim – which he achieved – was to make enough money from freelance journalism to keep himself while at university. He graduated with an MA with honours in economic science in 1915, and took an LLB with honours in economic history, statistics and mathematical economics, forensic medicine and administrative law in 1917. He taught for the Workers' Educational Association between 1915–18. In 1927 he was awarded an honorary LLD by the university.

In 1909 Graham had transferred his ILP membership to the West Edinburgh branch. Once at the university, he joined, and rapidly took office in, the university branch of the Fabian Society. He became a well-known figure, and in 1913 was approached by a deputation to stand as Labour candidate for the St Leonards ward in the town council elections. St Leonards was a slum area in the city centre, and in his election address Graham described housing as 'the primary problem': he advocated 'a vigorous and enlightened national and municipal policy' because private enterprise had 'broken down'. He also advocated better public healthcare, rating reform, a minimum wage, municipalisation of the trams and better recreation facilities. His Liberal opponent, Judge Macpherson, had been on the town council almost continuously since 1887, but after a vigorous campaign Graham was elected with 1316 votes to Macpherson's 992 and the Unionist's 213. He thus became the first university student to serve on the town council. As a councillor, over the next six years – he retired in September 1919 when it became clear that he could not combine the role with that of MP – he worked assiduously for the interests of his electors. He served on numerous committees, including that on public health. Given that he was still a student and had to support himself through freelance journalism, this was a very heavy burden of work indeed.

When the war came in 1914 Graham supported military action against Germany, although he opposed the tendency towards crass jingoism, and twice volunteered for service in the armed forces, only to be rejected on medical grounds. During the war he worked hard for the people of

Edinburgh, particularly as chairman of the Disablement Committee, and in battling for better war pensions. His prominence increased to such an extent that in late 1917 he was selected as prospective parliamentary candidate for the Edinburgh Central constituency, which included his own St Leonard's ward as well as St Giles and George Square. Edinburgh Central was a deprived and overcrowded area of poor housing and high levels of poverty. Edinburgh as a whole remained a relatively weak area for Labour; Central had been held by the Liberals since 1886 and there had never been a Labour candidate before. But in the December 1918 general election Graham fought with energy and verve against Joseph Dobbie, a Coalition Liberal. Graham made great play of his work with soldiers' dependants and the disabled; called for a strong League of Nations and an end to secret diplomacy; demanded limited home rule for Scotland; and advocated better social provision for old people and widows, higher wages, public ownership and control of land and key industries, and measures against profiteering. He also made a specific appeal to women voters, stressing the need for equal pay for equal work, and better housing. Most of this would have appealed to progressive and even some centrist Liberals, and Graham was to prove adept at maximising such linkages in his Edinburgh campaigns. Furthermore he made particular appeals to Jewish voters, for whom he held special meetings and to whom he stressed his support for a Jewish national homeland. He also employed techniques such as factory gate meetings, even though he found open-air speaking a trial, perhaps because of his small stature (he was 5 feet 6 inches tall). Dobbie's supporters tried to smear Graham's war record, but to no avail [Graham (1948) 70–4; ILP Papers, Reel 23] as he won the seat:

Edinburgh Central, 1918: electorate 30 867, turnout 45.2 per cent

W. Graham (Labour)	7161 (51.3 per cent)
J. Dobbie (Coalition Liberal)	6797 (48.7 per cent)
Majority	364 (2.6 per cent)

Graham's victory was widely seen as perhaps the most spectacular Labour success of the 1918 general election, but on the whole the results were disappointing for the party as it won only 57 seats. All the former ILP MPs, including Ramsay MacDonald and Philip Snowden, were defeated; indeed Graham was one of only three ILP MPs. But the domination of the Parliamentary Labour Party by rather dull and narrow trade union MPs left great openings for an articulate graduate such as Graham. Although his interests in pensions and the disabled – and for a time, Scottish home rule – continued, he was increasingly acknowledged as an expert on finance and economics and aroused admiration for his 'amazing memory': he was able to reel off figures and facts without the help of notes. In 1920–22 he chaired the Labour Party's Advisory Committee on Finance and Commerce (he later lost the position to Snowden). He additionally served as one of the five PLP representatives on Labour's National Joint Council, which included representatives of the party's National Executive Committee and the TUC General Council; he lost the position after the 1922 election brought back more senior figures. Even at that stage he was a right-winger in Labour terms, rejecting communism and direct action. Later, during the 1922 election, *The Times* described him as 'perhaps the mildest-mannered man who has ever proclaimed [sic] a capital levy'. Shortly after meeting him for the first time in February 1919, Beatrice Webb offered a characteristically sharp view:

[Graham] looks like an industrious and highly respectable bank clerk and seems at first sight insignificant and unattractive; but he is said to be a good administrator, a lucid speaker with considerable capacity for facts and arguments. He has the Fabian opinions of the late nineties, he dislikes big words and revolutionary sentiments: he prides himself on knowing more than the other Labour Members [of Parliament] – he is in fact a bit of a prig, but an honest and warmhearted prig [Cole (1952) 145].

Indeed his moderation became the subject of adverse comments and there were rumours in Central Edinburgh that he might switch to the Liberals. On 9 June 1919 the Central Edinburgh branch of the ILP passed a vote of confidence in him, but only by 36 votes to 25, and there was renewed criticism when he showed himself to be lukewarm about the Scottish rents agitation the following year [Dowse (1966) 62; McLean (1983) 171]. However as his reputation grew and Labour moderated its position after the excitements of 1918–20, Graham's position became increasingly in kilter with that of the party as a whole and he was readopted unopposed as the parliamentary candidate in February 1922. Graham's reputation as a moderate with a capacity for detailed work meant that the party called on him to serve on official bodies. In April 1919 he was appointed to the Royal Commission on Income Tax under Lord Colwyn. Also on the commission were Warren Fisher (head of the civil service) and the distinguished economist A. C. Pigou. The hard work that Graham put into the commission marked him out as an assiduous and expert individual, and many of the commission's recommendations were accepted, either at the time or subsequently. However Graham was no mere cipher and he joined with Fisher, Pigou and others in signing a reservation to the main report (March 1920), in which they called for cooperative societies' receipts to be exempted from income tax.

In September 1919 Graham was appointed to the Departmental Committee on Railway Agreements, again under Colwyn, which reported in February 1921; and in October he was appointed to the Speaker's Conference on Devolution, which reported in April 1920. From July 1920 he served under the former prime minister, H. H. Asquith, on the Royal Commission on Oxford and Cambridge Universities, which had been appointed in October 1919. The original Labour representative, Arthur Henderson, had resigned because of overwork; Graham, as one of the few Labour MPs to have any experience of university, was the obvious replacement, although in January 1922, just two months before the committee submitted its report, he admitted to Hugh Dalton that he knew 'nothing about Oxford and Cambridge' [Dalton (1986) 23]. In the final report, however, he did offer reservations in favour of greater powers to the universities against the colleges, and joined the vice-principal of Newnham College, Miss B. A. Clough, in proposing that full membership of Cambridge University be opened to women. All of this work did a great deal to establish Graham's reputation as one of Labour's most diligent and earnest figures.

Although his continuing financial reliance on freelance journalism (most notably for the *Edinburgh Evening News*) meant that he was heavily overworked, there could be no doubt that his star was in the ascendant. In a conversation with C. P. Scott in February 1922, Henderson mentioned Graham as one of four possible candidates (the others being MacDonald, Hugh Dalton and Tom Shaw) for the post of foreign secretary in a future Labour government [Pimlott (1985) 120]. However his first interest remained economics, and in 1921 he published his only full-length book, *The Wages of Labour*. This book confirmed his moderation: it called for the progressive improvement of wages by a gradual shift towards greater state intervention and control, and concluded with a condemnation of Marxists who called for the abolition of the wages system through revolution:

> Sad as the reflection may be, in wages, as in almost everything else, we are at the beginning rather than the end of civilization. Spectacular revolutions may provide orators and their audiences with a night's intoxication, but cold facts, impartial study, patient enterprise await the workers in the morning [Graham (1921) 160].

It was not surprising, in the light of these views, that he was associated for a time with the Whitley Councils movement, which espoused a conciliatory approach to industrial relations, or that he was chairman, from 1921–26, of the Industrial Fatigue Research Board (IFRB).

During this period Graham married Ethel Margaret Dobson of Harrogate, whom he had met in Edinburgh during the First World War. They rented rooms in Clapham before buying a house in Hendon in 1920. They were to have no children. He was still writing considerably (mainly, but not solely, on political matters) for various newspapers in order to supplement his parliamentary salary, and indeed when he travelled to Edinburgh he often took his typewriter with him so that he could work on the train. Although he enjoyed sport – he was a lifelong supporter of Heart of Midlothian FC, watched Arsenal and Tottenham when in London, and spent the occasional afternoon at cricket matches in the summer – he soon gained a reputation for being what would today be called a workaholic. Even on visits to The Oval, for example, he would take Blue Books or other official papers to read.

In the October 1922 general election, which followed the downfall of the Lloyd George Coalition, Graham held Central Edinburgh in a straight fight with a Lloyd George Liberal. He almost doubled this majority in the subsequent election in December 1923, when he again had a straight fight with a Liberal.

Edinburgh Central, 1922: electorate 30 970, turnout 71.8 per cent

W. Graham (Labour)	12 876 (57.9 per cent)
Sir G. McCrae (National Liberal)	9371 (42.1 per cent)
Majority	3505 (15.8 per cent)

Edinburgh Central, 1923: electorate 32 492, turnout 59.7 per cent

W. Graham (Labour)	13 186 (67.9 per cent)
T. Lamb (Liberal)	6225 (32.1 per cent)
Majority	6961 (35.8 per cent)

By now he had become somewhat out of sympathy with Labour's declared policy of imposing a capital levy to help pay off the war debt, which prefigured the party's shift towards a surtax (in which he would play a leading part) later in the decade. In his 1922 election address he expressed some support for guild socialism, declaring that in the large industries 'the future lies with a guild organisation', which, he argued, 'would avoid the weaknesses of State Socialism on the one hand, and the dangers and waste of existing industrial chaos on the other'. Soon, however, he moved away from this position and was increasingly attracted by the idea of public corporations. The 1922 election brought a large rise in the number of Labour MPs (to 142) and saw the return of many of the party's leading figures and 'experts', including, in Graham's own realm of finance and economics, Philip Snowden. The latter's seniority made it only natural that he should supersede Graham as the PLP's chief spokesman. Graham appears not to have resented this: indeed the two men soon formed a very strong relationship. Colin Cross says that Graham was 'the nearest thing Snowden ever had to a son' [Cross (1966) 198], while for Graham, whose own relationship with his mother was much closer than that with his father, Snowden might well have been something of a father substitute.

The 1923 election left the Conservatives without a parliamentary majority, despite being the largest party, and eventually the first Labour Government came to office with tacit Liberal support. Graham's expectations of the government were not high, but he did hope that it would last for at least a year, and would try to pacify Europe, cut food taxes and 'wasteful expenditure', launch a major housing programme to improve dwellings, help to relieve unemployment, and improve education and widow's pensions. He believed that Labour would then be in a position to call a further election, at which it would campaign for, *inter alia*, nationalisation of the mines and railways [*The Times*, 2 January 1924]. In the Government, Graham received the post he had wanted: Financial Secretary to the Treasury (in effect, number two to Snowden, who was made Chancellor of the Exchequer). There was general agreement that he acquitted himself well in the post: the leading Liberal, Sir John Simon, told one Labour backbencher that Graham was 'a first-class accountant in a failing business' [Toole (1935) 178], while Snowden wrote much later that he had been 'a conspicuous success' [Snowden (1934) II: 765]. By July 1924 the 'inner cabinet' was seeing Graham as the only junior minister with obvious cabinet potential [Cole (1952) 38]. But it was not to be, for the government fell that October over the Campbell Case. In private Graham was critical of MacDonald's handling of the affair, a view that turned him somewhat against the leader and therefore, in all probability, even closer to Snowden. In the general election that followed, Labour was soundly beaten and the Conservatives returned to power with a huge majority. In Edinburgh, Graham, fighting a Conservative for the first time, was safely re-elected:

Edinburgh Central, 1924: electorate 32 744, turnout 68.8 per cent

W. Graham (Labour)	13 628 (60.5 per cent)
A. Beaton (Conservative)	8897 (39.5 per cent)
Majority	4731 (21.0 per cent)

Graham's consolation for losing government office was to be sworn into the Privy Council. He also became chairman of the Public Accounts Committee, a position he held until 1929. His reputation for fiscal orthodoxy was enhanced when he broadly supported the return to the gold standard in April 1925, and he continued to work closely with Snowden in most areas. It was to a significant extent due to Graham's work that the party abandoned the capital levy and came to favour the surtax. In the run-up to the 1929 election he played a large part in planning the party's programme and manifesto [Dalton (1953) 173–4, 182]. In particular – along with Snowden, Tom Shaw and Sidney Webb – he drafted an immediate programme in early 1929. The central feature was an emerging programme of public works to reduce unemployment. Two features of this unpublished agenda are significant: it was drawn up prior to the launching of Lloyd George's 'We Can Conquer Unemployment' campaign, and it did not assume an overall parliamentary majority [see Report of the Sub-Committee on the First Session's Administrative and Legislative Programme, Passfield Papers IV 21; Williamson (1992) 40].

Some writers have depicted Graham as simply a cipher for Snowden. However too much can be made of his orthodoxy. While he continued to appear to be an orthodox free trader and was opposed to the introduction of safeguarding duties for lace in June 1925, he was not quite as firm on this point as Snowden. In August 1924 he had said that Labourites should not be slaves to free trade, and that 'he did not rule out the possibilities of a tariff in certain circumstances' [*The Times*, 19 August 1924]. A year later he wrote to the protectionist Colonial and Dominions Secretary, Leo Amery, proposing talks on 'a large empire policy', stating that he believed that 'on the basis of the Empire as a unit, we are much nearer to agreement than we imagine' [Boyce (1987) 89]. Significantly, he was appointed to the Research Committee of the Empire Marketing Board in January 1927. He also became increasingly interested in 'scientific' solutions to Britain's industrial ills. At first he believed that this could be done through the IFRB, making workers more efficient by granting them better working conditions; but in 1927 he began to favour the large-scale rationalisation of Britain's key industries and emerged as one of the driving forces behind Labour's industrial policy. Nonetheless he continued to believe that Britain's industrial and economic ills could only be resolved as part of a much larger programme to settle the international problems of war debts and reparations, excessive tariffs and the malfunctioning of the gold standard.

During this period Graham became a bigger player in his own right. In December 1924 he was elected to one of the 12 positions on the PLP Executive Committee, having taken eighth place. His popularity among his colleagues was illustrated by the fact that he finished second in the ballots of December 1925 and 1926, and third in the ballot of December 1927. With J. H. Thomas and James Maxton he served on a Labour Party committee appointed to look into MacDonald's handling of the infamous Zinoviev Letter (the committee exonerated the party leader). He also began to take a close interest in broadcasting. In August 1925 he was appointed to the Broadcasting Committee, which was headed by Lord Crawford and Balcarres. In March 1926 the committee recommended the establishment of a British Broadcasting Corporation. Graham made the keynote speech at a BBC conference on adult education in April 1928, but his awareness of the power of the new medium was not to be seen until early 1931, when as President of the Board of Trade he asked the BBC to broadcast his statement on the coal talks in South Wales so that it would reach the miners sooner than it might otherwise, and so end the dispute that was in progress there.

Graham narrowly missed one particular record: when the BBC made its first television transmission in September 1929, a letter from Graham was read wishing the new service well: if he had chosen to make the statement in person he would have been the first British politician to broadcast on television. Meanwhile other forms of public recognition included his appointment to the Medical Research Council in December 1924, and to the Royal Commission on the Court of Session in January 1926. Curiously, though, Graham remained a somewhat shadowy figure to the party at large. He appears to have taken no part in the party's annual conferences, and leading works on the party – such as the three-volume official tome, *The Book of the Labour Party* (1925) and Egon Wertheimer's *Portrait of the Labour Party* (1929) – ignored him altogether. Perhaps this was a result of his perceived lack of sparkle: as Beatrice Webb put it in 1927, while Sir Charles Trevelyan was 'worthy but dull; W. Graham [was] weighty as well as worthy but if anything duller' [Cole (1956) 138].

Dull or not, Graham sailed home in Edinburgh Central in the 1929 general election:

Edinburgh Central, 1929: electorate 40 975, turnout 69.3 per cent

Rt Hon. W. Graham (Labour)	16 762 (59.0 per cent)
H. Alexander (Liberal)	6745 (23.8 per cent)
J. H. Mackie (Conservative)	4889 (17.2 per cent)
Majority	10 017 (35.2 per cent)

The election resulted in the appointment of the second minority Labour Government, and – despite talk that he might be made Scottish secretary – Graham entered the cabinet as President of the Board of Trade. Three areas of his work in this position proved particularly significant. The first was international economic policy. Graham's preferred solution for Britain's economic ills – which intensified massively as the world recession hit Britain from late 1929 – was through the general resolution of the international problems of tariffs, war debts and reparations. On 3 September 1929 he became the first British economics minister to address the League of Nations Assembly in Geneva, where he called for a tariff truce of two to three years. Although a truce was eventually agreed the following year, few other countries, and no other great powers, adhered to it, and it was only of one year's duration. He also took part, with Snowden (Chancellor) and Henderson (Foreign Secretary), in the Hague conference on reparations in autumn 1929, where he secured concessions on the issue of Germany's payment of reparations in kind. With Snowden he also participated in the second Hague conference in early 1930. Later that year he chaired the Economic Advisory Council's Committee on the Chinese Situation, which called for a British loan to China to help British trade there. He also set up an Overseas Trade Development Council to boost British exports, and sent missions abroad to promote British trade.

The second significant area of Graham's work was the attempt to reorganise the coal industry. Nationalisation, Labour's preferred policy, was ruled out by the party's lack of a parliamentary majority, so Graham was left with the task of offering a reorganisation package. The Coal Mines Bill, published in December 1929, attracted heavy Liberal criticism and Graham was forced to make concessions to the Liberals in long drawn-out talks, where he was not helped by the incompetence of his first Minister of Mines, Ben Turner. The pressure became such that in February 1930 he collapsed during the debate on the third reading.

There were also serious difficulties with the Miners' Federation concerning the Labour Party's pre-election pledge to restore the seven-hour working day. Predictably the mine owners objected and pointed to the critical state of the industry. The Miners' Federation compromised initially on a seven and a half hour day and then more reluctantly on a Lords amendment allowing the option of a 'spreadover' – a 90 hour fortnight. The 1930 Coal Mines Act was in some ways weak and self-contradictory, but its creation of a Coal Mines Reorganisation Committee marked the point at which a British government first took direct responsibility for rationalisation.

Graham's third contribution was his attempt to rationalise Britain's other staple industries. He was appointed to chair a cabinet committee on the cotton industry (although he later relinquished the position to J. R. Clynes due to pressure of work). But progress through voluntary action was slow; and by August 1930 Graham was favouring compulsion. In April he told the cabinet that state financial assistance and protection might be the price of steel reorganisation, and was prepared to move towards nationalisation of the industry. But in neither case was the cabinet prepared to act.

More generally, this period saw two marked developments for Graham. The first was a degree of estrangement from Snowden and the latter's economic orthodoxy. This resulted partly from the issue of industrial reorganisation mentioned above, but also from the question of free trade. By mid 1930 there was a clear protectionist minority in the cabinet, including MacDonald, Thomas, Vernon Hartshorn and Christopher Addison, who tried to block the ratification of Graham's tariff truce. While they were thwarted by Snowden, it is clear that Graham was affected by their arguments. In June 1930 he told the leading Conservative MP, Sir Austen Chamberlain (with whom he had very good relations), that '[i]t sometimes seems as if there were a conspiracy against [British] trade. ... If you consent to join the suggested Three Party Conference on agriculture, I don't conceal that we shall have difficulty with Snowden, but you will find some men with very open minds' [Self (1995) 347]. By the time of the London Imperial Conference in October 1930 he favoured a quota for Empire wheat, a clear departure from free trade, and in a cabinet paper he criticised Snowden for taking such a hard line that he 'would play into the hands of the Tariff Reformers' [Drummond (1972) 68]. While he remained resistant to the idea of a revenue tariff, as advanced by Keynes and others, he had clearly moved from an adamantine free trade position. Thomas, the government's leading protectionist, later explicitly exempted Graham from his charge that most ministers had been 'riveted' to free trade, stating that his 'experience at the Board of Trade had convinced him of the necessity of changing our tariff system' [Thomas (1937) 205].

The second feature of the period was Graham's continuing rise up the party hierarchy. In early 1931 Snowden became very ill, and it was left to Graham, with the assistance of Sir Stafford Cripps (Solicitor-General) and F. W. Pethick-Lawrence (Financial Secretary) to do most of the work on the 1931 budget. Although Snowden recovered sufficiently to deliver the budget statement, Graham sat next to him with a copy of the speech so that he could take over should the Chancellor collapse. When Snowden began to talk of moving to the Lords, perhaps as colonial secretary, most observers within and outside the government firmly believed that the only realistic candidate to replace him was Graham. However Thomas was also interested in the post, and may have been favoured privately by MacDonald. Relations between Graham and the premier were now poor: it appears that Graham threatened to resign in November 1930, and MacDonald, who now thought him 'small and weak', might have accepted the resignation had the administration been in a stronger position [Williamson (1992) 103–4]. Snowden was determined not to allow Thomas to succeed him, and so held on in the hope that the succession could be made safe for Graham. In addition, by early 1931 he had replaced Clynes as one of the cabinet's 'Big Five'. When the cabinet established an economy committee in July 1931 to look into ways of rectifying the budget deficit predicted in the May report, it was Graham, not Clynes, who took the fifth place (with MacDonald, Snowden, Henderson and Thomas), although this also reflected the subject matter.

In the face of a predicted budget deficit of £120 million the Economy Committee had to act quickly. Along with other members of the committee, Graham was recalled from his holiday in Filey (his favourite resort) when the position of sterling weakened. Four meetings were held in mid August, prior to the first meeting of the cabinet on the nineteenth of the same month. Attempts were made to find an alternative to cuts, and particularly to the proposal for a cut in the rate of unemployment benefit. In the economy committee and in the cabinet, Graham voted for the proposition that a revenue tariff would be preferable to such a cut. This aroused the ire of Snowden, who told Graham bitterly: 'William, there shall be a Free Trade candidate next time in Central Edinburgh' [Dalton, P[olitial] D[iary], 27 August 1931, 153]. Graham was deputed to see the acting Liberal leader, Sir Herbert Samuel, to see whether the latter would back the government's more modest economic proposals independently of the Conservatives – the two had worked closely on the Coal Bill. However on this occasion Samuel could offer no hope of agreement. Graham's resistance to the larger package of cuts might have been tentative at first, but by the final weekend of the government's life he had emerged as a staunch opponent of further concessions to demands for economy, believing that 'the City [was] bluffing the Government' [Cole (1956) 282]. On 23 August he was one of nine ministers who opposed an unemployment benefit cut; this resistance to further economies meant the government had to resign. MacDonald remained in office to head a National Government, largely comprising Conservatives and Liberals, and the bulk of the Labour Party went into opposition. One of the few Labourites to follow MacDonald was Snowden [for Graham's account of the crisis see The Cabinet Committee and the May Report, Passfield Papers IV, Section 26].

In opposition, Graham's prestige within the party grew. He wrote a memorandum for leading colleagues stressing that the decisions made by the economy committee and the cabinet had been only 'provisional': while he probably believed this, some colleagues were rather sceptical. He also denied claims that the TUC General Council had attempted to dictate to Labour ministers. TUC opposition was presented 'with great moderation and restraint. ... At no time was there any suggestion of dictation; on the contrary the discussion was entirely friendly and constructive' [Cabinet Committee and the May Report]. When Henderson was elected to succeed MacDonald as leader on 28 August, Graham was elected joint deputy leader with Clynes. Graham, Dalton and Pethick-Lawrence took over as the party's main financial spokesmen. To some extent Dalton, himself an economist, found it easier to make the running, being less compromised by past closeness to Snowden and membership of the economy committee. But Graham chaired the party's new Finance and Trade Committee (which included Dalton, Cripps and Clement Attlee), whose work formed the basis of the later shifts in the party's economic policy. To a large extent this group took over control of the party from Henderson. Meanwhile Graham showed that, to a considerable extent, he remained a moderate. On 2 September 1931 he wrote privately that there was 'at the moment a serious danger of irresponsible talk and action', and that Labour must make sure that it advanced 'a constructive Socialist case' [Estorick (1949) 93]. He remained publicly committed to balancing the budget. His first – and in the event, only – major speech to a Labour party conference (on trade policy on 6 October), despite calling for an extension of state ownership of industry, aroused some criticism for its moderation [Labour Party Conference Report (1931) 195–198]. However Labour's opponents were not slow to portray him as an extremist who put party before country, and he did not help himself with the article he published in the Daily Express on 31 August. Although aimed primarily at rallying Labour spirits, it played into the hands of his critics:

What is described as the record of the Labour Government will be speedily forgotten. ... In an electorate approaching thirty millions there are now great, but essentially simple, mass movements; the trained students of politics and economics and the long view are in a hopeless minority. ... The next election will be fought, not by a Labour Government on an admittedly difficult defensive, but by a Labour movement united and eager. ... At one stroke, without an election, and with time to prepare for an election on unusually favourable ground,

[Labourites] have been relieved of [their] anxieties. Yesterday they dreaded a contest: to-day they are almost within sight of their clear majority in the House of Commons [cited in Bassett (1958) 202].

The consequential negative perception of Graham had a broader impact. In March 1929 he had been made a director of the Abbey Road Building Society. On becoming a minister he had had to relinquish the position, but had secured an understanding that, once back in opposition, he would be reinstated. Now, however, the society told him that this commitment would not be honoured, which meant the loss of a salary of around £1000 a year. In addition his hopes of resuming his career as a freelance journalist were largely dashed as most papers would take nothing from him. On top of the loss of his ministerial salary, such concerns can have done nothing to assuage the increasing depression he felt once the party's difficulties in opposing the new government became clear.

On 5 October 1931 the government called a general election. Graham's mood was pessimistic. His position in Edinburgh Central looked insecure from the start, and during the campaign he was mainly preoccupied with his efforts in that city, which prevented him from taking as high a profile in the overall campaign as the party's managers would have liked. The Conservative candidate was an able young advocate, J. C. M. Guy. Social change – including slum clearance – had reduced the population, and a disproportionate number of Labour voters had left. Graham found it hard to defend the actions he had taken in August, and his split with Snowden was held against him by many voters. Over the years he had built up a degree of cross-party support as a prominent Edinburgh man of whom the city could be proud: his moderation had enabled such support to flourish. Now it was a different story. When he tried to present himself as a defender of working-class interests by opposing welfare cuts, the Communist candidate, Fred Douglas, was there to remind voters of the extent of the cuts to which he had agreed, 'provisionally' or otherwise, while still a minister. His attempts to boost the record of the Labour government were unconvincing in a constituency where unemployment had soared. Furthermore Catholic voters were hostile to Graham for having supported the Labour government's allegedly anti-Catholic education policies.

Snowden, conducting a vitriolic anti-Labour campaign from 11 Downing Street, sent message after message to undermine Graham's arguments: within five minutes of Graham's election broadcast, for example, he was telephoning Treasury officials about his reply. When one of these messages was published in Edinburgh, according to one source Graham 'almost broke into tears' [Cross (1966) 316]. He ultimately became so tired of this losing battle that he announced on 22 October that he would make no further reply to any of Snowden's allegations. Worst of all, Graham could not be in Edinburgh on polling day, having had to return to London upon the sudden death of his father. In the event Guy won 17 293 votes to his 10 566 (Douglas lost his deposit), a majority of 6727. It was a crushing defeat.

Edinburgh Central, 1931: electorate 39 306, turnout 74.2 per cent

J. C. M. Guy (Conservative)	17 293 (59.3 per cent)
Rt. Hon. W. Graham (Labour)	10 566 (36.2 per cent)
F. Douglas (Communist)	1319 (4.5 per cent)
Majority	6727 (23.1 per cent)

In November 1931 Graham joined the stockbrokers Schwab and Snelling as an adviser on economic and financial matters: this at least gave him a living. He also visited Edinburgh Central to emphasise that it could be won back for Labour at the next election (a prediction that proved wrong). There was also the possibility that he would be nominated for a by-election when one became available, although he may have preferred to wait to try again in Edinburgh Central. However it was not to be. Shortly after Christmas he caught a chill. At first it did too seem too serious, for example on 31 December *The Times* published a letter from him about wheat quotas. But then he developed double pneumonia, and shortly before 10 p.m. on Friday 8 January he died at his home in Hendon. It was said that in his final delirium he moaned repeatedly of Snowden: 'Why did Philip do it? Why did Philip do it?' [Cross (1966) 316]. Indeed there were those who believed that he had died of 'heart-sickness' [Hamilton (1938) 409], but it may well be that sheer exhaustion from years of overwork had taken its toll. He was buried beside his father at Hendon Park Cemetery on 12 January 1932. He left £12 167 [*The Times*, 19 March 1932].

On hearing of Graham's death, Dalton was most fulsome in his praise of him, writing in his diary:

> This is a very great political loss. ... [O]n public grounds [it] is ruinous. He was only 44. ... He seemed to have the sure prospect of high office and great usefulness when we next came in. He had a combination of gifts very rare in politics – an immense power of mastery of detail; a clear grasp of Socialist principles; a tremendous – perhaps too great – capacity for work; courage, which had grown visibly in recent years and months; great patience, gentleness and courtesy. He always commanded confidence in his presentation of a case. He was a first-class colleague, perfect to work with. He never lost his temper. He erred, if at all, by excess of modesty. ... He is gone before any of our Old Men, be they wicked or virtuous. And he is gone just when our Movement most had need of him [Dalton (1953) 299].

More than 20 years later Dalton opined that if Graham had lived it was 'very unlikely that I should have become Chancellor of the Exchequer' in 1945 [Dalton (1953) 299–300]. It is, of course, impossible to tell; but it is clear that Graham would almost certainly have played a leading role in Labour politics in the 1930s, and probably the 1940s. And it seems possible that, as the influence of Snowden subsided and his own ideas continued to develop, he would have played a major part in the party's shift in economic thinking.

Writings: *Parliament, Legislation and Economic Science* (Birkbeck College Foundation Oration, 1931); *The Wages of Labour* (1921, revd edn 1924); Election Addresses: St Leonard's Ward (1913), Edinburgh Central (1918, 1922, 1923, 1924, 1929, 1931).

Sources: (1) MSS: Labour Party Conference Reports, 1918–32; The Cabinet Committee and the May Report, Passfield Papers IV 26. **(2) Newspapers:** *The Times*; *Edinburgh Evening News*; *The Scotsman*; *Edinburgh Evening Dispatch*; *Daily Herald*; *Daily Worker*. **(3) Other:** H. B. Lees-Smith (ed.), *The Encyclopaedia of the Labour Movement*, 3 vols (1928); E. Wertheimer, *Portrait of the Labour Party* (1929); *Dictionary of National Biography*, 1931–1940; Philip, Viscount Snowden, *An Autobiography* (1934); J. Toole, *Fighting Through Life* (1935); J. H. Thomas, *My Story* (1937); M. A. Hamilton, *Arthur Henderson* (1938); D. E. McHenry, *The Labour Party in transition, 1931–1938* (1938); G. D. H. Cole, *A History of the Labour Party from 1914* (1948); P. J. Grigg, *Prejudice and Judgement* (1948); T. H. Graham, *Willie Graham: The Life of the Rt. Hon. W. Graham* (1948); E. Estorick, *Stafford Cripps: A Biography* (1949); P. Ford and G. Ford, *A Breviate of Parliamentary Papers, 1917–1939* (Oxford, 1951); M. I. Cole (ed.), *The Diaries of Beatrice Webb, 1912–1924* (1952); H. Dalton, *Call Back Yesterday: Memoirs, 1887–1931* (1953); M. I. Cole (ed.), *The Diaries of Beatrice Webb, 1924–1932* (1956); R. Bassett, *Nineteen Thirty-One: Political Crisis* (1958); R. W. Lyman, *The First Labour Government, 1924* (1958); A. Briggs, *The History of Broadcasting in the United Kingdom, Volume I: The Birth of Broadcasting* (1961); A. Briggs, *The History of Broadcasting in the United Kingdom, Volume II: The Golden Age of Wireless* (1961); B. E. V. Sabine, *A History of Income Tax* (1966); C. Cross, *Philip Snowden* (1966); R. E. Dowse, *Left in the Centre: The Independent Labour Party, 1893–1940* (1966); R. Skidelsky, *Politicians and the Slump: The Labour Government of 1929–1931* (1967); O. Mosley, *My Life* (1968); T. Jones, *Whitehall Diary, Volume II: 1926–1930*, ed. K. Middlemas (1969); R. Rhodes James, *Memoirs of a Conservative: J. C. C. Davidson's Memoirs* *and papers, 1910–1937* (1969); H. J. Hanham, *Scottish Nationalism* (1969); D. Carlton, *MacDonald Versus Henderson: the Foreign Policy of the Second Labour Government* (1970); I. M. Drummond, *British Economic Policy and the Empire, 1919–1939* (1972); S. Koss, *Nonconformity in Modern British Politics* (1975); S. Howson and D. Winch, *The Economic Advisory Council, 1930–1939: A Study of Economic Advice during Depression and Recovery* (Cambridge, 1977); D. Marquand, *Ramsay MacDonald* (1977); B. Pimlott, *Labour and the Left in the 1930s* (Cambridge, 1977); M. Stenton and S. Lees, *Who's Who of British Members of Parliament, Volume III: 1919–1945* (1979); K. O. Morgan, *Consensus and Disunity: The Lloyd George Coalition Government, 1918–1922* (Oxford, 1979); I. McLean, *The Legend of Red Clydeside* (Edinburgh, 1983); W. Knox, 'William Graham', in W. Knox (ed.), *Scottish Labour Leaders, 1918–1939* (Edinburgh, 1984); B. Pimlott, *Hugh Dalton* (1985); H. A. Clegg, *A History of British Trade Unions since 1889, volume II: 1911–1933* (Oxford, 1985); B. Pimlott (ed.), *The Political Diary of Hugh Dalton, 1918–40, 1945–60* (1986); B. Pimlott (ed.), *The Second World War Diary of Hugh Dalton, 1940–45* (1986); I. G. C. Hutchison, *A Political History of Scotland, 1832–1924: Parties, Elections and Issues* (Edinburgh, 1986); W. Knox, *James Maxton* (Manchester, 1987); R. W. D. Boyce, *British Capitalism at the Crossroads, 1919–1932: A Study in British Politics, Economics and International Relations* (Cambridge, 1987); B. Supple, *The History of the British Coal Industry, Volume IV: The Political Economy of Decline, 1913–1946* (Oxford, 1987); K. Laybourn, *Philip Snowden: A Biography, 1864–1937* (Aldershot, 1988); A. Thorpe, 'The British general election of 1931', unpublished PhD thesis, University of Sheffield, 1988 (contains a case study of Central Edinburgh in 1931 that is not included in the published version); I. S. Wood, 'Hope deferred: Labour in Scotland in the 1920s', in I. Donnachie, C. Harvie and I. S. Wood (eds), *Forward: Labour Politics in Scotland, 1888–1988* (Edinburgh, 1989); P. Scannell and D. Cardiff, *A Social History of British Broadcasting, Volume I: Serving the Nation, 1922–1939* (Oxford, 1991); A. Thorpe, *The British General Election of 1931* (Oxford, 1991); P. Williamson, *National Crisis and National Government: Politics, the Economy and Empire, 1926–32* (1992); C. N. L. Brooke, *A History of the University of Cambridge, Volume IV: 1870–1990* (Cambridge, 1993); B. Harrison (ed.), *The History of the University of Oxford, Volume VIII: The Twentieth Century* (Oxford, 1994); R. C. Self (ed.), *The Austen Chamberlain Diary Letters, 1916–1937* (Cambridge, 1995); M. Dyer, *Capable Citizens and Improvident Democrats: The Scottish Electoral System, 1884–1929* (Aberdeen, 1996); N. J. Crowson (ed.), *Fleet Street, Press Barons and Politics: The Journals of Collin Brooks, 1932–1940*, (1998); N. Riddell, *Labour in Crisis: The Second Labour Government, 1929–1931* (Manchester, 1999); G. C. Peden, *The Treasury and British Public Policy, 1906–1959* (Oxford, 2000); Richard Whiting, *The Labour Party and Tatation: Party Identity and Political Purpose in Twentieth Century Britain* (Cambridge, 2001).

ANDREW THORPE

See also: †Arthur HENDERSON.

GREEN, Beatrice (1895–1927)
LABOUR PARTY ACTIVIST

Beatrice Green was one of the many women in south Wales to join Labour when the party extended individual membership to women. The numerous women's sections that were subsequently formed played a significant part in educating and training many women in south Wales. Green is representative of those women who remained nameless in the party's history, and in this respect she is typical of the many worthy women who have been neglected by historians of the party in Wales. Only her premature death saved her from total obscurity. In recollections and obituaries she has been presented as a remarkable figure whose political achievements deserve our attention. While she cannot be viewed as unique, this does not detract from the importance of her political contribution. It would be inaccurate to suggest that all the women who were active at the grass-roots level shared Green's talents for organising and public speaking, but she was by no means the only woman to possess these skills.

Beatrice Green, née Dykes, was born on 23 January 1895 in the bustling coalfield town of Abertillery in Monmouthshire, south Wales. She was the youngest of the three daughters and three sons born to William Dykes (formerly of neighbouring Abersychan) and Mary Ann Dykes (née Phillips, previously from Pontypool). William Dykes switched from iron puddling to coal mining at about the turn of the century following the closure of the local iron works. The family (which included Beatrice, her sisters Elizabeth and Margaret, and their three brothers, Thomas, William and Arthur) lived at various times in Ashfield Road, Gladstone Street and Cwm Street in Abertillery. Beatrice was educated locally in Abertillery, firstly at the Central School and later at Abertillery County School. Party politics does not appear to have been a subject that seriously concerned the Dykes family. In fact it would appear that Beatrice was the only member to develop an active interest in the Labour Party. For the Dykes household it was religion rather than politics that eterted the most powerful influence. The children were taken as babies to the nearby Ebenezer Baptist Chapel, and so began a long and close affiliation with Christianity.

Green's own connections with the chapel proved to be lifelong. She regularly attended the Sunday School as a child and it was there that she had her first taste of public speaking. She was baptised at the age of 17 and as a young adult continued to immerse herself in chapel matters. Through her work in the chapel she soon established herself as an effective communicator and organiser. She was among the people who, in the words of the minister, W. R. Lewis, 'carried out the difficult task' of grading the Sunday School [Ebenezer Chapel Annual Report, 1927]. The children were divided according to age and placed in one of four groups: nursery, primary, intermediate and senior. Green was also a founder of the chapel's 'Girl's Own Club', an all-girl club that was very similar to a youth club. Although there was a degree of religious education, it operated more on a social basis. Given that there were so few opportunities for girls to socialise at that time, this would have been a much welcomed facility, and the fact that there were usually 40–50 girls in attendance suggests that it was indeed a successful venture. Moreover because it was a chapel-organised group it would have been regarded as an acceptable way for young girls to pass their time when not helping with household tasks.

The years spent teaching the Sunday School's intermediate level earned Green a reputation as a remarkable story teller. She had the ability to reach and hold an audience with a style that was very much of her own making. A former Sunday School pupil later recalled how her teacher's face would radiate the content of her stories, and how she and the rest of her classmates had been mesmerized. Green's ability to make information clear to others was also exploited at chapel business meetings – she was often called upon when the content of the subject matter needed to be explained to those present. Likewise her ability to relay information in an easily understandable manner was invaluable during her short teaching career in various council schools in the area. However her marriage on 22 April 1916 to Ron Green, a local miner, forced her to give up the profession to which she was so obviously suited as women teachers were prohibited from continuing work after marriage. She returned briefly to teaching during the First World War, when women were required temporarily to fill the vacancies that arose when men were enlisted to fight.

Religion and education, then, were two of the guiding lights in Green's life, and both institutions reflected her concern for the welfare of humanity. By that time, socialism and nonconformity had become close allies for many activists in Wales. Many espoused a version of nonconformity that stressed the need for social morality and equality rather than a focus on the virtues and failings of the individual. For Green, their ideological basis combined to create an interest in public work that was concerned chiefly with the health, welfare and education of the working class. She took an active interest in the Abertillery District Hospital, which was built (funded by public subscription) in 1922. From its inauguration on 30 August 1922 she worked tirelessly as secretary of the hospital's Linen League. The league, which was made up of 40 or so local women, including both of Green's sisters and a number of Labour Party women, supplied the hospital's linen and provided washing services. They organised fund-raising events in order to purchase fabric and used their own sewing skills to make items such as sheets and pillowcases. During its first year of operation the league supplied over 1300 articles to the hospital, of which 800 had been made by the members themselves. Green's fellow workers attributed much of the league's success to her personally. In 1923 it was decided that membership of the league should entail an annual subscription and that the organisation should also serve as a social club, with regular social events for its members. As the league's representative on the board of management, Green was closely involved with much of the hospital's decision making. The league was consulted about new developments in the hospital, including David Daggar's proposal for a birth control clinic, to be opened in 1925. During the 1920s Green became a close friend of Marie Stopes, who was a fundamental figure in the clinic's formation. Green herself was a supporter of the clinic, although the league, like the local women's section, did not unanimously back its introduction to the hospital. The clinic operated for 16 months but was then forced to close due to intense opposition, led by the local clergy.

As Green's obituary in the local paper later maintained, it was her political work in which she was 'perhaps most interested' [*South Wales Gazette*, 21 October 1927]. It is difficult to pin down exactly when she began her association with the Labour Party. Abertillery was certainly a town where women were very much involved in activities that were closely connected to the party. A branch of the Women's Labour League was formed in the town in 1910, and in 1918 the decision to offer full party membership to women stimulated an increase in female involvement throughout south Wales. Under the new constitution the former league branches became known as women's sections, which were more closely affiliated to the party than their predecessors had been. The *South Wales Gazette* and *Labour Woman*, the official party magazine, portrayed the Abertillery women's section as a large and very active group during the 1920s, when Green was a member. Labour women's politics appealed to her because of their concern with matters related to health and welfare, particularly that of women and children.

Green remained true to her feminist convictions throughout her involvement in local politics. As she told a meeting of the Abertillery section in 1921, 'For too long the idea had been allowed to circulate that woman's place was in the home, and man's in the world. With the inadequate measure of franchise, woman was realising that politics had a direct bearing upon her home, and that she had to get out in order to put things right' [*South Wales Gazette*, 7 January 1921]. Nonetheless, 'No man, whatever his disposition, could know children like the women who bear them' [ibid.] Green, like the majority of Labour women in south Wales, did not call for a radical transformation of the gendered roles of men and women. However she and her counterparts believed that women should be encouraged to establish control over those aspects in which they were most closely involved. Hence women should not, Green maintained, remain passively in their homes waiting for the men in the political sphere to determine their fate. She supported women's participation in all aspects of the public sphere, and on equal terms with men. She backed the call for equal pay for equal work not only because financial inequality reinforced women's inferior status, but also because of 'the danger of cheap labour, and how it resulted in the social evil of our time' [ibid.] Her approach to Labour politics thus contained elements of both 'new' and 'equal rights' feminism.

During the 1920s Green established herself as a prominent member of the local Labour Party. During the early part of the decade she served as minute secretary for the Abertillery women's section for two consecutive years, and in the spring of 1921 was temporarily appointed as the section's secretary. During that time she was also chosen as one of the section's two Trades Council delegates, and in May 1920 was elected by the Trades Council to serve on the Executive Committee of the Divisional Labour Party. These positions provided her with valuable political experience and she was regularly commended for her work in them. In the autumn of 1920 the Abertillery women's section elected Green to attend the first conference of the Monmouthshire Labour Women's Advisory Council. It would appear that for the next few years the Linen League took up a lot of

Green's time and energy, especially during its early days. Furthermore the birth of her second son would have contributed to the slight lull in Green's front-line work for Labour from 1922–25.

In the summer of 1926 Green's stature as a political activist increased quite dramatically and she gained recognition at both the national and the international level, chiefly as a result of the mining crisis. As Marion Phillips, Green's friend and the national woman's officer, put it, 'she was marked out as a great woman leader for her sisters of the coalfield' [*Labour Woman*, November 1927]. Between 1921 and 1926 the bottom had fallen out of the British coal industry: the fall in domestic prices coupled with strong competition by German and American exporters had rendered Britain's own capacity to export coal largely ineffectual. The rising cost of British coal had brought with it an inevitable decline in demand, and consequently a rise in unemployment. In Wales the total number of insured workers without work rose from 13.4 per cent in December 1925 to 23 per cent in December 1927. The dominant themes of the south Wales coalfield in the 1920s were wage cuts, mass unemployment and extreme deprivation. The miners fought on alone after the nine-day general strike had ended, which meant that by the summer of 1926 the problem of poverty and hunger had escalated. Green's political motivation came from the suffering and distress that surrounded her. She feared for the future of the south Wales valleys, of which her own young sons were a part. She was concerned that they should receive an education that would enable them 'to get out of the trap of poverty which was closing round them in the valleys' [*Labour Woman*, November 1927]. With eight mines in the immediate Abertillery area and two more in nearby Crumlin, the poverty that Green saw was of a particularly acute nature, so along with numerous other Labour women in south Wales she threw her whole being into support for the miners and their families.

Green worked as part of the Labour women's network, the Women's Committee for the Relief of Miners' Wives and Children, to alleviate the hardship and distress being endured by the mining communities. The committee is thought to have drawn in approximately 5000 women, who undertook the work of 'an industrial Red Cross' in their respective parts of the country [Phillips (1927) ix]. As Marion Phillips maintained, 'they did it all the better because they were almost entirely working women who understood without explanation the conditions of those they visited' [ibid., 27]. The committee ensured that sick and invalid children were cared for, and set up sewing committees so that all the children in the various localities were adequately clothed. Adoption schemes were arranged, which involved sending children of the mining districts to stay with women in and around London. Green herself accompanied a party of children from south Wales who were to be adopted for the duration of the strike. She was also instrumental in the formation of a Maternity Relief Committee in Abertillery, which distributed food, milk, clothes, boots and blankets to those most in need. It was the committee's task to obtain the names of all pregnant women in the area and to ensure that they received extra food, as well as doing everything within the committee's means to make the expectant mothers as comfortable as possible. Ten shillings were allocated to each woman to purchase necessities before the birth of the child, and 30 shillings once the child had been born. The committee was successful in benefiting a number of women in the Abertillery area.

Green was one of three miners' wives from south Wales who, in an attempt to increase support for the miners and raise funds for the committee, travelled to London and other unaffected areas of Britain to publicise the facts from the coalfield. An interview with her in the July edition of *Labour Woman* revealed how the whole town of Abertillery was living on Poor Law Relief. She outlined exactly how much relief families were in receipt of and drew attention to the fact that most relief was given on loan, usually in the form of food tickets. She drew particular attention to the plight of working-class mothers struggling to make ends meet, and appealed to the readers to 'imagine what this means to the mother of a large family' [*Labour Woman*, July 1926]. Although most readers of the magazine, and many who attended public meeting on the matter, supported the miners they had no real conception of the extent of the problem until hearing about the situation from people with first-hand experience, including Green. Many present at the meetings were moved to make donations. Green's clarity of thought and the tactful way she dealt with information meant that she succeeded in pitching her speeches at the right level, which was an especially valuable asset at these venues. According to Marion Phillips, her 'simple dignity of diction' coupled with her 'delicacy of mind' enabled her to 'refrain from what people called sob-stuff lest she seem to exploit the tragedy of the mining areas, [and this] made her appeals all the more effective' [*Labour Woman*, November 1927].

As a speaker Green 'drew the very heart out of her hearers' [ibid.] and thus managed to appeal to a wide variety of people. The women's organiser for Wales, Elizabeth Andrews, recalled one incident during a trip to London that had made a lasting impression on Green's mind. 'It was an open-air meeting in a thickly-populated district. In the audience was a little ragged boy. He came near, tugged at her frock and said: "I ain't got a penny miss, but I will sing for you". He sang a popular song with such feeling that it carried away the meeting and the money thrown into the circle made a record collection' [Andrews (1951) 25]. It is unlikely that the child's response was in reaction to the content of Green's speech, but it is highly probable that the way in which she conveyed the information had much to do with the way he acted.

Green's strong belief and commitment, together with her calmness of spirit, carried her through the fund-raising trip to London. These attributes also created an image of her as a woman who was not easily fazed by what could at first have been perceived as difficult situations. One of her first public addresses in London took place in the midst of a series of boxing matches. For a young woman from the south Wales valleys, or indeed from any part of Britain, this would have been an extremely difficult and unusual experience. During the 1920s the developing leisure industry was generally a male-dominated domain, with sport, and boxing in particular, being even more so. Marion Phillips, who was accompanying her at the time, was 'struck with admiration at the way in which Mrs. Green appealed to those men for the people she represented; and her appeal was responded to with generosity' [*South Wales Gazette*, 23 December 1927].

Green's ability to adapt to and cope with new situations, together with her organisational and public-speaking skills, made her an obvious candidate for the delegation of miners and miners' wives that visited Russia in 1926. As Marion Phillips put it, 'when I was asked to suggest a miner's wife from Wales ... I proposed her name without hesitation' [*Labour Woman*, November 1927]. In August 1926 Green left her young family with their father and maternal grandparents in Duke Street, Abertillery, and set off on a two-month trip to Russia. The delegation, which was organised by the Miners' Federation, consisted of 19 representatives, of which six were women representing the Women's Committee for the Relief of Miners' Wives and Children. As guests of the Russian trade union movement, the group travelled all over Russia to speak on the plight of the British mining communities and to collect donations for their cause.

The experience proved to be highly inspirational for Green. According to Marion Phillips, 'Her Russian journey was a crowning happiness in her life. She blossomed under the friendly kindness of the Russian people, so vociferous and enthusiastic in their welcome' [*Labour Woman*, November 1927]. She flourished as a speaker and addressed huge crowds, which in many cases numbered thousands. At times the halls used for indoor meetings were not big enough to hold the crowd. At outdoor meetings 'it was impossible for us to see the edge of the crowd' [*Labour Woman*, November 1926]. The accounts of her trip that were published in *Labour Woman* revealed not only her ability to write, but also 'how good and just an observer she made' [*Labour Woman*, November 1927]. In her first account she dealt with the false impressions that had been created in Britain of the Russian people and to an extent had shaped her own preconceptions of them. In her words:

Instead of being met by crowds of bloodthirsty, bewhiskered hooligans with the inevitable bomb and dagger of our election posters we saw ordinary, warmhearted people, whose only excitement was caused by their desire to give us a really good welcome; the only risks we ever ran were those of being killed by sheer kindness [*Labour Woman*, November 1926].

Green was thus able to use this first-hand experience of life in Russia to make up her own mind about the country and its inhabitants. Moreover through her articles and the public addresses she gave on her return she was able to provide people in Britain with an alternative image of communist Russia.

Readers of *Labour Woman* enjoyed her effective writing skills. Her eloquently presented accounts of her visit provided an insight into Russian society. She had nothing but praise for the reconstruction that was in progress at the time of her visit. Her trip included visits to the salt mines at Liebrecht, the coal mines of the Donetz Basin and the oilfields of Grozny. In all three she found evidence of a constructive policy in operation and real attempts to improve the old conditions and raise the workers' standard of life. Of the coal mines she wrote, these 'were of special interest to us because they are a familiar feature of our own lives' [ibid.] Although reconstruction was incomplete, she noted that the workers were 'content because they know that the future is theirs' [ibid.] The situation in Russian coal mining was thus very different from the privately owned industry that Green had left behind in Britain, as were significant advances such as wage increases, paid holidays, free houses for workers and the development of public services.

She was equally impressed with what she saw as 'the complete emancipation of women' under the new regime of Soviet Russia [*Labour Woman*, December 1926]. She marvelled at women's acquisition of equal political, moral and social rights with men, and noted that in addition working women were assisted by paid maternity leave and crèche facilities. Demonstrating a particularly Western perspective on other cultures, she gave a vivid account of how the veiled women in some of the communities in the southern republic were being introduced to 'freedom of thought and action'; and learning that 'they were no longer subordinate creatures', illiterate and confined to the home. This, she pointed out, was not an easy transition and often meetings between women and 'strangers who had come to inform them of the new Soviet ideals and freedom of women' had to be arranged after dark and without the husbands' knowledge. In many cases the women were too shy to sit in the same room. Green referred to them as 'veiled, frightened women sitting in silence listening to a voice speaking through a hole in the door and gradually, very gradually, wakening to the idea that they were no longer subordinate creatures' [ibid.] From this, most women went on to join study circles and were taught to read and write. The message on Green's pages seemed to be that Britain, rather than fearing the Russians, should instead learn from them.

Having proved herself an efficient journalist, Green wrote regularly in *Labour Woman* on her return from Russia. Her monthly columns concentrated on aspects of child development and motherhood. These were fashionable subjects, as by the interwar period it was commonly held that good mothering skills were essential to the development of the future generation. The general consensus among the women of the Labour Party was that mothering was a career that, like any other, should have training and information attached to it. As Elizabeth Andrews put it, 'Motherhood, to a large extent, has been left to chance. Every other profession in life demands special education to be efficient' [*Colliery Worker's Magazine*, May 1925]. Green believed that women were equipped with an 'instinct' for mothering, but on its own this was not sufficient – 'Instinct does not supply us with all the knowledge necessary for the proper care and management of our children' [*Labour Woman*, March 1927]. She fully supported Labour women's campaign to educate and train women on matters related to childcare, and maintained that 'It behoves every mother and every prospective mother to apply herself to the acquisition of knowledge' [ibid.] Green's pages served as a vehicle for the provision of advice on rearing healthy, well-adjusted children.

Her articles were written in a simple and accessible style in order to reach her intended – predominately working class – audience. Her approach was informative rather than preachy, practical rather than patronising. The words were those of a working-class woman who knew of the problems surrounding child rearing at a time when economic difficulties ensured there were shortages of all kinds. Between January and October 1927 she advised working-class mothers on issues such as desirable sleeping patterns for babies, how to deal with disobedient children, child nutrition, family holidays and preparing children for school. She believed that if these were handled correctly from the earliest possible moment the result would be healthy future citizens. Her pages also included information on issues campaigned on by Labour women, such as the need for nursery provision and open-air schools. These articles encouraged readers to 'get busy in rousing their local authorities to a sense of their duties in these respects and to continue to press for action along these lines' [*Labour Woman*, January 1927].

Green herself was certainly a woman of action and remained so until her untimely death of ulcerative colitis at the age of 32 on 19 October 1927. She was not someone who was prepared to sit back and allow the injustices of the system to go unchallenged. If she was involved in an organisation, she immersed herself completely in its work. As the Reverend W. R. Lewis put it, 'She was always right in the centre of things. ... If she was in a movement she put all her energy and might into it' [*South Wales Gazette*, 21 October 1927]. As someone of perpetual motion who worked to benefit others, the ambulance that the people of Abertillery named after her was a fitting tribute. Her commitment to the causes in which she believed knew no bounds. At a memorial service for Green, Marion Phillips, referring to Green's political activism, described her as 'a woman who took a real interest in work – in fact, she worked too hard, and had given too liberally to the cause she loved' [*South Wales Gazette*, 23 December 1927]. In an obituary in *Labour Woman* Phillips drew attention to the part played by the harshness and uncertainty of the times in reducing Green's life: 'I believe that it was [this] anxiety added to present hardship which broke her physical resistance and brought her to this early and unexpected end. Her life is added to the long line of those whose fine texture is rent in the struggle against overwhelming odds' [*Labour Woman*, November 1927]. Although her political career had spanned a relatively short period, by the time of her death she had established an impressive political track record and would have had a promising future ahead of her in the labour movement. In Marion Phillips' opinion she possessed all the qualities required to become an excellent leader, qualities that in all probability would have ensured her a place in Parliament.

Writings: 'Woman in the State', report of an address given by Beatrice Green to the Abertillery Women's Labour Section, *South Wales Gazette*, 7 January 1921; 'Miners' Wives in Russia', extract of a letter written by Beatrice Green, *Labour Woman*, October 1926; 'British Miners' Wives in Russia – The Welcome They Received – What They Saw: What They Did', *Labour Woman*, November 1926, 169–70; 'British Miners' Wives in Russia – The Workers' Clubs: The Position of Women', *Labour Woman*, December 1926, 185–6; 'Care for the Toddlers', *Labour Woman*, January 1927, 2–4; 'Food, Sun and Air are the best Doctors', *Labour Woman*, February 1927, 18; 'The Women's Page – Contrasts in Soviet Russia', *Colliery Workers' Magazine*, February 1927, 39; 'Motherhood and Mothercraft', *Labour Woman*, March 1927, 36–7; 'Sleep, Baby, Sleep', *Labour Woman*, April 1927, 53; 'Naughty Children', *Labour Woman*, May 1927, 69; 'The Feeding of Children', *Labour Woman*, July 1927, 103; 'Choosing Food for the Children', August 1927, 127; 'Holiday-Time for Mother and Baby', *Labour Woman*, September 1927, 143; 'Going to School', *Labour Woman*, October 1927, 151.

Sources: (1) MSS: National Register of Marriages, Newport Public Library; *Ebenezer Chapel Annual Report* (1927). **(2) Newspapers:** *South Wales Gazette*, 1919–27; *Labour Woman*, 1919–27; *Colliery Workers' Magazine*, 1925–27. **(3) Other:** M. Phillips, *Women and the Miners' Lock-Out* (1927); E. Andrews, *A Woman's Work is Never Done* (1951); K. O. Morgan, *Rebirth of a Nation: Wales 1880–1980* (1981); C. Collette, *For Labour and For Women* (1989); P. Graves, *Labour Women* (1994); M. Douglas, 'Women, God and Birth Control: The First Hospital Birth Control Clinic, Abertillery 1925', *Llafur*, 6:4 (1995); C. Williams, *Capitalism, Community and Conflict: The South Wales Coalfield 1898–1947* (1998); D. Tanner, C. Williams and D. Hopkin (eds,), *The Labour Party in Wales 1900–2000* (2000); interview and correspondence with Keith Dykes, great-nephew of Beatrice Green.

LOWRI NEWMAN

See also: Elizabeth ANDREWS; Florence Rose DAVIES.

GREENWOOD, Arthur (1880–1945)
LABOUR PARTY DEPUTY LEADER AND CABINET MINISTER

Arthur Greenwood was born in Hunslet, Leeds, on 8 February 1880, the eldest son of William Greenwood, a painter and decorator, and Margaret Greenwood, née Nunns, of Dewsbury. Greenwood was one of the main bridges between the Labour Party of the founding fathers and the governing force it was later to become. In pre–1914 Yorkshire he heard Philip Snowden's famous lecture to socialists, 'the Christ that is to Be'. In 1945 he became lord privy seal in Attlee's government.

One of the main sources of momentum in Greenwood's early career was an interest in education, which had also played an important part in his own development. After attending St Jude's Board School, in 1893 he won a scholarship to Bewerley Street School, and two years later became a pupil teacher as this was the only means of continuing his schooling. He then won a teacher scholarship to the Yorkshire College, which he entered in 1899. His degree result, a BSc ordinary (second division), awarded in 1902, was not especially distinguished, but he did receive a prize certificate for exceptional work in education. This degree was translated into a BSc from Leeds University in 1905 to mark the college's transformation in status. Greenwood had stayed on as an associate of the university in 1902–3, taking courses in history and economics, the latter being taught by J. H. Clapham, who was head of department. He had also obtained his Board of Education certificate, and to fulfil the terms of his scholarship he spent several years teaching in various schools. He progressed to head of economics at Huddersfield Technical College and in 1913 joined the economics department at Leeds University.

Although Greenwood came to labour politics through the Fabian Society, he achieved prominence locally in connection with the Workers' Educational Association (WEA) and the Leeds municipal strike of 1913. Two figures common to both were Henry Clay and Sir Michael Sadler. The Leeds branch of the WEA was formed in 1907, but a decisive change in organization came in 1914 when Greenwood played a leading part in the creation of a district specifically for Yorkshire, rather than the larger north-western region in which the branch had previously operated. He was elected chairman of the district and Clay its treasurer. Greenwood was to remain chairman until 1945. He also taught a number of subjects, including economic and social history, to classes in south Leeds. He made a powerful impact on his charges: 'Greenwood's enthusiastic personality and complete identification with the cause of labour endeared him to his students ... they cherished for the rest of their lives an almost legendary memory of him' [Harrison (1957) 16].

Clay joined forces with Greenwood at the time of the Leeds municipal strike in 1913, when they pleaded for proper negotiating machinery for the employees. Their support for the strikers brought them into conflict with Sadler, who had been a supporter of the Leeds branch of the WEA from his arrival as Leeds University's vice-chancellor in 1911, (he had soon been made president). While Sadler was sympathetic to many of the problems faced by the working class, the rift came when he suggested that students from the university might act as volunteers during the strike to keep essential services going. Greenwood, Clay and Professor D. H. MacGregor opposed this, and it was one of the themes of Greenwood's article on the strike in the *Economic Journal* in March 1914. Sadler then parted company with the WEA, albeit temporarily.

Greenwood's desire to address a wider audience emerged through a number of articles on education. He published widely, not only in journals such as *The Child*, *The Crusade* and *Highway*, but also in more heavyweight publications such as the *Economic Journal*, the *Journal of the Royal Statistical Society* and the *Political Quarterly*. Education was a subject that fitted in well with the emphases of the early labour movement, where its value in helping citizens to develop their own characters so as better to serve the community could be stressed without difficulty. Although this point was brought out in Greenwood's essay on education in H. B. Lees-Smith's *Encyclopaedia of the Labour Movement* (1928), his arguments in the earlier publications were more specific. First, educational reform designed to help the adolescent (including an experimental open-air school in Bradford) had been frustrated by the pupils' need to keep working in industry. Second, he saw the need for a general rather than a narrowly vocational education for working-class children. Like many socialists Greenwood had a moral distaste for capitalism because it elevated material worth and utility above cooperation and public spirit. Greenwood's activities and writings began to place him within the intellectually respectable circles of the labour movement. His pamphlet of 1913, *The Health and Physique of Schoolchildren*, reiterated his views about the incompatibility of education and employment for young people. The fact that it was published by the Ratan Tata Foundation at the London School of Economics and its director, R. H. Tawney, wrote the introduction provides evidence of Greenwood's growing status among the intellectuals of the labour movement.

Greenwood's interests broadened when he left Leeds for London in 1914. He became secretary to the Council for the Study of International Relations and contributed to *The War and Democracy* (1914) with R. W. Seton-Watson, J. Dover Wilson and Alfred Zimmern. This project had links with Greenwood's earlier activities in that it arose out of the WEA summer schools that had been in action when war was declared. Greenwood contributed a chapter on the social and economic aspects of the war. While some of his hopes might have been overoptimistic – for example that the new democracy would generate a more enlightened public opinion on foreign policy – his sense that the war might encourage great strides in productivity as well as promoting an exercise in practical socialism was remarkably prescient. He also co-authored some study guides on the war, but his friend from his Leeds days, Henry Clay, seems to have contributed the major share. Another pamphlet, *The Reorganisation of Industry* (1916), emerged from a conference at Ruskin College, Oxford, featuring A. C. Pigou and Sidney Webb.

The war also brought developments in Greenwood's career. In 1916 he became a civil servant in Lloyd George's secretariat. At first he was assistant secretary to the Reconstruction Committee, and then he worked in the Ministry of Reconstruction from 1917–19. His minister, Christopher Addison, was impressed with his grasp of detail and administrative energy. With R. H. Tawney, he produced a report on adult education, and was also involved in the setting up of the Whitley Councils, which established negotiating procedures in the less well paid sectors of industry. The war heightened the optimism of labour on both the industrial and the political fronts. The Labour Party acquired a new constitution and programme in 1918, and expanded its electoral challenge in the 1918 general election and subsequent by-elections. The TUC reformed its structure; from 1921, its Parliamentary Committee became the General Council. One key issue was the relationship between the industrial and political wings of the labour movement. There were pressures both for unity and distinctiveness. How should these be resolved? Greenwood's experiences and outlook made him an advocate of more unity rather than less. He gave evidence for the Miners' Federation before the Sankey Commission in 1919, and later that year worked as a propagandist for the National Union of Railwaymen during their strike. On the party side he served on its commission on Ireland. His commitment to Labour Party–TUC cooperation was demonstrated in his secretaryship of a joint committee on the cost of living, which published three reports in 1921. The party secretary, Arthur Henderson, made the running in discussions on the formation of joint party–TUC departments; the policy was accepted by the TUC in September 1921 and three joint departments began their work on New Year's Day 1922, with Greenwood heading the Joint Research Department. He had been permanent secretary of the party's advisory committees on policy since March 1920.

In the immediate post-war period Greenwood had been involved with G. D. H Cole and the group in the Labour Research Department (LRD) in providing policy advice for the party. However the creation of the Joint Research Department effectively meant that the party distanced itself from the LRD, a shift that was welcomed by some Labour politicians on account of the latter's connections, through certain individuals, with the Communist Party. Greenwood was clearly committed to the Labour Party and its policies, and chose to work within the institutions of the labour movement. In the early months of the 1924 Government Beatrice Webb portrayed him as:

an old friend who has varied in his adhesion to Webbian philosophy from an early disciple-ship to a doubter of Webbian collectivism and then led away by G. D. H. Cole into 'workers' control'. Today he belongs again to the Fabian centre and his creed is not far removed from ours in substance, but more romantic in expression [Norman & Jeanne MacKenzie (1985) 20].

Under Greenwood's leadership the Joint Research Department had a record of solid achieve-ment. The alliance between party and unions necessitated application and effort, a commitment exemplified by Greenwood. This was more than a question of skirting around ideological and personal quarrels. Trade unionists were often quick to see the condescension that some middle-class 'thinkers' had brought to the Labour Party, along with their own ambitions for advance-ment, and it was easy for hard-working trade union officials to doubt the 'service' that some of the university men claimed to be providing when they took time off from their academic work. Greenwood was never the target of such criticism, and instead built up a loyal following within the trade unions.

However this rapport could not prevent the demise of the three joint departments. An element within the TUC had always harboured doubts about the arrangement, and these had been strengthened by the attitude of the 1924 Labour Government towards TUC priori-ties. A programme for a more independent position was presented to the 1925 TUC by its secretary, Fred Bramley, and in April 1926 the joint departments were terminated. Thereafter Greenwood became head of the party's research department, a post he held until 1943. One of his first tasks was to work with R. H. Tawney and an NEC subcommittee to produce a party programme, *Labour and the Nation*, which was presented to the 1928 party conference. He supplemented this in 1929 with a book-length exposition on party policy, *The Labour Outlook* [for material on the joint departments, their creation and abolition see Mckibbin (1974) 208–14; Minkin (1991) 18–20]. The Whitley Councils, which he had helped to establish, were intended to regulate trades where workers were relatively powerless. He also took an interest in industrial psychology and practical improvements in working condi-tions – lighting, ventilation and the like – which had attracted increased currency after the war. He sat on the Council of the National Institute for Industrial Psychology, as well as acting as honorary treasurer for the British section of the International Association for Labour Legislation. His involvement in the party's investigation into unemployment was reflected in his entry on the subject in the *Encyclopaedia of the Labour Movement* (1928). Part of the problem, especially with cyclical unemployment, was the difficulty of coordinating a private economy so that some production was held back in good times in order to provide work when the economy went into recession. His solution was to place more production under state planning. Like a number of others in the party, he saw inflation as damaging working-class interests. Indeed his explanation for unemployment was that it was a conse-quence of wages lagging behind rising prices, thereby reducing demand in the economy. Hence reducing unemployment was a monetary question of stabilising the price level. Although Greenwood cited J. A. Hobson's work in the bibliography of his entry in the *Encyclopaedia*, he did not mention that writer's thesis on the impact of inequality on pur-chasing power and therefore on employment, even though it provided both an ethical and economic critique of capitalism.

Alongside this activity, Greenwood developed his parliamentary career. He fought Southport unsuccessfully in 1918, but won Nelson and Colne in 1922. He retained that seat until 1931.

Southport, 1918: electorate 33 150, turnout 61.6 per cent

G. D. Dalrymple-White (Coalition Conservative)	14 707 (72.0 per cent)
A. Greenwood (Labour)	5727 (28.0 per cent)
Majority	8980 (44.0 per cent)

Nelson and Colne, 1922: electorate 43 914, turnout 83.2 per cent

A. Greenwood (Labour)	17 714 (48.5 per cent)
J. H. S. Aitken (Liberal)	11 542 (31.6 per cent)
F. N. Wainwright (Conservative)	7286 (19.9 per cent)
Majority	6172 (16.9 per cent)

Nelson and Colne, 1923: electorate 44 432, turnout 83.4 per cent

A. Greenwood (Labour)	17 083 (46.1 per cent)
J. H. S. Aitken (Liberal)	10 103 (27.3 per cent)
Sir A. Nelson (Conservative)	9861 (26.6 per cent)
Majority	6980 (18.8 per cent)

Nelson and Colne, 1924; electorate 44 871, turnout 85.6 per cent

A. Greenwood (Labour)	19 922 (51.9 per cent)
J. H. S. Aitken (Liberal)	18 479 (48.1 per cent)
Majority	1443 (3.8 per cent)

Nelson and Colne, 1929: electorate 56 465, turnout 82.8 per cent

A. Greenwood (Labour)	28 533 (61.0 per cent)
L. T. Thorp (Conservative)	18 236 (39.0 per cent)
Majority	10 297 (22.0 per cent)

With this kind of record he might have expected more than the post of parliamentary secretary to John Wheatley, Minister of Health in the 1924 government. However he himself became minister of that department in MacDonald's 1929–31 government. During his tenure he was responsible for a number of major welfare measures, including the Widows', Orphans' and Old Age Contributory Pensions Act of 1929, the Housing Act of 1930, and a town and country planning bill, which was put through by his National Government successor with little modification. Greenwood also discreetly intervened in what had been a major Labour Party controversy of the 1920s. Many activists, particularly in the Party's women's sections, had argued that a Labour government should permit publicly funded clinics to give advice on birth control. However this had been blocked by those who were concerned about the electoral consequences; they insisted that the party programme should not contain items that could appear divisive on either gender or religious grounds. Nonetheless in 1930 Greenwood circulated a memorandum to local health authorities stating that maternal and child welfare clinics could give birth control advice to women 'in cases of medical necessity'. The explanation for this limited shift in policy may involve two factors. First, the 1929 Local Government Act had replaced the percentage grant system to local authorities with a block grant, which had undermined the minister's ability to threaten specific programmes with withdrawal of funding. Second, Greenwood was under pressure from a number of local authorities on this issue – Labour women might have been unsuccessful in changing the party's national policy, but they did have an impact in specific communities [Graves (1994) 81–98, especially 97–8].

Perhaps as importantly for his later reputation, in January 1931 Greenwood came out against cuts in social services as a way of balancing the budget, insisting that he would 'die in the last ditch' in opposing them. This sentiment was widely shared, as became evident in cabinet meetings on 5 and 11 February, when MacDonald, Snowden and Bondfield failed in their attempt to secure emergency cuts in unemployment benefit. When in August 1931 the Labour cabinet considered demands for expenditure cuts in the context of the May report and the financial crisis, Greenwood was one of the first to oppose cuts in social expenditure. At the full cabinet's first consideration of the crisis on 19 August 1931, it appears that he aligned himself with George Lansbury and Tom Johnston. This opposition within the cabinet was strengthened the following day by TUC criticism of the government's proposals for economies. Along with his substantive opposition to cuts, Greenwood's political priorities required the maintenance of an effective party–union alignment. As the crisis deepened, on 22 August Greenwood joined Henderson, Lansbury and other dissenters in preparing a collective resignation should a cabinet majority support a cut in unemployment benefit. The following day he predictably voted with the minority who opposed a 10 per cent cut [for Greenwood's notes on the crisis see Notes on the Cabinet and the Crisis, Passfield Papers IV, Section 26].

In the 1920s Greenwood had extended his interests into industrial organisation and questions of unemployment. He was against the unchecked power of private capital in a democracy, and believed that the state and trade unions should have a greater say in the running of enterprises.

The only blemish in Greenwood's career so far was the one that was soon to undermine it – drink. At a dinner in 1925 Beatrice Webb, one of Greenwood's supporters, had noticed that Ben Spoor, the chief whip was under the influence of whisky, and Arthur Greenwood looked as if he was going the same way. In 1931 Greenwood faced the major challenge that confronted every Labour MP, namely the electoral disaster that year. This left the parliamentary party with a rump of mainly trade-union-sponsored MPs. Greenwood was defeated in Nelson, but he won in Wakefield in a by-election in April 1932 by the narrow margin of just over 300 votes, and this remained his constituency until his death.

Nelson and Colne, 1931: electorate 56 733, turnout 87.8 per cent

L. T. Thorp (Independent Conservative)	28 747 (57.7 per cent)
Rt Hon. A. Greenwood (Labour)	21 063 (42.3 per cent)
Majority	7684 (15.4 per cent)

Wakefield by-election, 1932: electorate 32 334, turnout 83.0 per cent

Rt Hon. A. Greenwood (Labour)	13 586 (50.6 per cent)
A. E. Greaves (Conservative)	13 242 (49.4 per cent)
Majority	344 (1.2 per cent)

Wakefield, 1935: electorate 33 215, turnout 84.9 per cent

Rt Hon. A. Greenwood (Labour)	15 804 (56.0 per cent)
A. E. Greaves (Conservative)	12 400 (44.0 per cent)
Majority	3404 (12.0 per cent)

Wakefield, 1945: electorate 32 721, turnout 80.3 per cent

Rt Hon. A. Greenwood (Labour)	14 378 (54.7 per cent)
H. Watson (Conservative)	8268 (31.5 per cent)

G. L. J. Oliver (Liberal)   3613 (13.8 per cent)

Majority   6110 (23.2 per cent)

Wakefield, 1950: electorate 53 763, turnout 87.3 per cent

Rt Hon. A. Greenwood (Labour)   25 996 (55.4 per cent)
H. Watson (Conservative)   15 925 (33.9 per cent)
S. J. Berwin (Liberal)   5022 (10.7 per cent)

Majority   10 071 (21.5 per cent)

Wakefield, 1951: electorate 54 529, turnout 85.3 per cent

Rt Hon. A. Greenwood (Labour)   27 100 (58.3 per cent)
M. Grant (Conservative)   19 398 (41.7 per cent)

Majority   7702 (16.6 per cent)

The early 1930s provided an opportunity for Greenwood precisely because the party had been so weakened by defeat. Lansbury, and in his absense through ill health, Attlee had to perform heroic feats in leading the opposition on such slender resources. Greenwood provided support in Parliament and from the Research Department. In 1934 the party published a pamphlet by Greenwood, *Immediate Steps Towards the New Order*, which dealt with schemes for national development on the domestic front and disarmament in foreign policy. In 1935 he became deputy leader. The leadership contest came after Lansbury's resignation and the general election, and Attlee, Herbert Morrison and Greenwood stood. Greenwood finished third on the first ballot, with Attlee winning 58 votes, Morrison 44 and Greenwood 33. Greenwood's supporters turned overwhelmingly to Attlee. When the latter triumphed in the second ballot, Morrison was furious and taunted Greenwood about his drink problem.

However Morrison did not stand for the deputy leadership, so this went to Greenwood. This partly reflected support from the trade unions – Ernest Bevin had encouraged him to stand, and trade union support helped him to prevail. A good deal of this support was based not on Greenwood's own strengths but on his opposition to Morrison, whom Bevin loathed. Greenwood was seen as credible enough to stand in opposition to Morrison, but not as sufficiently assertive to be his own man once office came his way. This dimension was also a feature of another, more secretive, strand of support for Greenwood. In 1938 Hugh Dalton, who had been Morrison's campaign manager, was shown notes from a meeting held at the New Welcome Masonic Lodge just before the 1935 leadership election. This had been organized by Scott Lindsay, secretary of the Parliamentary Labour Party, and had included Greenwood. His attraction as leadership candidate for this group was that he was biddable and would never stray out of line on important issues. As deputy leader Greenwood gave his backing to Attlee, who recalled in his autobiography that 'he gave me most loyal support and good counsel in the years to come' [Attlee (1954) 81].

There were blemishes, however. His susceptibility to drink was widely known and an obvious handicap. Many of his afternoons must have been unproductive. An NEC enquiry into the Research Department – which Greenwood ran – found that it was 'not, either administratively or psychologically, in a happy condition' [report as an appendix to the NEC minutes of 22 June 1938]. While Greenwood was relieved of much of the detailed work of the department, the report went out of its way to emphasize the debt the party owed him. What maintained his momentum in these unpromising circumstances were the problems surrounding Attlee's leadership of the party, which was competent but often appeared so uninspired that thoughts of replacing him frequently arose. Morrison was his major, but unsuccessful, rival. Greenwood was also occasionally mentioned as a possible replacement, and although he was never as credible an alternative as Morrison, this did help maintain his profile in the party. Where he did rise to the occasion was as an eventual critic of Neville Chamberlain's foreign policy, in which confidence had declined following the Munich agreement and the subsequent German seizure, in March 1939, of what remained of Czechoslovakia. This forceful position involved some shift in Greenwood's thinking on international affairs. He had previously endorsed the party's opposition to rearmament, and when the Parliamentary Labour Party's position shifted in July 1937 he had spoken out against it. Dalton, a leading advocate of the change, portrayed Greenwood as 'very halting and unhappy. ... He said mournfully it was all very difficult' [Dalton (1957) 136].

With Attlee ill in the critical days of August and September 1939, it fell to Greenwood to lead Labour's demand for a more resolute resistance to Hitler in the context of the Chamberlain government's earlier guarantees to Poland. Greenwood had not been noted as a parliamentary speaker on this big issue, although he had performed effectively on questions that touched his own areas of expertise, especially local government and the rating system. He had not been silent on foreign policy, and had participated in debates on Manchuria, Abyssinia and Spain. But his speech on Saturday 2 September 1939 was the high point of his career. The British government's response to Hitler's invasion of Poland had been muted on the Friday, and in Parliament on the Saturday Chamberlain seemed to be wavering and on the brink of making a renewed effort to appease Hitler. Encouraged by Leo Amery's call to 'speak for England', Greenwood provided a firmer line: 'I wonder how long we are prepared to vacillate at a time when Britain and all Britain stands for, and human civilisation, are in peril. We must march with the French' [Hansard, 2 September 1939, cols 282–3]. This stand continued as Greenwood played a central part in Labour's strategy of supporting the war effort but stopping short of giving its full support to Chamberlain.

While this account must give proper weight to Greenwood's achievements at this time, the more important point is that these were the exception. A great opportunity was presented to Attlee and Greenwood when they joined Churchill's war cabinet, as here was the chance for a new generation of Labour leaders to show that the fiasco of 1931 belonged firmly in the past, and that the work done when in opposition had produced personages who were capable of making a sustained and important contribution to government. However both failed to make their mark in the initial phase of the coalition, and although Attlee recovered somewhat it was up to Bevin and Morrison to rescue Labour's reputation. Nevertheless in the privacy of the war cabinet's early meetings, Greenwood intervened in a fashion that was reminiscent of his Commons speech of 2 September 1939. On 26, 27 and 28 May 1940 the five-member war cabinet met nine times. With France on the verge of collapse and the Dunkirk evacuation about to begin, the Foreign Secretary Lord Halifax raised the possibility of Mussolini acting as an intermediary in the exploration of peace terms between Britain and Germany. Churchill was thoroughly opposed to the idea, as were the two Labour members of the war cabinet. Attlee was characteristically laconic and the most vigorous backing for Churchill came from Greenwood. The outcome was uncertain, not least because the war cabinet's fifth member was Chamberlain. Churchill invited the Liberal Archibald Sinclair, a reliable supporter, to join the discussions. The decisive figure was Chamberlain, who gradually distanced himself from Halifax. His pivotal role reflected the dominance of the Commons by Conservative MPs; but at this critical moment for the newly formed Churchill coalition, Greenwood's interventions were significant and symbolized the commitment of Labour to Churchill's leadership and continuing resistance to fascism [for an account see Jenkins (2001) ch. 31; for the arguments from Halifax's position see Roberts (1991) chs 22 and 23].

Greenwood's longer-term contribution to the government was less significant. He was put in charge of the Production Council and the Economic Policy Committee, but he proved ineffectual and Churchill disbanded both bodies in January 1941. Greenwood then shifted to reconstruction policy, but he had no real authority or support and was sacked in February 1942. Thus he had fallen from membership of the war cabinet to loss of ministerial office in less than two years. The pressures of office, especially in wartime, highlighted his weaknesses, not least his alcohol consumption, and perhaps his indecisiveness. Nevertheless a more nuanced assessment can be made of his time as chair of the Reconstruction Priorities Committee. The committee had no executive powers and reconstruction issues were heavily overshadowed by military crises. Whatever Greenwood's administrative failures, he remained committed to the Labour Party's position that the war should provide the occasion for permanent economic and social changes. Hence the committee discussed the Uthwatt report on land use, launched the Beveridge inquiry and considered questions such as family allowances and post-war controls [Brooke (1992) 177–82; for a less positive view see Addison (1975) 167–8]. Subsequently he was made lord privy seal in the post-war Attlee government. He also chaired the cabinet's Social Services Committee, which was responsible for preparing plans for a national health service.

While Greenwood was dropped from the government in 1947 and his career as a significant ministerial figure was over, there was still a role for him in the party. After his dismissal in 1942 he had become chair of the Parliamentary Labour Party and had faced pressure from back-benchers who were uneasy about the compromises made by Labour ministers in the coalition. The post of party treasurer was largely meaningless in itself, but as MacDonald and Henderson had found, it was a useful stepping stone to higher things. The post had become vacant in 1943. Morrison had been a candidate, but Greenwood had entered the contest with the backing of the engineers. The railwaymen and Bevin's transport workers had also weighed in on his side. Greenwood may have won some support because of his dismissal by Churchill, but once again he had been a useful obstacle for others to place against Morrison's ambitions. He had been a reasonable choice for those in the trade unions who were concerned that a more aggressive and forceful figure such as Morrison would elevate the political side of the movement over the industrial side. With 1 253 000 votes Greenwood had headed the ballot. Morrison had come second with 926 000 votes and Glenvil Hall third with 519 000. With no second ballot, Greenwood had prevailed. Frustratingly for Morrison, a similar sequence was played out in 1953. Greenwood's health had further deteriorated in the interval, and he was clearly on his last legs. For Morrison, who had lost his place on the NEC the year before, the treasurership was an obvious route back to the heart of the party. He had powerful trade union backing from the miners, the municipal workers and the transport workers, now led by Arthur Deakin. However Greenwood had his own trade union support, plus a good deal of sympathy because of the pressure that had been put on him to resign. Given that the alternative was Morrison, Greenwood had the support of the left. Morrison, even if he had forced a contest and won, would have lost a good deal of sympathy and so he withdrew. In 1952–53 Greenwood also served as chairman of the party, but his life and career were moving to a close: he succumbed to pleurisy and died at his home in Hampstead on 9 June 1954. He left an estate valued at £7591 14s 3d.

Greenwood was made a privy councillor in 1929, a freeman of the city of Leeds and honorary doctor of laws by Leeds University in 1930, and a companion of honour in 1945. He refused a viscountancy in 1947. In 1904 he married Catherine Ainsworth, daughter of John Brown, a clerk, of Leeds. They had a daughter and a son, Anthony, who was a Labour MP from 1945–70 and held office in the Wilson governments in the 1960s.

Greenwood's career sheds light on the Labour Party in a number of ways. First, in its early phase it shows how much scope there was for a journalist-cum-intellectual to advance within the policy-making circles in the party. Greenwood's literary output does not convey the impression of a thinker of great force or originality, but he was interested in the right subjects and he convinced important people that his views and participation were worth having. He was probably too diffident and self-deprecating to carry himself to the very top in politics. He lacked the inherent immodesty of Attlee and the forceful character of Dalton, but in a sense this was by the way because drink was the more powerful solvent of any ambitions he may have had in his early career. His temperament may explain why he lasted so long in the party when his claim for high office had been so irretrievably spoiled: his character attracted no factions and his personality aroused no animosity. But his achievement did not rest solely on negative virtues. The most impressive aspects of Greenwood's career were the links and friendships he formed right across the labour movement. He was a successful party intellectual, trusted for and relied upon for his extensive knowledge of a number of topics relevant to working-class conditions. He was a prominent minister and built up a loyal following among MPs. He was liked within the trade union movement, and there was an international dimension too: representatives from the Polish Socialist Party attended his funeral. It was this ability to work within and draw together the many strands of the labour movement at a time when its horizons were constantly expanding that was his greatest contribution. He was loyal to the party and its members were loyal to him in return, although outsiders must have wondered how it was that he was elected to party offices in his declining years. Although the history of the party, especially for the post-1945 period, has been written around its factional and ideological conflicts, Greenwood's career shows the influence of loyalty and integration on party activities and relationships.

Writings: Essays on education and juvenile labour in *The Child* and *The Crusade* (1911); 'Blind alley labour', *Economic Journal* (1912); 'Some statistics of juvenile employment and unemployment' (with John Kettlewell), *Journal of the Royal Statistical Society* (June 1912); articles on the educational system in *The Highway* (1913, 1914); *Health and Physique of Schoolchildren* (Ratan Tata Foundation, 1913); 'Next steps in factory and workshop', *Political Quarterly* (September 1914); 'The school child in industry: a study of industrial fatigue' (WEA pamphlet, 1914); 'The Leeds Municipal Strike', *Economic Journal* (March 1914); *The War and Democracy* (1918); article on education in *The Parents' Review* (October 1916); *The Reorganisation of Industry* (1916); 'Health and industrial efficiency', *Journal of the Royal Sanitary Institute* (1925); 'Necessary conditions', *The Pilgrim* (October 1926); *The compulsory raising of the school leaving age* (National Union of Teachers/WEA, 1927); entries on education and unemployment in the *Encyclopaedia of the Labour Movement*, edited by H. B. Lees-Smith (3 vols, 1928); *The Labour Outlook* (1929); *Immediate Steps Towards the New Order* (1934); 'Commemorative Souvenir, 1914–1935', Workers Educational Association, Yorkshire District (N) (Leeds, 1935). Many of the Labour Party pamphlets produced during the interwar period, when Greenwood was in charge of the research department, would have reflected his considerable input.

Sources: (1) MSS: Greenwood's papers in the Bodleian Library, Oxford, contain draft memoirs, details of his private life and copies of publications, but no political correspondence. The collection of newspaper cuttings in the Labour Party Archive at the National Museum of Labour History (NMLH), Manchester, is helpful. The archives of Leeds University have material on his education there. Labour Party NEC Minutes, NMLH, Manchester; Passfield Papers IV/26, Notes on the Cabinet and the Crisis, BLPES. (2) **Other:** Hansard, 1939; Clement Attlee, *As It Happened* (1954); J. F. C. Harrison, *Workers Education in Leeds: A History of the Leeds Branch of the Workers Educational Association, 1907–1957* (Leeds, 1957); Hugh Dalton, *The Fateful Years* (1957); Ross Mckibbin, *The Evolution of the Labour Party 1910–1924* (1974); Lewis Minkin, *The Contentious Alliance: Trade Unions and the Labour Party* (1991); Norman and Jeanne MacKenzie, *The Diary of Beatrice Webb Vol. 4 1924–1943* (1985); Andrew Roberts, '*The Holy Fox'. The Life of Lord Halifax* (1991); Stephen Brooke, *Labour's War: The Labour Party During the Second World War* (Oxford, 1992); Pamela M. Graves, *Labour Women: Women in British Working-Class Politics 1918–1939* (Cambridge, 1994); Roy Jenkins, *Churchill* (2001). The printed diaries of Hugh Dalton and Beatrice Webb contain useful impressions of Greenwood, and there are helpful assessments in Ben Pimlott, *Labour and the Left in the 1930s* (1977); Paul Addison, *The Road to 1945* (1975); K. O. Morgan, *Labour in Power, 1945–51* (1984); Bernard Donoughue and G. W. Jones, *Herbert Morrison: Portrait of a Politician* (1973) is definitive on his clashes with Morrison over Party office. (3) **Obituary:** *Leeds Weekly Citizen*, 18 June 1954.

RICHARD WHITING

HALLS, Walter (1871–1953)
TRADE UNION OFFICIAL, LABOUR MP, COOPERATOR, NOTTINGHAM CITY COUNCILLOR

Walter Halls was born on 15 June 1871 in the east Leicestershire village of Tugby, seven miles west of Uppingham, to farm labourer William Halls and his wife Harriet, née Kelly. Halls was the eighth child of ten. The family subsequently moved to Gaulby, a village nearer to Leicester, and Halls went to the village school. He left at 12 to work on a farm. His early family life was marked by poverty and pessimism about the prospect of improvement.

> I was one of a family of 10 whose father never received above 18s a week, and I knew what it was to live in poverty when my father worked on the land. I remember a time, when a man who worked on the land dare not even let it be known that he was discontented with his lot. ... It was only in the family circle that a man allowed his discontent to be known. ... I remember as we sat at the fire, if we were talking about our lot and all that we had to put up with, my poor old mother, when she heard any person going past would say, 'don't talk so loud, or so-and-so may hear what you are saying' [*Hansard*, 25 July 1921, col. 107].

At the age of 18 Halls obtained a job in the Midland Railway goods department in Leicester. The initial wage levels were little better than in agriculture, but the post offered the chance of promotion; there was also paternalistic security with fringe benefits. Halls stayed with the goods department until December 1909; his final grade was that of checker. He joined the Amalgamated Society of Railway Servants' (ASRS) Leicester No. 1 Branch on 27 October 1896 during the expansion of union membership that marked the All Grades Campaign. He held several branch offices, including the secretaryship, and attended several of the union's Annual General Meetings as a delegate. These activities made him a locally prominent figure in the union. The All Grades campaign of the late 1890s failed, and under Richard Bell's leadership the ASRS followed a patient strategy of building up membership while avoiding local and often costly confrontations. Halls' temperament fitted this strategy. Many Leicester members were Midland Railway employees and the company strongly reflected the near-universal hostility amongst railway companies to union recognition. The modernisation strategy pursued by the new general manager of the company, Guy Granet, and the general superintendent, Cecil Paget, provoked opposition from many Midland men. Halls, as a cautious and painstaking branch official, would have been aware of such resentment.

At the union's AGM in December 1908 the delegates decided to increase the number of organisers. Four were to be elected: two for England and Wales, one for Scotland and one for Ireland. Halls was nominated by his own branch, supported by the neighbouring Wigston branch. An examination reduced the number of nominees to 17, including Halls. These were then balloted by the members. In the first ballot one candidate, J. N. Bell of Newcastle, was decisively ahead of the others, so the union executive declared him elected. Halls had finished in fifth place, and in the second ballot for the other three posts, with the candidates now reduced to 13, he again finished fifth. On a third ballot of six candidates he finished fourth. At that point he was fortunate; an attempt on the Executive to declare the first three elected was defeated, and by six votes to five it was decided to let the first four names go forward to a final ballot. In this decisive round Halls moved up to the crucial third place. His vote was 15 118 against the defeated candidates' 14 846. He was declared elected in December 1909 [ASRS Executive Minutes, December 1909].

The Executive next determined the allocation of organisational responsibilities, and Halls, having defeated an Irish candidate, was sent to Dublin. His official designation was Dublin local organiser, but as there were only six branches in the city he was also required to assist the Irish secretary, Nathan Rimmer, another Englishman who had previously been a locomotiveman on the Lancashire and Yorkshire Railway. The level of ASRS membership in Ireland was generally low. The Irish railway companies had not been involved directly in the 1907 settlement that had produced a system of Conciliation Boards for each company, but without union recognition. Acceptance of the new system by Irish companies was often slow.

When the August 1911 railway strike was called by the combined executives of the railway unions, the instruction was given to Irish ASRS members by the local full-time officials. Halls addressed a meeting of Dublin railway workers and advised them that a strike would take place from 6.00 a.m. the next day (Friday 18 August). His language was uncharacteristically vigorous: 'The law was made in the interests of capital, and they, in their struggle for freedom would not recognise that law which did not bind them morally' [*Irish Times*, 18 August 1911]. Yet beneath the rhetoric Halls showed some sympathy for a proposal to defer strike action for a day: 'he would like to fall in with the proposed compromise, but in view of the message of their leaders he thought he would be shirking his duty if he did not adhere to his advice' [ibid.] However, whatever his personal sentiments Halls' concern with solidarity and the authority of union procedures was dominant. After the strike Halls travelled to England and complained to the ASRS Executive about an Irish Executive member, Finnegan, who had supported the policy of delay [ASRS Executive Minutes, September 1911].

Railway workers in Dublin had been particularly responsive to the ASRS's strike call, and the rapid return to work and the setting up of the Royal Commission did nothing to assuage discontent about low wages. The situation was made even more explosive by the continuing conflict between employers and James Larkin's Irish Transport and General Workers' Union. On 15 September 1911 two checkers at the Great Southern and Western Railway depot at Dublin Kingsbridge refused to accept a consignment from a timber firm that was in dispute with Larkin's union. They were suspended. A walkout at Kingsbridge was followed by similar refusals to handle tainted goods by workers on the Great Northern, and the Midland and Great Western. The ASRS Executive moved to Dublin and met daily from 19 September. With the Royal Commission in session, union leaders were probably unsympathetic towards the dispute, but the unwillingness of the companies to cooperate in the search for a solution led the union to proclaim an Irish strike. However the strikers were limited largely to the Great Southern and Western system; elsewhere support was slight, and by the end of the month the union had effectively accepted defeat. The companies used the opportunity to victimise union activists [for details of the ASRS's response see ASRS Executive Minutes, September 1911; for a sense of one leader's unhappiness about the dispute, see J. H. Thomas, Evidence to the Royal Commission, 30 September 1911, especially paras 14030, 14036, 14041, 14055].

Halls' involvement in the dispute was essentially that of a grassroots organiser; he was active at Waterford and subsequently at Cork. The legacy of the strike was organisationally damaging as the purge of activists and the broader demoralisation led to a significant fall in the ASRS's Irish membership. Moreover the two disputes had revealed a serious problem for British trade union organisers who were seeking to build a strong membership in Ireland. In August Halls had conveyed a union instruction that Irish railway workers should strike as part of a national stoppage – the nation in this case being the United Kingdom. However a month later the ASRS Executive had declined to call out British railway workers in support of their Irish colleagues. As passions deepened over Irish Home Rule, the effectiveness of British unions as representatives of Irish working-class interests would become a divisive issue.

The formation of the National Union of Railwaymen (NUR) in 1913 meant that Halls would no longer be concerned with the problems of a British union official working in Ireland. Within the new union organisational districts and responsibilities were restructured, and Halls returned to the familiar world of the East Midlands, where he was placed in charge of the NUR's District No. 7, based in Nottingham. The war years saw a marked change in the NUR's status – state control of the railways, union recognition and greatly increased membership. Apart from his union work, Halls also played a role in the wider Nottingham labour movement. He represented both the Trades Council and the cooperative movement on the city's Food Control Committee. His support for the war was low key. He saw his role as protecting the interests of dependants of serving men: 'While his lads were serving in the forces, it was his duty and privilege to fight at home to defend the people's interests against the exploiters during the war period [*Northampton Daily Chronicle*, 11 November 1918].

Halls' pre-1914 politics remain obscure. While his subsequent political views contained strongly Liberal elements, the early commitment of the ASRS to political independence meant that such a union-centred figure would have endorsed a Labour identity. Edwardian Leicester politics at the parliamentary level demonstrated the apparent compatibility of the Liberal and Labour agendas, with Ramsay MacDonald being returned in three general elections as the beneficiary of a Liberal–Labour pact. Halls seems not to have been influenced by the ethical socialism of the Independent Labour Party. His political ambitions became evident during the war and at the end of 1917 he was nominated for one of two additional parliamentary candidacies to be sponsored by the NUR. There were 49 nominations, and while Halls polled well in the membership ballot he was unsuccessful. Instead he was adopted without sponsorship in the summer of 1918 as Labour candidate for Northampton.

The borough had previously returned two MPs (with one exception between 1885 and December 1910, these had been Liberals) but the recent redistribution had reduced Northampton's representation to one. Wartime Liberal divisions had also left their mark. The temper of Northampton Liberalism was indicated by the political identity of its candidate – the Coalition Liberal Charles McCurdy. His former colleague – H. B. Lees-Smith, a member of the Union of Democratic Control – had been discarded. There was no Conservative candidate. Halls could appeal to trade unionists and to a local tradition of radicalism that, prior to 1914, had contained a relatively strong Social Democratic element. The campaign was robust. McCurdy, backed by the local press, questioned Halls' patriotism: 'he was a member of the Pacifist and Revolutionary Party ... who by underhand means had got the Labour Party to leave the Coalition Government [*Northampton Daily Chronicle*, 11 December 1918]. Halls endorsed President Wilson's fourteen points on the peace settlement and insisted on the democratic credentials of the Labour Party. T. F. Richards, President of the National Union of Boot and Shoe Operatives, the town's dominant trade union, refused to speak for Halls because of the candidate's allegedly pacifist views. Given the prewar strength of Liberalism and the circumstances of the election, Halls' electoral performance was far from disastrous:

Northampton, December 1918: electorate 46 007, turnout 62.5 per cent

C. A. McCurdy (Coalition Liberal)	18 010 (62.7 per cent)
W. Halls (Labour)	10 735 (37.3 per cent)
Majority	7275 (25.4 per cent)

In his post-poll comments Halls claimed that the party alignment had been changed decisively:

The Liberal has the biggest Tory majority that has ever been obtained. ... We have achieved something in this fight that was worth doing ... we have got them both in one camp, and they will not shift from that in the fights of the future [*Northampton Daily Chronicle*, 30 December 1918].

The perception that the heightened post-war ambitions of the Labour Party would promote strategies for Labour's containment was significant. But in December 1918 such strategies were in their early stages. Much remained unclear, and Halls' own political career would be influenced decisively by the complexities and instabilities of the post-war party system.

As a district organiser he was thoroughly involved in the NUR strike of September/October 1919, and then in the local implications of the events of Black Friday in April 1921. Whilst the 1921 miners' lockout continued Halls was presented with another electoral opportunity. In May 1921 the Postmaster General, Alfred Illingworth, took a peerage, resulting in a by-election in the cotton textile seat of Heywood and Radcliffe. Illingworth had won the seat as a Coalition Liberal in 1918; in the changed circumstances of 1921 local Liberal acquiescence in a pro-government candidate was less likely. The Liberal Association agreed to find a candidate who was a 'sound exponent of Liberalism' [*Bury Times*, 18 May 1921]. The choice fell on a local Liberal notable, Cornelius Pickstone, who was a Congregationalist and head of a firm of bleachers and finishers. Beginning his campaign as a Liberal without prefix he moved to a more anti-government position. The Coalition Liberals were represented by Colonel Abraham England, head of a Manchester wholesale clothing business and possessor of a strong war record. England was backed by two Liberal clubs in the constituency and by the local Conservative organisation, complemented by the regional resources of the Coalition Liberals.

This failure to retain the united anti-Labour front of 1918 obviously gave encouragement to the local Labour organisation. Halls was adopted, this time with the benefit of NUR sponsorship. Yet the economic situation contained potential problems for a Labour candidate. The electorate included about 1200 locked-out miners, concentrated at Radcliffe. They were expected to vote heavily for Labour, although the selection of an NUR official could arouse negative sentiments about Black Friday. Many cotton workers had been laid off or reduced to short time by the coal crisis. It remained unclear how far they would blame the government, or alternatively the Miners' Federation, and by extension the Labour Party. Halls' campaign incorporated orthodox Liberal sentiments – free trade without reservation, and the need for a principled international policy. He attributed the coal crisis to the government's insistence on the export of German coal as reparation. His Irish experience was exploited in his support for Labour's Irish policy. Against England's hints that he was linked to 'socialist extremism', he insisted on Labour's constitutionalism. The *Manchester Guardian* went as far as to claim that the choice lay between three Liberals. 'He is not only not a firebrand. ... He talks in the self-same accents as Mr Pickstone of Free Trade, Ireland, peace, economy. In short, he will roar you Liberalism like any Asquithian dove' [*Manchester Guardian*, 6 June 1921]. This was perhaps exaggerated, but the continuities of style and policy were significant. Alongside these, Halls evoked a distinctively Labour appeal. 'As a worker and knowing the workers' needs and ideals he was ... the right man to represent the workers' [*Bury* Times, 4 June 1921]. The Labour campaign was lively and optimistic – 'England expects Halls to win' was one response to the Coalition Liberal's innuendoes about extremism. At the very end of the campaign Labour's chances were strengthened when wage negotiations between cotton employers and cotton trade unions broke down. Those cotton workers who were neither unemployed due to trade recession nor laid off due to the coal crisis suddenly found themselves locked out. Even the Coalition Liberal candidate suggested that the cotton employers had made a mistake. Liberal divisions and the immediate economic problems proved decisive:

Heywood and Radcliffe by-election, 1921: electorate 39 856, turnout 80.9 per cent

W. Halls (Labour)	13 430 (41.7 per cent)
A. England (Coalition Liberal)	13 125 (40.7 per cent)
C. Pickstone (Liberal)	5671 (17.6 per cent)
Majority	305 (1.0 per cent)

In the small Parliamentary Labour Party, Halls was a regular participant in Commons debates, and in his constituency he was regarded as a conscientious MP. Along with other NUR-sponsored MPs he supported the Third Reading of the Railway Bill against the opposition of the PLP in August 1921. This Bill amalgamated the railway companies into the 'Big Four'; it also provided the framework for a system of wage determination to which the union had already agreed. In contrast other Labour MPs opposed the legislation since it retained private ownership of the railways.

The November 1922 General Election was characterised by complex national alignments. The outcome was unpredictable, but in Heywood and Radcliffe the choice was simple – Labour versus the rest. The Liberal Association had adopted England as its candidate in June 1922. Pickstone supported him, and when the campaign began the Conservatives endorsed him as a Constitutional candidate. England emphasised Labour's 'extremism' and his opposition to the capital levy, while Halls defended the levy and again stressed his credentials as a workers' representative. The result demonstrated Labour's increasing support but minority status:

Heywood and Radcliffe, 1922: electorate 40 968, turnout 83.8 per cent

A. England (National Liberal)	19 016 (55.4 per cent)
W. Halls (Labour)	15 334 (44.6 per cent)
Majority	3682 (10.8 per cent)

After this defeat Halls indicated to the NUR Executive that he was unlikely to contest the seat in any future election [NUR Political Sub-Committee Minutes, 5 March, 13 September 1923]. The unexpected dissolution of Parliament in November 1923, however, caused him to change his mind. Initially the character of the election posed a problem for England. Since his victory he had had an understanding with the Conservatives that he would support the Conservative government except when Liberal principles were breached. But Baldwin's decision to fight an election on tariffs challenged this position. England responded by insisting on his free trade credentials, and treating Conservative protectionism almost as an aberration. Despite his free trade stand he once again obtained local Conservative support on constitutional grounds. In response Halls insisted that he was the better free trader. The constitutional strand in England's campaign perhaps led to Halls discussing the Soviet Union. He made the unexpected claim that 'the Bolshevik Government had done more to restore organisation and put the country on a sound and organised basis than any other Government in Europe'. More predictably he insisted that 'the development of the Russian market was the whole solution of European reconstruction'; above all, 'he as an Englishman was more interested in the government of England' [*Bury Times*, 5 December 1923]. The turnout was perhaps affected by fog on polling day, and it is possible that partisanship aroused by the tariff question marginally affected England's vote. A shift to Labour proved insufficient; victory seemed unlikely in a straight fight:

Heywood and Radcliffe, 1923: electorate 41 430, turnout 78.3 per cent

A. England (Liberal)	17 163 (52.9 per cent)
W. Halls (Labour)	15 273 (47.1 per cent)
Majority	1890 (5.8 per cent)

Upon his election to Parliament in 1921 Halls had ceased to be a union organiser, but after his 1922 defeat the union had paid him – and another defeated colleague – £400 a year for organising work. This was clearly an interim measure and after his second defeat he sought a permanent post. In March 1924 he asked the NUR Executive if he could be appointed to one of the seven new organisational posts without a ballot. This was not possible under the rules but he was excused the examination. When the ballot was held later in 1924 he headed the poll. He returned to his old post in Nottingham, and was involved in the General Strike and the subsequent problems of reinstatement. He retired from his organiser's post in June 1931.

Halls made an unexpected reappearance as a Labour candidate in the October 1931 election. J. H. Thomas's support for the National Government produced a vacancy for a Labour candidate in the two-member Derby constituency. The Derby Labour Party adopted Halls on 12 October 1931, to run in tandem with W. R. Raynes, who had previously partnered Thomas. The prospects were not good. The party agent had sided with Thomas and had apparently taken the canvassing records with him. In addition three councillors had left the Labour Group and the officials of the NUR's Derby No. 2 Branch backed Thomas. Moreover Thomas's electoral performance had consistently revealed a personal vote. He had topped the poll in every post-war election; in 1922 and 1924 he had been elected but Raynes had not.

Faced with these difficulties and the general political climate, Halls' and Raynes' task grew increasingly difficult. Halls attacked the bankers and Conservatives' plans for tariffs; he acknowledged that the budget must be balanced but insisted that the unemployed should have decent treatment. Furthermore he defended the right of married women to unemployment benefit:

> They could not blame married women for asserting their rights. ... He was not going to point the finger of scorn at a married woman who, with a husband in and out of work and paid an insufficient wage asserted her rights when she had been contributing to the fund [*Derby Daily Telegraph*, 20 October 1931].

Halls stated after the poll that in the last stages of the campaign he had 'misgivings', but that the extent of defeat had come as shock:

Derby, 1931: electorate   85 542, turnout 81.3 per cent (a double seat)

Rt Hon. J. H. Thomas (National Labour)	49 257 (35.4 per cent)
W. A. Reid (Conservative)	47 729 (34.3 per cent)
W. R. Raynes (Labour)	21 841 (15.7 per cent)
W. Halls (Labour)	20 241 (14.6 per cent)
Majority	27 416 (19.7 per cent)
	25 888 (18.6 per cent)

In 1929 Thomas had polled 39 688 as a Labour candidate and Raynes 36 237. Halls responded to the decline in Labour support by making what for him was an unusual political point: 'they had polled a good solid and reliable socialist vote. They had lost as much as they could possibly lose' [*Derby Daily Telegraph*, 28 October 1931]. A heightened emphasis on socialism was a characteristic Labour rejoinder to the disasters of 1931. Halls balanced this judgement with a less combative verdict: 'they all hoped that after the struggle was over the country would be able to go along as though nothing happened' [ibid.]

Halls became increasingly prominent in municipal politics. First elected to Nottingham City Council in 1919 and again in 1926, he became an alderman in 1929 and chair of the Education Committee in 1934. He served as Sheriff of Nottingham in 1937–38 and as Lord Mayor in 1941. He was an enthusiastic cooperator, serving on the Board of Management of the Dublin Industrial and Co-operative Society and then on the Board of the Nottingham Co-operative Society. He was president of the Nottingham Society from 1919–44 and a director of the Co-operative Press from 1933–42.

Halls married Jane Hanes of Sharnford in Leicestershire, the daughter of a postmaster. They had three sons and five daughters. He died on 20 October 1953, leaving an estate valued at £4405 2s 10d.

Respectability allied to a sense of class stood at the centre of Halls' politics. His desired society owed more to the culture of cooperation than to any explicitly socialist politics. In his 1923 election address he asked voters to believe in 'the possibility of building up a sane and ordered society based on a Co-operative Commonwealth to oppose the squalid materialism that dominates the world to-day'. A local journalist captured Halls' style in the Heywood and Radcliffe by-election.

> He possesses few of the arts which make a polished or cultured speaker, and he candidly told his audience that he did not. He is of the type of working-man who has made headway

amongst his own class by sincerity and commonsense ... if one missed polish or culture in his manner of speech one could find other good traits. He put his case forward plainly and effectively, and a note of honesty and frankness seemed always to be behind it [*Bury Times*, 4 June 1921].

Halls' emphasis on Labour decency was a significant strand in the party's post-1918 electoral appeal. His experiences in parliamentary elections illuminate the complex responses to the Labour challenge.

Sources: (1) MS: Amalgamated Society of Railway Servants Records, National Union of Railwaymen Records, Modern Records Centre, University of Warwick, includes annual reports and minutes of Executive, Executive Sub-Committee, annual and special general meetings. File MSS.127/NU/GS/3/25 contains biographies of officials, including that of Halls; Records of Derby Labour Party, Derby Public Library; Halls' 1923 election address and a few press cuttings, NMLH, Manchester; Ramsay MacDonald Papers, PRO. **(2) Newspapers:** *Manchester Guardian*; *Bury Times*; *Northampton Daily Chronicle*; *Northampton Daily Echo*; *Derby Daily Telegraph*; *Railway Review*; *Irish Times*. **(3) Other:** Report of the Royal Commission on the Conciliation and Arbitration Scheme of 1907 – Evidence, Command Paper 6014 (1912–13); G. W. Alcock, *Fifty Years of Railway Trade Unionism* (1921); Emmet Larkin, *James Larkin: Irish Labour Leader* (1965); Dermot Keogh, *The Rise of the Irish Working Class: The Dublin Trade Union Movement and Labour Leadership 1890–1914* (Belfast, 1982); Emmet O' Connor, *A Labour History of Ireland 1824–1960* (Dublin, 1992).

DAVID HOWELL

HARDY, George (1884–1966)
SYNDICALIST AND COMMUNIST

George Hardy was born on 26 July 1884 in Cottingham in east Yorkshire. His father, Robert Hardy, was a farm labourer of radical views who had rejected religion, but his mother Sarah, née Firth, was a practising Baptist from an educated middle-class family. Hardy later recorded the powerful impression that this conflict of beliefs had made upon him [Hardy (synopsis) 1]. Unfortunately he gave no indication as to whose precepts he had been brought up by, or whether he had taken sides in these disagreements himself as he grew older.

Hardy's family enjoyed relatively comfortable circumstances for agricultural workers, but at the age of 12 Hardy finished his education at the local church school and followed his father onto the land. When he was 16 he volunteered to fight in the Boer War – despite the objections of his father, an admirer of Lloyd George, who viewed the conflict as a war for gold – but was rejected on the ground of age. The following year, as he first evinced what would prove a life-long travelling instinct, the prospect of better wages and freedom from the long and exhausting hours of the agricultural labourer drew him to a shipyard in Beverley. There he joined his first labour movement organisation in the shape of the Gasworkers' Union, and also came across the hostile attitude of skilled workers towards unskilled workers such as himself. After losing his job he joined the regular army, where he proved a 'good soldier', being proficient in shooting and horse-riding. However by his own account he reacted against the bullying discipline and had a number of run-ins with his superiors. In 1906 he declined to extend his period of service. Following a spell of casual work in a tannery and having no intention of going back to the land, he emigrated to Canada.

Beginning in Toronto he took on a series of jobs – farm labourer, goods porter, boilermaker, moulder, teamster – while travelling west across the country. After a period in Edmonton,

Alberta, he eventually settled in Victoria, Vancouver Island, British Columbia, and it was there in 1908 that he made his first contact with revolutionary politics. Attending meetings and joining the Socialist Party of Canada (SPC), he began to build up his own Marxian library, obtaining books, pamphlets and journals by becoming a shareholder in Charles H. Kerr & Co., the Chicago publishers of Marxist literature. In July 1910 he was instrumental in forming a local Teamsters' union, of which he was appointed full-time organiser and elected president. The following year he had his first involvement in strikes, one of which he recalled as being successful and another as premature and ill-judged. In his memoirs, *Those Stormy Years*, he later claimed that by that time he had already broken with the SPC and its 'warped ideas of Marxism' as 'too "revolutionary" ... to take part in day to day struggles' [Hardy (1956) 36]. However in this respect, as in many others, reliance on Hardy's own recollections for details of his early life is not entirely satisfactory. Published in 1956, these were expressly intended for the edification of younger communists and adhered closely to the demands of the exemplary party life, always advancing from the lower to the higher stages of consciousness and hinging on the life-changing moment of allegiance to the communist party. In this respect they were strikingly similar in conception to the prototypical memoirs of Hardy's contemporary and sometime associate, W. Z. Foster, and their value as a historical source is inevitably circumscribed as a consequence.

This is especially evident in Hardy's account of his formative attachment to the Industrial Workers of the World (IWW), or Wobblies, into which he led his own union when exiting the American Federation of Labor (AFL) as a result of the aforementioned strike activities. The AFL was notorious as moderate, craft-based and hostile to socialistic agitators, while the IWW had quite a presence in Western Canada amongst miners, loggers and dock workers in the years immediately preceding the First World War [Leier (1990) 35–45; Palmer (1992) 187–8]. Nevertheless, from the perspective of the communist party loyalist of the 1950s, the IWW's vigorous dual unionism and suspicion of politics were like the syndicalist temptations of a misspent youth, to be recounted in Hardy's memoirs in a tone of self-criticism. In particular Hardy argued that the IWW's open advocacy of industrial sabotage and militant anticlericalism had alienated many workers and laid it open to attack by the state, while disaffiliation from the AFL was seen as having severed his own organisation from the main body of the local labour movement. However harsh the verdict of hindsight, Hardy was to spend the next ten years as an active and eventually a leading member of the IWW [Hardy (synopsis) 12–13; Hardy (1956) 28–39].

The proverbial Wobbly organiser was far more the roving agitator than a desk-bound functionary. Certainly such a pattern of activity seems to have attracted Hardy, though having married his first wife Edith around 1907 and having his first child Edna soon after, there are references in his memoirs to the difficulties this caused in the bringing up of a young family. Nevertheless in 1912, after six years in Canada, he recommenced his travels and after meeting with the IWW's leaders in Chicago was appointed as one of the union's general organisers. Accompanied by his wife and children, in this capacity he visited Australia, New Zealand and briefly South Africa. In Australia he made contact with local socialist organisations and spoke at public meetings in Melbourne and Sydney. In Gisbourne, New Zealand, he campaigned for socialist candidates in local elections and hoped to settle there, but his wife wanted to return to Canada. On arriving back in Victoria in the summer of 1913 he became involved in IWW support for striking miners on Vancouver Island [Hardy (synopsis) 14–15; Hardy (1956) 40–8; Fry (1998) ch. 3; Leier (1990) 38]. When war broke out in Europe he was involved in organising antiwar meetings, and in a curious echo of his earlier conflict with his father over the Boer War he tried unsuccessfully to dissuade his two younger brothers – who by this time, with the rest of his family, had joined him in Canada – from joining the British army. Their subsequent death at the front must have done a good deal to strengthen Hardy's growing internationalism. In October 1915 he left his family on his mother's farm and returned to Britain, ostensibly inspired by news of 'the rising revolt on the Clyde against conscription and the war', though this hardly seems likely at so early a date [Hardy (1956) 56–7]. What does seem credible is his report of the stagnation of the IWW in British Columbia, where his branch had disbanded in May 1914 and its library sent to an IWW branch in Sydney, Australia [Leier (1990) 45, 56 n. 26]. In Britain, partly as insurance against the possible introduction of conscription, he found work as a docker on the King George Dock in Hull, and became involved in a local branch of the No Conscription Fellowship (NCF), along with Fred Jackson, later a CPGB member who settled and died in the USSR. When the branch collapsed Hardy became active in a small IWW and anarchist-influenced group advocating direct action against conscription, which likewise was only short-lived.

Another of his wartime experiences was to leave a more lasting impression. While working in the docks Hardy was so stung by the boasts of Belgian sailors about Belgian rule in the Congo that he signed on a ship to see the country for himself. Very probably he was influenced by the prewar Congo reform agitation, which was currently receiving renewed publicity as a result of the antiwar activities of its main instigator, E. D. Morel, with whom Hardy was familiar in the context of the NCF and whose powerful exposé, *Red Rubber*, he had read. Like Morel before him, Hardy was profoundly affected by the brutality of Belgian colonial rule, which he ascribed not to any particular deficiency of the Belgians but to the barbarism of the capitalist system as a whole. In an article for the US publication *International Socialist Review*, for which he had formerly acted as a sales agent in Canada, he focused particularly on racism, which in the Belgian Congo was casually displayed in conditions of new slavery: 'The white population sleeps from 11 to 3 o'clock, but there is no respite for the natives, who toil until their bodies look as though they had been dipped in oil.' He continued:

The writer saw an officer go down into the hold of the ship and beat a native without mercy because he did not work fast enough in this heat. Another officer stood on the toes of a native worker who had squatted to rest during the rest period, and beat the bare legs of the native to make him draw his foot from beneath the hob nailed boots of the noble (?) white man [Hardy (1916)].

In his memoirs Hardy described the experience as 'deepening my feelings of revolt and schooling me in the ways of twentieth century imperialist barbarism' [Hardy (1956) 58–66].

When the British government introduced conscription in January 1916, Hardy returned to North America and quickly reimmersed himself in trade union activities. In Cleveland, Ohio, he worked in a shipyard and was secretary of the local Metal Workers' union branch, and then in early 1917 he was elected secretary of the Marine Workers' Industrial Union while working on the Great Lakes. Resigning from this position in 1917 to spend more time with his family, he was strongly criticised by Bill Haywood for abandoning the union at a critical time [Hardy (synopsis) 20]. In any case, he was almost immediately thwarted in this intention by the United States' entry into the war in April 1917. On 5 September 1917, IWW leaders were arrested and charged with subversion, a fate that Hardy only avoided by working on a ship in Alaska. For a time this allowed him to coordinate the prisoners' defence campaign from Seattle, but almost immediately he was himself arrested and remanded in Cook County Jail in Chicago. Subsequently he was tried with the other IWW leaders for sabotage and treason, and in August 1918 was given the relatively short sentence of a year and a day, to be served on a road-building gang at Leavenworth Penitentiary. He attributed his short sentence to the authorities' incomplete record of his membership and the letters of support he received from Britain and Canada [Hardy (synopsis) 25; Hardy (1956) 114]. Again conforming to the conventions of the communist memoir, Hardy was to describe his prison experiences as strengthening his certainty that the cause of the workers would prevail.

Hardy's incarceration coincided with the news of the Bolshevik revolution, and he later described how the dual impact of these events caused him to rethink some of the fundamental assumptions of his political philosophy. Alerted by his trial to the realities of state power, while in prison he had the opportunity to study writings such as Lenin's *Soviets at Work*, and claimed that these influences were reflected in an 'appeal' or 'open letter' to American workers that he had smuggled out of jail. This cannot be established definitively, for Hardy subsequently claimed that passages of a more 'political' orientation were removed from his text prior to publication [Hardy (1956) 119–20]. Even so, the fact that the published version positively ruled out any political role for the organisation, described the building of the union as 'the greatest of all questions', and squeezed a single passing reference to the Soviets in between the British shop stewards and French and Italian syndicalists, all give grounds for scepticism [Hardy (n.d.)].

In January 1920 Hardy attended the national conference of the British shop stewards' movement as IWW fraternal delegate, and must have raised some eyebrows if, as he later claimed, he supported the future Communist Party chairman MacManus against the antiparliamentarians. He had travelled to Britain to publicise the case of the remaining IWW prisoners, but he also attended the International Transport Workers' conference in Oslo. By the time he returned to North America he was committed to the revolutionary tactics of the Bolsheviks and supported the more political stance adopted by the main section of the shop stewards' movement in Britain. Despite his support for affiliation to the Comintern and the creation of a revolutionary trade union international, he was elected general secretary–treasurer of the IWW after its national convention in May 1920. By that time this was effectively an underground organisation, bitterly split over its relationship with the nascent American communist organisations.

Hardy also represented the IWW at a series of international conferences, debating the relationship between revolutionary trade unionism and communism, and at the International Syndicalist conference in Berlin in December 1920 he was among those who opposed a proposal to set up a separate syndicalist international. He also attended a meeting in Moscow to discuss the forthcoming inauguration of the new Red International of Labour Unions (RILU, or Profintern), which he welcomed as 'the most *virile* International ever launched on the industrial battlefield' [*Industrial Pioneer*, August 1921, 5]. By his own account he had already shed his earlier syndicalist preconceptions, but in his memoirs he still credited these encounters with the demolition – his own word – of his antiparliamentarianism by 'clear bolshevik discussion'. According to Dubofsky, it was at this time that he fell 'in love with "the future" he saw embodied in the Soviet Union'. Like Gallacher in his memoirs, he ascribed a special significance to his meeting with Lenin, although when Lenin asked him whether he was a communist he answered with a blunt 'No'. He also held that the IWW 'should keep strictly on the industrial field and ... not get mixed up in controversies with any political group' [Hardy (synopsis) 33; Dubofsky (1988) 463; Gallacher (1948) 7–21; *Industrial Pioneer*, June 1921, 6]. It was only after returning to the United States for the IWW's 1921 convention that Hardy took up the cudgels on behalf of political action and the formation of a Communist Party. When this was at last achieved in December 1921, he was one of its founding members. With his expulsion from the Wobblies the following year, his transition from syndicalist to communist, though rather more uncertain and protracted than he was later to depict it, was at last complete.

Somewhat conventionally for the genre, Hardy described this in his memoirs as the ending of his 'first lifetime' of 'trial and error' and the beginning of a new one committed to communism [Hardy (1956) 149]. Certainly it marked his transition to the status of a full-time functionary who would never again work in industry or be elected to any position from below. Instead he first took up work with the Anglo-Saxon Bureau of the Profintern in Berlin, and then, after attending the second RILU Congress in 1922, he served as head of the RILU's seamen's section in Hamburg. Consequently he was there in October 1923 to witness the failed communist insurrection in the city, which left 67 dead, and he was marked by the bitter enmity towards reformism that was such a feature of the German Communists. 'The Hamburg State is in the control of the Social Democrats', he wrote of the dockers' revolt that same summer, 'and their blood-thirsty chief of police was responsible for the deaths of our German fellow workers' [*Inprecorr*, 31 January 1924, 51]. Hardy was to retain a high regard for the German Communist Party, and during the political controversies of the late 1920s he urged the 'insular' CPGB to emulate its less temporising and conciliatory approach to reformism [RGASPI 495/100/68,

Hardy, 'statement', 25 November 1930]. In the meantime, however, the debacle of the German 'October' helped shift the Comintern's priorities to the steadier if more prosaic possibilities that the British labour movement seemed to offer. Perhaps reflecting this in a small way, Hardy returned to Britain in December 1923 to establish what proved to be a lifelong connection with the CPGB. That, however, may not have been evident at the time. Arriving as an emissary of the International, in this case the Red International of Labour Unions, Hardy immediately experienced the first of a long series of disputes with leading British Communists in which the dramas of centre and periphery were played out in rancorous and highly personalised ways.

His instructions on arriving in Britain were to 'eliminate the deficiencies in the old RILU Bureau', dating from 1921, and he remained in the country to help launch the bureau's successor body, the National Minority Movement (NMM), as an unofficial opposition within the trade unions [RGASPI 495/100/413, Hardy to CPGB Political Bureau, 25 February 1927]. In the process he came into conflict with William Gallacher, the Clydeside militant who had been charged with this responsibility after the Comintern's British commission of July 1923, but hitherto had neglected it in favour of work with his parliamentary contacts. In Gallacher's memoirs there is only a mild reference to 'a smartly dressed young fellow with an engaging manner and a somewhat decisive way of deciding and doing things', whom Gallacher humoured by straightening out his files and typing his own letters [Gallacher (1948) 47]. That hardly does justice to the bitterness of the affair. According to Hardy's assessment three years later, Gallacher was 'not only grossly negligent ... but [also] ... incapable as a leader and organiser'; and when at the start of 1924 Hardy tabled his own proposals for the bureau's reorganisation, and was himself proposed as its organising secretary, Gallacher 'flew out at this as [a] concealed attempt to replace him' and insisted that he could no longer work with the interloper. This was a 'Dismal scene like the murdering of a baby', commented R. Palme Dutt, whose account of the meeting this was. The upshot was that Hardy remained in Britain, Harry Pollitt was persuaded to step into Gallacher's shoes – a development for which the latter gave a wholly implausible explanation in his memoirs – and in August 1924 the Minority Movement was formally inaugurated at a conference in London. Its president was Tom Mann, its general secretary Pollitt and its organising secretary Hardy. Gallacher was moved to other duties with the insult still rankling [Hardy to CPGB Political Bureau, 25 February 1927; WCML, Dutt to Salme Dutt, 31 March 1924; RGASPI 495/100/155, CPGB Political Bureau minutes, 20 February and 11 March 1924].

In all this work there is no reason to believe that Dutt's high regard for Hardy's 'practical sense and industry' was not vindicated [Dutt to Salme Dutt, 31 March 1924]. Roderick Martin has described Hardy as 'a rather blustery character' who, as its secretary, never really succeeded in getting the Transport Workers' Minority Movement off the ground [Martin (1969) 48]. Nevertheless, as Pollitt's capable deputy Hardy played a full part in what Martin characterises as a period of 'initial success' for the NMM, and during Pollitt's year-long imprisonment from October 1925 – the critical year of the General Strike – he handled the responsibilities of acting secretary without any apparent costs to the movement's effectiveness. Indeed it was at that time that Hardy obtained his highest level of seniority within the British party, being co-opted onto the Central Committee and made a substitute member of the Political Bureau. Among other responsibilities, in the 1924 general election he was sent to North Battersea to strengthen the 'communist' content of Shapurji Saklatvala's campaign [RGASPI 495/100166, CPGB election commission report, 1924], and in February–March 1926 he was one of the British delegates at the sixth plenum of the Comintern Executive – effectively an interim Comintern minicongress. On this latter occasion he put forward a strong defence of the pragmatic methods by which the CPGB was then achieving its apparent success within the trade union movement. 'If a comrade's influence as a trade union official is to be of the least practical value he has to be practical', he argued. 'He must deal with the things that the workers want, leading them step by step' [*Inprecorr*, 25 March 1926].

Working closely with Pollitt, Hardy gave every sign of having been assimilated into the ways of the British party. This was especially apparent in connection with the General Strike and miners' lockout, in the course of which Hardy took a robust line of opposition to the more 'leftist' positions adopted by the Russian trade unions and the Profintern chief, Losovsky. Less than a week before the general strike he even counselled against indiscriminate attacks on right-wing union leaders and commended the work of relative 'lefts' such as Alonzo Swales and Ben Tillett. 'We are endeavouring to be ... practical and to have the workers look upon the Minority Movement as a serious constructive organisation during this crisis', he wrote [RGASPI 534/7/33, Hardy to Losovsky, 29 April 1926]. Subsequently he warned against the 'ill-advised' pronouncements on the TUC by the Russian trade unions and Losovsky, and declined to disseminate these on behalf of the Minority Movement. 'Your presumption that the bourgeoisie are in love with sheltering the capitulating General Council is wrong', he wrote to Lososvsky, pointing out that they had never been expected to take a 'revolutionary lead' [RGASPI 495/100/359, Hardy to Losovsky, 24 July 1926; 534/7/32, Hardy to Central Council of Trade Unions of the USSR, 24 June 1926]. Up to that point there is little evidence of any serious political differences between Hardy and the rest of his British colleagues.

This equable state of affairs was brought to an end by what was depicted as a personal and political indiscretion of some magnitude on Hardy's part. In the early British Communist Party there was a strong tinge of revolutionary puritanism (as personified by Gallacher), which in matters of sexual conduct was reinforced by organisational pragmatism. Though largely unconcerned with the private liaisons of its functionaries, the party reacted strongly to any behaviour that might alienate either party members themselves or the wider circles they sought to influence. Ted Lismer, a Sheffield engineer and Minority Movement activist, and Sid Elias, then the Tyneside organiser of the CPGB, were two early communist officials whose extramarital affairs led to their being removed from their positions [CPGB biographical database]. Another was Hardy, whose alleged indiscretions provided Gallacher in particular with what Hardy described as his 'first opportunity' for retribution [RGASPI 495/100/413, Hardy statement, 17 March 1927].

The details of the case can be briefly summarised as follows. Until the 1920s Hardy appears to have enjoyed a politically companionate marriage, and we know that two of his children, George and Iris, were brought up as communists and inducted into the Young Pioneers. However his memoirs were again conventional in generally passing over his domestic circumstances, a reticence reinforced in Hardy's case by the break-up of his marriage in circumstances that were hardly admissible in a text intended for emulation. In 1925 or 1926 he began a relationship with a King Street party worker, Paddy Ayriss – who later married the poet and sometime CPGB Head of Education, Douglas Garman – which one suspects would have passed without comment but for the announcement in the latter part of 1926 that Ayriss was pregnant with Hardy's child. One cause of concern was that, as the party's confidential stenographer, Ayriss was acquainted with its 'most intimate' affairs, and if she was in any way 'embittered' she had the capacity to cause it considerable damage. Another and better founded anxiety concerned the reaction of Hardy's wife, who had begun to turn up at the CPGB headquarters 'threatening to create disturbances' and dangling the prospect of exposure in the press. To avert this Hardy and Ayriss were hastily shipped off to Moscow (the British party suggested China), and arrangements were put in place to support Hardy's family directly from his salary. This suggested lack of confidence in his sense of personal responsibility, together with the refusal of any mandate upon which he might formally represent the party in Moscow, left Hardy with a burning sense of grievance [RGASPI 495/100/357, CPGB secretariat to J. T. Murphy, 19 October 1926, Albert Inkpin to Murphy, 19 November 1926; 495/100/359, CPGB Politburo to Losovsky, 10 December 1926; 495/100/419, CPGB Political Bureau minutes, 4 February 1927; Drew (2000) cites RGASPI 534/7/32, Inkpin to Losovsky, 16 December 1926].

While Hardy, like Lismer, regarded such measures as representing 'the narrowest petty-bourgeois conception of sex relationships', party officials justified them on grounds of expediency rather than personal morality. 'We can believe that it may be difficult for comrades in other countries to understand how it is that personal and domestic matters of this description should cause a Party scandal', they wrote to Losovsky, 'but we can assure you that the general outlook and psychology of the workers (and even the Party members) in this country ... is such that if the matter had been allowed to go on a scandal would have resulted' [RGASPI, CPGB Politburo to Losovsky, 10 December 1926; 495/100/413, Hardy to Comintern 'British' [Anglo-American?] secretariat, 17 March 1927; 495/100/514, Hardy to CPGB Politburo, 5 October 1928]. This was not an entirely fanciful prospect. Only three years later the marital difficulties of another party activist, Bob Lovell, attracted national press attention, necessitating an official party statement dismissing the press reports as a deliberate attempt to undermine Lovell's political effectiveness [NMLH CP/DISC, Bob Lovell, CPGB Political Bureau statement, 26 January 1929]. The difference in timing was nevertheless significant, for in 1926 the CPGB was still very much committed to maintaining its standing with mainstream trade union opinion, whose 'psychology' the letter to Losovsky cannot be said to have misrepresented. In revolutionary Moscow, on the other hand, a very different view was taken and in 1927 Hardy was unanimously vindicated by the Comintern's Political Secretariat and confirmed as the Minority Movement's official representative to the Profintern.

Repudiated by his own party, Hardy once again took on the colouration of his new environment, and as an international functionary he came to identify more closely with the International than with the national section he ostensibly represented. Probably this was assisted by the shift to 'Class against Class' and the Profintern's promotion of revolutionary trade unionism on lines that may not have been entirely uncongenial to the former Wobbly. He had after all celebrated the migratory groups of lumber workers, farm workers, miners and seamen as the 'most revolutionary workers' in America and the most ready to get involved in 'a fight' [Industrial Pioneer, May 1921, 12]. Moreover in the context of seamen's trade unionism, with which Hardy was particularly concerned, not only were communists already opposed to Havelock Wilson's reactionary National Union of Seamen, but the general disregard and contempt for colonial seamen provided a further case for revolutionary alternatives that clearly linked up with Hardy's earlier experiences in the Congo. This was reinforced when he spent the winter of 1927–8 in China working with the Pan-Pacific Trade Union Secretariat, established in Hankou, with Tom Mann in attendance, in May 1927. For a time Hardy functioned as the body's acting secretary in place of the American Earl Browder. If nothing else the experience underlined both the need to reach beyond traditional working-class constituencies, in this case to peasants and 'semi-proletarians', and the contrast between the Profintern – as 'the only real international trade union centre ... embracing oriental as well as occidental workers' – and the International Federation of Trade Unions, which Hardy described as 'only an appendage of European imperialism' and bearing direct responsibility for the 'white terror' against the Chinese workers [Pan-Pacific Worker, 1 November 1927, 9–13; 1 March 1928, 11–19]. Once again the subject is omitted from Hardy's memoirs, where a misleading impression is created of the linear development and maturation of his trade union views. In reality Hardy emerged as one of the fiercest British critics of 'yellow' trade unionism, denouncing even the International Transport Workers' Federation, led by the Dutch left-winger Edo Fimmen, as a 'social fascist international' indistinguishable from the general reformist drift towards 'open fascism' [Hardy (1930) 7–10, 13–14].

Hardy's criticisms of the CPGB, which sometimes were only slightly more moderately phrased, were to focus above all on the role of Harry Pollitt. Hitherto relations between the two appear to have been largely untroubled, and Hardy recorded that Pollitt had expressly dissociated himself from the action taken over his personal affairs [Hardy to CPGB Politburo, 5 October 1928]. However as Minority Movement secretary, Pollitt had long expressed a certain distrust of the Profintern leadership and in 1928, though free from the demands of conventional employment, he made no attempt to attend the Fourth Profintern Congress in Moscow, held not long before the Comintern's Sixth Congress. Hardy, on the other hand, attended both congresses, and following the decision that he should be allowed to return to Britain he arrived back in London with a Comintern mandate in September 1928.

Up on his arrival in Britain he discovered that most of his letters embodying Profintern directives had been binned by Pollitt without their contents being relayed to the Minority Movement executive. 'I was told that "any suggested organisational changes or instructions emanating from that end [meaning the Profintern EC] will be resisted from here" ', he reported indignantly of his efforts to communicate the same information in person. To his obvious disgust he was not restored to his old authority within the NMM, and in preference to him Pollitt delegated business even to the 'office girl' – probably either Dora Cox or Doris Allison, experienced party activists to whom Hardy would not have referred so dismissively had they been men. To make matters worse the old personal charges against Hardy had evidently been resuscitated by Gallacher and Dick Beech, the latter, like Hardy, a former syndicalist and seamen's activist. All in all the mission was something of a fiasco. Initially it had been intended that Hardy would work in Britain on a long-term basis, and his own ambitions were clearly evident in his suggestion of an Organising Bureau under the leadership of someone with a knowledge of the movement internationally as well as in Britain. Frustrated at every turn, it was of his own volition that in November that year Hardy returned to Moscow and his seat on the Profintern General Council. 'I feel I cannot', he said, 'be humiliated by any such contemptuous depreciation of myself for another day' [RGASPI 495/100/514, Hardy to CPGB Politburo, 5 October 1928; 495/100/498, CPGB Politburo minutes, 6 November 1928; 495/100/481, CPGB delegation, sixth Comintern congress, executive members' minutes, 1 August 1928].

Almost immediately he returned to China. Recommencing work with the Pan-Pacific Trade Union Secretariat, Hardy and Ayriss also functioned as members of the Comintern's Far Eastern Bureau, working directly with the leadership of the Chinese Communist Party, along with representatives of the Comintern such as the German Eisler and the Pole Rilski. Though we have little information on what must have been largely clandestine activities, it is clear that the confirmation of Hardy's standing and capacities contrasted markedly with the reception he had had in Britain, and this evidently strengthened his identification with 'centre' against 'periphery'. The connection with China was to remain a significant one for Hardy, who was to become secretary of the China Campaign Committee in the late 1930s and in 1951 to experience the 'supreme happiness' of witnessing the triumph of the revolution at first hand [Hardy (1956) 194–213, 245–9; Hardy, Synopsis, 37–9; RGASPI 495/100/914, Hardy, Statement, 4 January 1933, Studer, *Un parti sous influence*, 530–2].

Hardy returned to Britain at the end of 1930 and resumed the tussle over the formation of a revolutionary seaman's union that had contributed considerably to the ill-feeling of his previous visit. 'Seamen for you!', Pollitt had told him then, 'with a characteristic domineering wag of the head' [RGASPI 495/100/514, Hardy to CPGB Political Bureau, 5 October 1928]. The suggestion was not in fact an unreasonable one. Hardy's involvement with the organisation of this sector dated back to the early 1920s, and as early as 1924 the inadequacy of traditional unions on a national basis had been a theme in his propaganda for a 'United International of Transport Workers' [*Inprecorr*, 1 May 1924, 295–6]. In 1925 he had actively supported the Amalgamated Marine Workers' strike, and when that union had folded the following year he had remained at the fore in expounding the case for a 'fighting seamen's union', ideally in the form of a seamen's section of the Transport and General Workers' Union [Clegg (1985) 384–5; Hardy (1927) 24–9.) At the Sixth Comintern Congress, where Hardy's return to Britain had been agreed, the objective of a revolutionary seamen's union had been formally endorsed, and presuming that it meant the opportunity to set up this union under his own direction, Hardy now willingly acquiesced in Pollitt's proposal [Hardy to CPGB Political Bureau, 5 October 1928; Worley (2002) 123]. But in fact, as the next three and a half years were to show, Pollitt had very little intention of promoting a breakaway union, and the instant Hardy left the country he secured the CPGB's endorsement of recruitment to the seamen's section of the TGWU, at last established with the disaffiliation of the NUS from the TUC [Hardy to CPGB Politburo, 5 October 1928; RGASPI 495/100/498, CPGB Politburo minutes, 6 and 13 November 1928; Worley (2002) 129–30].

With Hardy out of the country the issue of a new union appears to have remained in abeyance. However it resurfaced almost immediately on his return. Installed as head of the Seamen's Minority Movement (SMM) and then as chair of the Hamburg-based International of Seamen and Harbour Workers (ISH), Hardy was strongly placed to push for what was now intended to be Britain's third 'revolutionary' breakaway union. In his memoirs this agitation is attributed to 'Trotskyite' elements in the ISH, such as the German Albert Walters, and it is true that Hardy was troubled by attacks on the ISH by 'Trotskyist' elements associated with Beech [Hardy (1956) 216–17; RGASPI 495/100/914, Hardy statement, 4 January 1933]. Nevertheless, as Hardy himself put it in 1932, he was 'always a convinced supporter of such a rev-olutionary seamen's union ... ready to do everything necessary to accomplish this ... in full con-formity with the directions of the RILU'. In 1928 and 1930 he put the RILU's case in categorical terms, and in January 1932 directly rebutted Pollitt in suggesting that the conditions for estab-lishing such a union were rapidly developing [Hardy to CPGB Political Bureau, 5 October 1928; Hardy, Statement, 25 November 1930; RILU Magazine, February 1932, 68–71]. It is true that after the disastrous failure of that month's seamen's strike, Hardy warned against the 'mechani-cal' formulation of such a demand [RILU Magazine, April 1932, 345–7]. Nevertheless, when immediately afterwards he was levered out of the SMM in favour of the 'reformist opportunist' Fred Thompson, his long catalogue of grievances again included Pollitt's 'entirely negative atti-tude' towards new unions and the prevailing 'right-opportunism ... that reduces our Party trade union work to the narrow basis of trade union politics' [RGASPI 495/100/836, Hardy to CPGB Political Bureau, 8 July 1932; 534/7/52/98–109, Hardy's statement on his removal as SMM secre-tary, 25 September 1932]. Though legend has it that it took the Comintern agent Valtin to liquid-ate the idea of the revolutionary union, Valtin's memoirs are unreliable if not malicious. His allegations that Hardy and Thompson were running International Seamen's Clubs in British ports and in Freetown in Sierra Leone for their own personal profit, and that their wives were dressing like fashionable country club regulars on the proceeds, have not been corroborated [Pelling (1958) 70–1; Valtin (1941)]. The reality was that the union had proved a non-starter because of the persistent refusal by Pollitt in particular to attempt put the policy into practice.

It was during this period that Hardy's relations with the CPGB reached their lowest point. Although he both asserted and sought advantage from his outsider status, he was not oblivious to the personal isolation that was both its cause and effect. In a long memorandum drafted after his return to Britain in 1930, he had struck a note of undisguised contempt for the CPGB's congenital reformism, whether displayed in Pollitt's 'undisguised MacDonaldism', Gallacher's 'social democratic demagogy' or the party's neglect of unorganised workers and the anticolonial struggle. What is particularly instructive is the way in which he linked the CPGB's orientation towards labour-movement respectability with its supposed disregard for the authority of the International. 'The British comrades must have done forever with their insularity', he wrote.

> Their disrespect for 'foreign comrades' must cease. They must be told that other comrades
> from other countries see clearly the general political problems before the British Party,
> clearer than some of the British Party leaders, although they may never have entered Britain.
> Such comrades can help the British Party to overcome its lingering opportunist tendencies. ...
> I myself, born in the British Isles, having a fairly good experience in the British trade union
> movement, was even regarded as an intruder when sent by the ECCI and Profintern
> [RGASPI 495/100/68, 'Statement of the impressions of Comrade Hardy regarding the situ-
> ation within the CPGB', 25 November 1930].

Presumably Hardy envisaged himself as one of the 'good practical workers from other countries' who should be sent to guide the work in Britain, but his nomination by the Profintern as the NMM's joint secretary was successfully resisted by Pollitt precisely because it posed a threat to the control of the organisation [RGASPI 495/100/754, Pollitt to R. Page Arnot, 23 January 1931]. Blustery and authoritarian though he seemed, once in Britain Hardy's ambitions were consistently thwarted by this resistance to working under him, and although he bore the authority of the Profintern, this, far more than that of the Comintern, was more or less openly defied. Though the experience took a heavy personal toll, it is characteristic of the toughness expected of the leading party cadre that little sign of this can be found in Hardy's own correspondence. Instead it was, Paddy Ayriss who, in September 1932, sent the Profintern a 'purely personal' letter describing Hardy's deep distress at the thought 'that he has simply been thrown off and that our Party has no more use for him'. By that time he was being treated by a Communist doctor, R.W. Dunstan, and Ayriss pleaded that he be found a place in a sanatorium, if only to head off his plan to start a new life. 'His heart and soul is in our movement and this dreadful isolation is having a terrible effect on his nerves', she wrote. 'And naturally I feel very strongly about this, as I have to leave him in this state of mind, wondering whether he will be there when I return' [RGASPI 534/7/52, P. Ayriss, undated letter enclosing statement by Hardy of 25 September 1932; 495/100/833, 'Andrew' to Jimmy Shields and John Mahon, n.d.]. Behind the machismo of tough adversaries such as Pollitt and Hardy, one can gain a glimpse of the vulnerability that came of investing so much of one's self in the movement. This again was not the sort of subject to be broached in a party memoir, and the probability that Hardy received the necessary treatment must to some extent be inferred from the fact that he went on to fulfil a number of party responsibilities both in Britain and for the International. None of these, however, were of the top rank.

In 1935 Hardy was briefly the CPGB's Tyneside organiser, and the following year he was nominated by the CPGB as the Comintern's 'special instructor' to the South African Communist Party (CPSA). With somewhat ambivalent feelings about yet again receiving his marching orders, Hardy based himself in Johannesburg and Cape Town, where he worked closely with the CPSA leadership to secure the adoption of the Comintern's popular front line and the isolation of Trotskyists and sectarians. In his draft notes for his autobiography, Hardy observed that he was actually congratulated by the Comintern – 'a thing that rarely happened ... unless one did an excellent job'. But in fact the Comintern's initial satisfaction with how Hardy had interpreted his mandate was soon reversed and further frustration ensued. It was argued that he had shifted the focus of the CPSA's work too firmly onto white workers at the expense of work with the black population. Having reported on his mission in Moscow and sat on a committee established by the CPGB to oversee the CPSA's operations, Hardy's resumption of his work in South Africa was subsequently vetoed by the Comintern in late 1937 [Drew (2000) 183, 190; John (2001)].

Returning once again to Britain, Hardy was sent to 'reorganise' the leadership of the CPGB's Midlands district and drafted on to the party's Control Commission to help vet recruits for the International Brigade. The tragedy of the Spanish Civil War was in his case also a matter of great personal grief. Though we know little of his relations with his children by his first marriage, we do know that they were brought up as Communists and that his path crossed that of his daughter, Iris, who after working for Russian Oil Products took up employment in Comintern agencies in Moscow in 1932 [Iris Hardy, personal file]. His son, also named George Hardy, was a printer, an antifascist activist and a keen cycling member of the British Workers' Sports Federation. George volunteered for the International Brigades in February 1937 – before his father was involved with the recruits – and was killed on the Aragon front in April 1938. Writing to Moscow soon afterwards, Pollitt argued that there were 'urgent personal reasons' why Hardy should be given a change of work, and with a reaffirmation of the Comintern's veto on his return to South Africa, he was appointed organiser of the China Campaign Committee. He remained there until political tensions surfaced in the aftermath of the Nazi–Soviet pact.

In the mid 1940s Hardy worked as a CPGB industrial organiser in Merseyside, but shortly after the war he and his second wife, Dorothy Coulthard, moved to Sussex, where he became the party's district secretary. His roamings over five continents now completed – instead he held party branch positions successively in Brighton, Croydon and South Norwood – his status

became that of revered party veteran whose travails were unsuspected by the younger generation. Although he appears to have struggled with some of his administrative responsibilities, he
enthralled party schools and YCL gatherings with stories of his international experiences and
renditions of old Wobbly songs. Appointed to the party's International Affairs Committee, he
also chaired its West Indies Subcommittee, which provided one of the principal inputs into
party affairs of black activists such as Claudia Jones, whose difficulties as an 'outsider' in the
CPGB perhaps bore some comparison with Hardy's own. Though conspicuously loyal in most
respects, Hardy's continuing impatience with insular or nationalistic attitudes had a last airing in
1957, when, along with the West Indies Committee as a whole, he sided with Palme Dutt and
others in criticising the 'paternalistic' and ambiguous formulations on post-colonial relations in
the CPGB programme, *The British Road to Socialism* [CPGB West Indies committee 1957; *Daily
Worker*, 18 March 1957]. Remaining active to the last in the pensioners' movement, Hardy died
in Sussex on 24 May 1966, leaving an estate of £2617.

In 1932 Hardy spoke of the allegation sometimes made against him that he had 'not grown up
with the British movement'. This, he commented,

> expresses precisely the fogged insularity which is traditional in the British working class move-
> ment ... it is just because of my wider experience and my willingness to utilise the experiences
> arising out of the struggles of all countries that makes me totally free [of] the imperialist
> ideology that expresses itself so often even in our own Party [Hardy's statement on his
> removal as SMM secretary].

Hardy's great political strength was this genuine strain of internationalism, which remained
clearly evident from the time of his early opposition to the First World War and his trip to the
Congo in 1916. His weakness was that this international experience was largely acquired as a
functionary of the Comintern and its ancillaries – it was 'wider' in the geographical but not the
political sense, and he had no real involvement in workplace or industrial struggles to offset his
dependence on the International. Rather than the seamless party myths so carefully fostered in
his memoirs, it is the fraughtness of the relationship between the national and the international
in communist history that his life so clearly reveals.

Writings: 'Blacks and whites in the Congo', *International Socialist Review*, December 1916,
414–16; *Open Letter to American Workmen* (Chicago, n.d., 1919?); *The Struggle of British Seamen*
(1927); *A Fighting International of Marine Workers* (Hamburg, 1930); *Those Stormy Years* (1956);
contributions to *One Big Union Monthly*; *Industrial Pioneer*; *Pan-Pacific Worker*; *Inprecorr*; *RILU
Magazine*; *Communist Review*; *Workers' Weekly*; *Daily Worker*.

Sources: (1) MSS: Synopsis of early chapters of proposed autobiography, CPGB archives,
NMLH; Iris Hardy, Personal File, 1952, NMLH; CPGB West Indies Committee, recommenda-
tion to Commission on the British Road to Socialism, 1957, NMLH CP/Cent/Comm/1/5; Dutt
correspondence, WCML; Comintern and Profintern archives (*fondy* 495, 534), Russian State
Archive for Socio-Political History (RGASPI), Moscow. **(2) Other:** William Z. Foster, *From
Bryan to Stalin* (New York, 1937); William Gallacher, *The Rolling of the Thunder* (1948); Henry
Pelling, *The British Communist Party. A historical profile* (1958); Roderick Martin, *Communism
and the British Trade Unions 1924–1933. A study of the National Minority Movement* (Oxford,
1969); H. A. Clegg, *A History of British Trade Unions Since 1889. Volume 2: 1911–1933*
(Oxford, 1985); Melvyn Dubofsky, *We Shall Be All. A History of the Industrial Workers of the
World* (New York, 1988); Mark Leier, *Where the Fraser River Flows. The Industrial Workers of the
World in British Columbia* (Vancouver, 1990); Bryan Palmer, *Working-Class Experience.
Rethinking the History of Canadian Labour 1800–1991* (Toronto, 1992); Brigitte Studer, *Un parti
sous influence. Le parti communiste suisse, une section du Komintern 1931 à 1939* (Lausanne,
1994); *Tom Barker and the IWW*, recorded and edited by E. C. Fry (Melbourne, 1998, available

at iww.org.au/history/ tombarker); Allison Drew, *Discordant Comrades. Identities and loyalties on the South African Left* (Aldershot, 2000); Matthew Worley, *Class Against Class. The Communist Party in Britain between the wars* (2002). **(3) Unpublished papers:** Sheridan John, 'From fraternal solidarity to Comintern hierarchy: the changing nature of relationships between South African and British communists', delivered at the 'People of special mould?' conference, University of Manchester, April 2001. **(4) Personal information:** Monty Johnstone, Dorothy Thompson.

Acknowledgement. This research was carried out as part of the CPGB Biographical Project at the University of Manchester, funded by ESRC award number R000 23 7924.

ANDREW FLINN
KEVIN MORGAN

HASTINGS, Sir Patrick Gardner (1880–1952)
LAWYER, LABOUR MP, ATTORNEY GENERAL

Sir Patrick Hastings was one of the most prominent lawyers of his generation. While his parliamentary career and significant involvement with the Labour Party spanned less than four years, this included office in the 1924 Labour Government and a central role in the events that precipitated its defeat in the House of Commons.

Hastings was born in London on 17 March 1880. His father, Alfred Gardner Hastings, was a solicitor whose career ended in disaster. As Hastings later recalled, in his family 'bankruptcy ... was not a misfortune, it was a habit' [Hastings (1948) 5]. Beatrice Webb noted that 'he had a horrid upbringing, – his father, a wealthy solicitor and leading Wesleyan, having been convicted of gross embezzlement of clients' fortunes and sentenced to ten years' penal servitude' [N. and J. Mackenzie (1985) 19–20]. Hastings' mother, Kate Cormyns Carr, was a pre-Raphaelite painter. Educated at a preparatory boarding school and then at Charterhouse, family crisis led to the end of his formal schooling at the age of 16. With his mother and elder brother he then lived in a financially precarious and nomadic fashion in Corsica, France and Belgium. After 18 months he became involved in fruitless prospecting for gold in north Wales. The outbreak of the South African War led to his enlistment in the South African Yeomanry and two years of active service.

Despite his very limited financial resources, on his return from South Africa Hastings committed himself to a legal career. Admitted to the Middle Temple, he managed through strict economy and part-time journalism to save the £100 required for his call to the Bar in 1904. His earliest legal work was carried out for Charles Gill, who had a large criminal practice. Two years later he found a seat in the chambers of Sir Horace Avory; when Avory moved to the bench in 1910, Hastings took on the chambers. Through guile and industry he acquired a secure position; he rapidly became recognised as a busy lawyer with a growing reputation. Rejected for military service in the 1914–18 war as medically unfit, he took silk in 1919. His technique owed much to Avory's example. He made no notes on his briefs and upon conclusion of the case he expunged the material from his memory.

Senior judicial posts conventionally required a political background since they were the gift of the Prime Minister. Arguably this at least partly explains Hastings' developing interest in politics. His initial attachment was to the Liberal Party, and in the 1918 election he seemed likely to be Liberal candidate for Ilford. However, discouraged by the party's divisions, and perhaps doubtful about its credibility as a party of government, he abandoned his candidacy and subsequently shifted his attachment to the Labour Party. The reasons for this choice arguably had more to do with Hastings' career plans than with any ideological commitment. The Conservative Parliamentarians included many lawyers amongst their number; the Liberals were a shambles. Labour might have seemed to be a party with a governmental future, and most decisively perhaps, the Parliamentary Labour Party and the aspiring Labour candidates included few lawyers. Beatrice Webb's acerbic portrait of Hastings supports this assessment:

> an unpleasant type of clever pleader and political arriviste, who jumped into the Labour Party just before the 1922 election, when it had become clear that the Labour Party was the alternative government and it had not a single lawyer of position attached to it … an unsavoury being: destitute of all the higher qualities of intellect and without any sincerely held public purpose [N. and J. Mackenzie (1985) 19–20].

Another assessment, written in the mid 1930s by John Paton of the Independent Labour Party (ILP), is suggestive, especially given Hastings' approach to briefs. Paton spoke with Hastings at a Lanarkshire ILP meeting. The latter's contribution was a full-blooded denunciation of capitalism, decorated with Marxist language and demonstrating detailed knowledge of the labour movement. Yet these qualities induced scepticism

> after a time, I became aware of what seemed a certain mechanical quality about the speech; as it proceeded to its conclusion it flowed somehow too effortlessly. I remembered he had ample experience in mastering a brief, and that his political secretary was from the Clyde and a member of the ILP [Paton (1936) 164].

Paton's suspicions were seemingly confirmed as they travelled back from the meeting to Glasgow. Hastings listened to Paton's lengthy presentation of a point of difference between the Labour Party and the ILP. His response was a question: 'By the way, Paton, what exactly *is* the ILP? [ibid.]

Whatever his motives, Hastings was an attractive recruit for a party that was keen to broaden its social base. He became the Labour candidate for the Tyneside constituency of Wallsend; this was strongly working class and included sizeable contingents of miners and shipyard workers. The seat had been won in 1918 by Matt Simm: once an ILP propagandist, Simm had broken with the party because of its opposition to the 1914–18 war. His success had come as a candidate of the National Democratic Party, 'a patriotic labour' organisation, and he had benefited from the coalition coupon. In the uncertain alignments that followed the Coalition's collapse, Simm went into the November 1922 election as a supporter of Lloyd George. He faced not only Hastings but also a Conservative (C. W. Lowther) and a Liberal.

Hastings appealed to the working-class identity of most electors, and repelled attacks by his opponents on Labour's proposal for a capital levy. Simm seemed far removed from the context that had previously strengthened him: Lloyd George's appeal had declined and, Simm's reliance on such 'patriotic labour' figures as Havelock Wilson and 'Captain' Tupper seemed anachronistic. With the contest effectively being between Hastings and Lowther, the votes of unionised workers, already experiencing the effects of the depression on their trades, were perhaps decisive.

Wallsend, 1922: electorate 37 001, turnout 82.2 per cent

P. G. Hastings (Labour)	14 248 (46.8 per cent)
Hon. C. W. Lowther (Conservative)	11 425 (37.6 per cent)
T. G. Graham (Liberal)	2908 (9.6 per cent)
M. T. Simm (National Democratic Party)	1840 (6.0 per cent)
Majority	2823 (9.2 per cent)

In his maiden speech Hastings raised the controversial question of the capital levy in a relatively uncontroversial fashion. A tribunal should consider the policy; in his view it was an issue not of politics but of economics. Such a shift from partisanship did not reduce the Conservatives' hostility towards him. He was characterised in class terms as a renegade, an assessment that strengthened his standing within the Parliamentary Labour Party [see Beatrice Webb's conversation with Tom Johnston in Cole (1956) 243].

Hastings' most significant intervention during his first term in Parliament arose from the Irish Civil War and involved actions in the Commons and the courts. The Irish Free State government was concerned to reduce Republican activity in Britain. The British government was sympathetic but initially considered that Republicans should be arrested only if they had broken British laws. Extradition would require the Irish government to issue warrants for specific offences. However on the night of 10–11 March 1923, 119 Republican suspects were arrested, transferred to Dublin by destroyer and cruiser, and interned in Mountjoy prison. The deportations provoked strong criticism of the government in the Commons [*Hansard*, 12 March 1923, cols 1151–98]. Hastings' intervention [ibid., cols 1166–71] included a claim that he would subsequently utilise in the courts: the action was illegal since the creation of the Irish Free State had effectively nullified the legislation under which the deportations had been carried out.

This argument was developed when one of the deportees, Arthur O'Brien, applied to the High Court for a writ of *habeas corpus*. O'Brien acknowledged that he was the representative in London of the Irish Republican Government, but stressed that he had been born in England, had resided there for over twenty years and had never lived permanently in Ireland. The deportation had been carried out under a regulation made under the Restoration of Order in Ireland Act 1920. Hastings' argument elaborated on his Commons position:

> when the ... Act was passed the Imperial Government was having great difficulties about the maintenance of order in Ireland. ... There were specific mentions of the Lord Lieutenant and the Chief Secretary and his Forces. ... The Government seems to have acted as though what had happened in 1922 had had no effect on the position, and as though the regulations were still in force. His submission was that they were implicitly repealed, as the state of affairs in which the Act of 1920 was passed had ceased to exist [*The Times*, 11 April 1923].

His argument was not upheld by the High Court, but the case then proceeded to the Court of Appeal, with Hastings in opposition to Attorney General Sir Douglas Hogg. This time the judgment went in favour of O'Brien. Hastings' argument was effectively upheld by Lord Justice Bankes and his colleagues: 'since the establishment of the Irish Free State an order cannot lawfully be made by the Home Secretary for the internment of a person in the Irish Free State' [*The Times*, 10 May 1923]. The government appealed to the House of Lords, but by a majority decision the law lords decided they had no competence on the issue. The result was an Indemnity Act awarding compensation to the deportees. The chastened Home Secretary commented: 'these scoundrels got some £50 000 or more between them' [William Bridegeman, cited in Williamson (1988) 164].

This legal and political victory strengthened Hastings' claim to office in a Labour government. The opportunity came unexpectedly with Baldwin's decision to risk his majority with a Protectionist appeal in late 1923. This time the Wallsend contest was a straight fight between Hastings and Lowther. The latter was a Protectionist, which was an advantage for Hastings in his attempt to secure Liberal support. However the president of the Wallsend Liberals urged a Conservative vote against the capital levy and the former MP, Simm, backed protection [*Newcastle Journal*, 5 December 1923]. Hastings combined attacks on tariffs with affirmations of his socialist faith and insistence that unemployment was the result of the pursuit of profit [*Newcastle Journal*, 23 November, 3 December 1923]. In two Newcastle constituencies straight fights meant two Labour losses as the Conservatives and Liberals came together; but in Wallsend Hastings seemingly secured the majority of Liberal voters, an achievement acknowledged by the local Conservative newspaper [*Newcastle Journal*, 8 December 1923].

Wallsend, December 1923: electorate 38 435, turnout 75.6 per cent

P. G. Hastings (Labour)	16 126 (55.5 per cent)
Hon. C. W. Lowther (Conservative)	12 950 (44.5 per cent)
Majority	3176 (11.0 per cent)

Hastings became Attorney General in the 1924 Labour Government; the appointment brought a knighthood and, for the first six months, routine business. But by the end of July there were rumbling of the crisis that would lead to the parliamentary defeat of the administration – the Campbell case. The context was the complex relationship between the Labour Party and the Communist Party. The attitude of the latter towards the Labour Government had become increasingly hostile. On Labour's side there were those who wished to make a decisive break with the Communist Party, not least on electoral grounds, and others who wished to have no enemies on the left and shared at least some opinions with the communists.

On 25 July 1924 an article entitled 'The Army and Industrial Disputes: An Open Letter to the Fighting Forces' appeared in the Communist *Workers' Weekly*, written by the editor, J. R. Campbell. This noted not only that wars between armies involved workers killing each other but also that soldiers had frequently been employed against strikers. The conclusion was emphatic:

> let it be known that neither in the class war nor a military war will you turn your guns on your fellow workers, but instead will line up with your fellow workers in an attack upon the exploiters and capitalists, and will use your arms on the side of your own class [*Workers' Weekly*, 25 July 1924].

The circulation of the newspaper was small, but its content provided ammunition for Conservative backbenchers who were keen to embarrass the Labour Government over 'Bolshevism' and Labour Party–Communist links. Questions were asked of a Home Office Minister on 29 and 30 July [*Hansard*, 29–30 July, cols 1890, 2060–1]. On the latter day Hastings was informed of the article by the Director of Public Prosecution (DPP). He decided that the article was an incitement to mutiny and instructed the DPP to initiate an appropriate prosecution under the Incitement to Mutiny Act 1797. A warrant for Campbell's arrest was issued on 2 August and the matter was reported in the press. Three days later Campbell was arrested, charged and released on a bail of £200. His case was predictably taken up in the Commons by left-wing Labour MPs.

Hastings was questioned on 6 August by John Scurr, George Buchanan, James Maxton and Thomas Dickson. The gist of their questions was that Campbell's sentiments were widely shared within the Labour Party [*Hansard*, 6 August 1924, cols 2928–30]. Following these exchanges Hastings met with his backbench critics. They emphasised the Attorney General's political vulnerability, Campbell had an excellent war record; they claimed that he was only the acting editor. Moreover the prosecution would mean severe backbench criticism of Hastings. After this meeting Hastings discussed the case first with the Solicitor General, Sir Henry Slesser, and then the Director of Public Prosecutions, Sir Guy Stephenson. The latter confirmed the statements about Campbell's editorial status and war service, while Slesser expressed doubt about the validity of a prosecution under the 1797 Act.

At that point the issue was restricted to Hastings, the Solicitor General, the DPP and a few backbench critics, but the politicisation of the issue inevitably brought in other ministers. MacDonald, who was preoccupied with the inter-Allied conference currently meeting in London, had not been formally approached about the matter although he had learnt about it from an Admiralty junior minister, Charles Ammon. After Hastings' meeting with Stephenson in MacDonald's Commons room, MacDonald told Hastings that he thought the prosecution ill-advised. The cabinet met at 6 p.m. on 6 August. Hastings was present for the latter part of the discussion, which was muddled and rather incoherent in its outcome. Tom Jones, acting as cabinet secretary in the absence of Sir Maurice Hankey, took notes on the exchanges [Middlemass (1969) 287–90]. Hastings seemed ready to continue with the prosecution, but also offered a way out: the prospect of a letter from Campbell indicating that he was only the temporary editor. Jones' notes suggest that this was the preferred strategy. 'Attorney-General – I'll accept his letter – reply being we had to take cognisance reluctantly' [ibid., 290]. This outcome was confirmed in the official cabinet minute drafted by Jones, which reported Hastings' suggestion of a letter from Campbell and that in that eventuality 'steps could be taken not to press the prosecution ... if the Cabinet so desired'. The Cabinet's formal conclusions were twofold:

(a) That no public prosecution of a political character should be undertaken without the prior sanction of the Cabinet being obtained:
(b) That in the particular case under review the course indicated by the Attorney-General should be adopted [quoted in Marquand (1977) 367].

The official minute could be read to give the impression that the prosecution was dropped on the decision of the cabinet, but in fact, as Jones' rough notes make clear, the initiative came from Hastings. The general issue concerning prosecutions of a political character was a separate decision based on a proposal by J. H. Thomas [Middlemass (1969) 289]. Hard-pressed ministers about to go on holiday did not query the ambiguity. Hastings saw the DPP and the assistant DPP the following morning (7 August) and told them that the prosecution should be dropped. Six days later it was duly withdrawn. The Treasury counsel, Travers Humphreys, used a phrase that further muddied the waters. It had 'been represented' that the article had not been intended to undermine the allegiance of servicemen, but merely to oppose the use of troops in industrial disputes. The character of such representations remained obscure; no letter had arrived from Campbell. One predictable conclusion was that the representations had come from within the Government – a political intervention in the judicial process. The Communist Party's reaction was jubilant: 'Working Class Agitation Forces Government Surrender' [*Workers' Weekly*, 15 August 1924].

Hastings' contribution to the muddle of the Campbell case was significant. He had embarked on a prosecution that raised sensitive political issues without any consultation and despite the fact that his experience of Labour Party sentiments was limited. Having met with some party criticism, he grew concerned about the viability of the prosecution's case, and perhaps about the political cost to himself and his colleagues of proceeding. The prospect of a letter from Campbell was crucial to the cabinet's decision to support his proposal, yet he initiated the abandonment of the prosecution without obtaining such a letter. The immediate consequence was the phrase 'been represented'; the longer-term one was a political crisis.

The Government's clumsy response laid it open to attack. A senior Conservative, Sir Kingsley Wood, tabled two parliamentary questions, one asking Hastings why the prosecution had been dropped and the other asking MacDonald about his part in the affair [*The Times*, 20 September 1924]. A Liberal lawyer, Sir John Simon, subsequently raised the question of Travers Humphreys' statement. The threat of an antigovernment majority was emerging. The broader context was also significant. Many Liberals were opposed to the government's policy towards the Soviet Union, which had resulted in a commercial treaty and a general treaty. The Campbell case fitted in well with an attempt to construct an anti-Labour parliamentary majority around the theme of Bolshevism and Labour 'extremism'.

The Commons met on 30 September 1924 to debate the Irish Free State Bill, which was an attempt to resolve the dispute over the boundary between the Free State and Northern Ireland. Sir Kingsley Wood's two questions were taken before this debate. Hastings' answer stressed Campbell's temporary status as editor and his war record, and suggested that these factors might result in a failed prosecution. He insisted that he had 'received no representation ... of any kind whatsoever relating to the matter from the defendant, or from any person whatsoever'. Apart from the Solicitor General, 'no member of His Majesty's Government suggested or even knew of the proposal until I myself informed them of it' [*Hansard*, 30 September 1924, cols 8–12]. The Communist Party's response was to ridicule this account:

> This article ... was not copied out of another publication. It was ... written on the specification of the editor for a special anti-war number of our paper. It was not a wild and irresponsible statement inserted in the paper by a young and inexperienced editor. It was a cold, deliberate statement of the Party position inserted by the editor, Comrade Campbell, who is a responsible member of the political bureau of the Party [*Workers' Weekly*, 3 October 1924].

This response was at most an irritant. In the Commons Hastings had held the line in a potentially embarrassing situation, but MacDonald, when responding to Wood's second question, reacted disastrously. Wood's question referred to the possibility raised by the Communist Party that MacDonald could have been summoned to act as a defence witness. The implication was that he wished to avoid this situation; the Communist Party's argument might have been that in the past MacDonald had expressed similar views to those of Campbell. The Prime Minister's reply was later described by Sir Maurice Hankey as 'a bloody lie' [Middlemass (1969) 296].

> I was not consulted regarding either the institution or the subsequent withdrawal of these proceedings. The first notice of the prosecution which came to my knowledge was in the Press. I never advised its withdrawal, but left the whole matter to the discretion of the Law Officers, where that discretion properly rests. I never received any intimation, not even a hint, that I should be asked to give evidence. That also came to my attention when the falsehood appeared in the Press [*Hansard*, 30 September 1924, col. 16].

This reply did not lead to an immediate broadening of the issue and the initial press comments were largely critical of Hastings alone [*The Times*, 1 October 1924; *Manchester Guardian*, 1 October 1924]. However the Conservatives then tabled a censure motion on the Government's handling of the Campbell case, and this was followed by a Liberal amendment asking for the establishment of a select committee.

The attitude of most ministers was belligerent. The Cabinet decided on 6 October to oppose the Liberal amendment, along with the censure motion. Hastings was the only minister prepared to offer a less political form of inquiry: by a royal commission, a judge or the judicial committee of the Privy Council [Marquand (1977) 374]. Instead ministers hoped to divide the Conservatives and Liberals, and to defeat the amendment and censure motion in turn.

The debate on 8 October was prefaced by a personal statement by MacDonald acknowledging that his previous explanation had been misleading. The first ministerial contribution to the debate came from Hastings, who recounted in a skilful fashion the events of 6 August [*Hansard*, 8 August 1924, cols 602–7]. He provided an explanation of Travers Humphreys' statement to the magistrates concerning the abandonment of the case:

> The statement which I [Travers Humphreys] made on 13 August to Mr Leycester the magistrate was, as I believed, the statement which the Attorney-General desired should be made, although the language used was, of course, my own. The expression which apparently I used 'it has been represented' referred to the representations or statements in the House of Commons and elsewhere at public meetings ... and to nothing else [ibid., col. 613].

Having picked his way through these complexities, Hastings powerfully attacked the core indictment of his critics by pointing out that there were ample precedents for law officers consulting the cabinet about cases that involved political concerns. This point, was subsequently emphasised by a Labour backbencher, Herbert Morrison: 'He is in all Governments a politician, and surely, this doctrine of legal exclusiveness as far as the Attorney-General is concerned is a new doctrine which seems to have been specially saved up for the Labour Government' [ibid., col. 661].

The Conservatives' decision to support the Liberal amendment meant the Government's defeat and an election in which the Soviet Treaties and the Campbell case were linked to a rhetoric of anti-Bolshevism that was given additional power by the appearance of the Zinoviev letter. Hastings faced a new Conservative opponent in Wallsend, Sam Howard, a populist who was keen to pursue the anti-Bolshevik theme: a Labour government would be 'under the deliberate dictation of a foreign power' [*Newcastle Journal*, 13 October 1924]. Although Hastings was prepared to claim that socialism was the only cure for unemployment, he sharply differentiated his politics from those of the Soviet regime:

I hate the Russian methods of revolution. I thoroughly dislike their methods of government. … All that I am concerned about is my country. As a business proposition I want two things. I want to live in peace with Russia, and I want Russia which is the biggest country in Europe to buy the goods which the people in England are wanting to make to sell to them [*Newcastle Journal*, 18 October 1924].

Once again the absence of a Liberal candidate raised the question of the choice that would be made by Liberal voters. The turnout increased by almost 10 per cent, with the Conservative campaign, both national and local, strengthening the party's support.

Wallsend, 1924: electorate 38 598, turnout 85.4 per cent

Sir P. G. Hastings (Labour)	17 274 (52.4 per cent)
S. Howard (Conservative)	15 672 (47.6 per cent)
Majority	1602 (4.8 per cent)

Both Hastings, in his autobiography, and his principal biographer, claim that he never spoke again in the Commons [Hastings (1948) 249; Hyde (1960) 160]. This is inaccurate; he made some interventions during 1925 and 1926. For example on 6 March 1925 he spoke on a bill introduced by the Conservative backbencher Frederick Macquisten, The measure proposed a shift in the rules governing union members' payment of the political levy, replacing the need to 'contract out' with the requirement to 'contract in'. Hastings insisted that Conservative speakers had failed to provide evidence that those who contracted out were subject to victimisation and insisted that 'hon Members opposite do talk about this class war' [*Hansard*, 6 March 1925, col. 869]. His last Commons intervention was on 4 February 1926 in support of a Labour amendment advocating public ownership of essential services. Shortly afterwards he resigned his seat. His relationship with MacDonald had been distant since the Campbell case, which had underlined his peripheral position in Labour politics.

The ending of Hastings' political involvement was followed by a highly prestigious and lucrative law career, primarily at the common law bar. Some cases attracted considerable publicity, but much of his work was of a commercial character. His effectiveness owed much to his capacity to present complex issues in language that was comprehensible to jurors, and also to his forceful cross-examinations. A contemporary recalled him at the height of his powers:

A great and forceful personality with an alert and agile mind, a man of great resource and great resilience and of great courage and determination. I was fascinated by the expressions on his face – anger, surprise, incredulity, disdain – and knew them for what they were, and what they were intended to be. They were meant for the jury and were indeed more eloquent than words [Lord Birkett, Foreword to Hyde (1960) xiv–xv].

Two of Hastings' later cases had a political content. On the evening of 23 April 1928 two Metropolitan policemen arrested a man and a woman in Hyde Park and charged them with an indecent offence under the Park Regulation Acts. The man was Sir Leo Chiozza Money. A former Liberal MP and an economist, Chiozza Money had been one of the Miners' Federation nominees to the Sankey Commission and had been a Labour candidate. The woman, Irene Savidge, was employed by the Standard Telephone Company in north London. When the case came to court the magistrate listened to the police evidence and to Chiozza Money, and then dismissed the case. Questions were asked in the Commons about policemen and perjury, and the Home Secretary, Sir William Joynson-Hicks, asked the Director of Public Prosecutions to investigate.

The DPP instructed a Metropolitan Police officer, Chief Inspector Collins, to interview the principal figures. On 15 May 1928 Irene Savidge was taken from her workplace to Scotland Yard and subjected, on her account, to a lengthy and intimidating interrogation. The consequence was strong Commons pressure for an inquiry; as with the Irish deportation affair, a leading role in this was played by the Labour MP Tom Johnston [*Hansard*, 17 May 1928, cols. 1216–20, 1303–39]. The government appointed a tribunal consisting of Sir John Bankes (who had heard the Irish deportees' case in the Court of Appeal), J. J. Withers (Conservative MP for Cambridge University) and H. B. Lees-Smith (Labour MP for Keighley). Hastings appeared for Irene Savidge. He carefully led her through her account of her treatment at Scotland Yard, and then subjected Chief Inspector Collins to a characteristically robust cross-examination. In his closing speech Hastings extended the issue beyond the specifics of the case to the broader question of police procedures in such investigations. In particular he emphasised the lack of safeguards that might have allowed an agreed version of the police interview. This absence helped to produce a divided report. Bankes and Withers accepted the police version; Lees-Smith endorsed the claims of Irene Savidge [for the Commons debate on the report see *Hansard*, 20 July 1928, cols 803–94]. The Tribunal members did agree, however, on the need for the reform of police procedures.

Harold Laski, professor of political science at the London School of Economics, called Hastings' cross-examination of Collins 'the most brilliant thing I have ever heard in a court of law' [quoted in Kramnick and Sheerman (1993) 517]. In November 1946 Laski personally experienced the effectiveness of Hastings' cross-examination in the Laski libel trial, which raised important issues about British society and politics in the 1940s (see Special Note below). At one moment in the searching cross-examination Laski managed to draw blood:

Q ... are there any privileged in the Socialist Party?
A. Why indeed, Sir Patrick, when you were a member –
The Lord Chief Justice: No, Mr Laski.
Sir Patrick Hastings: Do not be rude.
[*The Laski Libel Trial* (1947) 94].

As Laski's leading counsel, G. O. Slade KC commented, 'I think I should at least have said "Touché" if that answer had been given to me' [ibid., 362].

Clearly Hastings' Labour past was something he wished to forget; arguably his attacks on socialism during the trial were not just for the benefit of his client, but also reflected the extent to which this one-time relative outsider had become a defender of traditional values. He felt that future prospects were bleak with the inevitable advance of socialism. 'All the refinement and charm associated with luxury and cultured wealth had gone, and it will never come back' [Hastings (1948) 288].

Success in the Laski case was Hastings' last legal triumph. His health was already problematic, as indicated by the fact that his quixotic attempt during the war to serve as an intelligence officer at Fighter Command headquarters had ended on medical grounds. He suffered a stroke in 1950 whilst visiting a son who was farming in Kenya, and died in London 26 March 1952. He left an estate valued at £14 532 8s. He had married Mary Ellenore, daughter of Lieutenant-Colonel Frederick Leigh Grundy, in 1906. They had two sons and three daughters.

Hastings' professional successes were not based on intellectual curiosity. His reading was limited largely to law reports and thrillers, with Edgar Wallace being a favourite. He wrote several plays, some of which were performed commercially and one, *The Blind Goddess*, was made into a film. Professionalism and clarity formed the basis of his triumphs. Politically he was a transient figure. The Campbell case showed the limits to his understanding of the Labour Party. More broadly his brief political career illustrated one element of Labour's search for a broader social base and, as government seemed a feasible ambition, for legal talent. His rapid exit from politics contributed to the belief within the party that most lawyers could not be trusted, an assessment seemingly confirmed in August 1931 when three of the Labour government's legal officers supported the National Government.

Writings: *The Autobiography of Sir Patrick Hastings* (1948); *Cases in Court* (1949). Published plays: *Scotch Mist* (1926); *The Blind Goddess* (1938).

Sources: (1) Speeches and Answers to Questions in *Hansard – House of Commons Debates, Fifth Series*: vol. 159, cols 976–83, 30 November 1922, maiden speech; vol. 161, cols 1166–71, 12 March 1923, Irish deportations; vol. 175, cols 1890, 2060–1, 29–30 July 1924, initial questions on Campbell case to Home Office ministers – also written question at col. 2085; vol. 176, cols 2928–30, 6 August 1924, Hastings' responses to questions on Campbell case, col. 3090, 7 August 1924, further response by Hastings; vol. 177, cols 8–16, 30 September 1924, replies to private notice questions by Sir Kingsley Wood – Hastings cols 8–12, MacDonald cols 14–16; vol. 177, cols 512–17, 8 October 1924, MacDonald's correction of his answer to Wood on 30 September, debate on Campbell case, cols 581–704, Hastings at cols 596–618; vol. 181, cols 866–9, 6 March 1925, Macquisten's bill; vol. 191, cols 465–9, 4 February 1926, final Commons speech, Opposition amendment to address – public ownership of essential services. **(2) Official Law Reports:** Secretary of State for Home Affairs v. O'Brien (1923), 2KB. 361 (1923) AC 6C3 (Irish Deportees). **(3) Other:** John Paton, *Left Turn* (1936); Sir Henry Slesser, *Judgment Reserved* (1941); *The Laski Libel Action* (1947); Margaret Cole (ed.), *Beatrice Webb's Diaries 1924–32* (1956); Richard Lyman, *The First Labour Government 1924* (1957); Patricia Hastings, *The Life of Patrick Hastings* (1959); H. Montgomery Hyde, *Sir Patrick Hastings. His Life and Cases* (1960); Keith Middlemass, *Thomas Jones. Whitehall Diary Volume 1 1916–1925* (1969); F. H. Newark, 'The Campbell Case and the First Labour Government', *Northern Ireland Legal Quarterly 20* (1969); David Marquand, *Ramsay MacDonald* (1977); Norman and Jeanne Mackenzie (eds), *The Diary of Beatrice Webb Volume 4 1924–1943: The Wheel of Life* (1985); Philip Williamson (ed.), *The Modernisation of Conservative Politics. The Diary and Letters of William Bridgeman 1904–1935* (1988); Isaac Kramnick and Barry Sheerman, *Harold Laski. A Life on the Left* (1993); Eunan O' Halpin, *Defending Ireland. The Irish State and its Enemies Since 1922* (Oxford, 1999). Political and legal events can be followed in *The Times* and Hastings' election campaign in the *Newcastle Journal*. For profiles see S. V. Bracher, *The Herald Book of Labour Members* (1923); *Dictionary of National Biography Supplement 1951–1960*, entry by Anthony Lejeune, pp. 465–7 (Oxford, 1971).

DAVID HOWELL

Special Note: The Laski Libel Trial

The Laski libel trial of November/December 1946 arose from an incident that took place during the 1945 general election. Harold Laski, professor of political science at the London School of Economics, member of the Labour Party's National Executive, Party chairman for 1945–6, spoke extensively on behalf of Labour candidates during the campaign. On 16 June 1945 he spoke in Newark market place in support of the Labour candidate for Newark: Air Vice-Marshal Hugh Vivian De Crespigny, who was a very recent recruit to the party. The meeting was well attended and until the final minutes it was without incident. Laski spoke for about 45 minutes and the candidate for about 15 minutes. As the audience was beginning to disperse an exchange took place between Laski and a member of the audience that became the subject of an item in one of the two local newspapers, the *Newark Advertiser*. The presentation of Laski's response to the intervention became the subject of the libel action. The item was located on a different page from that presenting the preceding speeches.

'REVOLUTION BY VIOLENCE'
Professor Laski Questioned

There were some lively exchanges between Mr Wentworth Day and Professor Laski following the latter's speech in Newark Market Place on Saturday night. Mr Day asked the Professor why he had openly advocated 'revolution by violence' in speaking at Bishop's Stortford and Bournemouth during the war – 'whilst most Englishmen were either fighting or being bombed at home', and why he (Professor Laski) had spent the whole of the last war lecturing in America. If he were unfit, why did he not join the Red Cross?

Rejected

Professor Laski replied that he was twice rejected in this country during the 1914–18 war and had medical certificates to prove it. He also attempted to enlist in Canada, and he then went to Harvard University, and he had a certificate from the Medical Officer of the British Army in New York of his inability to be accepted on medical grounds. 'That was said about me in the House of Commons ... and if you look at Hansard for 29th November, 1944, you will see an ample and generous apology made to me for being as insolent as you are in suggesting it now' [Laski's dating was mistaken; the apology was made on 14 December 1943].

Reference to Violence

As for violence, he continued, if Labour could not obtain what it needed by general consent, 'we shall have to use violence even if it means revolution'. When people felt it was the moment for great experiment, for innovation, because when war is over people so easily forgot – especially those who had the power in their hands – that was the time for experiment. Great changes were so urgent in this country, and if they were not made by consent they would be made by violence, and judging by the temper his questioner had displayed he would be perfectly naturally one of the objects of violence when it came.

Mr Day submitted to the Professor that when general consent was against him he substituted revolution.

Professor Laski said it did not lie in the mouth of any member of the Tory Party, who helped to organise mutiny in the British Army over Home Rule in 1914 to discuss the question of violence. When a situation in any society became intolerable – and when 25 per cent of the people had inadequate nutrition it did become intolerable – it did not become possible to prevent what was not given by generosity being taken by the organised will of the people.

Not an Asset

Mr Day: 'You are precisely the sort of bloodthirsty little man, full of words, who has never smelt a bullet, but is always the first to stir up violence in peace.

'We expect serious constructive thought from the Chairman of the Labour Party, but since you have consistently attacked everyone and everything from Mr Churchill to the leaders of your own party and the constitution of this country, and have been disowned by Mr Attlee only this morning, how can anyone take you seriously? I suggest that you are not an asset to the Labour Party but a liability' [*Newark Advertiser*, 20 June 1945].

The underlined words provided the ground for the subsequent action. The exchange became a lead story in the Beaverbrook press – the *Daily Express* and the *Evening Standard* – on the same day. These two presentations also drew on an earlier account in the *Nottingham Guardian* (a morning daily) on 18 June. This took the form of a letter to the editor and suggested a rather different sequence; by implication the incident occurred during Laski's speech, and he was clearly presented as the initiator of the exchange:

SIR – Attending a meeting in the Newark Market Place on Saturday night I was horrified to hear Prof. Harold J. Laski, Chairman of the Socialist Party, when enumerating reforms he wanted to see, declare: 'If we cannot have them by fair means we shall use violence to obtain them'. A member of the audience immediately challenged him and said: 'You are inviting revolution from the platform'. Prof. Laski replied: 'if we cannot get reforms we desire we shall not hesitate to use violence, even if it means revolution'. I think the widest publicity should be given to this statement, for I feel that electors all over the country should know what is really behind the Socialist mind. Seated on the platform was the Socialist candidate, Air Vice-Marshal Champion de Crespigny. I should like to know if this gallant gentleman does really associate himself with this statement, which he also heard.

Yours faithfully,
H. C. C. Carlton

The candidate sent a response to the *Nottingham Guardian* denying that Laski had ever made the statement and affirming his own commitment to constitutional government. The letter was never published apparently because by then the matter was *sub judice*; Laski took out a writ against the *Nottingham Guardian* and the *Daily Express* on 20 June and the *Evening Standard* and the *Newark Advertiser* two days later. In a statement issued through the Press Association late on 19 June – and therefore specifically in response to the publication of Carlton's letter – Laski insisted that his words, at the meeting had been 'entirely different'.

What I said was: 'It was very much better to make changes in time of war when men were ready for great changes and willing to make them by consent through the urgency of war, than to wait for the urgency to disappear through victory, and then to find that there was no consent to change what the workers felt an intolerable burden. That was the way that a society drifted to violence. We had it in our power to do by consent that which in other nations had been done by violence' [*Laski v. Newark Advertiser Co Ltd and Parlby* (Daily Express, London, n.d. but 1947), hereafter Transcript, Intro., p. 9].

This theme had been central to Laski's wartime politics. He claimed a radicalisation in wartime Britain that not only permitted but also necessitated revolution by consent. 'Our problem is whether we can use the dramatic opportunity of war to lay the foundations of a new social order' [*Nation*, March 1941]. Failure would mean the loss of a rare opportunity for peaceful transformation; frustrated radicalism in a post-war context could easily lead to violent confrontation.

This diagnosis combined with Laski's often polemical style to complicate his relationship with those Labour Party leaders who were committed to the Churchill Coalition. Laski articulated the views of those who insisted that Labour ministers were too cautious; radical measures were justifiable on socialist grounds and would strengthen the war effort. In response Labour ministers pointed to the lack of a parliamentary majority for such measures and deprecated the division of opinion in a national emergency.

Through the seniority rule Laski, the radical gadfly, became Party Chairman during what proved to be an election year. His insistence on respect for party policy led to further conflict with the party leadership and his consequential depiction as a bogeyman by sections of the

Conservative press. In such a context the deployment of anti-Semitism was always a possible strategy. The *National Review* made an early bid for this territory:

> Anything less like the British working man than an international Jew could not well be imagined, and yet Mr Harold Laski presided at the big meeting of the Socialist Party on 11 December. It is said that every nation has the Jews it deserves. We do not know what we in England have done to deserve Mr Laski, but there he is, sneering at us and decrying us and our very English Prime Minister, but though he has so much contempt for this country, with no thought of returning to the country, whichever it was, that his parents came from and with no idea about the land he happened to be born in, save to make a revolution in it [*National Review*, January 1945].

In fact Laski's father had been born in Middlesbrough and had become an extremely successful Manchester cotton merchant and a leader of the city's Jewish community. His grandfather had arrived in England as a child after leaving Poland in 1831 [Kramnick and Sheerman (1993) 9–11]. Laski's views, and more covertly his identity, subsequently became prime targets in the election campaign, especially in the Beaverbrook press. The initial focus was on the forthcoming Potsdam conference, involving Churchill, Stalin and Truman. Since this was scheduled to begin during the period between the British election on 5 July and the counting of the votes 21 days later, Churchill invited Attlee to attend. Laski's response was to assert the primacy of the party over policy, including foreign policy. Intended as a warning against bipartisanship, the intervention raised the spectre of a party caucus headed by a red intellectual. Churchill raised the issue in an election broadcast; in the *Daily Express* the depiction was 'Gauleiter Laski'. This was the prelude to the meeting in Newark market place and the attempt to present Laski as a 1945 equivalent of the Zinoviev letter. There was also a local prelude. At a meeting on the evening prior to Laski's Newark speech the Newark Conservative candidate, Sidney Shephard, had linked Laski to the use of 'violence'. Shephard referred to Laski's Bishop's Stortford and Bournemouth speeches, which he claimed had publicly advocated revolution by violence. This was 'thoroughly un-British. ... No one can respect such loud-mouthed nonsense' [*Newark Advertiser*, 20 June 1945]. This was an overture to Wentworth Day's subsequent intervention.

These two presentations of Laski's alleged views were not unrelated. The claims about Laski's speeches in Bishop's Stortford in November 1941 and in Bournemouth the following month were in newspaper reports reproduced in the *Handbook for Speakers* prepared by the Conservative Party for the 1945 election. Wentworth Day acknowledged in his evidence that he had drawn Shephard's attention to the extracts [Transcript, p. 235]. Carlton's characterisation of Wentworth Day as 'a member of the audience' was, as Carlton himself knew, misleading. Wentworth Day was acting as Shephard's publicity adviser, as he had done in the 1943 by-election that had first returned Shephard to the Commons. The initial link between candidate and questioner was possibly a shared interest in field sports. Shephard, a successful industrialist, had acquired the trappings of the squirearchy and had served as a master of fox hounds; Wentworth Day had similar sporting interests and had been editor of *The Field*. During the 1945 election Wentworth Day stayed with Shephard at Elston Hall.

In fact Wentworth Day's political involvements were often highly controversial. His work as a journalist had involved a variety of employers, including Beaverbrook; his connection with the *Daily Express* was utilised by him in the Laski affair. During the 1930s he had worked for that rich and eccentric sponsor of right-wing causes, Lady Houston, and following her purchase of the *Saturday Review* he had become its editor. Its columns resonated with British nationalism and anticommunism, with contributors praising Mussolini but attacking Hitler. Its style reflected Wentworth Day's sense of himself as a High Tory concerned to recover a Merrie England eroded by liberals, socialists and rootless cosmopolitans. The National Government under Ramsay MacDonald was a political hybrid that threatened to marginalise genuine Toryism. Backed by Lady Houston's funds, he intervened in by-elections – for example in East Fife and

Ashford in early 1933 – to pose a Tory alternative to National Government weakness. By his own account these interventions involved claims against MacDonald that could be euphemistically described as inaccurate. He branded him a 'traitor' during the 1914–18 war and suggested that he had taken money from Russia during the war to foment strikes and revolution [Day (1958) 145–9].

His penchant for exaggeration was subsequently evident when he stood as Conservative candidate for Hornchurch in the 1950 and 1951 elections. The seat had been won for Labour in 1945 by the left-winger Geoffrey Bing. Although Wentworth Day radically reduced Bing's majority in 1950 and marginally in 1951, he failed to take the seat. A critic saw his appeal as far removed from the Conservatism espoused by the post-war party leadership. His meetings involved stepping from 'the atmosphere proper in a British election to the political jungle of the most backward American states or Latin American republics. ... Mr Day uses figures with the abandon of a child who calls any distance a hundred miles. Many of his statements would not stand the test of reference to a newspaper file' [Mervyn Jones, *New Statesman*, 18 February 1950].

Wentworth Day's aggressive campaigning appealed to some within his local party, but his characterisation of Sir Stafford Cripps as a 'white sepulchure' and a 'cadaverous humbug' brought protests that went beyond electoral partisanship [*Hornchurch and Upminster News*, 20 and 27 January 1950]. Some of his party activists grew critical of his unreliability. A Central Office Agent (8 November 1950) noted his 'originality and pugnacity', and a later communication characterised him as 'the most extraordinary personality ... the sort of man one is not accustomed to dealing with ... quite clearly a fairly slippery customer' [CCO 1/8/346, Conservative Party Archive].

Wentworth Day's dismissal of the Hornchurch party leaders as 'small time crooks' [ibid.] was not the first time his relationship with a local Conservative Association had become conflictual. In 1946 he had sought the Conservative candidacy for South East Essex but had failed to make the short list; he believed his exclusion had been due to his two divorces. He addressed a meeting of Shoeburyness Women Conservatives and presented his views on the issue. He then prepared a report of the meeting for the local press that indicated strong support for him amongst his audience. The branch officials alleged serious inaccuracies and accused him of stirring up trouble in the branch [for this controversy see *Southend Standard*, 12 and 19 September 1946]. As a later examination will demonstrate, this controversy – coming just two months before the libel trial – had features in common with the Laski affair.

Wentworth Day, however, was not the defendant; this position was occupied by Cyril Everard Parlby, proprietor of the *Newark Advertiser*. This was an independent newspaper, contrary to the claim in one study that it was part of the Beaverbrook chain [Kramnick and Sheerman (1993) 486]. Parlby had been born in Newark, the son of a schoolmaster, and had served his time on the *Leicester Mail*. During the 1914–18 war he had fought with the Royal Garrison Artillery and lost an arm during action in Belgium. After demobilisation he had returned to Newark to work with an uncle, J. C. Kew, proprietor of the *Advertiser*. In 1930 Parlby had succeeded as editor and managing director. He had also entered local politics, sitting on the town council from 1932 as an independent – a man of generally conservative views he felt that his position as a newspaper proprietor and editor precluded any formal party affiliation. Twice wartime mayor, he was a local notable, an individualist whose achievements suggested determination to conquer adversity. Close to Sidney Shephard, his view of local society and of his newspaper's role in it had an affinity with Wentworth Day's Toryism: 'Like many other country paper of its kind, it has in it, the yeoman spirit of England – that spirit of sturdy independence which informs the whole history of our countryside' [*Daily Mail*, 3 December 1946].

Having presented the principal figures in the affair, an attempt will now be made to reconstruct the complex chain of events by which the crucial report came to appear in the *Newark Advertiser*. As a prelude it is useful to consider the first public reference to the contested statement by Laski: the letter in the *Nottingham Guardian* of 18 June 1945. Henry Carlton was a

Conservative member of the Nottinghamshire County Council. Two days before the Newark meeting he had met Wentworth Day after a village meeting for Sidney Shephard, the Conservative candidate, who had mentioned the forthcoming visit by Laski. Carlton travelled some distance to the Newark meeting and had another brief conversation with Wentworth Day. Carlton denied any foreknowledge of Wentworth Day's intentions; the question of whether informal social networks facilitated a conspiracy designed to entrap Laski was implied repeatedly by his lawyers but evidence proved predictably elusive. What was acknowledged, however, was that Carlton did not write the letter that appeared over his name.

The speed of its publication was striking; a remark allegedly made at a meeting on Saturday night was printed in the letter column of a newspaper on Monday morning. Carlton contacted a *Nottingham Guardian* reporter called Wilson early on Sunday. He told Wilson about Laski's comments; on the basis of this conversation Wilson produced a draft and they met on Sunday evening in Nottingham. Carlton signed the letter, discussed its contents on the phone with the editor and the latter agreed to its publication. Whatever Carlton's insistence on the 'shocking' character of Laski's remarks, this concoction was an overtly political intervention. The circumstances of the letter's conception probably help to explain its departure from the agreed order of the events [Transcript, pp. 272–82].

The provenance of the *Newark Advertiser* report was more complicated, although a partisan element was once again apparent. The newspaper had its own reporter at the meeting. James Opie, a Cornishman, was highly experienced and, as the evidence demonstrated, a very competent writer of shorthand. He was at the corner of the lorry that served as the meeting's platform. He was accompanied by a reporter from the town's other newspaper, the *Newark Herald*. Both men took shorthand notes of the speeches; only James Opie took a note of the heated exchanges between Laski and Wentworth Day. This exercise was difficult; the protagonists were excited and some of the crowd were becoming angry. The resulting note was not verbatim but it was lengthy and was accepted within its limitations as accurate. Opie's note on the critical part of the exchange was:

> I turn now to your second question. This is a war in which most of the people have been called upon to make tremendous sacrifices, and all through the war Mr Churchill and those in the Conservative Party who stand by Mr Churchill have said with the greatest possible emphasis that there is nothing that is too good for the people of the country. They always say that in war-time. And I said – that means 'I said at Bournemouth and Bishop's Stortford' – 'that if that is the case, when people feel it is the moment for great experiment, when they feel the time for innovation is possible, that that is the time to experiment, the time to make innovations, because when the war is over people so easily forget, especially those who have the power in their hands. And I say that exactly as at the end of the Napoleonic wars we had the opportunity to do great things for the British people and did nothing for them, so, having tried in the 1914 war and again in a second war to do something for the British people, and let that moment pass, when the war is over our chance of making great changes by consent will pass away. Great changes are so urgent in this country that if they are not made by consent, they will be made by violence' [Transcript, p. 28].

This transcript was an accurate presentation of Laski's wartime emphasis on revolution by consent. Its contents falsified a claim made in the *Daily Express* on 20 June that the shorthand note included the following statement: 'Mr Laski said that if Labour could not obtain what it needed by general consent, we shall have to use violence even if it means revolution.'

James Opie used his shorthand notes to produce copy for the forthcoming edition of the *Newark Advertiser*. On the morning of Monday 18 June he summarised the speeches and after lunch he conducted the same exercise for the subsequent exchanges. He had discussed the topic with Cyril Parlby that morning, when the decision had been made to separate the report of the speeches from that of the Laski–Wentworth Day confrontation. Parlby also told his reporter that there would be additional material on the confrontation. Cyril Parlby had been present at the Saturday night meeting and had heard the gist of Wentworth Day's question; he had heard some, but not all, of Laski's reply:

I heard him use the word 'violence'. I heard him refer to his 'insolent friend', and I am convinced that he used the word 'revolution' and the word 'revolution' at that time I thought was used in conjunction with 'violence'. I also heard him point to Mr Wentworth Day in a very threatening attitude and say: 'You will be one of the first objects of violence when it comes'. … The last utterance I believe by Mr Laski was a quotation from Burke which I did not catch [Transcript, p. 180].

Later that evening Parlby phoned Wentworth Day at the Conservative candidate's house: 'I asked Mr Wentworth Day if he would let me have a copy of the questions he had put and also a report of his version of what happened' [Transcript, pp. 180–1]. Wentworth Day took these to the *Advertiser* office on Monday 18 June whilst James Opie was producing his own version. In contrast to the reporter's detailed account, Wentworth Day's submission was brief. Apart from his concluding reflections on 'a bloodthirsty little man', it comprised his initial two-part question followed by:

Professor Laski replied that he had volunteered for service in the 1914/18 war, but had been rejected, and that as for violence, if Labour could not obtain what it needed by general consent 'we shall have to use violence even if it means revolution' [Transcript, p. 230].

Parlby stated that he felt the report was accurate:

I read it through, and from what I had heard myself it sounded a very fair summary of what had happened. I was particularly desirous of getting the correct questions. I drew attention to that particular sentence which is now complained about, but Mr Wentworth Day was quite confident about that and I in my own mind was confident from what I had heard, because I thought it was simply explanation and amplification of what had been said in the Bournemouth and Bishop's Stortford speeches, the thing seemed to be just the same [Transcript, p. 181].

This assessment was made despite Parlby's earlier acknowledgement that he had heard only fragments of Laski's comments.

Moreover the press reports of the Bishop's Stortford and Bournemouth speeches did not make identical claims. The Bishop's Stortford report in the *Herts and Essex Observer* was equivalent to the disputed report in the *Newark Advertiser*, and was rejected by Laski as an inaccurate representation. In contrast the report of the Bournemouth speech in the *Daily Echo* was acknowledged by Laski as fair. The former report contained the following sentence: 'Their choice was very simple: to begin social transformation by general consent now or do it by violence after the war'. In contrast the Bournemouth report read 'we have a choice of revolution by consent now or revolution by violence after the war'. The difference between 'do' and 'have' was central to Laski's position [for texts see Transcript, pp. 50–1, and for Laski's comment see p. 69].

When James Opie noted the discrepancy between his shorthand note and Wentworth Day's typescript, Parlby reassured him:

I pointed out to him that I had been to the meeting, and that from the fragments I had heard I was of opinion that that sentence should be in – and also on the Monday morning I had seen the letter in the *Nottingham Guardian* from Mr Carlton and that further reinforced my view that those words had been used knowing the *Nottingham Guardian* to be a most careful paper and that anything that appeared in the *Nottingham Guardian* would be very carefully edited [Transcript, p. 182].

Opie's response was that it had been impossible to hear everything but that those words had 'probably' been used. He then prepared a composite copy adding three elements from Wentworth Day's version: the latter's version of the question asked, Laski's alleged reference to the use of violence and 'the bloodthirsty little man' passage. The remainder of the resulting article was provided by Opie's original copy, with headlines and subheadings provided by Parlby (For Opie's evidence see transcript pp. 205–27).

In order to consider the subsequent legal processes, a starting point must be the Statement of Claim made on behalf of Laski on 9 July 1945. This had two key elements. The words of the report:

a ... were false and malicious.

b ... by innuendo ... meant and were understood to mean that Mr Laski had declared his intention to commit and to conspire with others to commit the crimes of treason, treason felony, sedition, riot and breach of the peace if the policy of the Labour Party should not be put into operation by constitutional means and that Mr Laski was guilty of treason felony. (Transcript. p. 11)

The initial defence claimed that the words did not mean what was pleaded in the innuendo and that the report was fair and accurate. Its statements of fact were true or a fair and accurate report of the proceedings at the public meeting. Its statements of opinion were fair comment. In April 1946 the defence was amended; it was pleaded that the words of the report were true in substance and in fact. The effect of the amendment was to broaden the defence. Whilst one element remained the insistence that the report was a fair and accurate account of what had happened at the meeting, the defence now also embraced the innuendo, claiming that 'The Plaintiff has used substantially similar and/or revolutionary words and expressions on diverse occasions in speeches, in discussions and in his published writings'. The trial could now include not just consideration of what had been said on a Saturday night in Newark market place, but also an extensive debate on the meaning of Laski's prolific publications [see Transcript, pp. 86–91, and for the cited claim, pp. 23–4].

The two legal teams included lawyers of great repute and contrasting styles. The senior for Laski was G. O. Slade KC, a leading expert on libel law, supported by Sir Valentine Holmes KC. Slade in particular had expert knowledge of the law. Neither man engaged in courtroom drama: Slade was notable for 'his careful, fair and cautious mind', while Holmes had 'nothing theatrical about him' [*The Times*, 20 November 1956 and 12 February 1962]. Such discreet images were wholly foreign to the figure who dominated the defence. Sir Patrick Hastings KC had been Attorney General in the first Labour government, but his left-wing politics were now very much in the past and he had become one of the most successful common law pleaders of the interwar years. His legal knowledge was modest compared with that of Slade, but in style, theatricality and populist rhetoric he was unique.

Initially the expectation was that all four cases would be considered together, but the *Newark Advertiser* case came to stand first. Each side suggested sharp practice. The defence suggested that the plaintiff had selected the smallest of the four newspapers in the hope that the costs of the action would pressurise the defendants into an apology; instead the Beaverbrook press supported the *Newark Advertiser* [see Transcript, pp. 169–70]. In contrast the counsel for the plaintiff suggested that this prioritisation was at Hastings' suggestion [ibid., p. 186]. Such a strategy would perhaps appeal to sentiment for the 'small man' in a way that would not be possible if the defendants included a national newspaper.

Hastings made a successful pretrial application for the hearing to be held before a special jury. This option was available to both sides on the ground that the material to be considered was of great complexity. The qualification for a special juror was economic – presumably this was deemed a significant indicator of intellectual capacity. The common juror qualification for London in 1946 was the occupation of premises with a rateable value of £30; for a special juror the equivalent qualification was £100. Hence this special jury of seven – five men and two women – was drawn from a social class that was much less likely than the population as a whole to have voted Labour in 1945. Moreover in the post-war climate of austerity they were unlikely to have much sympathy for the nuances and complexities of socialist discourse.

The use of a special jury in the Laski case produced subsequent criticism by some left-wing Labour MPs, and its abolition in 1949 indicated the increasing belief within the legal profession that the provision was anachronistic. Abolition of the provision was endorsed in a House of Lords debate by the presiding judge in the Laski trial [*Hansard*, vol. 161, 8 March 1949, cols 192–5]. The Lord Chief Justice, Lord Goddard, had been appointed in 1946 by the Attlee government and was known as an advocate of capital punishment and other severe penal measures; his instincts were impeccably conservative. He also had some personal experience of political campaigning: in the 1929 election he had stood unsuccessfully as an independent Conservative in the blue chip South Kensington constituency.

The plaintiff's trial strategy was narrowly centred on the claim that Laski had not said 'if Labour cannot obtain what it needs by general consent, we shall have to use violence'. Apart from Laski, ten witnesses supported this negative claim. They ranged from Hugh Vivian de Crespigny, now Governor of Schleswig-Holstein, to local Labour Party officials, one Communist and men of no party. Hastings' technique in each case was simple: to cite other comments, ask if the witness had hèard them, and on receiving a negative response to indicate that Laski had admitted making the cited statement. The advocate drew the obvious conclusion: 'Quite possible you did not hear a great deal of what he said?' [Transcript, p. 158].

The defence produced two witnesses, as well as Carlton and Wentworth Day, in support of the claim presented in the *Newark Advertiser* article. Richard Breene, the acting British consul in Trebizond, was not present in court and his evidence was taken in Istanbul. In June 1945 Breene, after service in Special Operations and then as liaison officer with Tito's partisans, had been billeted near Newark. A graduate of Queen's Belfast, he had a limited acquaintance with Laski's writings and had been present at the later stages of the meeting. He claimed that Laski had responded to heckling by Wentworth Day with the comment 'If the Labour Party does not obtain the reforms desired, it may be necessary to use violence', and then added 'if that means revolution or words to that effect'. The claim was more ambiguous than that made in the article – 'we' had become 'it'. Breene claimed that he had been sufficiently struck by the statement to make a note of it, and subsequently to write to the *Daily Express*. Yet his recall of the exchanges was not perfect. He suggested in cross-examination that Laski had said that 25 per cent of the population were starving. 'I had actually come from a starving country, and I was rather amazed by his saying that 25% of the population were starving here' [Transcript, p. 268]. In fact Laski's reference, as demonstrated in Opie's shorthand note, was to 25 per cent of the population suffering from 'inadequate nutrition' [ibid., p. 29]. Even 'a witness of intelligence and education', in Goddard's words [ibid., p. 385], could recollect inaccurately.

The second defence witness – Bertram Spinks, who worked in a Newark shoe shop – contrasted thoroughly with the acting consul. This 'extremely modest member of the public' [Transcript, p. 290] offered a similar version to that printed in the article: 'If Labour cannot get power by consent, we must use violence to get it' [Transcript, p. 286]. Beneath his claim lay sentiments that were deaf to Laski's distinction between revolution by consent and by violence:

As a man in the street, Mr Slade, the word 'revolution' and the word 'violence' sound different. I am an ordinary member of the public, and they are horrible words to use at any time. I look upon it that violence is to take things by force and I look upon 'revolution' as a word meaning to overthrow the existing authority [Transcript, p. 290].

For this witness what Laski admitted saying, as represented in the Opie shorthand note – 'Great changes are so urgent in this country that if they are not made by consent, they will be made by violence' – was not significantly different from the sentence in dispute.

This occlusion offered a bridge to the second strand in the court hearing, a theme taken up by Hastings and for which Laski's legal team seemed ill prepared. This strategy was based on the amended defence of April 1946 to the effect that Laski's use of the disputed or similar words was long established. The effect of this argument might have been to reduce the credibility of Laski's claim for damages. Even if the jury found that he had not spoken the alleged words on 16 June 1945, their acceptance of a claim that such words reasonably represented his long-standing position would indicate that any inaccuracy in a specific newspaper report could not be deemed to have damaged his reputation. More radically the defence might have hoped that an exploration of Laski's publications would strengthen the credibility of the claim that the disputed words had indeed been spoken by him. The centrepiece of this strategy was Hastings' lengthy cross-examination of Laski. Subsequently Laski recalled this experience in a manuscript published after his death:

> You are then handed over to that same counsel whose life has so largely been passed in pricking men until they bleed. He performs his war dance about you like a dervish intoxicated by the sheer ecstasy of his skill in his own performance, ardent in his knowledge that, if you trip for one second, his knife is at your throat. He makes a pattern from bits and pieces picked with care from a pattern of life you have been steadily weaving for a quarter of a century to prove either that you never meant what you intended, or that you lacked every element of skill to give the world the sense of your intent. He moves between the lines of sarcasm and insult. It is an effort to tear off, piece by piece, the skin which he declares no more than a mask behind which any man of understanding could have grasped the foulness of your purpose. He treats you not as a human being, but as a surgeon might treat some specimen he is demonstrating to students in the dissecting room ['My Day in Court', *Atlantic Monthly*, November 1952].

Laski had frequently suggested in his writings, as he had indeed at the Newark meeting, that if majoritarian pressures for radical change were frustrated by resistance from capitalists and their allies, then the outcome could well be change through violence. He also insisted that this should be prevented if at all possible; the constructive alternative was his 'revolution by consent'.

Hastings attempted to blur the distinction between analysis and exhortation. Laski's suggestion that change through violence was a possibility became a claim that violence was inevitable, and then a suggestion that a claim of inevitability was effectively a willingness to justify violence as a route to radical change. Laski attempted to defend the crucial distinction:

> I take the view that the maintenance of social peace and the avoidance of violence is one of the most vital things at which our society can aim. ... This is at no point ... exhortation. Every part of the material that you have quoted is careful, and I hope accurate, diagnosis; and I think that you put me in an unfair and an unjustifiable position by asking me to accept diagnosis as exhortation [Transcript, p. 93].

Laski's arguments were rendered more complicated by his having changed his view about the likelihood of revolution by consent. As noted earlier, he believed that the upheavals and challenges of the war had strengthened the possibility of such a route to change. In contrast his view in the 1930s had been much more pessimistic. The collapse of the second Labour Government in 1931, mass unemployment and the growth of fascism had all supported a bleaker thesis, as presented in his 1933 book *Democracy in Crisis*. This text belonged very much to the post-1931 debate among the Labour left on whether socialism was attainable by constitutional means. It provided significant material for Hastings' cross-examination.

In his cross-examination Hastings attempted to portray Laski's view as dangerous not simply by dissecting his writings but also through a broader and less precise association of him with 'force, violence, revolution' [Transcript, p. 176], spectres that might haunt members of a special jury in their straitened circumstances of late 1946. This fed into the peroration to his opening for the defence:

> They can decry what to some people are the holiest feelings they possess. They can sneer at some of our old institutions, which have been the glory of our Empire: Law, Justice, all that we hold dear. He thinks nothing of them. ... But rude as he is, if anybody says one word about him, so thin is his skin that he flies to the Tribunal of Justice which he so utterly despises. Look at him. He is the man who comes here and says: 'I come to my country for justice. For God's sake do not look and see what I have said about it before by any chance, but now let us forgive and forget. I come for justice, the justice I say I shall never get, the justice that I despise in this hopelessly effete country'. He says: 'Away with all your religion.' [Transcript, pp. 77–8]

The characterisation of Laski as un-English, rootless, cynical and hypersensitive verged on the anti-Semitic. It had strong affinities with a portrayal of him by Wentworth Day that was introduced by Slade in his cross-examination to demonstrate that this key defence witness had been actuated by malice:

> He seemed to find so much solace in the revolutionary standards of less happy countries and so little comfort in the Britain which his ancestors had adopted as a place of profitable residence ... Professor Laski appeared on a sort of French Revolution cart. Fitted with a microphone instead of a guillotine, dressed in a tight-fitting hip-slinky overcoat of the sort that dance band leaders wear. ... For the best part of an hour he sprayed us with an oleaginous stream of rhetorical oratory [Wentworth Day, quoted in Transcript, pp. 250–1].

Here the anti-Semitic elements are more evident, yet Slade's attempt to discredit the witness might have been far less effective than Hastings' populism, which utilised the same sentiments, albeit more discreetly. The contrast was again evident in the counsels' closing speeches: Hastings brief and dismissive of Laski – 'this rubbish' [ibid., p. 311]; Slade, lengthy, thorough and careful but not entering into the wider territory raised by Hastings. The problem for the plaintiff was that what was really on trial in Hastings' presentation, and plausibly in the eyes of the jury, was the legitimacy of left-wing socialism and its compatibility with a conservative sense of Englishness.

Laski saw the Lord Chief Justice as the embodiment of such an identity. As Goddard began his summing up with a discussion of the principles of freedom of discussion, Laski felt he was 'back in some pleasant lecture room of an Oxford College where an elderly don is retelling the details of some ancient trial decided long ago'. However for Laski this image was rapidly shattered: 'He makes his point ... but they are always your opponent's points'. At root Laski saw Goddard as embracing the sentiments presented by Hastings:

> The judge not only hates the opinions you hold, but will explain to the jury that they are dangerous opinions. And since, at your opponent's instance, the jury is a 'special' jury, you know how unlikely it is that they will have an atom of concern for anyone with dangerous opinions. What, you swiftly see, is the real issue at stake is not what was said at some place on a definite occasion, but the fact that you hold unpopular opinions which both judge and jury are convinced it is bad to hold and worse by far to express ['My Day In Court', *Atlantic Monthly*, November 1952].

Or as Goddard insisted: 'when you are using the words "revolution" and "violence", Members of the Jury ... it is at least desirable, is it not, to make it very clear what you do mean? Young people are often apt to be inflammable' [Transcript, p. 383].

The jury took only 40 minutes to find for the Defendants. They did so on the ground that the *Newark Advertiser* article was a fair and accurate report. The broader question of Laski's published writings was not addressed directly, although the lengthy exchanges between the plaintiff and Hastings might well have had a significant influence on the verdict. With regard to Goddard's role in the case, there was a curious aftermath. Following Goddard's death in 1971 there was considerable debate in the columns of *The Times* concerning his record as Lord Chief Justice. These exchanges were in response to an obituary that was characterised by some as too benign and as failing to note Goddard's reactionary views. Two contributors to the debate were critical of Goddard's behaviour in the Laski trial, at which both had been present [see Bernard Levin's article and John Redfern's letter in *The Times*, 8 and 12 June 1971]. Yet a letter from H. Philip Levy [*The Times*, 12 June 1971] presented a very different view of Goddard's reaction to the case. Levy recounted a conversation between Goddard and Laski's brother Neville – both were members of the Inner Temple – in June 1965. A statement of Neville Laski's account was subsequently reproduced in Fenton Bresler's 1977 biography of Goddard. This claimed that whatever the nature of Goddard's summing up, the verdict was unwelcome to him:

> I did not agree with the finding of the Jury. I thought [a defence witness's name omitted] was lying throughout and I did not like any of the evidence for the Defence. I gravely considered where there was anything I could do, but as a Jury was involved I was helpless. I have been unhappy about this case always and often think about it. I can say that it has been on my conscience. I do want to add that your brother was not a good witness. He could not answer simply 'yes' or 'no' and made long speeches. Slade was no match for Pat Hastings [quoted in Bresler (1977) 177].

Despite the complexities of the evidence two propositions can be reasonably maintained. The first concerns Harold Laski. The words attributed to him on that night in June 1945 were in contradiction to the political position he had developed over a lengthy career both as an academic and as a member of the Labour Party. Hastings' attempt to demonstrate otherwise depended on exaggeration, distortion and populist rhetoric. Whatever its impact on the jury, it does not survive serious textual analysis. The second proposition concerns Wentworth Day, who was the source of the disputed sentence. Everyone acknowledged that he was a thorough partisan. Minimal attention was paid to his wider career, which had been marked by exaggerated statements and claims by others that he was unreliable. In particular the Southend affair shortly before the trial contained striking parallels with his actions in June 1945 – his preparation of copy for a local newspaper, with that copy containing statements that were rejected by those to whom they were attributed [briefly referred to by Slade in Transcript, p. 254].

For Laski the verdict was devastating, but donations poured into a Labour Party fund to meet his costs. Over $6300 was raised in the United States and the total amount came to £14 000–£2000 more than the costs. Yet the image of Laski as the cosmopolitan revolutionary endured. More than four decades later the defendant's son suggested that most of Laski's costs had been paid by the Polish Communist Party [Kramnick and Sheerman (1993) 543]. Despite the financial support and expressions of sympathy, many of those who were close to Laski believed that he was never the same again. The pain, in his eyes, of being branded a liar was accompanied by an increasingly bleak political outlook. Once hopeful about the prospects for progressive politics in the United States, his optimism was undermined by an increasingly virulent anticommunism. He also despaired about the increasing grip of Stalinism on Eastern Europe; as with many on the left, the Czech coup and the death of Jan Masaryk were defining events for Laski. Although he remained strongly committed to the Labour Party, Ernest Bevin's foreign policy, not least that on Palestine, brought further disillusion. In September 1947 he felt that the radical moment had passed. He wrote to his American friend, Felix Frankfurter, 'I am feeling that I am already a ghost in a play that is over' [quoted in Kramnick and Sheerman (1993) 564]. Yet the economic and social reforms carried out by the Labour government could be seen as a kind of 'revolution by consent'. In February 1950 he was back on the hustings; but exhausted and ill he died on 24 March.

If the trial could be seen as emblematic of the post-war decline in the optimism of the Labour left, it also revived the spirits of the Conservative right. Letters poured into the *Newark Advertiser* office. A local newsagent rejoiced – 'the little man has not been squashed'. A more expansive verdict came from another correspondent:

You must feel very satisfied that you have struck so good a blow against all that the real Britisher hates. Lack of freedom to act and trade and speak as he wishes – may the time soon come when pointless controls – Bureaucracy and nationalisation of everything will cease [Letters to Cyril Parlby, proprietor of the *Newark Advertiser*, 3 December 1946, Laski file].

Such sentiments energised the post-war revival of the Conservative Party. Whilst one strand in the party's platform for the 1950 and 1951 elections emphasised acceptance of the post-war economic and social settlement, another demanded 'set the people free'.

Cyril Parlby's congratulatory letters included one from a neighbouring town by a correspondent who like Parlby had recently been mayor. His values were similar to those of Parlby: 'I hope your courage will inspire others to fight these enemies of freedom'. Such rhetoric would later become very familiar; Alfred Roberts' daughter Margaret would soon graduate from Oxford.

Sources: (1) Transcript: *Laski v. Newark Advertiser Co Ltd and Parlby (The Laski Libel Action Verbatim Report)* (1947). **(2) MSS:** Correspondence on Laski Libel Action, File, *Newark Advertiser*, Newark; Conservative Party Archive, Bodleian Library, University of Oxford, Material on Wentworth Day's Hornchurch candidacies, CCO 1/8/346. **(3) Newspapers:** *Daily Express*, 16, 18, 19, 20, 21 June 1945, 3 December 1946; *Daily Mail*, 3 December 1946; *Hornchurch and Upminster News*, 20, 27 January 1950, 3, 10, 17 February 1950, 5, 12, 19, 26 October 1951, 2 November 1951; *Hornchurch, Dagenham and Romford Times*, 8, 15, 22 February 1950, 10, 17, 24 October 1951; *National Review*, January 1945; *Newark Advertiser*, 11 November 1942 (material on C. E. Parlby), 19, 26 May 1943, 2, 9 June 1943 (by-election), 30 May 1945, 6, 13, 20, 27 June 1945, 4 July 1945, 4, 11 December 1946, 2 December 1953 (portrait of Sidney Shephard); *Newark Herald*, 23 June 1945; *New Statesman*, 18 February 1950, piece by Mervyn Jones; *Nottingham Guardian*, 18 June 1945; *Southend Standard*, 12, 19 September 1946; *The Times*, 8, 12 June 1971. **(4) Writings by Harold Laski:** *A Grammar of Politics* (1925); *The Dangers of Disobedience and Other Essays* (1930); *Democracy in Crisis* (1933); *Liberty in the Modern State* (Harmondsworth, 1937); Preface to Victor Gollancz (ed.), *The Betrayal of the Left* (1941); 'Revolution by consent', *Nation*, March 1941; *Reflections on the Revolution of Our Time* (1943); 'On Being Suddenly Infamous', *New Statesman and Nation*, 14 July 1945; 'My Day in Court', *Atlantic Monthly*, November 1952; 'On Being A Plaintiff', in Kingsley Martin, *Harold Laski: A Biographical Memoir* (1953), **(5) Biographies of Laski:** Kingsley Martin, *Harold Laski 1893–1950. A Biographical Memoir* (1953); Granville Eastwood, *Harold Laski* (1977); Isaac Kramnick and Barry Sheerman, *Harold Laski: A Life on the Left* (1993); Michael Newman, *Harold Laski* (1993). **(6) Other:** James Wentworth Day, *Harvest Adventure* (1948); Patrick Hastings, *Cases in Court* (1949); James Wentworth Day, *Lady Houston OBE The Woman Who Won The War* (1958); Arthur Smith, *Lord Goddard My Years With The Lord Chief Justice* (1959); Patricia Hastings, *The Life of Patrick Hastings* (1959); H. Montgomery Hyde, *Sir Patrick Hastings. His Life Cases* (1960); Fenton Bresler, *Lord Goddard* (1977); Richard du Cann, *The Art of the Advocate* (Harmondsworth, 1986); Stephen Brooke, *Labour's War. The Labour Party During the Second World War* (Oxford, 1992). **(7) Obituaries:** *The Times*, 25, 29 March 1950 (Laski), 20 November 1956 (Sir Valentine Holmes), 12 February 1962 (G. O. Slade), 6 January 1983 (Wentworth Day); *Essex Chronicle*, 7 January 1983 (Wentworth Day). **(8) Interview:** Roger Parlby (son of defendant and present at the hearing).

DAVID HOWELL

HOLMES, James Headgoose (1861–1934)
RAILWAY TRADE UNION OFFICIAL

James Headgoose Holmes (the middle name appears on his death certificate but not on his birth certificate) was born on 19 March 1861 at Frampton near Kirton in south Lincolnshire. His mother was Maria Holmes; no father's name is given on his birth certificate. His formal education in a rural community was limited. He later claimed to have become a ploughboy at the age of nine, and two years later to have run away to sea for a brief period. He recollected that the captain 'cultivated his moral side by the aid of his rope and his mental side by making him read and copy articles from newspapers and commit passages to memory' [*Doncaster Gazette*, 4 October 1934]. He subsequently returned to the land, but his agricultural employment ended when he was dismissed after an attempt to organise a strike. Following a spell in a stables, he joined the Great Northern Railway Company at Spalding in 1882. Holmes had become a member of the uniformed working class; he would be subject to authoritarian management, but an authoritarianism tempered by paternalism for the 'good company man'.

In all probability Holmes' employment on the Great Northern was the result of complex railway geopolitics. In 1882 railway activity at Spalding increased because of new construction that represented a major bid by the Great Eastern Railway to break out of its heavy dependence on rural East Anglia. The Great Eastern, in a joint venture with the Great Northern, expanded northwards from rural Cambridgeshire, across Lincolnshire and into South Yorkshire. The Great Eastern's objective was the Yorkshire coalfield. Decision making in railway company boardrooms and the consequential alliances and rivalries affected employment prospects in rural areas; the companies could employ former farm workers at little more than the agricultural wage.

The 1880s were a period of relative railway expansion and Holmes achieved rapid promotion. Regular advancement meant several changes of workplace within the Great Northern system. Beginning in Lincolnshire, he then moved to the West Riding. By 1891 he was a first-class signalman working an eight-hour day and receiving 26 shillings a week at Retford in Nottinghamshire on the Great Northern mainline. His signalling post was at a strategic point on the company's network, so Holmes was clearly a competent young signalman and positively regarded by the Great Northern management. He was also a committed trade unionist; he had joined the Amalgamated Society of Railway Servants in either 1883 or 1884. In the mid 1880s the union was weak and there appears to be no surviving evidence of Holmes' early involvement. But at Retford he was president of the ASRS branch, a vigorous campaigner for reduced working hours and against company tyranny.

Holmes was also an active Liberal. The location was significant. Retford was part of the Bassetlaw constituency, much of which was rural and as yet largely untouched by the eastward expansion of the Nottinghamshire coalfield that would transform the seat's politics from the 1920s. Until 1929, with the sole exception of 1906, Bassetlaw was a Conservative seat. This was not simply a matter of the balance between urban and rural voters. The rural districts were dominated by the great estates of the Dukeries: Welbeck, Clumber and Thoresby. For the Liberals of the towns, the rural electorate seemed to be under the influence of aristocrats and the church. The constituency seemed designed to strengthen the darkest suspicions of Gladstonian radicals.

The Bassetlaw candidates in the 1892 general election fitted partisan stereotypes. The sitting MP, Sir Frederick Milner (Eton and Christ Church), was opposed by J. T. Yoxall, a Methodist and from 1892 General Secretary of the National Union of Teachers. Holmes played a very active part in this election. He had recently spoken at the inaugural meeting of the Retford Branch of the Labour Electoral Association, a firmly Liberal body, and campaigned for Yoxall. Soon after the election Holmes became the subject of an alleged victimisation case. Following an acknowledged breach of signalling regulations he was downgraded. He was required to transfer but turned down two options, one with lower pay and the other with lower pay and longer hours. His refusal meant his dismissal; the consequence was political controversy.

Retford Liberals could readily assimilate Holmes' treatment to the rhetoric of landlord tyranny that rationalised their electoral failures in Bassetlaw. Holmes underlined such sentiments at a meeting called to protest his dismissal:

The company did recognise politics and did so in such a manner as to reduce the Liberals and allow the Tories to do just as they liked. ... The Tories were the enemies of the working man ... he stood there as a victim of Tory tyranny. ... What he objected to was having been dismissed for holding opinions. ... He hoped that working men would recognise that without combination they were the helpless victims of a tyrannising party [*Retford and Gainsborough Times*, 29 July 1892].

Holmes had allegedly been punished for asserting his independence – 'he had dared to be a man' [ibid.] Here was the appeal of Gladstonian Liberalism to self-respecting working men, the emphasis on individual rights as against arbitrary authority, the necessity for collective action as a means to individual self-development.

The details of Holmes' dismissal were revealed when he unsuccessfully took legal action to recover the earnings he had lost during the period of suspension that preceded his dismissal. The Great Northern stressed the seriousness of Holmes' offence and its own political neutrality. However there was evidence, not refuted effectively by the company, that Holmes had been the victim of differential treatment. The incident involved what appeared to have been a fairly common breach of the formal regulations in order to facilitate the flow of traffic. Holmes' claim of political discrimination appeared to be without foundation; but arguably the Great Northern took the opportunity to downgrade and then rid itself of an employee who was a highly visible union activist. Significantly the local campaign against Holmes' dismissal did not include a characterisation of him as a victimised trade unionist – probably an indication of the dominant political discourse in a country town.

The Retford branch of the ASRS applied successfully to the union executive for Holmes to be paid a protection grant of £50 as a victimised member. The branch case combined trade union and political arguments:

In his capacity as branch chairman he protested to the station master against the excessive hours some of our members had to work, and the tyranny of some of the intermediate officials towards them. Through his efforts the shunters obtained meal hours and Sunday pay. He was instrumental in establishing a branch of the Society at Newark, as one result of his persistent advocacy of the Society. More recently his activity at the General Election seems to have given great offence, and is believed to be the real cause of the dismissal [General Secretary's Report, 8 August, ASRS Records 1892].

After July 1892 Holmes never again worked for a railway company. His Retford sympathisers collected £170 for him, but the ASRS Executive's upholding of his victimisation claim proved much more significant. The verdict meant that whatever his employment he could retain an ASRS card and could be active in the union. He could serve as a delegate to the union's annual general meeting and could stand for election to full-time posts. When Holmes utilised these opportunities he enjoyed the valuable resource of his identity as an officially recognised victim.

In fact Holmes' next job was relatively lucrative. He worked for the Singer Sewing Machine Company, where promotion brought him a salary of £450 a year and a move to Doncaster. There he re-emerged both as an ASRS activist and a Liberal partisan. The latter is important not least because of the link of the union's Doncaster No. 1 Branch with the foundation of the Labour Representation Committee. The resolution carried at the 1899 Trades Union Congress for a conference on labour representation was moved by Holmes as an ASRS delegate; its origins lay in the Doncaster branch. The branch member responsible, T. R. Steels, was certainly sympathetic to the Independent Labour Party, and probably a member. This has led to speculation that the resolution from its origins to its realisation in the LRC was a key strand in the ILP leadership's strategy of establishing a broad alliance with the trade unions rather than a socialist fusion with the Social Democratic Federation. Whatever the validity of this claim, Holmes cannot be placed neatly within a pragmatic ILP plot to win over Lib-Lab trade unions not through the failed method of frontal attack, but by being flexible and utilising union concerns with procedure and precedent. Holmes' Doncaster politics – and indeed his position in the ASRS – do not fit readily into such an interpretation.

An appreciation of the nature of Doncaster politics in the 1890s is an essential starting point. This market town had become a railway junction and a major site for the construction of loco-motives. Growing employment in the traffic grades and in the workshops meant that railway companies, especially the Great Northern, dominated the local labour market. But unionisation remained weak amongst railway employees. Trades Council membership was small, with the ASRS being the largest affiliate with the balance provided by a mixture of craft and general unions. As yet the Yorkshire Miners' Association played no part in Doncaster politics; that awaited the eastward expansion of the Yorkshire coalfield. One of the prime instruments for independent labour initiatives – the Trades Council – was therefore weak, and there was little evidence of socialist politics.

Holmes, arriving in the mid 1890s, was clearly politically ambitious. His involvements were three fold: the ASRS, the Trades Council and the Liberal Association. He also rapidly secured election to the Board of Guardians. His account of his work there combined Labour and radical Liberal concerns. He successfully promoted a fair wages clause and also championed a classic denominational cause:

He fought hard along with other friends for giving Nonconformists a right to hold religious services in the Workhouse ... there were some who were brought up in Nonconformist schools and churches, and who were compelled to seek the shelter of the Workhouse – and if their social rights had been taken away from them that was no reason why they should be deprived of their religious rights and liberties as well [*Doncaster Gazette*, 16 October 1896].

His political identity became a cause of controversy on the Trades Council. When he stood unsuccessfully for the Town Council in the autumn of 1896 he was supported by his union, but because of his Liberal affiliation did not gain the formal backing of the Trades Council. The dif-ferences became more acrimonious in the spring of 1897. Holmes was returned unopposed to the Board of Guardians after a Liberal withdrawal, but three Trades Council candidates were defeated. Holmes was criticised for displaying both Liberal and Trades Council candidates' addresses in his window. He responded by confirming his support for the Liberals – at least for the moment. 'He would still stick to the Liberal flag until they had better men to work for him than there were in the Council' [*Doncaster Chronicle*, 16 April 1897]. Holmes quarrelled with an ASRS delegate whose comments suggest that subsequent characterisations of Holmes' politics have been misleading: 'When Mr Holmes received any opposition from a person on that Council he duped him as an ILP man' [ibid.]

Holmes' backing for the Liberals was sometimes qualified by the rider that in principle he would prefer to back a Labour candidate, but as yet this was not feasible. His support for the unsuccessful Doncaster Liberal candidate in the 1895 election came with the claim that an inde-pendent Labour initiative would be preferable, but would require '1 man [*sic*] 1 vote' and the payment of MPs. Whether Holmes' preference for independence meant thorough indepen-dence of the Liberal Party remained obscure. In a town where Labour organisation was weak, he sought and secured Liberal support. His political identity remained strongly Liberal; he was certainly not the 'militant socialist' presented by Clegg, Fox and Thompson [Clegg *et al.* (1964) 313].

This judgement is strengthened by an appreciation of his position within the developing, if sometimes ambiguous, factionalism of the ASRS. The union's dominant figure in the early and mid-1890s was its General Secretary, Edward Harford, a committed Liberal. Having come to office with the union in a weak position he had led it cautiously through years of rising member-ship and growing self-confidence. By the late 1890s his position was coming under pressure from his Executive and at the annual general meeting. Some opposed his Liberalism on a variety of political grounds; his careful industrial strategy also attracted criticism. In 1897 the critics were given their opportunity. A stoppage in February amongst Newcastle goods workers on the North Eastern produced familiar complaints about Harford's flexibility towards the companies and lack of enthusiasm for members' initiatives. Harford succeeded in producing an agreement with the North Eastern, the only major company to recognise the union. But at the concluding meeting in York Harford appeared drunk, a consequence it seems of a mixture of whisky and medication. At that year's AGM the critics secured enough votes to dismiss Harford by 35 to 20. Significantly Holmes was a vocal supporter of Harford [Report of Mr Edward Harford's Case at the Annual General Meeting, ASRS Reports, 1897]. In part this support was an acknowledge-ment of Harford's lengthy service to the union; it also demonstrated sympathy with the difficult situation faced by Harford in the North Eastern dispute. His position indicated that he was not aligned with any independent Labour or socialist section within the union.

Certainly Holmes' sympathy for the deposed general secretary appears to have done him no harm with union activists. At the 1898 AGM delegates elected him to a full-time Organiser's post under the new General Secretary, Richard Bell. Holmes became responsible for Bell's former territory: Wales and the west of England. Relations between the two men deteriorated rapidly. The basic difference between them was not political – Bell was essentially a Liberal who entered the Commons in 1900 as one of the first LRC MPs, but subsequently reverted to his formal Liberal allegiance. Rather the clash was over industrial strategy and style. Bell was concerned to continue Harford's policy of gradually developing the union's organisation rather than risking its existing strength in localised disputes. The strategy reflected Bell's conciliatory style; he believed that the cultivation of positive relationships with companies was essential. In contrast Holmes' rhetoric, rather than his policies, could seem radical. George Alcock, the first historian of the union, claimed that Holmes was 'the most effective platform speaker the ASRS had. Humour, pathos, irony, scorn, invective mingled with his gift of speech. His audiences have laughed and cried in turns' *Railway Review*, 12 October 1934].

Another assessment suggested that while Holmes' style persuaded railway workers to join the union, the consequences could be uncomfortable for cautious officials. The expectations of the new recruits could be a challenge to the latter's priorities; 'Holmes was all right to have a drink with, but if he went on the platform he would set the world on fire ... he was *the organiser*' [*Railway Review*, 5 October 1934]. Such sentiments ran contrary to Bell's strategy and his wish to develop firm centralised control over union activities. His verdict on Holmes' activities was con-demnatory:

> From the time of his appointment ... his conduct was almost one continuous violation of the Society's rules and a repudiation of all authority. In each of these movements in his district ... he acted directly contrary to the rules and the instructions of the E.C. [Taff Vale v. ASRS Agenda for SGM, January 1903, ASRS Reports, 1903].

This assessment came after the conclusion of the Taff Vale case but it was not simply the product of legal defeat. From the early months of Holmes' appointment, Bell's letters to him were critical and Holmes' responses were characteristically combative:

> Now I shall not be dictated to by you in that manner, so you can drop that style at once. ... I would not allow my late employer to write to me in that strain, and I am certain I shall not allow you to do it. There is [*sic*] limits to human endurance and so far as your letters to me are concerned the limits are nearly reached [Holmes to Bell, 21 May 1900, MSS 127/AS/TU/3/19/2, ASRS Records].

This poor interpersonal relationship was one strand in the complexities of the August 1900 Taff Vale strike. The Taff Vale Railway was the principal and profitable carrier of coal from the central section of the south Wales coalfield to the port facilities in Cardiff. Its manager, Amman Beasley, took the typical railway company stance against union recognition. Nonetheless Holmes had been relatively successful in strengthening the union's position amongst Taff Vale employees, and there was hope that the increased coal traffic generated by the South African war would make the company more responsive to pressure for improved wages and conditions. An initial campaign by union activists in the winter of 1899–1900 proved anticlimatic; Bell intervened to delay a threatened strike, and support then declined. In August 1900 militancy revived as railway workers' wages remained stagnant in the face of rising prices, and a signalman and union activist called Ewington appeared to be suffering victimisation by the company.

Holmes' rhetoric strengthened the resolve of the Taff Vale unionists. When he drafted some copy for the union newspaper, the *Railway Review*, one remark was deleted by the editor: 'There is nothing I would like better than to measure swords with this Taff Vale dictator' (that is, Beasley). Yet along with his rhetoric he could be sagacious. Insisting that this was the moment to demand their rights, he nevertheless urged all employees to give due notice and to strike together, thus avoiding breach of contract. Equally he diluted the demand for union recognition to his being allowed to accompany an all-grades deputation to meet Beasley. This was rejected by the company, as was his subsequent proposal that both parties agree on an arbitrator.

The strike movement was in breach of ASRS rules in that the union executive had not given its approval for a stoppage. When the executive met in special session on 19 August 1900 it was decided, after a long discussion and by seven votes to five, that the strike be supported. Some executive members – and certainly Bell – felt that their hand had been forced by Holmes' actions. In fact as the executive agonised in London, Holmes was insisting at a Pontypridd mass meeting that the strike would go ahead. Arbitration would be before 'the tribunal of rusty wheels and rusty rails' [Bagwell (1963) 215].

Despite Holmes' earlier advice the stoppage involved several strikers breaching their contracts. It lasted 11 days and there was abrasive picketing, some of which was the result of strike breakers being imported from the National Free Labour Association. On two occasions Holmes was injured when attempting to protect strike breakers from pickets. The strike achieved none of its objectives, and but for the legal consequences it would have counted as one more failed local movement. During the strike the company served writs against Bell, Holmes and the ASRS. Given the existing understanding of the law, the granting of Taff Vale pleas against named individuals was expected, but the granting of the injunction against the union came as a surprise. Reversed on appeal, the original judgment was confirmed in the Lords in July 1901. A few months later the company filed for damages.

This legal defeat deepened the divisions within the ASRS. Bell was determined that Holmes' defence should be separated from his own and that of the union. He informed two sympathetic branches that Holmes had been in breach of union rules and they accordingly asked the Executive to refuse to pay the latter's defence costs. When the Executive rejected this proposal they obtained an injunction preventing the union from funding his defence. In response a 'Holmes Defence Fund' was set up, with J. H. Thomas as secretary. The sum raised – £1172 11s 6d – more than covered Holmes' legal expenses.

The final legal hearings took place in December 1902. The result was the payment by the ASRS of £23 000 damages to the Taff Vale Railway. With costs the total expense to the union came to £42 000. Mr Justice Willis was relatively positive about Bell's role but was highly critical of Holmes – his actions were 'impossible to excuse' as he had encouraged law breaking. 'Nobody can doubt that it was in his mind that the men should strike and break their contracts' [Taff Vale Railway v. Amalgamated Society of Railway Servants, Bell and Holmes, December 1902, MSS 127/AS/TV/7/LE/10/1].

The final act came at an ASRS special general meeting in January 1903. Bell claimed that primary responsibility for the debacle lay with Holmes:

I was opposed to the movement right from the beginning to the end, and on the 17th August, at the request of the President of the Board of Trade, I went to Cardiff with a view to preventing the strike taking place. I was then told by Mr Holmes that the movement was independent of the society and I should not interfere [*Railway Review*, 9 January 1903].

An attempt to dismiss Holmes was defeated by 35 votes to 18, so instead he was censured: 'Mr Holmes has been very indiscreet on some occasions' [*Railway Review*, 16 January 1903]. Holmes thereafter became a conventional ASRS organiser. Transferred back to Doncaster in 1906 and taking responsibility for northern England, he became committed to the Conciliation Boards established following the agreement of 1907. His previous rhetoric remained but his strategies were now thoroughly conventional. In retrospect he was unenthusiastic about the character of the 1911 strike, which had been driven by the actions of rank and file members:

take the railwaymen's strike of 1911 – a strike for no purpose except in sympathy with the demand for the reinstatement of the men out on strike in Liverpool. Yet the final settlement of this had to be through negotiations by men who were in no way in association with its origin [Letter, *Doncaster Gazette*, 2 June 1916].

As a consequence of the 1913 amalgamation, Holmes became an official of the National Union of Railwaymen. His political position remained an amalgam of radical Liberal and Labour sentiments. When moving the vital resolution at the 1899 TUC he declared himself to be 'on the side of those who view with distrust both the great political parties in their relation with labour questions'. Trade unionists should 'obtain the balance of power so that they might dictate their own terms to either Liberals or Conservatives' [*Manchester Guardian*, 7 September 1899]. He was a member of the ASRS delegation at the foundation conference of the Labour Representation Committee (LRC) his response to the conference's decisions was enthusiastic. The LRC's policy would be 'independence without isolation – the formation of a definite Labour group with latitude to negotiate and co-operate with other parties' [*The Labour Pioneer. Cardiff*, April 1900]. The spectre from the past was the Barnsley by-election of October 1897, when the Yorkshire Miners Association had backed a Liberal coal owner despite the presence of an Independent Labour Party candidate, Pete Curran. Holmes believed that the formation of the LRC could mean an end to such destructive contests:

If this resolution does nothing else, it puts a stop to that sort of thing and shows a united front ... a labour platform in harmony ... it will have given birth to a movement ... that will create a new party that can enfold all the best and most advanced men of the radical party [ibid.]

The significance of this hope is unclear. Holmes was writing for a newspaper subtitled 'the Organ of the Cardiff Socialist Party', but his frequent contributions never mentioned socialism. An attack on Liberal cowardice targeted Liberal ambiguities over the South African war and not Liberal failures with economic and social questions [The Labour Pioneer. Cardiff, August 1900]. In many respects Holmes remained a radical Liberal, disillusioned with the recent record of the Liberal Party and hoping that an effective political organisation for the labour movement might facilitate some realignment of anti-Conservative forces.

This appraisal is compatible with Holmes' actions in the 1900 general election. He spoke for one LRC candidate, Richard Bell, despite their acrimony over union affairs. He spoke for neither LRC candidate in south Wales – Keir Hardie and John Hodge – nor for the south Wales miners' leader, W. J. Abraham (Mabon). Instead he crossed the Severn to support the successful Liberal candidate for Gloucester, Russell Rea, the vice-chairman of the Taff Vale Railway. This cannot be characterised as an eccentric action by Holmes. Rea was endorsed by Richard Bell, and by James Sexton of the National Union of Dock Labourers. He was presented as a progressive employer isolated on the Taff Vale board by his willingness to meet union representatives and his support for a conciliation scheme. Holmes combined his recommendation with an unfamiliar claim about his own political identity:

> His desires were not those of a party politician, as he himself was a socialist, but he was bound to tell the truth, and give credit where credit was due. He did not think they would get the opportunity again of voting for such a democratic and suitable candidate as Mr Rea, who was a true friend of the workers [*Gloucester Journal*, 29 September 1900].

The context was a speech to the Gloucester Trades Council. The claim not to be a party politician was a significant element in the LRC's appeal; the old partisan cries had divided the workers and should be ignored. Instead Labour should reward its friends and punish its enemies – although its friends generally proved to be Liberal. Nevertheless alongside this conventional argument Holmes' claim to be a socialist was, in terms of his own politics, anomalous.

Subsequent electoral interventions found Holmes exploring the variable and complex spaces available to Labour in pre-1914 contests. Unlike Bell, whose quarrel with the LRC divided the union, Holmes remained firmly with independent Labour. He fought three seats, each without success, and his campaigns demonstrated the repertoires open to pre-1914 Labour candidates. In January 1906 he stood in East Birmingham, where the adversary was not so much Conservatism as Chamberlainite Unionism. He obtained the best result by any anti-Unionist candidate in the city between 1886 and 1914:

East Birmingham, January 1906	Electorate 14,469 Turnout 77.9 per cent.
Sir J. B. Stone (Conservative)	5928 (52.6 per cent)
J. Holmes (Labour)	5343 (47.4 per cent)
Majority	585 (5.2 per cent)

Arguably he was aided by the constituency's employment structure: the municipal gas works, a railway carriage works and a significant concentration of railway workers. Official Liberalism had demonstrated its electoral weakness in the city for almost two decades; a Labour candidate could therefore claim to offer a more effective challenge to Unionist dominance. Holmes was nevertheless willing to share a platform with a Lib-Lab candidate from another Birmingham seat, an action that produced criticism from some supporters not on grounds of principle, but because any association with a discredited Liberalism would weaken the necessary appeal to working-class Unionists [see LRC Letter Files 28/180–181 for the exchanges between H. Wilson and Ramsay MacDonald on 25 and 27 November 1905].

In his speeches Holmes made little reference to the LRC. Instead he presented himself as essentially a trade union candidate with no party ties:

> He was run by the Amalgamated Society of Railway Servants, and the only condition they laid down was that on conditions affecting the trade union movement and outside the society he must be guided by the Parliamentary Committee of the Trades Union Congress in measures they promoted in the interests of trade unionists. ... Apart from that his society gave him a free hand in the House of Commons to deal with legislative matters in accordance with the desires of the constituency he represented [*Birmingham Daily Post*, 6 January 1906].

His claim that he was 'tied to no party' [*Birmingham Daily Post*, 30 December 1905] was flavoured with defence of the rights of white labour in the Transvaal. His attacks on the Conservative Government's support for the use of Chinese labour at the behest of the Rand capitalists utilised familiar stereotypes. His opponents followed 'not only the Chinese pigtail ... but the German–Jew gang as well' [*Birmingham Daily Post*, 5 January 1906]. Holmes' campaigning coalition incorporated radicals, the ILP and trade unionists. The labour appeal proved more effective than concurrent Lib-Lab and ILP interventions elsewhere in the city.

Holmes' second parliamentary contest, a by-election in West Hull in November 1907, posed very different strategic problems. The constituency was dominated by a Liberal ship-owning family, the Wilsons, who had supplied successive MPs. The maritime economy and the defeat of dockers' unionism in the 1893 strike had helped to weaken the local labour movement, but Labour's national prospects seemed relatively promising. Pete Curran's victory in Jarrow and Victor Grayson's triumph in Colne Valley gave an exaggerated sense of Liberal vulnerability. The Hull Trades and Labour Council was keen to contest. The initial favourite for the candidacy was William Walker, a Belfast Carpenters' official and three times the Labour candidate for North Belfast. He was backed by the Hull ILP, but under pressure he had expressed Unionist sympathies in his Belfast campaigning and the Irish section in the Hull labour movement was hostile towards him. Holmes defeated Walker by 76 votes to 33 despite the opposition of the local ILP. One party member claimed that Walker had been 'persecuted' for his opinion on Home Rule, and Holmes was 'a tool to further that work' [R. Dawson to James Middleton, Labour Party General Correspondence, 21/248]. Holmes responded by claiming that one reason for his adoption was that he was not a socialist [*Eastern Morning News*, 27 November 1907].

The Hull vacancy coincided with the 1907 railway crisis and the consequential agreement on an elaborate system of Conciliation Boards. This outcome was irrelevant for most Hull railwaymen, who were employed by the North Eastern and had already achieved union recognition. Faced with indifference and sometimes hostility from his union members, Holmes abandoned his initial commendation of the scheme. This question was, however, marginal to his campaign, which focused on the alleged iniquities of the Wilson family: poor employment conditions and links with the National Free Labour Association. Yet in other respects Holmes' programme seemed compatible with liberalism. Keir Hardie's Merthyr colleague, the idiosyncratic Liberal industrialist D. A. Thomas, backed Holmes as 'a radical'. The *Manchester Guardian* claimed that Holmes' programme would be endorsed by 100 Liberal MPs [for this support see *Hull Daily Mail*, 29 November 1907]. Holmes' poll was creditable, especially given the lack of Labour organisation. The affair could be seen as a contest within the Liberal, or at any rate progressive, family in a community where official liberalism could seem insensitive to labour and broad radical demands.

Kingston Upon Hull West. by-election, 29 November 1907	Electorate 20,583 Turnout 75.4 (per cent)
Hon. G. G. Wilson (Liberal)	5623 (36.2 per cent)
Sir G. C. T. Bartley (Conservative)	5382 (34.7 per cent)
J. Holmes (Labour)	4512 (29.1 per cent)
Majority	241 (1.5 per cent)

Holmes' final parliamentary candidacy was at Crewe in July 1912. The underlying issue was strategic. How far should – or could – the balance between Liberal and Labour MPs, as established in the 1910 elections and underpinned by the two parties' secret understanding, be revised? Prior to January 1910 the North Staffordshire seat of Hanley had been held by a Lib-Lab miner, Enoch Edwards, he had then joined the Parliamentary Labour Party following the affiliation to the party of the Miners' Federation of Great Britain. When Edwards died in mid 1912 the Liberals entered the by-election. The Labour Party had an immediate chance to respond to this 'aggression' when a vacancy occurred in the adjacent Crewe constituency. This seemed a natural seat for Holmes. Crewe town was the headquarters of the London and North Western Railway and the company employed about 6000 workers. However, only 1000 held ASRS membership. The union did not organise in the locomotive works, some Crewe ASRS activists were committed to Liberalism and ASRS members signed the Liberal candidate's nomination papers. Moreover over a third of Crewe electors lived in smaller industrial villages and rural areas.

Beyond emphasising the need for workers to represent workers, Holmes found it a struggle to offer a distinctive position. The developing alliance between the National Union of Women's Suffrage Societies and the Labour Party was evident in Holmes' demand for the political equality of men and women, a position he had also taken at Hull. But he faced a Liberal claim that a vote for him was wasted and effectively pro-Conservative. Recent events in the railway industry – the 1911 strike and its consequences – were not discussed. Instead the central issues – Home Rule and national insurance – divided the electorate into progressives and Conservatives. A disastrous Labour poll at Hanley during the Crewe contest damaged Holmes' credibility and Liberal fears that the seat could be lost proved well founded:

Crewe, 26 July 1912   Electorate 15,927 Turnout 88.1 (per cent)

E. Craig (Conservative)	6260	(44.6 per cent)
H. L. Murphy (Liberal)	5294	(37.7 per cent)
J. Holmes (Labour)	2485	(17.7 per cent)
Majority	966	(6.9 per cent)

'Awfully bad', commented Arthur Henderson [Henderson to Middleton, 28 July 1912, LP/HEN/08/1/57].

Holmes strongly supported Britain's involvement in the 1914–18 War: he spoke at recruitment meetings, paid some of the cost of publishing a pro-enlistment sermon by the minister of the Doncaster Free Christian Church and offered to return to railway employment in order to free a younger man for military service. His position did not always produce a sympathetic response from union members, and when he proposed the suspension of the guaranteed week to deal with heavy traffic 12 NUR branches asked for his removal from office. Holmes' patriotic zeal was evident within his own family as two of his married sons attested under the Derby scheme; however a third said he had a conscientious objection to joining the army. Holmes' response was robust: 'there was no room in England for conscientious objectors who took the protection of the country' [Barnsley Chronicle, 8 April 1916]. The son subsequently attested.

A public presentation of Holmes' prowar credentials occurred when on 31 March 1916 he was accused at Barnsley Magistrates Court of an offence under Section 27 of the Defence of the Realm Act; allegedly he had 'made certain statements likely to cause disaffection to His Majesty or likely to prejudice the recruiting, training, discipline, or administration of His Majesty's forces'. The incident had occurred in a railway brake van at Wombwell near Barnsley on 6 January 1916. Holmes had been amongst a party on the way to inspect the site of a recent accident when he had become involved in a heated argument with a Midland Railway locomotive inspector called Mills. The dispute had concerned the introduction of military conscription; Holmes, along with his union, had been opposed to the proposal. The Military Service Bill was about to be debated in the Commons, and on the day of the argument the Trades Union Congress was meeting to discuss the question. Mills had subsequently reported the confrontation to the authorities, alleging that Holmes had been opposed to all enlistment and would have accepted a German invasion. In his evidence Holmes claimed that he had voiced his opposition to conscription and defended the voluntary principle, to which Mills' response had been that he 'ought to be shot'. The discussion had then become heated; Holmes acknowledged, 'I must admit I lost my temper'. He suggested that Mills' allegations had been based on his dislike of the union and of Holmes personally. The magistrates found Holmes guilty. The penalty was a £25 fine or two months' imprisonment. The fine was paid by members of the NUR [for detailed accounts of the case see Doncaster Gazette, 7 April 1916, and Barnsley Chronicle, 8 April 1916].

The hearing revealed a further aspect of Holmes' politics (arguably by 1914 his involvement in Labour politics had left its mark on his political identity):

When the Socialist Party took exception to the war he severed his connection with it, and supported Mr Henderson and other members of the Party that supported the Government. He would still be a Socialist of a more moderate type but for the action of the Socialists [*Doncaster Gazette*, 7 April 1916].

Moderation accurately describes his position on the wartime disputes within the NUR: he extolled the virtues of conciliation and condemned Direct Action; he was unsettled by the growing radicalism among sections of the union, feeling that this could undermine recent advances.

The only hope, industrially or politically is for a sane educated democracy guided by reason, appealing to the higher instincts, not by brute force ... Strikes have always been, and always will be, a failure to obtain industrial or political liberty [Letter, *Doncaster Gazette*, 21 July 1916].

These sentiments were evident in Holmes' oratory during the 1919 railway strike. It was thought that Lloyd George might attempt to portray the stoppage as potentially revolutionary, but Holmes, speaking in Doncaster, insisted that it must be an orderly affair. 'He wanted them to protect the property of the Companies – they were not Bolsheviks' [*Doncaster Gazette*, 10 October 1919]. After the settlement he urged the strikers to unite in the re-establishment and reconstruction of the finest country in the world – 'Merrie England' [*Doncaster Gazette*, 1 October 1919].

Holmes spent the final year of his union career at the NUR's London headquarters and retired in 1922. When the union held its AGM at York in July 1924, he was a speaker at the delegates' dinner. As the Labour Party legitimised its arrival in office by constructing an appropriate past, the events of 1899–1900, stripped of their ambiguities, were an important ingredient. On 1 October 1934 Holmes died at his home at 16 Brunner Road, Brentham, Ealing, Middlesex. He was survived by his wife Elsie May and by two sons and a daughter. Two other sons had been killed on active service. His funeral was at Westminster Cemetery in Hanwell. The service was taken by the Reverend Percy Jones, retired minister of the Doncaster Free Christian Church and author of the pro-enlistment sermon endorsed by Holmes in 1915. Holmes left an estate of £6476 3s 2d.

The emergence of the Labour Party involved two critical contributions by Holmes: the successful presentation of the ASRS resolution at the 1899 TUC, leading to the establishment of the Labour Representation Committee; and (unintentionally) the strengthening of the unions' commitment to the LRC that came out of the Taff Vale strike and the subsequent legal case. Conventional narratives have often presented Holmes as a socialist and a militant. In 1900 he was certainly not in any serious sense the first, and his militancy was typically restricted to his platform pyrotechnics. Indeed an exploration of Holmes' actual positions gives valuable insights into the complexities of late Victorian and Edwardian labour politics.

Sources: (1) MSS: MRC WU, NUR Collection, correspondence and MSS re Taff Vale, 127/AS/TV; PRO, Taff Vale Company File, RAIL 1057/1791; NMLH, Labour Party Records. **(2) Newspapers and Periodicals:** *Doncaster Gazette* 1890–99, 7 April 1916; *Doncaster Chronicle* 1890–99; *Retford and Gainsborough Times*, 29 July 1892; *The Labour Pioneer. Cardiff* (The Organ of the Cardiff Socialist Party), 1900; *Gloucestershire Journal*, 29 September 1900; *Eastern Morning News*, 27 November 1907; *Hull Daily Mail*, 29 November 1907; *Barnsley Chronicle*, 8 April 1916; *Doncaster Gazette*, 4 October 1934; *West Middlesex Gazette*, 6 October 1934; *Railway Review*, 5 and 12 October 1943; **(3) Other:** TUC Report of Proceedings (1899); G. W. Alcock, *Fifty Years of*

Railway Trade Unionism (1922); P. Bagwell, *The Railwaymen* (1963); H. A. Clegg, Alan Fox and A. F. Thompson, *A History of British Trade Unions Since 1889: Volume 1 1889–1910* (Oxford, 1964); D. Howell, *Respectable Radicals: Studies in the Politics of Railway Trade Unionism* (Aldershot, 1999).

DAVID HOWELL

See also: †Richard BELL; †Edward HARFORD; †Walter HUDSON.

HORRABIN, Winifred (1887–1971)
SOCIALIST, WRITER, JOURNALIST

Winifred Horrabin was born Winifred Batho on 9 August 1887 in Sheffield. She was the fourth of the six children (three died in infancy) of Arthur John Batho (*circa*.1856–91) and his wife Lilian, née Outram (*ca*. 1859–1938). Both of her parents were from working-class families that were nonconformist in their religious sympathies. Arthur Batho was a postal telegraph clerk. The family attended the Wicker Congregational Church in Sheffield and Arthur Batho was an independent minister and president of the Telegraph Bible Class. In his thirties he developed tuberculosis and journeyed to South Africa on the *SS Durban* in the desperate hope of regaining his health. He was joined a year later by his family, but shortly after, in May 1891, he died from a tubercular haemorrhage.

After her father's burial at Graff-Reinet the young Winifred returned to Sheffield with her mother and siblings. The family lived with Henry Outram, Winifred's maternal grandfather, until his death in 1894, when they took a house at 176 Springvale Road. Winifred was a precocious child – her mother said she could read before the age of four. In Sheffield she attended the Central School from about 1902–6 and then Sheffield Art College from 1907, where she met and fell in love with James Francis (Frank) Horrabin (1884–1962). The attraction was cemented by shared political sympathies. They were both guild socialists – Winifred once recording that this came about 'via William Morris Art and Ruskin'. Frank Horrabin was employed as staff artist for the *Sheffield Telegraph* between 1906 and 1909, and then as art editor for the *Yorkshire Telegraph* between 1909 and 1911. Winifred started a biography of the South African novelist and socialist commentator Olive Schreiner (1855–1920), and a play, 'Victorian Love Story: Beloved Good', inspired by Thomas Carlyle's love for Jane Welsh and drawing upon their love letters, which were published in 1909. Her interest in Schreiner developed partly because of her unresolved sense of loss after her father's death and partly because of the political sentiments she shared with Schreiner. She came to identify closely with Schreiner's feminism, calling *Woman and Labour* 'the very Bible of the pre-war feminist movement'. Her interest in Thomas Carlyle may be attributed to his influence on members of the late Victorian/Edwardian British left, such as Frank Horrabin and herself. The unpublished manuscript of this play is an oversentimentalised fictional account of the mutual dedication of Carlyle and Jane Baillie Welsh, and her interest was as much in the role played by Jane Baillie Welsh in Carlyle's life.

Winifred became a member of the Women's Social and Political Union, working with Adela Pankhurst. In 1909 she disrupted a speech being given at a Liberal Party meeting in Sheffield's Albert Hall by Winston Churchill. She had drawn the short straw and later noted her shock, as up till then she had been 'an ordinary rank-and-file art student member'. She also noted her fear, recalling that stewards at Liberal Party meetings had previously demonstrated more energy than liberalism, throwing women down stone staircases and breaking their legs. She seated herself by an aisle and cried 'votes for women' twice before fleeing. An aunt in the audience stabbed her in the leg as she ran away. Always a person who lacked confidence, Winifred later said of this incident: 'I had done it. I had really done it. Nobody was more surprised than I was in that surprised excited audience' [Brynmor Jones Library MSS, DWH/1/63]. The *Sheffield*

Independent called it the 'complete failure of [an] unsexed woman'. More painful for Winifred was the accusation of other women that her performance in no way matched the efforts of Adela Pankhurst, and her mother's verbal dismissal: 'That just serves you right'.

In 1911 Frank Horrabin answered an advertisement in the *Clarion* for a staff post with the *Star*, and the couple married on 9 August 1911 before relocating from Sheffield to London. He later worked for the *News Chronicle*, creating for the paper the cartoon characters of Japhet (son of Noah) and Happy (a bear). For the *Star* he created the characters of office girls Dot and Carrie, and this cartoon strip was still appearing at the time of his death. In London the Horrabins threw themselves into the activities of the Labour College movement, becoming members of the Plebs League. The Plebs League had been founded in 1908 by students at Ruskin College whose mission statement was to 'bring about a definite and more satisfactory connexion between Ruskin College and the Labour Movement'. Instead, desire to see 'education of the workers ... controlled by the workers' resulted in the establishment of the Central Labour College in London through an inaugural conference on 8 September 1909, with George Sims as first secretary and editor of *Plebs*, the organ of the Labour College movement.

The Horrabins were totally committed to the cause of the Plebs League and the Labour College. Winifred Horrabin designed and embroidered the Labour College banner (the torch of knowledge surrounded by three words – Educate, Agitate, Organise) and they became very friendly with George Sims. Winifred Horrabin later said of him that 'He was a great man ... the first Marxist I ever met' [Obit., *Plebs* 35:11 (1943)]. She became infatuated with him and he clearly had an influence on her political opinions during this period. She left behind her days as a suffragette, subscribing instead to the opinion of *Plebs* that male and female workers needed to work together against 'producers'; seeking the female vote amounted to collaborating with capitalism. The other influence at that time was H. G. Wells. In a paper given to the Fabian Society at the behest of Wells in 1912 – 'The Futility of Feminism' – Horrabin argued that the abolition of private property was the only means of releasing women from economic slavery and gender hierarchy. These views were repeated in 'Is Woman's Place the Home?', written in 1913 and published by the Socialist League in 1933. Typically for a woman of her generation, Horrabin came under pressure from the labour movement to place her socialism ahead of her feminism; her diaries reveal a woman who sometimes pondered the consequences of this choice. 'I want to see women come in, free and fearless, to a full participation in the collective purpose of mankind', she told the Fabian Society in 1912. But in 1947 she confided in her diary that 'women seem to me to have a long way to go before they become human beings in their own right' [Horrabin Papers].

Between 1913 and 1922 Winifred and Frank Horrabin lived at 127 Hamlet Gardens, Ravenscourt Park, Hammersmith, near the office of the Plebs League. Winifred formed the Women's League to promote the education of women workers and four issues of *Plebs* ran articles on women. In 1914 George Sims went off to war and the Horrabins became joint editors of *Plebs*. The war affected support for the Plebs League and Winifred wrote an article to rekindle the support of working women by arguing that while they paid for the war with the blood of their men, bishops' daughters played golf. There is 'only one war – class war' she told them; if women did not become class conscious they would become 'capitalism's biggest asset in breaking strikes and undercutting labour'. Her aim was the admission of women into men's trade unions and from there to the Labour College. She became honorary secretary of the Plebs League and coorganised with her husband fund-raising events and dramatic performances in the evenings. The aim was to bring the plays of George Bernard Shaw to the working classes. The Horrabins also turned to writing educational texts to promote their message, and in 1917 they jointly published *What Does Education Mean to the Workers?* Frank Horrabin threw his cartographic skills into cheap textbooks and the popular *Plebs Atlas*. Ostensibly the Plebs League aspired to equal education for male and female workers, and *Plebs* ran articles stating the aim of the league was 'the extension of educational facilities to women on the same basis as men ... imply[ing] a conscious recognition of the equality of the sexes'. However, both in the rules of the Labour College and in the *modus operandi* of the Horrabins' marriage, sexual equality was never realised. The Central Labour College never became coeducational and remained a male residential college. Male trade union membership remained the route for scholarships and women were effectively excluded from all but day classes.

During the First World War Horrabin began what turned out to be an unsuccessful career as a novelist. Her archive includes the manuscript of 'After Which War?', a novel she worked and reworked her whole life until it was finally called 'This Year ... Next Year ...? Sometime ... Never'. The subtitle was 'A Wartime Love Story by Winifred Horrabin'. As with her play about Thomas and Jane Carlyle, this novel indicates that Horrabin was a frustrated writer of romance. The main characters, Madeline and Richard Denton, are loosely based on the Horrabins themselves. A third character, Terry, fights employers in his home of Bermondsey and is closely modelled on George Sims. Her infatuation with Sims (as well as unresolved emotions about her father) seems evident in the text – 'It was all one to him: nights on the veld, nights in Flanders, or the picket line in a strike'. Terry falls in love with Madeline and has a brief affair with her while his best friend Richard is away at war. The story line may reflect Horrabin's unrequited love for Sims or it may be confessional (much of her fiction had an autobiographical element). Some of the dialogue in 'After Which War?' is asinine, but the novel has humanitarian elements and is pacifist in a way that reveals the genuinely committed and likeable nature of Horrabin herself. Even in fiction her essential socialism never rested.

When Frank Horrabin joined the Queen's Westminster Rifles in 1917, Winifred took over as editor of *Plebs* for a year until his return. Frank remained editor until 1932 and during these years Winifred was a regular contributor of articles. *Plebs* turned its attention to international socialism, reflecting a shift in the political direction of the Horrabins themselves. In an article in May 1918, Winifred argued that European industrialists were part of a 'War Party' and in this way she wedded her international socialism and pacifism. She described the way in which fund raising for the Plebs League and writing for *Plebs* were contributing to her joint cause: 'It is a privilege to be able to help keep going part of the revolutionary press of the world' [*Plebs*, 12:4 (1918)]. Her articles of the 1910s and 1920s all demonstrate a total belief that the dictatorship of the proletariat would result in 'economic freedom', so that 'neither Dictatorship nor Proletariat shall ever exist again' [*Plebs*, 10:12 (1919)].

During the 1920s the Horrabins were part of a circle of left-wing socialists who lived for at least some of the year on the Essex estates of Lady Warwick. Thus they had connections with prominent members of the Communist Party such as Harry Pollitt (the Horrabins joined the party in 1921 but left in 1924, and she later admitted that she was only 'a sort of Marxian'). Other members of their circle included H. G. Wells, Conrad Noel and Robert Blatchford. In 1920 Wells' *Outline of History* appeared, illustrated by Frank Horrabin, whose career in this period accelerated. The Noah Family in the *News Chronicle* was turned into a series of books – *Japhet and Fido* (1922), *Mr Noah* (1922), *More about the Noahs* (1922) and *The Japhet Book* (1925) – and the characters Dot and Carrie in the *Star* also appeared in book format (1922). The National Council of Labour Colleges was founded in 1921, bringing the Plebs movement to maturity. In *Working Class Education*, written jointly by the couple and published by the Labour Publishing Company in 1924, the Horrabins expressed their opposition to the university extension movement, arguing once again the need for a close connection between working-class education and the labour movement. However an attempt by Winifred in the 1920s to establish (with the help of Lady Warwick) a residential college for women workers failed.

In about 1924, probably during a Plebs League summer school at Cober Hill, Frank Horrabin began an extramarital affair with Ellen Wilkinson, 1891–1947, a trade unionist, Labour MP for Middlesbrough (1924–31; Jarrow 1935–47) and a leader and significant figurehead of the 1936 Jarrow March. At the summer school Wilkinson had given a lecture on 'Modern Workshop Methods', and a report on the summer school in the July 1924 issue of *Plebs* includes one of Frank Horrabin's cartoons, featuring himself standing next to Ellen Wilkinson, with Winifred Horrabin to the other side of Wilkinson. A second summer school in Blackpool was arranged in

August 1924; again Ellen Wilkinson was a plenary speaker and there is evidence of Frank Horrabin's growing attachment. The pattern was repeated at summer schools in 1925. The consequences of the affair on the marriage and working partnership of Winifred and Frank Horrabin were immediate – articles by Wilkinson began to appear in *Plebs* and Winifred Horrabin's role in the magazine diminished. She wrote fewer topical and theoretical articles and took more of a secretarial role, reporting on the movement and fundraising for it in 'The Plebs Page'.

In 1926 Wilkinson arranged for Winifred Horrabin to accompany John Beckett MP on a Red Aid delegation to Russia and Poland. This left Wilkinson free to work with Frank Horrabin during the general strike. Together they met with George Lansbury and came and went from the Broxted estate of Lady Warwick. He illustrated articles written by Wilkinson for *Plebs* and was in her company when she accosted Ernest Bevin in Eccleston Square and called him a 'spineless coward'. Throughout the miners' lockout, Frank Horrabin travelled with Ellen Wilkinson addressing dozens of regional meetings, especially in the west, north-east and the Midlands. Winifred Horrabin had been told of her husband's affair with Ellen Wilkinson just before her departure for Russia, and during her trip she received letters from Frank begging forgiveness and understanding and telling her that he wished she could share in the excitement of the general strike activity. She retaliated by having a brief sexual affair and he responded with desperate pleas for her return [private papers].

In Russia Winifred and her colleagues were entertained by the Society for Cultural Relations. She met N. K. Krupskaya, later consigning her impressions to a chapter in an unpublished autobiography: 'large yellowish face with prominent pale eyes' [DWH/1/63]. In Poland she acted as Beckett's secretary at a show trial of dissidents set up by Marshal Pilsudski. She recorded in her diary that the minister of justice had assailed them for two hours with a lecture on how the tales of persecution were 'nonsense' [DWH/3/31; Beckett (1999)]. Upon her return to England Winifred increasingly found herself reduced to a supporting role while her husband cow-rote articles with Wilkinson for *Plebs* on subjects such as 'The Plebs Point of View'. Winifred wrote articles calling for support for the Labour Party. In this way she supported her husband, who had decided to follow Wilkinson into parliamentary politics. Wilkinson took over Winifred's old role of writing articles for *Plebs* on subjects such as 'The Advance of Women' [*Plebs*, 21:8 (1928)]. Frank Horrabin became Labour MP for Peterborough in 1929, but lost his seat in the 1931 election. His affair with Ellen Wilkinson was superseded in 1932 by an affair with his secretary, Margaret Victoria McWilliams, the wife of a travelling salesman. Again Winifred Horrabin was asked to keep her faith in the marriage and she remained with her husband.

In 1932 Winifred Horrabin's brother, Harold Batho, who for years had collaborated with Frank Horrabin on the Japhet cartoon strip, died from injuries sustained during the First World War. His death confirmed Winifred's pacifism and deepened the strength of her international socialism and antifascism. She told the National Conference of Labour Women in 1932 that the international working classes should strive to resist war, choosing starvation over employment in munitions factories in their collective effort to destroy the war plans of capitalist producers. Once again her political interests followed that of her husband, who had abandoned his editorship of *Plebs* and was pursuing anti-imperialist politics. He became editor of the *Socialist Leaguer* and the *Socialist*, and collaborated with Rita Hinden, Margaret and G. D. H. Cole and Arthur Creech Jones to form the Fabian Colonial (later Commonwealth) Bureau.

The 1930s were very productive for Winifred Horrabin. She completed a draft of her biography of Olive Schreiner in 1936 and commenced a career in journalism. She was film and book reviewer for *Tribune* from 1937–45 and contributed travel writings, social commentaries and short stories to journals such as the *New Clarion*, *The Miner* and *Time and Tide*. From 1944 she wrote weekly for the *Manchester Evening News* under the *nom de plume* Freda Wynne. However from the late 1930s she suffered a series of personal tragedies that left her with long-term depression: her novel was rejected by publishers; her mother died on 20 May 1938, the anniversary of the death of her father; and in 1939 she had a hysterectomy following what was probably polycystic ovarian disease. At the outbreak of war she moved to Oxford at the suggestion of her husband, only to discover that he wanted her out of London not for her own safety but so that he could cohabit with Margaret McWilliams. In 1942 he asked for a legal separation and she was devastated. She sought psychoanalytical treatment in Oxford and the insights she gained from this were channelled for the remainder of her life into autobiographical jottings about the loss of her father, her tense relationship with her mother and her perpetual torment over the loss of her husband. Her diaries reveal a woman who was genuinely perplexed that marital love had not prevented her husband from falling in love with other women. Later in life she came bitterly to resent having chosen not to have a child because her husband had always said that she was 'too precious to risk in childbirth'.

Winifred worked for part of the Second World War making Spitfire parts in a factory. She eventually granted her husband a divorce and the *decree nisi* was issued on 13 October 1947. However it was more than two years before she could bear to leave the family home at 92 St John's Court in Finchley Road and sell the Little Bardfield cottage in Essex. In 1950 she moved to Jamaica for six months to ease her unhappiness and threw herself into writing. On her return she moved to Blackheath, where she lived in a flat in The Paragon through the 1950s. There were further personal tragedies. Her older brother Arthur (Artie) Denton Batho died in 1951, leaving her without family. In the 1960s she moved from the Paragon to a tiny flat in Blackheath and kept herself occupied with local art classes. She continued to write short articles and book reviews for journals. She also continued drafting and redrafting her novel, her play about Carlyle and her biography of Olive Schreiner. The biography of Schreiner is her best work. It is detailed and well written. Her play on Carlyle is her worst. It is a vicarious tale of a man's adoration for a clever political woman and totally devoted wife. Her constant reworking of this play at the end of her life is sadly juxtaposed with her fruitless attempts to understand the breakdown of her marriage through repetitive entries in her diaries. As late as 1953 she wrote in her diary '66th birthday. Ye gods feel 30. Cannot think I am an old woman. An old woman living alone with Frank the husband of another woman.' More productively, at the end of her life she compiled a series of autobiographical essays entitled 'Collage: The Summer of a Dormouse', in which she recalled her suffragist work with Adela Pankhurst and her involvement in left-wing politics during the 1920s and 1930s. These essays remain as a testament to a long life devoted to socialism. They contain many recollections of influential left-wing figures such as Robert Blatchford, H. G. Wells, Robin Page Arnot, Frances Evelyn (Lady Warwick), Rita Hinden, Harold and Frida Laski and Sidney and Beatrice Webb. There is a delightful short essay on a lunch visit by Jawahalal Nehru.

Winifred Horrabin's main legacy was her dedicated work for the Labour College movement and her ceaseless personal campaign against all inequality and injustice, but especially when directed against women. Her unpublished biography of Schreiner is an important source. 'An Old Fashioned Socialist Manifesto', written *circa* 1925 (not published), listed her goals as the establishment of a socialist state with no prime minister or political accommodation, the abolition of the House of Lords, the socialisation of industry, including banks, no inheritance of capital, no free trade and the transfer of wealth from production into the hands of the workers [DWH/2/7]. In her final years she moved to Dorking, where she died on 24 June 1971. In Horrabin's obituary for *Tribune*, Elizabeth Thomas described her as a 'witty', 'sparkling' human being with a 'vocal sense of injustice'. Her small estate and papers were bequeathed to Robert Alfred Blatchford, who later entrusted them to Chris Barker, a mutual friend who arranged for their deposit in the Labour Archives of Hull University. Winifred Horrabin was cremated at Randall's Park Crematorium on 30 June 1971. She left no children and her husband predeceased her in 1962. She left £185.

Writings: 'Victorian Love Story: Beloved Good' (unpublished play *ca* 1910–1960s); 'Olive Schreiner: a biography' (unpublished biography *ca* 1910–1960s); articles, reviews and editorials in *Plebs* (1911–32); 'This Year ... Next Year ...? Sometime ... Never (unpublished novel,

1914–1960s); *What Does Education Mean to the Workers* (1917); *Working Class Education* (with Frank Horrabin) (1924); film and book reviews in *Tribune* (1937–45); film and book reviews in *New Clarion, The Miner, Time and Tide, Manchester Evening News* and other papers (1930s–1960s); 'Collage: The Summer of a Dormouse' (unpublished autobiography containing short stories and autobiographical vignettes, *ca* 1960s).

Sources: (1) MS: Horrabin Manuscripts, Brynmor Jones Library, University of Hull. **(2) Other:** *Plebs* (1909–); *The Labour Who's Who, 1927* (1927); W. W. Craik, *The Central Labour College, 1909–29* (1964); J. P. M. Millar, *The Labour College Movement* (1979); P. M. Graves, *Labour Women: Women in British Working Class Politics, 1918–1939* (1994) Francis Beckett, *The Rebel Who Lost His Cause: The Tragedy of John Beckett MP*, (1999) **(3) Obituaries:** *CGP* (1971); *Tribune*, 2 July 1971.

Amanda Capern

JONES, Ernest Charles (1819–69)
CHARTIST LEADER

Ernest Jones, the last Chartist leader, was born in Berlin on 25 January 1819. He was the only son of Major Charles Jones (*ca* 1776–1843) and his second wife Charlotte, née Annesley (1779–1845). Jones' childhood and early adulthood provide few obvious pointers to the radical political vocation of his later years. His father was a veteran of the French wars, serving in the XVth (King's) Hussars and seeing active service in the Peninsular campaign and at Waterloo. In 1815 he became *aide-de-camp* to the commander of his regiment, Ernest Augustus, Duke of Cumberland, the fifth son of George III, then resident in England, and, following the death in childbirth of Princess Charlotte in 1816, possible heir to the throne after the Prince Regent. When the Duke of Cumberland went to Berlin at the end of 1818, Charles Jones, now remarried, returned with him, but was less happy in peacetime service and retired on half pay in 1821 to an estate in Reinbek, Holstein. Ernest Jones, a precocious child, was doted on by his parents. He was educated at home – in his adolescent years by two Lutheran pastors – before being sent to the Ritterakademie, Luneburg, in 1836. A volume of his verse, *Infantine Effusions*, was published in Hamburg in 1830 and the same year a poem of his appeared in *Ackermann's Juvenile Forget-me-not*.

After an unhappy start in Luneburg, where he was bullied, Jones completed his studies in 1838 and in the summer the following year the family returned to England. They settled near Baker Street, where Jones took up his literary aspirations once more. A mythical tale, *The Wood Spirit*, was published by Boone at the beginning of 1841, and various poems, reviews and articles appeared in *Court Journal, Metropolitan Magazine* and the *Morning Post*. The Jones family resumed their place in fashionable court circles. Through Lady Catherine Stepney, the widow of a groom to the Duke of York, Jones was introduced to Bulwer Lytton, the Strickland sisters and the Wordsworths. He was presented to the Queen by the Duke of Beaufort at a levee in 1841, and in the same year entered the Middle Temple to study for the Bar. He was called three years later. He also became a devotee of the London stage, befriending leading tragedians and theatrical managers of the day. Between 1841 and 1843 Jones himself penned seven dramas. In June 1841 he married Jane Atherley (1818–57), the daughter of Edward Gibson Atherley and his wife Jane, née Stanley, and a niece of Edward Stanley, MP for West Cumberland. Despite a whiff of scandal – at the time of their marriage Jane was already expecting their first child – Jones seemed set for a happy and successful career as a minor dramatist, well-connected in the fashionable London scene.

However, during the next three years Jones was beset by a series of misfortunes in both his private life and his literary career. None of his dramas was taken up by the major London theatres; an attempted newspaper, espousing 'Conservative' politics was stillborn; and he was unable to secure a more regular berth on the *Court Journal*, to which he had contributed poetry and translations. In 1843 his father died in a shooting accident, leaving the family in straitened financial circumstances. Jones sought a widow's military pension for his mother, but to no avail, and then in 1844 she fell seriously ill, eventually dying in 1845. In the autumn of 1844, in what proved to be a disastrous financial gamble, Jones sought financial security through the purchase of a large estate at Kearsney Abbey, near Dover in Kent. The house and estate, which included a number of working farms and separate residences, had been modernised and improved by the vendor and was valued at £70 000. Jones bought it for £57 000 and within a month had sold off part of the property. By the start of 1845, however, he had run into problems with his mortgagors and the whole property fell into receivership when he was declared bankrupt. The family gave up their London home in Bayswater and moved to a cottage in Hampstead, from where Jones spent much of the rest of the year pursuing Hutton Annesley, his deceased mother's brother, for fraudulent conveyance of their father's estate. This proved inconclusive. For the first time in his life Jones was forced to seek his own living. He offered his journalistic services to the Anti-Corn Law League and applied to be the auditor of Essex district, before becoming secretary to the Leek and Mansfield Railway Company in September 1845. He also continued to write during 1845, now turning his attention to poetry, completing *Corayda* (not published until 1860), *Lord Lindsay* (published in 1848) and *My Life*. The latter – a melodramatic ballad telling the tale of an aristocratic youth who gave up his fortune to devote himself to the people – was published by Newby in the autumn of 1845.

At the beginning of 1846, encouraged by Irish friends and his best friend Archer Gurney (then lecturing on behalf of the protectionist cause), Jones began to take more interest in the contemporary political scene. He gave a copy of *My Life* to the Chartist *Northern Star* and in May 1846 he was invited to become Chartist delegate for Limehouse. He was presented to the movement as a renegade from the governing classes and his poetry became an essential bridge between his gentlemanly status and his working-class audience. 'Democratic' poems by Jones were published regularly in the *Northern Star* during the summer and autumn of 1846, and in October MacGowan, the publisher of the *Star*, brought out Jones' *Chartist Poems* in a penny edition (later republished as *Chartist Songs and Fugitive Pieces*). Jones' attachment to the Chartist cause was in part a marriage of convenience. It gave him an outlet for his poetry and employment on the *Star*, and provided Feargus O'Connor with a willing deputy at a time of increasing tension within the Chartist leadership. One of Jones' first public acts as a Chartist came in August at a Leeds Chartist conference, when he backed the expulsion of O'Connor's fiercest critic, Thomas Cooper, at that time the Chartist 'poet laureate'. But in a short time Jones became committed to the movement, not only putting his literary talents at its disposal – especially in evidence in the *Labourer*, which he and O'Connor began publishing in 1847 – but also lecturing up and down the country on political matters, as well as on poetry. Jones' cosmopolitan background was also helpful. He joined George Julian Harney's Democratic Committee for the Regeneration of Poland (soon becoming its chairman) and later the Fraternal Democrats, where he befriended Karl Marx and Friedrich Engels.

In the general election of July 1847, Jones contested the constituency of Halifax. Although he only polled 280 votes, standing alongside the Nonconformist radical Edward Miall, he helped split the local Liberal camp, much to the embarrassment of the sitting Whig MP and Chancellor of the Exchequer, Charles Wood. By the time of the revival of popular protest at the beginning of 1848, Jones enjoyed a prominent position as a Chartist leader, alongside O'Connor, Harney and McDouall. He spoke at meetings in London during February, served in the Chartist convention as delegate for Halifax, and in March was part of a three-man Chartist team sent to Paris to congratulate the new republican government. At Kennington Common on 10 April he spoke alongside O'Connor. Despite the dissolution of the convention after the presentation of the national petition, Jones continued to speak in London and Scotland. After one such meeting – on 4 June in Bishop Bonner's Fields, London – a small riot erupted and a week later Jones was arrested in Manchester under the Crown and Government Security Act for incitement and for using seditious language at the London meeting (he had called for Lord John Russell to be transported, and looked forward to the day when the green flag flew over Downing Street). The trial took place in July and Jones was found guilty. In a long speech delivered before the sentence was passed, he defended his actions and appealed to the customary right of public meeting, but he received a two-year term nonetheless.

Jones' imprisonment in the Westminster House of Correction was the subject of much controversy. He complained that he was treated as a common criminal – placed in solitary confinement, forced to pick oakum, denied visits from his wife, and denied books and writing materials. On his behalf Lord Dudley Coutts Stuart, Joseph Hume and Feargus O'Connor raised questions in Parliament about his treatment. Whilst prison conditions were undoubtedly harsh, particularly when cholera raged in 1849, Jones exaggerated his suffering. Regular payments to the prison authorities ensured that he never had to pick oakum (the supply of which ran out anyway in 1849), and on several occasions he was given pen and paper, making rather dubious his repeated claim that the poetry he composed behind bars was written in his own blood. But his imprisonment added to his reputation, and on his release in the summer of 1850 supporters in London and Halifax greeted him as a martyr to the cause.

To the disappointment of his wife Jane, Jones resumed his Chartist activities. In the autumn of 1850 he went back on the road in an attempt to breathe new life into the flagging fortunes of Chartism, and in May 1851 a periodical, *Notes and Poems to the People*, commenced publication. In it Jones published all his prison poetry (much of which was later included in *Corayda*), *De Brassier*, a novel set in 1848 with, some critics alleged, O'Connor as the eponymous demagogue, and a protofeminist series of tales, *Woman's Wrongs*. Jones distanced himself from other Chartist leaders, including O'Connor, arguing that the movement should remain separate from other radical groups, notably the 'Manchester school' of free traders, about whom he was especially scathing. He effectively displaced his rivals in the 1851 elections to the Chartist National Executive, and for the rest of the decade the fortunes of the wider movement became inseparable from his efforts. In 1852 he began publishing the *People's Paper*, which was a natural successor to the *Northern Star* (featuring contributions from Karl Marx) but at its peak reached a weekly circulation of only 3000 copies.

Jones unsuccessfully contested Halifax again in the 1852 election, and in 1854 organised another Chartist convention in the shape of the 'Labour Parliament' (See below). He was also particularly active in the republican exile politics that flourished in London in the aftermath of the European revolutions, translating and publishing German and French pamphlets and articles. But he was never financially secure in the 1850s and applied for insolvency again in 1851. The *People's Paper* never paid for itself or properly supported Jones and his family, which now included four sons. He produced two penny dreadfuls – *The Maid of Warsaw* and *The Lass and the Lady* – to raise income, and tried to revive publishers' interest in his backlist of poems. Exploiting the mood of the moment during the Crimean War he produced two collections, *The Emperor's Vigil* and *The Battle Day*, which brought some critical acclaim. In 1857 he repackaged some of his poetry from the *Notes to the People* as *The Revolt of Hindostan*, and this too was well received.

In February 1858 Jones made one final effort to revive Chartism, this time allying with the radicals at a conference in St Martin's Hall in London. The move was controversial. Marx and Engels were particularly critical, and George Reynolds, the publisher of *Reynolds' Weekly News*, publicly voiced his suspicion of Jones' motives. Jones brought a libel action against Reynolds, which he won in 1859, and the details of the case – relating to Jones' financial hardship in the 1850s – provoked considerable sympathy both in the London press and amongst the remnants of Chartism in the north-west, where a public subscription was launched to support Jones, now a widower (Jane had died in 1857). After the closure of the *People's Paper* in 1858 he started up a series of short-lived papers, the principal feature of which was the demand for manhood suffrage. He contested Nottingham in the 1859 election, but came bottom of the poll. Public interest following the libel case of 1859 guaranteed the success of another collection of poems, *Corayda* (1860), but the same year Jones returned to the Bar, initially in London and then, from October 1860, mainly in the police courts and assizes of Manchester and Liverpool. He had a busy practice, mainly as a defence barrister in cases involving petty theft, bastardy claims, prostitution and assault. Often acting with W. P. Roberts, he also took on workers' cases, notably those of Barnsley miners, Manchester brickmakers and employees at John Bright's family firm of carpet manufacturers. He settled permanently in Manchester, residing in Higher Broughton, and married for a second time in December 1867 to a local woman, Elizabeth Darbyshire.

Gradually Jones began to take part in local Manchester politics, speaking at meetings on the American Civil War and the Schleswig Holstein question. In 1864 he participated in the reform conference in Manchester, which heralded the start of the parliamentary reform campaign outside London. From the autumn of 1866 he was employed full-time by the Reform League and he gave up his Manchester practice. He was an important addition for the new generation of parliamentary reformers, for not only was he a seasoned speaker but he also represented an authentic link with the Chartist years. Historians of Chartism tend to read Jones' oscillation towards more mainstream Liberalism as either apostasy or pragmatism, but in many respects his new-found popularity attested to the revival of radical Liberalism in the 1860s. Two episodes brought him back into the public spotlight: his defence of the Fenian prisoners in November 1867, for which he was singled out for praise by the judge; and his 1867 best-selling pamphlet reply to the scholar J. S. Blackie on the historical credentials of democracy.

In demand as a public speaker, Jones was also sounded out in 1868 as a Liberal parliamentary candidate for Carlisle, Dewsbury, Edinburgh, Halifax and Manchester. He opted for the new constituency of Dewsbury and then for Carlisle, but gave way in both cases when other radical Liberals emerged to contest the seats. He contested Manchester instead, polling 10 662 votes but coming fifth behind the three elected MPs. However an election petition against Hugh Birley, one of the Manchester candidates, was filed and in January 1869 in a test ballot the Manchester voters chose their candidate to fight the seat in the event of a by-election. Jones was selected ahead of the free trade veteran, Thomas Milner Gibson. Tragically, on the eve of perhaps his greatest success Jones fell ill with pleurisy, and on 26 January 1869, the day after he turned 50, he died at his home in Manchester. Four days later a procession of several thousand people accompanied his coffin from his home to Ardwick Cemetery, where he was buried. Jones was survived by his second wife and four sons, one of whom, Llewellyn Atherley Jones (1851–1929), emulated his father by becoming a leading labour lawyer, as well as MP for North-West Durham from 1885 to 1914.

Writings: Five main collections of Jones' poetry were published in his lifetime: *Chartist Poems* (1846); *The Battle Day* (1855); *The Emperor's Vigil* (1856); *The Revolt of Hindostan; or the New World* (1857) and *Corayda* (1860). Most of this poetry was originally published in either the *Northern Star* in 1846–7, the *Labourer* (1847–8) or the first volume of *Notes to the People* (1851), where many other poems by Jones can also be found. There were two smaller collections of poetry: *Rhymes for the Times* (1852) and *Songs of Democracy* (1856–7). Editions featuring Jones' poetry published after his death include: *In Memoriam. Ernest Jones* [James Mosley, comp.], (1879); A. H. Miles, *Poets and Poetry of the Century* (1891); Y. Kovalev, *An Anthology of Chartist Literature* (1956); Peter Scheckner, *An Anthology of Chartist Literature: Poetry of the British Working Class, 1830s–1850s* (1989). Four novels by Jones were published: *The Wood Spirit* (1841; 2nd edn 1855); *The Maid of Warsaw* (1853); *The Lass and the Lady* (1855); *Woman's Wrongs* (1855). The newspapers and periodicals with which Jones was principally concerned were: *Northern Star* (1846–52), *Labourer* (1847–8), *Notes to the People* (1851–2; repr. 1967); *People's Paper* (1852–8); *London News* (1858); *Chartist Circular* (1858); *Cabinet Newspaper* (1858–60); *Penny Times* (1860); *Weekly Telegraph* (1860). Many of Jones' lectures and speeches were published separately in cheap editions, including: *The Trial of Ernest Jones* (1848); *The Right of Public Meeting* (1848); *Canterbury versus Rome* (1851); *Evenings with the People*

(1856–7); *The Slaveholders' War* (1863); *The Danish War* (1863); *Oration on the American Rebellion* (1864); *Democracy Vindicated* (1867); *Labour and Capital* (1867); *The Politics of the Day* (1868); *The Horrible Inquisition of Rome* (1880). The Central Library in Manchester has the most comprehensive collection of Jones' published work.

Sources: (1) MSS: Jones kept a fastidious hold on his papers. Diaries, legal notebooks, sketch albums, volumes of his verse, business accounts and family correspondence (including that of his father, mother and his first wife) remained intact despite a life of constant moving and disruption. Unfortunately the bulk of his papers were broken up in the decades after his death and today are scattered amongst a number of libraries. The principal holding is in the Seligman Collection at the Library of Columbia University, New York. This contains most of Jones' family correspondence, his school records, business, legal and literary papers relating to the 1840s and 1850s, and correspondence concerning his Reform League activities in 1866–7. Most of the material in the Seligman Collection is now available in Britain on microfilm in the Dorothy Thompson Special Collection in Staffordshire University Library. The remainder of Jones' family papers, which passed to the economist J. E. T. Rogers, are in a microfilm collection held at the Brynmor Jones Library, University of Hull. Jones' diary (1839–47), legal notebooks (1862–5), manuscript poems, election ephemera, photographs and miscellaneous items relating to the memorial committees established after his death are all held by the Central Library in Manchester. Chetham's Library in Manchester houses a revealing set of letters between the imprisoned Jones and his wife in 1848–50, as well as correspondence with Jones' working-class supporters in 1859 and 1867–8. There is an album of Jones' sketches and verse from the late 1840s in the British Library (Add. MS 61,971). Other significant holdings of Jones' personal papers are in the National Library of Wales, Aberystwyth, and the International Institute for Social History, Amsterdam. Manuscript materials relating to Jones' political activities are much less extensive. The fullest and perhaps best-known series is Jones' correspondence with Karl Marx and Friedrich Engels – much of it in German – kept originally in the Marx-Engels Institute in Moscow. Most of this has now been translated and published in the relevant volumes of the *Collected Works of Marx and Engels*. Microfilm copies of the originals, obtained by Dorothy Thompson in the 1950s, are now available in the Dorothy Thompson Special Collection. The other principal collection of Jones' political correspondence can be found in the papers of the Reform League, in the George Howell collection, Bishopsgate Institute Library, London. The Bishopsgate Institute also holds the large collection of miscellanea relating to Jones and compiled by Howell in the course of preparing his biography. Otherwise papers relating to Jones and late Chartism are limited to minor items in the following collections: Robert Owen and George Jacob Holyoake (both in the Co-operative Library, Manchester); letters to Thomas Allsop and others in Yale University Library; Joseph Cowen, Tyne and Wear Archives; the Frederic Harrison papers, British Library of Political and Economic Science; and the East Midlands Collection, University of Nottingham Library. Letters relating to Jones' literary activities can be found in the papers of the Royal Literary Fund in the British Library, for which see Thomas W. Porter, 'Ernest Charles Jones and the Royal Literary Fund', *Labour History Review*, 57 (1992), and also in the Bulwer Lytton papers, Hertfordshire Record Office. One other source deserves mention: Jones' prison years are extensively documented from the prison authorities' point of view in Home Office files in the Public Record Office (HO 12/2/81) and the London Metropolitan Archive (WA/GP/1849/9–10). **(2) Other:** Jones has long eluded a full biography. In the years after his death there was a spate of short accounts by Frederick Leary (1887); A. B. Wakefield (1891) and D. P. Davies (1897). All these biographies drew uncritically on a pamphlet entitled *Ernest Jones: Who is he and what has he done?*, dictated by Jones himself and published as a riposte to his opponents in Manchester in 1867. The first independently researched biography of Jones was that commissioned by the Jones memorial committee in 1892, undertaken by George Howell. Howell was unable to find a publisher, although the work was serialised in the *Newcastle Chronicle* in 1898.

Ella Twynam completed a life of Jones in the 1920s, but this too remained unpublished, although parts of it found their way into G. D. H. Cole's chapter on Jones in his *Chartist Portraits* (1941). After the Second World War Jones attracted interest from a new generation of Marxist historians. John Saville drew together extant published materials on Jones' political activities in the 1850s and 1860s in his *Ernest Jones: Chartist* (1952), whilst Dorothy Thompson became the first historian to use the Seligman collection. Part of her research on Jones was included in 'Halifax as a Chartist Centre' (typescript, *ca* early 1950s, jointly written with E. P. Thompson). Since then, however, interest in Jones' political career has been confined to two unpublished theses: Thomas W. Porter, 'The political thought of Ernest Charles Jones' (PhD thesis, University of Northern Illinois, 1972) and A. D. Taylor, 'Ernest Jones: his later career and the structure of Manchester politics, 1861–9' (MA thesis, University of Birmingham, 1984), some of which was included in his ' "The best way to get what he wanted": Ernest Jones and the boundaries of liberalism in the Manchester election of 1868', *Parliamentary History*, 16 (1997). By contrast Jones' poetry has received more attention, notably in Ulrike Schwab, *The Poetry of the Chartist Movement: A Literary and Historical Study* (1993) and Anne Janowitz, *Lyric and Labour in the Romantic Tradition* (1998). See also Miles Taylor, *Ernest Jones and the Romance of Politics, 1819–69* (Oxford, 2003).

MILES TAYLOR

See also: †George Julian HARNEY; John Bedford LENO; †Robert George GAMMAGE; †Edward Owen GREENING; †Abel HEYWARD; †Edward HOOSON.

Special Note: The Labour Parliament, 1853–4

The social, and especially the socialist, aspect of Chartism became programmatically most explicit in the post–1848 period of 'late Chartism', based upon the movement's predominant commitment to 'the Charter and Something More'. This commitment was most marked among George Julian Harney, Ernest Jones and their supporters, and derived considerable sustenance and inspiration from the revolution in France in 1848. Jones, increasingly the dominant figure in late Chartism and at that time the English protégé of Marx and Engels, was successful in his attempt to commit the 1851 Chartist convention to a 'blueprint for a "socialist" democratic state in which the land, co-operative endeavour, credit and welfare provision were all to be nation-alised prior to "the complete adjustment of the labour question" ' [Belchem (1996) 100; Saville (1953) 35–45]. However the new programme 'failed to revivify the movement'. The present and the future of the labour movement seemingly lay more with the cooperatives, moderate trade unions, friendly societies, mutual improvement societies and other collective agencies of working-class respectability and self-help than with 'the Charter and Something More' [Belchem (1996) 100]. It was in this context of further attempting to revive 'the movement' in an increasingly unpromising environment that Jones and his supporters turned, in the late summer and autumn of 1853, to the idea of a 'labour parliament', standing at the head of a national 'mass movement', as the means of labour's salvation.

The extensive industrial conflict of 1853 and early 1854, and especially the protracted 'Ten Per Cent' dispute in the cotton industry in Preston, provided the immediate context and inspira-tion for the creation of the labour parliament. Employers in Preston refused to concede not only the cotton operatives' demand for a 10 per cent increase in wages, but also their own mastery over workplace matters to collective organisations and representatives of their workers. The mass suffering accompanying the industrial conflict in Preston was grimly depicted by Charles Dickens in *Hard Times* (1854). As the press and other contemporary sources made plain, workers in many other sectors of the economy than cotton sought to recoup their wage and union losses of the late 1840s by fighting for increases and recognition during the period of good trade in 1853 and 1854. For their part, however, employers throughout the country were equally determined to resist union recognition, pay rises and any attempt to reduce their power and control over the workplace. The result was widespread and very acrimonious industrial conflict in, for example, cotton, coalmining, shoemaking, carpet weaving, building and frame-work knitting, and even among constables in the London police service [for examples see *People's Paper*, 9, 16 July, 27 August, 17 September, 1, 8, 22 October 1853].

The significance of this wave of industrial conflict is hard to exaggerate. First, it reawakened memories of the severe crisis in class relations and the general strike of 1842 [Dutton and King (1981); Kirk (1985) ch. 6; Jenkins (1980)]. Second, it brought to the fore questions about the relative merits of and the relationship between workers' militancy and moderation, pragmatism and 'utopianism', and trade unionism and politics. Third, much as in 1842, it engendered very real and widespread fears among workers and labour activists, both political and industrial, that capitalist tyranny was once again on the ascendancy nationally – a form of tyranny that sought nothing less than complete mastery and the destruction of organised labour. For example Jones' *People's Paper* declared on 3 December 1853, 'There never was a time when working men had greater cause to complain of the tyranny exercised towards them than at the present.' Fourth, labour had to prepare itself thoroughly for the impending and probably decisive clash with capital. As the Chartist R. G. Gammage counselled in his speech to supporters of the mass movement at a meeting in Manchester in late November, 'The crisis is fast approaching when the great battle must be fought between Capital and Labour. Prepare for that crisis, so that when it comes your efforts may be crowned with a glorious victory' [*People's Paper*, 26 November 1853]. Jones had expressed very similar sentiments earlier in the month: 'You cannot sufficiently estimate the importance of the struggle – defeat the "masters" now, and the social revolution is virtually accomplished. The victorious workers would achieve "the ascendancy in the social scale", "a victory such as a people never gained before" ' [*People's Paper*, 5 November 1853].

It was in his opposition to 'the mass movement of the rich' that Jones conceived of his new mass movement of the people, the workers, to be headed by 'a mighty delegation from all trades' [Saville (1953) 54; *People's Paper*, 26 November 1853]. Seeking to halt and reverse the chaos, confusion and destruction wrought among workers and their organisations by the increasingly successful capitalist offensive of 1853, this new movement would, of necessity, be mass-based and national in character, organisation and scope. It would seek to organise all sections of the national labour force in order successfully to overcome the divisions, isolation and sectionalism that had manifested themselves so disastrously in the past in labour's struggles and that were once again in evidence. For example colliers in Wigan were largely isolated from workers elsewhere in waging their fight against their employers, while the dyers of Manchester enjoyed only limited support from the all too often 'aristocratic' trades. Similarly Jones believed that success in Preston required 'the unity and support' of 'all trades', 'not in the north alone, but from Plymouth to Inverness' [*People's Paper*, 27 August, 5, 12 November 1853].

Under the heading 'A Parliament of Labour', in the 12 November issue of the *People's Paper* Jones called for delegates from all the trades to 'assemble in the centre of action, in Lancashire, in Manchester, and remain sitting until the victory is obtained'. In fact he had already addressed a 'large amalgamated committee' of trades in Manchester, which had 'divided into wards' and set up 'an organised system of subscription' for the locked-out or striking workers in Preston and elsewhere. It was this committee that was to take the lead in calling the meeting to create the mass movement and the labour parliament. The latter, as declared by the London Chartist and labour parliament delegate James Finlen, would comprise 'the representatives of the poor' who 'worked for the poor', in marked contrast to 'the representatives of the rich' in Parliament, who 'worked for the rich' [*Manchester Guardian*, 15 March 1854].

In November 1853 handbills were put up in Manchester calling working men to a meeting in the People's Institute in the factory district of Ancoats. The declared purpose of the meeting was to create a mass movement of the people, a national organisation of working men to secure financial aid for those locked out in Lancashire. The *Manchester Guardian* was not impressed. An editorial of 23 November declared that the proposed national organisation amounted only to 'a perpetual begging-box in every part of the country'. In complete contrast the *People's Paper* of 26 November highlighted 'the most significant importance' of the meeting. For it would both 'inaugurate the march of freedom at the head of a united people' and 'decide whether the People's Movement shall be rescued from chaos and confusion' to enter 'a new stage'.

The leaders of the mass movement, complete with their denunciations of 'grasping capitalists' and 'capitalist tyranny and thraldom', were similarly depicted by the *Manchester Guardian* as parasitic opportunists and self-seekers. All too eager to exploit the naivety and hard-won earnings of the workers, they were seen to comprise 'a numerous and hungry body of agitators, secretaries, delegates and other people who are glad enough to live well without working' [*Manchester Guardian*, 23 November 1853]. Yet seemingly mistaken as to their true interests – especially the misguided and sometimes wilful interference by trade unions and other artificial or unnatural combinations in the laws of supply and demand – between five and six hundred working men, as estimated by the *Guardian*'s reporter, attended the meeting on Sunday 20 November. They were doubtless keen to learn details of the handbills' promise that laid before them would be 'the means of victory and the plan of action'.

The main speakers at the meeting – Edward Hooson (wiredrawer, Chartist and close friend of Ernest Jones), Jones himself, the Stockport Chartist James Williams, William Hill (cardroom operatives' representative and Stalybridge Chartist) and Gammage – provided these details. Thus without wishing to 'interfere with the present trades unions and combinations of working men', the proposed national organisation and mass movement of the people sought to harmonise, conjoin and strengthen their actions in order 'to centralise and confederate the strength of the whole body of the working classes'. In such a way the problems of sectionalism, isolation and lack of support for workers' actions would be overcome [*Manchester Guardian*, 23 November 1853; *People's Paper*, 26 November 1853]. The speakers were particularly keen to highlight their shared belief that sectional bodies such as the trade unions, acting locally or even regionally and often in isolation or with limited support, could not bring about complete and lasting improvement and social transformation. Furthermore they declared that the mass movement would mobilise workers not only to provide financial support to locked-out or striking workers, but also to demand a share of profits and, even more ambitiously, by means of active support for self-employment and co-operation, to end wage slavery and the 'thraldom of capitalists'. In keeping with the general spirit of the movement for 'The Charter and Something More', this combination of immediate and limited and more ambitious and transforming goals was characterised by Jones as 'the new aspect the labour question had assumed' [*Manchester Guardian*, 23 November 1853; *People's Paper*, 26 November, 31 December 1853]. In the *People's Paper* on 31 December 1853, Jones unambiguously expressed his continuing belief in the primary need to achieve political power, and stressed that 'without political power, every other effort would prove unavailing, and end in ultimate disappointment'.

However, in the manner of late Chartism, the movement was deemed to require a more explicit social programme to accompany its political demands and to link the political and the social more closely than had been the case prior to 1848. For example in August 1853 Jones had declared that the labour movement was 'taking a higher and deeper scope – it is taking a wider sweep', and was advancing and striking against capitalists and capitalism on several fronts: 'as we advance on the political path, let our flanks be guarded by our gallant Labour allies – let the Trades' Unions and the Short Time Committees continue their goodly work' [*People's Paper*, 27 August 1853]. In October 1853 he referred to 'the two-edged political and industrial sword for our battle'; and declared that, as 'the people's true programme', 'if you stick to that you'll conquer' [*People's Paper*, 8 October 1853]. Jones and his colleagues in the mass movement did not wish to draw undue attention to the political nature of the labour parliament. This was because of their fear that in so doing they would antagonise and scare away potential trade union support. As we shall see below, some trade unionists in Preston and elsewhere were suspicious of and hostile towards the labour parliament on account of its political character and improper interference in what was seen as a purely social or wages question. However we shall also observe that matters were more complex, with leading trade unionists and many members supporting it financially, morally and physically.

Jones and his colleagues were only too well aware of the potential pitfall of highlighting the political to the perceived detriment of the social among potential trade union supporters. After all they fully realised that, notwithstanding important bonds of unity, relations between trade unionism and Chartism had at times been problematic, especially after 1842 when Chartism's formerly hegemonic influence over the movement had declined [Sykes (1982); Thompson (1984)]. Contrary to the view expressed by Saville, Jones did not fail to 'appreciate the crucial role of the trade unions in the labour movement' [Saville (1953) 55]. However, while acknowledging that the unions had an important part to play in the resurrection and development of a many-sided movement, Jones was acutely aware of and opposed to the divisive and isolating effects of sectional trade unionism. At the general level, moreover, Jones was attempting to pull off the very delicate balancing act of getting all shades of opinion within the movement to work harmoniously together and to unite under the umbrella of the labour parliament and the mass movement – much in the way that they had united, for a time at least, under the banner of Chartism. Thus it was for largely tactical and pragmatic rather than ideological reasons that Jones played down the political aspect of his scheme. Above all it was the establishment of a labour parliament – 'a gigantic Labour Union, to raise a national subscription ... for rendering the present lock-out and strikes victorious ... and for devising the means of independent self-employment for the wage-slave' – that constituted the means to the national renewal of labour's self determination, unity and advancement [People's Paper, 31 December 1853].

In terms of labour's renewal and advancement, the November meeting was seen by the People's Paper and even the hostile Manchester Guardian as a success. It endorsed the combination of immediate and long-term aims expressed by the main speakers, and on a practical level it elected a committee to 'make all necessary arrangements for the calling of the Labour Parliament'. The committee was to call meetings, correspond with interested parties, receive and distribute subscriptions in support of locked-out and striking workers, and urge working men throughout the country to call public meetings in order to elect delegates to the forthcoming labour parliament. Special importance was attached to the formation of amalgamated committees of the trades in each district in order to promote more integrated action and support [Manchester Guardian, 23 November 1853; People's Paper, 12, 26 November 1853, 3 December 1853].

Jones encouraged his supporters to 'have the courage and perseverance to play it to the end'. He believed that the privileged classes were already trembling at the thought of the labour parliament. The mass movement committee, made up of Hooson, Edward Clark Cropper (a joiner and cabinet maker), John Teer (a dyer) and other activists recruited predominantly from skilled and craft occupations quickly and efficiently set about its business [Manchester Guardian, 23 November 1853; People's Paper, 26 November, 3 December 1853]. It published regular reports of its activities and declared its financial receipts and expenditure in the People's Paper. Reference to the pages of the latter between December 1853 and the end of the first week of March 1854, when the labour parliament began its sitting, certainly suggests that for the most part, the committee shared, Jones' confident expectations. To its credit the People's Paper did report disagreements among trade unionists over the pros and cons of the labour parliament. For example some of the delegates to the National Association of United Trades in London and most of the weavers' delegates in Preston were resolutely against the political nature of the labour parliament. However these dissenting voices were opposed, by other members of the same organisations and by Jones himself [People's Paper, 24, 31 December 1853; Dutton and King (1981) 60–1]. Furthermore there were reports of trade-union-inspired meetings of support for the labour parliament, such as the 'great meeting' at Nottingham in January, 'convened by a committee of Trades' Unions, and 'consisting of numerous members of every branch of trade'

[*People's Paper*, 4 February 1854; see also 7 January 1854]. Finally, the newspaper highlighted meetings at which support was expressed for both the Preston operatives and the proposed labour parliament in numerous localities, including parts of London, Birmingham, Stockport, Norwich and Manchester [*People's Paper*, 7, 28 January 1854]. Thus by early March, and notwithstanding the committee's repeated pleas for increased energy and a little more aid on the part of its supporters, expectations were high. According to the, albeit partial, *People's Paper* a solid basis of support had seemingly been laid for the formation of the labour parliament [*People's Paper*, 10, 24, 31 December 1853, 21 January 1854, 25 February 1854, 4 March 1854; Dutton and King (1981) 59].

The labour parliament sat in Manchester from 6–18 March 1854. Initially 37 delegates from sections or bodies of the working classes, including two 'delegates of observation', assembled in the People's Institute. Karl Marx, Louis Blanc and M. Nadaud (stonemason and 'eminent French Republican exile') were elected as honorary delegates. Nadaud attended and conveyed to the meeting the support of Proudhon and Victor Hugo, while Marx and Blanc sent letters of support. The delegates began by indignantly refuting charges levelled in the press – and directed especially at the working classes and trade union committees – that the labour parliament had 'nothing but a political object in view'. They then got down to the business of endorsing and putting into practice the goals set out at the November meeting [*Manchester Guardian*, 8 March 1854; *People's Paper*, 18 March 1854].

The raising of a national subscription, with an estimated target of £5 million per year and graduated according to earnings, was to provide the financial bedrock. The subscription would enable effective support to be given to all workers who were locked out or on strike. Jones hoped that the highly paid would show sympathy with the low paid, and thus avoid sectional and divisive 'aristocratic' temptations. Regret was expressed about the human and financial costs incurred by strikes, but the intransigence and aggression of capital towards the claims of labour meant that they were 'unfortunately necessary'. The national subscription would also provide the means, via the purchase of land, factories and machinery, to achieve independent and remunerative self-employment and cooperative production. A department would also be set up for the regulation of labour. This would guarantee workers a fair wage and a share in the profits of their cooperative enterprises.

The delegates also endorsed a programme of labour legislation, embracing 'due restriction of the hours of labour', the limitation of female labour and the abolition of child labour, and 'a cessation of the tyrannical system' of fines, discharge notes and truck, 'the silent system in factories' and 'locking operatives up in the same', and 'all the inhuman machinery of oppression now in exercise against the employed in all branches of industry'. Five departments were created, each charged with a specific area of responsibility – agriculture, manufacture, distribution, regulation, and strikes, lockouts and legislation – in order to provide the organisational framework and expertise necessary to the successful realisation of the parliament's goals. Finally, the labour parliament would house the offices of its executive committee in London and would 'meet not less frequently than once in each year' [*Manchester Guardian*, 8, 11, 15, 22 March 1854; *People's Paper*, 11, 18, 25 March 1854; Saville (1953) Appendix IV].

The labour parliament's plan of action, in keeping with the sentiments expressed in Manchester in November 1853, amounted to nothing less than a wide-ranging and ambitious blueprint for the immediate improvement of the position of the worker and for thoroughgoing socialist 'emancipation from the curse of wage slavery' by means of self-employment and cooperative production [*People's Paper*, 11, 18, 25 March 1854]. Significantly, it met with public approval and seemingly unlimited enthusiasm from two of the most prominent contemporary thinkers on the left, Blanc and Karl Marx. Blanc's letter to the delegates warned that the pursuit of strikes would 'lead back to slavery through hunger', but commended them on their plan to raise a subscription for the purpose of self-employment of workers [*People's Paper*, 18 March 1854]. Although far more circumspect in private correspondence with Engels, in his letter to the labour parliament, Marx was warm in his praise and extremely ambitious in his expectations of the work of that body [Saville (1953) 238]. Thus the organisation of 'the labouring classes on a national scale – such, I suppose, is the great and glorious end aimed at by the Labour Parliament'; and 'The mere assembling of such a Parliament marks a new epoch in the history of the world. The news of this great fact will arouse the hopes of the working classes throughout Europe and America' [Saville (1953) 274–5]. Jones' claim was even loftier. He declared that they had witnessed in Manchester 'the organisation of the greatest movement the world had ever seen' [*Manchester Guardian*, 15 March 1854].

The most important question facing the departing delegates in mid March was whether the high hopes would be realised. According to the *People's Paper*, the early signs were auspicious. Five delegates were appointed as the provisional executive committee, while three of them, as 'mass movement missionaries', were 'to start with all possible speed, and agitate the country' [*Manchester Guardian*, 22 March 1854; *People's Paper*, 25 March 1854). Subsequently 'mission-aries' Robinson, Williams and Finlen, aided by Teer in Manchester and Jones and his colleagues in London, toured Lancashire, Yorkshire, the north, the Midlands and the west to establish branches of and raise subscriptions for the movement. Their reports, published in the *People's Paper*, were initially encouraging [see for example *People's Paper*, 8 April 1854]. However reference to other sources, such as *The Times* and the *Manchester Guardian*, reveals silence rather than corroborating or conflicting evidence on this matter.

Jones had earlier received a rebuff when he had been refused permission by the chair to speak at a mass meeting in support of the Preston workers in mid March. However he subse-quently received a written apology from the secretary of the Amalgamated Committee of the Cotton Operatives in Preston for this 'unmerited insult'. The same letter also expressed 'confidence in the members constituting the Labour Parliament' [*People's Paper*, 18 March 1854]. Furthermore it is evident that, notwithstanding continued opposition on the part of the powerloom weavers' central committee to the political nature and outside interference of the labour parliament in the Preston dispute, many of the key leaders in Preston were now con-vinced by Clark Cropper's denial of 'a political object in view' and affirmation that 'our only object was to bind the Factory Operatives together in one fraternal union' [*People's Paper*, 21 January 1854; Dutton and King (1981) 59–61]. This was shown by the fact that the two most prominent leaders in Preston, George Cowell and Mortimer Grimshaw, along with five of their leadership colleagues, were elected honorary members of the labour parliament [Saville (1953) 272; Dutton and King (1981) 59–61].

Yet the fortunes of both the Preston operatives and the labour parliament were soon to suffer a catastrophic decline. In late April, Jones desperately warned those in Preston that 'National organisation alone can save you. The Mass Movement is your only anchor of salvation ... Take my warning ere it is too late! [*People's Paper*, 29 April 1854]. A week later it was indeed too late! The operatives were starved of sufficient funds to continue their struggle and the eight-month Preston dispute, involving some 26 000 workers, came to an end. Reductions in cotton workers' wages 'were enforced throughout Lancashire and Cheshire' [Kirk (1985) 250–1; Dutton and King (1981) ch. 10; *People's Paper*, 6, 13 May 1854]. As an editorial in the *People's Paper* declared on 6 May, 'The accumulated gold of the employer [had] proved stronger than the accu-mulated pence of the employed.'

The *People's Paper* attributed the industrial defeats in Preston and elsewhere to workers' insufficient adherence to the principles and practices of national organisation and support. For only a national union could emancipate labour. Furthermore the leaders in Preston had demon-strated that their commitment to the labour parliament lacked resolve and consistency. According to Jones, when the employers perceived signs of division and a change of course on the part of some leaders formerly sympathetic to the labour parliament, they cried 'We are safe – and the Preston operatives are in our grasp' [*People's Paper*, 6 May, 1854). However much we debate the truth of the *People's Paper*'s claim that leadership weakness and betrayal caused the defeat of the Preston operatives, there is no doubt that the fortunes of the labour parliament plummeted dramatically in the wake of industrial defeat. While the executive committee of the mass movement continued to provide reports on the formation of new branches during June, the pages of the *People's Paper* were increasingly devoted to the attempted revival of Chartism [*People's Paper*, 20 May, 10, 17, 24 June, 5, 26 August 1854].

The inflated ambition of the labour parliament's goals and the rapid and precipitous nature of its fall would suggest to many that it had no real place from the very outset and certainly not in the future, in an increasingly sectional post-Chartist labour movement that was more concerned with digging in and establishing a defensive base and limited presence within capitalism than in the latter's transformation. The failure of the labour parliament and/or Jones' socialist goals is attributed to changing socioeconomic and political conditions and the alleged weaknesses in Jones' personality. Primary attachment to the societal factor in the failure of socialism is clearly seen in the thesis advanced by G. D. H. Cole in the 1940s that the 'conditions of the time', and 'not … defects of his own', accounted for the fact that Jones 'failed utterly' to transform British society [Cole (1965) 349–50].

R. G. Gammage, the first historian of Chartism, explained Jones' failure, in terms of his matchless impudence and trickery. Jones was portrayed as having duped Gammage and other Chartists into participating in the labour parliament on the promise that it would deliver both political and social change. However Jones' alleged abandonment of the notion that political change must precede effective social change, indeed abandonment of the political altogether during the period of the labour parliament and his embrace of the primacy of the social, alienated Gammage and like-minded Chartists. It was seen by Gammage effectively to have guaranteed the failure of the labour parliament [Gammage (1969) 394–5].

In his 1953 study of Jones, Saville offered an explanation that combined both points of emphasis but, much in the manner of Gammage's account, attached priority to the personal factor. Thus while Saville set the failure of the labour parliament against the broad if somewhat sketchy backcloth of the growth of the more defensive and reformist labour movement highlighted by Cole, it was Jones' lack of political realism – his rejection of the primacy of the political and other 'gross errors of judgement', especially his anti-trade unionism and his hyperbolic claims and expectations on behalf of the 'wildly unpractical and utopian' labour parliament – for which he is most severely taken to task [Saville (1953) 54–5]. Saville's conclusions largely echo those made by Gillespie in 1927 that, during the transitional mid Victorian years, the notion of the labour parliament was impractical, vague and visionary, and necessarily abortive [Gillespie (1966) 56].

The view shared by Gillespie and Saville has subsequently become the dominant historiographical commonsense. Moreover as impractical and necessarily abortive, as alien to the increasingly limited ambition or reformism of mid Victorian labour, and as a social as opposed to a political movement, the labour parliament has barely figured in more recent accounts of post-Chartist radicalism. Indeed in the vast majority of these accounts it merits no more than a single, brief reference [for example Harrison (1965) 56; Taylor (1984) 6; Belchem (1996) 109; Hewitt (1996) 252]. In some of them, and especially those whose focus is primarily or entirely on politics, it has disappeared altogether [for example Cole (1965); Biagini and Reid (1991); Ashton *et al.* (1999)]. The most recent study of early trade unionism refers to Jones' general opposition to the trade unions ('lamentable fallacies'), but not to the labour parliament [Chase (2000) 218, 221]. In sum, the labour parliament is either entirely absent from or appears as a mere footnote in the current scholarship.

A convincing case can be made both for the treatment of the labour parliament as a subject worthy of historical investigation, and for the centrality of the societal factor to its rise and decline. Furthermore a specific focus upon the labour parliament, set within its full historical context, continues to raise important questions about our knowledge and understanding of the neglected but crucial period of transition from Chartism to reformism. For it was the mid Victorian decades, rather than the late 1830s and early 1840s – the years of Chartist hegemony – that saw the firm establishment of the reformist British labour traditions of trade union strength, voluntarism, self-reliance, pragmatism, sectionalism, and limited and gradual but real labour-movement and working-class advancement (however restricted to the more regularly employed, respectable and predominantly male sections of the working class), as well as suspicion of theory, especially theory of a revolutionary and/or utopian kind.

The labour parliament experiment developed out of the massive industrial and class conflicts of 1853 and early 1854. The nature and aims of these very important conflicts demand further historical investigation. Jones and other leaders, including hard-headed veterans of Chartism and trade unionism and leading intellectuals of the day, maintained that this workplace conflict, complete with extensive working-class suffering, provided a highly favourable context in which to create an institution, the labour parliament, that would unite the political and industrial wings of the movement. The labour parliament would also offer an attractive and effective combination of immediate and long-term aims and objectives that would eventually transform British society in a socialist way.

Both the delegates to the labour parliament and the latter's executive committee displayed strong trade-union connections and allegiances [*People's Paper*, 26 November 1853, 11, 18 March 1854; *Manchester Guardian*, 23 November 1853]. Moreover in promoting the benefits of national unity and organisation the members of the labour parliament were appealing to a well-established tradition of intertrade cooperation, which had been particularly strong in the 1842 strike and among Chartists in general [Sykes (1982); Chase (2000) chs 6, 7]. Workers on strike or locked out during 1853 and 1854 were conscious of the benefits of cooperation and the dangers of division and isolation. The raising of mass subscriptions and the policy of selective strike action contributed greatly to the success of the campaign for a 10 per cent wage increase for the cotton operatives of Stockport in the summer of 1853, while Wigan's colliers suffered from the lack of wider, coordinated support and action [Kirk (1985) 248–9; *People's Paper*, 27 August, 5, 12 November 1853]. We have also seen that, although limited in its appeal and receiving a mixed reception from those involved in the industrial conflicts in Preston and elsewhere, the labour parliament received more support from those within the movement, including trade unionists, than is suggested by conventional wisdom.

It is of course difficult to determine the extent to which working-class support for the labour parliament embraced not only the demand for greater unity and organisation, but also socialist transformation. The continuing failure of late Chartism to attract mass support for its social aspect suggests it did not. However there is no doubt that the revival of industrial conflict in 1853 and 1854 did lead to a heightened sense of class identity [Dutton and King (1981) chs. 3–5; Kirk (1985) ch. 6]. It was in this context, of course, that support for the labour parliament mounted. However the rapidity with which both the labour parliament and mass industrial conflict subsequently collapsed, combined with dwindling support for Chartism and the accelerated movement of Chartists into liberalism, strongly suggest that socialism was a fleeting and minority concern among workers in the 1850s. Nevertheless the issues raised – relations between those locked out or on strike in 1853 and the proponents of the labour parliament, and the nature of the political consciousness displayed by all the participants – also merit far more intensive and extensive historical investigation than has so far been attempted.

The labour parliament, as both a social and an intellectual movement, was firmly grounded in national and international radical traditions. Above all it grew out of the late Chartist concern with 'the Charter and Something More'. Influenced by the French revolution and the social thought of Louis Blanc [Saville (1953) 234; Finn (1993) 68], it also occupied a novel place in the tradition of the 'radical convention' in British history [Parssinen (1973)]. For unlike earlier examples of the radical convention, such as the Chartist National Conventions of 1839, 1842 and 1848, which met to prepare the petitions to parliament and to consider ulterior measures, it was primarily social rather than political in character. However, like most of the preceding conventions it was keen to highlight its identity as a radical association rather than a subversive antiparliamentary force. Jones rebuffed fears and charges of illegality. He claimed, in the pages of the *People's Paper*, that while it was not necessary to 'bow to the technicalities of the law', the proposed parliament would constitute a conference, much in the manner of those held by 'the

Peace Society', the 'Wesleyan Reformers and other analogous bodies', and 'must sit, and place itself in communication with Government and with the Parliament of faction' [*People's Paper*, 12 November, 31 December 1853].

Moreover in articulating their notion of an alternative system of political economy to that held by the advocates of *laissez-faire* capitalism the delegates to the labour parliament were, to a significant extent, expressing continuity with the views of the early nineteenth-century socialist 'critics of the market' [Thompson (1988)]. There is a mistaken but widespread assumption that in the mid-century context of the decline of Chartism and the growth of reformism and liberal radicalism, alternative socialist notions of political economy more or less disappeared.

The story of the labour parliament illustrates the wide range of ideas and practices that influenced workers during the 1850s. In the opinion of Jones, in a very real sense the future development of the labour movement was more open ended in 1853 and early 1854 than blanket application of the adjectives 'defensive' and 'reformist' to this period would suggest. Simultaneously, however, the opportunities and choices available were not limitless. In the wake of the defeat of the third Chartist petition in 1848, it is not surprising that organised workers increasingly turned – in their trade unions, the cooperative and friendly and mutual improvement societies – to social rather than political means as the preferred, but not only, way of achieving their goals. In setting up the labour parliament Jones was reflecting, and attempting successfully to relate to, the growing importance of 'the social'. Yet he did so pragmatically rather than in the manner of a blinkered ideologue.

Attachment to the principles of democracy, openness and honesty, so marked a feature of earlier working-class movements, also figured prominently in the labour parliament experiment. For example provision was made for the election of all officers of the mass movement, of delegates to the labour parliament and of members of the executive committee. The fact that elections were to be conducted by and for 'working men' pointed to the central gender limitation in the preferred democratic system. The secretaries or managers of the labour parliament's five departments were also to be elected by their respective (presumably male) workers. In the event of complaints or disputes arising, 'the operatives shall have the power of dismissing the manager and electing another by a majority of not less than three-fourths of their number'. Strict attention was paid to the proper safeguarding of the subscriptions raised and to the public declaration of receipts and expenditure [*Manchester Guardian*, 11, 22 March 1854].

The labour parliament holds an enduring importance and fascination for the historian of mid-Victorian labour that has not been adequately reflected in the historiography. When set in its proper historical context, the labour parliament was far less wild, impractical and divorced from mainstream working-class movements and traditions than we might at first suppose. The tragedy of the labour parliament experiment and the key to its failure, lay not in Jones' personality defects but, as claimed by Cole, in the 'conditions of the time' [Cole (1965)]. The child of a wave of strikes, the labour parliament could not survive long after defeat in Preston and elsewhere. The period of the labour parliament not only casts light upon neglected alternative and minority labour movement traditions and largely unfulfilled possibilities, but also suggests that we must more carefully scrutinise the grand narrative of mid-Victorian labour's mainstream reformism.

Sources: (1) Newspapers: *Manchester Guardian*, August 1853—August 1854; *People's Paper*, January 1853—December 1854. **(2) Other:** C. Dickens, *Hard Times* (1854); J. Saville, *Ernest Jones: Chartist* (1953); G. D. H. Cole, *Chartist Portraits* (1965); R. J. Harrison, *Before the Socialists: Studies in Labour and Politics 1861 to 1881* (1965); F. E. Gillespie, *Labor and Politics in England 1850–1867* (1966); R. G. Gammage, *History of the Chartist Movement* (1969); T. M. Parssinen, 'Association, Convention and Anti-Parliament in British Radical Politics, 1771–1848', *English Historical Review*, 88 (1973) 504–33; M. Jenkins, *The General Strike of 1842* (1980); H. I. Dutton and J. E. King, *Ten Per Cent and No Surrender: The Preston Strike 1853–1854* (1981); R. Sykes, 'Early Chartism and trade Unionism in South-East Lancashire', in

J. Epstein and D. Thompson (eds), *The Chartist Experience: Studies in Working-Class Radicalism and Culture 1830–1860* (1982); A. D. Taylor, 'Ernest Jones: his Later Career and the Structure of Manchester Politics 1861–9' (MA thesis, University of Birmingham, 1984); D. Thompson, *The Chartists: Popular Politics in the Industrial Revolution* (1984); N. Kirk, *The Growth of Working Class Reformism in Mid Victorian England* (1985); N. Thompson, *The Market and its Critics: Socialist Political Economy in Nineteenth Century Britain* (1988); E.F. Biagini and A. Reid (eds), *Currents of Radicalism: Popular Radicalism Organised Labour and Party Politics in Britain 1850–1914* (1991); Margot Finn, *After Chartism: Class and nation in English radical politics 1848–1874* (Cambridge, 1993) J. Belchem, *Popular Radicalism in Nineteenth-Century Britain* (1996); M. Hewitt, *The Emergence of Stability in the Industrial City: Manchester 1832–67* (1996); O. Ashton, R. Fyson and S. Roberts (eds), *The Chartist Legacy* (1999); M. Chase, *Early Trade Unionism: Fraternity Skill and the Politics of Labour* (2000).

Neville Kirk

JONES, Thomas (Tom) (1908–90)
TRADE UNIONIST, SOCIALIST, SPANISH REPUBLICAN VOLUNTEER

Tom Jones, also known as Tom 'Spain' and Tom 'the Union', was a coal miner, trade unionist, socialist and Spanish Republican volunteer. He born on 13 October 1908 in Ashton-in-Makerfield, Lancashire, to a Welsh family, the second of the three children of William Jones, a coal miner, and his wife Mary, née Clayton, a kitchen maid. Jones moved to the Wrexham coalfield as a child. His father had earlier left Wrexham to work in the Lancashire coalfield, but returned to North Wales in 1915 due to the health of his wife. After an elementary education Jones followed his father into the mines at the age of 14, working at Hafod Colliery in Rhosllannerchrugog and two years later at Bersham. Jones' father had been active in the minimum wage strike in 1912, although he held no official position in the union. Tom Jones developed an early interest in politics, taking advantage of his industrial environment and the informal opportunities for self-improvement that coalfield society provided.

The north Wales coalfield in this period had a volatile industrial relations culture. The main miners' union, the North Wales Miners, Association (NWMA), found it difficult to recruit and sustain a cohesive membership base [Lerry (1968) 29–39]. The village of Rhosllannerchrugog was the strongest sector of mining unionism, with members exhibiting the kind of solidarity that had developed in the south Wales valleys. In contrast the collieries in the southern section of the coalfield exhibited little radicalism. Black Park was characterised by paternalism and deference, although there was a small core of socialists who worked hard to establish the union at particular collieries in Chirk. In the neighbouring Flintshire coalfield, union organisation was even more sporadic, until the miners at Point of Ayr were organised by Edward Hughes, who in 1897 had become the first agent of the union. By 1918 the NWMA had organised a significant proportion of miners and established a central fund and offices in Bradley Road, Wrexham.

The Labour Party in Wrexham was reliant on the miners for support, and had difficulty spreading its influence beyond the coalfield. A small Independent Labour Party (ILP) branch had been formed in the town in 1897, but by 1914 it still had no more than a dozen members. The Trades Council played a more prominent role in pushing for labour representation. Because of a redistribution of parliamentary seats, the new constituency of Wrexham was created out of the old Denbighshire seat in 1918. Hugh Hughes, the miners' agent, contested the election but was heavily defeated. In the 1922 general election Hughes gave way to Robert Richards, an adult education lecturer who won the seat for Labour.

Unlike areas in the south Wales coalfield, working-class education was built on tenuous foundations. Outside of Rhosllannerchrugog there were no miners' libraries. The Workers'

Educational Association (WEA) initiated courses in 1909 in Wrexham, led by R. H. Tawney, but they failed to attract large numbers of miners. However Jones found that the workplace provided significant educational experience. A retrospective interview in the *Western Mail* made it clear that life in the mines had left an indelible imprint on him: 'Rhos was a university not a village, you would have men studying Greek and holding intelligent debates during their breaks underground' [*Western Mail*, 18 October 1973]. But this did not translate into a political shift in terms of the district union. The successive leadership elections in the NWMA were largely bereft of factionalism and the union's industrial policies were marked by pragmatism and moderation.

The 1921 lockout was a formative experience for Jones. He felt that the government was continually undermining the pay and conditions of miners, and when he started work in 1922 he became fully involved in the subsequent struggles between the union and the coal owners. In the 1926 general strike and subsequent miners' lockout, Rhosllannerchrugog became an area of acute distress and Jones played an active role in picketing and political demonstrations. He became a socialist after hearing a rousing speech by A. J. Cook at the Wrexham racecourse the same year. The north Wales coalfield was divided throughout the lockout. The leadership of the NWMA retained their loyalty to Cook and the MFGB, but by August significant numbers had returned to work at Llay Main, the biggest colliery. The union was further debilitated by the formation of a company union at Point of Ayr in Flintshire, which survived until 1944. Jones and most other miners at Rhos stayed out until the bitter end, with many falling victim to blacklisting and intimidation.

Due to the decline in the coal industry after 1926 many Wrexham miners migrated to the United States, settling in the coalfields of Pennsylvania. Jones considered such a move, but instead opted to join the army, enlisting in the Royal Welch Fusiliers. Initially attracted by the promise of adventure, he was quickly disillusioned. On discharge after a year, he re-entered the coal industry at Bersham and resumed his interest in the politics of the trade union movement. He was elected to the lodge committee, which faced a falling membership and declining funds. He became chair of the Rhos Labour Party, which included A. R. Jones of the cooperative movement and James Idwal Jones, the future Labour MP for Wrexham. Tom Jones moved between the various collieries in Wrexham and in 1930 became a delegate to the Wrexham Trades Council after completing a number of courses offered by the National Council of Labour Colleges (NCLC) and the WEA. Education led to his further politicisation and he was encouraged to read Mark Starr's *A Worker Looks at History* (1927).

The failure of the Labour Government in 1931 pushed Jones towards the Communist Party, but although he met Harry Pollitt he refused to join the organisation. While politically sympathetic, he was critical of the perceived atheism of the Soviet Union, which stood in opposition to his Welsh Methodism. Along with the prominent Welsh Christian Communist, J. Roose Williams, Jones travelled by bicycle through the villages of north-east Wales spreading the socialist gospel. On arrival Jones would ring a bell to announce an impromptu political meeting. Williams remained a Communist and a Christian throughout his life, enjoying a long personal friendship with Jones.

In 1932 the Labour Party was still finding it difficult to reach beyond the miners. In the Denbighshire County Council elections the same year the party was only able to muster 17 seats out of the total of 88. The pragmatism of Jones and others helped to ensure that the Communist Party remained a minority concern across the coalfield. Trade union activists were aware of the moderation of workers in mining, textiles and steel production, and could see that their organisational efforts would be seriously threatened by association with Communists. Within the mining industry and the factories organised by the TGWU, the influence of Communists was negligible. The party initiated recruitment drives throughout the decade, but was unable to capture any local leadership positions in the main unions.

The north Wales district of the Miners' Federation of Great Britain (MFGB) became increasingly radicalised in the 1930s. Local owners were held responsible by the union for the Gresford disaster of 1934, in which 266 perished. A five-week stoppage at Bersham a year later led to violent clashes between pickets and police, with blacklegs being imported from other parts of the coalfield. Jones and other miners who were members of the military reserve armed themselves with rifles and prepared to build barricades on Johnstown Road. They were only dissuaded from more violent action by the calming influence of the local police, who were sympathetic to the miners' cause. The district union was also moving towards a coalfield-wide stoppage to gain representation at the Point of Ayr Colliery, where the company union represented most workers. Jones played an active part in these campaigns. Impatient with the caution of local district leaders, he moved closer to the politics of Arthur Horner and Aneurin Bevan.

Jones was secretary of the Rhos Peace Council, but when the Spanish Civil War broke out he became convinced that international support for the republicans was the only way to stop the spread of fascism. He now had little time for pacifism and felt that the fascist threat could only be deterred with force. Through his involvement with the Rhos Labour Party, Jones organised an Aid to Spain meeting and invited Aneurin Bevan to speak. He also felt that he should set an example locally and therefore decided to travel to Spain to promote the republican cause. On the advice of Bevan, he contacted Arthur Horner of the South Wales Miners' Federation (SWMF). Through contact with the largely Communist-controlled Anti-Fascist Committee, arrangements were made for his passage to Spain. He left Victoria Station on 3 April 1937, under the scrutiny of the CID men who were patrolling the boat train. He was arrested in Paris and had to endure the harsh conditions of a French jail. After a short hunger strike the authorities offered him a passage home, which he refused. Upon his release he was given 48 hours to leave the country. Avoiding further arrest, he booked a ticket to Marseilles, where local trade unions arranged his journey to Barcelona [Jones, autobiography, 7]. The only other north Wales volunteer, a trade unionist from Colwyn Bay, returned to Britain after the French experience.

Along with other international volunteers picked for their military background, Jones served in an elite antitank battery. He was the only British member of a special multinational company of machine-gunners, consisting of Poles, Italians, Canadians and Americans. He was involved in intense fighting on the Ebro River, defending a line of hills in support of a Spanish brigade. The battle on the Ebro, which began in July 1938 and ended in November, was the largest conflict of the war and one that signalled sure defeat for the republican forces. There were numerous casualties on both sides: the nationalists lost around 6000 and the republicans many more through death, desertion or capture. Lewis Clive, a British socialist councillor, was a notable International Brigade casualty [Carr (1993) 225–6]. In a clash on 7 September, Jones' company was repeatedly shelled for eight hours, the left flank gave way and the company was surrounded. Aerial bombardment had already killed a significant number and a ground attack followed. Nationalist troops surrounded the remaining volunteers, who fought on until all their bullets had been dispensed. The nationalists then responded to the volunteers' cries for mercy by throwing grenades. As the enemy approached the remaining volunteers raised their hands in surrender, but were mercilessly mown down by machine-gun fire. Jones received a bullet in the thumb, and two more grazed his left leg; he was further immobilised by grenade shrapnel tearing muscles in his right arm. The nationalist troops immediately moved on without checking for survivors. Jones, who had lost a large amount of blood, thought that he would die on the battlefield but a passing nationalist patrol spotted him and put him under arrest. He was first interrogated and then taken to the prisoner of war hospital in Bilbao. A month later the International Brigades were withdrawn.

On 21 September Jones was transferred to a prison in Saragosa. In his unpublished autobiography he catalogues the appalling conditions he faced while imprisoned:

The people in charge of the dormitories were regular convicts and assassins who were in prison for rape, robbery, and murder. The lice and bugs were in complete command of the bodies, clothes, and mattresses of the prisoners ... there was only one lavatory for 350 prisoners. The same conditions applied to the women prisoners as to the men, many women prisoners had their heads shaved and suffered other indignities [Jones, autobiography, 8].

Jones was particularly appalled by the confiscation of his Bibles: the Catholic guards refused to let him read them as they were Protestant versions. On 2 January 1939 he was sent for trial and sentenced to death. At that stage he felt that such an outcome would be a release:

> I didn't worry much about the death sentence at the time because I was so very hungry and miserable with the lice and the bugs that were attacking my underfed body. During the time I was in the death cells, men and women were taken out and shot everyday [ibid., 10].

On 5 March 1939 the death sentence was commuted to 30 years' imprisonment and Jones was transferred to Burgos, where the conditions were a little better. In Burgos Jones shared a cell for 12 months with an Irish republican, Frank Ryan, who gave Jones a share of the clothes and provisions he received from supporters. Ryan's work in teaching Spaniards English and other subjects greatly impressed Jones, and he later claimed that 'Ryan is the most honourable and bravest men I have ever come across ... a man all the Irish and Ireland can be proud of, he is another James Connolly' [ibid., 15]. Jones never accepted the subsequent claim that Ryan was sympathetic to the Germans during the Second World War.

Jones was presumed dead for a long time as his family had not heard from him and a witness reported that he had been shot through the heart in the battle of the Ebro. His parents received a death certificate and a memorial meeting was held in Bangor; a poem was composed by T. E. Nicholas to honour his memory. Death insurance was paid by the Co-op but it was not spent – his family and others were convinced that he was still alive as they had received letters from released captives who claimed he had been seen after the date on the death certificate [Letters in Jones Papers, D/JO/25]. This was confirmed when a nurse who was looking after Jones released his details to allies of the republican cause. When Jones' whereabouts was established there were initiatives from the north Wales coalfield to secure his release. The local solicitor and veteran socialist Cyril O. Jones tirelessly campaigned for his return. Cyril O. Jones, who had been an activist in north Wales since before the First World War, was the legal representative for the NWMA and an organiser of agricultural workers in Shropshire. Tom Jones received money, chocolate, tea and coffee from Cyril O. Jones, who became the intermediary between the Spanish authorities and Jones' family. Robert Richards, the Labour MP for Wrexham, also made representations in the House of Commons and pressured the Foreign Office and the Spanish Embassy, but to no avail. Intense campaigning by local supporters and the SWMF, along with Will John, the Labour MP for Rhondda West, finally secured his return to Britain in April 1940, the last International Brigade member to come home. The release of the final prisoners also owed much to a trade agreement signed by the British and Spanish governments.

When Jones arrived back at Paddington Station he was met by a welcoming party. However the event was marred by the absence of his mother, who had died at Christmas after tirelessly campaigning for his release. Jones continued to denounce the Spanish regime and put considerable energy into locating the whereabouts of Frank Ryan. He sent letters to Members of Parliament and various trade unions to press for Ryan's release. 'I am home again, but I cannot be happy until Frank Ryan gets home as well. It is my duty, and it is also yours, to get all democratic and working class organisations to demand the release of Ryan' [Jones, autobiography, 7].

Not everyone was happy with Jones' return. At that stage of the war the Soviet Union had still not committed itself to the cause of the allies, thus ensuring that members of the Communist Party and fellow travellers came under sustained attack in the local press. Jones responded to press allegations that he was a fifth columnist by claiming that 'if Soviet Russia did enter the war on the side of the allies I should be the first to welcome her. I love my country better than any other ... and all my political activity during the last twelve years has been directed towards making it a better place for the working people' [*Wrexham Leader*, 16 June 1940]. His experiences in Spain had not pushed him towards the Communist Party and he remained a centre-left member of the Labour Party. Early in the Second World War he had voiced support for Churchill and was critical of those on the left who were uneasy about the prospect of hostilities.

It was at about that time that Jones started work on his autobiography. He was unable to write for protracted periods owing to the injuries he had sustained in the Spanish conflict, so he dictated his reminiscences to his wife Rosa Thomas, whom he married in 1942 with whom he had two sons and two daughters. Rosa also threw herself into politics and became a leading figure in the East Flintshire Labour Party.

Jones did not return to the mining industry, but kept up his trade union work as a member of the TGWU. Between 1940 and 1945 he worked in the chemical industry, joining Monsanto in Cefn Mawr. Aiming to rise through the ranks of the union, he became an official of the union in north Wales in April 1945 (as organiser of the Shotton regional office) after being interviewed by Arthur Deakin. He then took charge of the Wrexham district, relishing the prospect of union work back on his home patch. In 1953 he took over from Huw T. Edwards, who had earlier replaced Deakin as officer of the union's Shotton office on Deeside. Jones fitted neatly into the shoes of Edwards, who had been a critic of Deakin and a follower of Aneurin Bevan; nevertheless the TGWU remained in the grip of the rightwing throughout this period.

Although politically to the left of Deakin, Jones seemed a popular choice and Deakin probably favoured the selection of both Edwards and then Jones because they shared a background of trade union activity in north-east Wales. The appointment of Jones goes some way towards challenging both the view that Deakin was an intolerant person and his alleged obsession about ensuring the positioning of union place-men to curtail the rise of communism in the unions and Bevanism in the Labour Party. Deakin retained his affection for the north Wales district and expressed his feelings in a letter to Jones confirming his appointment:

The responsibilities that you are called upon to undertake are very great. You will appreciate that with my long association with the region ... I have an immense pride in the union, its traditions, and the place it has won for itself in the minds of the people in the six counties of north Wales [Deakin to Jones, Jones Papers, D/JO/78].

Once at the helm of Region 13 of the TGWU, Jones knew that following Deakin and Edwards would be a difficult task. He immediately threw himself into the job and attempted to replicate the 'kingmaker' role of his predecessors. Deakin had been instrumental in promoting the parliamentary career of Eirene White in East Flintshire and Jones worked hard to persuade a former Liberal, Megan Lloyd George, to stand in West Flintshire. However she declined the offer to fight for Labour in such a Conservative constituency. Jones also lectured on a number of WEA courses and became a deacon of the Welsh Congregational Chapel in Connah's Quay. The TGWU in north Wales provided prominent social roles for its leaders: the union had a larger representation than the National Union of Mineworkers (NUM) in the region and both Edwards and Jones took centre stage when national and local political issues were discussed in the media.

On the industrial front Jones faced an increasingly restive rank and file, culminating in the Wrexham bus strike during October–November 1953. Jones informed Deakin that the drivers were contravening the national agreement and striking without the sanction of the union. At a rowdy meeting members had condemned the national leadership and refused to return to work. After some arm-twisting they reluctantly returned, but Jones' resolve had been tested and a number of branches had voiced sympathy with the disgruntled drivers [Report on Wrexham Bus Strike, Jones Papers, D/JO/79]. Deakin was keen to ensure that the industrial relations culture of Region 13 remained consensual – he had earlier reprimanded Huw Edwards for his failure to settle negotiations quickly in the John Summers Steel Plant in Shotton. With Jones at the helm on Deeside, Deakin continued to keep a watchful eye over the TGWU in north Wales.

After the death of Deakin on May Day 1955 the 'cold war culture' of the TGWU began to thaw. This enabled regional officials to press their political ideals without having to be wary of the parameters of the left–right division within the labour movement. Jones immediately took advantage of this to challenge Plaid Cymru and its call for independent Welsh trade unions. He viewed the party as generally anti-union and only concerned with the rural interests that formed the core of its support. His experience with the TGWU had strengthened his commitment to union amalgamation, and he felt that 'trade unions in the modern world have to be large and powerful in order that they might negotiate on equal terms with big business and large employers' [*Wrexham Leader*, 12 June 1951]. Jones was astute enough to realise that Plaid Cymru largely took votes from Labour, which would allow the Conservatives to take a number of seats in marginal constituencies, particularly Flintshire.

Jones also showed his aversion to the nationalists by attacking calls for Welsh devolution of the unions and the Labour Party. He worked closely with D. Caradog Jones, a lecturer in the Extra-Mural Department at the University of Manchester, in writing letters to the press emphasising the impracticability of a Welsh parliament: economically it would lead to a fall in living standards, and politically the north would be dominated by the south [D. Caradog Jones to Tom Jones, 7 February 1956, Jones Papers, D/JO/83]. The north's resentment of the dominating influence of the south was a significant feature of the Welsh labour movement. The political differences between those in the north and south coalfields were stark, with the north Wales miners generally being averse to the Communist leadership of the south. In the case of the TGWU the issue was more complicated, as Region 13 also organised workers in England, especially in Ellesmere Port and elsewhere on Merseyside.

A more practical problem for Jones was not political ideology or institutional change, but that unemployment in rural areas would weaken union membership. He viewed both the government and employers as villains who were conspiring to ensure that north Wales suffered underinvestment, a claim that seemed lost on Plaid Cymru. In a speech to TGWU local activists in 1955, Jones stressed that it was a 'scandal that Welsh workers live in fear of unemployment and poverty whilst workers are being imported from Italy, Ireland, European mainland, and West Indies' [Jones Papers, D/JO/96]. There had already been debates in the local coal industry relating to the employment of foreign labour, although overt racism remained minimal in local political discourse.

Jones' remedy for the precarious economic position of rural areas was industrialisation and inward migration from England, a policy that attracted the wrath of the nationalists. In a circular distributed to TGWU members in 1957, Jones argued that 'it is obvious that in north Wales we have ample room for much more industry and people ... the present level of industrialisation must be trebled and the population ... increased by at least one million' [Jones Papers, D/JO/99]. His experience in Spain had made him hostile to all forms of nationalism, and in his view the anti-English strand in Plaid Cymru had fascist overtones. A more concrete formulation of Jones' ideas can be found in his article 'Land of Our Fathers – But what about our Sons?', which was published in the *Transport and General Workers' Record* in October 1957. He stated that since 1921 only two of the six north Wales counties had increased their population, and that displaced workers from Birmingham would be an ideal choice for staffing government-induced industrial development in rural areas. He expressed a firm belief in state-led modernisation, anticipating a more planned economy once the Labour Party was returned to power. Within the TGWU Jones supported the unilateralist position on nuclear weapons, a position promoted by Frank Cousins, the union's general secretary since 1956.

Throughout the 1960s Jones retained his belief in the ability of the Labour Party to transcend the constraints of the market. In a speech to the Wrexham Trades Council in 1963 he made a plea for state intervention: 'until we get a planned national economy with proper distribution of industrial policies, the Wrexham district, like every other area, must actively join the stupid rat-race to attract and demand industries, or once again become a depressed area with all its unhappy consequences' [Jones Papers, D/JO/118]. However Harold Wilson's Labour Government failed to deliver, and in some areas even followed a policy of deindustrialisation. Much to the dismay of Jones and other local union leaders, the coal industry in north Wales was almost totally eradicated in 1966–68.

In his address to the Welsh Council of Labour in 1968, Jones reaffirmed his belief in socialism and rounded on media critics of the party:

The present crisis, like all previous economic crises throughout this century, is a crisis of the capitalist system ... One of the main reasons the Labour Party came into being was to change the economic system, in an evolutionary way, from an unplanned capitalist system to a planned democratic society ... If we are to bring about democratic socialism then we must, as the late Nye Bevan stated, capture the commanding heights of the economy [Jones Papers, D/JO/135].

The language of struggle and solidarity littered the public utterances of Jones, but in industrial matters he remained a pragmatist and resisted rank and file pressure for internal union change. In one speech he stressed that 'strikes are not an intelligent method of settling disputes' [Jones Papers, D/JO/96]. Trades councils throughout Wales were increasingly questioning the policies of the TUC Regional Advisory Committees, which were dominated by trade union establishment figures. The tensions between the trades councils and the Regional Advisory Committees in north and south Wales reached a climax in 1966, leading to a TUC inquiry into the problems. The trades councils, along with the South Wales NUM, were increasingly calling for a Wales TUC. The North Wales Advisory Committee was vociferous in its opposition. Jones once again attacked the nationalists for promoting separatist institutions, adding that both unions and employers were completely different in the north and south. The trades councils became more prominent when they were granted representation on the Regional Advisory Committees. Within the TGWU itself, pressure for reorganisation mounted due to the scale of industrial closures, and in 1969 it dismantled the north–south structures and organised on an all-Wales basis. The domination of the south was checked by the appointment of Jones as the first TGWU all-Wales secretary, a post he held until his retirement in 1973 [Osmond (1977) 115–22].

In the early 1970s, Region 13 of the TGWU fought to save jobs in the massive British Steel plant in Shotton, which went on to shed labour throughout the decade. Jones was at the forefront of this campaign, seeking wider alliances with trade union leaders in the south. Numerically the TGWU was still the most prominent union in Flintshire and Denbighshire, with around 24 000 members, but its plan for joint action with the south was limited by the distance, both ideological and geographical, within the Welsh labour movement. The National Union of Mineworkers (NUM) in the north was increasingly critical of southerners' domination of bodies such as the Welsh Economic Council [Gildart, *North Wales Miners* (2001) 141]. Jones pressed on with joint meetings that eventually led to the formation of the Wales TUC in 1974. He worked closely with Dai Francis of the South Wales NUM, who became founding chairman of the body. Jones had reluctantly accepted the policy of devolution that was being promoted by trade unions in Wales, but retained his aversion to the nationalism of Plaid Cymru.

In 1962 Jones was awarded an OBE, and in 1974 a CBE. The Spanish government in exile had also remembered the service he had rendered and honoured him by making him a Knight of the Order of Loyalty. In 1976 he was invited by Tony Benn, then Secretary of State for Energy, to become a member of the Merseyside and North East Wales Electricity Board, which he accepted. The University of Wales awarded him an honorary MA in 1989. He died at his home in 2 Blackbrook Avenue, Hawarden, Flintshire on 21 June 1990. His son Kieth Jones followed in his footsteps, becoming a research officer with the TGWU, based in Cardiff.

Tom Jones was a committed socialist who was impatient with political factionalism on the left. His political journey was characterised by the pit, the community and republican Spain. He was far more comfortable in the TGWU after the death of Deakin, and under Frank Cousins' leadership he was able to press his internationalist perspective more assuredly. Away from the world of union work he was an avid reader and DIY enthusiast, although his capacity for such work was limited by the injuries he sustained in Spain. Throughout his life he retained his enthusiasm for politics. The increasingly materialistic nature of British society and the part that the working class played in perpetuating this troubled him. In many ways he represented a dying breed of Welsh Labour figures who had fused a Christian ethos with a socialist politics that saw a positive role for trade unions in governmental decision making and the Labour Party as a vehicle for working-class emancipation.

Writings: An incomplete autobiography of Jones, which he started on his return from Spain in 1940, can be found in the Flintshire Record Office, Hawarden, D/JO/35. He also wrote occasional pieces for union publications such as 'Land of our fathers – but what about our Sons?', *Transport and General Workers' Record*, October 1957.

Sources: (1) MSS: Tom Jones Papers D/JO/1–175, Flintshire County Record Office, Hawarden; Wrexham ILP Papers 1906–17, Denbighshire County Record Office, Ruthin; Huw T. Edwards Papers, National Library of Wales, Aberystwyth; Roger Eatwell, 'Wrexham Independent Labour Party, Trades Council and Divisional Labour Party 1903–1951', unpublished manuscript, Denbighshire Record Office, NTD/589. **(2) Newspapers and Periodicals:** *Wrexham Leader*, 1945–79; *Liverpool Echo*, 2 May 1955; *Birmingham Mail*, 12 August 1957; *Transport and General Workers' Union Record*, 1957; *Chester Chronicle*, 30 April 1960; *Western Mail*, 18 October 1973. **(3) Other:** Huw T. Edwards, *It was my Privilege* (Denbigh, 1957); Huw T. Edwards, *Hewn From the Rock* (Cardiff, 1967); G. G. Lerry, *The Collieries of Denbighshire: Past and Present* (Wrexham, 1968); John Osmond, *Creative Conflict: The Politics of Welsh Devolution* (Dyfed, 1977); Hywel Francis, *Miners Against Fascism: Wales and the Spanish Civil War* (1984); Ronald Fraser, *Blood of Spain: An Oral History of the Spanish Civil War* (New York, 1986); Jane Pugh, *A Most Expensive Prisoner: Tom Jones, Rhosllannerchrugog's Biography* (Llanwrst, 1988); Raymond Carr, *The Spanish Tragedy: The Civil War in Perspective* (1993); Francis Beckett, *Enemy Within: The Rise and Fall of the British Communist Party* (1995); Duncan Tanner, Chris Williams and Deian Hopkin (eds), *The Labour Party in Wales 1900–2000* (Cardiff, 2000); Keith Gildart, 'Militancy, Moderation, and the Struggle against Company Unionism in the North Wales Coalfield, 1926–44', *The Welsh History Review*, 20:3 (2001) 532–64; Keith Gildart, 'Co-operation and conflict: Episodes from the North Wales Coalfied, 1925–35', *Historical Studies in Industrial Relations*, 12 (Autumn 2001) 27–56; Keith Gildart, *North Wales Miners: A Fragile Unity, 1945–96* (Cardiff, 2001); Personal information, Kieth Jones, Research Officer, TGWU, Cardiff.

KEITH GILDART

See also: Huw T. EDWARDS; †Edward HUGHES; †Hugh HUGHES.

KNIGHT, George Wilfred Holford (1877–1936)
LABOUR AND NATIONAL LABOUR MP

George Wilfred Holford Knight was born on 23 April 1877 at 61b Swinbrooke Road in the Kensington district of London, the eldest son of George Thomas Knight, a tailor, and his wife Alice Maud Mary Knight, née Woodward. He was educated at private schools in London and left full-time education at the age of 16 to work as a clerk in local government. In the evenings he attended courses run by London University and then switched to studying for a career in law. He was called to the Bar of the Middle Temple in 1903 and practised on the south-eastern circuit and the Surrey and South London sessions. He was senior counsel to the Royal Mint at the Central Criminal Court in 1911–30. He took silk in 1930 and became recorder of West Ham in the same year. Among his colleagues at the Bar he had the reputation of being a reformer: in 1913 he was the first to advocate the admission of women to the English Bar, earning him the nickname 'Portia's champion', and for many years he argued for the creation of an Imperial Bar Council, to meet periodically in London.

As a young man Knight became an active member of the Liberal Party and stood unsuccessfully for the Wokingham seat (East Berkshire) in the January 1910 general election. His Conservative opponent was Ernest Gardner, a former mayor of Maidenhead and long-serving alderman on the Berkshire County Council. At the count Gardner polled 8132 votes to Knight's 4095. Knight supported the Progressive Party on the London County Council and served as a poor law guardian for Paddington from 1903–9.

After the outbreak of war in August 1914, Knight volunteered for the army but was rejected as unfit for military service, whereupon he enlisted in the Special Constabulary and served in the Metropolitan Police's Headquarters Detachment for the duration of the war. When conscription was introduced in 1916 Knight received his call-up papers. He could have avoided the draft without great difficulty by attending the army medical examination, instead he chose to make a stand on the issue of conscription. Accordingly he appeared before the Military Service Tribunal in Acton in July 1916, where he stated that he was opposed to conscription on moral and religious grounds. He was, however, granted exemption by the tribunal because he had already been declared unfit for military service and it was recommended that he should carry on with his normal civilian duties and continue his service with the Special Constabulary. He afterwards claimed that he had not been exempted from military service as a conscientious objector, and legally this was correct, although he had chosen to object to the introduction of conscription. Knight had taken up a position that many people found difficult to understand and it caused him considerable trouble when he stood for Bromley in the 1918 general election as an Independent Liberal and Progressive candidate; during the campaign he was freely charged with having been a 'conchy'. His opponent had served as a junior minister in the wartime coalition government and had been awarded one of Lloyd George's 'coupons'. After this defeat Knight decided that the Liberal Party was a spent force in British politics and he joined the Labour Party.

Bromley, 1918: electorate 40 709, turnout 52.0 per cent

Rt Hon. H. W. Forster (Coalition Conservative)	16 840 (79.5 per cent)
G. W. H. Knight (Liberal)	4 339 (20.5 per cent)
Majority	12 501 (59.0 per cent)

During the 1920s Knight served on the Labour Party's Legal Advisory Committee and represented several trade unions in the courts. He stood unsuccessfully as the Labour candidate for North Southwark in the London County Council elections in March 1922, and in August the same year he was the Labour candidate at a parliamentary by-election in South Hackney. The by-election had been caused by the expulsion from the House of Commons of the sitting MP, Horatio Bottomley. He had won the seat as an independent in 1918, and the Labour Party was contesting the seat for the first time. Lloyd George's Coalition Government was losing its popularity with the electorate and many political commentators found it difficult to forecast the result. The Coalition Conservative candidate was C. C. A. L. Erskine-Bolst. He had a good war record, having served on the Western Front as a captain in the Black Watch, and Knight was thrown on the defensive during the campaign, having to explain the line he had taken on conscription during the war. However he did not buckle under pressure and ably propounded Labour's policies, although Herbert Morrison – then a prominent member of the Hackney Labour Party – believed that Knight had made a mistake in attacking Horatio Bottomley. Although Bottomley had been convicted of fraud he still had a number of supporters in the constituency who resented any criticism of their former MP [Morrison (1960) 91].

Hackney South by-election, 18 August 1922: electorate 32 262, turnout 56.3 per cent

C. C. A. L. Erskine-Bolst (Coalition Conservative)	9118 (50.2 per cent)

G. W. H. Knight (Labour)   9046 (49.8 per cent)

Majority   72 (0.4 per cent)

This was a creditable performance by Knight considering that, as the Labour Party's National Agent reported to the NEC, 'there was not a shred of effective organisation in the Division' and 'evidence of corrupt methods was abundant' [quoted in Donoughue and Jones (1973) 104].

Knight fought the same constituency in the general election later that year. By this time the Lloyd George Coalition had been replaced by a Conservative government, with Bonar Law as Prime Minister. Law decided to go to the country to seek endorsement for his new government, and he was successful in achieving this.

Hackney South, 1922: Electorate 33 284, turnout 70.0 per cent

C. C. A. L. Erskine-Bolst (Conservative)   14 017 (60.2 per cent)
G. W. H. Knight (Labour)   9 276 (39.8 per cent)

Majority   4 741 (20.4 per cent)

The result in Hackney South was disappointing for the Labour Party after the narrowness of the by-election defeat, although there was no criticism of Knight and the assumption of most local party members was that he would remain their candidate. Hence there was some surprise when on 8 October 1923 it was reported in the Hackney local press that Knight had been selected as the Labour candidate for Swindon. The reason why Knight switched constituencies is not clear. He had proved to be an able and energetic campaigner and had not been involved in any local party factionalism: there is no evidence that he would have failed to be reselected to fight the seat for a third time. In the event Herbert Morrison – not without some local opposition – was selected as Knight's successor and he won Hackney South in the general election of 6 December 1923, while at Swindon Knight came second to a Conservative barrister. There are critical references to Knight's behaviour in Swindon in Hugh Dalton's diary. These refer to his ambition for office and willingness to drop the capital levy proposal to secure Liberal votes.

Halford Knight ... had told MacDonald that he lost on Capital Levy, tells me that all ex-Liberals were vindictively tracked down and kept out by Liberal machine ... (I hear later that he went to the Liberal leader at Swindon and offered to drop Capital Levy if they would support him). He then goes round telling several people including deaf Mrs Wedgwood, that he hopes it will be realised that the Solicitor-General need not be in the House, and that the Law Officers should include a common and a criminal lawyer. (I hear later that he said at public meetings at Swindon that if he were returned, he would be a Law Officer). He and Bennett are a fine pair of throw offs from the Liberals! [Pimlott (1986) 36].

Dalton suffered his third election defeat in December 1923 and that setback arguably made this portrait more jaundiced.

Swindon, 1923: electorate 33 787, turnout 82.8 per cent

R. M. Banks (Conservative)   12 625 (45.1 per cent)
G. W. H. Knight (Labour)   9 121 (32.6 per cent)
W. L. Rocke (Liberal)   6 231 (22.3 per cent)

Majority   3 504 (12.5 per cent)

Thus Knight failed to win a seat in the Commons for the nine months that the first Labour Government spent in office, and when the next general election was held on 29 October 1924, after the fall of the Labour Government, he fought Plymouth Devonport. Here his opponents were the barrister Leslie Hore-Belisha, standing for the Liberals, and the solicitor Samuel Gluckstein, standing for the Conservatives.

Plymouth Devonport, 1924: electorate 33 159, turnout 84.4 per cent

L. Hore-Belisha (Liberal)	11 115 (39.7 per cent)
S. Gluckstein (Conservative)	10 534 (37.6 per cent)
G. W. H. Knight (Labour)	6 350 (22.7 per cent)
Majority	581 (2.1 per cent)

Knight was elected to the House of Commons upon his seventh attempt, when he caused one of the upsets of the 1929 general election by defeating the venerable Lord Henry Cavendish-Bentinck in Nottingham South.

Nottingham South, 1929: electorate 42 920, turnout 80.4 per cent

G. W. H. Knight (Labour/National Labour)	14 800 (42.9 per cent)
Lord Henry Cavendish-Bentinck (Conservative)	14 252 (41.3 per cent)
C. L. Hale (Liberal)	5 445 (15.8 per cent)
Majority	548 (1.6 per cent)

For several years Knight had harboured ambitions to be Solicitor-General – he had canvassed for the post in a letter to Ramsay MacDonald in 1924 – and there was speculation in the press that he would be appointed as such in the newly formed Labour Government. Instead MacDonald chose J. B. Melville, and when Melville resigned in 1930 he was replaced by Stafford Cripps. Knight never became a law officer nor achieved any other ministerial office.

Knight proved to be an active backbencher. In his maiden speech in the Commons on 5 July 1929, during the debate on the address, he praised the Labour Government's devotion to world peace, or more specifically its intention to sign the Optional Clause of the Statute of the Permanent Court of International Justice, binding it to submit all disputes, with certain reservations, to the court's arbitration. He tried on several occasions to bring about a reform of the divorce laws by making the certified lunacy of a spouse a ground for divorce, and supported the simplification of divorce law embodied in the Marriage Acts Amendments Act of 1934. He worked closely with various ramblers' associations and in 1932 had the satisfaction of steering a Rights of Way Act through the House of Commons. He also took a sympathetic interest in the work of the Round Table Conferences, designed to offer India a larger measure of self-government. He had visited India in the 1920s as part of his campaign to secure an Imperial Bar Congress, and had met Gandhi and gained some insight into the problems of the subcontinent.

Although an energetic backbencher, Knight was hardly a well-known public figure until his role in the political events of the summer of 1931 thrust him into the national spotlight. On 31 July 1931 Parliament adjourned for the summer recess without any awareness of an impending crisis. The economic position of the country was difficult but far from critical. Philip Snowden, the chancellor of the exchequer, had assured MPs that he had the financial situation under control. The May report, published on the day Parliament adjourned, gave a bleak assessment of the budgetary position; the majority report supported radical cuts in public expenditure. Ministers' discussion of the report was shaped by a financial crisis threatening the abandonment of the gold standard. Knight was as surprised as most other Labour backbenchers when it was announced on 24 August that the Labour Government had resigned and been replaced by a National Government, with Ramsay MacDonald as Prime Minister. The following day MacDonald sent a letter to all Labour MPs informing them that this action had been forced upon the government, and expressing the hope that they would reserve judgement until all the facts were made public.

The Labour Party was thrown into turmoil by MacDonald's actions, and meetings of party members were held across the country to discuss the political situation, with Labour opinion gradually hardening against the National Government. On 28 August the Parliamentary Labour Party assembled for the first time since the formation of the National Government, with members of the National Executive of the Labour Party and the General Council of the TUC in attendance. The meeting discussed the crisis, elected Arthur Henderson leader of the Labour Party, and confirmed that the party would oppose the National Government. Knight resented the attendance of TUC members at a PLP meeting: he believed their presence was designed to put pressure on Labour MPs to conform to the TUC's wishes [*Nottingham Evening Post*, 2 September 1931].

In Knight's own constituency the monthly meeting of the South Nottingham Labour Party's executive committee was due to convene on 2 September 1931. It was expected that Knight would attend and discuss the political situation with local party members, but instead he sent a telegram: 'Regret cannot leave London today awaiting Government proposals. Only test satisfaction of national necessities. Repudiate dictation by caucus of officials.' Meanwhile he told a reporter: 'I believe in the interests of the country all men and women of goodwill should give to the difficulties of the Government their sympathetic attention' [*Nottingham Evening News*, 2 September 1931].

On 8 September Parliament reassembled after its summer recess and MacDonald asked for a vote of confidence. Knight was one of 12 Labour MPs who went into the lobby in support of the National Government, and in his speech in the Commons debate on the National Emergency Bill, held on 29 September, he infuriated his former colleagues when he referred to abuses of the Unemployment Insurance Act by 'spongers' and suggested that Jenny Lee, then the MP for North Lanark, was the right person to lead this 'mob' [of 'spongers'] at the anticipated general election [*Hansard*, 29 September 1931, col. 246].

By this time Knight had already been deselected by his constituency party. The South Nottingham Labour Party's executive committee had held a special delegate meeting on 13 September with Knight in attendance. On the eve of the meeting Knight had said to reporters: 'My choice is not in doubt. I stand by my duty as a Member of Parliament, acting with a free mind. I shall support the only available Government to resolve the nation's difficulties. The Labour Party has degenerated into a business run by its paid officials' [*Nottingham Evening News*, 12 September 1931]. Knight spoke for 25 minutes at the meeting, and after hearing his views the delegates passed a resolution: 'This meeting disassociates itself from the policy of Mr Holford Knight and requests him to resign as Member for South Nottingham.' In another resolution the delegates pledged their loyalty to the Labour Party and instructed the executive committee to take steps to select another candidate [Minutes of South Nottingham Labour Party, 13 September 1931].

After the meeting Knight told a local reporter: 'As I expected, the delegates stand by the machine: I stand by the country'. When asked if he would resign he replied 'No', and added that he had received many letters of support from the general public [*Nottingham Evening News*, 12 September 1931]. A fortnight later Knight announced that at the next general election he would stand as a National Labour candidate, and when Parliament was dissolved on 7 October, with polling to take place on 27 October, Conservative Central Office put pressure on the local Conservative Association to support Knight, in accordance with the agreement between pro-Government parties. Knight was duly adopted as the National Labour candidate for the South Nottingham constituency on 14 October at a meeting presided over by the chairman of the local Conservative Association. A. R. Ellis, a trade union official from Bradford, had been selected to fight the seat for the Labour Party, and after an election campaign notable for the rowdiness of its public meetings, Knight was returned for Nottingham South:

Nottingham South, 1931: electorate 43 104, turnout 77.6 per cent

G. W. H. Knight (National Labour)   22 852 (68.3 per cent)

A. R. Ellis (Labour)	10 583 (31.7 per cent)
Majority	12 269 (36.6 per cent)

Despite the 1931 split, Knight never regarded himself as someone who had betrayed his principles. A year after the formation of the National Government he observed: 'There are Members of this House, supporters of the Prime Minister, who have not abated their attachment to the principles and policies of the previous Government but who are prepared in the interests of the nation, at this moment to support a general national Administration' [*Hansard*, 26 May 1932, col. 591]; and two years after this, in another speech in the Commons, he pointed to the general improvement in living standards since the formation of the National Government and argued that this justified his support for it [*Hansard*, 20 November 1934, col. 54].

Few of his former colleagues on the Labour benches would have agreed with him, for in several speeches in the Commons Knight had defended the means test, although, he argued, he wanted to see it administered in a more humane way, and in order to establish uniformity across the country he wished to see it removed from the hands of local authorities and administered by a special commission set up for the purpose. His support for the means test, expressed in an abrasive style, antagonised many Labour MPs and Knight had some bitter exchanges on this topic with Aneurin Bevan and James Maxton, among others.

Knight was a Londoner: he was born in the capital, resided in it throughout his life, and most of his social activities took place in it. He was a Freeman of the City of London, a Knight of the Knights of the Round Table Club, a member of the Wheelwrights' Company and a member of the Reform Club. He was keenly interested in the theatre, and was deputy chairman of the National Theatre Appeal Committee and a member of the Drama League Council. He was particularly fond of Shakespeare and rarely missed a performance at the Old Vic. He supported the use of Regent's Park for open air theatrical productions and was concerned about the impact of entertainment tax on the British theatre.

In April 1935 there was a demand from some members of the South Nottingham Conservative Association that they should be allowed to select a Conservative candidate to fight the seat in the next general election, whereupon Conservative Central Office promptly intervened and asked the association to honour the National Government's interparty agreement. With some reluctance local Conservatives agreed to continue to support Knight as the National Labour candidate. However when Parliament was dissolved on 25 October, Knight suffered a heart attack and had to withdraw. After a few months' rest he appeared to have made a good recovery and talked of returning to politics, but on 1 April 1936 he was admitted to London's St John and Elizabeth Hospital suffering from thrombosis. He died in hospital on 26 April 1936, leaving an estate of £749 12s 8d. Knight had been a member of the Church of England and had taken an active interest in church affairs. As a layman he had delivered a series of addresses on religious topics to the congregation of St Martin-in-the-Fields and his funeral service was held in that church. Knight was survived by his wife, Christine Hilda (née Logan) of Bedford Park, Croydon, whom he had married in 1908 when she was 18. There were no children.

Writings: *Advancing Woman* (1921): various papers in *Contemporary Review* and *Fortnightly Review*; articles in *Manchester Guardian, Nation,* and *Westminster Gazette.*

Sources: (1) MSS: MacDonald Papers, PRO; Minutes of South Nottingham Labour Party 1931, Nottingham County Archives Office; Records of the University of London. **(2) Newspapers:** *Acton Gazette*; *Bromley Record*; *Nottingham Daily Guardian*; *Nottingham Evening News*; *Nottingham Evening Post*; *Hackney and Kingsland Gazette*. **(3) Other:** Hansard (1929–35); *Who Was Who* (1929–40, 1941); R. Bassett, *Nineteen Thirty-one Political Crisis* (1958), Lord Morrison of Lambeth, *An Autobiography* (1960) A. Marwick, *Clifford Allen – the open conspirator* (1964); Bernard Donoughe & G. W. Jones, *Herbert Morrison Portrait of a Politician* (1973). F. W. S.

Craig, *British Parliamentary Election Results 1885–1918* (1974); C. Bell (ed.), *The National Government 1931* (1975); F. W. S. Craig, *British Parliamentary Election Results 1918–49*, revd edn (1979); M. Stenton and S. Lees (eds), *Who's Who of British Members of Parliament, 1919–45* (Brighton 1979); Ben Pimlott (ed.), *The Political Diary of Hugh Dalton, 1918–1940, 1945–1960* (1986); A. Thorpe, *The British General Election of 1931* (Oxford, 1991). **(4) Obituaries:** *Nottingham Daily Guardian*, 27 April 1936; *The Times*, 28 April 1936.

ARCHIE POTTS

LAWSON, Hugh McDowall (1912–97)
COMMON WEALTH AND LABOUR MP

Hugh McDowall Lawson was born in Leeds on 13 February 1912, the second of the four children of John Lawson, a successful chemist's manager, and his wife Faith, née Clokie. Faith Lawson, who was from a Methodist family in Castleford, made a living as an art teacher. The Lawson family moved to West Bridgford in Nottingham in 1914, where John was recruited by Sir Jesse Boot, the founder of Boots Pure Drug Company. The Lawsons became influential members of the local Methodist community. Politically they were staunch Liberals. John Lawson was a member of the National Liberal Club, but held a seat on the West Bridgford Urban District Council as an independent. As a successful businessman he was suspicious of socialism, but retained an ethical commitment to social progress and held most of the lay offices in the Methodist church.

Hugh Lawson attended Nottingham High School, and by his own admission did not show much early promise. His gift was oratory, no doubt strengthened by his formative experiences in the church. As a Methodist he was actively involved in study groups, weekend conferences and Sunday schools. After high school he attended University College Nottingham (which awarded degrees from London University), and obtained a BSc in Civil Engineering in 1932. His social values were revealed when he was the only student to vote for a motion to allow women to stand for the office of union president. After completing his education he was articled to the borough water engineer in Preston, where he served a two-year apprenticeship. From 1935–7 he held posts in Daventry and Bromley in Kent, and then joined the Nottingham City Engineer's Department. He was to retain a strong link with Nottingham and its people for the rest of his life. In 1940 he joined the army and was posted to Gibraltar, where he worked on the construction of defences. He returned to Britain in 1943.

During the 1930s Lawson's ideals were primarily driven by his Methodism and he showed only a limited interest in politics. He joined the University of London branch of the Labour Party in 1935, but because of his employment outside London was not an active member. Nonetheless he paid his dues regularly and enthusiastically read the party literature. A far more important phase of politicisation came when he joined the Left Book Club. It was John Strachey's *The Theory and Practice of Socialism* (1936) and the work of Norman Angell that convinced him of the importance of the socialist cause. From 1937–9 he was also an active member of the League of Nations Youth Group, where he spoke regularly at the fortnightly meetings. Lawson remained an inactive member of the Labour Party as he felt that all his energy should be directed at fighting fascism. The prospect of war was the most pressing problem for Lawson, and he saw Labour as an inadequate vehicle for channelling anti-fascist activities. He was involved in a number of anti-appeasement demonstrations, including a large rally at White City in London that attracted many students.

Lawson's conception of socialism was firmly rooted in his religious beliefs: 'acceptance of the Christian gospel implies the acceptance of the idea of the brotherhood of man, and to me that means that I've to try and make the world a brotherly place and that for me means being a socialist' [Questionnaire for Common Wealth completed by Lawson, Lawson Papers 9/46]. His marriage to Dorothy Louisa Mallinson in 1937 cemented his commitment to Methodism and radical politics. She had been born in Llangollen and was the daughter of Reverend T. Harold Mallinson, a Methodist minister. They had met at a local service, over which Reverend Mallinson had presided. Dorothy Mallinson was also interested in politics and became a member of the 1941 Committee and the Anglo–Soviet Friendship Committee. She was to play an active role in the Common Wealth Party, holding positions at the branch and district level. Lawson's elder brother, John, confirmed the family connection to Methodism by becoming a minister in Grantham in the same period.

Common Wealth was a merger between two organisations that had been formed to channel dissent, thereby seeking to transform British policy during the war: the 1941 Committee, and Forward March. The 1941 Committee was an *ad hoc* think tank promoted by Edward Hulton the owner of *Picture Post*. Forward March was epitomised by the figure of J. B. Priestley, whose radio broadcasts during the war did much to boost morale. This group was a bottom-up organisation formed in response to the publication of books by Sir Richard Acland, the Liberal MP for Barnstaple, who was increasingly critical of the politics of the established party system. Acland became the driving force behind Common Wealth. He expounded his ideas for a new Britain – a mixture of Christianity and Socialism – in a series of publications that converted many to the Common Wealth cause. The cornerstones of the new party's policies were public ownership, reform of the electoral system and morality in politics [Calder (1969) 548)]. George Orwell, writing in the *Observer*, provided a succinct summary of the Common Wealth programme: 'capitalism must be scrapped forthwith but Britain must go Socialist under her own steam and in a way that accords with her past traditions. Nationalisation of industry – yes, class warfare – no, imperialism – no, patriotism – yes, collaboration with Russia – yes, imitation of Russian methods – no' [quoted in Davison (1998) 105]. But perhaps the most significant rallying call for Common Wealth was the publication in December 1942 of the Beveridge Plan for social reform, which envisaged a comprehensive system of social security. The party felt that immediate implementation of the plan would provide a socialist foundation for British post-war society. This policy gained much support in the climate of general pessimism that followed the fall of Tobruk.

Common Wealth attracted a membership of around 15 000 at its peak. It was divided into about 300 branches and recruited largely amongst the middle class. Geographically it drew significantly on disaffected voters in London and Merseyside, along with rural areas where the Labour vote was traditionally weak. As an avowed socialist party, it had to compete with Labour, the Communist Party and the Independent Labour Party (ILP) in promoting a programme of common ownership. It was at an advantage in that these parties, except for the ILP, continued to support the wartime electoral truce. However on many occasions Common Wealth would avoid using terms such as socialism and Marxism, which aroused suspicion about its true purpose amongst others on the left. Because of the nature of its membership and the personal fortunes of some of its supporters, it was able to produce high-quality propaganda that aided its cause in electoral contests.

Lawson was exposed to the appeal of the party while stationed in Gibraltar, and he was particularly influenced by the writings of Acland. He corresponded with the MP in 1940 and poured praise on Acland's vision of a new Britain, as set out in his book *Unser Kampf* (1940).

You set out a system of moral ideals and political aims which (sic) I am in complete agreement. I am passionately convinced too, that unless they are realised now, it will mean the destruction of nearly everything of value in Western civilisation. ... The world needs a higher morality and a more scientific and economic political system [Lawson to Acland 23/2/40, Lawson Papers 9/1].

Acland responded to Lawson by asking him to establish a group in Nottingham to discuss his ideas. This was thwarted by Lawson's immediate activities in the army, but in Gibraltar

Lawson's belief in Acland's politics led to him becoming a member of Common Wealth in November 1942. He organised Common Wealth discussion groups and could sense an emerging radicalism in the forces, which he felt would generate support for socialist measures in the post-war period. The party was having a significant impact in the forces and was well represented in the Cairo 'parliament' in 1943. This body had started life as a British forces discussion group, but caused a furore when it was banned by the authorities. It was in this context of popular radicalism at home and overseas that Common Wealth ideas flourished. In Gibraltar Lawson produced a number of political articles for *The Rock*, a local magazine. He brought together a number of political sympathisers in the Gibraltar Garrison Literary and Debating Society, where he held the position of treasurer and later became warden of the club's premises. The society soon became the centre of cultural activities, and like its counterpart in Cairo it established a mock parliament. This was dominated by socialists, and Lawson was made a member of the cabinet and eventually prime minister. He combined this role with talks on Common Wealth policies, as a small number of his peers were party members. His most prominent role was as question master on a 'brains trust' discussion programme that was broadcast on local radio.

Lawson returned to Britain in June 1943 and was initially stationed in Edinburgh, where he attended Common Wealth meetings and was made chairman of the North and Central Edinburgh branch. This branch had wide support amongst the local working class, there being strong links between Labour members and Common Wealth. On briefly returning to Nottingham some months later he threw himself into work for the party. He volunteered his services as a parliamentary candidate and was accepted by the national leadership. His candidature was recommended by the East of Scotland executive, who had noticed his skills as an organiser and orator. In his statement to the National Committee he proclaimed his belief in Christianity and socialism. At the time he was buying a house in Nottingham, which prompted a defensive statement: 'it is at present let to a tenant, but mortgage repayments exceed rent, so I am not really a capitalist' [Personal information, Lawson Papers, 9/47–63].

A cluster of effective individuals at the top of the party were now campaigning vigorously for Common Wealth representation in Parliament. With Acland as president, R. W. G. Mackay as chair and Tom Wintringham as vice-president, the party had already won a dramatic by-election in Eddisbury in April 1943, when John Loverseed defeated his opponents in a largely rural constituency. But the problem for the party was that its organisation and ideology rested on fragile foundations. The leadership was divided over whether its political activity should be a temporary substitute for the Labour Party, or whether it should attempt to become a permanent presence. C. A. Smith, formerly of the ILP, wanted it to become a viable alternative to other parties of the left, whereas Ronald Mackay wanted affiliation to Labour [Duff (1971) 4]. Before the end of the war Lawson, along with Acland, prevaricated over the future of the party, although both eventually, left and committed themselves to the post-war policies of Clement Attlee's Labour Government.

After the success of Loverseed in Eddisbury, Lawson indicated that he would like to stand in Nottingham as he was a well-known figure locally and could draw on an effective circle of Methodist allies. In his personal testimony that accompanied his letter of request for a Common Wealth candidature, he declared that he was 100 per cent committed to the ideals of the party. Lawson also revealed that he was also keen to campaign against anti-Semitism and anti-feminism. He was eventually selected to stand for Common Wealth in the Yorkshire constituency of Skipton in late 1943, after the offer had been declined by Desmond Donnelly, who went on to become a Labour MP. The vacancy was due to the death of the sitting Conservative MP, G. W. Rickards. The local Labour and Liberal Parties remained pledged to the electoral truce, providing an opportunity for an independent advance. Forward March had established a small branch in Skipton two years previously; it was quite active – holding meetings and distributing pamphlets – and had an office on the High Street. One leading member, M. Forster, was headmaster of the local grammar school and typical of the kind of individual the party attracted. The constituency was one of the largest in England, with numerous townships and villages and a widely scattered electorate. Much of it covered the Yorkshire Dales and included a number of discontented farmers who were aggrieved about the level of government financial support for converting pasture into arable land. The party mobilised significant support during the campaign, organising numerous well-attended rallies. Tom Driberg, who had won Maldon in June 1942 as an independent candidate, threw his weight behind Lawson's candidature when the latter confirmed that he had been a supporter of the republican cause in Spain and that Common Wealth was a socialist party. To the distress of figures in the national Labour Party, Lawson's chance of success was significantly strengthened when he gained the backing of Bradford Labour Party and the Skipton Trades Council. Lawson was still a member of the London University Branch of the Labour Party, a dual membership that was true of many Common Wealth figures and helped candidates to convince wavering Labour supporters that they were committed socialists. Members of the local Labour Party often appeared on the platforms of both Lawson and the independent candidate, Joe Toole, causing confusion about the likely result of the contest. Toole had once been lord mayor of Manchester and Labour MP for Salford South. W. V. Titherington, an influential Labour Party and trade union figure, spoke at several of Lawson's meetings in support of his candidature. Lawson also gained the support of the local branch of the National Farmers' Union. Farmers were initially hostile to the Common Wealth policy of common ownership, which had been depicted by local Conservatives as a programme of confiscation. But Common Wealth did well in countering this propaganda and quelling fears by declaring its commitment to compensating landowners in the event of nationalisation. Lawson also gained the support of the National Federation of Old Age Pensioners, which was keen to see the immediate implementation of the Beveridge Plan [*Yorkshire Post*, 7 December 1943].

Common Wealth started to campaign early, producing a number of pamphlets and sending many organisers into the constituency. A mass meeting in the local cinema was addressed by J. B. Priestley, who claimed that Lawson made an ideal candidate; he was young and had an unblemished record of military service [*Manchester Guardian*, 3 January 1944]. Lawson's opponents targeted Acland and stressed that his plan for common ownership would lead to financial ruin for farmers in the constituency. The vote for the left was threatened with fragmentation when Toole entered the fray. The latter felt that Common Wealth was disrupting the unity of the Labour movement, and aware of the power of this allegation Lawson announced that he would not contest the seat in the future if the local Divisional Labour Party or Trades Council decided to choose a candidate [*Bradford Observer*, 5 January 1944]. The local press was generally hostile to Lawson's candidature and felt that Toole's view of Common Wealth was accurate. Lawson responded with a number of letters in which he claimed that 'he was going into the dales and preaching democratic socialism and the need for radical change in our society in villages where there has been no political activity for years' [*Yorkshire Post*, 15 December 1942]. It was certainly true that Common Wealth was ploughing a lonely furrow, as the Communist Party remained unwilling to break the electoral truce. The Skipton branch suggested that all the parties, including the Conservatives, should meet to discuss Common Wealth's challenge to electoral unity. The Communist Party had been suspicious of Common Wealth because of its affluent membership base and its criticism of the Soviet Union and on many occasions had attacked it as antisocialist. A comprehensive critique of the party, Robin Page Arnot's *What is Common Wealth?* (1943), claimed that the party could well become fascist. Within Common Wealth there were emerging criticisms of its overtly socialist stance. Eric Troward, a member of the party's South East Regional Committee, resigned and argued against a vote for Lawson, claiming that the party had 'degenerated into a dangerous sort of hybrid communism' [*Yorkshire Observer*, 21 December 1943]. The party leadership was also attacked by the left, with some members becoming increasingly suspicious of the role of the business tycoon Alan P. Good, who was the main financial backer for its election campaigns.

The battle for Skipton generated a great deal of interest locally and nationally. Lawson made much of his military experience and his youth, arguing consistently for a policy of full employment, common ownership and the immediate introduction of the Beveridge Plan. The party invested a great deal of time and resources in the contest, with Acland and others making great use of the motor car and the loudspeaker. Lawson was heavily dependent on the Labour vote, and the electorate generally viewed Common Wealth as socialist. Acland recalled that Toole, standing as independent Labour, could not compete with their policies and had to resort to 'musical hall jokes and a certain amount of Beveridge'. In later years Desmond Donnelly, amongst others, felt that the appeal of Common Wealth in Skipton was largely dependent on Acland's personality. Acland could generate a 'certain messianic zeal', whereas Lawson was 'not a first rate speaker'. Donnelly also felt that the party generated suspicion amongst trade unionists because 'of the presence within its ranks of a good deal of anti-Labourism among do-gooding middle class people' [Calder interview with Desmond Donnelly, 15 December 1965, Common Wealth Papers, 14/113–6]. The personal wealth of Alan P. Good, Ronald Mackay and Sir Richard Acland did nothing to dispel this view of the party being dominated by people who were not familiar with the working class. Nonetheless Lawson was elected.

Skipton, 7 January 1944: electorate 49 608, turnout 54.9 per cent

H. M. Lawson (Common Wealth)	12 222 (44.9 per cent)
H. Riddiough (Conservative)	12 001 (44.0 per cent)
J. Toole (Independent Labour)	3 029 (11.1 per cent)
Majority	221 (0.9 per cent)

With an election team based in the constituency from the first day of the contest, the campaign had cost the party well over £1000, the bulk of the expenditure being met by the national office. Lawson returned to his military unit in Scotland before moving to the constituency, residing at 2 Otley Street, Skipton. There was some controversy when the forces attempted to stop him attending political meetings outside Skipton. This related to an order, passed in 1940, forbidding serving members of the army from speaking outside their constituencies and the House of Commons. Lawson was introduced to the House by Acland and John Loverseed, the victor of Eddisbury.

Donnelly's criticism of Lawson was mostly directed at his inexperience, but when the latter entered the Commons he competently articulated Common Wealth policy in terms of questions and interventions. His maiden speech was on agriculture, and he criticised the policies of the government that had led to bad feeling amongst farmers. Many farmers had been unhappy with the government for not raising prices to offset the wage increases awarded to farm labourers. Lawson suggested that the tide was turning politically towards socialism, as a notoriously conservative section of the electorate had voted for Common Wealth in Skipton. He articulated his views further in an article titled 'The Lesson of Skipton':

A majority of the people of Britain are now convinced of the failure of the capitalist system, very few of them will challenge the statement that the private ownership of the means of production and the private profit motive in industry has produced frustration, unemployment and poverty in the past, still fewer believe that this system will work satisfactorily in the future … I know that the Labour and Socialist movement is failing in its duty now if it does not with the most vigorous insistence impress upon the people that the only hope of decent conditions after the war, of full employment, of Beveridge, and yes, of the continuation of democracy and lasting peace is the achievement of a Socialist Britain, and the decent burial of the rotting corpse of the capitalist system (*Edinburgh Clarion*, March 1944).

The problem for Lawson and other members of Common Wealth was choosing a political vehicle that could deliver the new Britain. In February 1944 R. W. G. Mackay had written to Lawson and argued that his success in Skipton had provided evidence that there needed to be unity on the left. He wanted to form a committee to prepare for the next general election and was already moving towards throwing his lot in with Labour [Mackay to Lawson, 28 February 1944, Lawson Papers, 9/76]. By its own admission, Common Wealth was a party divided between idealists and realists. The former were committed to the ethical principles of the party and were wary of links with other parties, while the latter were inclined to see the organisation as a short-term alternative to Labour and as a campaigner for the rapid introduction of socialist measures. The relationship with the Labour Party was to be the major dilemma for the party in the run-up to the general election of 1945. In April 1944 a Common Wealth delegation, led by Acland, attended a *Daily Worker* unity conference organised by the Communist Party. Mackay called for unity in all constituencies when attacking the record of the Conservatives. However the Communist Party preferred a more reserved approach and was opposed to a direct attack on the Coalition until the war was over. Within Common Wealth there was intense pressure from Mackay and others for formal affiliation with Labour. The issue reached a climax at a special conference held in October to discuss the question of Labour affiliation. Lawson spoke in favour:

> if the [Labour Party] is going to be a revolutionary body we must go in with them ... We believe that socialism can only come through revolutionary means ... If the Labour Party says in no unmistakable voice that it intends to do the right thing, and there is a considerable part which means it, we could go in with some chance of success [Report of Special Conference, 8 October 1944, Common Wealth Papers, 9/588].

The problem for the party was that Labour was indifferent to Common Wealth affiliation. This situation was reinforced when in late 1944 a number of Common Wealth figures applied for party membership. The Common Wealth MP for Eddisbury, John Loverseed, announced his conversion to Labour, but was not able to carry many with him from his local branch. Loverseed had been quite ineffective as an MP: he had spoken infrequently in the House and the national office had received a number of complaints about his failure to keep speaking engagements. In contrast Lawson remained convinced of the Common Wealth cause, and in a letter to a friend in the RAF he stressed that 'what we are going to do is not yet fixed but you can be quite sure that we are not going to lose heart or wind-up the organisation' [Lawson to W. O. Taylor, 18 December 1944, Lawson Papers, 11/466].

Lawson's positive view of the party's future was dashed in early 1945 when the national chairman, R. W. G. Mackay, resigned and applied for Labour Party membership. This was not surprising; Mackay had always been close to Labour and was keener on affiliation than Lawson and Acland. In the face of this development the party announced that it would continue because the Labour Party was not socialist. While it would support Labour in some constituencies, Common Wealth would be standing candidates on a programme of 'full socialism'. Others in the party were calling for the organisation to be wound up. Sybil Wingate, a member of the national committee, left after the party voted to continue. Lawson felt that in the coming election, Common Wealth was better equipped to capture middle class votes as it was not associated with the trade unions and refrained from using the rhetoric of class. In a letter to a party member he reiterated his view that 'people of this type see the contradiction and frustration of capitalism, just as much as the boiler-maker or the miner' [Lawson to W. O Taylor, 2 February 1945, Lawson Papers, 11/460].

Lawson's position as an MP was threatened when the Skipton Divisional Labour Party announced that it would be standing its own candidate, J. P. Davies, in the forthcoming election. Labour Party activists did not want Common Wealth opposition in Parliament and were keen for a clear Labour majority. Lawson had made a firm commitment not to stand against the wishes of the local labour movement. However he did not want to relinquish the seat and hoped that a deal could be done so that he could stand again in a free run against the Conservatives and the Liberals. In a letter to a local newspaper he stated that 'if the DLP officials are willing to put the principles of socialism before organisational pride and interest there is no reason at all why it should not happen' [*Yorkshire Observer*, 28 November 1944]. He then went further and made a personal appeal to the prospective candidate. He argued that Common Wealth should have been consulted before the selection of the candidate in order to promote socialist unity. Lawson was aware of the political sensibilities of the constituency and felt that he was in the best position to generate the support of non-Labour voters. He was clearly regretful of the promise that he had made to the DLP before his election and closed the letter with an appeal that the party should think again: 'Please do not think that I am asking you to withdraw now; all I am saying is that in my opinion it is unsafe to assume that the very best thing for the socialist cause is for me to withdraw now' [Lawson to J. P. Davies, 14 March 1945, Lawson Papers, 12/536–8]. Local Common Wealth members in the constituency played their part and started a petition to pressure the DLP to think again and support Lawson as a socialist candidate. This proved futile and in the general election Lawson became the Common Wealth candidate for West Harrow.

Lawson was widely regarded as a very good MP. He lived in the constituency and held regular meetings, and in the House of Commons he spoke frequently in debates and made numerous interventions in discussions on government bills. In an article in the *Common Wealth Review* he set out his views of what he thought was the central task of an MP: 'The most important job of a Socialist MP today is to challenge the existing order, and neither the friendly atmosphere of the House of Commons nor the individual hardships of his constituents should be allowed to distract him from this' [*Common Wealth Review*, April 1944]. Here we see his impatience with the politics of Labour and its commitment to the war coalition. Nonetheless he felt that after the war Labour would provide the best hope for common ownership. He continued to proselytise the ideas of Common Wealth across the country and was a particular draw in local party branches, although there were occasional complaints to the national office that his speaking style was 'meek and mild' and he did not do enough to attack the Tories [Letter from Newcastle CW to National Office, 2 November 1944, Common Wealth Papers, 9/494].

The question of affiliation to the Labour Party, which had been discussed at the Common Wealth conference, was finally put to rest when Labour decided to apply the same principle that had been adopted in the case of the Communist Party. It would not accept affiliation from other parties, but individuals were free to join if they were prepared to accept the constitution of the Labour Party. This path had been followed by R. W. G. Mackay, who now argued that the work of Common Wealth was finished. James Walker, a steelworker and right-wing member of the Labour NEC, invited its members to join the Labour Party, stressing that Common Wealth 'was a party founded by a rich man in order that he should become a political leader, with views based on Marks and Spencer, unable to contribute anything to the Labour movement' [*Common Wealth Review*, January 1945]. The party remained buoyant despite a number of defections to Labour. It continued to publish pamphlets and held some large meetings. Lawson wrote a regular column in the *Common Wealth Review* on developments in the armed forces. This lively publication included articles from a number of political figures, including Fenner Brockway, Willie Gallacher and George Orwell. Lawson was aware that the radicalism in the forces that had done much to boost support for the party was on the wane. A Common Wealth member stationed in the Middle East informed Lawson that the troops 'are not socialist by any means. They are merely rather disgruntled and still pro-Churchill to a great extent, but mainly just wondering whether anything can make a difference either way' [W. O Taylor to Lawson, 25 February 1945, Lawson Papers, 11/466].

With the Labour Party pushing for the maximum number of seats, Common Wealth had to define its brand of socialism and explain the differences between the two organisations. Lawson and Acland had been isolated figures in the House of Commons, and the *Common Wealth Review* insisted that while 'their attendance in the House is higher than the majority of members … they need reinforcement'. However this seemed unlikely as Labour was promising to implement the cornerstone of Common Wealth's policy, namely full implementation of Beveridge's recommendations. But Common Wealth was encouraged by the election of Ernest Millington at the Chelmsford by-election in April 1945. Churchill reacted to the result by saying Millington was 'a member of a disintegrating political fragment whose equipment for dealing with the intractable problems the war will leave is a portfolio of grandiose aspirations and untried theories' [*Daily Herald*, 28 April 1945]. Despite Churchill's attack, Millington retained his seat in the general election that took place later that year.

Lawson made a number of speeches in West Harrow during his 1945 campaign, emphasising the distance between Labour's and Common Wealth's policy. He argued that Labour was constructed as a reformist party that only believed in 'half measures' in eradicating capitalism. His commitment to the more radical strand of socialism espoused by Common Wealth was emphasised in his earlier rejection of a plea by the local Labour Party to resign from the party and stand as a Labour candidate. His principles prevented him from making the switch and he now worked for the withdrawal of his Labour opponent to avoid splitting the left-wing vote. Lawson and Joan Thompson, the Labour candidate, signed a joint request for a conference of the Labour and Common Wealth executives to decide who should stand – both agreed to abide by the decision. The document was submitted to the national agent of the Labour Party, but to little effect. Thompson was reprimanded for acting unconstitutionally by signing the document, while the local party was told to reject calls for Common Wealth's policy of left-wing unity and to campaign solely for the Labour Party. Lawson felt that this was proof that the responsibility of splitting the socialist vote rested with Labour [Draft of speech, Common Wealth Collection, 12/283/4]. The contest then degenerated, with both parties attacking each other in the press and on the street. Lawson unsuccessfully campaigned around the five core principles of Common Wealth: vital democracy, common ownership, security and equality, colonial freedom, and world unity. He had become increasingly impatient with a section of Common Wealth membership who wanted to compete against Labour candidates in seats that the party could not win. C. A. Smith, formerly of the ILP and now Mackay's replacement as chairman, was the most vociferous advocate of this approach. At the 1945 conference Lawson attacked Smith and argued against such hostility to Labour [*Common Wealth Review*, May 1945].

West Harrow, 1945: electorate 73 174, turnout 78.4 per cent

N. A. H. Bower (Conservative)	28 617 (49.9 per cent)
Mrs B. J. K. Thompson (Labour)	18 961 (33.0 per cent)
Sir H. W. Young (Liberal)	7 364 (12.8 per cent)
H. M. Lawson (Common Wealth)	2 462 (4.3 per cent)
Majority	9 656 (16.9 per cent)

Lawson's commitment to Common Wealth, and in particular to Acland, remained pronounced even after Labour's success in the general election. On 3 August 1945, in a letter to Acland, Lawson expressed his trust in Acland's capacity for leadership: 'I know you are a prophet, Richard, and even if my senses told me that you were leading us into the wilderness or over the cliff I would still gladly follow' [Hilson and Melling (2000) 164]. Acland was clearly an immense figure in the party and Lawson, among others, was attracted to his messianic zeal. Orwell also recognised Acland's ability for leadership and felt that he had 'the single-mindedness of a dictator, but not the vulgarity, perhaps not even the toughness' [Orwell in Davison (1998) 105].

With the landslide victory of Labour, Common Wealth suffered a membership haemorrhage. In August 1945 Acland advised the Executive Committee to press for the dissolution of the party and for Common Wealth members to join Labour immediately:

If we go on, even for as little as six months, we will not continue to be an organisation of the same quality as we have been before. Inevitable forces will very quickly turn us into a small and rather bitter sectarian group, mercifully opposed to the Labour Party as a whole, and snarling and yapping about its heels. The existence of such a group will not accelerate the initiative of the good Socialists within the Labour Party. It will retard and thwart it [Common Wealth Memorandum, August 1945, Acland Papers, 471/5].

In September, Lawson and his wife sent a letter of resignation to the Skipton Branch. This move was based on Acland's decision to leave and join Labour, after which the party had voted by 119 votes to 89 to continue as a separate organisation under C. A. Smith. Lawson remained an important figure in the civic life of Nottingham. In 1948 he was appointed deputy chief engineer and surveyor for the council, a post in which he remained for 25 years. In 1950 he again attempted to enter Parliament, but was defeated in Nottingham Rushcliffe. A further campaign in Kings Lynn in 1955 ended his political ambitions.

Nottingham Rushcliffe, 1950: electorate 60 868, turnout 87.8 per cent

M. Redmayne (Conservative)	27 497 (51.5 per cent)
H. M. Lawson (Labour)	20 860 (39.0 per cent)
Mrs E. F. Stallabrass (Liberal)	5 065 (9.5 per cent)
Majority	6 637 (12.5 per cent)

King's Lynn, 1955: electorate 51 867, turnout 78.2 per cent

R. Scott-Miller (Conservative)	20 949 (51.6 per cent)
H. M. Lawson (Labour)	19 611 (48.4 per cent)
Majority	1 338 (3.2 per cent)

Lawson retained his commitment to Methodism, but in later years he and his wife were drawn to the Quakers and joined the Religious Society of Friends. His work for Nottingham Council included a major development plan that led to an extensive road-building scheme. Showing an early concern for environmental issues, he was responsible for the construction of an incinerator that utilised the heat generated to supply warmth to local houses and shops. With the reorganisation of local government in 1973, he was appointed director of leisure services. He retired in 1976 after almost 40 years of service with Nottingham City Council.

Lawson represented a radical tradition that led him from Methodist activism to a short parliamentary career as a left-wing socialist. He was typical of the kind of individual that the Common Wealth party attracted: a grounding in Christian ethics, a military background and a belief in a socialism that transcended social class and industrial politics. His most important contributions as an MP came when he supported the introduction of Child Benefit and worked hard to ensure that it was paid direct to the mother. Lawson was also very close to his constituents. He introduced the idea of weekly surgeries so that constituents would have maximum contact with their MP. In later life his politics underwent a shift to the right and he eventually joined the Social Democratic Party. This organisation also tried to forge a path between the politics of Labour and the Conservatives, seeking to attract a constituency similar to that canvassed by Common Wealth 40 years earlier. His life did not revolve solely around politics and he enjoyed camping, walking and joinery. He described himself as short, fat and dark, although pictures of him during his electoral campaign in Skipton tell a different story – of a young, smart soldier, keen to build a better Britain based on socialist principles. Dorothy Lawson died in 1982, and Hugh Lawson died on 23 March 1997, leaving an estate valued at £331 053.

Writings: Lawson wrote numerous articles in forces publications such as *The Rock*. He also regularly contributed to *Tribune* and *Common Wealth Review*.

Sources: **(1) MSS:** The Hugh Lawson Papers are held in the University of Sussex Library and form part of the Common Wealth Collection Boxes 9–13; Richard Acland Papers, University of Sussex; Mass Observation Archive, University of Sussex. **(2) Newspapers and Periodicals:** *Manchester Guardian*; *Daily Worker*; *Bradford Observer*; *Yorkshire Post*; *Yorkshire Observer*; *Daily Herald*; *Daily Mail*; *Daily Mirror*; *Common Wealth Review*; *Common Wealth Year Book*; *World News and Views*; *Hansard*, 1942–45. **(3) Other:** Richard Acland, *Unser Kampf* (1940) Robin Page Arnot, *What is Common Wealth?* (1943); Angus Calder, *The People's War: Britain 1939–45* (1969); Peggy Duff, *Left, Left, Left: A Personal Account of Six Protest Campaigns 1945–65* (1971); D. L. Prynn, 'Common Wealth – A British Third Party of the 1940s', *Journal of Contemporary History*, 7: 1–2 (1972) 169–79; Chris Cook and John Ramsden (eds), *By-Elections in British Politics* (1973); M. Stenton and S. Lees, *Who's Who of British Members of Parliament Vol. 3 1919–1945* (Sussex, 1979); Bill Davidson, 'The Cairo Forces Parliament', *Labour History Review*, 55: 3 (1990) 20–6; Paul Addison, *The Road to 1945: British Politics and the Second World War* (1994); Tony Benn, *Years of Hope: Diaries, Letters and Papers 1940–62* (1994); Kevin Jefferys, *War and Reform: British politics during the Second World War* (Manchester, 1994); John Callaghan, 'Common Wealth and the Communist Party and the 1945 General Election', *Contemporary Record: Journal of Contemporary History*, 9: 1 (1995) 62–79; Peter Davison (ed.), *The Complete Works of George Orwell Vol. 12: A Patriot After All 1940–41* (1998); Peter Davison (ed.), *The Complete Works of George Orwell Vol. 15: Two Wasted Years 1943* (1998); Peter Davison (ed.), *The Complete Works of George Orwell Vol. 16: I have Tried to Tell the Truth 1943–44* (1998); Mary Hilson and Joseph Melling, 'Public Gifts and Political Identities: Sir Richard Acland, Common Wealth, and the Moral Politics of Land Ownership in the 1940s', *Twentieth Century British History*, 11: 2 (2000), 156–82; *Who's Who*, 1991. **(4) Obituary:** *Independent*, 21 May 1997.

KEITH GILDART

See also: †W. J. BROWN; R. W. G. MACKAY; †Tom WINTRINGHAM.

LENO, John Bedford (1826–94)
CHARTIST, RADICAL, POET

John Bedford Leno was born on 29 June 1826 in humble circumstances at Bells Yard, Uxbridge in Middlesex, the eldest son of John and Phoebe Leno (née Bedford). At the time of his birth Leno's parents were in service: his father was a footman to a local landowner; his mother had been a lady's maid and she still undertook needlework. After a fruitful period of tuition at a dame school run by his mother, Leno's formal education was brief. Aged eight, he started at a preparatory school but was soon expelled, ostensibly for absenteeism. The real reason for this punishment, Leno felt, was social class: coming from a poor background, his presence lowered the tone of the school. He was then sent to the national school, but again made little headway and had to leave when his father lost his job. Thus by his twelfth birthday Leno had begun to earn his own living in a series of demanding jobs – cow minder, firework maker, rope spinner and rural postboy – all of which were poorly paid. However he soon discovered his talents as an actor, singer and poet, and supplemented his meagre income by entertaining fellow workers with songs and impromptu recitations.

In early 1839 Leno's artistic talents impressed a local printer and stationer, who engaged him as an apprentice printer for seven years. As a journeyman, Leno found the company of and conversations with fellow apprentices very stimulating, but fell particularly, under the spell of Henry Kingsbury, a free trader, and Fred Farrell, a Chartist. Like them he became a life-long autodidact in the best tradition of the thinking and self-improving artisan. He also retained a great zest for life's pleasures. He had an attractive personality, which made him a firm favourite among fellow social drinkers, singers and snuff-takers in the Uxbridge taverns of the late 1840s. An expert gambler, he earned his beer money in his apprenticeship days from winnings at card and dice games in the Falcon public house, where he also operated as a master of ceremonies. At other times he sang at local 'free and easy' evenings in local taverns, including one where his father became a publican. Leno's outgoing nature is further underlined by his enthusiasm for the game of cricket and his membership in adult life of the Clown Lodge of Royal Antediluvian Order of Buffaloes.

At the earliest opportunity Leno, like his brother Frederick, joined the Chartist movement, becoming secretary to the Uxbridge branch of the National Charter Association and helping with the establishment of a new branch in the nearby royal town of Windsor. Within days of the end of his apprenticeship in 1846, his master was made bankrupt and Leno was forced to move on. He found work briefly in Windsor and then at Eton, where he was employed in the college's printing office for approximately 12 months. Towards the end of 1847 he was forced to leave because of his Chartist activities in the workplace. He next tried to find work by moving to London in 1848, taking with him his new wife Sarah (née Thrift), who was ten years older than himself and the daughter of a small farmer in Harefield. The Lenos found life hard going in the capital; they barely had enough money to rent a few unfurnished rooms and had to sleep on the floor. Although he did not participate in the Chartist mass demonstration on Kennington Common on 10 April 1848, six weeks later he was beaten by a policeman for standing his ground whilst discussing the Irish question at a mass meeting on Clerkenwell Green.

Faced with even bleaker economic prospects, Leno decided to look for work further afield and became a tramping artisan. His wife returned to Uxbridge to live with relatives. He tramped over 1000 miles, first through the Midlands and then in Kent, picking up a little work here and there, and often living literally hand to mouth. In early 1849 he returned to Uxbridge where, pressed by friends, he organised a very successful one-man benefit concert at the town hall. Supplemented by donations from his old Eton workmates, Leno made £40, which allowed him to set up his own small printing press and office in a chair-maker's workshop in Windsor Street. With a few friends from the Young Men's Improvement Society in Uxbridge and aided by his wife in the print shop, he started a small political magazine, *The Uxbridge Pioneer*, in February 1849. This was the offshoot of an earlier manuscript newspaper, *The Attempt* (1846), of which he had been both a founder and a joint editor. The first number of the *Pioneer* had hardly been printed before a split occurred amongst its producers. Leno, together with fellow Chartist and poet Gerald Massey, eschewed the *Pioneer*'s moderation and in April 1849 published the first edition of the *Uxbridge Spirit of Freedom and Working Man's Vindicator*, a Chartist journal known for its militancy and republican slant.

Towards the end of 1850 Leno settled with his wife and young family in London. Gerald Massey, who had left Uxbridge in December 1849, persuaded Leno to join him and other arti-sans in working to help Charles Kingsley's group of Christian socialists to foster cooperative ventures among working men. Leno became the working manager in charge of the Working Printers' Association in John Court, Fleet Street. The work was not always certain and the pay even less so, but Leno, a life-long agnostic, gave valuable service to the Christian socialists over the next three years. Alongside Kingsley, Thomas Hughes and F. D. Maurice, he served on their central board of management, which set up more workers' associations in the building and footwear trades. Leno's first poem – 'A Plea for Cursing' – was published in the Christian social-ists' eponymous weekly journal in November 1850. However misgivings on the part of the journal's editor, J. M. Ludlow, about the degree of realism in the poem prompted Leno to seek a more sympathetic publisher for his first volume of protest verse, *Herne's Oak and other Miscellaneous Poems*, which appeared in 1853. At the same time, by speaking on the Chartist platform, engaging in its committee work, printing Chartist stationery for Ernest Jones and writing poems for the *People's Paper*, Leno established himself as a leading London Chartist for the remaining years of the movement. As a member, too, of Harney's Society of Fraternal Democrats, he supported a new initiative from October 1850: the National Charter and Social

Reform Association, whose purpose was to take the Chartist movement in a socialist direction. This aspiration, however, was met by the policies of Ernest Jones and a revival in the fortunes of the National Charter Association after Jones' release from prison. Leno wholeheartedly supported Jones until the spring of 1858.

Although he stood unsuccessfully for the Chartist Executive in the 1850s, Leno was active on a number of Chartist committees based in London. His areas of involvement included the financial guarantee of Julian Harney's *Friend of the People* (1851), a welcome meeting with Louis Kossuth (1854), protests in Hyde Park against the Sunday Trading Bill (1855), the public funeral of Feargus O' Connor (1855), a reception for the return of John Frost (1856), the 'Propagandists' radical-intellectual circle (1858), agitation against Palmerston's Conspiracy to Murder Bill (1858) and opposition to Louis Napoleon's visit to England (1858), for which Leno personally printed 10 000 copies of a hostile handbill. However by May 1858 Leno had declared against the swelling tide of class collaboration that was leading Ernest Jones into negotiations with bourgeois radicals. With George Wheeler, James Finlen and other left-wing activists, Leno founded the National Political Union for the Obtainment of the People's Charter. They published a short-lived monthly paper, *The National Union*, in which they attacked Jones and his new allies. Its demise in 1860 marked Leno's last formal links with the Chartist movement.

Thanks to two sponsors, the former Chartists T. M. and G. W. Wheeler, who now ran a flourishing insurance agency, Leno had sufficient wherewithal in 1860 to set himself up in business as a master printer and small-scale publisher. He lived first at 56 and then at 132 in the poorer end of Drury Lane. Besides regular printing work for the Wheeler brothers' Friend-in-Need, Life and Sick Assurance Society, he was strategically positioned to respond quickly to the demand for printed material by the nearby theatres of renown. He continued to play a prominent part in the network of advanced radicals and socialists who gathered in the 1860s to debate issues such as the struggle for the vote, trade unionism, internationalism and cooperative activity. They met at such venues as the Cogers' Discussion Hall in Shoe Lane, the John Street Institution and the Windsor Castle tavern in Holborn. In 1861, in a competition organised by George Potter's Progressive Carpenters' Union, he wrote a prize-winning pamphlet, *An Essay on the Nine Hours Movement*, in support of the London building workers' aims, and then in 1863 broadened his campaigning interests on behalf of the trades to include the exploitation of women. The result was another acclaimed pamphlet, *Tracts for Rich and Poor: No 1 Female Labour*.

On the issue of the American Civil War (1861–5), Leno supported the South. Like a small number of ex-Chartists, such as Thomas Dunning and Patrick Matthew, he was not proslavery, but from his perspective as an ultra radical internationalist he was deeply suspicious of strong centralised government and condemned the hypocrisy of middle-class abolitionists who employed 'white working-class slaves' in their factories and yet sought their support in the North's stand against black slavery.

A great deal of Leno's energy in the early 1860s was channelled into editing, printing and publishing ventures. In 1861 Leno's friend Edward Truelove published his *King Labour's Song Book*, in which he portrayed labour as the only legitimate source of all wealth; another collection, *The Poetic Magazine*, appeared in 1863. Both turned out to be successful literary works. Leno was also kept busy with all aspects of the production of *The Westminster News* (1863–4), the first attempt by anybody to establish a local newspaper in that district, and with *St. Crispin's Journal* (1868–75), a shoemakers' trade journal. The press-work experience gained in Westminster helped Leno to campaign vigorously on behalf of John Stuart Mill during the Westminster election of 1865. In 1862 he published *A Memoir of Thomas Martin Wheeler*, a biography of that Chartist leader by William Stevens. Leno became a member of the International Working Men's Association in 1864 and editor of its newspaper, the *Workman's Advocate*, a year later. In this capacity he came to know Karl Marx, who was one of the paper's directors. Leno's prominence in the cause of radical internationalism was further underlined by his friendship with foreign exiles such as A. Herzen and G. Eccarius, cemented through his membership of the National League for the Independence of Poland (1863) and the Garibaldi

Reception Committee (1864). These spheres of activity overlapped with his chairmanship of the Universal League for the Material Elevation of the Industrious Classes (1864–5), a self-improvement group, and involvement in the Working Men's Shakespeare Tercentenary celebrations on Primrose Hill (1864), at which George Howell proposed the idea of the Reform League (1865).

Leno became extremely prominent in all the Reform League's London-based activities: For example, he helped to found new branches in Bloomsbury and Uxbridge; spoke regularly at campaign meetings; became a member of the League's powerful Executive Council; played a prominent role in the successful agitation over the right to public assembly in Hyde Park (1866–7); joined Reform League deputations to lobby government ministers in person; and was an editor of the League's new paper, *The Commonwealth* (1866), formerly the *Workman's Advocate*. Although Leno figured as a very important bridge between late Chartism and the Reform League in the metropolitan reform community, he never identified too closely with its middle-class leaders and policies. His defence of workers' rights, his active consideration of forming a Fenian–Reform League alliance in 1867 if ministers did not concede to working-class demands, and his general hostility to capitalist economics illustrate both the fragility of the mid-Victorian Liberal consensus and the links that existed between Chartism and late-nineteenth-century socialism. Radicals such as Leno were committed to the long-term goal of bringing about a fundamental change in the nature of society. Dedicated to the toilers of all nations, another volume of his poems, *Drury Lane Lyrics*, was published in 1868 in the wake of the Reform League's victory in securing the vote for many urban workers.

Over the next 20 years Leno was extremely active in printing, politics, press work and poetry. As well as maintaining his small printing office, he started to sell second-hand books in nearby Holywell Street, and opened seven shops to sell peat to the London poor as the price of coal had become prohibitive. In politics he declared his support for the new French Republic and joined the Manhood Suffrage League, the programme for which embodied socialist–Chartist traditions of the 1850s. He received in excess of £100 for his labours as an election agent for an old friend, the Radical Liberal George Howell, who stood unsuccessfully in Aylesbury in 1868, and much later for the Liberal candidate John Rickman, who fared likewise in Uxbridge in 1885. By the mid 1870s he was aiding Joseph Arch's fledgling National Union of Agricultural Labourers, the experience of which undoubtedly inspired the next collection of poems, some of which were in local dialect: *Kimburton: A Story of Village Life* (1875). By this point Leno's talents as a poet had been noted by the Hotspur Club, an influential cultural association of middle-class north countrymen working in London in the professions, party politics and the literary world; they invited him to their gatherings to give readings of his poems and sing songs from his extensive repertoire.

Leno's involvement in political journalism continued. He published a radical paper, *The Anti-Tithe Journal* (1881), and for a short while was sub-editor of the Reverand Henry Solly's labour weekly, *Common Good* (1880). By the late 1880s he was a contributor to and supporter of William Morris's *Commonweal*, the journal of the Socialist League, and W. E. Adams' radical paper the *Newcastle Weekly Chronicle*. Leno's versatility as an author was further underlined by the publication in 1874 of his brief history of Temple Bar, London, and of a practical handbook describing the skills needed to produce hand-made boots and shoes. The eighth impression of this technical compendium was still available in 1949. Between 1876 and 1888 Leno certainly had his fair share of life's misfortunes. At work, both his printing and book-selling businesses hit hard times, and in order to survive financially he was forced to sell his proprietorship of *St. Crispin* to the owner of *The Boot and Shoe Trades Journal*. At home, he was faced with the death of his eldest son and then his wife; his own health, too, began to decline.

It was above all as a poet that Leno left his mark on the history of the nineteenth-century labour movement. William Morris, a great admirer, published Leno's protest poems in the columns of his *Commonweal*. Among the best known and most inspirational were 'Herne's Oak', 'Song of the Spade', 'Judge Not a Man', 'Wild Flowers' and 'The Crowded Court'. For these and many others Leno won popular acclaim in Europe and the United States, and he came to be referred to as the 'Burns of Labour' and the 'Poet of the People'. In the space of three years, following the successful publication of an enlarged edition of *Kimburton* (1889), Leno published two poetical works: *The Last Idler* (1889), which depicted the overthrow of capitalism, and *The Aftermath* (1892), in which his unfinished autobiography prefixed the anthologies. Around the same time he also published – for a specifically local audience, and in penny broadside form – *The Bells of Uxbridge*. In 1889, when ill health rendered him unable to work, members of the Hotspur Club raised a subscription for him of £60–£70. The grateful Leno was able to receive from this sum a weekly pension of 10 shillings. This was supplemented in 1893 by Gladstone's decision as prime minister to award him a gratuity of £50 from the Royal Bounty Fund. Between them the two funds kept Leno in relative comfort until his death, at the age of 68, on 31 October 1894 in Uxbridge, where he had retired in 1892. He was buried in the family grave in Uxbridge Cemetery on Monday 5 November before a large gathering of family, friends and admirers from many parts of the country.

At the time of his death Leno had one son, William, living in Australia, and three daughters – Sarah, Sophia and Caroline – all living in London. In his will Leno left each of them a house in St Andrew's Terrace, Hillingdon, and, collectively, the lease on his property in Booksellers Row in London; they also inherited all his copyrights. Leno's personal effects were valued at £162 10s 3d, £50 of which was to be divided between another five beneficiaries. In 1895 a gravestone was erected in Uxbridge Cemetery by members of the Hotspur Club and other friends.

Writings: (1) Books: *Herne's Oak and other miscellaneous poems* (1853); *King Labour's Song Book* (1861); (ed.) *The Poetic Magazine* (1863); *Drury Lane Lyrics, and other poems* (1868); *Kimburton, a story of village life* (1875, repr. 1889); *The Last Idler, and other poems* (1889); *The Art of Boot- and Shoe-making. A practical hand-book* (1892, eighth impression, 1949); *The Aftermath with Autobiography of the Author* (1892, repr. 1986 without the poetry from the original). **(2) Pamphlets:** *An Essay on the Nine Hours' Movement* (1861); *Tracts for Rich and Poor, No. 1 – Female Labour* (1863); J. Bonel (pseudonym), *The History of Temple Bar, the City Golgotha* (1874); *The Bells of Uxbridge* (n.d., c.1890). **(3) Periodicals:** *The Attempt* (1846–53); *The Uxbridge Pioneer* (1849); *The Uxbridge Spirit of Freedom and Working Man's Vindicator* (1849); *The Westminster News* (1863–4); *St. Crispin* (1868–c.1874); *The Anti-Tithe Journal* (1881).

Sources: (1) MS: Minute Books of the Executive of the Reform League (1865–6, George Howell Papers, Bishopsgate Institute, London). **(2) Newspapers and Periodicals:** *The Christian Socialist* (1850–1); *Red Republican* (1850); *Friend of the People* (1851); *People's Paper* (1853–7); *The National Union: a Political and Social Record* (1858); *Bee-Hive* (1863–7); *Workman's Advocate* (1865); *The Commonwealth* (1865–6), particularly 6 October 1866, 'John Bedford Leno'; *The Common Good* (1880); *The Commonweal* (1889–90); *Newcastle Weekly Chronicle* (1888–9), particularly 3 March 1888, 23 February, 23 March, 6 April, 14 December 1889, 5 April 1890 for Leno and the Hotspur Club, 16 November 1889 'Chartist Poets', 23 May 1891 'The Gathering of Contributors', 11 April 1896 (supplement) 'Some Men I Have known' by Robert Applegarth; *Justice*, 12 August 1893, 'John Bedford Leno'; *Guardian*, 22 November 1893, 'Home News'; *Hillingdon Mirror*, 26 September 1967, 'Famous people of the Borough: J. B. Leno'. **(3) Books:** R. G. Gammage, *The History of the Chartist Movement, from its Commencement down to the Present Time* (1854–5, repr. 1969); H. Solly, *These Eighty Years*, vol. 2 (1893); H. B. Bonner, *Charles Bradlaugh. A Record of his Life and Work* (1908); C. E. Raven, *Christian Socialism* (1920); F. Boase, *Modern English Biography*, vol. 6 (1921, repr. 1965); W. H. Brown, *Charles Kingsley. The Works and Influence of Parson Lot* (1924); F. E. Gillespie, *Labor and Politics in England 1850–1867* (1927); A. R. Schoyen, *The Chartist Challenge* (1958); R. Harrison, *Before the Socialists* (1965); F. M. Leventhal, *George Howell and Victorian Working Class Politics* (1971); J. T. Ward, *Chartism* (1973); M. Ashraf (ed.), *Political Verse and Song from Britain and Ireland* (1975); D. Jones, *Chartism and the Chartists* (1975); D. Kynaston, *King*

Labour (1976); M. Ashraf, *Introduction to Working Class Literature in Great Britain, Pt. 1, Poetry* (1978); D. Vincent, *Bread, Knowledge and Freedom. A study of Nineteenth Century Working Class Autobiography* (1981); D. Goodway, *London Chartism 1838–1848* (1982); J. Burnett, D. Vincent and D. Mayall (eds), *The Autobiography of the Working Class. An Annotated Critical Bibliography*, vol. 1 (1984); D. Thompson, *The Chartists* (1984); C. Godfrey, *Chartist Lives* (1987); U. Schwabe, *The Poetry of the Chartist Movement. A Literary and Historical Study* (1987); I. Armstrong, *Victorian Poetry: Poetry, Poetics and Politics* (1993); M. Finn, *After Chartism Class and Nation in English Radical Politics, 1848–1874* (1993); E. and R. Frow (eds), *Radical and Red Poets and Poetry* (1994); J. Breuilly, G. Niedhart and A. Taylor (eds), *The Era of the Reform League: English Labour and Radical Politics, 1857–1872 Documents selected by Gustav Mayer* (1995); J. Newsinger, *Fenianism in Mid-Victorian Britain* (1995); D. Shaw, *Gerald Massey: Chartist, Poet, Radical and Freethinker* (1995); O. Ashton and S. Roberts, *The Victorian Working Class Writer* (1999); O. Ashton, S. Roberts and R. Fyson (eds), *The Chartist Legacy* (1999). **(4) Articles:** E. J. Humphreys, 'An Uxbridge Radical', *Uxbridge Record*, 6 (November 1965) 7–10; S. Coltham, 'Working Class Newspapers in 1867', *Victorian Studies*, 13 (December 1969) 159–180; C. Kett, 'The Uxbridge Spirit of Freedom – 1849', *Uxbridge Record*, 32 (Autumn 1979) 12–13; D. Vincent, 'Love, Death and the Nineteenth Century Working Class', *Social History*, 5:2 (May 1980) 223–47; A. Taylor, ' "Commons-Stealers", "Land-Grabbers" and "Jerry-Builders": Space, Popular Radicalism and the Politics of Public Access in London, 1848–1880', *International Review of Social History*, 40: 3 (December 1995) 383–407. **(5) Theses:** C. Kett, 'John Bedford Leno: A Consideration of One Man's Involvement in various Nineteenth Century Working Class Campaigns and Organisations' (BSc in Government, Politics and Modern History, Brunel, 1980, copy in Central Library, Uxbridge); T. Randall, 'Towards a Cultural Democracy: Chartist Literature, 1837–1860' (D.Phil., University of Sussex, 1994). **(6) Research Notes:** J. Bellamy, J. B. Leno file, 1977–95 (includes biographical information, correspondence with descendants, press cuttings, several pamphlets, copy of Leno's will), Staffordshire University Library Special Collections Unit. **(7) Obituaries:** *The Boot and Shoe Trades Journal*, 17 November 1894; *Justice*, 17 November 1894; *Middlesex and Buckinghamshire Advertiser, Uxbridge, Harrow and Watford Journal*, 17 November 1894; *Newcastle Evening Chronicle*, 2 November 1894; *Newcastle Weekly Chronicle*, 10, 17 November 1894.

OWEN ASHTON

See also: †Robert APPLEGARTH; †Thomas Joseph DUNNING; †George HOWELL; Ernest JONES; †Benjamin LUCRAFT.

MACKAY, Ronald William Gordon ('Kim') (1902–60)
LABOUR MP, COMMON WEALTH PARTY CHAIRMAN, EUROPEAN FEDERALIST

Ronald William Gordon Mackay, commonly known as 'Kim', was born in Bathurst, New South Wales, Australia, on 3 September 1902, the fifth child of Alexander William Gordon Mackay and his wife Mary, née Knight. Both parents came from strongly Methodist families. His father was the Irish-born governor of Bathurst gaol and his mother was the Tonga-born daughter of J. E. Moulton, a Methodist missionary in the South Pacific. After showing early educational promise, Kim Mackay attended Sydney Grammar School in 1915–19 and later the University of Sydney, where he gained his LLB in 1926 and an MA hon. in education in 1929. He was admitted to the Supreme Court of New South Wales in 1926 and worked as a member of the Sydney law firm Sly and Russell. He married Mary Barker Hassall on 21 February 1928 at the chapel of St Paul's College, University of Sydney; the marriage produced two children but ended in divorce. While completing his education, Mackay founded the *New Outlook*, a fortnightly publication of politics and economics. He wrote articles attacking, amongst other things, militarism and the Versailles Treaty.

Mackay seemed set for an academic career when he gained a part-time post as a lecturer in history at St Paul's College (1926–32). While he continued to practice law, his greater interest was in the field of economics and he developed a keen mind for business and an acute sense of the problems of political economy. He steadily built up a publication profile, beginning with *The Industrial Arbitration Act of the Commonwealth of Australia* (1928) and *Some Aspects of Primary and Secondary Education* (1929). In 1932 he helped to establish the Australian Institute of Political Science (AIPS), through which body he argued for reform of the Australian constitution. The AIPS held numerous summer schools and founded the journal *Australian Quarterly*. Mackay became an active figure in the Australian labour movement, and on a business trip to Britain he formed lasting links with a number of British labour activists. He was particularly close to Sir Stafford Cripps and other figures on the Labour left. After some persuasion by Cripps, Mackay moved to England in 1934, establishing a reputation as a practising lawyer and socialist. He was part of a thriving law firm operating under the name of Oppenheimer, Vandyk and Mackay. Before his permanent move to Britain, Mackay had been a regular visitor. He made contacts with the Frome Divisional Labour Party through Cripps and financially contributed to their funds. With the support of Cripps he was selected as the divisional party's parliamentary candidate in 1933. However, as he was still not a permanent resident in Britain, the Labour Party NEC refused to endorse his candidacy. A year later, the NEC shifted its position as Mackay had now settled permanently and he was duly endorsed as the prospective Labour candidate for Frome [Frome Divisional Labour Party Records 1933–4, microfilm 97561, NMLH].

Mackay's organisational ability was recognised by party notables when he successfully developed a very active and efficient Labour machine in the constituency. Frome had been a Labour seat in the 1920s, but electoral defeats had caused the local movement to become increasingly demoralised. Mackay was selected to fight the seat for the party in the 1935 general election. He campaigned for a strong League of Nations and an end to conflict between states. He criticised both left and right for facilitating the rise of fascism and for the ineffectiveness of the League. His goal was the creation of a world government based on the principles of the League, which would act as its protective force. He pointed out at numerous meetings the failure of the British government to support the League with any real commitment, thereby facilitating the drift towards war in Europe [*Somerset Standard*, 25 October 1935]. He fought the election on a socialist programme calling for common ownership of key industries, land and the productive resources of the country. The local press appealed for voters to support the government by voting for Mavis Tate, the National Conservative candidate. An editorial in the *Somerset Standard* claimed that Mackay was an

extremist ... he is the terror and despair of even the fastest shorthand writer. But that he is an extremist is proved, not only by his own political utterances, but by the fact that his political debut in England was made under Sir Stafford Cripps, of whom many members of his own party are distinctly afraid [*Somerset Standard*, 8 November 1935].

Mackay's use of socialist rhetoric was typical of many Labour candidates in 1935. While he insisted that the Labour Party would abolish capitalism, he was a critic of the Soviet Union and the politics of the Communist Party. His campaign was weakened in the final week of the contest when he was struck down with gastric influenza.

Frome, 1935: electorate 51 582, turnout 82.5 per cent

Mrs M. C. Tate (Conservative)	19 684 (46.3 per cent)
R. W. G. Mackay (Labour)	18 690 (43.9 per cent)
P. W. Hopkins (Liberal)	4177 (9.8 per cent)
Majority	994 (2.4 per cent)

In the late 1930s Mackay became disillusioned with the timidity of the Labour Party and the electoral truce that was agreed at the outbreak of war. He remained close to Cripps, who had been expelled from the party in 1939 for advocating a popular front. He kept close council with others in the Labour Party through his work as a member of the Advisory Committee of the Fabian Colonial Bureau, which had been established in 1941. With the outbreak of the Second World War Mackay was posted to the Ministry of Aircraft Production. This post took him on a number of trips overseas, including to the United States, where he advocated an increase in war production. This direct role in the war effort led Mackay to criticise the electoral truce and the willingness of Labour to conceal its criticisms of government policy. He resigned from the Labour Party and searched for a left-wing alternative that could harness the popular radicalism that had been generated by concern for a more democratic and egalitarian society. This was deepened by a belief that military setbacks reflected the shortcomings of a traditional elite. But Mackay retained his links with the Labour Party through his active membership of the Clerical and Administrative Workers' Union. He was also busy securing his position in the world of business, taking positions on the boards of a number of large firms.

In 1942 Mackay fought in the Llandaff and Barry by-election as an independent socialist, spending £1200 of his own money. The vacancy was due to the death of Patrick Munro MP and the 1941 Committee had invited Mackay to stand. (The 1941 Committee had started as a discussion group, led by J. B. Priestley. The group subsequently merged with Forward March to form the Common Wealth Party.) The Llandaff and Barry Labour Party also supported Mackay. When explaining to the local press his reasons for resigning from the Labour Party, he argued that the electoral truce must be terminated so that the war could be prosecuted more effectively. He was disappointed that there seemed to be unequal sacrifices for the war effort and called for the conscription of wealth. Most importantly, he argued for a clear statement of peace aims from the national government. Nonetheless there were tensions within the left in respect of his candidacy. At a meeting of the Communist Party in Llandaff, Arthur Horner, the south Wales miners' leader, attacked the presence of independents in by-elections, insisting that all national government candidates must be supported. The Communists felt that unity was paramount to the maintenance of maximum production during hostilities, a position they had adopted when the Soviet Union had entered the war [*Barry Herald*, 22 May 1942]. The Conservatives used the press to highlight Mackay's business associations and distributed a number of leaflets that they hoped would deter Labour voters from supporting such an extravagant candidate. However Mackay had the support of Vernon Bartlett, an independent MP who argued that the electoral truce was in need of reappraisal. Mackay fought an energetic campaign but was unsuccessful:

Llandaff and Barry by-election, 10 June 1942: electorate 82 232, turnout 41.5 per cent

C. H. A. Lakin (Conservative)	19 408 (56.8 per cent)
R. W. G. Mackay (Independent Labour)	13 753 (40.3 per cent)
R. M. R Paton (Independent)	975 (2.9 per cent)
Majority	5655 (16.5 per cent)

During the campaign Mackay aired his ideas on the new Europe that he hoped would emerge when the war was over. In a letter to the prime minister he stated that he stood 'not for a return to a national sovereignty, but for a federation if possible of Western Europe, as a first step towards world peace; the second step is World Federation' [Mackay Papers, 24/23, LSE]. The issue of Europe was to be his main political interest throughout his career. His book *Federal Europe* (1941) was read widely and remains one of the most credible proposals for federation to emerge after the downfall of France. For Mackay, the dilution of sovereignty in the context of a developing federation could facilitate socialism. He set out his beliefs in a letter to the *Manchester Guardian*:

A federation of Europe would abolish the national economic policies of 25 states, and would make it possible to plan production and distribution, and to provide improved standards of living and social security for the European peoples ... if we want peace, extend the territory of organised liberty at the end of the war, by creating, not a league of states with disarmament, but a federation of states, like the United States of America, with plenty of force to preserve order throughout the federation [*Manchester Guardian*, 19 August 1941].

In June 1942 he contributed financially to Tom Driberg's successful campaign in the Maldon by-election. It was in this context of emerging radicalism, expressed through a variety of initiatives, that the Common Wealth Party appeared. Mackay had no doubt been attracted to the 1941 Committee's policy on a federation of European states. Desmond Donnelly, an early supporter of Common Wealth and later a Labour MP, retrospectively viewed the party as a combination of 'leftist militants and middle class do-gooders' [Donnelly interview with Calder, CW papers, 14/113–6]. Mackay probably represented both wings as he was a respected intellectual, independently wealthy, and committed to democratic socialism. Sir Richard Acland was the figurehead of the new organisation, which went on to to enjoy electoral success in Eddisbury, Skipton and Chelmsford. Although Mackay had resigned from the Labour Party because of its stance on the electoral truce, he had never lost his commitment to its democratic socialist ideals. He joined Common Wealth in 1943, and as national chairman he transformed its chaotic organisation. On arrival he found that the office staff were largely incompetent due to lack of training. He immediately developed a reorganisation plan. The first tasks were to streamline the internal structure and transform the party from an idealistic pressure group into an efficient electoral machine. Mackay took control of the office, receiving a lump sum of £500. He wanted a tightly run organisation that could coordinate the activities of the various branches of the party in order to maximise its chances in by-elections when they arose. He introduced a coherent system of thorough door-to-door canvassing and detailed records [Common Wealth Papers, 14/4–10]. This system provided the foundation for what would later be called the 'Reading system', which Mackay developed with Ian Mikardo when they were neighbouring MPs for Reading in the early 1950s.

According to Angus Calder, Mackay had the total support of Acland but was held in suspicion by others in the party. Acland expressed his belief in Mackay's abilities in his diary in April 1943: 'Thank God Mackay has come and I can give up worrying about organisation, and get back to my job of propaganda' [quoted in Calder (1968) 150]. The newspapers often referred to Common Wealth's by-election campaigns as 'Acland's circus', but the resources and planning that went into the party's organisation were essentially down to Mackay. The members of the election team were nicknamed 'Mackay's Trained Seals' and they took their tactics from a pamphlet he produced in 1943: *Common Wealth Election Handbook*. In another publication, *Coupon or Free? Being a Study in Electoral Reform and Representative Government* (1943), Mackay promoted his arguments for proportional representation. Throughout the book he criticised Conservatives, socialists and Liberals for failing to reform the undemocratic structures of the British system of government.

Mackay might have transformed the organisation of the party but he caused tensions in some branches. Those in the London region were critical of his wealth and affluent lifestyle, and felt that he was merely a careerist who was set on gaining a prominent position in the Labour Party after the war. This view was reinforced by Mackay's association with Alan Good, a wealthy businessman who, along with Acland, supplied the party with the bulk of its funds. Good was a director of numerous firms and had amassed a six-figure personal fortune by the age of 35. He was almost solely responsible for bankrolling Mackay's grand plans for the national office, although Mackay himself personally rented the premises he owned in Bloomsbury to the party for a nominal sum [Calder (1968) 57]. Sybil Wingate, a member of Common Wealth's national committee, claimed that the factionalism within the party stemmed from the different directions in which individuals wanted to push the organisation. Mackay was convinced that the overtly

Marxist posturing associated with Joe Thomas of the London region was restricting the organisation's popular appeal. He outlined his reservations about Marxism in a revised edition of
Federal Europe:

> However cogently the Marxist may argue, it is difficult to accept the proposition that a change
> in the economic system must come before a change in the political system. However bad he
> may argue capitalist democracy in Britain is, it is nevertheless a democracy which can be con-
> verted from capitalism to socialism, if the people of Britain desire to convert it [Mackay
> (1941) 68].

Amongst the prominent figures in the party, Mackay was seen as the most efficient. Wingate felt
that others, including Acland and Tom Wintringham, were no match for his superior debating
skills and powers of persuasion, and that while Mackay saw Common Wealth as a vehicle for
socialism, it was only one component of a broad coalition of progressive forces. When it became
clear that Labour was not interested in Common Wealth's affiliation and was likely to be the
dominant left-wing party after the war, Mackay's choice was settled [Calder interview with
Wingate, Common Wealth Papers, 14/263–4]. According to Calder, the three principal figures
in Common Wealth viewed the party differently: Acland saw it as a distinct party; Wintringham
viewed it as an organisation of different classes working together in a popular front; and
Mackay felt that it provided a temporary repository for radicalism while the Labour Party
adhered to the electoral truce [Calder (1968) 2]. The policies that Mackay had promoted in
Common Wealth stayed with him through his years as a Labour MP, notably proportional representation, federalism, devolution and the abolition of the House of Lords.

Despite the factional criticism that Mackay often faced, he was re-elected chairman in 1944.
C. A. Smith, who replaced Mackay after he rejoined the Labour Party, felt that the national
committee harboured a certain resentment towards Mackay's superior organisational and intellectual ability, but remembered him as a sound individual who was always sincere: 'unlike
Acland who was a chronic poseur ... always thinking of his own image ... Mackay was, in my
experience frank and business like, easy to get along with. He was rich, lived well, and had some
unconventional luxuries of the type that aroused envy masked as disapproval' [Calder interview
with Smith, CW Papers, 14/388–9]. The attacks on Mackay were just one symptom of the factionalism that was emerging within Common Wealth, and the party became increasingly weakened by the outpourings of disgruntled members. For example Eric Troward, a former member,
accused the party of being nothing more than a communist organisation. Perhaps more damaging was the perception of fascist involvement in the party. While this allegation is difficult to
substantiate, John Beckett of the British Union of Fascists did join one of the London branches
upon his release from prison [Calder (1968) 193]. Mackay himself came under pressure from
the Christian wing of the party, which felt that he was diluting the moral strand in its programme in favour of electoral opportunism. He had already offered to resign from the chairmanship in November 1943, complaining to friends that he was receiving no loyalty or
cooperation from other members of the national committee, but had been dissuaded from
doing so by Wintringham. It was clear to both Acland and Wintringham that Mackay was
holding the party together through his organisational expertise and commitment to the cause.

The idealism that Mackay initially displayed when he first entered Common Wealth was frustrated when it became clear that the Labour Party was unwilling to agree to amalgamation.
Mackay worked for closer links with the Fabians and then the Communist Party, but the discussions led to nothing. A more successful partnership was worked out with the Independent
Labour Party, which had tried to broker a third way between social democracy and communism
since its break with Labour in 1932. The debate on closer links with the Labour Party caused
Mackay gradually to distance himself from Common Wealth. In October 1944 he attacked the
anti-affiliationists and argued that 'Hugh Dalton, Herbert Morrison, Jim Griffiths and others
were all better Socialists and more capable leaders than most of the people in Common Wealth'

[Calder (1968) 288]. In an attempt to pave the way for Common Wealth's affiliation to Labour, Mackay arranged a meeting with Sir Stafford Cripps and Ellen Wilkinson in November. However the attempt proved futile as Mackay was told that the only option available to Common Wealth members was to join Labour as individual members. He then worked to convince the more obdurate members of Common Wealth that it was political power that mattered. He grew gradually more impatient with those on the left of the party who wanted autonomy and rapid change in the British political system. In the *Common Wealth Review* he argued that:

> Democratic politics was a slow process. The alternative was revolution. In democracy you had to learn to suffer fools gladly ... you have first to convince the country before you introduce changes. ... Don't slate the Labour leaders and say they're all a bad lot ... surely our job was to bring more democracy into the Labour Party and help to make it clearly socialist [*Common Wealth Review*, 1, 9, November 1944].

Mackay wanted a career in politics and argued at successive Common Wealth conferences for closer ties with Labour. On numerous occasions he stated that the party only existed because the Labour Party was not providing effective opposition to the government. Nonetheless until his resignation in January 1945 he worked hard for the party by producing propaganda and refining the ability of head office to organise electoral campaigns. He envisaged a broad coalition of left-wing forces that would come together to ensure that the Conservative Party was seriously weakened by the end of the war:

> The Tories must go! And let the forces of the left, the Labour Party, the ILP, the Communists and Common Wealth, and any other socialists that there are, come together by affiliation or otherwise, and create a united socialist movement which, when the war is over will secure a socialist House of Commons and a socialist peace [News sheet of Merseyside Region of Common Wealth, Common Wealth Papers, 4/114].

The party showed no hard feelings towards Mackay when he left, and it continued to occupy Mackay's Gower Street premises free of rent for a year. All his energy was now directed towards ensuring Labour's success in the general election of 1945. He was selected to fight for the seat of North West Hull, which he succeeded in wresting from Sir A. Lambert Ward.

Kingston-Upon-Hull North West, 1945: electorate 37 247, turnout 76.9 per cent

R. W. G. Mackay (Labour)	13 944 (48.7 per cent)
Sir A. L. Ward, Bt (Conservative)	10 450 (36.5 per cent)
H. S. Freemantle (Liberal)	4235 (14.8 per cent)
Majority	3494 (12.2 per cent)

In his maiden speech to the Commons, Mackay called for United Nations control of strategic locations such as the Suez and Panama Canals, and declared that Britain had a role to play in spreading democratic ideals, as opposed to territorial conquest:

> Bigness is not greatness, and we do not rely for our important place in the world today on the fact that we have a lot of territory and a lot of people to control. This is not it at all. It is the contribution in political ideas which this country can make to the world which makes its greatness, and the contribution this country is making is the contribution of showing, that by powerful change, it is possible to secure a real Socialist Government. It is that which other countries in the world are now beginning to realise, and it is that contribution that we are making today [*Hansard*, 7 May 1946, col 878].

Mackay was a very effective parliamentary speaker and used his intellectual ability and oratorical skills to defend the policies of the Labour government. Nonetheless he remained a critic of the government's moderation. In early 1947 he became a member of the Keep Left group – he was a keen advocate of the nationalisation of essential industries and aligned himself with the left on economic issues. His grasp of economics and the fact that he was managing director of a business that employed 3000 workers strengthened his credibility in debates. His sympathies clearly lay with the radical socialist wing of the Labour Party and he supported further nationalisation to deal with the ailing British economy in the late 1940s. However he directed most of his energy into campaigning for his long-term goal of a federal Europe, and pressed his parliamentary colleagues to lobby for a policy of federalism to advance socialist ideals throughout the globe. He felt that European unity would ensure independence from the superpowers and prevent future wars [Schneer (1988) 65]. He broke with Conservative federalists when he realised that they viewed federalisation merely as a tool to suppress the Soviet Union. When he signed the *Keep Left* pamphlet in 1947, he did so from a third-way position, attacking the politics of both the United State and the USSR.

Federalists across Europe had come together in the European Union of Federalists under the leadership of Winston Churchill in 1946. This body was superseded two years later by the European Movement. Much to the dismay of Mackay, the Labour Party was not as enthusiastic about Europe as socialists on the continent. Mackay was elected chairman of the Europe Group of the Parliamentary Labour Party in 1947. Crossman and Foot were also members, and the group contained over 80 members at its peak. Mackay and John Hynd were vice-chairmen and Christopher Shawcross was secretary. They established links with socialists abroad and met with the ILP, which had been arguing for federalism since the war. Divisions soon appeared within the group. The federal issue was a difficult one for British socialists, as Mackay found out when he canvassed MPs on the left of the Labour Party. Some felt that it would weaken the Soviet Union and force Europe into a closer alliance with the United States. Others, such as Tom Braddock, felt that the project would serve to perpetuate capitalism and were reluctant to support any initiative that was promoted by the Conservatives [Braddock to Mackay, 1 April 1948, Mackay Papers, 7/1 LSE]. Indeed the federalist movement in Britain was a cross-party group consisting of socialists, Liberals and Conservatives. Mackay remained determined to promote the European ideal and the issue dominated his political work both inside and outside Parliament. In May 1948 he delivered a lengthy speech on the subject to the Commons:

> Surely, the time has arrived for people in this country and in Europe to realise that democracy in a small area where there are a lot of democracies is an unstable form of government ... there are people who want to buy British textiles and cannot afford to do so. If we had a common currency for Europe we would not have this problem ... A common European currency would remove all problems of foreign exchange, import licences and balance of payments [*Hansard*, 5 May 1948, cols 1288–90].

Throughout 1948 there was a hardening of the divisions within the Labour Europe Group on, amongst other things, the situation in Eastern Europe, particularly the communist coup in Czechoslovakia. The final straw was when Churchill established the Movement for a United Europe. Mackay faced the wrath of the Parliamentary Labour Party when he attended the Interlaken and then the Hague Conference on federation; both meetings were criticised by the party leadership, who felt that Churchill and the Conservatives would dominate the agendas. The Europe Group of Labour MPs dissolved, but Mackay continued to campaign for cross-party support for federalism [Schneer (1988) 66–72].

When a Council of Europe was eventually established it was a toothless body that frustrated the federalists. Mackay wanted to create a federalist structure and to convert the assembly that had been formed by the Council into a legislative body. He again called on old friends such as Alan Good to raise funds for his European project. Mackay himself donated over £1000 and sought 'private Marshall Aid' to ensure that a federal union would stop communist expansion and war [Mackay to Alan Good, 11 May 1949, Mackay Papers, LSE 8/1]. He also felt that Europe needed to provide an alternative to Soviet communism and American capitalism. For Mackay the battle was between communism and social democracy, and this battle could only be won through a formal policy of federation. He outlined his thoughts in a number of speeches during his time in the House.

The prosperity of the United States comes not primarily from her large resources or the intelligence of her population but from her large markets. Europe has comparable resources if the 17 states receiving Marshall Aid were taken as one area and not as 17 independent states ... if there were a common currency for Europe ... trade in Europe would be much freer and would inevitably increase [Draft Speech, Mackay Papers, 7/2 LSE].

In 1949 Mackay was among the British delegates to the European Consultative Assembly in Strasbourg. His commitment to the federal ideal ensured that he was selected as chairman of the European Parliamentary Union. The weakness of the federal movement was that its aims were contested, with only Mackay having few reservations about the policy. The Conservative MP Duncan Sandys felt that the initiative should be primarily directed towards inhibiting the Soviet Union and providing scope for common defence initiatives to prevent communist expansion. Mackay had worked closely with Sandys, and confided in him his frustration with Labour's aversion to the European project. In one letter he told Sandys that 'there was such hostility to Europe in the Labour Party that it was becoming a difficult subject to raise' [Mackay to Sandys, 14 December 1950, Mackay Papers, 9/9 LSE]. He later broke with Sandys when it became clear that the Conservatives were not totally committed to the project and merely viewed it as a strategy to ensure cooperative defence strategies amongst European states. Although Mackay was no fan of the Soviet regime, he did feel that if a federal Europe was to be successful it needed the cooperation of communist countries. He argued that the Soviet Union should be allowed to enter the federation once the country had embraced democratic ideals.

In the House of Commons Mackay became increasingly concerned with this issue, prompting the Conservative MP Peter Macdonald to refer to him as the 'fanatical federalist' [Mackay Press Cuttings File, LSE 9/12]. In 1949 his aims and ambitions for Europe were laid out in his *Western Union in Crisis: Economic Anarchy or Political Union?* (1949). With the intensification of the Cold War, Mackay felt that federalism would provide the best guarantee against future wars. He held the pragmatic view that 'the purpose of federation is to bring together people of diverse types in such a way that they can keep their diversity in matters which are not common to all the peoples, and give it up in matters which are' [Mackay (1949) 84–5]. He became impatient with the Labour Party's suspicion of federalism and argued that it would not be able to deliver socialist policies if it continued to believe that the British economy could withstand the booms and slumps of global capitalism. For Mackay, the improved standard of living that the British were beginning to enjoy could only be maintained if the European states merged their resources and planned their economies according to need.

In 1950 Mackay drafted his plan for Europe, in which he envisaged a strong assembly and committee of ministers. He called for the transfer of power over defence, foreign affairs and currency, which for him was the ultimate aim of federation. He formulated a similar plan for Africa, which was viewed as unworkable by both left and right, although it did gain the support of Fenner Brockway. Rita Hinden felt that Mackay's naivety about African matters did not bode well for his policy of federation. As she pointed out to him in a number of letters, Africa consisted of regions at different stages of development, and many parts of the country had no tradition of democratic politics [Hinden to Mackay, 15 September 1950, Mackay Papers 15/2 LSE]. For all his intellectual training, Mackay's views on world government were seen by some in the labour movement as rather simplistic, but he remained committed to the project and it increasingly dominated his political persona.

Following the redistribution of constituencies in 1950, Mackay became MP for North Reading, where he worked closely with Ian Mikardo. Mikardo later remembered Mackay as a 'left-wing socialist, a technocrat, generous spender and generally a marvellous man' [Calder interview with Mikardo, CW Papers, 14/147–8]. Mackay contested Reading again in 1951 but was defeated.

Reading North, 1950: electorate 39 261, turnout 86.8 per cent

R. W. G. Mackay (Labour)	15 681 (46.0 per cent)
Sir J. S. V. Marling, Bt (Conservative)	15 154 (44.5 per cent)
J. M. Derrick (Liberal)	3238 (9.5 per cent)
Majority	527 (1.5 per cent)

Reading North, 1951: electorate 39 681, turnout 86.8 per cent

F. M. Bennett (Conservative)	17 378 (50.4 per cent)
R. W. G. Mackay (Labour)	17 076 (49.6 per cent)
Majority	302 (0.8 per cent)

Mackay's allies in the labour movement felt that his political career was hindered by his preoccupation with the European issue. His position within the Labour Party was also perhaps weakened by criticisms of his business interests and lifestyle. Above all he put national interests above the party when campaigning for European federation: 'even if it is a capitalist federation, or a federation of capitalist states, it will still provide an organisation which will remove war from Europe' [Mackay (1949) 150]. In 1953 he retired from the political scene due to ill health. He continued to write articles and books and provided a state of the nation address in his pamphlet *Whither Britain* (1953). He still saw federalism as the only solution to Britain's economic problems:

> Today there is no happy future for any small country, either politically or economically; politically because it cannot defend itself without external help – and that applies most of all to Great Britain; economically because a decent living standard means higher real wages, an increase in productivity and raw materials which we cannot provide on our own [Mackay (1953) 41].

He eventually came to the view that the European issue should not have divided the parties and called for statesman-like decisions to guarantee future stability and prosperity. He optimistically felt that the British people would ultimately vote for a federal Europe in a referendum. In an obituary in *The Times*, Lord Boothby later referred to the driving force behind Mackay's political commitment: 'the cause was European unity, under the leadership of Britain: and to it he gave his time, his immense energy, his money, and ultimately – his – life' [*The Times*, 16 January 1960].

Mackay was one of the first generation of European federalists in the Labour Party. His interest in economics and his experiences in Australia and the United States convinced him that a federal system of government would avert future wars by reducing the power of the nation state. His preoccupation with the viability of the European project was seen by some of his contemporaries as naive, but understandable in the context of the prewar rise of fascism and the conflicts between East and West in the post-war period. He enjoyed the good life but was a committed socialist with brilliant organisational skills. As a wealthy individual he was not opposed to people making money, but supported high taxes to finance social services. He appeared prosperous and self-confident, with his silvery grey hair and his ability to talk intellectually and at length on many subjects. His life was largely focused on politics, although he did find time for the odd game of golf and a drink in the Reform Club. A series of heart attacks eventually led to his death on 15 January 1960. He left an estate of £7449 19s 1d. He was survived by his second wife – Dorean Mary, née Armstrong, whom he had married on 15 August 1946 – and his son and daughter from his first marriage.

Writings: Mackay wrote many books, articles and pamphlets, the most important of which are; *The Industrial Arbitration Act of the Commonwealth of Australia* (1928); *Some Aspects of Primary and Secondary Education* (1929); *Federal Europe: the Case for Federation* (1940) Revised edition 1941; *Peace Aims and the New Order* (1941); *Common Wealth Election Handbook* (1943); 'Labour and the General Election', *Town Crier*, 11 December 1943; 'Why not a Socialist Government in 1944?', *Left*, January 1944; *Coupon or Free: A Study in Electoral Reform* (1944); *You Can't Turn the Clock Back* (1948); *Britain in Wonderland* (1948); *Western Union in Crisis* (1949); *Heads in the Sand* (1950); *Whither Britain* (1953); *Towards a United States of Europe* (1961).

Sources: (1) MS: Mackay left an extensive collection of personal papers. His Common Wealth years are covered in the University of Sussex's Common Wealth Collection, which includes periodicals, reports, correspondence and interviews by Angus Calder with numerous members of the party. A large collection of papers relating to Europe, divided into 112 files, is deposited in the library of the London School of Economics. Correspondence between Mackay and L. G. Curtis can be found in the Bodleian Library, Oxford. Letters to Victor Gollancz are held in the Modern Records Centre at the University of Warwick. Letters on federalism to the *Manchester Guardian* newspaper are kept in the John Rylands Library, University of Manchester; Frome Divisional Labour Party Records, 97561/1, National Museum of Labour History Manchester. **(2) Newspapers:** *Somerset Standard* 1935; *Barry Herald*, 1942; *Hull Sentinel*, 1945; *Manchester Guardian*, 1945–50; *The Times*, 1948; *News Chronicle*, 1948; *Sunday Observer*, 1948; *Reading Standard*, 1950–1. **(3) Other:** *Hansard*, 1945–51; Angus L. Calder, 'The Common Wealth Party 1942–45', (unpublished DPhil, University of Sussex, 1968) is an invaluable source of information on the individuals involved with the Common Wealth Party; Peggy Duff, *Left, Left, Left: A Personal Account of six protest campaigns 1945–65* (1971); M. Stenton and S. Lees, *Who's Who of British Members of Parliament Vol. 3 1919–1945* (1979); D. W. Urwin, *Western Europe since 1945: A Short Political History* (1981); Jonathan Schneer, *Labour's Conscience: The Labour Left 1945–51* (1988); *Australian Dictionary of Biography Vol. 15 1940–1980* (Melbourne, 2000); *Who Was Who*, 1951–60. **(4) Obituary:** *The Times*, 16 January 1960.

KEITH GILDART

See also: Hugh LAWSON; †Tom WINTRINGHAM.

MIDDLETON, Lucy Annie (1894–1983)
LABOUR MP AND SOCIALIST PROPOGANDIST

Lucy Annie Middleton was born on 9 May 1894 in Keynsham, the third of the four children of Sidney Cox, a wire drawer, and his wife Ada, née Britten, both of whom came from a rural working-class background. Lucy attended the local elementary school and then won a scholarship to Colston Girls' School in Bristol. She went on to train as a teacher at Bristol University and for ten years worked in a variety of schools in the West Country. At the same time she became increasingly active in local socialist politics and remained committed to the labour movement for the rest of her life. She later claimed in an interview that the hardships endured by her parents to give their children an education, and the loss of young men from her village during the First World War, had made her determined to enter politics to 'make the world a better place ... these were the two things that made me join the Labour Party – poverty and war' [*The News*, 21 July 1978].

Middleton joined the Independent Labour Party (ILP) in 1916 and became secretary of the Keynsham branch. She worked closely with Walter Ayles, a Bristol councillor and conscientious objector, to develop a programme of municipal socialism for the city. She attended the ILP's annual conferences, and in 1924 spoke on disarmament and grants for divisional councils. In the early 1920s she held a variety of posts in local Labour Party organisations, including the vice presidency of the Frome Divisional Labour Party, and travelled all over the West Country making speeches and organising local branches. Despite the tensions and difficulties she encountered, she later looked back on these years as 'among the happiest and most rewarding years of my life' [*Labour Woman*, July 1971]. Her time as a local socialist propagandist seems to have had a formative influence on her attitudes towards labour politics. This is clear in her tribute to the Halifax activist Sara Barker:

> I still believe that really to know the Labour Party one has to start at the bottom and work one's way through service to the ward, the Constituency Party, District and Regional Organisation, gathering all the time knowledge and experience, giving and receiving comradeship at every level, culling understanding and a sense of history [*Labour Woman*, April 1969].

In the mid 1920s Middleton devoted most of her time to the other main interest of her life – the achievement of peace and international understanding. She was appointed secretary of the No More War movement in 1924, a post she held for eight years. She also edited *The New World*, a monthly journal devoted to international and peace issues, and was described as 'the best woman speaker on peace subjects in this country' [Middleton Papers, MID 117 (5), typescript, 1935]. At the same time she took a course in publicity and advertising and qualified as an advertising consultant. She became a member of the Institute of International Affairs and developed a good understanding of economic questions in relation to the needs of developing nations. Her expertise in international and colonial issues was given recognition when she was invited to become a political adviser for the Hindu minority at the Round Table Conference on Indian affairs in 1932, an honour that was not given to any other European.

During the early 1930s the focus of Middleton's activities began to shift. She devoted more of her time to Labour Party politics and, after acting as an assistant election agent on two occasions, stood unsuccessfully as a candidate for Paddington South in 1931 and for Pudsey and Otley in 1935:

Paddington South, 1931: electorate 51 651, turnout 61.4 per cent

E. A. Taylor (Conservative)	27 206 (85.7 per cent)
Miss L. A. Cox (Labour)	4532 (14.3 per cent)

Majority 22 674 (71.4 per cent)

Pudsey and Otley, 1935: electorate 56 245, turnout 76.0 per cent

C. G. Gibson (Conservative)	22 107 (51.7 per cent)
J. C. Smuts (Liberal)	10 682 (25.0 per cent)
Miss L. A. Cox (Labour)	9977 (23.3 per cent)

Majority   11 425 (26.7 per cent)

Middleton gained the support of well-known figures in the labour movement, including George Lansbury, Katharine Bruce Glasier and Margaret Bondfield, who wrote that 'your splendid and loyal work for peace should commend you to all right thinking citizens' [MID 137 (5), Election Leaflet, 1935]. She also became a national propagandist for the Labour Party and it was during this time that she met the party's assistant secretary, James (Jim) Smith Middleton. It is clear from the surviving letters that the couple developed a close relationship as early as 1931, while Jim was still married to his second wife. After his wife's death in 1935 Jim and Lucy were married at Caxton Hall, Westminster on 1 May 1936 in a ceremony witnessed by Lucy's sister Eveline and her close friend Walter Ayles. The couple did not have children and at first there was a difficult relationship between Lucy and her stepdaughter Margaret, Jim's daughter from his second marriage. By 1936, however, they appear to have been reconciled and the letters between them became far more friendly and supportive.

After their marriage the Middletons spent the rest of their lives working for the cause of the Labour Party. Their shared interests and political commitment formed the basis of an extremely close and happy relationship. Jim Middleton claimed that 'everything about us seems to chime. We have the same interests, we share and share in mind and thought, openly and frankly. There is never a jar or misunderstanding' [Bloomfield Typescript, MID/9]. Lucy Middleton continued to seek a career in politics and in 1936 was adopted as a parliamentary candidate for Plymouth Sutton, the seat held by Nancy Astor. When offering her the candidacy the secretary of the local party referred to the need to 'fight the Astor influence, therefore a strong candidate is essential' [MID 51 (13), 3 June 1936]. Apart from the Astors, Middleton faced other difficulties because the constituency was not well organised and lacked energetic leadership. By 1937 this was to change. The propaganda committee was reformed with a new membership, a full-time agent was appointed and Thomas Hendy took over as secretary. He was confident that with time Labour could win in Sutton and that Middleton was the candidate to do it. The two became firm friends and Hendy set about organising regular meetings for Middleton to address, kept her informed of local issues and put considerable energy into gaining new ward members.

Middleton spent as much time as she could in the constituency and finally achieved success in the Labour victory of 1945, joining 20 other Labour women MPs. Her husband, who had retired in 1944, acted as her election agent and gave all the help he could in subsequent years to further her career. In her election manifesto she emphasised the importance of avoiding future wars through an international peace organisation that would deal with 'economic and social, as well as political justice between nations' [election address]. She also focused on a question of considerable local interest – the need for more and better houses, since Plymouth had suffered so badly in the Blitz. This had compounded the housing shortage that had already been apparent in the interwar years. It is hardly surprising, therefore, that the reconstruction of cities after the devastation of war and the development of peace and international understanding became her two main interests as an MP.

Plymouth Sutton, 1945: electorate 41 493, turnout 71.9 per cent

Mrs L. A. Middleton (Labour)	15 417 (51.6 per cent)
L. D. Grand (Conservative)	10 738 (36.0 per cent)
Miss J. A. Gaved (Liberal)	3695 (12.4 per cent)
Majority	4679 (15.6 per cent)

Middleton acted as chairman of the All-Party Committee on War-Damaged Areas and concentrated on helping those who did not get their claims in on time. She had personal reasons for her involvement with bombed areas: her sister, brother-in law and their child had been killed in an air raid, and her closest friend in West Country politics, Tom Hendy, had died when fire watching. Middleton was also a member of the committee set up to examine parliamentary estimates and served on the standing committees for the National Health Bill and the Town and Country Planning Bill, which had considerable importance for Plymouth. When she was criticised by her political opponents during the 1955 election campaign for not speaking up enough in Parliament to urge the government to get on with building more houses, her answer revealed something of her style as an MP and the methods she used to get things done. As chair of the committee looking into war-damaged areas she met with all the relevant ministers and their parliamentary secretaries, but preferred not to raise the issues in the Parliament since baiting ministers could be counterproductive and it was important to ensure that they never said no in public [MID 50/32, notes for a speech].

As an MP Middleton was able to reinforce and extend her international connections. She was particularly keen to 'build a bridge of friendship' with the German people, who, she was convinced, wanted the chance to rebuild their shattered towns and economy on a basis of peace with the rest of the world [MID 50/38, typescript]. During the war she had attempted to maintain links with German émigrés and in 1942 established an International Women's Group, which included two German socialists. After 1945 she became a member of the executive of the British section of the Inter-Parliamentary Union and travelled to several European cities to attend its conferences. In Rome and Stockholm she presented a report on legislation for the welfare of mothers, including family allowances and the protection of women in industry. She also went on two extensive visits to Germany. In 1948–49, at the invitation of socialist women's organisations, she spoke to social democrats in major cities. On this occasion she was accompanied by her husband, but in 1949 went alone on behalf of the Foreign Office to speak to German women in each centre and to contact men and women engaged in social and political work in the Western Zone. In 1950 she formed an all-party women's committee to invite the Bürgermeister of Berlin, Louise Schroeder, to Britain on a state visit, and she acted as the official hostess for the government on this occasion.

Middleton was a conscientious constituency MP, but lost her seat in the general election of 1951 when a combination of boundary changes, a swing to the Conservatives and arguably the absence of a Liberal candidate ensured her defeat. She contested Plymouth Sutton again in 1955, but was unsuccessful:

Plymouth Sutton, 1950: electorate 66 711, turnout 86.4 per cent

Mrs L. A. Middleton (Labour)	27 512 (47.8 per cent)
Hon. J. J. Astor (Conservative)	26 588 (46.1 per cent)
K. H. B. Major (Liberal)	3 541 (6.1 per cent)
Majority	924 (1.7 per cent)

Plymouth Sutton, 1951: electorate 66 894, turnout 85.4 per cent)

Hon. J. J. Astor (Conservative)	28 908 (50.6 per cent)
Mrs L. A. Middleton (Labour)	28 198 (49.4 per cent)
Majority	710 (1.2 per cent)

Plymouth Sutton, 1955: electorate 71 367, turnout 78.9 per cent

Hon. J. J. Astor (Conservative)	30 051 (53.4 per cent)
Mrs L. A. Middleton (Labour)	26 241 (46.6 per cent)
Majority	3810 (6.8 per cent)

This marked the end of Middleton's parliamentary career, but she remained active in labour politics and public life. She travelled throughout the country with her husband, speaking to local labour groups, and they both continued to attend Labour Party annual conferences. Between 1958 and 1968 she was also a director and foundation chairman of War on Want. As her husband's health deteriorated Middleton took time out from her political work to nurse him. He died from heart disease on 18 November 1962.

After her husband's death Middleton immersed herself in a variety of activities connected with the labour movement. At various times she had engaged in journalism; for example in the early 1920s she had written short articles for *Bristol North Forward*, and in the 1940s had published and edited *Labour Candidate*, a journal of the Society of Labour Candidates. Now that she had more time she wrote frequently for *Labour Woman*. The themes of her articles ranged from debates on current political questions such as education, health and social security, to book reviews and biographical sketches of female pioneers. She had always had an interest in the history of the labour movement, believing that a sense of history should inform political practice, and from the late 1960s she helped to found local history groups, corresponded regularly with the editors of the *Dictionary of Labour Biography* and became vice president of the Trade Union, Labour and Cooperative Democratic History Society. She also helped to organise the centenary celebration for James Ramsay MacDonald and helped to arrange an exhibition of Robert Owen memorabilia at Congress House.

Middleton had a long-standing interest in the women pioneers who contributed to socialist and labour politics and inspired future generations to take up the cause. When in 1945 she had been invited by *Labour Woman*, along with the other successful female Labour MPs, to write a message to party workers, the theme of her piece had been the debt they owed to the pioneers who established the Women's Labour League and the tradition of public service. Her later biographical sketches of Labour women continued in the same vein. Writing of Marion Phillips, chief woman officer of the Labour Party in the interwar years, Middleton concluded that Labour women were still carrying on the tradition Phillips had established of 'keen political education, devoted public service and ... courageous exposition of our Socialist beliefs' [*Labour Woman* (January 1969) 6]. Middleton subsequently edited a collection of essays, *Women and the Labour Movement* (1977), which was a celebratory volume on the various ways in which women had contributed to the development of labour politics. It had the official approval of the Prime Minister, Jim Callaghan, who took the opportunity in his foreword to the book to point out that 'throughout its life the Labour Party has been identified with the advancement of women's rights'. He hoped that the book would inspire a new generation of women to become active in labour politics.

The book received mixed reviews. Its emphasis on legislation and formal institutions seemed out of tune with the interests of the feminists of the 1970s and their preoccupation with challenging sexism, consciousness raising and sexual liberation. Its loyalty to the Labour Party and roll of honour of labour women pioneers meant that it lacked a critical edge and a sense of debate. On the other hand it was seen as raising useful questions and drawing attention to the importance of women at a time when they were still neglected in mainstream histories of the socialist and labour movements. In Barbara Castle's view it provided a springboard for the Labour Party to do something more positive to increase the number of women involved in politics, including a stipulation that there should be at least one woman on every shortlist at selection conferences for parliamentary and local government candidates [*Labour Weekly*, July 1977].

The mixed reactions to the book mirrored Middleton's own complex attitudes towards gender issues. In common with many women of her generation she did not emphasise women's rights or seek to challenge gender inequalities in an explicit way. When standing as a candidate in Plymouth against Lady Astor she had claimed that she was fighting 'not as a woman, but as a socialist', and had never wavered from her loyalty to the Labour Party [*Daily Herald*, 25 March 1938]. She had urged women to support the Labour Party because it gave precedence to the home, the mother and the child, and also sought to deal with poverty and war, which were both women's questions. In her 1945 election manifesto she had argued that she would not be satisfied until every 'Plymouth housewife' had a modern, well-equipped home that would free her from drudgery and enable her 'to take her full place as a citizen while efficiently discharging her duties to her family'.

On the other hand she had been keen to encourage women to take a more prominent role in politics and to stand for elected positions at the local and national levels. This view had been shared by her husband who, when thanking his wife for all her help, had argued in his retirement speech that 'we should remember that women are personalities, that they lead their own lives and have their own ideas. There should be many more of our women in the forefront of our movement' [*Labour Woman*, 1 May 1964]. Lucy was proud of her own achievements in the labour movement. She had been asked to be the candidate for Plymouth Sutton just before her marriage and later claimed that 'I felt it would be the last time I would be asked to do anything political in my own recognisance. I was very happy it happened that way, because I was sure it was my own reputation. Not that I wasn't proud of my husband and all that he had done, but I was very glad they invited me when I was Lucy Cox' [*The News*, 1 October 1977]. Her own success, however, tended to cause her to blame women for their own inactivity and she failed to identify structural barriers that prevented more active participation, or suggest ways in which these could be overcome.

Middleton remained active in local labour politics until almost the end of her life. At various times she was chairman and then vice president of the Wimbledon Divisional Labour Party and in her eighties still chaired the Merton Labour Women's Council. She lived to see the opening of the Middleton Room at Labour Party headquarters, and despite suffering from cataracts she, continued to attend meetings until the age of 87. In October 1983 failing health meant that she had to be admitted to Wandle Valley Hospital, Carshalton, where she died on 20 November from a cerebral thrombosis and Parkinson's disease. Her estate was valued at £64 027.

Writings: Middleton contributed numerous articles to newspapers and magazines. She authored one book, *Women in the Labour Movement* (1977).

Sources: (1) MS: Middleton Collection, Ruskin College Library; C. M. Bloomfield, 'James Smith Middleton', typescript, MID/9; Independent Labour Party, Annual Conference Reports. (2) **Newspapers:** *Daily Herald*, 25 March 1938; *Labour Woman*, 1 May 1964, January 1969, April 1969, July 1971; *Labour Weekly*, July 1977; *The News*, 1 October 1977, 21 July 1978.

JUNE HANNAM

MURRAY, John (Seán) (1898–1961)
COMMUNIST PARTY OF IRELAND GENERAL SCRETARY

Seán Murray was born on 15 June 1898 to Patrick Murray, a farmer at Laney, Cushendall, in the predominantly Catholic glens of Antrim, and his wife Mary Ann née Gore; the last of their four children, after Mary Ann, Kate, and Margaret. On 18 June he was baptised in St Mary's Catholic Church in Cushendall. Christened John, he was known as John to his neighbours and used the name on most official documents, but was otherwise called Seán. Murray was educated locally at Glenaan national school, until at 11 years of age he left to work on the family farm. Later he attended evening school in the winter months, and began to study Irish history.

Murray joined Sinn Féin in 1917 and became secretary of the local cumann. In April 1919 he enlisted in the Irish Republican Army (IRA), and was briefly officer commanding the local company. In 1920 he was arrested while on his way to join an IRA flying column, and was interned in Crumlin Road jail, Belfast, and in the Curragh. Following the Anglo-Irish truce in July 1921 he was released and returned home. In March 1922 he attended the convention in Dublin at which the IRA withdrew its allegiance from the pro-Treaty Provisional Government. It was here that he met Peadar O'Donnell and became his closest friend and confidante.

After emigrating to Glasgow in December 1922, Murray worked as a labourer and made his first contact with Communism. He attributed his initial interest in socialism to reading James Connolly. Moving to London in 1924, he became secretary of the London branch of Jim Larkin's Irish Worker League, the Irish affiliate of the Communist International and successor to the first Communist Party of Ireland (CPI, 1921–4). In 1925 he joined the Communist Party of Great Britain (CPGB), and was soon organizer of the CPGB's Islington branch, a member of the party's London District Committee, a delegate of the National Union of Distributive Workers to London Trades' Council, and editor of a Communist rank-and-file paper in the union. During the 1926 General Strike his lodgings were raided by the Special Branch. Through the CPGB he was employed by the All-Russian Co-operative Society Ltd (ARCOS) and, after ARCOS was closed in May 1927, he worked in the London depot of Russian Oil Products.

On 11 December 1927, Murray arrived in Moscow as one of ten CPGB members enrolled in the second intake of the International Lenin School, the Comintern's 'cadre-forge'. While delegated by the CPGB, he was part of the Comintern's design to Bolshevize a corps of Irish comrades who would return home to build a party, as Larkin was ensuring that the Irish Worker League functioned intermittently as nothing more than a personal soap-box. Murray was among the first Irish students to arrive. With a good party record – an advantage denied those delegated by the Irish Worker League – he was also regarded as the most trustworthy, and admitted to the All-Union Communist Party (Bolsheviks) on 20 February 1928. Like all students at the Lenin School, he was obliged to adopt a pseudonym, and took the name 'James Black'. An early school report noted: 'Murray. Worked well and has made progress. Good attitude to party and social work. Still shows confusion on some questions, and should make a bigger effort to understand the fundamentals of Leninism' [RGASPI, International Lenin School report on Murray, 495/218/10–5]. Later he was judged 'very capable, very active', and commended for 'independence of thought', and 'a good grasp of Marxist-Leninist methods' [McLoughlin (1997) 67]. Murray himself claimed to have acquired a working knowledge of Russian. With James Larkin Jr. and four other anglophones, he undertook his *praktikum* in the summer of 1929 in Daghestan, where the group noted the growing food shortages and were shocked by attitudes to women in the predominantly Muslim society. Later they holidayed in Leningrad and the Ukraine. The *praktikum* required students to do administrative work for the departments of the Executive Committee of the Comintern (ECCI). From October 1929, Murray and Larkin Jr. were assigned to a group in the ECCI's Anglo-American secretariat dealing with agrarian problems. They were entitled to attend meetings of the secretariat, which handled ECCI business with all anglophone countries.

As an initial step towards reconstructing an Irish party, a Comintern commission under Tom Bell was activated in Dublin in September 1929. By December Bell was urging the release of Murray and others from Moscow. Students in the Lenin School had been subjected to the general party purge of 1929, and Murray – possibly because of his friendship with Larkin Jr. – was excluded from discussions on Irish policy. However, when Murray and Larkin Jr. returned to Dublin in July 1930, both were entrusted to make the Comintern's first contact with Larkin Sr. since his breach with Moscow in early 1929. Embittered, Larkin refused to back the new initiative, though neither did he tender opposition. Murray commenced full-time party work, and in November 1930 the Communists formed the Revolutionary Workers' Groups (RWG). The next four years were a time of hope and stress, when Communists had some prospect of a major accretion of strength from republicans, and the Catholic church instigated a climate of intolerance that lingered until the 1960s. Within southern Ireland at least, this would be the most successful phase of Communism, and of Murray's career. On Bell's recall in 1931, he was appointed to the secretariat of the RWG. His first notable success was to reissue the weekly *Workers' Voice*. The paper had been suspended from June to September in late 1930, and again in December 1931, due to anti-communist pressure on the printer, financial problems, and government censorship. Publication resumed in April 1932, with Murray as supervisory editor, and circulation reached 2000 in July. By November RWG membership had risen to a peak of some

340 in a dozen groups around the country. Murray also developed the intellectual side of the movement. Irish Communist publications had been confined to newspapers up to 1931, when Workers' Books and, in 1933, Sphinx Publications, issued Marxist studies of Irish history and politics, and offered a catalogue of revolutionary literature by Connolly, Marx, Engels, Lenin, socialist novelists, Bolshevik historians, and anti-fascists, together with thirty or so pamphlets on the Soviet Union. In 1932 the RWG opened Connolly College in Dublin as a workers' study centre. One issue of a theoretical journal, the *Irish Communist*, appeared in September 1934.

In contrast with the two previous Irish leaders of Communism, Roddy Connolly (1920–23) and Larkin (1924–29), Murray proved to be a diligent disciple of Comintern procedures and directives in a time of tortuous tactical fine-tuning. He and Larkin Jr. had returned to Dublin in 1930 with instructions that the 'Class against Class' policy, hitherto restricted to social democrats, should be applied *in extenso*. When the new line alienated republican sympathisers, Moscow rebuked the Irish comrades, and ordered a more fraternal policy towards anti-imperialists. Over the next five years, further modifications of Comintern policy allowed the Communists to edge closer to republicans, to Murray's satisfaction. In September 1931 he was a delegate to the inaugural convention of Saor Éire, an IRA-sponsored socialist movement, and was consulted on its programme. Following the election of a Fianna Fáil government in February 1932 and the start of the 'economic war' with Britain, Murray pleaded for a further revision. In June he argued in Moscow that de Valera was confronting British imperialism and could not be dismissed as 'social fascist'; rather Communists should challenge Fianna Fáil's leadership of the struggle. Accommodating Murray in theory rather than in tactics, the Comintern endorsed a fresh emphasis on anti-imperialism, with the proviso that reformists remained 'social fascist'.

In 1933 Murray yielded to Comintern demands for the transformation of the RWG into a party, despite the heightening anti-communist atmosphere, and a fall in membership to about 250. The second CPI was founded in June at a secret conference in Dublin. Murray was elected general secretary, and his pamphlet, *The Irish Case for Communism*, adopted as the basis of the CPI's manifesto 'Ireland's path to freedom', not without some criticism from those who wanted to prioritize class struggle. The manifesto envisaged the fight for Communism growing out of the national struggle and included the sub-heading 'National liberation leads to social liberation'. Introducing it, Murray remarked that in the past 'we did not see clearly that it was necessary to change the class leadership of the national struggle' [*Irish Workers' Voice*, 17 June 1933]. Hopes of affecting this policy were raised by the Republican Congress, a coalition of some 8000 radicals, launched in 1934 after leftists decamped from the IRA. Fortuitously, Moscow approved a switch from 'united front from below' to 'united front' tactics just before the Congress's inaugural convention, and as a CPI delegate to the convention, Murray declared: 'you cannot smash capitalism until you get rid of British imperialism' [Republican Congress, 13 October 1934]. The Republican Congress promptly split over strategy and sank into rapid decay, ending the CPI's last chance of winning a mass base.

From 1933 to 1935 Communists found it dangerous to hold public meetings in Dublin. In the city's municipal elections of June 1933, Murray finished bottom of the poll with 75 votes, and Larkin Jr., the CPI's only local councillor, lost his seat. In October 1933, Murray was arrested in Belfast and served with an exclusion order from Northern Ireland. When he returned to Belfast the following week he was sentenced to one month's hard labour. Until 1941 he was unable to enter Northern Ireland openly, though he slipped back to Cushendall occasionally to see his family. In 1934 he visited Moscow, and from Russia travelled to the United States, where he attended the national convention of the Communist Party in Cleveland, Ohio, and lectured widely under the auspices of the party, collecting funds to keep the CPI afloat. Murray was again in Moscow in 1935 for the seventh world congress of the Comintern. Supporting the popular front policy, he told the congress that the CPI had committed errors of a sectarian and opportunist nature, and made the mistake of bracketing de Valera in the same camp as the imperialists; now they would try to stimulate opposition to de Valera's vacillation in the struggle against British imperialism. His pamphlet, *The Irish Revolt: 1916 and After*, written for the twentieth anniversary of the Easter Rising, called for 'a united labour movement joined to all that is virile in the national cause'.

The popular front line did not arrest the CPI's decline. The *Workers' Voice* ceased production in June 1936, and was replaced in July with a cheaply produced four page weekly, the *Worker*, which Murray edited and for which he wrote much of the copy. However the Spanish Civil War briefly generated something of a popular front climate on the far left. In October, Murray helped to found a branch of the Left Book Club in Dublin. The *Worker* became the leading anti-Franco publication in Ireland. And Murray, O'Donnell, and Bill Gannon were the main organisers of Irish enlistment in the International Brigades. Murray and Bill's sister, Margaret, were later married in Dublin. In March 1937, the CPI allied with the revived Republican Congress and the Socialist Party (Northern Ireland), replacing the *Worker* with the weekly *Irish Democrat*, until differences with the Socialist Party and financial problems caused the alliance and the paper to fold in December. By now, interest in Spain was abating, the CPI muster had fallen to around 100, and Moscow was calling in the CPGB for rescue work. Describing the party's state as 'catastrophic', the British consultants blamed Murray's leadership and his failure to apply the popular front line. In reality no mainstream political organization in Ireland wished to be associated with Communism. The CPI's latest paper, the *Workers' Republic*, 'a monthly journal of labour and progressive opinion', collapsed in August 1938 after four issues.

The Anglo-Irish Treaty of April 1938, which ended the 'economic war' and transferred naval bases in Éire from British to Irish control, delivered another blow to Murray's standing with Moscow. Whereas Murray denounced the Treaty in *Inprecorr* for ignoring partition, and claimed it entailed a pro-British foreign policy, the Comintern reckoned it would ensure Irish neutrality in the event of an Anglo-German assault on Soviet Russia. In January 1939 the CPI fell in step, and announced its broad support for the Treaty and Fianna Fáil. That same month the Communist Party branch in New York's fifth district was named after Murray in tribute to his 'brilliant courageous leadership'. By contrast, a CPGB report to Moscow in March commended Murray's 'unquestioned devotion', but added that 'he has shown neither political leadership nor organizing ability' and lacked the confidence of the members, especially in Belfast. While recommending his replacement as general secretary, it acknowledged that there was no obvious successor. Murray was dropped from the Comintern's payroll, on which he had held the nominal post of Irish correspondent of the New York *Sunday Worker*, and ceased to be a full-time party worker.

The CPI effected a minor recovery in 1939–40, issuing a readable, and ardently pro-Soviet, little paper, the *Irish Workers' Weekly*, from April 1939. 'Nazis can never be our allies', it declared on 5 August, quoting one of Murray's speeches. On 26 August, it welcomed the Molotov-Ribbentrop pact with the headline, 'Soviet Union's policy strengthens peace'. The party carried on with anti-fascist propaganda until October 1939. With some dissent and a few resignations, the war was then accepted as 'imperialist'. Murray continued to speak against fascism on occasion, and condemned an IRA statement welcoming German aid. Though much used as a lecturer and speaker at regular street meetings in Dublin, Murray's status was evidently diminished. He was not mentioned in a history of party newspapers in the *Workers' Weekly* in 1940. In March 1941 the *Workers' Weekly* announced that Tommy Watters had become party general secretary with no acknowledgement of Murray. Wartime circumstances were placing a severe strain on the CPI. The Comintern noted in December 1940 that its only knowledge of the CPI came from articles by Murray in *Inprecorr* and the *Sunday Worker*. The Irish government interned about a dozen Communists in 1940, and the Northern government arrested leading Communists and suppressed the *Workers' Weekly*. In the spring of 1941, the Belfast branch considered dissolution. The Nazi invasion of the Soviet Union plunged the southern CPI deeper into crisis, but rescued the northern wing. On 10 July 1941, under pressure from the CPGB, eleven of the twenty members in the Dublin branch, the only unit south of the border, voted to 'suspend' party activity in Éire. Covertly, southern Communists were to enter the Labour Party to work for a Labour-Fianna Fáil coalition that would bring Ireland into the war. The intent was to avoid public confrontation with the state's near universally popular neutrality, and propagate a pro-war policy in Northern Ireland.

Now in favour with Stormont, the Communist Party, Northern Ireland (CPNI), as it eventually came to be called, got Murray's exclusion order lifted on 8 October 1941 with the aid of Independent Labour MP Jack Beattie. Murray moved to Belfast to work as a labourer on building sites, and later in Harland and Wolff's shipyard. The CPNI's absolute commitment to the war effort, coupled with the phenomenal enthusiasm for things Soviet, caused membership to mushroom to 1000 by 1943. As editor of the party's organ *Unity* (1942–6), Murray endorsed its pro-war, pro-Stormont policy. In a public lecture in Dublin in 1943, he offered some gentle criticism of Irish neutrality. He was not well regarded within the CPNI's wartime leadership. His republican past was out of line with its increasingly partitionist stance. Some wrote him off as 'deadwood' for his record in the late 1930s, or frowned on his drinking habits. Conversely, others deplored the neglect of his talents. O'Donnell, who thought him too unassuming, was incensed that he was not given a full-time job by the party.

During the war the Murrays lived with Michael McInerney, the CPNI's full-time industrial organizer, and his family at 260 Limestone Road, in the house of a party member in the Royal Air Force. Afterwards they obtained a house at 32 Lincoln Avenue, which was to be his final address. On his father's death at an advanced age in the 1950s, Murray rented out the farm, keeping the farmhouse for his own occasional use. He remained friendly with relatives and neighbours from the glens, and was sensitive to rural social snobbery; telling one party comrade not to mention in such company that he worked as a labourer, and to order bottles of stout, not pints of porter.

In the mid 1940s, Murray attempted to extend himself as a writer. O'Donnell frequently commissioned him to ghost write editorials for the *Bell*, a radical liberal magazine of literature and social comment, paying him five guineas a time. Murray also submitted a story on rural life to the BBC in Belfast, and tried to get articles into the *Irish Times* through Michael McInerney, who joined the paper in 1946. One at least was published under the name 'John Gore Murray'. His party journalism continued as Belfast correspondent of the *Daily Worker*, and contributor to the *Irish Review*, the *Irish Socialist Review*, the *Irish Workers' Voice*, and the *Northern Worker*. O'Donnell said of his style: 'He would write only on the current, concrete situation, and write brilliantly, but he had a strange reluctance to reveal or uncover his mind except in conversation'.

Membership of the CPNI had begun to fall sharply in 1944, and had withered to 172 by 1949. A purge of the party leadership in 1946 facilitated Murray's political recovery, and for the rest of his life he served as party chairman, secretary, and finally chairman again. In 1950 he was appointed CPNI national organiser, a position he held until his death. He was also a member of the first Irish delegations to international Communist conventions since 1935; attending a conference in Moscow to mark the fortieth anniversary of the Bolshevik revolution in 1957, the twenty-first congress of the Communist Party of the Soviet Union in 1959, and the world congress of Communist and workers' parties in Moscow in 1960, where he responded to differences between the Soviets and Chinese by issuing a statement on behalf of the Irish delegates in support of the former.

Under Murray's leadership, CPNI policy inched towards anti-partitionism. His private papers reveal his republicanism, but he moved slowly in deference to party opinion and the party's electoral constituency. In the 1949 general election, the CPNI's 'Facts for speakers and canvassers' advised that a socialist Northern Ireland was the safest way to maintain the link with socialist Britain. Murray's strategy was to build a practical unity among communists initially. In 1952 he helped to create a joint council of the CPNI and the Irish Workers' League (founded by communists in Éire in 1948 and renamed the Irish Workers' Party in 1962), with a view to the adoption of common policies and discussion on the promotion of Irish unity. His last significant contribution was to draft the CPNI programme, 'The Irish way to socialism', in 1958. Not without controversy, the programme argued for the primacy of the struggle for socialism, with national unity coming afterwards. In 1962 'The Irish way to socialism' – much revised and extended after discussion with the CPGB and its Irish expert, Desmond Greaves – was formally adopted by the CPNI and published as *Ireland's Path to Socialism*. Simultaneously, the Irish Workers' Party published its programme *Ireland Her Own*. The northern and southern parties merged in 1970 as the third CPI. Murray took ill in March 1961, and died in the Royal Victoria Hospital, Belfast. He was survived by his wife Margaret. They had no children. On 30 May he was taken from the Belfast Co-operative Society rest rooms on the Shankill Road for burial in Dundonald cemetery (plot B5). The headstone read: 'Seán Murray, Republican, Socialist, Foundation Member, Communist Party, Born 15 June 1898, Died 25 May 1961, Remembered by his wife, Comrades and friends'. Some 300 people from all sections of the labour movement, with representatives of various communist parties, attended the funeral, at which there were renditions of Connolly's 'Rebel song', 'The blue hills of Antrim', and the 'Internationale'. In 1963 Willie Gallacher unveiled a memorial stone over the grave.

Murray had his critics, but the assessment of Peadar O'Donnell, one of twentieth century Ireland's greatest agitators, deserves respect:

His greatest strength was a vast reservoir of ideas and an enlightened sanity in the most dreadful situations ... a great Fenian ... His strongest conviction was that the working class must lead the struggle for freedom ... he had the wonderful gift of convincing everyone, particularly young people and women, that they had something especially important to contribute to the working class movement. [McInerney (1974) 97–9].

Writings: No bibliography exists of Murray's extensive writing for newspapers and journals. His published pamphlets were: *The Irish Case for Communism* (RWG, Dublin, 1933); *Ireland's Path to Freedom* (Sphinx Publications, Dublin and *Labour Monthly*, London, 1933); *Ireland's Fight for Freedom and the Irish in the USA* (Workers' Library Publishers, New York, 1934); *The Irish Revolt: 1916 and After* (CPI, Dublin, 1936).

Sources: (1) MSS: Seán Murray papers, Public Record Office of Northern Ireland, Belfast; University College, Dublin Archives, Seán MacEntee papers, 'Notes on Communism in Saorstát Éireann (supplement)', P67/528; Russian State Archive for Social and Political History (Rossiiskii Gosudartsvennyi Arkhiv Sotsial'no-Politicheskoi Istorii, RGASPI), Seán Murray, cadre file, 11 August 1932, 495/218/1; International Lenin School report on Murray, 495/218/10–5. **(2) Other:** Republican Congress, 1934; Michael McInerney, *Peadar O'Donnell: Irish Social Rebel* (Dublin, 1974); Mike Milotte, *Communism in Modern Ireland: The Pursuit of the Workers' Republic Since 1916* (Dublin, 1984); Barry McLoughlin, 'Proletarian academics or party functionaries? Irish communists at the International Lenin School, Moscow, 1927–37', *Saothar*, 22 (1997) 63–79; Stephen Bowler, 'Seán Murray, 1898–1961, and the pursuit of Stalinism in one country', *Saothar*, 18 (1999) 41–53; Interviews with Andrew Boyd and Joe Deasy.

EMMET O'CONNOR

READE, Arthur Essex Edgeworth (1902–71)
COMMUNIST, TROTSKYIST, LABOUR PARTY CANDIDATE, NATIONAL LABOUR ACTIVIST

Arthur Reade was born at 24 Bolton Street, Piccadilly, London, on 22 January 1902. His father, Essex Reade – an international banker of independent means – came from an Anglo-Irish background and had strong professional connections with Latin America. Reade's mother, Sheelah Chichester, was a granddaughter of the Earl of Galloway. Reade's early life was spent in London and at two summer residences: Wrotham Rectory in Kent and a house near

Shillingstone in Dorset. After his father's death in 1908 he travelled in Europe with his mother and sometimes stayed with his aunts in Suffolk. He attended Gibbs Preparatory School in Sloane Street, London, and Stonehouse Preparatory School in Broadstairs, Kent. In 1915, when he was 13 years old, he was sent to Eton, where at the end of the war he encountered 'the queer revolutionary feeling of the time' recorded by his contemporary, George Orwell, who remembered 'it was all the fashion to be a Bolshie as people then called it'. He experienced a range of socialist ideas through the radical Eton Political Society, fostered by the young Earl De La Warr [Orwell (1937) 129–30; Smith (1969) 137–9].

Reade's subsequent studies at the University of Strasbourg in 1919–20 brought him into contact with the revolutionary unrest that had swept through Germany to Alsace-Lorraine. At that time he took his first steps in journalism with articles for the *Daily Mail*. On his return to London, attendance at labour movement meetings reinforced his growing commitment to the left, and when he went up to Worcester College, Oxford, in October 1920 to study history he already regarded himself as a socialist. With the zeal of the neophyte, he was soon playing a prominent part in the University Labour Club and the smaller, more radical Socialist Society. By January 1921 he was editor of a journal, *The New Oxford*, which was associated with the Labour Club. He was also moving from adherence to the Independent Labour Party (ILP) towards identification with direct action and the politics of the infant Communist Party of Great Britain (CPGB).

Reade was always a rebel. His new allegiance was sustained by the intense social conflicts in Britain after the cataclysm of 1914–18, by the extremes of affluence and oppression he witnessed in London and Suffolk, by the romance of the Russian Revolution and by his fierce opposition to Britain's role in Ireland. He was influenced by the Communists he met through the University Socialist Federation (USF), which had come under the control of the CPGB through the efforts of Rajani and Clemens Palme Dutt and of Mary Moorhouse – former Guild Socialist, friend of Ellen Wilkinson and Comintern courier. He was particularly close to Charles Gray, the brilliantly precocious secretary of the Oxford Socialist Society who was studying history at Balliol and who had been influenced by his predecessor as Brackenbury Scholar at the college, the young Communist Andrew Rothstein. Reade also worked with two Cambridge undergraduates and lifelong members of the CPGB: Allen Hutt and Maurice Dobb, to whose journal, *Youth*, he contributed a regular 'Oxford Letter'.

Black Friday (15 April 1921, when the leaders of the railway and transport unions retreated from industrial action in support of their partners in the Triple Alliance – the locked-out miners) was a key event in Reade's conversion to Communism. Without consulting his comrades in the Labour Club, he put together an issue of *The New Oxford* that in rich invective attacked the trade union and Labour Party leaders for their role in Black Friday and asserted that Communism offered the only viable future for British workers. In the consequent furore Reade resigned the editorship and proclaimed his intention to produce a Communist journal for students that would completely eclipse *The New Oxford*.

The Free Oxford burst like a firecracker over the university in the long, hot summer of 1921. Reade's rustication for failing his exams simply provided him with more time to devote to the journal. Its six issues, which ran into 1922, took up university matters and scathingly criticised the administration of the vice-chancellor, Lewis Richard Farnell, an unbending Victorian who had been in Oxford since the 1870s, latterly as Rector of Exeter College. There were poems and criticism from the future CPGB member Edgell Rickword, the Queens College student and published novelist Louis Golding, and the future novelists and short story writers Richard Hughes and A. E Coppard. The political coverage was largely 'party line', with contributions from two ornaments of the Communist International – Karl Radek and Eugen Varga – and the leader of the Red International of Trade Unions, Alexander Lozovsky. Nearer home, there were controversial articles by the socialist clergyman Conrad Noel and the ethical socialist Edward Carpenter, as well as pugnacious debates with the former Liberal and soon to be Labour MP Arthur Ponsonby, and the partisan of the Russian revolution Gerald Gould of the *Daily Herald*.

The Free Oxford had an instantaneous and extensive impact. It was sold in all British universities and on the continent, and even reached the United States. Reade – a striking figure, powerfully built, 6ft 3ins tall and with a luxuriant red beard and a strong attachment to the corduroy trousers, clay pipes and heavy beer drinking that were *de rigeur* for 1920s Bohemians – was lionised by the small university left. Like several of his Eton and Oxford contemporaries, he was gay in his youth. He eagerly embraced an active social life and delighted in disregarding convention. He was criticised and lampooned in the mainstream student journals, *Cherwell* and *Isis*. He was also under police surveillance as a dangerous revolutionary and soon attracted the hostile attention of the vice-chancellor. Farnell opposed all student political activities, but considered socialism to be particularly abhorrent and Bolshevism quite beyond the pale. He had recently banned Labour Club meetings that were to be addressed by George Lansbury and Bertrand Russell. Appalled by *The Free Oxford*'s advocacy of 'Russian Bolshevism, the Red Terror, obscene licentiousness and the bitterest class hatred … gross insults against the authorities', Farnell bludgeoned the Worcester College dons into submission [Farnell (1934) 297]. Reade was sent down from the university in December 1921 while Gray, who received greater support from his tutors at Balliol, was rusticated for two terms.

Partly because of Reade's flair and his extensive press contacts, the expulsion stimulated a media storm. The *Daily Herald* declared Oxford 'home of the inhumanities'; for the *Daily Express* Farnell was a 'modern Canute'; for the *Saturday Review* he was the architect of 'a modern inquisition'; and for the *Daily News* he was the perpetrator of 'an academical pogrom'. Publications as different as the *Spectator* and the *Manchester Guardian* followed the *Evening Standard* in regretting the vice-chancellor's overreaction to 'merely youthful exuberance', praising Reade as 'a young man not yet 21, willing to undergo any sacrifice for his principles' [*Manchester Guardian*, 18, 24 January 1922].

A statement by the officers of the Oxford Union and three of the four political societies condemned Farnell and attracted wide publicity. The chancellor of the university, Lord Curzon, wrote to *The Times* to disavow any responsibility. Reade received messages of support from the CPGB leader, Arthur MacManus, and from Harry Pollitt, although the proletarian party itself, which was somewhat uneasy about such a bourgeois issue, did little openly to campaign on the question. The tempest quickly subsided and 19-year-old Reade was left to pick up the pieces.

He spent the next year working as a freelance journalist, writing poems – one appeared in *Oxford Poetry 1922* – and an unpublished novel, studying Marxism and attempting unsuccessfully to resurrect *The Free Oxford* and pay off its debts. Inside the party he was a junior member of Palme Dutt's faction, which, disaffected with the existing leadership, espoused a more thoroughgoing Bolshevisation of the CPGB. As an *aide-de-camp* of the party's leading intellectual, Reade was involved in a wide range of party work. In 1923 he shared in the Herculean and unpaid labours on the party paper, the *Workers' Weekly*, and Dutt's *Labour Monthly*, which were soon to break his mentor's health. There is no mention of Reade in the official party history, *Forging The Weapon: The Struggle of the Labour Monthly, 1921–1941* but it is clear from the papers of Robin Page Arnot (who together with Dutt and the foreign editor of the *Daily Herald*, W. N. Ewer, shared control of the *Monthly*, from the memories of the London party activist Arthur Siffleet who recalled Reade as Dutt's 'right-hand man') and from the Young Communist League leader Harry Wicks that Reade succeeded Joan Beauchamp as the journal's business manager in early 1924. By that time he was a member of the party's London District Committee and served as its training officer, running classes across the south-east.

Reade had always intensely admired Trotsky as a man of action and military genius, a coruscating polemicist and a brutal political thinker. Of course this was far from unusual in the young CPGB, particularly among youths and intellectuals. 'Trotsky', Reade had remarked in *The Free Oxford*, 'whether as leader of the Red Armies or as the brilliant and biting controversialist, gives the revolution its inspiration.' He had mused with awe: 'Perhaps our imagination is dazzled by the grandeur of Trotsky's attitude' [*The Free Oxford*, 26 November, 1921 p. 4]. Crucially he was no conformist, and unlike many in the CPGB he read widely, scouring not only the official Communist press but also socialist journals from France, Germany and the United States. In this context he studied the controversy over the Left Opposition, which developed in Russia from late 1923.

Reade tested out his ideas in classes he conducted for the Young Communist League (YCL). He also acquired background information from a first-hand source. A chance encounter with Andreychine – a supporter of the Russian opposition who worked in the Soviet delegation in London, which was headed by Trotsky's close friend, the Bulgarian Bolshevik Christian Rakovsky – led to Reade being briefed in depth on the political situation in Russia. In November 1924, on instructions from the International and on the basis of a statement drafted by its representatives in London, the CPGB leadership condemned unread Trotsky's preface to his *1917, The Lessons of October*, which was seen as reopening the controversy. They went on to declare their 'implicit faith' in the International and the Russian party leadership. Reade came out as their solitary vocal opponent.

Others were uneasy. The London District Committee could not see the need for urgency and objected to the Political Bureau and the Party Council condemning Trotsky before more information was available and the matter had been discussed in the districts. At the London Aggregate called in response to this mild dissension, a motion to adjourn until more information was available was defeated by the relatively narrow margin of 81 votes to 65. Only Reade spoke out. In the face of the thunder of the party's big guns – J. T. Murphy, Andrew Rothstein and Page Arnot – he moved an amendment to the leadership resolution. In this Reade not only endorsed the London district's criticism of the Party Council's condemnation of Trotsky on the basis of inadequate information, but also went much further: he expressed emphatic solidarity with the Left Opposition in their fight in the Russian party against bureaucracy, as well as congratulating their supporters in the French, German and other parties. The Russian leaders and the International, he argued with ardour, had suppressed Trotsky's arguments while Lenin's dying criticism of the leadership *troika* – Kamenev, Zinoviev and Stalin – had vindicated Trotsky's blistering aspersions on their political qualities. Reade justified his position with lengthy quotations from the international socialist press and from Lenin's testament. However the CPGB's almost uniform adherence to orthodoxy – a tendency that already distinguished it from Communist Parties in many other countries – won out. Reade's resolution was heavily defeated, attracting on different estimates 10 or 15 votes.

Reade immediately became *persona non grata* with the party leadership. While those who had been audacious enough to request more information attracted opprobrium – 'they have a terrible deal to learn before they become real Communists' [*Workers' Weekly*, 23 January 1925] – Reade was singled out for denouncement. He was dismissed as a romantic and a Bohemian; he had failed to overcome his Eton and Oxford background and had demonstrated his 'anti-party attitude' by reading Lenin's testament. He was removed from the District Committee by the Political Bureau and pressure was put on branches that asked him to speak. He was also refused permission to visit Russia and subjected to petty harassment. In April 1925 his appeal to the Control Commission was rejected in a report that also questioned whether he should be allowed to remain in the party. That same month he was dismissed from his post on the *Labour Monthly*. He was barely 23 years of age but his career in the CPGB was over. There was negligible support for his views in the party and at its 1925 congress Trotskyism was irrevocably pronounced a political deviation and disease.

Reade was the first British communist to call himself 'a Trotskyist' when forcefully disassociating himself from those he regarded as Trotsky's non-communist admirers – such as Morgan Philips Price, Raymond Postgate and Frank Horrabin – around the *Plebs* journal and *Lansbury's Labour Weekly* [*Plebs*, 17, 8, August 1925]. Apart from arguing his case inside the CPGB, he made no attempt to develop an organised opposition, which in the circumstances would almost certainly have been an impossible task. His influence endured only through the youthful party activist and future Trotskyist Harry Wicks, who attended his classes and never forgot his arguments. Although he remained a party member until 1928, Reade's Bohemian side reasserted itself. He spent much of the next three years travelling in the Balkans and Greece with Charles Gray, living in Athens with Evelyn Waugh's 'friend of the heart' Alastair Graham, developing his interest in Hellenism and Greek politics and discussing Trotskyism with the Russian consul in Athens. Reade's biography of the Greek political titan Venizelos was almost completed, but like so much of his writing it was never published. The interest in Albanian history and politics that his travels stimulated in him was consummated only in articles for the *Daily Mail*.

Reade's inheritance, finally acquired after litigation against his mother, was quickly dissipated on travel, stock exchange speculation and an exuberant social life, whereupon he returned to the path of respectability. In 1928 he joined the Labour Party, where the MacDonald leadership smiled on new middle-class recruits. Reinvented in the Douglas Fairbanks/Oswald Mosley mould and active in the ILP, he was selected to fight the Abingdon division of North Berkshire in the 1929 general election. This was a scattered farming constituency and Conservative-held seat. On what was for Labour tough terrain, Reade mounted an imaginative and popular challenge under the banner 'Reade for Merry England'. In the first fortnight of his campaign he spoke at 63 meetings, setting up his platform in towns on market days or simply motoring up to village greens and orating from the wingboards of his car. The *Reading Mercury* noted that 'Mr Reade has a pleasing, far reaching voice and has attracted good audiences', while the *North Berks Herald* reported that 'All the candidates found it difficult to get a hearing with perhaps the exception of Mr Reade' [*Reading Mercury*, 18 May 1929; *North Berks Herald*, 31 May 1929]. He expounded the ILP's plans for the nationalisation of mines and better old age pensions, and advocated increased government support for farmers, guaranteed prices and better wages for farm labourers. The old Reade also spoke out in favour of reversing Baldwin's hostile policy towards the Soviet Union and declared his opposition to all forms of censorship. Reade was personally congratulated by MacDonald on his performance.

Abingdon, Berkshire, 1929: electorate 36 758, turnout 80.8 per cent

R. G. C. Glyn (Conservative)	14 094 (47.4 per cent)
E. A. Lessing (Liberal)	11 896 (40.1 per cent)
A. E. E. Reade (Labour)	3712 (12.5 per cent)
Majority	2198 (7.3 per cent)

Labour needed lawyers and Reade a living, so in January 1930 he joined the Inner Temple and spent the next three years reading for the Bar. However he clashed with Arthur Henderson at the 1929 Labour Party conference over the Executive's control of candidates' election addresses, and as the crisis of 1931 developed he resigned from the Labour Party. In *The Fascist Movement in Britain* (1972), Robert Benewick states that Reade joined Mosley's New Party, which was launched in March 1931 and initially possessed a small constituency on the Labour left. It has proved impossible to assign specific authority to this statement or to obtain corroboration for it, apart from a vague and confused reference by Reade's old pupil in the Young Communist League, Harry Wicks. On Reade's own account, he rejoined the Labour Party only to become disillusioned once more with its stance on rearmament and the threat of fascism. By 1936 the politically volatile Reade had once again defected from the Labour Party. This time he decamped to MacDonald's National Labour Group, where he was reunited with an old contemporary, the Earl De La Warr, and two figures who had influenced him in his early days at Oxford, Kenneth Lindsay, MP for Kilmarnock, and Malcolm MacDonald, MP for Ross and Cromarty and Secretary of State for the Dominions.

Having broken with MacDonald twice (in 1921 and 1931), Reade had come full circle. But his past still intruded. In 1934 Farnell published his memoirs, *An Oxonian Looks Back*, in which he injudiciously raked over the ashes of *The Free Oxford* affair. Flexing his muscles as a newly qualified barrister, Reade issued a writ for libel. Farnell subsequently died, but the matter was settled to Reade's satisfaction by the removal of the offending passages from the text, the payment of his costs and, in response to Farnell's dislike of Germans, a small sum in damages to a charity that helped Germans to study in British universities.

Reade practised as a member of the Central Criminal Bar and subsequently the South Eastern Circuit Bar and the London Sessions Southside. A chance encounter with Harry Wicks in Kleinfelds, a Bohemian pub in Soho frequented by a variety of Communists, fascists and the polymath magician Aleister Crowley, led to a renewed interest in Trotsky. In the face of the Moscow trials, Reade wrote supportively to *The Times* and *The Spectator* and at greater length in the National Labour press. He also provided legal advice to the Committee for the Defence of Leon Trotsky. Unlike his fellow barristers D. N. Pritt and Dudley Collard, who shamelessly whitewashed the show trials, he remained a critic of Stalinism. But this evolution had taken him far from Marxism. While he retained his old identification with the leader of the Russian revolution and creator of the Red Army, it was as 'an old fashioned bourgeois believer in individual liberty' that he declared, 'I should be proud to do anything I properly can to secure justice for Leon Trotsky who I regard as the most superb warrior in the cause of the working people in modern history' [Reade to Wicks, Haston papers, University of Hull, DJH18/4, 2 December 1936].

Reade had matured as a man of the centre. Rejecting the class war, describing himself as a radical social reformer and praising the tradition of teamwork for which the National Government stood in Britain, he became secretary of the Inns of Court branch of the National Labour Group and prospective parliamentary candidate for East Bristol – Stafford Cripps' constituency and a stronghold of the Labour left. Lacking coherence and the resources and will to build a new party, National Labour remained a small, disparate ginger group. During its brief existence its members ranged from extinct volcanoes of the left, such as the former Communist J. T. Walton Newbold, through experienced politicians in new incarnations, such as the pioneer of the University Socialist Federation, absolutist conscientious objector and former chairman of the ILP, Clifford Allen, now Lord Allen of Hurtwood, to the declining but resilient Jimmy Thomas. For Reade it was another lost cause. The 1940 general election never came. National Labour was increasingly a small fig leaf for Conservative rule, and not surprisingly it failed to survive the war.

Another curious incident occurred in 1938, when three articles signed 'Arthur Reade' appeared in the *British Union Quarterly*, a journal of the British Union of Fascists. Attributed to an Englishman resident in Italy, they criticised the dark designs of international finance, praised Nordic racial consciousness, depicted communism as a Jewish creation and sought to appropriate William Morris for national socialism. As Reade was in England at that time and was relatively prominent as a National Labour candidate, writing in its press and signing articles and documents 'Arthur E. E. Reade', it is unlikely that he authored these pieces, particularly in light of the views expressed. Nonetheless this matter, as with so much about Reade, is intriguing. His restlessness and appetite for adventure certainly remained unimpaired. Agitated by Munich, he joined the Officers' Emergency Reserve. When he was not called up he enlisted in the army in spring 1940 and was soon promoted to sergeant. A year later, after much string-pulling and circumvention of his MI5 file, he joined the intelligence services. He was appointed to the infant, unorthodox Special Operations Executive (SOE) in the Mediterranean and eventually became head of administration. Caught up in the Byzantine politics of the Rustum Buildings (the SOE headquarters in Cairo), he fell foul of the notorious Brigadier Mervyn Keble, who designated his vendetta 'Operation Oxford'.

Quite improbably, for he was over 40, a poor swimmer and had no experience of marine sabotage, and moreover knew the true identity of most active SOE agents, Reade was chosen by Keble to blow up the damaged HMS *York*, which the Germans were trying to refloat in Suda Bay. Reade duly landed on Axis-occupied Crete in November 1942, but his mission proved impossible. One of his experienced colleagues later recalled: 'The Brigadier must have known that the suicidal enterprise was doomed in advance to failure, so I could only conclude that he was less interested in destroying a top-priority target than in getting rid of a junior officer with whom he was on bad terms' [Fielding (1954) 106]. Reade saw action in Crete before a furious Keble ensured he was sent back to England in disgrace. However a nine-month wrangle and protracted representations by Cripps and Philip Noel Baker MP resulted in his exoneration and promotion to major.

Reade's war ended in Germany, where he worked for the War Crimes Commission until the end of the 1940s. His rootlessness and wanderlust continued: he spent 1950–53 as a resident magistrate in Kenya and then practised as a barrister in another of the decade's trouble spots, Cyprus, before retiring to Jersey in 1963. He died on 12 December 1971, leaving an estate valued at £3417.

Reade was married twice – to fellow barrister Bettina Morel in 1934, and to Cynthia Fowler, a lecturer in English literature, in 1948. Each marriage produced three children, but one child from each marriage died young. Reade was a flamboyant, mercurial, generous, caring character whose political impulsiveness was reflected in shifting allegiances, which was more common than is often thought in the first four decades of the twentieth century. He had his share of bad luck, and political stamina was not one of his virtues; he found it difficult to reconcile his appetite for life, laughter, wine, song and convivial company with the austere demands of political discipline. He will be best remembered for the events of 1924–25. His Daniel-like, prescient indictment of the degeneration of the revolution in Russia still stands in impressive contrast to the silences, apologetics and complicity in despotism of successive generations of communist intellectuals.

Writings: Articles in the *Daily Mail, The New Oxford, The Free Oxford, Youth, Workers' Weekly, Labour Monthly, The News-Letter, The Challenger.*

Sources: (1) **MSS:** Palme Dutt Papers, Hutt Papers, Communist Party Archive, NMLH; Page Arnot Papers, Haston Papers, University of Hull; Oxford University archives, Bodleian Library; Pollard Papers, Bodleian Library; Russian State Archive of Socio-Political History (RGASPI), Moscow. (2) **Newspapers and Periodicals:** *North Berks Herald; Oxford Mail; Reading Mercury,* 1929; *British Union Quarterly,* April, July, October 1938. (3) **Other:** A. E. E. R., 'Trotskyism, etc', Letters, *Plebs,* 17 (8 August 1925); C. H. Gray, 'Albania and Italian Imperialism', *Plebs,* 19 (4 April 1927); Labour Party, *Report of the 29th Annual Conference, The Dome, Brighton, September 1929* (1929); M. P. Ashley and C. T. Saunders, *Red Oxford: A History of the Growth of Socialism in the University of Oxford* (Oxford, 1933); L. R. Farnell, *An Oxonian Looks Back* (1934); George Orwell, *The Road to Wigan Pier* (1937); X. Fielding, *Hide and Seek* (1954); B. Pearce, 'Early Years of the Communist Party of Great Britain' (1958), in M. Woodhouse and B. Pearce, *Essays on the History of Communism in Britain* (1975); B. Pearce, 'The Last Years of the University Socialist Federation', *Bulletin of the Society for the Study of Labour History,* 4 (Spring, 1962) 45–6; G. Smith (ed.), *The Letters of Aldous Huxley* (1969); R. Benewick, *The Fascist Movement in Britain* (1972); M. Davie (ed.), *The Diaries of Evelyn Waugh* (1976); M. Upham, 'The History of British Trotskyism to 1949', unpublished PhD dissertation (Hull, 1980); I. MacDougall (ed.), *Militant Miners* (Edinburgh, 1981); J. Mabro, *'I Ban Everything'. Free Speech and Censorship In Oxford between the Wars* (Oxford, 1985); S. Bornstein and A. Richardson, *Against the Stream: A History of the Trotskyist Movement in Britain 1924–38* (1986); A. Beevor, *Crete: The Battle and the Resistance* (1991); N. West, *Secret War: The Story of SOE* (1992); H. Wicks, *Keeping My Head: The Memoirs of a British Bolshevik* (1992); J. McIlroy, 'New Light on Arthur Reade: Tracking Down Britain's First Trotskyist', *Revolutionary History,* 8:1 (2001) 2–48; J. McIlroy, 'The Young Manhood of Arthur Reade', in J. McIlroy, K. Morgan and A. Campbell (eds), *Party People, Communist Lives* (2001). (4) **Personal information and papers**: Julian and Viola Reade, Keith Gildart, David Howell, Brian Pearce.

JOHN MCILROY

RICHARDSON, Reginald John (1808–61)
CHARTIST

Reginald John Richardson was born in the Manchester area in 1808. While no information has come to light on his family background and formative years, it is known that as an 11-year-old boy he witnessed the Peterloo massacre, and it was from that day in 1819 that he later dated the origin of his political career. At 14 he became a bonded apprentice to a carpenter and joiner, a trade that he followed well into the 1830s. Richardson was married in about 1833 and some time after that he and his wife Elizabeth established a newsagency cum bookshop in Chapel Street, Salford. An industrial accident had forced him to give up his trade, but he maintained close links with the Carpenters' and Joiners' Union, being appointed a trustee of Carpenters' Hall in Manchester after it was built in 1838–39.

Richardson's newsagency continued in business for many years, during which time he also worked as a newspaper editor, lecturer, pamphleteer, publican and eventually building surveyor. Richardson's first foray into public life came in 1826 when he spoke at meetings in connection with a series of riots by power-loom weavers; he later achieved national notoriety by moving an amendment for universal suffrage during a massive public meeting in Manchester at the height of the Reform Bill crisis in 1832.

Richardson's career in politics and unionism gained momentum during the 1830s. By January 1838 he was secretary of both the South Lancashire Anti-Poor Law Association and the Executive of the Manchester Trades' Council. In April 1838 he was a leading figure in the reformed Manchester Political Union and spoke at the first Chartist demonstration on Kersal Moor in September, when he was elected as a Manchester delegate to the Chartists' national gathering, the General Convention of the Industrious Classes. For the remainder of 1838 he represented the Manchester and Salford Chartists at numerous major meetings across Britain. At about that time he was described as being 'of middle stature and robust frame, with light hair, in some profusion, and bushy reddish whiskers, meeting under his chin' [*Operative*, 3 March 1839].

At the Convention Richardson was a vocal delegate, with one of his speeches forming the basis of a well-known pamphlet on the constitutional right to bear arms. In July 1839 he resigned as a delegate following a succession of disputes with his Manchester constituents over his salary, but by that time he was also increasingly at odds with the Manchester Chartists on questions of policy. In particular he opposed the inclusion of a National Holiday or general strike among the proposed 'ulterior measures' to be enacted should the National Petition be rejected by the House of Commons. Despite his opposition to the National Holiday, Richardson was arrested in early September 1839 and charged with sedition and conspiracy, and in April 1840 he was sentenced to nine months' imprisonment.

In early 1839 Richardson had attempted to interest radical MP John Fielden in the formation of an organisation entitled the Constitutional Society for Promoting Political Instruction, but this came to nothing. In his prison cell he again turned his attention to organisation and composed a detailed plan for a national Chartist body, which he published as part of the debate leading up to the formation of the National Charter Association in July 1840. He also wrote a pamphlet entitled the *Rights of Women*, which made a case for single women and widows to be given the vote, as well as a series of lengthy essays on the condition of hand-loom weavers. When Richardson was released in December 1840 he declared that 'he was a radical reformer of the old school of Major Cartwright and Henry Hunt [and] they might persecute him till doomsday, but he would never alter' [*Northern Star*, 2 January 1841].

A mark of his continuing popularity among sections of the Chartist movement was his nomination to the NCA Executive after his release, but he did not contest the poll the following year. In February 1841 he represented Burnley at a national conference, and in March he embarked on a lecture tour authorised by the South Lancashire NCA delegates. In June 1841 he was nominated for the borough of Perth, but he was unable even to secure victory at the show of hands over the sitting Tory MP, George Fox Maule, the treasury solicitor. By that stage Richardson's relations with the mainstream Manchester Chartists had again soured as a result of allegations of personal vindictiveness, favouritism and financial mismanagement. Pleading heavy debts, Richardson left Salford in October 1841 to become editor of the *Dundee Chronicle*, a post he held for six months.

Richardson's split with the majority of Chartists in south-east Lancashire became further evident in April 1842 when he openly advocated an alliance with middle-class radicals by attending the Complete Suffrage Conference in Birmingham. By mid 1842 he was back in his native Salford, where he established a 'Tract Library'; he also became a regular contributor to and later shareholder in Bronterre O'Brien's *British Statesman*. During 1843 he published a detailed analysis of the parliamentary opponents of the repeal of the Corn Laws, suggesting that the intransigence of the 'Monopolist Majority' strengthened the case for parliamentary reform. Although he had often clashed with leaders of the Anti-Corn Law League, he remained a strong advocate of Corn Law repeal. Later in 1843 he promoted an Anti-Corn Law petition on the Salford Police Commission, the local government body of which he had been an elected member since 1839.

In addition to the Police Commission, Richardson was active in a variety of local government forums, including the Salford Select Vestry and elections for Manchester churchwardens. Although he remained active in Chartism after 1842–43, his attention shifted primarily to local affairs, being involved in a range of organisations from the Vestry to the Ancient Foot Paths Association. In mid 1844 he was instrumental in initiating the campaign for public parks that resulted in the creation of Peel Park in Salford, although his attempts to have working men represented on the steering committee were unsuccessful.

In 1848 Richardson was involved in ill-fated moves to establish a joint working and middle-class movement based on Joseph Hume's 'Little Charter', and was a strong advocate of Chartist principles in the nascent People's League, formed in mid 1848. In 1858 he joined George Wilson, the former chairman of the Anti-Corn Law League, in promoting a new Reform Association, but ill health prevented him from being very active. Appearing before a parliamentary committee in 1854, Richardson summed up his career with the claim that he had been involved 'in every movement that has taken place amongst the working classes since I can remember' [PP, *Report from Select Committee on Public Houses* (1854) 196]. When he died in 1861 he left a widow and three young children, as well as several grown-up children.

According to a prison inspector who interviewed him in 1840, Richardson's 'temper is so low that he began to quarrel with the other Chartists as soon as he arrived', a pattern that was repeated throughout his stormy public career. Historians too have had little positive to say about him. For Mark Hovell, Richardson was a 'wordy, pedantic, logic-chopper of the worst description' [Hovell (1918) 91]; for David Jones he was a 'bore' and a 'garrulous antiquarian' [Jones (1975) 23]; while Dorothy Thompson, quoting Lloyd Jones, has drawn attention to his 'rude provincialism' [Thompson (1971) 87–8]. Richardson was undoubtedly an obstreperous person and could be painfully self-righteous, but his truculence was indicative of a fierce independence. When assessing Richardson's place in nineteenth-century radicalism, his independence stands out as his most important quality. Although he often advocated an alliance with middle-class radicals, he always insisted on strict equality, and as such he was a major contributor to the development of the tradition of independent radicalism that characterised Chartism in Lancashire.

Writings: *South Lancashire Political Almanac* (1838); *Englishman's Manual* (1839); *State Secrets* (1839); *The Rights of Englishmen to Have Arms* (1839); *The Rights of Women* (Edinburgh, 1840); *Political Almanac for 1841; the Annual Black Book* (Manchester, 1841); *The Corn Laws and Equal Taxation* (1841); *Richardson's Popular Emigration Guide to the United States* (1842); *An Exposure of the Banking and Funding System* (1842); *Blue Book of the Commons* (Manchester, 1847); *Annual Black Book and Political Almanac for 1848* (Manchester, 1848).

Sources: (1) MSS: Volume of Cuttings and Other Material Relating to Reginald John Richardson, Archives Department, Manchester Public Library; Home Office 20/10, Report upon the Treatment and Condition of the Prisoners Convicted of Political Offences at Present Undergoing Imprisonment in the Gaol and House of Correction at Kirkdale (October 1840). (2) Newspapers: *Northern Star*, 1838–52; *British Statesman*, 1842; *English Chartist Circular*, 1841–44; *Operative*, 1839. (3) Other: M. Hovell, *The Chartist Movement* (Manchester, 1918); D. Thompson, *The Early Chartists* (1971); D. Jones, *Chartism and the Chartists* (1975); J. Ridley, 'Richardson, Reginald John', in J. O. Baylen and N. J. Gossman (eds), *Biographical Dictionary of Modern British Radicals Vol. 2* (Sussex, 1984); E. and R. Frow, Introduction to a facsimile edition of Richardson's *Rights of Women* (Salford, 1986); P. A. Pickering, *Chartism and the Chartists in Manchester and Salford* (Basingstoke, 1995).

PAUL A. PICKERING

See also: James SCHOLEFIELD; James WROE.

ROYCE, William Stapleton (1857–1924)
LABOUR MP

William Stapleton Royce was born on 13 December 1857 in Spalding, Lincolnshire. His mother was Rebecca Royce; no father's name was given on the birth certificate. Rebecca Royce subsequently married a millwright. Royce was brought up in a growing family and was educated at Willesby School and at William Pretty's Commercial School. The latter was considered educationally superior to the British School and was attended largely by the sons of the local middle class. Royce's education was relatively basic: a grounding in reading, writing and arithmetic. As a member of a large family his education ended at the age of 13 and he was apprenticed to a joiner in Spalding, Christopher Harrison. Royce found the prospects uncongenial and broke his apprenticeship after two years. He moved to London and with the help of an uncle eventually found work on the construction of the General Post Office in St Martins-le-Grand. Still dissatisfied he left England in 1876 for South Africa.

Railway construction in the Cape Colony had been given a boost by the discovery of diamonds at Kimberley. The Cape Colony government was keen to recruit British workmen; Royce accepted the offer of a free passage and a three-year contract. He was employed on the construction of a line in the Eastern Cape from East London to Queenstown; his task was essentially to train and supervise African and 'coloured' labour. He enjoyed the social life of the relatively small European community. By the end of his contract he had saved £200. He went into partnership with James Lang as a contractor, the first of a number of partnerships, including Royce and Wise, and Royce and Warren.

The first contract for Royce and Lang was the construction of a reservoir near Queenstown. They also built churches. Royce was subsequently involved in bridge and railway construction and in the building of the presidency at Bloemfontein in the Orange Free State. From 1882 he was accompanied on his travels by his wife, Emma Broedlet. Her father, a Dutch missionary, had moved to South Africa in 1861.

Royce returned to Lincolnshire for a visit in 1888, and then went back to South Africa, this time to Johannesburg. The fortunes of the Transvaal Republic had been transformed by the discovery of gold on the Rand. Initially Royce worked as a manager of the Golden Kopje Mine, but then secured contracts for public buildings and for a section of the railway from Germiston to Pretoria. The formation of the Netherlands South African Railway Company in 1887, with considerable German capital, indicated the Transvaal Government's wish to free itself of dependence on British-based facilities. In the early 1890s a line was slowly constructed from Pretoria to Delagoa Bay, offering the prospect of an outlet for the Rand's products through Portuguese territory. Royce and Warren were responsible for the construction of a difficult section of the line involving the Eland Tunnel, where the line ascended to the Highveld. The line was formally opened by President Paul Kruger on 2 November 1894. A Pretoria newspaper commented:

> Regardless of malaria, summer floods or heavy frosts of the high veld, their work was carried out in a magnificent manner by the chief contractors. Messrs Royce and Warren, who, especially in the tunnel work, and the final construction from Middleborg to Balmoral, achieved record results for [the] time and quality of the work they put in [Ould (1925) 86].

Royce and his growing family subsequently established a permanent base in England. From 1895 he shuttled between England and South Africa, but his railway projects were halted by the start of the South African War in October 1899. He spent the war in England, but from 1902 reverted to his prewar existence. While day-to-day involvement in railway construction was left to his sons, he regularly visited South Africa. He also developed his Lincolnshire interests. He acquired the Hall at Pinchbeck, just to the north of Spalding. He extended and modernised the house and developed a reputation as an improving landlord. The country house, the large motor car with a liveried chauffeur, the identity of the local boy turned public benefactor; this was the William Royce of the years before the First World War.

His economic successes and his achieved social status indicated that he could be a credible parliamentary candidate. His imperial experiences suggested a likely affinity with Edwardian Conservatism, and Royce agreed to stand as the Conservative candidate for Spalding. This decision signalled the end of his South African activities. He completed his work there in 1909 and realised his South African investments, apparently valued at £100,000.

Royce fought Spalding as a Conservative in both 1910 elections. The seat, formed in 1885, had often been marginal, but had been held very decisively by the Liberals in 1906. Apart from Spalding town, the seat was rural, mostly fenland – the part of Lincolnshire known as Holland. Nonconformity was relatively strong, which provided the basis for a significant Liberal presence. Royce's 1910 campaigns emphasised tariffs and imperial development. He opposed Home Rule for Ireland as tending towards the dismemberment of the Empire. In the January election he attacked the land tax proposals in the 1909 budget as a burden on agriculture. He viewed the House of Lords as a 'bulwark of the constitution' [*Spalding Guardian*, 3 December 1910], not least because it could prevent a hasty and damaging decision on Home Rule. He endorsed the campaign for naval dominance.

These core Conservative sentiments were flavoured with some populist and modernising elements. He supported better transport facilities in agricultural districts, the expansion of allotments and smallholdings, the removal of the pauper disqualification for old age pensions, the introduction of national insurance against both illness and unemployment, and reform of the second chamber on a democratic basis. He repeatedly referred to his local origins – 'I am a man of the people' [*Spalding Guardian*, 8 January 1910]. In the December campaign he referred critically to the post-war political settlement in South Africa and stated that the Afrikaner influence remained too strong: 'I believe in British rule and not Boer rule ... in the Free State ... a great majority of the English officials were put down by the Dutch officials who had taken their place' [*Spalding Guardian*, 10 December 1910].

Both 1910 elections were keenly fought and the Liberal majority declined sharply from its 1906 level: 16.2 per cent. Royce felt that he had been beaten by the votes of agricultural workers.

Spalding, January 1910: electorate 13 645 turnout 78.2 per cent

F. W. S. Maclaren (Liberal)	5527 (51.8 per cent)
W. S. Royce (Unionist)	5148 (48.2 per cent)
Majority	379 (3.6 per cent)

Spalding, December 1910: electorate 13 645 turnout 76.3 per cent

F. W. S. Maclaren (Liberal)	5335 (51.3 per cent)
W. S. Royce (Unionist)	5070 (48.7 per cent)
Majority	265 (2.6 per cent)

Royce was subsequently invited to be Conservative candidate for North Manchester and for Gorton, but refused as he preferred to stay in South Lincolnshire. During the 1914–18 war he served on the tribunal for Spalding Rural District Council (set up under the Military Service Act), was a member of the Holland War Agricultural Committee, and a special constable. He seemed likely to contest any post-war election as a Conservative. There is certainly no evidence that the war years witnessed any significant revision of his political views.

The redistribution of constituencies that accompanied the wartime extension of the franchise meant the end of the Spalding seat. It was effectively replaced by Holland with Boston – the old Spalding constituency with a few rural additions, and more significantly the inclusion of Boston. The latter had previously been a separate borough seat and had been won by the Conservatives in both 1910 elections. Despite this urban addition the new seat contained one of the highest concentrations of agricultural employment in Britain – over 54 per cent of employed adult males aged 12 and over in 1921, according to one assessment [Kinnear (1981) 119].

Royce announced his resignation as prospective candidate in February 1918. His claim was that the old seat no longer existed, and he showed no interest in securing the nomination for its successor. When the Holland with Boston Conservative Association was formed in August 1918, Royce was unanimously chosen as president, and in early September was elected chair of a sub-committee entrusted with finding a candidate. Two men, one the sitting MP for Boston, declined to be considered, so the Conservative Central Office list was examined. Royce subsequently favoured Patrick Hannon, secretary of the Naval League, but some local Conservatives felt that his Roman Catholicism would be a handicap. One unnamed member instead suggested the Director of Vegetable Supplies at the Ministry of Food, Major E. A. C. Belcher. On 5 November 1918 Belcher and Hannon met the subcommittee; its members and then the Association's executive unanimously backed Belcher. Royce was in the chair for this rejection of his preferred candidate. When a Special General Meeting of the Conservative Association endorsed Belcher on 13 November 1918, Royce was absent. Six days later he resigned from the presidency of the Association. Almost immediately there were quickly substantiated rumours that Royce would shift to the Labour Party and offer to be its candidate.

This was a local political sensation. Royce had played a major part in strengthening south Lincolnshire Conservatism, both in its formal organisation and in the development of a support-ive local newspaper, the *Lincolnshire Observer*. Until November 1918 he had seemed to be a committed Conservative. His unwillingness to contest the new constituency had not seemed to indicate any political disagreement, since he had played a leading role in the search for a new candidate. Certainly his prewar campaigns had contained some deviations from conventional Conservatism. In 1910 he had supported agricultural trade unionism, and claimed 'I am no friend of heredity' [*Spalding Guardian*, 1 January 1910]. This Liberal newspaper had suggested that Royce's deviations were just vote catching: 'Do you really think that Mr Royce talks the same in his Tory-committee rooms as he does at his village meetings?' [ibid.] At the time Royce had claimed that for him tariffs were decisive for his political allegiance; later he had empha-sised Liberal attitudes towards the Empire, as evidenced during the South African War [*Boston Guardian*, 7 December 1918]. Whatever the distinctiveness or otherwise of Royce's Conservatism, it is hard to avoid the conclusion that the rejection of his preferred candidate on religious grounds was crucial. There were significant parallels between Royce and the Irishman, Patrick Hannon. The latter had worked with Sir Horace Plunkett on schemes of cooperation amongst Irish farmers, and between 1905 and 1909 he had been employed as an agricultural specialist in Cape Colony. He too had returned to fight the 1910 elections on a tariff reform and big navy platform. Royce had quarrelled with his Conservative Association because it would not adopt someone who stood for his type of Conservatism. Hannon subsequently became MP for Birmingham Moseley, a Commons 'character', a significant industrialist and for many Labour MPs the epitome of Conservatism. Yet his former champion in Holland with Boston now became the Labour candidate.

Royce's first step was to meet local Labour Parties, first in Spalding, then in Boston and finally in Sutton Bridge in the far east of the constituency. The Spalding meeting was held on 16 November 1918, before Royce's formal resignation of the Conservative presidency. A week later, on 23 November, Royce met the Divisional Party. He said he accepted the party's national programme, and if elected would take the Labour Party whip. His name then went forward to the party's National Executive Committee for endorsement, which was given on 27 November. Royce had also spoken to trade union representatives, most notably agricultural workers, whose strength had grown significantly during the war, and railway workers, who were often central to Labour's political growth in rural areas.

Royce's election address barely mentioned the Labour Party. He praised the patriotism of the working class and claimed that this 'pointed out to me the only possible path of duty viz – a clear association with the party that identifies itself with their ideals'. His views on the peace settlement involved opposition to secret diplomacy, punishment of the guilty and reparations. 'Germany must pay.' He emphasised decent treatment for servicemen who had defeated 'a brutal and treacherous enemy'. Much of his address dealt with post-war reforms – housing schemes under state control, land reform, expansion of educational opportunity and public works as a contribution to reconstruction. His examples focused on rural issues; his reform proposals were presented as a national programme. The same vision informed his agenda for industrial relations.

> An era of class strife, of strikes, of wage disputes, and of embittered relations between Capital and Labour must be avoided. The people are as weary of strife as they are of economic injustice. There must be more comprehensive machinery and a better ordered system of representative bodies in all the well organised industries. Where organisation is lacking, Parliament must insist that wages are maintained relatively to the cost of living, and must resist every attempt to depress the working-class standard of life [*Boston Guardian*, 7 December 1918].

In his campaign speeches Royce emphasised that the war had strengthened the claims of labour to decent treatment and political representation. One aspect of his own wartime activities was linked to the Labour rhetoric of fairness in such a way that it evoked rural class tensions:

> He had been Chairman of the Recruiting Committee, and in that capacity he had expressed the opinion that the farmers should not be immune from military service. (Applause). When the farmers had said they had made great sacrifices and had sent their men, he had said 'Is it not the men who are making the sacrifice? What about your sons'? (Applause) Was he to be punished for that? Was he to be punished because he had denounced the profiteers? (Cries of 'No' and 'That's the stuff to give'em) [*Boston Guardian*, 14 December 1918].

Belcher received the coupon, indicating that he was the approved candidate of the Lloyd George Coalition. Royce insisted that he and indeed the Labour Party were supporters of Lloyd George, but preferred to maintain their autonomy. The third candidate, A. G. V. Peel, had become Liberal MP for Spalding in October 1917; he had been unopposed under the wartime electoral truce. In the Commons he had voted against the government in the Maurice Debate in May 1918 and opposed the temporary withdrawal of the vote from conscientious objectors. Despite his war service he was precisely the kind of Liberal who was vulnerable to the rhetoric of the 1918 election.

Holland with Boston, December 1918: electorate 40 004, turnout 55.2 per cent

W. S. Royce (Labour)	8788 (39.8 per cent)
E. A. C. Belcher (Coalition Conservative)	7718 (35.0 per cent)
Hon. A. G. V. Peel (Liberal)	5557 (25.2 per cent)
Majority	1070 (4.8 per cent)

This result stood out amongst out amongst the otherwise modest number of Labour victories. Royce's standing in the constituency and the distinctive nature of his appeal – he claimed to be consistent in many ways with his position in 1910 – were crucial. Yet he was also the beneficiary of the wartime strengthening of rural trade unionism that provided a basis for Labour organisation. In the adjacent King's Lynn constituency Labour was only 366 votes short of victory in 1918; there the candidate, unlike Royce, benefited from the absence of a Liberal. Labour also polled well in another adjacent seat, Rutland and Stamford.

The November 1922 election was notable for attempts by opponents to link Royce with the alleged extremism of the Labour Party. In particular he was faced with the question of the capital levy. Royce's response was to claim loyalty to his party, a right to his own and his constituents' judgement on any proposal for a capital levy, and insistence on the stability of his own political views:

> I have pledged myself that if the measure is introduced I will have no lot, parcel or truck with it until I have come down to my constituents and consulted them. When you read my election address you will find there is nothing Bolshevist about it. It is largely moulded on my election address of 1910, and it is practically the same on which you returned me at the last election [*Lincolnshire Free Press*, 7 November 1922].

Royce's appeal remained strongly that of a community notable. An advertisement proceeded by rhetorical questions to a predictable answer: 'Who knows Your Needs Best? A Tory from Warwickshire? A "Wee Free" from Surrey? Or your neighbour, your advocate, your friend? Do not waste your vote on a carpet bagger!!' [*Boston Guardian*, 11 November 1922]. The result of the election was a disappointment to those who had expected Royce's personal vote to decline once the uncertain alignments of 1918 had ended:

Holland with Boston, November 1922: electorate 41 516, turnout 76.9 per cent

W. S. Royce (Labour)	12 489 (39.1 per cent)
Sir H. W. C-R Fairfax-Lucy Bart (Conservative)	11 898 (37.3 per cent)
E. S. Agnew (Liberal)	7535 (23.6 per cent)
Majority	591 (1.8 per cent)

Royce's final contest, in December 1923, was a straight fight with a Conservative. Once the advocate of tariffs, Royce now proclaimed himself to be a free trader. He claimed that his earlier views had been shaped by his South African experiences and that the prewar proposals had been essentially a scheme of colonial preference. In fact in 1910 Royce had advocated tariffs as a means of both reducing unemployment and raising revenue. For him, wartime experience suggested that the Baldwin Government's tariff proposals would be futile. His position was sufficient to secure the public support of some local Liberals and of the Liberal candidate defeated in 1922. His constituency reputation also ensured support from across party lines, and a group labelling themselves 'Royceites' campaigned for him. Once again he distanced himself from specific elements of Labour's position. He had not voted for Philip Snowden's Commons motion on socialism in 1923, and was dismissive of its value. 'I considered it both inopportune and a waste of good time' [*Spalding Guardian*, 1 December 1923]. His advocacy of public ownership was limited to coal mining and railways – the latter probably drew on his South African experience, where state-funded railways had played a decisive part in the development of agriculture and mining.

In the absence of a Liberal candidate, Holland's Liberal voters either split their support between the two candidates to Royce's advantage or abstained.

Holland with Boston, December 1923: electorate 42 220, turnout 68.8 per cent

W. S. Royce (Labour)	15 647 (54.1 per cent)
A. W. Dean (Conservative)	13 331 (45.9 per cent)
Majority	2366 (8.2 per cent)

Royce's election campaigns and his parliamentary activities focused heavily on agricultural problems. His Maiden Speech on 14 February 1919 presented an agenda of rural modernisation, including small holdings, better housing, railway nationalisation (with a consequential reduction of transportation rates for agricultural produce) and the building of light railways under local authority control in rural areas [*Hansard*, 14 February 1919, cols 496–501]. As the hopes of post-war reconstruction faded, Royce became concerned with the threat to the living standards that agricultural workers had achieved under wartime government control. In the summer of 1921, as part of its broader policy of decontrol, the Lloyd George Government repealed the Corn Production Act and its system of Wages Boards. Royce attacked the government for effectively abandoning the agricultural labourer. He accurately predicted wage reductions and a drastic weakening of agricultural trade unionism. His relationship with farmers in his constituency was close and he understood their unhappiness with wages boards:

I have a good deal of sympathy with men, who have been accustomed all their lives to be practically free from all control in the matter of arrangement of wages with their workers, when they find that the question of the rate of wages that must be paid to their employees is fixed by an independent authority [*Hansard*, 25 July 1921, col. 71].

Yet he also appreciated farm workers' memories of poverty and exploitation.

In the second winter of the War, in my own village, labourers were receiving 18s a week. In the winter time the farmers took 3d a day off them, and at that time the farms were doing remarkably well. If that spirit is to be applied in future, how do you expect anything like an agreement can be come to between the workers and the farmers? [*Hansard*, 4 July 1921, col. 90].

When the 1924 Labour government introduced legislation to restore Wages Boards, Royce was a strong advocate of the need for a Central Wages Board. Local committees would be affected by a basic inequality of power; farm workers would be reluctant to present their case vigorously.

He is living on the farm, and possibly any difference of opinion on the board might be translated onto the farm and disagreement might ensue. ... The employer goes to such a board with much greater powers that can operate outside the board than the agricultural labourer [*Hansard*, 2 June 1924, cols 977–8).

Royce's South African experiences left their mark on his parliamentary activities, and in 1922 he became the first chairman of the Parliamentary Labour Party's Commonwealth Group. Other participants included George Lansbury, Tom Johnston and Harry Snell. In some fundamental respects Royce did not share the principled egalitarianism that characterised several Labour colleagues on imperial issues. For example he thought that each case for the broadening of political representation should be examined on its merits:

'If you are going to apply the same principle to a country like Ceylon with its 40 per cent of educated population as to another country like South Africa where there is no education at all, it is so absurd'.

His expectations of change were paternalistic and segregationist:

I do think that by wise administration, by encouragement and by education, you can bring these people up not to the same level – you will never mix black with white – but that on parallel lines they can attain the same degree of civilisation. It is not, however, by teaching them too much civilisation in the earlier stages that you can bring them to the desired level; their progress must be slow [*Hansard*, 11 August 1920, col. 484].

While he criticised the severe limitations on black representation in the Union of South Africa, he highlighted the Europeans' sense of vulnerability:

The white man who lives in South Africa with his wife and family realises that he has to live with these people. It is a trouble to him. Their number is greatly in excess of his own and he is always possessed of very considerable fear [*Hansard*, 30 July 1919, col. 2229].

Such sentiments inspired him to defend the Coalition's Colonial Secretary, Lord Milner, against the criticisms of Labour MPs, most notably the former Liberal Josiah Wedgwood. A debate on the treatment of Chinese workers engaged to mine phosphates on the Pacific island of Nauru saw Royce's perhaps most emphatic parliamentary intervention on the question of ethnicity and justice:

It seems to me that the nigger [*sic*] or the Chinaman is looked upon as somebody who ought to be preserved, while we intend to take no care of our own people. We import Chinese into this country, they enter into competition with our own people, and they are a source of trouble to our social order. We are quite unconscious of what is going on under our nose [*Hansard*, 3 March 1924, col. 1120].

This characterisation owed something to Royce's South African experiences and the Edwardian controversy about the importation of indentured Chinese labour to the Transvaal. 'I have seen those Chinese slaves come into Johannesburg and engage every cab at the railway station, whilst my wife and I have had to carry our luggage up to the hotel' [ibid.] He also contrasted the internationalism of some Labour and Liberal MPs with their alleged lack of concern for British agricultural workers.

The distinctiveness of Royce's views requires precise elaboration. His South African experiences had clearly affected his position, but some aspects of it were also articulated by other Labour MPs. For example E. D. Morel's attacks on the French military occupation of the Ruhr utilised hostile images of African troops, and John Wheatley frequently attacked internationalists who were insensitive to inequalities within their own society. Royce's political positions were often distinctive within the Labour Party but his sentiments sometimes linked with those of colleagues. Moreover this affluent backbencher was not stylistically at odds with the bulk of Labour MPs. As T. P. O' Connor observed:

In appearance there was nothing to suggest that he came from a different class or different conditions from those of the other members of the Labour Party. You heard with some surprise that this Labour member was a very rich man. If he looked a little rough, he belonged to a class that required the iron jaw and ready fist to get there [T. P. O' Connor, quoted in Ould (1925) 125 – originally in *Daily Telegraph*].

This shared style was complemented by a self-education that was similar to that of many Labour MPs. His knowledge of Shakespeare was extensive, and he also cited Emerson, Burns, Froude, Carlyle and Ben Johnson as influential.

In June 1924 Ramsay MacDonald offered Royce the Governership of Tasmania. After consulting his family, on 23 June he travelled from Spalding to London intending to accept. From King's Cross station he caught a bus to Westminster – he died on the journey. His funeral in Pinchbeck involved many from the labour movement, alongside representatives of the institutions of rural Lincolnshire. Noel Buxton, the Agricultural Minister, was present, along with local party activists and William Holmes of the National Union of Agricultural Workers. Royce left an estate valued at £131 355.

The consequent by-election was fought for Labour by Hugh Dalton. Prior to his acceptance of the candidacy he had pondered the extent to which Labour's victories in the constituency had been successes for Royce rather than for the Labour Party. 'At first I refuse on the ground that it was a personal vote, not Labour at all' [Dalton (1953) 149]. But having decided to fight, Dalton was enthused by the rural support. 'Spirit in the villages very fine and fearless. Splendid young men leading the agricultural workers here' [ibid.] He felt that Boston and Spalding were the weak spots; in contrast the national agent, Egerton Wake, felt that the party had little real presence outside the towns [Labour Party NEC, 2 September 1924]. Although Dalton found the organisation businesslike, he hinted at a lack of party propaganda under Royce; 'I made quite an ordinary speech, but they have never heard anything like it before' [Dalton Diary, July 1924]. He also met the former MP's wife: 'Mrs Royce is a queer creature ... says to young men in her village, but for the Labour Party you would be going around with broken boots' [ibid.] As an outsider Dalton found it difficult to counteract claims by the Liberals and the *Spalding Guardian* that he was hostile to religion, even though Royce had been able to deflect charges of Bolshevism. His verdict was typically dismissive 'Lincolnshire yokels weren't inoculated yet against this kind of thing' [ibid.]

The by-election result was close, suggesting that the Labour Party's strength in the constituency had not been wholly dependent on Royce's candidacy:

Holland with Boston by-election, 31 July 1924: electorate 42 220, turnout 77.2 per cent

A. W. Dean (Conservative)	12 907 (39.6 per cent)
E. H. J. W. Dalton (Labour)	12 101 (37.1 per cent)
R. P. Winfrey (Liberal)	7596 (23.3 per cent)
Majority	806 (2.5 per cent)

Thereafter Labour's electoral strength declined. In the October 1924 general election the party's vote fell to 10 689 (32.8 per cent), and in a March 1929 by-election a Liberal gained the seat, with a further Labour fall. In the general election two months later Labour fell to third place. Only in March 1966 did it ever again come close to victory.

The above suggests the centrality of Royce's social standing and political style to the three unlikely Labour victories. However this should be balanced against other factors that might have weakened Labour's appeal: the decline of agricultural trade unionism, the consolidation of Labour as a predominantly urban party and the Liberal revival in some parts of rural England in the second half of the 1920s. Yet the latter revival was particularly marked in Holland with Boston, providing a further testimony to the degree to which Royce shaped the constituency's politics between 1918 and 1924.

Royce secured electoral victories for a relatively new party by means of an electioneering style that had been common in the nineteenth century. He claimed political support on the basis of his social mobility and current position. He sought consensual solutions to national problems and claimed that his record as a modernising landlord was relevant to the challenge of post-war reconstruction.

His political position within the Labour Party was distinctive. It owed nothing to any form of socialism, nor to trade unionismn nor liberalism. He claimed a consistency in his politics: from tariff reformer and imperialist with a commitment to social reform – a democratic Toryism – through to Labour MP specialising in agricultural and imperial questions. This claim belonged to the election platform; the truth was more complex. His concern with modernisation became flavoured with labour themes, particularly the plight of agricultural workers; and his call for the abandonment of tariffs probably owed most to expediency. Yet his support for Lord Milner at the Colonial Office highlights a continuing theme in his politics – a concern with national and imperial efficiency that did not shy away from state intervention and involved significant social reform. His insistence on the protection of the standards of 'white' labour might appear heterodox in a party influenced heavily by an internationalism that was based on radical liberalism and ethical socialism, but the demand would not have been unorthodox in either the South African or the Australian Labour Party.

Sources: (1) MSS: Labour Party National Executive Committee Minutes, NMLH Manchester; Hugh Dalton Diaries, British Library of Political and Economic Science. **(2) Newspapers:** *Boston Guardian*; *Lincolnshire Free Press*; *Lincolnshire Observer*; *Spalding Guardian*. **(3) Other:** Charles W. Ould, *William Stapleton Royce: A Memoir with an Introduction by J. H. Thomas* (1925); George Lansbury, *My Life* (1928); Thomas Johnston, *Memories* (1952); Hugh Dalton, *Call Back Yesterday Memoirs 1887–1931* (1953); Henry Pelling, *Social Geography of British Elections 1885–1910* (1967); P. S. Gupta, *Imperialism and the British Labour Movement 1914–1964* (1975); Michael Kinnear, *The British Voter* (1981); Dulcie Edwards and David Cox, *My Village – Pinchbeck* (Spalding, 1986); *Pinchbeck Past and Present* (Spalding, n.d.).

DAVID HOWELL

SANDHAM, Elijah (1875–1944)
LABOUR MP, INDEPENDENT LABOUR PARTY ACTIVIST, INDEPENDENT SOCIALIST PARTY PRESIDENT

Elijah Sandham was born in Chorley, Lancashire on 17 September 1875, the son of James Sandham and Isabella, née Thorpe. His father began a small shuttlemaking and repair business at the rear of his home on the east side of the town. During the late nineteenth century the cotton industry expanded in Chorley, and as a result James Sandham's business grew rapidly. Premises were acquired at Sherbourne Street Mill and the business diversified into bobbin making, and subsequently into the manufacture of a wide variety of wooden products as a bulwark against the vicissitudes of the cotton trade. Both Elijah Sandham and his brother James entered the business.

As a young businessman Sandham became involved in local politics. The Chorley constituency, created in 1885, was strongly Conservative. It included an extensive rural area, and this agricultural vote together with the Lancastrian tradition of popular conservatism helped to make this a safe Conservative seat throughout the pre-1914 period. To a significant degree, such popular Conservatism was an expression of religious/ethnic identities, with Anglican voters backing Conservative Unionism against the claims of immigrant Irish Catholics. In Chorley the Conservative vote was further strengthened by a significant number of indigenous Catholics who were likely to vote Conservative on the issue of denominational education. The Conservative predominance was compatible with the occupational dominance of cotton textiles. In 1921 in Chorley town, 22 per cent of the male and 31 per cent of the female adult population were employed in the trade. The concomitant figures for the Chorley Rural District were 16 per cent and 69 per cent respectively.

Sandham was active in the Chorley Conservative Club and the Chorley East Ward Conservative Committee, as well as being a principal officer of the Chorley Habitation of the Primrose League. His Conservatism was typically partnered by involvement in the Church of England: his early political connections were made through St James Church in Chorley, and he also had a long-standing connection with the Boys' Brigade. When Lord Balclarres successfully defended his seat against the Liberals in the general election of 1906, Sandham assisted Balclarres' election agent. In November 1906 he won a seat in Chorley's East Ward. As a young local businessman he was viewed as a rising star within local Conservatism. He entered the Town Council keen to promote the more efficient provision of municipal services. His interventions became notable for their confrontational character, not least with fellow Conservative councillors, whom he alleged were guilty of administrative incompetence and financial malpractice. This practice of denouncing alleged dishonesty and sharp practice would mark his political career.

Confrontations became increasingly acrimonious during 1907, when Sandham began to focus on the need for social improvements in the East Ward and accused other Tory councillors of inertia. Perhaps significantly, Sandham lived close to his business in the ward that he represented, in contrast with many of his Conservative colleagues, who lived outside the town. The pivotal moment for Sandham came when he presided over an Independent Labour Party (ILP) meeting in the Chorley Co-operative Hall, with Katherine Glasier as the principal speaker. He announced that he had resigned from the East Ward Conservative Committee, quit the Conservative Club in Chorley and declared his conversion to socialism. He summed up his position in one word – 'brotherhood', in which 'men were one man, suffering and rejoicing together, that each touched all and all touched each' [*Chorley Guardian and Leyland Advertiser*, 21 September 1907]. In his conversion speech this idealism was combined with an attack on social inequality and poverty.

Having joined the ILP, Sandham established branches in Chorley and later in neighbouring Coppull and Leyland. In 1910 he became treasurer of the ILP's Lancashire Division. The party's organisation had recently developed a divisional structure. The Lancashire Division had a sizeable membership and provided Sandham with a strong base for his subsequent career. He became well known for his fiery socialist oratory in Chorley's flat iron market; his daughter, May, later commented that this was one of the ironies of her father's life [Budge (1972) in Bob Edwards Papers, Box 4, NMLH, Manchester]. As a young Tory he had heckled socialist speakers with whom he now shared platforms.

Predictably the Chorley Conservatives attacked him for his political apostasy, but despite this he retained his council seat as a Labour representative in successive elections. This must have owed something to his high personal standing as a businessman and representative, but he was also famous for his outspokenness and volatility: he received many censures and suspensions, and on one occasion was physically ejected from the council chamber. His obituary in the local press portrayed him as the 'stormy petrel' of municipal life [*Chorley Guardian and Leyland Advertiser*, 12 May 1944].

An alternative view was of 'Lijah' waging a lone crusade in the face of the Tory machine to bring about municipal improvements. Reportedly, he was crucial to the provision of public baths, two primary schools, a day nursery, the extension of free milk provision in schools and to expectant mothers, a new hospital extension and a hospital for the treatment of tuberculosis, together with a scheme for post-war municipal housing. In fact Sandham's confrontational style hid a capacity for political manoeuvre and dialogue. He courted support from potential allies amongst Liberal and independent councillors. His business connections facilitated support on specific issues from individual Conservatives. One tactic was regularly to challenge the composition of important council subcommittees, claiming that they were the preserve of an inner circle of Tory councillors; Sandham could then woo those who were excluded, including some Conservatives. The result was the forging of a series of effective *ad hoc* alliances through which he could gain crucial votes in favour of specific improvements.

Sandham stood as Chorley's first Labour parliamentary candidate in the December 1918 general election. This candidacy was bound to be difficult as Chorley's durable Conservatism had been strengthened by the party's unambiguously prowar position. In contrast Sandham's involvement with the ILP laid him open to accusations of pacifism and pro-German sympathies. The immediate circumstances of the election – military victory, the continuation of the Lloyd George Coalition and the issuing of the Coalition coupon to the Conservative candidate, Douglas Hacking – compounded his problems.

The Labour challenge was also affected by tensions within the party's own organisation. The decision to form the Chorley Divisional Labour Party (DLP) was taken at a meeting on 18 February 1918. Although the meeting comprised 36 delegates from 18 organisations claiming to represent 15 000 members, the initiative effectively came from the Amalgamated Society of Engineers (ASE), which was particularly strong in Leyland, and from local branches of the Lancashire and Cheshire Miners' Federation (LCMF). However the principal trade union strength was provided by the textile unions. Sandham was favoured as candidate by the ASE and the Chorley branch of the National Union of Clerks, but the textile unions had significant reservations – this difference was apparent when the DLP was formally founded at a meeting in March, and was deepened by the miners' branches, which proposed two possible candidates from the LCMF.

The uncertainty caused Sandham to indicate that unless the issue was resolved, he would seek the nearby Rossendale candidacy. Prior to the first annual meeting of the Chorley DLP in April 1918, a meeting of the Chorley Textile Workers' Federation formed a committee with the objective of providing candidates from within the textile unions to contest both municipal and parliamentary elections. This marked the birth of the textile union caucus, which proved capable of exercising considerable influence over Labour nominations in Chorley for many years. The Textile Workers' Federation also resolved that 'Any candidate for Chorley must be a recognised official or member of a bone fide trade union' [Chorley Guardian and Legland Hundred Advertisers, 6 April 1918]. This declaration could be seen as an attempt to exclude Sandham – an ILP member and a businessman.

Yet the DLP meeting on 27 April 1918 revealed that he had support from engineering and rubber workers, clerks, shop assistants, printers and farm workers. His nomination by 52 votes to 30 came only after much wrangling between his supporters and the textile unions. The Chorley branches of the Operative Spinners' Association and the Bleachers' Association nominated two of their own officials as alternative candidates.

Although Sandham's ILP membership might have been objectionable for some patriotic trade unionists, the disagreements were much more indicative of trade union sectionalism. The Labour Party's 1918 constitution and the formation of DLPs was accompanied by heightened optimism about Labour's electoral prospects in the context of a greatly widened franchise and expectations of partisan realignment. In this context trade unions sought increased political representation and pursued nominations in what were hopefully winnable seats. Given the dominance of textile employment in much of the Chorley constituency the textile unions' concern to secure the nomination was predictable.

During the electoral campaign the relationship between Sandham and the textile unions remained distant. He addressed only one meeting sponsored by them – a poorly attended meeting at the Weavers' Institute. His reception from an audience of women weavers was frosty, despite his claim to champion the rights of women workers and voters. When Sandham characteristically became involved in a campaign squabble with a prominent Conservative councillor who was also a Roman Catholic, some textile union leaders queried his political judgement. Although Sandham took care to court Catholic opinion throughout his council career, this row over the parochial question of the Conservative's appointment to the town's Housing and Planning Committee threatened to heighten religious tensions and lose Catholic votes.

Inevitably Sandham's ILP activities produced claims that his patriotism was questionable, whilst his business activities permitted the allegation that he paid his employees less than trade union rates. His statement that 'the world is my country, and humanity is my religion' was an implausible vote winner in December 1918. However it should be noted that Sandham favoured Germany paying reparations to Belgium and other invaded territories. He also supported the punishment of the Kaiser as a deterrent against future acts of aggression [*Chorley Guardian and Leyland Advertiser*, 7 December 1918]. Faced with attempts to identify him with Bolshevism, Sandham insisted that 'He did not believe in Bolshevism but in Parliamentary action' [*Chorley Guardian and Leyland Advertiser*, 14 December 1918]. A contemporary suggested that Sandham had strong support in the mining community of Coppull and in his own Chorley East Ward, but his defeat was decisive [see *Chorley Guardian and Leyland Advertiser*, 21 December 1918 for an assessment of his support].

Chorley, 1918: electorate 35 370, turnout 54.5 per cent

D. H. Hacking (Coalition Conservative)	13 059 (67.7 per cent)
E. Sandham (Labour)	6222 (32.3 per cent)
Majority	6837 (35.4 per cent)

After his defeat Sandham attacked his critics, insisting that it had been the cavilling of his personal and political allies on both left and right that had turned a difficult task into an impossible one. He also suffered setbacks in municipal politics. Blocked from further participation in the council subcommittees that he had utilised to promote his reform agenda, he also failed to be elected as alderman. Sandham, it seemed, had upset too many people. He remained on Chorley Council until 1929 but his profile was much reduced. Arguably he had achieved much of what he had set out to accomplish in 1907, and the development of more thorough Labour Party organisation meant that he was no longer the only party representative on the council.

The immediate post-war period also saw a turning point in Sandham's domestic and business lives. He moved with his family out of the grime of Chorley's east side to the rural and comparatively palatial surroundings of the 'Nightingales' in Heath Charnock. His involvement in the family business was reduced, with his brother James becoming more prominent. In Chorley he remained politically active, building an ILP institute on land adjacent to his business premises. This 'Steeley Lane Institute' became a focal point for education and recreation away from the attractions of the public house. One of his preoccupations at the institute was the promotion of Esperanto.

During the 1920s Sandham became much more prominent in the national ILP. His base was the party's Lancashire Division, which was second only to Scotland in terms of divisional membership. In 1924 he was elected to the National Administrative Council (NAC) as the Lancashire Divisional Representative. He entered the NAC in the context of vigorous and sometimes confused debate on the party's post-war role. The 1918 Labour Party Constitution, by permitting individual membership through Divisional Labour Parties, had posed a major challenge to the ILP. The latter was no longer the principal means by which individual socialists entered the wider Labour Party. One response to this challenge was associated with Clifford Allen, a pacifist and ethical socialist. He wished the ILP to become a socialist think-tank for the wider Labour Party, producing carefully researched statements that the Labour Party could adopt and a Labour government could implement. Allen was a successful fundraiser, and his achievements in this area permitted a major expansion of ILP activities, including study groups to develop policies.

Yet Allen's strategy was always controversial within the ILP; many members were concerned not with detailed policies but with traditional propaganda work. Some of them increasingly mistrusted Allen's admiration for MacDonald and his high-profile metropolitan connections. Tensions were exacerbated when some ILP members reacted critically to the record of the 1924 Labour Government. Sandham was very much in the anti-Allen camp – he had challenged Allen for the chairmanship at the 1924 ILP conference. Allen, who was often scathing about the quality of some NAC colleagues, bracketed Sandham with Walter Ayles and Fred Longden as opposition that could be disregarded. However arguments within the NAC became more heated and Allen resigned the chairmanship in October 1925.

Thereafter the ILP leadership gradually became more thoroughly left wing. A party document on the living wage, published in 1926, was ambiguous in its political implications. Under James Maxton the ILP provided a radical interpretation of its popular characterisation: 'Socialism in Our Time'. Sandham was a thorough supporter of this shift to the left and a reliable ally of Maxton on the NAC. In July 1928 NAC members divided over Maxton's sponsorship of the Cook–Maxton Manifesto campaign, a crusade for socialist revivalism outside the institutions of the ILP. Critics stressed the lack of consultation; a majority within the NAC were prepared to back Maxton. Whatever the procedural niceties, this indicated a more fundamental political split between left and right. Sandham voted with the majority.

Along with his increased prominence in the ILP, Sandham sought once more to enter Parliament. In the 1924 general election he stood in Liverpool Kirkdale. Liverpool – with its religious sectarianism, working-class Conservatism and maritime economy – had been a weak area for the Labour Party [See Waller (1981); Davies (1996)]. However the recent electoral signs were more encouraging. In February 1923 the party gained its first seat at a by-election in Edge Hill; 15 months later a second by-election victory was achieved in West Toxteth. Kirkdale had long been a cockpit for religious antagonisms. The constituency's two wards, Kirkdale and St Domingo, had a reputation for militant Protestantism [see Davies (1996) 292, 311–13]. The sitting MP, John de Fonblanque Pennefather, typified many in Liverpool Conservative politics: he was a partner in a firm of cottonbrokers, a landowner and former master of the fox hounds, as well as a reliable defender of Ulster and critic of the Vatican. A vigorous opponent of the capital levy, he argued that unemployment could be reduced by assisted emigration [Waller (1981) 308, 505]. Sandham's performance in the 1924 election suggested that if the dominance of Conservatism in Liverpool was weakening, at least in Kirkdale older loyalties remained strong.

Kirkdale, 1924: electorate 32 262, turnout 73.7 per cent

J. de F. Pennefather (Conservative)	14 392 (64.6 per cent)
E. Sandham (Labour)	9369 (39.4 per cent)
Majority	5023 (21.2 per cent)

In May 1929 Labour achieved a significant electoral advance in the city, doubling its representation from two to four. One of the gains came in Kirkdale, where Sandham had a new Conservative opponent:

Kirkdale, 1929: electorate 40 646, turnout 72.9 per cent

E. Sandham (Labour)	15 222 (51.3 per cent)
R. Rankin (Conservative)	14 429 (48.7 per cent)
Majority	793 (2.6 per cent)

Sandham entered the Commons as an exponent of ILP rhetoric. His style was captured by a not unsympathetic colleague:

His body is massive and slow moving. So is his speech. So is his thought. In our present Parliamentary situation Sandhams are invaluable. On minds like this, cozening threats, wheedlings, sophistries, produce no effect whatsoever. He doesn't argue. He gets his outlines right and crunches steadily along, impervious to every form of blandishment and intimidation. … Like the rest of us, he has the defects of his qualities. In his case, like that of some of the Clyde men, his defect is a complete unwillingness to recognise the necessity of having regard to either strategy or tactics [W. J. Brown, *New Leader*, 13 June 1930].

During his campaign he had defended the possibility that Parliament could be used by the working class; by the time of his maiden speech he had become less optimistic:

I said that in the past politics may have been a game played by the orthodox political parties with marked cards and a loaded dice, and that, if this were so all the more reason for people like myself to go to the House of Commons to attempt to humanise politics. ... I have been wondering since I entered this House how soon there would be an alteration in the atmosphere, which has not impressed me. I believe we could do more of a practical nature in a city council in a day than we can do here in a week [*Hansard*, 11 July 1929, cols 1203–4].

In fact Sandham's position was that significant improvement in working-class conditions necessitated the abolition of capitalism. This made him an increasingly thorough critic of a minority Labour government facing rising unemployment; but it also rendered him ineffective in debates on alternative economic policies. The debate on free trade and protection was 'merely a question of Tweedledum and Tweedledee so far as the working classes [are] concerned' [*Hansard*, 13 March 1930 col 1613].

Such fundamentalism was given more force in Sandham's case because of his commitment not just to the ILP but also to its distinctive policies. When Margaret Bondfield introduced revised rates of, and qualifications for, unemployment benefit in November 1929, these were viewed critically by many in the Parliamentary Labour Party. The critics extended beyond the established left, and many of them sought adjustments through negotiation. Maxton and the ILP left, including Sandham, were the core of a much smaller group who opposed the Labour Government in the division lobby. This episode was a significant step in the deterioration of relations between the ILP and the Labour Party. Maxton and his allies had attempted to mobilise all Labour MPs with an ILP link to oppose the proposals, but most of them were Labour MPs first and ILPers second and had refused to follow his lead. During 1930 the ILP Parliamentary Group was reconstructed, with membership restricted to those who were prepared to back ILP policy in Parliament even when this was at odds with Labour Party policy. Sandham was amongst the 18 MPs who were prepared to make this commitment.

This episode meant that the ILP critics had become an identifiable faction within the PLP, acting as a left-wing opposition to an increasingly beleaguered administration. In October 1930 they moved a socialist amendment to the King's Speech; in July 1931 they voted repeatedly against the Anomalies Bill, which was the product of a deal between the Government and the Trades Union Congress on the question of eligibility for unemployment benefit. Sandham participated regularly in these activities, but very much as a foot soldier. Others – James Maxton, George Buchanan, Fenner Brockway, Fred Jowett – made the speeches.

Sandham's contribution to parliamentary pyrotechnics was typical of his penchant for muckraking. In July 1930 the ILP MP John Beckett had scandalised respectable opinion by seizing the mace. On Saturday 26 July 1930 Sandham spoke at a meeting of the ILP's Lancashire Divisional Council:

The sheer stupid tradition of this ghost house has got most of the Members in its deadly grip. Labour Members can receive bribes to help pass doubtful Bills in the interests of private individuals; Labour Members can get stupidly drunk in this place; but none of these things are against the sacred traditions of this House, in fact they are in keeping with them. It is known that Labour Members accepted money from money lenders and other interests, and it is known that Labour Members of Parliament get drunk in this House [*Manchester Guardian*, 28 July 1930].

For Sandham the contrast was between this alleged acquiescence in corruption and the treatment of Beckett: 'Immediately John Beckett touches the sacred symbol, the gilt toy, all the pack are in full cry. They are as righteously indignant as would any tribe of savages be if somebody had desecrated the temple of their favourite medicine man' [*Hansard*, 29 July 1930 col 310].

The Manchester speech was raised as a question of privilege by the Conservative MP Earl Winterton [see Winterton (1953) 162–3]. Sandham was called before the Committee of Privileges but refused to provide evidence of his claims. The Committee found Sandham guilty of a gross breach of privilege in making allegations outside the Commons; in addition his statement that the acceptance of bribes was in keeping with the traditions of the House constituted a gross libel upon the House as a whole [Report of the Committee of Privileges, 30 July 1930]. Although members of the ILP Group defended him in the Commons, there was some criticism within the ILP of his speech. Fenner Brockway felt that such allegations deflected attention from the left's basic cause and aroused maximum prejudice [*New Leader*, 1 August 1930]. However the beleaguered ILP Parliamentary Group felt compelled to give support to any of its members, whatever the reservations of some about the advisability of a specific action by an individual on his own initiative.

The parliamentary isolation of the ILP Group indicated the growing estrangement of the ILP and the Labour Party. The core of the problem was the refusal of ILP MPs to endorse the standing orders of the Parliamentary Labour Party since this would prevent the expression in the division lobby of distinctive ILP policies. The consequence was that Sandham and other ILP Group Members fought the 1931 election without Labour Party endorsement. In Kirkdale, Sandham not only faced the problems arising from the collapse of the Labour Government and the power of the National appeal, but also experienced a revival of religious sectarianism.

Curiously, in 1929 Sandham – an ILP candidate in a predominantly Protestant seat – had been unique amongst the city's Labour candidates in supporting the Roman Catholic position on the funding of denominational education. In January 1931 the Catholic Labour MP John Scurr successfully moved an amendment to his own government's Education Bill. This would defer the Bill and its raising of the school leaving age until denominational schools were given sufficient funding to resource the additional facilities required. Sandham voted with the Government; three other Liverpool Labour MPs sided with the rebels. On this occasion Sandham the rebel was Sandham the party loyalist. As well as this national contretemps, the Labour organisation in Liverpool split in 1930 over the city council's sale of the site of a former workhouse for the construction of a Catholic cathedral. Claims of Catholic political influence aroused Protestant militancy. The Reverend H. D. Longbottom, having expressed his preference for a 'poison germ factory' rather than a Catholic cathedral, entered the 1931 Kirkdale election as a Protestant Party candidate [Waller (1981) 324]. He indicted the Conservatives for abandoning Protestant concerns, and blamed Irish immigration for unemployment and poor housing. Having won the Saint Domingo ward in the 1930 municipal elections, and with his party polling credibly in the Kirkdale ward, his poll in October 1931 was predictably strong.

Kirkdale, 1931: electorate 40 862, turnout 77.5 per cent

R. Rankin (Conservative)	14 303 (45.2 per cent)
E. Sandham (Independent Labour Party)	9531 (30.1 per cent)
Rev. H. D. Longbottom (Liverpool Protestant Party)	7834 (24.7 per cent)
Majority	4772 (15.1 per cent)

The shifts in voting compared with 1929 were complex, and which of the other two candidates Longbottom harmed more is unclear.

Even after the Labour Party lost office, and was decimated in the 1931 general election, the dispute between the ILP and the Labour Party continued. The conflict over PLP Standing Orders was only one aspect of this dispute; there were also serious arguments about the policy and attitude of the larger organisation. For Sandham these two aspects could not be separated as he viewed the ILP's organisational vigour as a central part of its traditional commitment to socialism. He personally tended to support a split from the Labour Party, but was worried about the impact of 'irresponsible' elements within the party. In the public arena of party conferences Sandham was circumspect about outlining his position: at the Blackpool conference in early 1932, against the vocal call for a strong lead from above, he argued that the delegates should make up their own minds.

When the ILP did split from the Labour Party in July 1932 at a specially convened conference in Bradford, the decision was eagerly endorsed by Sandham, who later recalled his enthusiasm at the prospect of an 'end of careerism and foolish stunting' [*Labour's Northern Voice*, May 1934]. However within the ILP many believed that the split signalled a break with a reformist past and the building of a new revolutionary policy: this strategy was promoted not only by the pro-Communist Revolutionary Policy Committee (RPC) but also by a majority of the leadership of the ILP. Sandham, as the Lancashire Divisional Chairman and NAC representative, became the leading figure in opposition to this approach. He believed in the 'paramount importance' of democracy whilst the new policy of the ILP questioned the role of Parliament. He also believed in the basic efficacy of the established organisations of the labour movement, such as trades councils, whilst the ILP proposed to champion new 'workers' councils' [*Labour's Northern Voice*, February 1933; NAC Minutes, June 1933]. Behind these disputes lay the ILP's desire to work in a united front and eventually to form a united organisation with the Communist Party. After attempting some joint activity in late 1932, Sandham and the leadership of the Lancashire Division came down firmly against any form of cooperation with the 'alien' Communist Party. In this they were supported by the organisers of a number of other divisions, including Scotland, the North-East, Yorkshire and East Anglia, plus a substantial proportion of the rank and file members of the ILP. However only in Lancashire was the leadership completely united in its opposition to what had become official party policy.

During 1933–34 Sandham led both the defence of the Lancashire Divisional Council and the attack on the RPC – the London-based ILP faction that was leading the drive towards the new policy and closer cooperation with the Communist Party. On the NAC Sandham found himself increasingly isolated. Sympathetic figures such as the General Secretary, John Paton, later Labour MP for Norwich, resigned from the party. Increasingly truculent in his position, Sandham often could not muster the support of even those who shared his suspicions of the united front and the 'new revolutionary policy'. At a fractious meeting in June, when the new policy in the wake of the recent annual conference was debated, he found himself alone in calling for an immediate end to the United Front with the Communist Party; he also criticised the way in which ILP policy discussion had become 'poisoned' by talk of revolution by force [NAC Minutes 24–25 June 1933].

The decisions taken at the ILP annual conference in March 1933 in Derby were a major blow to Sandham, the Lancashire Divisional Council and their supporters. The 'new revolutionary policy', its stress on workers' councils and a reduction in the emphasis given to parliamentary struggles in the ILP's strategy were all endorsed by the conference. Even more worrying for Sandham was the endorsement not only of the united front, but also of the ultimate aim of merging with the Communist Party. Sandham wrote that the ILP's distinctive appeal lay in its 'democratic appeal to all that is decent, honest and essentially peace loving in the well educated, technically skilled workers of Britain'. With the abandonment of this strategy at the Derby conference and the rush 'into the arms of the CP', he feared that the ILP was becoming redundant [*Labour's Northern Voice*, July 1933]. Sandham, along with the ILP's Lancashire Divisional Organiser and ILP veteran J. T. Abbott, decided to create an organised faction, the Unity Group, to oppose these tendencies. They received support from across the ILP, particularly in East Anglia, where the literary critic John Middleton Murry was an important figure in the local ILP and the national Unity Group. However the Group's organisational focus remained on Lancashire, where in June the Divisional Council requested all branches to cease co-operating with the Communist Party. At the Divisional Conference in September, a motion moved by Sandham that the United Front was 'quite definitely killing our identity as a party, whilst frittering away valuable energy and finance in a resultless activity' was passed by 31 to 26. At the ILP's 1934 Annual Conference the Lancashire Division, in a motion moved by Sandham, called for a complete reversal of the 'new revolutionary policy' [Labour's Northern Voice, February 1934]. However instead of heeding the Lancashire Division's calls for the reversal of the policy the 1934 ILP conference decided to reorganise the party's structure in line with the principles of democratic centralism.

For the Unity Group this was a step too far; led by Abbott, a member of the ILP since 1894, resignations flooded in and a new political party, the Independent Socialist Party (ISP), was established on 13 May 1934 (see special note below). Sandham's role in the formation of the ISP is rather enigmatic. He had been at the forefront of the Unity Group and was seen by those establishing the ISP as its natural leader, yet he was absent from all the ISP's foundation meetings. It is possible that illness played a part in this. However Sandham felt a strong loyalty to the ILP and clearly found it difficult to break with his political home of 24 years. At the 1934 ILP conference he had declared unequivocally that he would remain a member of the ILP. At the special divisional conference of the party, called to reconvene the decimated Lancashire ILP Council on 26 May, Sandham's attitude was declared as 'undecided' and he was invited to the conference. However that conference made clear how untenable Sandham's position was when it adopted without dissent a resolution that Sandham's views did not reflect the views of the membership, and called for a ballot to elect a new divisional representative to the NAC.

In his letter of resignation from the party Sandham expressed his disappointment with the ILP. He acknowledged that disaffiliation had been a risk but had hoped that 'another section of my most deeply respected comrades ... would be able to steer the ILP past the dangers of sham revolutionism on to the tremendous role which they expected the ILP to play when it had complete political freedom'. He attributed the failure of the ILP in this task not to the RPC but to the leadership, including Maxton, who had 'unexpectedly sided with [the] Communistically minded'. He finished by claiming that he did not really consider himself to be leaving the ILP as 'the Party which calls itself this, until it is finally absorbed into the Communist Party, is not the ILP which I joined and in which I have had the honour to serve' [Labour's Northern Voice, July 1934]. When Sandham joined his comrades in their new party he declared that he was joining the 'ISP because it [was his] deepest conviction that the spirit of the ILP must be kept alive'. He criticised the ILP for becoming a 'sectarian backwater stuck in stultified truths of half a century before', and set out a stall for the ISP in appealing to the 'higher level of education of British workers' and to 'man's reason' [Labour's Northern Voice, August 1934].

Perhaps with one eye on the absence of Sandham at its foundation, the ISP had decided to elect only a provisional committee. At its first formal conference in September 1934 Sandham was elected as the first full chairman of the new organisation. The ISP maintained a significant low-key presence, centred primarily on Lancashire although branches were established elsewhere, most notably – inspired by Middleton Murry – in London. Sandham remained the figurehead for the organisation and when the ISP reconsidered affiliation to the ILP shortly before the Unity Campaign of 1937 it was Sandham who took the lead in the negotiations with Maxton and the ILP. However Sandham's health problems, which had begun in 1934, were becoming more acute so he allowed Abbott to take on the bulk of the practical organisation of the new party. In 1938, despite being too ill to attend the ISP annual convention, he was re-elected party chairman. It was only at the following convention, which he was again unable to attend due to ill health, that he resigned as the party's leading figure.

Sandham moved to Blackpool, where he died on 7 May 1944. His funeral took place at Carleton Crematorium near Blackpool on 11 May 1944. He left an estate of £238 10s 6d. Sandham's first wife, Alice, had died in 1906, but his second wife, Charlotte Ellen, and his two sons and two daughters from the first marriage survived him. One daughter, May, was a member of Chorley Town Council, serving from 1929 and was mayor of Chorley in 1953–54. Through the ILP Guild of Youth she met and married Bob Edwards, who served with the Republicans in Spain, was an ILP candidate on three occasions and was chairman of the ILP from 1943–48. From 1947 he was secretary of the Chemical Workers' Union, and served as Labour MP for Bilston from 1955–87. Sandham's son Ernest Thorpe Sandham lived in Chorley and later in Ormskirk. He was a representative for a firm of undertakers and monumental masons. Herbert Sandham entered the family business and served as Labour councillor on Chorley Town Council.

During his brief parliamentary career Sandham appeared to be an inflexible and ineffective figure. 'A curious cross-grained creature ... [who] can no more behave than he can live the life of a fish' was Ramsay MacDonald's assessment in the aftermath of the privileges affair [MacDonald to Charles Sixsmith, 7 August 1930, PRO 30/69 1176]. He found the Commons uncongenial and the performance of the Labour Government disillusioning. These experiences strengthened the penchant for rectitude, revolt and recrimination that had been evident in his earlier Chorley career. Yet as a municipal politician he arguably showed some capacity for bargaining that was lost in later years. Easily dismissed as an eccentric, he bore the self-improving and deeply ethical tendencies that were common amongst socialist pioneers in communities that could offer little encouragement. His later choices – the increasingly radical ILP, disaffiliation, the ISP – were one ethical socialist's response to the problem of political choice in a period dominated by the alternatives of the Labour Party and the Communist International.

Sources: (1) MSS: BLPES ILP Archive; P. L. Budge, 'May Edwards Councillor 1929–35' (1972), unpublished manuscript in Bob Edwards Papers, Box 4, ILP Pamphlets and Reports 1908, ILP Lancashire (Area 10) Divisional Council Minutes, ILP, NMLH Manchester; Ramsay MacDonald Papers, PRO. **(2) Newspapers:** *Manchester Guardian*; *Daily Herald*; *New Leader*; *Chorley and District News*; *Chorley Guardian and Leyland Hundred Advertiser*; *Chorley Standard and District Advertiser*; *Labour's Northern Voice*. **(3) Other:** *Hansard* 1929–31, *Morris's Directory of Chorley* (1895); *Chorley Directory* (1895); *Census of England and Wales* (1911, 1921); *Kelly's Directory of Lancashire with Gore's Liverpool* (1898); *Who Was Who 1941–50*; Earl Winterton, *Orders of the Day* (1953); R. E. Dowse, *Left in the Centre* (1966); Henry Pelling, *Social Geography of British Elections 1885–1910* (1967); J. Hill, 'Working Class Politics in Lancashire 1885–1906: A regional Study in the Origins of the Labour Party' (unpublished PhD thesis, University of Keele, 1971); L. B. Nattrass, 'The Governing Elite in Chorley 1854–1914' (unpublished MA dissertation, University of Lancaster 1974); D. T. Denver and H. T. G Hands, 'Politics 1924–74', in *The History of Lancashire County Council 1889–1974* (1977); Ben Pimlott, *Labour and the Left in the 1930s* (Cambridge, 1977); P. J. Waller, *Democracy and Sectarianism: A Political and Social History of Liverpool 1868–1939* (Liverpool, 1981); J. Jupp, *The Radical Left in Britain in the 1930s* (1982); Sam Davies, *Liverpool Labour – Social and Political Influences on the Development of the Labour Party 1900–1939* (Keele, 1996); G. Cohen, 'The Independent Labour Party 1932–1939 (unpublished DPhil thesis, University of York, 2000).

STEPHEN CATTERALL
GIDON COHEN

See also: †Campbell STEPHEN; †Dorothy JEWSON; †George BUCHANAN; †Fred JOWETT.

Special Note: The Independent Socialist Party

The Independent Socialist Party (ISP) was formed on 13 May 1934. It stumbled into existence at a conference convened by the disgruntled leadership of the Lancashire Division of the Independent Labour Party (ILP). In July 1932 the decision of the ILP to disaffiliate from the Labour Party had been supported by large sections of the Lancashire ILP. Although the subsequent membership loss was substantial, it remained less in the north west than in many other parts of Britain. Disaffiliation was a clear statement of incompatibility between the ILP and the

Labour Party, but its positive content was more ambiguous. For some, most notably the London-based Revolutionary Policy Committee (RPC), it signalled the need to formulate a new revolutionary policy with particular stress on developing a close working relationship with the Communist Party and the Communist International. For others disaffiliation was a more reluctant decision and was taken to give the ILP, especially the parliamentary ILP, the space to follow its own socialist path in an uncompromising fashion. This latter position was dominant in the Lancashire Division of the ILP.

Following disaffiliation the RPC gained significant ground within the ILP in terms of support and influence over policy. In 1933 the party adopted a new revolutionary policy based on working towards the creation of workers' councils, with a consequent reduction in the place of Parliament in the party's strategy. By 1933 the controversial committee, which would disband to join the Communist Party in 1935, was gaining ground outside London, including establishing a foothold in the Lancashire ILP. At the suggestion of leading opponents of the RPC in London the Lancashire ILP established the Unity Group to defend the traditions of the ILP and prevent Communist takeover. The leadership of the Unity Group and of the Lancashire Division were effectively at one with Elijah Sandham, the divisional chairman and representative on the National Administrative Council (NAC), ably assisted by Tom Abbott, the divisional organiser. The central concern for the Unity Group was the relationship between the ILP and communism. Whilst not against the 'revolutionary' label, the Group steadfastly opposed the ILP pursuing a United Front policy with the Communist Party unless the Labour Party and the unions could be brought on board. Given that those in the mainstream of the labour movement were never likely to agree to common action with the Communists, the Unity Group wanted to withdraw completely from the United Front. On 20 June 1933 the Lancashire Divisional Council circulated a letter to the division's branches announcing that their participation in the United Front had ceased, and urging them to end their joint activities with the Communist Party. This was directly contrary to the national policy of the ILP.

Opposition to the United Front and the ILP's new policy, and consequently support for the Unity Group, was not restricted to Lancashire. The East Anglian Division, whose membership was concentrated in Norwich, was an increasingly significant component of the post-disaffiliation ILP. There was considerable support for the Unity Group within the Division, centred on the influential figure of John Middleton Murry, the literary critic and sometime close friend of D. H. Lawrence. Using the columns of his literary and, in the early 1930s, increasingly political journal *The Adelphi*, and in his book *The Necessity of Communism* (1932), Middleton Murry promoted the ideas of ethical communism. He believed that the ILP could promote ethical communism only if it remained independent of both the failed gradualism of the Labour Party and the subservient politics of the Communist Party. The Norwich branch declared the end of its cooperation with the United Front at the same time as the Lancashire Division (June 1933). A manifesto opposing the new politics of the ILP was presented by Middleton Murry to a specially convened divisional conference in October. Although the manifesto was rejected it attracted considerable support, including by the divisional chairman, George Johnson, and the conference rejected both the United Front and the NAC's proposals for a reduced role for Parliament in the ILP strategy [Division 5 Council, 1 June 1933; Minutes of Division 5 special conference, 15 October 1933; *New Leader*, 3 November 1933]. Prominent members of other divisions were also sympathetic to the Unity Group. The Scottish Division was the largest and most influential section of the ILP in the 1930s, and its organiser, James Carmichael, and the Divisional Council were opposed to continuing the United Front. Similarly, in the north-east the organiser Mark Simpson and the Executive of the Divisional Council opposed cooperation with the Communist Party. After the 1933 ILP conference in Derby, Simpson and Carmichael joined with the Lancashire organiser and Unity Group leader Tom Abbott to write to the NAC calling for an end to the United Front [NAC Minutes, 24–5 June 1933].

In a rather romantic fashion the Unity Group constructed a past for the ILP in which the party had encouraged democratic debate and divisional autonomy, and the group now saw these principles as under threat. The Power for Socialism fund, an outgrowth of the 1933 Special Effort Fund, led to increasing demands being made on divisional finances to support the top-heavy party centre – special venom was reserved for the organisers of the ILP journal, the *New Leader*. The Unity Group contrasted the financial drain caused by the party's paper nationally with the local success of the Lancashire ILP newspaper and Unity Group mouthpiece *Labour's Northern Voice*, edited by Samuel Higgenbotham. The Lancashire Divisional Council, crying foul at what it perceived as an attempt to replace divisional autonomy with centralised control, refused to contribute to the compulsory fund unless the funding of the *New Leader* was reconsidered (NAC Minutes, 13–4 May 1933, 24–5 June 1933). Of even greater concern for the Unity Group were the decisions of the 1934 ILP conference to increase party discipline and the power of the central executive in-line with the principles of democratic centralism. Behind these points lay the fundamental issue of the ILP's ideology. Unity Group supporters in the Manchester City branch proposed a resolution to the 1934 York conference to commit the ILP firmly to ethical democratic socialism:

> In a country where the industrial working-class is in a majority, a socialist regime can only be firmly based on the enlightened democratic assent of the majority of people. It is therefore an essential part of the work of a Socialist organisation to propagate not merely 'Collectivism' as an economic necessity (for in this the 'National Socialists' and Fascists will be equally successful), but Socialism as an ethically superior social system. Thus the ILP's propaganda must not be merely economic and addressed to the political intelligence of workers, but also idealistic and addressed to their humane intelligence, as was the practice of Keir Hardy [*sic*] and the pioneers of the ILP [ILP Conference Report, 1934].

The rejection of their proposals for ethical socialism, the moves towards democratic centralism, the continuation of the united front with the Communist Party and the prominence of the RPC were too much for some leading members of the Unity Group. After the York conference Tom Abbott, the divisional organiser and one of the longest-standing members of the Lancashire ILP, announced his resignation from the party, citing as his reason the wholesale change in the nature of the party in the short time since disaffiliation:

> York is the 'next step' in the stage of carrying the ILP into the CP. It is the inevitable consequence of the toleration by the NAC – evidently unable to meet its task after the break with the Labour Party – of the RPC with its alien outlook, secret organisation and purse, which soon poisoned the stream of life flowing through the ILP with its fellowship and comradeship which had grown over the past 42 years, and gave such historic results [*Labour's Northern Voice*, May 1934].

Abbott's resignation was accompanied by those of other high-profile members of the Lancashire Division, including Samuel Higgenbotham, the editor of *Labour's Northern Voice*, Arthur Mostyn, the cartoonist at *Labour's Northern Voice*, and Stephen Shaw and Roger Shackelton of the Nelson Weavers.

Although frustrated with the ILP, the reasons for disaffiliation from the Labour Party, which had led to the decision in 1932, weighed heavily on the minds of those in the Unity Group. When they met on 13 May to discuss the future, a group led by Samuel Higgenbotham proposed rejoining the Labour Party. This move would strongly depend on a positive assessment of the prospects of the Socialist League, the left-wing Labour organisation led by Sir Stafford Cripps and consisting largely of ex-ILPers who had chosen remain with the Labour Party in 1932. However the majority of the conference, led by Tom Abbott and Arthur Mostyn, were in favour of forming a new party. Thus the Independent Socialist Party (ISP) was born.

At its foundation the ISP developed a policy based on the idea of revolutionary socialism as 'an ethically superior social system'. It affirmed that the 'change from Capitalism to Socialism involves a revolution', but insisted that this transition 'can only be accomplished by the enlightened democratic assent of the majority of the people' [ISP Papers]. *Labour's Northern Voice*, previously the journal of the Lancashire Division of the ILP, now adopted a position of formal independence, although in reality it was, in the initial period, the voice of the ISP. Robert Dowse, in his influential history of the ILP, has suggested that the ISP was the result of Elijah Sandham's personal fiefdom in the Lancashire ILP, and that it was personal attachment to Sandham that drove many into the new party. Thus it is particularly significant that Sandham was not present at the ISP's foundational conference. It is possible that illness played a part in his absence, but it seems more likely that he had serious doubts about leaving the ILP. A central facet of Sandham's defence of his Unity Group was its ultimate loyalty to the ILP. In contrast to Abbott's threat to leave the ILP, just a month before the ISP was formed Sandham had unequivocally stated that he would remain in the ILP. Inevitably, together with all his supporters outside the party, Sandham did resign, but not until more than a month after the ISP's formation.

Perhaps with one eye to the absence of Sandham, at its initial conference the ISP did not appoint a full committee and only appointed a provisional chairman, Wilfred Picken, later a National Union of Distributive and Allied Workers (NUDAW) official and executive member of the Manchester Borough Labour Party (BLP). The first annual convention of the ISP was held in Manchester on 29–30 September 1934, with Sandham, Abbott and John Middleton Murry as speakers. The convention set up a constitution, elected a General Council, and carried a small number of resolutions that indicated the primary interests of the ISP. The party's constitution was based on the 1922 constitution of the ILP, which gave the ILP the opportunity to portray the new party as backward looking [*New Leader*, 7 September 1934]. Sandham was elected chairman and Tom Abbott the general secretary, whilst Harry Ponsonby (a director of Stockport County football club and an ILPer of 27 years' standing) was elected treasurer. These three officers were joined on the ISP General Council by Stephen Shaw (Nelson), Miss Morris (Ashton), W. Entwistle (Blackpool), John Middleton Murry (Norwich) and W. L. Thorpe (East Manchester) [*Labour's Northern Voice*, November 1934].

The convention passed three important resolutions: the first supported the attempted move towards socialism by groups within the Labour Party; the second stressed the constitutional methods of the ISP; and the third called for the socialisation of the cotton industry (*Labour's Northern Voice*, October 1934). In many ways these three resolutions summed up the basic position of and important questions faced by the ISP. The first resolution reflected the intense interest that the ISP had in the Labour Party and the close relationship that some were trying to forge with the larger party. The second resolution indicated the enduring interest in constitutional and ethical socialism and the continuity between the ISP's position and the politics of the early ILP. The third resolution indicated the only real links the ISP had with an industrial base, namely in cotton. When the ILP had disaffiliated from the Labour Party it had retained some influence over the Nelson Weavers, with four of its members holding official positions. When these four refused to work for Labour Party candidates in local and national elections they were dismissed from their positions. Two of the four, Stephen Shaw and Roger Shackleton, left the ILP in 1934 and formed an ISP branch in Nelson. With Shaw sitting on the new General Council of the ISP, and given the interest of other ISP members in the cotton industry, it was scarcely surprising that the cotton industry and unions appeared frequently on the list of concerns of the ISP

The ISP's positions only made real sense when connected to contemporary debates in the Socialist League. For example the ISP argued – in a manner similar to Sir Stafford Cripps in his 'Can Socialism Come by Constitutional Means?' [Cripps (n.d.)] that only a democratically elected Labour government that was ready 'to enforce the will of the people' could be successful in bringing about a socialist transformation. The ISP envisaged a much closer relationship between itself and the Labour Party than the disaffiliated ILP had permitted. It decided that although the party would remain outside the Labour Party, branches would be allowed to apply for affiliation to the Labour Party and individual membership of the larger organisation would be permitted [*Labour's Northern Voice*, October 1934, January 1935]. Many in the ISP attempted to rejoin the Labour Party, and initially some were successful. The Altrincham Labour Party even nominated leading ISPer Arthur Mostyn as its parliamentary candidate in the early months of 1935. However Labour's National Executive quickly quashed the candidature and declared that ISP members were not permitted to stand for Labour [Labour Party Organisation Sub-Committee, 20 February 1935; Labour Party Conference Report 1935, 29]. Then, at the 1935 Labour Party conference, when Mostyn's attempt to stand for the Labour Party was debated, the conference agreed with the NEC's proposal that the ISP be declared a proscribed organisation [Labour Party Conference Report (1935), 139–40]. Within the Labour Party the distinction between ILP and ISP was not appreciated, and even if it was understood it was not considered relevant. Based to a certain extent on this confusion between the two organisations, the ILP was proscribed in the same debate, which had significant implications for the party when it tried to negotiate reaffiliation in 1938–9 and again in the immediate post-war period.

The objections by the Labour Party to the ISP dealt the group a huge blow. Many of the members had grown frustrated at their isolation within the ILP, which had forced them towards the Communist Party, and the denial to the ISP of joint membership with the Labour Party left them even more isolated. The frustration was especially great for those who argued with Mostyn that being outside the Labour Party was 'bad revolutionary tactics' [*Labour's Northern Voice*, January 1935]. It was inevitable that unless there was a rapid turn in events many ISP members would drift back to the Labour Party. The main hope of avoiding such a decline was for the Socialist League to be forced out of the Labour Party and join the ISP. The ISP was thus keenly interested in the progress of the Socialist League. At the Party's Southport conference in 1934 the League had proposed a series of far-reaching changes to Labour's planned election programme. Every one of the League's proposals was heavily defeated. For the ISP this was a signal for the Socialist League to take a definite stand and not rule out action that would result in it being forced out of the Labour Party. However the leaders of the Socialist League saw things rather differently and chose to change their tactics at a conference at the end of November 1934. This was described as 'a clear turning point for the Socialist League' and amounted to a concentrated effort to turn the league into a mass organisation. For the ISP the League's decision to remain within the Labour Party was a great disappointment, and even something of a betrayal. They argued that the League's decision showed that its leaders had been 'brought to heel because they value affiliation to the Labour Party more than their ability to voice their convictions' [*Labour's Northern Voice*, January 1935].

The ISP's failure to work out a satisfactory relationship with the Labour Party led to fractious internal disputes. Whilst subsequent commentators, including Robert Dowse (1966), have described the ISP as a purely Lancashire party, ISP branches could be found in Nottingham, Aberfan, Hastings, Maidstone and beyond. In the late 1930s there was even a branch in Sierra Leone, although given the branch's interest not only in conditions in Sierra Leone but also with the niceties of the Lancashire cotton industry, this was presumably the result of the departure of one of the party's members to West Africa. Of much greater significance for the party as whole was the existence of a London ISP, which was very different in composition and focus from the Lancashire ISP (which mainly consisted of former ILP members) and was built almost entirely on the personal reputation of John Middleton Murry. Middleton Murry set up an interesting experiment in communal living – the Adelphi Commune, founded at 'The Oaks', in Langham, Essex, lasted from 1934–37, when the property was used to house Basque refugee children. In the tradition of ethical socialism, Murry stressed socialist actions as a practical form of socialist propaganda. Although even Middleton Murry quickly came to see this experiment as a failure it did attract into the ISP a significant number of individuals who had had no connection with the ILP and bore none of the marks of the extended dispute with the Labour Party. Middleton Murry and his associates were initially very taken with the down-to-earth, working-class,

Lancashire ex-ILPers. For example Richard Rees described Tom Abbott as a 'real tough old nut' who was concerned with being the 'guardian of the true socialist faith' [Richard Rees to John Middleton Murry, Richard Rees Papers, 10 June 1933]. However after the establishment of the ISP an enmity quickly developed between the middle-class, literary ISPers and the Lancashire leadership of the party. Shortly after the foundation of the party Middleton Murry wrote that the ISP would amount to something only because of the involvement of him and his associates. After a trip to the United States in early 1935 Middleton Murry became much more sympathetic to the Labour Party and withdrew his support for the ISP as an independent organisation:

> When one sees the utter futility of 'radical' politics in America, how every understanding Socialist would give his eyes to have even the rudiments of a British Labour Party here, one gets a sense of proportion. ... If the ISP doesn't want to become a simple socialist society well and good but I don't intend to belong to anything else [Middleton Murry to Rees, Richard Rees Papers, 14 February 1935].

On Middleton Murry's return serious disputes began between the London and Lancashire branches over the appropriate ISP – Labour Party relationship. When it became clear that the Lancashire ISP was determined to keep the organisation going as a political party, Middleton Murry decided to end his increasingly 'intolerable' activities on behalf of the ISP. The *Adelphi* magazine was founded by Middleton Murry and funded by Rees as a journal to give a voice to visionary young writers. From 1931 it had been filled with political articles supporting first the ILP and then the ISP, but in 1935 it made a conscious return to more literary concerns. At the beginning of March 1936 Middleton Murry resigned his position on the General Council of the ISP. In May 1936, at the ISP's third annual convention, the party rejected a motion from its London branch to seek affiliation to the Labour Party, whereupon Middleton Murry left the ISP and rejoined the South Norfolk Labour Party. The London branch quickly folded and with it the ISP's chances of making a significant impact outside Lancashire.

The ISP had earlier decided that it would put forward candidates in parliamentary or local elections if the circumstance warranted. However the conditions were never right and the party never fielded candidates at either the national or the local level. In the 1935 general election it urged its supporters to vote Labour. Nevertheless the party issued a manifesto, founded on two 'rock bottom truths'. First, capitalism was in decline and this would involve war and the withdrawal of hard-won concessions from the working class. Second, any remedy that sought to maintain private ownership of national resources, including evolutionary socialism, was doomed to failure. The ISP thus proposed a twelve-point programme based on the abolition of private ownership and the democratisation of government and other branches of the executive, as well as equality and organised resistance to war [Independent Socialist Party, General Election Manifesto, November 1935].

After the effective closure of the London branch of the ISP and the departure of the RPC from the ILP, the ISP turned its attention to cooperating with the organisation from which it had recently split. In May 1936, following a decision at the third ISP annual convention, Sandham and Abbott met with ILP chairman James Maxton to make arrangements for a united front with the ILP, particularly on the question of war with Germany. These talks were ongoing throughout the Unity Campaign between the ILP, the Communist Party and the Socialist League. In 1937, when the Unity Campaign faltered, prompting the Socialist League to dissolve itself to prevent expulsion, the ISP attempted to use the incident to stimulate its involvement with other groups. For example the ISP General Council issued a statement on socialist unity that confirmed its position outside the Labour Party and pointed to the failure of the Unity Campaign: 'Its [the unity campaign's] net result is that the Independent Labour Party and Communist Party are still officially banned by the Labour Party, and the Socialist League has had to dissolve so that its members may remain inside the Labour Party' [undated ISP leaflet].

According to the ISP this situation called for concerted action for socialism, and there was no way in which the Labour Party could provide such a lead: '[The Labour] Party, despite genuine revolutionary elements within its ranks, has at present no realistic programme of Socialist advance in face of the increasing danger of war, fascism, and intensified unemployment' [ibid.]. The answer, according to the ISP, was 'to link all British Socialists in an organisation with Socialism as its only objective' [*Labour's Northern Voice*, August/September 1937].

After the failure of the Unity Campaign the ISP again approached the ILP to request joint activity. The ILP was prepared to send its chairman, secretary and a Lancashire representative to a meeting with the ISP, but the ISP had second thoughts and repeatedly postponed the meeting. Then in August 1937 a specially convened ISP conference decided it was 'not an opportune moment to open up another Unity Campaign' [ISP papers]. Further approaches were made to the ILP at the outbreak of war, when some elements of the ISP, particularly in Nelson, considered rejoining the ILP.

In 1938 Elijah Sandham was too ill to attend the ISP's annual convention and in 1939, when he was again ill for the convention, he retired as chairman. He was replaced by Comrade Stevenson. The outbreak of the Second World War brought something of a change to the ISP's line. Before the war there had been considerable feeling within the party that pacifism was the only clear-cut reason for the existence of the party, so in March 1939 the ISP had joined with the ILP, the Society of Friends and some members of the Labour Party in setting up the 'Manchester No Conscription Fellowship'. When war broke out the party made a direct comparison with the 1914–18 War and refused to accept the 'deluded' story that 'the issue is not one of conflicting imperialisms, but is the simple one of reason against brute force'. It insisted that 'Socialists cannot accept this blank denial of all the historical evidence and can give no support to a war, which (like that of 1914–18) will settle nothing and will leave the economic causes of war untouched' [*Labour's Northern Voice*, October 1939]. The ISP argued that the only alternative to fascism and war was socialism, and thus presenting an effective opposition to the war could only be done from within a socialist party. In accordance with this logic the ISP changed its previously rather sympathetic attitude towards the Labour Party and called on all socialists immediately to join one of the socialist parties that was opposed to the war; that is, itself, the ILP, the Socialist Party of Great Britain or the Socialist Labour Party [*Labour's Northern Voice*, September 1939].

In 1939 the Communist Party's Lancashire District blamed its failure to recruit trade unionists on the ISP, or more specifically *Labour's Northern Voice*, which carried reports of the Manchester and Salford Trades Council. In addition to its involvement in the No Conscription Fellowship, the ISP was also, perhaps surprisingly, involved with the Trotskyist-influenced Socialist Anti-War Front, which included ISP members on its provisional committee. However despite its hope that the war would spark a socialist revival the ISP's fortunes did not pick up. The party faced increasingly serious financial difficulties, particularly after the departure of John Middleton Murry and Richard Rees, who had donated significant amounts of money. By the middle of the war the situation had become desperate, and *Labour's Northern Voice* was reduced to selling off back issues to chip shops in order to stay afloat. Elijah Sandham died in 1944 and the active life of the party did not last much longer. It continued in purely formal terms with Tom Abbott as chairman, but when he died in 1951 the remaining few members finally decided to end the ISP. The final act of the organisation was to write a letter to the Labour Party informing them that the ISP could be removed from the list of proscribed organisations as it no longer existed.

Contemporary commentators and historians have ignored the ISP in almost equal measure. Its adherents were limited and its direct influence was probably no larger than its meagre membership would indicate. Yet the ISP was not without significance. The left-wing politics of the 1930s, so frequently portrayed as a straightforward battle between Communism and the Labour Party, was in fact much more complex as other organisations proliferated. For example in 1932 the ILP was five times the size of the Communist Party, although by the end of the decade it was a fraction of its former size. The internal struggles that led to the formation of the ISP give significant insights into the reasons why the ILP declined so rapidly. Perhaps more importantly the ISP was independent of the Labour Party, the Communist Party and the ILP not only organisationally but also in terms of ideology. The ISP's struggle to synthesise revolutionary and ethical socialism reflected an important concern of many in the Labour movement, yet the complexities of the debate were often hidden by organisational loyalties. The debates within the ISP in Lancashire and London, although not attracting a significant number of adherents, were representative of a least a part of this wider current of thought within the British labour movement.

Publications: 'Socialist Unity' (n.d.); ISP Manifesto (1935); 'What is Socialism?' (n.d.); 'Behind Rearmament: Preparing for Fascism in Britain' (n.d.)

Sources: (1) **MSS:** Records of the Independent Labour Party, London School of Economics; Labour Party Archive, NMLH, Manchester; ISP Material, WCML Salford; Richard Rees Papers, UCL. (2) **Newspapers:** *Adeplhi*, 1931–36; *Controversy* 1933–34; *Labour's Northern Voice*, 1932–51; *New Leader*, 1932–51; *London RPC Bulletin*, 1932–34; *The Times*, 1934. (3) **Other:** John Middleton Murry, *The Necessity of Communism* (1932); John Middleton Murry, *The Necessity of Pacifism* (1937); Fenner Brockway, *Inside the Left: Thirty Years of Platform, Press, Prison and Parliament* (1942); F. A. Lee, *John Middleton Murry* (1959); R. E. Dowse, *Left in the Centre: The Independent Labour Party 1893–1940* (1966); Geoffrey Mitchell (ed.), *The Hard Way Up: The Autobiography of Hannah Mitchell* (1968); Ben Pimlott, *Labour and the Left in the 1930s* (Cambridge, 1977); Andrew Flinn, 'Prospects for Socialism: the character and implantation of working class activism in the Manchester area, 1933–41' (unpublished PhD thesis, University of Manchester, 1999); Gidon Cohen, 'The Independent Labour Party 1932–1939' (unpublished DPhil thesis, University of York, 2000); Stafford Cripps, 'Can Socialism Come by Constitutional Means?' (n.d.)

GIDON COHEN

SARA, Henry Thomas William (1886–1953)
INDUSTRIAL UNIONIST, ANARCHIST, COMMUNIST, TROTSKYIST

Henry Sara was born on 24 August 1886 at 51 Essex Street, Islington, London, the son of John Henry Sara, a draper's assistant from Falmouth, Cornwall, and his second wife, Amy Maude Sara, née Smith. Sara had little formal education and from an early age worked in an ironmongery store after school. In the early years of the twentieth century he was employed as a glassblower, as a process block-maker and for six years as a brewery engineer. He also worked in a property office and as a cinema projectionist. Like most working-class socialists of his generation he was self-taught; more unusually, he was intellectually self-reliant. From boyhood he was an omnivorous reader. He took a keen interest in labour history, popular science, Darwinism and the literature of free thought and secularism. He devoured the plays of Shaw and the novels of Eugene Sue. He studied everything he could lay his hands on in connection with telepathy, theosophy, spiritualism and the supernatural. He delighted in magic, at which he was adept, and was an enthusiast of silent films, boxing and later speedway racing. Throughout his life he was a bibliophile and an avid collector of socialist books and pamphlets.

His first acquaintance with socialist ideas came from Robert Blatchford's weekly newspaper *Clarion*. However in 1905 he became interested in Indian self-government and began to question Blatchford's social patriotism, which was confirmed when the *Clarion* joined H. M. Hyndman in denouncing the growing 'German menace'. He met members of the Socialist

Labour Party (SLP) and read its paper, the *Socialist*, but was critical of its dependence on the American thinker Daniel De Leon and its dogmatic emphasis on the role of the party. Nevertheless he admired De Leon's economic writings and credited the *Socialist*'s serialisation in 1908 of *Wage Labour and Capital* with his initiation into Marxism. He became a partisan of industrial unionism, as propagated by the Advocates of Industrial Unionism, established in August 1907 and animated by the SLP, although formally independent of it. Sara's socialism was nurtured in the eclectic, ecumenical, libertarian, syndicalist milieu of North London by an invisible college of proletarian autodidacts. He was influenced by Advocates such as Leslie Boyne, an Islington gas worker, and W. G. E. Smith, a local sheet-metal worker, as well as anarchists, particularly the painter Victor Beacham and the turbulent Walthamstow activist Walter Ponder, who congregated in the electrical engineering shop of the Italian anarchist Errico Malatesta in Upper Street, Islington.

In 1908 Sara joined the Industrial League, which had broken away from the Advocates and taken most of the latter's London membership. The League opposed SLP control, indeed any connection with political parties in the work of organising workers on industrial lines 'into one big union'. With E. J. B. Allen as editor of its paper, the *Industrialist*, and Boyne as general secretary, it insisted that the economic organisation of workers should take precedence. It declared that it was in principle neither in favour of nor opposed to parliamentary action, but the demonstrative use of Parliament should only be discussed after the revolutionary industrial union had been established. Intended to curtail disputation, this formula led to the secession of branches that wanted a decisive antiparliamentary line.

Sara was a member of the Islington branch. Led by Smith, it attracted up to 200 members to its meetings on subjects such as internationalism, industrial unionism and anarchism, and antimilitarism at the Secular Hall, Essex Road, and organised speakers at Clerkenwell Green, Highbury Corner and Parliament Hill. At the end of 1908 Sara became business manager of the *Industrialist*. He was responsible for producing and circulating pioneering pamphlets such as A. B. Elsbury's *Industrial Unionism: Its Principles and Meaning* (1909) and Allen's *Revolutionary Unionism* (1909). He expanded his international interests, followed syndicalist developments in France and North and South America and studied both Marx and the anarchists Bakunin and Kropotkin.

The League held joint meetings with anarchist groups and enrolled anarchists in its ranks, although Ponder was expelled in 1909 for exploiting the organisation for anarchist purposes. It strengthened its constitution to condemn 'the futility of parliamentary action' in response to anarchist agitation and the climate of the times. By 1911 the expulsion of Allen and the League's acceptance of a charter as the British branch of the Industrial Workers of the World (Chicago faction), which opposed De Leon, suggested a loss of élan and independence. Sara's interest in anarchism was intensified by a growing friendship with its most vigorous British proponent, Guy Aldred, who studied industrial unionism and spoke at league meetings. When the *Industrialist* was forced to suspend publication in 1912, he offered the league space in his own journal, the *Herald of Revolt*. Sara assisted Aldred during the 'Savarkar affair'. When Madanlal Dhingra, a student influenced by the Indian nationalist Vianyak Savarkar, assassinated the political secretary to the secretary of state for India, the Free India Society's journal, *The Indian Sociologist*, was suppressed by the courts. Aldred printed it and suffered imprisonment for his pains. Under Aldred's influence Sara began to question the centrality of industrial unionism. He terminated his two-year membership of the League and moved into the orbit of the self-styled 'Minister of the Gospel of Revolt'.

While Sara did not share Aldred's extravagant declaration that ultimately there was no difference between industrial unionism and orthodox trade unionism, he no longer saw the former as a panacea. He came to believe that organisation was secondary to consciousness. Once propaganda had transformed workers' consciousness, revolutionary action would follow spontaneously, with direction being provided by local communist propaganda groups if necessary. Capitalism would collapse. Meanwhile strikes, the eight-hour day and industrial unionism were all palliatives and potential distractions. Freed from the tyranny and partiality of party politics, the socialist gospel would embrace all shades of opinion – Marx as well as Bakunin – for Sara subscribed to the view that Marx was an anarchist and that communism means anarchy. He styled himself a communist or marxian anarchist.

The *Herald of Revolt*, established by Aldred in 1910, drew on the anarchist tradition and published the writings of Bakunin, Kropotkin, Emma Goldman and Voltairine de Cleyre. It also reprinted the work of British radicals such as the pioneer of press freedom Richard Carlile, discussed industrial unrest and explored feminism, birth control and sexual politics. It carried reports of the work of local communist groups, played a significant part in the campaign against the deportation of Malatesta in 1912 and relentlessly publicised the connections between H. M. Hyndman's stake in the Colt Gun and Carriage Company and his bellicose politics. By 1913 Sara was a prolific contributor and was increasingly involved in editing the paper. He moved from Pentonville Road in Islington to the flat that Aldred shared with his companion, Rose Witcop, in Richmond Gardens, Shepherds Bush. All three believed in sexual equality and free unions. The serious, studious Sara began an affair with Witcop, 'a tall, pale Jewess, with an oval face and dark, wide luminous eyes ... with a grand romantic air, like a Conrad revolutionary' [Fox (1930) 54–5].

Rose was the younger sister of Milly Witcop, companion of the German Rudolf Rocker. With Kropotkin in retirement, Rocker was the doyen of metropolitan anarchism. Centred on the clubs in Jubilee Street and Charlotte Street, the journals *Freedom* and *Workers' Friend*, Henderson's 'Bomb Shop' and Karl Lahr's Holborn bookshop, it was a cosmopolitan world in which the Shepherds Bush *ménage a trois* became a colourful cameo. Aldred's 'missions' strengthened the spread of communist propaganda groups in London and Scotland. Sara was increasingly popular as an open air propagandist at Finsbury Park, Clapham Common, Putney Embankment and the Grove in Hammersmith, where he spoke on Marxism, revolutionary organisation, the value of the vote, antimilitarism and spiritualism. He gained a reputation for well-researched contributions and as 'a calm dispassionate debater' [Howard (1916) 94].

In 1913 Sara became secretary of the Revolt League, established to coordinate the activities of the communist groups. Like many such groups its existence was shadowy. Attempts to arrange debates with the Socialist Party of Great Britain, Guy Bowman's Syndicalist League and the Anti-Socialist Union proved unfruitful. More productive was the North London Daily Herald League. Formed the same year, it provided a vibrant meeting place for most of the tendencies on the revolutionary left and Sara became one of its best known orators.

When the *Herald of Revolt* was relaunched in June 1914 as the *Spur* – 'because the workers need a spur' – Sara was assistant editor. In its pages he argued the socialist case against the European War: it was a war for profit that would divide workers and provide capitalism with a new lease of life. He produced detailed reports of the activities of the armament combines, and took to task those socialists, notably Hyndman and Kropotkin, who supported the war as well as militant trade unionists who sought to exploit it. The only course of action, he argued, was point blank refusal to participate in militarism or aid the war effort in any way.

Sara, who was in the front line of the fight for free speech, was arrested and convicted three times in the first weeks of the conflict. On 28 September 1914 Sara – '28 years of age, a well-dressed man described as an engineer' – appeared before the South West London Police Court. The magistrates were told: 'when the police removed the speaker Sara jumped on the platform and said to the crowd: "This meeting will continue. The police inspector has no right to stop a public meeting. I'll carry on. ..." The speaker's remarks were against the King, the Government and the people' [*Spur*, October 1914]. With the introduction of conscription legislation in January 1916 the attitude of the police and patriotic crowds hardened. Sara reinforced his growing reputation for fearlessness, urging the Herald League, whose meetings were being broken up, to resist intimidation. He offered to speak at any place at any time: 'I think we were all surprised at the change that had occurred in him ... he had developed into the passionate orator. Many a time after he had finished speaking I have seen khaki armleteers shamefacedly slip their badges into their pockets and then demonstratively cheer him to the echo' [Howard (1916) 94].

The war engaged Sara fully, emotionally as well as intellectually and at the age of 30 it provided his greatest test. In February 1916 he returned his conscription papers, stating he could not serve because of his socialist opposition to the war. The Hammersmith tribunal held that it had no power to grant exemption for an objection based on political grounds. He was arrested on 3 April, taken before the South West London Police Court and sentenced to a month's imprisonment as an unlawful absentee. When he stated that his occupation was public speaker the magistrate told him the sooner his mouth was closed the better. The military authorities refused to allow him to serve his sentence or communicate with friends and he was immediately taken into army custody. Despite poor eyesight he was pronounced medically fit and taken to the Harrow Road Barracks of the 3rd (Reserve) Battalion London Regiment, where he was badly beaten and forcibly dressed in uniform. After refusing to parade he was again beaten, transferred to Hurdcott Camp, court martialled and sentenced to 28 days in Parkhurst Military Prison on the Isle of Wight. Returned to Hurdcott in May, he again refused to obey orders and served a further sentence in Parkhurst.

The case attracted wide publicity. It was raised in the House of Commons by Joseph King, the Liberal MP for North Somerset, and the Labour Party's Philip Snowden. Harold Tennant, the Liberal Under-Secretary of State for War, promised a report but then announced that reports on individual soldiers could not be provided. Sara was transferred to Wormwood Scrubs and taken before the Central Tribunal, which accepted that as a conscientious objector he was entitled to perform alternative work under the Home Office scheme. As an absolutist who believed that nothing should be done to aid the state, he refused. He was again court martialled in October 1916 and January 1917, when he was sentenced to two years and transferred to Exeter Prison.

He endured his imprisonment stoically – 'che sara sara', as he wrote to his friends. A fellow prisoner, R. M. Fox, recorded with surprise that Sara had developed a sense of humour. He took inspiration from Rosa Luxemburg, Karl Liebknecht and, he insisted, the thousands of nameless Germans who were fighting against the war. His resistance was simple and adamantine: 'conscience is not to be bargained with' [Sara (October 1917) 154]. He became suspicious of the No Conscription Fellowship's attempts to play the system and extend exemptions. He felt isolated and at times disheartened: 'To fight with the minority is always hard, when the odds are against you obstacles seem great, greater perhaps than they are in reality but that is little consolation' [Sara (January 1919) 110]. He grew worried about his own weakness when, along with other long-term prisoners, he was transferred in September 1918 to Wakefield gaol and offered concessions. But the absolutists remained intransigent. They introduced a system of self-government, affirmed 'the inviolable rights of conscience' and refused to accept any work that would facilitate the war.

At the end of his sentence Sara again refused to put on khaki and again endured rough treatment. In an article in the *Herald of Revolt* he remarked: 'Two and a half years of bitter struggle', and at the end a disgusting retort, "You are a coward of the deepest hue", [Sara (January 1919) 110]. In October 1918 he was once more court martialled. It was not until he went on hunger strike in February 1919 that he was finally released, and only then under the Cat and Mouse Act, which enabled the authorities to recall him at any time.

Sara emerged from his ordeal stronger and more self-sufficient. His moral stature was enhanced and he enjoyed a growing reputation in the labour movement. He plunged into propaganda, speaking all over the country for the Herald League, the SLP, the British Socialist Party and, in particular, anarchist groups throughout Scotland and Sylvia Pankhurst's Workers' Socialist Federation (WSF) in London. He was an enthusiast for the Russian revolution. Where he had earlier deprecated party organisation, he now considered Pankhurst's organisation as the germ of a new libertarian, antiparliamentary communist party. The minute books of the WSF record Sara's attendance at meetings of the Bow branch in 1919. He was also active in the WSF-influenced East London Workers' Committee.

In the summer of 1919 a fellow absolutist, Harry Thompson, whom Sara had befriended in Wakefield Gaol, invited him to spend a few weeks at the holiday home of his sister and her businessman husband, Connie and Percy Taylor, at Hawkshead in the Lake District. Their son, the future historian, A. J. P. (Alan) Taylor, later recalled the 'magnificent open-air orator with a tremendous voice'. He reflected:

> Henry Sara talked Marxism all the time. ... [He] was extremely handsome, despite a wall eye. He was well over six feet tall, with curly black hair and a powerful physique. He had winning ways. ... Indeed he had already acquired a harem of feminine admirers in London. He now won my mother. She fell passionately, although of course, platonically, in love with Henry Sara and remained in love with him for the rest of her life [Taylor (1983) 54].

Connie became a fervent supporter of Sara's politics. For his part Sara exerted a powerful and to some extent underacknowledged influence on the young Alan, being instrumental in extending his interest in politics and history and stimulating his brief sojourn in the Communist Party of Great Britain (CPGB). In turn Percy was always on good terms with Sara and became a militant pillar of the Independent Labour Party in North Lancashire. Thus for Sara it was a happy encounter. Until Connie's long, final illness in the early 1940s she provided Sara with a home for part of the year, gave him money and bought his suits.

But this lay in the future. What urgently exercised Sara in 1919 was the relationship of the antiparliamentary, libertarian tradition of socialism from below – in which he had spent a good part of his 33 years – to the Russian revolution and the development of the Third International (Comintern). He interpreted the revolution and its extension by the Comintern through the prism of his own politics, emphasising the centrality of insurrection, workers' councils and their antagonism towards Parliament. He participated in the short-lived Communist League formed in 1919 as a loose amalgam of dissident SLP branches, the WSF and Aldred's communist groups, whose paper was now entitled *The Spur – To Communism*. He took another small step towards party when he moved into the orbit of Pankhurst's Communist Party (British Section of the Third International, BSTI), although there is no evidence that he became a member. He was caught up in the same dilemma as Pankhurst: how to reconcile a passionate belief in the necessity of the Comintern with a profound antipathy to its emerging insistence on parliamentary action and affiliation of its British section to the Labour Party. Like many other communists he pondered whether to give his allegiance to Bolshevism. In the summer of 1920 he was still speaking for the Scottish anarchist groups. Russia – and perhaps their relationship with Rose Witcop – precipitated Sara's final break with Aldred [Caldwell to author, 7 December 1999]. Like most anarchists, Aldred made Parliament the litmus test and was increasingly concerned about the strengthening of the state and growing authoritarianism in Russia.

Sara was not yet ready to turn away from what would become the submerged tradition of left-wing communism and embrace 'official communism'. Prison had made him more careful, cautious and methodical. But despite doubts about its policy he chided critics: 'If there is *not* a Communist International very soon, the time is not far distant when there will not be a Soviet Government' [Sara, January 1921]. He determined to see for himself what the International and the Soviet government were doing. In January 1921, as the CP (BSTI) threw in its lot with the CPGB, he sailed for Russia.

In five hectic months he visited not only Moscow and Leningrad but also Samara, Tashkent and Samarkand. He toured factories, schools and soviets. He spoke with Comintern functionaries, ordinary communists and anarchists, and even unearthed Jacob Miller – 'Peter the Painter' of the siege of Sydney Street notoriety. Whether he travelled with or encountered Witcop, who was in Russia in 1921 to raise money for Aldred's Anti-Parliamentary Federation, remains unclear. But his already intimate relationship with the CPGB was evident in a letter from a party representative in Moscow to the Comintern. It noted that while he had refrained from joining, 'There is no question ... as to his loyalty to

the movement. He was always in great demand as a lecturer by the branches of our organisation. He has given years of work for the cause. His record and influence is such that he would
be undoubtedly an acquisition to our forces in Britain' [RGASPI, 495/100/42, Tom Quelch to
Kobetsky, 12 April 1921].

In an account written for the *Dreadnought* on his return to London, Sara evoked the vitality of
the revolution, its very real problems and the urgency of international solidarity. His conclusion
– despite doubts about the Bolsheviks' crushing of the sailors' revolt in Kronstadt in
March 1921 and Pankhurst's ejection from the CPGB in September 1921, which had laid to rest
the hope some had held for a left-wing faction – was that sustaining the Russian revolution was
the priority for socialists, and that the revolution was best nourished from inside its official
representative party. The working-class militancy of 1919–20 was in retreat across Europe,
together with illusions of a revolutionary situation arising in Britain. Left communism was
waning and, as the next few years would demonstrate, its organisational prospects were brittle.
It was as a reluctant recruit who could see no alternative that Sara joined the CPGB in late 1922
or early 1923. Within a few months he was debating with Pankhurst at Essex Hall on the competing virtues of the Third and Fourth Internationals, the left-wing council communist grouping
with which Pankhurst was associated (led by the Dutch critic of Lenin, Herman Gorter, and not
to be confused with Leon Trotsky's movement of the same name).

The CPGB made extensive use of Sara as a propagandist. In 1922 he toured the United
States and Canada, lecturing on his experiences in the Soviet Union. The following year the
CPGB districts urged the branches to engage him to speak on Russia, with the proviso that
for open-air meetings he would expect a share of the collection. His hallmark was the lantern
lecture, bred of his days in the cinema and facilitated by slides from his travels, which he pio-
neered while others persevered with chalk and talk. As well as Russia his other specialities
were the Lives of Lenin, Luxemburg and Liebknecht, and the revolution in China. He also
lectured widely on Marxism, labour history and current politics. His other significant arena
was the National Council of Labour Colleges, a passion that united the extended Taylor
family: Connie became secretary of the Preston Labour College, later the North Lancashire
Labour College, while Percy lectured and wrote in the NCLC journal, *Plebs*, on the cotton
industry. As the 1920s wore on, Alan commenced lecturing with Sara and defended the
Comintern against Raymond Postgate in *Plebs*. Sara was in demand as a tutor and often
spent most of the winter season at the Taylors' Preston home, taking classes in Lancashire
and Yorkshire. Two or three times a year Connie would visit London, where Sara would take
her to the theatre and restaurants at her expense. In 1924 the couple, accompanied by Alan,
toured France and Germany, where they encountered a wide variety of politicians although
the highlight was a performance by the great clown Grock. In 1925 the trio travelled across
Russia, meeting Kamenev and Litvinov, hearing Zinoviev speak and returning with their
dedication to the Soviet experiment refreshed and reinforced.

Sara was a member of the CPGB's St Pancras branch and then from 1925 the Tottenham
and Wood Green local branch. He was also a member of the Hornsey Labour Party and sat
on its executive committee from 1924 until he was expelled in 1926. He was a popular CPGB
member and was active in party causes and a periodic contributor to its press, although he
always regretted the fact that he never wrote as well as he spoke. He was a member of the
Central Agit-Prop Committee, but the was on the whole, on a long leash. In 1925, for
example, he was elected to the London District Committee but was excused service because
of his other commitments. He could be a difficult customer and was enduringly critical of
many in the leadership for their activities before and during the war, for he never accepted
that militancy was a substitute for antimilitarism. In 1932 Willie Gallacher, whom he had
always valued lightly, opined that Sara had never been a Communist. He was certainly never
a Communist in the sense that Gallacher was as he never absorbed Bolshevization, still less
Stalinism. Rather he maintained a sturdy intellectual independence. He held himself aloof
from involvement in the burgeoning machine, particularly after he was asked to keep an eye

on former anarchist comrades Charlie and Esther Lahr, who had left the party in the early 1920s. Nonetheless he became a well-known figure in the CPGB.

> I was aware of his history and his deep interest in the labour movement ... and he was quite unusual, even though he was an orthodox Communist for a whole period. He had an unusual interest in the Trotskyist movement. He was one of the few people, I'd never seen anyone before, who had a little tiny button, which he got on one of his trips to Russia in 1921 or 1922 with a photograph of Trotsky in it. It was the only one I'd seen. He also had a sculpture by Claire Sheridan of Trotsky [Wicks interview with Richardson].

All in all Sara was an austere figure and was perceived even by Communists who shared his working-class background as 'an intellectual' [Dowdall interview with Richardson], one whose outsiderism suited the leadership as well as himself. In 1926 he spoke all over the country during the miners' lockout, sharing platforms with Arthur Cook. The following year he was despatched by way of Moscow and Vladivostok to represent the CPGB at the Fifth Congress of the Chinese Party – held at Hankow in April–May 1927 – in order to permit Tom Mann, who was on a Red International of Labour Unions delegation to China, to represent the Minority Movement. In China he saw at first hand the consequences of Stalin's and Bukharin's subordination of the Chinese party to the Kuomintang and its disastrous and stubbornly sustained misreading of Chiang Kai Shek. He would later complain bitterly about the Russians' attempt to scapegoat the party leader, Chen Duxiu, who had simply executed their policy. However, speaking as a delegate to the CPGB's ninth Congress in Salford in October 1927, he was critical only of those party members who failed to understand the importance of China to world revolution.

Sara was one of 25 CPGB candidates in the May 1929 General Election, standing in Tottenham South. He faithfully elaborated the new 'third period' line that capitalist crisis and working-class radicalisation had transformed Labour into the third capitalist party, hermetically sealed from proletarian pressure, and demanded a revolutionary workers' government. He paid the price and lost his deposit. The seat was won by his old comrade in the Herald League, the Islington French polisher Fred Messer:

Tottenham South, 1929: electorate 45 970, turnout 67.5 per cent

F. Messer (Labour)	14 423 (46.4 per cent)
P. B. Malone (Conservative)	9701 (31.3 per cent)
W. Stonestreet (Liberal)	6407 (20.7 per cent)
H. T. W. Sara (Communist)	490 (1.6 per cent)
Majority	4722 (15.1 per cent)

Perhaps the New Line stirred the old Sara, revived his leftism and fanned his resentment of labour fakirs and what he saw as men on the make. He contributed titbits to the *Daily Worker* that paid off old scores against the ex-ILP absolutist Clifford Allen and the ex-SLP impossibilist E. E. Hunter. But as he demonstrated when rebuking the CPGB novelist Harold Heslop for employing denunciation rather than textual criticism to dismantle Postgate in the *Communist*, he was essentially a man of argument, exactitude and tolerance. As such he cannot have been happy with Stalin's proscription of Luxemburg in 1931 or the British leadership's witch hunting of the ideas of Arthur Horner, J. T. Murphy, Maurice Dobb and Tommy Jackson between 1930 and 1932.

On his way to China Sara had become embroiled in an obscure argument with Petrovsky, the Comintern representative in Britain, over trade union policy. His first real brush with the party leadership, however, came in 1930 when, as part of the work of discrediting the fallen Bukharin, his differences with Lenin were magnified by the Russian leaders and their national epigones. Nonetheless Sara provided the *Communist Review* with a positive estimation of the new British edition of Bukharin's *Imperialism and World Economy*. When it was unfavourably reviewed in the *Daily Worker* he wrote to the paper contradicting Hugo Rathbone's verdict that there was a fundamental antagonism between Lenin and Bukharin over imperialism. The leadership switched the controversy to the *Communist Review* and encouraged Rathbone to expand and 'sharpen' his response to Sara and discredit his original piece. The real point in this engagement between the proletarian autodidact who remembered the past and respected truth and the orthodox, bourgeois intellectual who reflected the present power struggles in the USSR, was the fundamental antagonism Stalin felt towards Bukharin. Lenin had never regarded the very real differences he had with Bukharin as sufficient to merit his silencing, stigmatisation or exclusion, indeed he had contributed a commendatory introduction to the first edition of the book, which until 1929 was generally accepted as a classic Bolshevik text. But Bukharin's approach and, Rathbone suggested, Sara's, was no longer permissible in the evolving Stalinist order.

Sara read Trotsky, studying not only earlier works such as *Where is Britain Going?* but also 'The Draft Programme of the Communist International: A Criticism of Fundamentals', published in English in January 1929. He found the 'third period' claim that the Labour Party, ILP and trade union leaders were going over to fascism disturbing and unsustainable. The new leadership was proving no better than the old in reversing the party's fading fortunes. His belief, which had solidified in 1921–22, that the leaders of the Comintern and the CPGB could take the world revolution forward was foundering. He was still considered sufficiently acceptable to be sent to Vienna in August 1931 on behalf of the Friends of the Soviet Union, although he was arrested and deported from Austria. By that time he was a member of the opposition group led by Reg Groves and Stewart Purkis. He met them in 1929 and gradually strengthened his involvement, although it was only in 1932, when he moved from Crouch End to south-west London, that he became a member of the Balham group of the party. Groves later recalled Sara's 'eloquent, resonant voice and a commanding platform manner, incisive, informed in debate and discussion [he] brought much to us in the way of knowledge of Marxism, socialist theory and labour history. His critical faculty had been toughened by early associations with anarchist ideas and the stricter industrial unionist groups, by his experience during the 1914–18 war' [Groves (1974) 19–20].

The group's ideas were disparate, to a degree contradictory and certainly still evolving. Opposition to the leadership's 'right-wing' resistance to the Comintern line in 1929 gave way to resentment about the Comintern's disastrous dictation and its espousal of 'socialism in one country' by 1931. Their belief that the new leadership of the CPGB was missing opportunities and their concern about the parlous state of the party was sustained. But their continued advocacy of 'third period' nostrums, such as the priority of organising in the workplace as opposed to organising in the trade unions, coexisted uneasily with their newly acquired support for the united front, which had been stimulated by their experience of working with the ILP in South London and by studying Trotsky's writings on Germany. Meetings with Trotsky's emissaries Albert Glotzer and Max Shachtman produced only limited clarification of their politics, which in early 1932 remained at some distance from the conceptions of the International Left Opposition.

Sara's pivotal confrontation with the CPGB leadership was characteristically bound up with his revulsion at its 'unreal propaganda and cheap demagogy'. On 20 March 1932, when he was speaking at the St Pancras branch on the 'war danger', that had obsessed the party for the previous five years, he held up the previous day's *Daily Worker*, which blazoned and attempted to justify the headline 'The World War Has Begun'. He 'asked his audience what sort of reply would be received were he to go down into the street and ask the passers-by whether they were aware that "world war has begun"?' [Sara (1939) 4]. Party leader Harry Pollitt received a report of Sara's speech and observed on behalf of the Political Bureau (PB): 'This opportunist poison must be plucked out of the Party and all who disseminate it ruthlessly fought as objectively helping the war preparation of the imperialists by the doubts and confusions they create in the Party' [*Daily Worker*, 6 April 1932].

Sara was now a marked man. The secretariat wrote to him asking for clarification of his comments. He retorted that they had already been sufficiently apprised about what he had said to denounce him demagogically and requested a copy of the report on which they had based their condemnation. In protracted correspondence he defied their instruction to put what he had said into writing. At the PB there was discussion of his expulsion, concern about the platform that his NCLC work provided and, when the *Communist* (anonymously circulated by the Balham group) appeared in May with a reprint of Trotsky's *Germany: The Key to the International Situation*, suspicion that Sara was involved. Two stormy south London aggregates and a confused meeting between the London District Committee, Bill Rust from the leadership and the Balham group failed to resolve matters.

The affair moved to a close in August when, in response to a request to discuss the German situation, Groves, Sara and Harry Wicks were invited to meet the London district secretary, R. W. Robson. Instead they were confronted by Pollitt, Gallacher and Kay Beauchamp. Sara's prompt exit, explaining that he had been invited to meet Robson not Pollitt, provided a stay of execution. While Groves and Wicks were expelled, he escaped with suspension. The respite was brief. On 8 September 1932 he was expelled from the CPGB for membership of 'an Anti-Party grouping'. The letter of dismissal stated that the final straw was the publication in the September issue of *Plebs* of his extended, laudatory review of the first volume of Trotsky's *History of the Russian Revolution*. Sara was aware that Pollitt was trying to avoid publicity about Trotskyism in the party: 'the article in *Plebs* was written deliberately (by arrangement with the Editor) as a challenge to the Communist Party – which I knew would lead to my expulsion, so that the membership could be made aware of the grounds of my expulsion' [MRC MSS15B/3/S, Sara to W. Hill, 12 August 1941]. His exit from the party was as calculated as his entrance.

In Trotskyism he sought a purer Marxism, based on a united front of working-class parties, political transformation in Russia and world revolution. He supported Trotsky's verdict that its performance in respect of Germany had rendered the Comintern beyond repair. He viewed this as enhancing the argument for developing the British Trotskyist group, the Communist League, as an open organisation, albeit carrying out factional work inside labour movement bodies, including the ILP. He did not share Trotsky's belief in the potential of the ILP and opposed the International Left Opposition's advice that the league should enter the ILP *en masse*. Such an approach, he pointed out, would mean sacrificing the League's new paper, the *Red Flag*, withdrawing members from the fruitful work they were still carrying out in the CPGB and putting the group's future in the dubious hands of the ILP. At the League's December 1933 conference he successfully moved that wholesale entry be rejected. He argued that Trotsky was more enamoured of the ILP than the tiny Communist League; Trotsky did not adequately appreciate developments in Britain, particularly the difficulty of revolutionary work inside the ILP. The refusal of the minority who supported Trotsky to accept the vote resulted in British Trotskyism's first split.

In this context, and with the Comintern's turn towards a united front, depriving the Trotskyists of their best card, his hopes for an independent Communist League evaporated. However there were small successes. When the CPGB and its satellite, the International Labour Defence, refused to campaign over the imprisonment of Chen Duxiu, the former secretary of the Chinese Communist Party who had embraced Trotskyism, Sara was able to draw on the goodwill he had accumulated with Tom Mann during their encounter in Hankow. Mann's signature on a circular protesting about the imprisonment influenced Jack Tanner, Dick Beech, Alex Gossip, John Jagger and other prominent left-wing trade unionists to add their names to those of James Maxton and Fenner Brockway. Furthermore there was still a trickle of recruits from the CPGB and the ILP. But by early 1934 sales of the *Red Flag* were in decline and the League was wracked by internal divisions. There was some resentment about the behaviour of Groves, his monopolisation of international contacts and what some saw as his overemphasis on the British dimension. Still advocating independent organisation, Sara was less than impressed by the suggestion that the group prioritise work inside the Labour Party. In May 1934 he resigned from the Communist League.

Unlike most of his comrades Sara had an alternative outlet in the National Council of Labour Colleges (NCLC). As well as maintaining his base in Lancashire he had become popular in south Wales, where the NCLC organiser and future general secretary of the Labour Party, Len Williams, helped with the sale of the *Red Flag* and tweaked Stalinist tails by presenting the best students with copies of Trotsky's *History*. Even when CPGB stalwart Charlie Stead succeeded Williams in 1936, he proved unable to resist NCLC general secretary J. P. M. Millar's sponsoring of Sara. The latter's appointment as full-time winter tutor was branded as 'provocation' by the party's Agitprop Committee, which remonstrated forcefully with the hapless Stead.

To the CPGB's chagrin Sara was able to take Trotskyist politics into the NCLC. Statements such as 'The June Tutors' Council meeting listened with interest to Comrade Sara outlining the attitude of the Left Opposition (Trotskyism) and agreed to devote another evening to certain problems which cropped up in discussion' [*Plebs* (July 1933) 167] were guaranteed to cause apoplexy in King Street. Throughout the 1930s Sara contributed to *Plebs* in restrained, scholarly style, crossing swords on several occasions with fellow proletarian autodidact Tommy Jackson, who was increasingly marginal to the party but its man in the NCLC. But if all this strengthened anti-Stalinism among British workers, it did little to expand organised Trotskyism.

By 1936 Sara had returned to the fold. He was reunited with his old comrades from the Balham group in a looser organisation, the Marxist League, which worked inside the Labour Party and the Socialist League. He rigorously raked through the fictions and fables traducing Trotsky and the mendacities of the Moscow trials, and remarked of Stalin's attorneys the Pollitts and Pritts, who slavishly justified them: 'Like the gangs who used to concoct anti-Soviet forgeries with faked documents for circulation in the capitalist press, their work teems with stupid errors' [Sara (January 1937) 2]. He was one of the tiny band who put all their energy into the Committee for the Defence of Leon Trotsky in 1936–37. He was on the platform at the handful of big meetings the Committee was able to mount at Essex Hall and the Memorial Hall in Farringdon. He also addressed gatherings of the ILP, NCLC and Left Book Club. He worked with C. A. Smith, editor of the ILP's *Controversy*, priming him with anti-Stalinist ammunition. When the CPGB published a competitor, *Discussion*, he commented: 'I find that really amusing. Particularly when one knows that the thing they fear most is discussion and controversy' [MRC MSS 15/3/1/63, Sara to Smith, 22 August 1937].

His earlier concerns about the Soviet state had proved prescient. The trials left him with mixed feelings: of vindication – in the trials' unmasking of the nature of the Stalinism he had escaped – and demoralisation – the sense that for many this was the bleak terminus not only of 1917 but of the entire project of revolutionary socialism. He reflected:

> Frame-ups against active revolutionaries in capitalist countries are bad enough but when the frame-ups can be staged in a country where a people have thrown off their oppressors things must be infinitely worse ... the harm done to the cause of International Socialism through the Moscow trials of the alleged Trotskyist Zinoviite Terrorist Centre will be felt for many a long day. Its main value – but at what price? – is to expose still more clearly, to all who have the sense to see, what tremendous harm is being done to the working class movement through the bureaucracy of Stalinism [Sara (October 1936) 3].

With the majority of the Marxist League, Sara supported the fusion with C. L. R. James' Marxist group in the ILP in early 1938. He welcomed the formation of the Fourth International in the autumn of that year, chaired the foundation conference of its affiliate, the Revolutionary Socialist League (RSL), which brought together the majority of British Trotskyists, and served on its executive. Looking back on what had happened to Communism in the 1930s, on events in Russia and on the Comintern's role in China, Germany, Spain and Britain, he succinctly observed: 'Stalinism betrays the revolution, destroys the faith of the workers and makes socialism a mockery' [Sara (April 1938) 4].

Thereafter, together with his old comrades from the Balham group, he drifted away from mainstream Trotskyism. Like them, his impatience with *ersatz* Leninism and revolutionary posturing was enduring. He opposed the war as imperialist, arguing in the Labour Party in south London and in the Royal Arsenal Co-op that the struggle for peace was inseparable from socialist advance. His involvement with Groves and Wicks in the Socialist Anti-War Front, which was criticised as pacifist by most Trotskyists, led to a breach in 1939 with the RSL leadership, around Denzil Harber. Nonetheless he spoke with Fenner Brockway at the Trotsky Memorial Meeting in September 1940, commending Trotsky's murderers and their apologists, such as J. R.Campbell, to 'the execration of humanity'. He was now 54 years of age. He had travelled far from his political roots, but remained faithful to the vision of workers' self-emancipation and the belief in the power of the word in which he been nurtured. He was captured for posterity at Clapham Common one Sunday morning in 1940, much as he had been in 1914:

> he began with four or five of us around his platform … there was a sizeable crowd around an Economic League speaker. Sara boomed out in measured tones, 'Travelaars in Indiaah … tell a tale … of Indian fakirs … who … throwing a rope into the air … make it stand the whole length … suspended from nothing'. In this manner he spoke about mass hypnotism and the Economic League speaker's attempt to practise it. In five minutes or less he had stripped the audience away from the Economic League and they were gathered around him [Hunter (1997) 36–7].

He was still working in the Labour Party, although his bid to become parliamentary candidate for Wimbledon in 1941 proved unsuccessful. Connie Taylor was terminally ill and in May 1942 Sara married Eleanor Pembrook, a Tooting woman 17 years his junior. In the winter of 1941–42 he acted as NCLC tutor for south Wales, and in March 1942 he was appointed to the full-time post of South London divisional organiser, with the brief to develop classes with trade union bodies and members of the Labour Party and the cooperative movement. Following surveillance of its revolutionary socialist opponents the CPGB recorded that 'Henry Sara, ex-Party member and a virulent Trotskyist, is now an NCLC organiser in London. George Phippen, the other London official is very much under his influence and facilitates the work of the Trotskyists as NCLC lecturers' [NMLH, CP/CENT/ORG/13/4, Report on Trotskyite Activities, May 1943]. But Sara was a teacher, not an organiser, and problems disguised by wartime dislocation emerged into the open as the post-war era dawned. J. P. M. Millar, who was intensely loyal to the Labour government, demanded greater efficiency, a more contemporary, 'constructive' approach, more union affiliations and more students in order to win the relentless competition with the state-aided Workers' Educational Association.

In the face of Sara's alleged failure to develop courses, Millar claimed that the appointments committee had doubted his capacity as an organiser. He attempted to involve Sara in alternative work: training new tutors and marking correspondence courses, interspersed with periodic reviews of his student figures. Conflicts between organisers and the Stakhanovite Millar were a regular occurrence. But the anti-authoritarian Sara compounded matters by acting defiantly, drumming up support from London NCLC activists and requesting permission to stand for Wandsworth Borough Council. In the face of harassment he hung on, but Millar's persistence paid off. Despite support from divisional delegations and the Organisers' Association, he was dismissed in February 1948. At that year's NCLC conference an emergency motion calling for his reinstatement was ruled out of order on the ground that the dismissal of staff was an administrative issue and beyond the remit of NCLC democracy.

That was Sara's last battle: his life as an activist was drawing to a close. Connie Taylor, whom he visited to the last, died in 1946. Her son recorded that he and Sara were her only mourners and that the 60-year old Sara felt that life had finally caught up with him. According to Taylor,

Connie had left Sara a small annuity. Nonetheless he was forced to take a poorly paid post as a temporary post office worker. He remained active in Wandsworth Labour Party, kept in touch with British and American Trotskyists and in 1951 and 1952 regularly reviewed books for the ILP's *Socialist Leader*. He disparaged Lysenko and his British disciples, excoriated 'Stalin's Empire' and 'Red Imperialism', and wrote favourably of Tony Cliff's early work on Eastern Europe. In the autumn of 1952 he contracted lung cancer. He died aged 67 on 19 November 1953. Most of the mourners at his funeral were members of the Balham group. He left an estate valued at £442 6s. 2d.

Sara was representative of the irreconcilable, antistatist strain in the autodidactic, propaganda-driven tradition of early-twentieth-century socialism, which insisted that workers must secure their emancipation through direct action. He always maintained this position, and unlike many other pre-1914 irreconcilables never succumbed to the imperatives of the burgeoning but degenerating Russian state. He embraced official Communism reluctantly, and when he realised it was a *cul-de-sac* his deep and direct knowledge of other communisms helped him to find another path. In the midst of wartime martyrdom he complained about how hard it was to fight with the minority – but he always did so. Apart from his years in the CPGB, he stood with the minority of the minority, the real underdogs.

Sara was a Trotskyist when it was hardest to be a Trotskyist: when Trotskyism was weak and persecuted, yet arguably at its most inspiring as a compelling critique of Stalinism at midnight in the century. Even here he was fully an individual: his early years as a syndicalist and anarchist sustained an inherent independence; he was never comfortable in disciplined organisations; and his early self-education taught him to trust his own judgement. In the end he could find no place in the transformed labour movement. He possessed an unbending political rectitude. If, in more personal terms, as Alan Taylor asserted, he exploited his appeal for women he did so, as Taylor also suggested, with a certain innocence and loyally sang for his supper. If at times he felt that the world owed him a living, it was so that he could turn his entire energy to winning the world for the working class.

Writings: (1) Articles in the *Herald of Revolt*: 'The Limit', October 1912; 'Revolution and the Strike', November 1912; 'What Makes War?', December 1912; 'Berkman's Memoirs', February 1913; 'Theosophy', 'The Workers and the War', March 1913; 'Industrial Unionism', April 1913; 'Our Policy Stated', May 1913; 'Fly Away Gill', June 1913; 'We Must Have Eight', July 1913; 'Are Strikes Reformist?', September 1913; 'Are Anti-Socialists Mad?', October 1913; 'Hyndman's Confession', December 1913; 'Blasphemy!', December 1913; **(2) Articles in the *Spur*:** 'Daniel de Leon', June 1914; 'The Luxury of Poverty', July 1914; 'Most and Tucker', August 1914; 'Armaments and Profits', October 1914; 'The War on Nietzsche', November 1914; 'Behind the War', December 1914; 'The Two Classes', February 1915; 'Playing the Game', April 1915; 'The Present Socialism', May 1915; 'Sorgue!', June 1915; 'Below the Surface', August 1915; 'Notes and Queries', February 1916; 'The Yellow Streak', July 1916; 'A Moral Outlook', October 1917; 'The Wakefield "Concession"?: A Diary', October 1918; 'Recognition', December 1918; 'Uncowed Conscience', January 1919; 'The Logic of War', February 1919; 'A Plaint of Peace', April 1919; 'They Speak for Themselves', May 1919; 'The Force of Parliament', July 1919; 'Direct Action', August 1919; 'Who Are The Communists?', January, 1921. **(3) Other articles:** 'The Grief And Glory of Russia', *Workers' Dreadnought*, 23 July 1921, 6, 13, 27 August 1921; 'The March Past', *Communist Review*, March 1926; 'The Class War', *Communist Review*, April 1926; 'Further Jottings on R. W. Postgate', *The Communist*, May 1928; 'An Anarchist With A Temper', *Sunday Worker*, 14 October 1928; 'Dietzgen – The Tanner Who Confounded The Pundits', *Sunday Worker*, 9 December 1928; 'New Light on Chartism', *Communist Review*, January 1930; 'The Leisure Class', *Communist Review*, February 1930; 'About Marx and Engels', *Daily Worker*, 15 February 1930; 'The Revolutionist: A Glance at the Past of a Labour Hack', *Daily Worker*, 9 April 1930; 'The Stage of Imperialism', *Communist Review*, April 1930; 'A Communist Textbook', *Communist*

Review, May 1930; 'Laying the Ghost of Karl Marx', *Plebs*, May 1930; 'Organised Capitalism: Rathbone Replies to Sara', *Communist Review*, September 1930; 'Communist education', *Daily Worker*, 2, 3 October 1931; 'Trotsky and the Russian Revolution', *Plebs*, September 1932; 'Trotsky on the Revolution', *Plebs*, May 1933; 'William Gallacher: Notes for Autobiography', *Red Flag*, June 1936; 'The Deportation of Mrs Muhsam', *Red Flag*, September 1936; 'Trotsky's Traducers', *Red Flag*, October 1936; 'The Novobirsk Trial', *Red Flag*, January 1937; 'Behind the Popular Front', *Red Flag*, March 1937; 'Marxism and MacDonaldism', *Plebs*, March 1937; 'Maxim Gorky, Lenin and Trotsky', *Red Flag*, May 1937; 'Needs or Deeds – A Rejoinder', *Plebs*, August 1937; 'China and the Comintern', *Controversy*, October 1937; 'Histories of the CPGB' *Controversy*, December 1937; 'The Prince of Anarchists', *Plebs*, March 1938; 'Murder in Moscow: Another Gigantic Frame Up', *Fight*, April 1938; 'Could Be Improved: Engels on Capital', *Plebs*, April 1938; 'Soviet Purge Continues', *Fight*, June 1938; 'Jackson versus Sara', *Plebs*, June 1938; 'Japan: Weakest Link in the Chain', *Controversy*, August 1938; 'Engels on Capital', *Plebs*, August 1938; 'The Chinese Revolution', *New Leader*, 21 October 1938; 'Pollitt and the Party Line', *Call of the Socialist Anti-War Front*, November 1939; 'Not State Capitalism', *Left*, January 1940; 'Is Anarchy The Answer?', *New Leader*, 26 August 1944; 'Warfare and Words', *Plebs*, December 1944; 'Frederick Engels', *Plebs*, September 1945; 'Science and Heredity', *Socialist Leader*, 24 March 1951; 'Pathways in Science', *Socialist Leader*, 23 June 1951; 'Marx, Hegel and Russia', *Socialist Leader*, 16 February 1952; 'The Peasants and Marx', *Socialist Leader*, 29 March 1952; 'Stalin Said No', *Socialist Leader*, 5 April 1952.

Sources: (1) MSS: Sara–Maitland Papers, Wicks Papers, MRC, University of Warwick; Aldred Papers, Mitchell Library, Glasgow; Communist Party Archive, NMLH; NCLC Papers, National Library of Scotland; Russian State Archive of Socio-Political History (RGASPI), Moscow; Harry Wicks, interview with A. Richardson, 11 March 1978; Steve Dowdall and Daisy Groves, interview with A. Richardson, n.d. but 1982 (in author's possession). **(2) Other:** Parliamentary Debates, Fifth Series, Commons, 1916, vols LXXXI, LXXXII; P. Howard, 'Henry Sara: An Appreciation', *Spur*, June 1916; 'Henry Sara Stands in Tottenham', *Workers' Life*, 19 April 1929; R. M. Fox, *Drifting Men* (1930); R. M. Fox, *Smoky Crusade: An Autobiography* (1938); G. Aldred, *A Call to Manhood: 26 Essays* (1944); R. Groves, 'Farewell To A Rebel: The Life and Death of Henry Sara', *Socialist Leader*, 28 November 1953; G. Aldred, *No Traitors' Gait* (1963); R. Groves, *The Balham Group: How British Trotskyism Began* (1974); B. Holton, *British Syndicalism, 1900–1914* (1976); R. Challinor, *The Origins of British Bolshevism* (1977); J. Quail, *The Slow Burning Fuse: The Lost History of British Anarchism* (1978); A. J. P. Taylor, *A Personal History* (1983); K. Weller, *Don't Be A Soldier! The Radical Anti-War Movement in North London, 1914–1918* (1985); S. Bornstein and A. Richardson, *Against The Stream: A History of the Trotskyist Movement in Britain, 1924–1938* (1986); John Taylor Caldwell, *Come Dungeons Dark: The Life and Times of Guy Aldred* (Barr 1988); M. Shipway, *Anti-Parliamentary Communism: The Movement for Workers' Councils in Britain, 1917–1945* (1988); C. Tsuzuki, *Tom Mann, 1856–1941: The Challenge of Labour* (1991); H. Wicks, *Keeping My Head: The Memoirs of a British Bolshevik* (1992); A. Sisman, *A. J. P. Taylor: A Biography* (1994); B. Winslow, *Sylvia Pankhurst: Sexual Politics and Political Activism* (1996); B. Hunter, *Lifelong Apprenticeship: The Life and Times of A Revolutionary* (1997); M. Davis, *Sylvia Pankhurst: A Life in Radical Politics* (1999); K. Burk, *Troublemaker: The Life and History of A. J. P. Taylor* (2000). **(3) Obituaries:** *Socialist Leader*, 28 November 1953; *Plebs*, January 1954. Information and papers from J. T. Caldwell, A. Campbell, T. Crawford, J. Greenway, A. Richardson, J. Quail, K. Weller and C. Wrigley.

JOHN MCILROY

See also: †Walter AYLES; Arthur READE; † W. H. THOMSPON.

SCHOLEFIELD, James (1790–1855)
CHARTIST

James Scholefield was born in 1790 to Daniel and Rebecca Scholefield in Colne Bridge, near Huddersfield, Yorkshire. Of his childhood and upbringing no information has come to light, but we do know that at some point before 1809 he moved to Manchester to live and study at the Salford Academy of Sciences, run by the Reverend William Cowherd, a theologian, polymath and founder of a schismatic Swedenborgian sect known as the Bible Christians (Cowherdites). Ordained as a minister in this sect in 1813, Scholefield served at Christ Church in Hulme until 1823, when he founded the Round Chapel in Ancoats, another Manchester suburb, where he preached until his death in 1855.

Scholefield's religious heritage was a rationalist heterodox theology and an intense notion of public duty that led him into a myriad of reform causes. He was a life-long advocate of teetotal-ism (serving as an official in a branch of the Manchester Temperance Society during the 1830s and 40s), and a founding member of the Manchester Vegetarian Society in 1847. Like Cowherd, he was renowned as an apothecary and doctor (at one time he listed his occupation as 'Surgeon'). He earned his reputation for healing during the cholera epidemic that swept through the squalid cellars of Ancoats in 1833, and one of his patented remedies was still on sale in Ancoats in 1904. Scholefield also shared with Cowherd a deep commitment to education, and like his mentor he worked as a lecturer and operated a school at his chapel for many years. In the 1850s he was involved in the controversial Lancashire Public Schools Association.

Scholefield's radical creed took shape amid the suffering and discontent that followed the French wars. By January 1817 he had been brought to the attention of the Home Office as an 'Ultra-Radical Huntite', and he was present at Peterloo in 1819. Scholefield condemned the actions of the Yeomanry Cavalry and those who supported them, and he signed a declaration of protest condemning the 'unexpected and unnecessary violence' of the Yeomanry Cavalry against peaceful protesters [*Manchester Observer*, 11 September 1819]. He was appalled by the attitude of clergymen in other churches, many of whom, Dissenting as well as Anglican, had signed a Loyal Address, and he deliberately flaunted his opinions against them. When on the first Sunday after the massacre the doors of the Anglican Sunday schools were barred to all children sporting radical insignia – green ribbons and white hats – the doors of Scholefield's Sunday school were thrown open in a gesture of defiance specifically to cater for them. Most provocative of all was his action when a preacher in the Wesleyan Connexion published a Patriotic Sermon on the text 'Let every soul be subject unto the higher powers': Scholefield responded by publishing a pamphlet in which he identified the Bible as a source of radicalism that went further even than the writings of Tom Paine. 'For of all the Books that ever were written, none ever flew so full in the face of oppression, and pleaded for justice, mercy and truth, so boldly and repeatedly, as the Bible', he wrote. 'In short the Bible is the Book of all books in the World, considering its inspiration, and its doctrines, as eminently worthy of being entitled – RIGHTS OF MAN!' [Scholefield (1819) 8]

In October 1819 Scholefield set up a subscription at his chapel 'for the benefit of the Unfortunate Sufferers' at Peterloo, and as a witness to the massacre he testified on behalf of Henry Hunt at his state trial in March 1820. During the second half of 1820 Scholefield was prominent among the local 'friends of Queen Caroline', and he toured Lancashire preaching sermons for her deliverance. This commitment to popular radicalism continued into the 1830s. In 1833 he succeeded with other radicals in denying the Anglican Church in Manchester a church rate for the first time. In March 1835, following Hunt's death, Scholefield hosted a meeting of radicals who determined to erect a monument to Hunt's memory (as chairman of the Hunt Monument Committee, Scholefield's perseverance was instrumental in the completion of a monument overlooking his churchyard in Ancoats). Later in 1835, when Feargus O'Connor visited Manchester for the first time to address the inaugural meeting of the Manchester Radical Association, it was Scholefield who came forward to welcome him. This was the beginning of a friendship with the man who bestowed upon him the title 'Chaplain of the Manchester Chartists'.

Scholefield was on the platform at the first Chartist rally on Kersal Moor in September 1838, and was elected to the council of the Manchester Political Union the following month. He was often called upon to chair large public meetings and dinners. His chapel served as the venue for the national conference during the Plug Plot riots, which convulsed large parts of Lancashire, Cheshire and the Midlands in 1842, and although he was not a delegate he was arrested and tried for sedition and conspiracy, but acquitted. He claimed that his brush with the law cost him £150 and this strained his relationship with some Chartists, including O'Connor. By 1846, however, Scholefield had again, to use O'Connor's colourful phrase, 'buckled on his Chartist armour', becoming a leading supporter of the People's Hall in Ancoats and a promoter of the Chartist Land Company. In the 1820s he had promoted a working-class building society, and he was a supporter of a Christian Chartist cooperative on Chat Moss in the early 1840s.

Scholefield's close connection with the local community in Ancoats led him into an extensive career in local government. He successfully sought public office on four occasions. Between 1833–36 and 1839–42 he served the people of Ancoats as an elected member of the Manchester Police Commission. Despite his vehement opposition to Manchester receiving a Charter of Incorporation in the late 1830s on the ground that it was a reform that did not go far enough, he was elected as a town councillor for two terms (1847–53). As a local politician he did not articulate grandiose schemes for urban reconstruction of the sort made famous later in the century. Like William Cobbett and other popular radicals of the day he associated taxation with 'old corruption', and consequently was opposed to giving local government either the power or the revenue for reform on a grand scale. Thus his objectives as a Police Commissioner and subsequently as a local councillor were immediate, practical and piecemeal: paving streets, installing sewers, erecting streetlights. He took this role seriously, attending all but six meetings during his six years on the borough council.

Known for his philanthropy, Scholefield assisted churchwardens in distributing poor relief. He continued his opposition to the introduction of the New Poor Law long after others had given up. He was also an opponent of persecution in Ireland, the standing army and the Corn Laws, and attended the Anti-Corn Law League's National Conference of Ministers in August 1841. He kept up the pace of his reforming activities until his death in 1855. Towards the end of his life he played a leading part in the Manchester Vegetarian Society and was one of the most prominent local leaders of the 'Short Time' movement for reduced working hours.

In 1851 Scholefield was a founding member of the Manchester branch of the Parliamentary and Financial Reform Association (PFRA), which embraced the twin objectives of extending suffrage and cutting government spending as a prelude to a reduction in taxation. As the product of an alliance between middle- and working-class radicals, the PFRA provoked a split in the ranks of Manchester Chartism and led Scholefield to quarrel with some of his former colleagues. Although he remained a close friend and supporter of Feargus O'Connor, Scholefield's support for the PFRA signalled, as with other Chartists, his transition to the ranks of nineteenth-century liberalism. It was also a reflection of his commitment to practical reform that did little to dent his popularity in working-class Ancoats, a popularity that remained 'second to none': 'The people felt that his sympathy for them was genuine', recalled one commentator, 'and that his expression of it was prudent as well as courageous' [*Middleton Guardian*, 12 April 1890].

In 1821 Scholefield had married Charlotte Walker and over the next 14 years they had eight children. At a time when the mortality rate in Manchester was the scandal of the age, the register of Scholefield's chapel records his family tragedy: – the death of his three youngest children and his wife (aged 30) in the space of four months in 1835. Few could doubt his qualification to minister to the labouring poor in Ancoats. In physical terms he was described as a 'good-looking, even corpulent man' who was never wanting 'in activity and animation' [*Middleton Guardian*, 29 March 1890]. He died in 1855.

Scholefield's significance was greater even than his local reputation. Firstly, he was an example of the powerful influence of religious forms of radicalism on the Chartist movement. Secondly, his long career demonstrates some of the continuities in nineteenth-century radicalism and rescues individual reform movements from the isolation in which they are sometimes studied. Finally, he exemplified the ease with which many Chartists moved into the ranks of mid-nineteenth century liberalism, and by helping to ensure that it was a radical creed made it the repository of a great deal of Chartist aspiration for a better world.

Writings: *Letters, etc. On Religious Subjects* (n.d.); *The Second Lecture on the Creation of Man, Delivered at Christ Church, Ancoats* (n.d.); *Remarks on the Sermon, Adapted to the State of the Times, Preached by the Rev. John Stephens, In the Methodist Chapel, Oldham Street, Manchester* (Manchester, 1819); *A Reply to the Address to the Labouring Classes of Manchester and Salford; Together With Remarks on the Letters on the Subject of the Auxiliary Bible Society* (Manchester, 1821); *Select Hymns for the Use of Bible Christians; By the Late Rev. W. Cowherd, With an Appendix by the Rev. James Scholefield, Christ Church, Every Street, Ancoats* (Manchester, 1841); *An Address of the Members and Friends of the Bible Christians, Assembling at Christ Church, Every Street, Manchester* (Manchester, 1845). Scholefield also published an abridged edition of a vegetarian cookbook and contributed articles on various subjects to a range of newspapers and journals, often using the pseudonym 'S'.

Sources **(1) MS:** Register of Christ Church, Every Street, Manchester Public Library Archives Department. **(2) Newspapers:** *Northern Star*, 1838–52; *Middleton Guardian*, 1890. **(3) Other:** W. E. A. Axon, *A History of the Bible Christian Church Salford* (Manchester, 1909); W. R. Ward, 'Swedenborgianism: Heresy, Schism or Religious Protest?' in D. Baker (ed.), *Schism, Heresy and Religious Protest* (Cambridge, 1972) 303–9; P. J. Lineham, 'Restoring Man's Creative Power: the Theosophy of the Bible Christians of Salford', in W. J. Shiels (ed.), *The Church and Healing* (Oxford, 1982) 207–23; P. A. Pickering and A. Tyrrell, ' "In the Thickest of the Fight": The Reverend James Scholefield (1790–1855) and the Bible Christians of Manchester and Salford', *Albion*, 26 March 1994, 461–82; P. A. Pickering, *Chartism and the Chartists in Manchester and Salford* (Basingstoke, 1995).

PAUL A. PICKERING

See also: Reginald John RICHARDSON; James WROE.

SMITH, Henry Norman (1890–1962)
LABOUR MP, CO-OPERATOR, JOURNALIST, SOCIAL CREDITER

Henry Norman Smith (known as Norman) was born in Swindon, Wiltshire, on 31 January 1890, the son of Enoch Smith, a solicitor's clerk, and his wife Elizabeth, née Hopkins, both of whom had an agricultural background. His great grandfather had been a Romany Gypsy who earned money from prize fighting. His great grandmother was a practising clairvoyant. His parents were supporters of the Conservative Party, but played little part in formal political campaigns. Smith was educated at his local elementary school and regularly attended Sunday school. He proved an able pupil during his time at Swindon High School and later Swindon College. He showed an interest in politics and was elected 'Tory prime minster' in mock elections in his final year. On completing his education he was apprenticed to the local Great Western Railway Works. He was averse to this work from the outset and wanted to fulfil his childhood ambition of becoming a journalist. It was in the railway works in Swindon where he was first exposed to the politics of the labour movement: during meal breaks he would listen to the arguments of local trade unionists and political activists. He was quickly converted to the socialist cause. A major influence on the young Smith was Robert Blatchford's *Merrie England*. He joined the Independent Labour Party in 1907 and rapidly became the leading propagandist in his workplace. He was viewed as a rather eccentric figure by his fellow apprentices, combining his blue overalls with a red tie and making regular speeches on a soapbox.

After leaving engineering in 1912 Smith began a career in journalism. He first worked on a publication in Belgium, where he lived in a room above a local bar. At the weekends he helped the proprietor to serve drinks and prepare food. After a number of other short-term appointments he joined the staff of Messrs Iliffe and Sons, publishers of *Autocar* magazine. During the First World War he served with the British Expeditionary Force in France, where he was seriously wounded. He remained overseas until 1918. After the end of hostilities he was again able to practice his journalistic craft, in line with his political beliefs, when he obtained a position on the left-wing *Daily Herald* in early 1919. At that time the paper was controlled by a committee, consisting of George Lansbury, Frank Hodges, Alfred Barnes and others from the labour movement. For the next 11 years he travelled widely with the newspaper, reporting on a variety of stories and becoming a well-known figure in Fleet Street. He also provided copy for *Reynolds News* and *John Bull*. He rose quickly through the ranks at the *Daily Herald*, becoming sub-editor, then parliamentary lobby correspondent and then news editor. In the last position he was the highest-paid staff member under the editor, commanding a salary of £15 per week [Labour Party Records, LP/DH/444, NMLH]. Smith became a regular figure in the House of Commons press gallery, where he made numerous political contacts. Within the labour movement there were some criticisms of the independence of the *Daily Herald* during Smith's period of employment. Arthur Henderson felt that if possible it was imperative for all journalists employed on the paper to be close to the Labour Party. Ernest Bevin echoed this view in his memorandum on the weaknesses of the paper, drafted in 1925:

> In politics it is difficult to know where the *Daily Herald* stands. Probably it is due to the party itself, but there has been no real attempt, so far as I can see, to get the party to use it as a medium for conveying the official or semi-official policy, outside the articles of MacDonald, and instead of these articles being placed in a readable position, they seem to me to be scraggily set up. In other words it is a hotch-potch between the *Daily Mail* and *Daily Mirror* in make-up [LP/DH/461, NMLH].

Smith was advised to improve the paper and draw it more closely to the politics of the Labour Party. One important role he took on was as journalistic companion to the Labour leader, Ramsay MacDonald, on his national tour during the 1929 general election campaign. Soon after the election he travelled with MacDonald to the United States and Canada to cover the naval negotiations. He remained personally and politically close to MacDonald until the latter's decision to lead the National Government in 1931. In his position as parliamentary lobby correspondent Smith was able to press his views on economic questions in discussions with Labour politicians. He later recalled that Philip Snowden 'used to be icily sarcastic with me on the occasions when I suggested to him that banks created the funds they lent' [Smith (1944) 50].

Smith was already a committed advocate of social credit. This system of finance was the brainchild of a Scottish engineer, Major Clifford Hugh Douglas, who first published his economic ideas in 1919 in the *English Review* and in *The New Age* under the editorship of A. R. Orage. The articles led to some serious consideration by socialists, but most rejected them as naive and unable to alter the balance of power in capitalist society. Douglas's theory was relatively simple: under the capitalist economic system there was a shortage of purchasing power, but this could be rectified by creating a national dividend to supplement wages so that consumers could buy the abundance of goods that were produced without going into debt and being at the mercy of bankers who controlled the money supply [Douglas (1969) 5]. Only a minority of socialists were sympathetic to social credit. The National Guilds League had a significant social credit strand, but by 1921 the ideological thrust of that organisation was being directed by the majority communist faction [Kenney (1939) 287]. Nevertheless in the climate of economic uncertainty that followed the crash of 1929, social credit ideas began to be eagerly discussed as an alternative both to current capitalism and to the Communism of the Soviet Union.

In 1930 Smith left the *Daily Herald* to take up a post with the Co-operative Press, where he was asked to improve the quality and circulation of its house journals. He established the Co-operative Citizen series of publications in conjunction with the London Co-operative Society's Political Committee. He settled in Sevenoaks, Kent, and immersed himself in the local labour movement. He used his extensive contacts in the cooperative and trade union movements in order to promote himself as a potential parliamentary candidate. With the resignation of Albarn Gordon as prospective parliamentary candidate for the Faversham Divisional Labour Party in 1931, Smith seized his chance and was duly selected. The main focus of his campaign was unemployment. He argued in favour of the traditional Labour ideal of social ownership, but felt that such a programme could provide only a temporary solution to economic problems and advocated a social credit policy as a necessary step towards the institution of socialism. He told the *East Kent Gazette* that it was the 'Bank of England, not Parliament that controls the economic destiny of Britain. Parliament is a pawn in the hands of international finance' [*East Kent Gazette*, 18 July 1931]. He fought an energetic campaign in Faversham, but was defeated in a straight fight with a Conservative:

Faversham, Kent, 1931: electorate 53 733, turnout 72.2 per cent

A. Maitland (Conservative)	25 568 (65.9 per cent)
H. N. Smith (Labour)	13 226 (34.1 per cent)
Majority	12 342 (31.8 per cent)

Smith's prominent role in the Kent labour movement ensured that he was the Faversham representative at successive Labour Party conferences. He used this forum to press his social credit philosophy and consistently attacked both left and right within the party for clinging to financial orthodoxy.

The politics of social credit had been a minority interest for British radicals until the early 1930s, but slowly became more prominent as the policies promoted by left and right seemed unable to deal with the problems affecting the international capitalist economy. The founder of the political movement for social credit in Britain was John Hargrave, a charismatic eccentric who led a break from the Boy Scouts in 1921. He went on to become a prolific writer, faith healer and inventor of the navigation system used on the Concorde aircraft. He became the founding member of the Kibbo Kift, a youth organisation that attracted a number of socialists because of its advocacy of world peace, antimilitarism and the importance of rural life for the self-improvement of the masses. Other members included the Pethick-Lawrences, H. G. Wells and Carl Cullen of the Independent Labour Party. The dominant left-wing group within the Kibbo Kift was made up of socialists from the London cooperative movement, who were also mostly members of the Labour Party. It was probably through his involvement with this group that Smith was first drawn to social credit ideas. In 1923 the Kibbo Kift was subjected to pressure by two opposing forces, each determined to steer it in a particular direction: the more conservative members wanted to slow the growth of membership in order to maintain internal cohesion, while the more political group, led by the feminists, cooperators and the future Labour MP John Wilmot, wanted to turn the movement into a mass membership organisation [Drakeford (1997) 59].

The Kibbo Kift formally adopted social credit as policy in 1927, when it was added to the third clause of the organisation's covenant. By that time many socialists, including John Wilmot and Carl Cullen, had left the organisation; the cooperative movement severed its ties in 1924. With the weakening of the socialist tendency within the Kibbo Kift, advocacy of social credit became its main concern, and in 1931 it changed its name to the Green Shirt Movement for Social Credit. Smith had little contact with the Green Shirts as he was more sympathetic to the non-party Social Credit Secretariat, established by Douglas in 1933 as a pressure group to promote social credit policies. It produced a newspaper, *The Social Crediter*, and organised courses and conferences. Douglas himself became critical of this group after trying to control it in a dictatorial fashion. He wanted supporters to renounce their party affiliation if their local candidate would not adhere to social credit policies. The various groups had enjoyed autonomy and cross-party support and Douglas's intervention led to dissension, factionalism and expulsion. Outside the secretariat, Hargrave was the most prominent exponent of social credit [Reckitt (1941) 173–4]. Another body, the Social Credit Co-ordinating Committee, based in North Yorkshire, attracted social credit activists, but the movement remained relatively disconnected, with each faction claiming to hold the most accurate interpretation of Douglas's ideas. Smith's principal task was to press for the acceptance of social credit ideas by the Labour Party so he remained aloof from the various groups, save for speaking at the odd conference of the Secretariat and the Co-ordinating Committee.

Advocates of social credit were disturbed by the degree of distress in industrial areas and claimed that they had the solution to the problem of 'poverty in the midst of plenty'. At the annual conference of the Labour Party in Leicester in 1932, Smith attacked not only Philip Snowden but also the supposedly iconoclastic Bevin, arguing that the party leadership had not learned the lesson of 1931:

> The simple truth is that Bevin, like the National Executive, is steeped in financial orthodoxy. During the first 24 years I was in this Movement Snowden kept us in the path of financial orthodoxy, and that path led straight to the disaster of 1931 ... The simple truth is you cannot socialise industry unless you socialise credit ... The National Executive's financial policy is useless, because it does not rid industry of the burden of usury ... I ask the National Executive to pour into the petrol tank of our Socialist planning the necessary fuel of Socialist credit which alone can energise our policies and render our democracy secure [Labour Party Conference Report (1932) 191].

The Labour Party was increasingly concerned about the growth of social credit ideas: Douglas was having some success in propagating his ideas overseas and the Green Shirts had become more visible on public demonstrations. The latter spoke at a number of unemployed meetings and attended the large antifascist rally in Hyde Park on 2 April 1933. They often faced violence from fascists, who branded them Communists, and hostility from Communists and members of the ILP, who viewed them as fascists. By now the Green Shirts had established a headquarters at 35 Old Jewry in London and a month later they published the first addition of *Attack!* This publication was aimed at mobilising the masses in favour of social credit. The party's rallying cry, which it used when addressing street demonstrations and disrupting opponents' meetings, was sharp and direct: 'Open the National Credit office! Issue the National Dividend! Apply the Scientific Price!' The Communist Party saw the Green Shirts as a threat to its recruiting ambitions amongst the working class and stepped up its practice of breaking up meetings and threatening social credit advocates with violence [Drakeford (1997) 133–43]. At the Labour Party conference in Hastings in autumn 1933, Smith moved a resolution in favour of social credit, but it was defeated.

> Our policy of nationalisation, essential though it be, does nothing whatever to enable the mass of the people to buy more goods. Indeed, it might have, and probably would have in the beginning, exactly the contrary effect. This is an age of mass production. Therefore you must have mass consumption [Labour Party Conference Report (1933) 176].

The National Executive of the Labour Party responded to the challenge of social credit by setting up a subcommittee to look into Douglas's ideas. The findings of the committee, which consisted of Evan Durbin, Hugh Gaitskell and W. R. Hiskett, were published in 1935 in a pamphlet entitled *The Labour Party, Socialism and Social Credit*. The members of the Social Credit Secretariat were invited to meet with the subcommittee to discuss their proposals for economic reform. The invitation was declined, but the committee was able to garner a discussion with social credit advocates through correspondence in the periodical *New Age*. Along with others, Smith attended some of the meetings. Labour remained unconvinced and felt that not only was Douglas not a socialist, but also that the ideas he proposed were overtly simplistic. Undeterred, Smith and others defended attacks on social credit at the 1935 Labour Party conference in Brighton. In response Hiskett reiterated the views of the subcommittee:

I appeal to those members of the Labour Party who are superficially attracted to Social Credit, not to be misled by the fact that Social Crediters sometimes steal our thunder and use our terminology. Economic power can only come from the control of real things, and the belief that a new social order can come through any jugglery with figures or tokens is a complete and dangerous delusion [Labour Party Conference Report (1935) 227].

Smith and the small band of social creditors were now labelled 'currency cranks'; a phrase used by John Strachey in his attack on Douglas's economics in his pamphlet *Social Credit: An Economic Analysis* (1936). Social credit advocates were often shouted down in meetings and wrongly accused of being under the spell of the 'mysterious' Hargrave. The movement was now spreading beyond the Green Shirts, with discussion and reading groups emerging across the country. The Green Shirts changed their name to The Social Credit Party of Great Britain (The Green Shirts) in 1935 and decided to fight an electoral campaign on the sole issue of Douglas's economics. The first fight was South Leeds, where Wilfred Townshend, the son of an unemployed miner, gained a respectable 3642 votes but Labour regained the seat it had lost in 1931 [Drakeford (1997) 165–77]. Smith stood again for the Labour Party in Faversham and was expected to do well against Maitland, his Tory adversary. He spoke at a number of large meetings but felt that the conservatism of the rural areas of the constituency would make it difficult for Labour to succeed: fear of Tory landowners was still very much evident in the constituency. Smith later recalled gaining favourable vocal support from farm labourers who nevertheless displayed Conservative posters in their windows – they were afraid to show overt support for Labour as they lived in tied cottages and could easily be evicted if their landlords felt slighted by their apparent political independence [*Nottingham Co-operative Herald*, March 1945]. In the event, Smith polled well but failed to unseat Maitland.

Faversham, Kent, 1935: electorate 56 664, turnout 74.0 per cent

A. Maitland (Conservative)	22 881 (54.6 per cent)
H. N. Smith (Labour)	19 060 (45.4 per cent)
Majority	3 821 (9.2 per cent)

Smith continued to face criticism from the left, both within and beyond his own district, owing to his association with the social credit cause. Maurice Dobb, the Cambridge Communist economist, placed social credit firmly in the tradition of fascist movements in Italy and Germany, and he attacked Smith for being a social crediter first and a socialist second:

Norman Smith relegates Socialism to the position of something which merely 'remains our goal' and 'would take a long time', while in the forefront, and as something separate from it, he places his Social Credit proposals as competent to increase the standard of life by some 40 per cent and abolish poverty [Dobb (1936) 23].

Smith was sympathetic to the Green Shirts and their advocacy of social credit through direct action, but he remained uncomfortable with Hargrave's leadership cult. Some years later, in an article in *Tomorrow*, he claimed that:

Many of John Hargrave's Green Shirts were exceedingly likeable human beings, even if their uniforms and their heel-clicking did at times make the public think them a little ridiculous.

Their propaganda was of a high order, and some of Hargrave's own writings have borne the mark of excellence. But the British public just won't stand for anything that looks like the 'Leader' idea [quoted in *The Message from Hargrave*, no. 453 (November 1946), Kibbo Kift Archive, YMA KK/183, LSE].

In 1937 the government passed the Public Order Act. This was primarily aimed at disrupting the activities of the British Union of Fascists, but its ban on the wearing of military-style uniforms also diluted the visual presence of the Social Credit Party. The social credit movement more generally was dissolving into warring factions, with Douglas attacking Hargrave and many members drifting away because of the latter's authoritarian leadership. The urgency of the proposals also fell on deaf ears because production was increasing and unemployment beginning to fall. The authorities still viewed the Green Shirts with suspicion and the latter remained under surveillance by the police and the secret service. In 1940 Smith's own house was raided by five plain-clothes officers, who undertook a detailed search. He was questioned about financial notes in his pocketbook and his political affiliations. He subsequently claimed that 'in the end, they took away a number of political documents that were about as seditious as a racing calendar' [*Reynolds News*, 28 July 1940].

Smith continued to attend social credit discussion meetings and began to research economic theories in preparation for his book *The Politics of Plenty* (1944). He was now editor of *The Illustrated Carpenter and Builder*, and in one issue of the magazine he claimed that 'So complete has been the boycott of Social Credit ideas by press, radio and political parties in this country that the general public knows hardly anything about them' [*The Illustrated Carpenter and Builder*, 9 October 1942]. In *The Politics of Plenty* Smith aimed to popularise social credit ideas and question the fundamental assumptions of economic thought. He provided a critique of economic orthodoxy and a plan for an improved system of finance through social credit. He also made space for an attack on the limitations of Labour socialism, which ensured that the book would command a readership beyond the political left and was generally well received. He pointed out that:

Too many socialists still think in terms of taking from the rich to give to the poor, too many socialists still bother their heads about how to share out equally the existing little cake, when they ought instead to be planning to make the cake itself much bigger [Smith (1944) 43].

The book became required reading within the restricted world of social credit study groups. Potential allies on the left remained unconvinced. G. D. H. Cole felt that purchasing power was affected not only by the pricing system and any improvement in the livelihood of the working class could only come through socialism [Cole (1944) 316–17]. Smith was convinced of the efficacy of social credit, but also remained committed to the Labour Party. He was selected to fight South Nottingham as a Labour and Co-operative candidate in the 1945 general election. The *Nottingham Co-operative Herald* gave Smith glowing coverage, claiming that he was 'never a yes man, always an original thinker and fearless spokesman of the people, he may be relied upon to put South Nottingham on the parliamentary map' [*Nottingham Co-operative Herald*, March 1945]. He addressed a number of large meetings across the constituency, making populist attacks on banks a central aspect of his speeches. In the event he took the seat, defeating S. F. Markham with a majority of 4550:

South Nottingham, 1945: electorate 39 989, turnout 75.9 per cent

H. N. Smith (Labour and Co-op)	15 316 (50.4 per cent)
S. F. Markham (National)	10 766 (35.5 per cent)
R. J. R. Blindell (Liberal)	4 272 (14.1 per cent)
Majority	4550 (14.9 per cent)

The Social Credit Party welcomed Smith's election to the Commons as a major advance. However the movement in general had declined significantly, with John Hargrave leading the party in an increasingly autocratic and bizarre manner, and littering his texts with mystic references. He published a weekly bulletin, *The Message from Hargrave*, which was merely a directive to party members. Hargrave and the social credit movement were given renewed confidence with the election of Smith and felt that his success would be the first stage in the acceptance of social credit ideas in the British political system.

> If this sudden and unexpected sweep to the left brings with it the opportunity for Mr Norman Smith, MP (Social Credit, Labour) to make his voice heard ... and to ease the Labour Party away from its economic conservatism and its Work complex, why then a ray of hope for the future will have penetrated the world darkness ... Norman Smith, however, is well aware of the shortcomings of the Labour Party ... This General Election has returned the first Social Credit advocate to the British House of Commons. As a party, we must do everything in our power to assist Mr Norman Smith, MP ... At the earliest opportunity we must send other Social Credit men into the House to support him ... We hope and believe that Mr H. Norman Smith will prove to be a real Social Credit champion. Good luck to the first Social Credit MP in the House of Commons [*The Message from Hargrave*, 3 August 1945, Kibbo Kift Archive, YMA KK/183, LSE].

In the Commons, Smith held to his economic beliefs and cut a rather isolated figure. In his maiden speech he attacked the emerging Bretton Woods agreement. He criticised the United States for exporting its obsession with capitalism to Europe, and argued that accepting US help 'would be placing a bludgeon in the hands of persons not necessarily in this country who might desire to hammer the present Labour Government in the way the last Labour Government was hammered by financial influences outside this country' [*Hansard*, 20 August 1945, cols 372–8]. Hargrave was delighted with Smith's performance and reported in his weekly message that it was 'a splendid fighting speech, with punch and vigour, that warms the hearts of all members of the Social Credit Party' [*The Message from Hargrave*, 7 September 1945, Kibbo Kift Archive, YMA KK/183, LSE]. Subsequently Smith voted against the US loan in December 1945.

Smith was critical of what he saw as the economic conservatism of the Attlee government, and felt that the front bench was dominated by persons who slavishly followed a liberal economic philosophy. He was equally critical of the left and their talk of the class war. In line with the thinking of most social credit advocates, he argued that the real division in Britain was not between the classes, but between the few people who controlled finance and the rest of the community. Smith called for a war of independence, starting in the House of Commons, to free the country from the shackles of American capitalism. He welcomed nationalisation as a socialist, but felt that this would not provide a long-term solution to economic problems. 'The ownership of the instruments of production confers very little economic power indeed, and is in fact completely subordinate to the control of the means of distribution, which is finance' [Smith (1944) 76]. The socialisation of credit was the only immediate remedy. Smith was increasingly seen throughout Parliament as a rather eccentric figure who was obsessed with his own interpretation of economic questions. MPs were often confused by his detailed speeches on international finance. Viscount Hinchingbrooke, MP for Dorset, was typical in his assessment: 'I have never been able to understand whether the Hon. Member for South Nottingham is one of those people who understands finance or not. At times, it appears to me that he both does and doesn't' [*Hansard*, 13 March 1946, col 1125]. Smith himself seemed to be unsure about his ability as an economic thinker. He told the Commons that 'I happen to be fascinated by the topic of finance, whether I understand it or not, I do not know' [*Hansard*, 29 October 1946, col 518]. He responded to attacks from the left with a critique of Marxism and a call for the establishment of a National Credit Account:

Karl Marx died 66 years ago, and Marxism is as dead as the dodo. What is wrong with the country is not that the employers rob the workers at the pay table, but that the price system fleeces the consumer at the retail counter [*Hansard*, 7 April 1949, col 2258].

Smith saw Labour's nationalisation policies as beneficial, but only to workers and especially those organised into trade unions. What was really needed was a 'consumers policy, not a workers' policy' [*Co-operative News*, 12 June 1948]. The strengthening of Britain's relationship with the United States incensed Smith:

I recoil in disgust from the prospect of having thrust on me at all times American comic strips, American canned food, American music, American films, and the American accent. I am British, I like being British, and I want to remain British ... We differ widely from the Americans in such vital matters as political maturity and social conscience [*Tomorrow*, August 1946].

Although Smith used every opportunity to raise the issue of social credit, he soon faced criticism from Hargrave and the Social Credit Party. They felt that his attempt to marry social credit with socialism was unworkable. They still referred to him as the 'Mighty Smith', but the weekly directive from Hargrave gradually began to question his understanding of Douglas's economic principles. Nevertheless he continued to campaign against the power of international financiers. This coloured his perception of the Palestine question:

Zionism is a bad thing. What is Zionism but the expressed belief of certain fanatical Jews that they are the chosen people, who ought to have a national state in Palestine ... This belief of the more fanatical Jews is a belief backed by big money in various parts of the world, particularly in the United States [*Hansard*, 26 January 1949, col 1001].

Towards the end of the 1945–51 Government the Social Credit Party came to see Smith as a hindrance to its cause and attacked his belief that nationalisation represented the first step towards social credit economics. In his new publication the *Commons Commentary*, Hargrave now referred to him as 'the Little Simpleton'. The party only continued to report Smith's speeches in order to 'expose the glaring technical mistakes' and 'dangerous propaganda weaknesses of his near Social Credit expositions' [*Commons Commentary*, 16 June 1950, Kibbo Kift Archive, YMA/KK 183, LSE]. But the Social Credit Party was now a spent force. Hargrave contested Stoke Newington in the 1950 general election but gained a mere 551 votes. A year later an extraordinary meeting was called and the decision was taken to dissolve the organisation. Meanwhile Smith worked hard to convince socialist MPs that he was not a slavish follower of Hargrave, or indeed Douglas. 'They brand me a 'Douglasite, which I am not, because I am a Socialist ... the fact that I accept some of his financial analysis does not make me a Douglasite' [Smith to Ellis Smith, 10 January 1954, Ellis Smith Papers, U294/C194/1].

Smith retained his seat in South Nottingham in the 1950 general election, although he felt himself lucky to be returned because of the changing socioeconomic character of the constituency: there was now an almost equal balance between Labour and Conservative supporters, with a large proportion of home-owners and affluent working-class people. His majority was reduced further in the 1951 election.

South Nottingham, 1950: electorate 45 864, turnout 85.4 per cent

H. N. Smith (Labour/Co-operative)	18 806 (48.1 per cent)
W. R. Rees-Davies (Conservative)	17 165 (43.8 per cent)
E. G. Watkins (Liberal)	3182 (8.1 per cent)
Majority	1641 (4.3 per cent)

South Nottingham, 1951: electorate 46 413, turnout 84.5 per cent

H. N. Smith (Labour/Co-operative)	19 844 (50.6 per cent)
W. R. Rees-Davies (Conservative)	19 362 (49.4 per cent)
Majority	482 (1.2 per cent)

Smith advocated monetary reform to the end of his parliamentary career, claiming that 'there is no future for socialism in this country so long as we have to depend upon international banking' [*Hansard*, 14 November 1952, col 1334]. He continued to call for the socialisation of credit and was seen by many as a one-issue MP. In a debate on the Finance Bill in 1951 he claimed that:

No amount of nationalisation, no matter how intrinsically good it may be, and no amount of Socialist expedients, however innately good they may be, can be made permanently effective unless and until there is public control over the flow of money from start to finish [*Hansard*, 8 May 1951, col 1844].

He held the seat until 1955, when – primarily due to boundary changes – he lost it to the Conservative D. M. Keegan by more than 7000 votes:

South Nottingham, 1955: electorate 65 449, turnout 78.3 per cent

D. M. Keegan (Conservative)	29 145 (56.9 per cent)
H. N. Smith (Labour and Co-operative)	22 092 (43.1 per cent)
Majority	7 053 (13.8 per cent)

In retirement Smith lived in Rustington, Sussex. He was now largely content to enjoy his hobbies: astronomy, motoring, gardening, gourmet food, a drink in the local pub an the horses. He continued to write the occusional letter to the newspapers and retained his interest in social credit ideas. In 1922 he had married Clare Louise Ody, daughter of Joseph Ody, an agricultural worker. He died on 21 December 1962 and left £8038.

H. Norman Smith was an exponent of a neglected tradition in the British labour movement. Social Credit was taken seriously by socialists in the 1930s, but typically as something that had to be discredited. For example influential thinkers such as Durbin and Gaitskell were mobilised to challenge the claim that it could solve the problems of poverty and capitalist crisis. Yet a few socialists felt that Social Credit complemented rather than challenged their politics. As an advocate of Social Credit, Smith remained critical of the limitations of Labour socialism. The banks were the major power brokers and democratic power could not be fully exercised unless this problem was solved. The introduction of social credit policies would be the first step towards a socialist society.

Social Credit stands-up, despite the sneers and jeers of politicians who will not take the the trouble to understand it simply because it does not square with their own pre-conceptions ... The main obstacle to its acceptance by the public is the pre-occupation of politicians with outmoded controversies, particularly those based on the obsolete concepts of Marx [*Tomorrow*, September 1946].

Although Smith often referred to himself as a misfit, apart from his rather eccentric economic views he was a typical ethical socialist, driven by a sense of English radicalism and populist democracy. In a speech in the House of Commons he once declared:

I am an Englishman. I believe in trying to combine in this country the ideal of social justice with individual freedom. I believe that the future peace of the world depends upon the creation and the maintenance of a political entity in the world which shall not be Communist or Capitalist, but shall be Social Democratic [*Hansard*, 22 October 1947, col 205].

262   (Henry) Norman SMITH

Writings: As a journalist Smith wrote various articles for a wide range of publications, most notably the *Daily Herald* and cooperative publications. He also produced a number of pamphlets. His thoughts on economic and political questions could be found in articles in *Tomorrow* throughout 1946. His most important publication was his book *The Politics of Plenty* (1944).

Sources: (1) **MSS:** The complete records of the Social Credit Party of Great Britain are deposited in the British Library of Political Science at the London School of Economics, YMA KK 1–29; there is a small collection of social credit pamphlets in the National Museum of Labour History, Manchester (NMLH); Labour Party Conference Reports and *Daily Herald* Files, NMLH; Papers of Social Credit Secretariat, Keighley, Yorkshire; Papers of Ellis Smith MP, Salford Local Studies Library. (2) **Newspapers and periodicals:** *Faversham Mercury*, 1931–35; *Co-operative News*, 1948; *Nottingham Co-operative Herald*, 1945; *Nottingham Guardian*, 1945–55; *Nottingham Evening News*, 1945–55; *Nottingham Evening Post*, 1945–55; *The Times*, 1962; *East Kent Gazette*, 1931–35; *Daily Worker*, 1935–50; *The Illustrated Carpenter and Builder*, 1942; *Daily Express*, 1948; *Tomorrow*, 1946; *Hansard*, 1945–55. (3) **Other:** C. H. Douglas, *Social Credit Principles* (1924); Oswald Mosley, *Revolution by Reason* (1925); Labour Party, *The Labour Party, Socialism and Social Credit* (1935); W. R. Lester, *Poverty and Plenty: The True National Dividend, The Pros and Cons of Social Credit* (1935); Clive Kenrick, *The Case for Social Credit* (1935); W. R. Hiskett, *Social Credit or Socialism: an Analysis of the Douglas Credit Scheme* (1935); Rev. Hewlett Johnson, *Social Credit and the War on Poverty* (1935); John Strachey, *Social Credit: An Economic Analysis* (1936); Maurice Dobb, *Social Credit Discredited* (1936); W. R. Hiskett and J. A. Franklin, *Searchlight on Social Credit* (1939); Rowland Kenney, *Westering: An Autobiography* (1939); Maurice B. Reckitt, *As it Happened: An Autobiography* (1941); G. D. H. Cole, *Money: Its Present and Future* (1944); John Hargrave, *Social Credit Clearly Explained* (1945); Bryan W. Monahan, *An Introduction to Social Credit* (1967); C. H. Douglas, *Fifty Years of Social Credit 1919–1969* (Mexborough, 1969); C. H. Douglas, *Economic Democracy* (1974); Frank Matthews, 'The Ladder of Becoming: A. R. Orage, A. J. Penty and the Origins of Guild Socialism in England', in David E. Martin and David Rubinstein (eds.) *Ideology and the Labour Movement: Essays Presented to John Saville* (1979) 147–99; Michael Stanton and Stephen Lees, *Who's Who of British Members of Parliament Vol. 4 1945–1979* (1981); John L. Finlay, *Social Credit: The English Origins* (1972); Wilfrid Price, *Social Credit and the Leisure State* (1981); Walter Van Trier, *Every One A King: An Investigation into the meaning and significance of the debate on basic incomes with special reference to three episodes from the British inter-war experience* (Leuven, 1995); Mark Drakeford, *Social Movements and their Supporters: The Green Shirts in England* (1997); Frances Hutchinson and Brian Burkitt, *The Political Economy of Guild Socialism and Social Credit* (1997); Peter Barberis, John McHugh and Mike Tyldesley, *Encyclopaedia of British and Irish Political Organisations: Parties, Groups and Movements of the Twentieth Century* (2000); *Who Was Who 1961–1970*; (4) **Obituaries:** *The Times*, 29 December 1962; *Nottingham Evening News*, 28 December 1962; *Co-operative News*, 5 January 1963.

KEITH GILDART

See also: †Alfred Richard ORAGE.

SMITH, Rosina (Rose) (1891–1985)
COMMUNIST PARTY ACTIVIST, ORGANISER, JOURNALIST

Rosina Smith was born in Putney, London, on 10 May 1891. Also known as Rose, she was the eldest daughter and second of the seven children of Samuel Ellis and Sarah, née Gardiner. Samuel Ellis was a potter and an active trade unionist; Sarah Ellis's family were Bristolians and the extended family included many ship's carpenters and stonemasons. Most of Rose's childhood and adolescence were spent in Whittington Moor, an industrial community on the edge of Chesterfield. Her formal education was relatively extensive for an Edwardian working-class girl. A two-year Minor County Scholarship supported her from the age of 12 to 15 at the Clay Cross Science School. Subsequently she joined the local pupil-teacher training scheme and passed the Pupil Teachers' Examination in 1907. Two years later she obtained the Preliminary Certificate, qualifying her for university entrance. However her family could not afford the fees and for much of the next ten years she worked as an infant teacher, first in Chesterfield and then in Windsor.

Smith's politicisation occurred during the dramatic prewar years of industrial conflict and suffrage agitation. During the 1911 railway strike she witnessed the setting ablaze of Chesterfield railway station. In 1909–10 she joined the local branch of the Social Democratic Federation (SDF), which in 1912 became a major element of the newly founded British Socialist Party (BSP). There she associated with people who were active in trade unions and sympathetic to industrial syndicalism. This socialist involvement led to her commitment to the concept of class struggle and the materialist conception of history. This was complemented by her commitment to the cause of women's emancipation after reading Olive Schreiner's *Women and Labour* (1911). Rose believed that better training opportunities for women and women's entry into the labour market were prerequisites for their liberation. Therefore she welcomed the prewar increase in the level of women's unionisation.

Her quest for political understanding led to her attendance at the political science tutorial class organised by the Workers' Educational Association (WEA) at the Chesterfield Settlement. In 1913–14 she attended summer schools at Balliol College, Oxford. Her fellow students included sympathisers with the more radical educational doctrines of the Central Labour College, an influence that perhaps hastened her rejection of the WEA's liberal pluralism.

The war divided the Chesterfield BSP. Smith felt politically isolated in her opposition. In 1916 she married a fellow socialist, Alfred Smith, a Sheffield house decorator and sign painter. When her husband was conscripted she had to take work in a local munitions factory because of the meagreness of her dependant's allowance. Shocked by her experiences on the shop floor she organised her workmates into a trade union. The Bolshevik Revolution was for her a magnificent achievement and she subsequently became an uncritical supporter of the Soviet Union; in her view any opposition or criticism of anything said or done in Moscow was a betrayal of Marxism–Leninism.

In 1919 Smith and her husband settled in Mansfield. Their twin sons Ted and Percy were born the following year. She was active in a broad range of labour movement institutions and attended local classes run by the National Labour College on Marxist economics and industrial history. By 1925 she was secretary of the Mansfield and District Labour College, organising evening courses and weekend and day schools on industrial and welfare matters. She was a delegate to the Mansfield Trades Council and active in the Women's Co-operative Guild.

Most significantly Smith and her husband were members of the Mansfield branch of the Communist Party from its formation in 1922. She was its first treasurer, but as a housewife with two small children she appears to have been given full membership only in 1923. At the same time, with dual membership still permitted, she was a member of the Mansfield Labour Party. Inevitably her political activities in Mansfield were heavily influenced by the disputes in the locally dominant coal industry. She assisted the local branch of the Miners' Minority Movement, and during the 1926 dispute played a leading part in maintaining morale amongst striking miners and their families. She led miners' wives in demonstrations, picketing and street committees against the spread of blacklegging. She was also involved in negotiations over Poor Law relief for strikers' families.

The Nottinghamshire Miners' Association emerged from the 1926 defeat in an appalling state, faced with the Spencer Union and denied recognition by the coal owners. Many Nottinghamshire miners were in neither union. Rose Smith believed that the miners had been betrayed by the Labour Party and the TUC and that an effective revolutionary party was urgently needed. She therefore welcomed the Communist Party's shift to 'Class against Class'. In the 1929 election she stood as the party's candidate in the Mansfield constituency. Her performance was characteristic of that of many Communist candidates in that election:

Mansfield, Nottinghamshire, 1929: electorate 59 735, turnout 81.2 per cent

C. Brown (Labour)	28 416 (58.6 per cent)
W. Collins (Liberal)	10 517 (21.7 per cent)
S. R. Sidebottom (Conservative)	9 035 (18.6 per cent)
Miss R. Smith (Communist)	533 (1.1 per cent)
Majority	17 899 (36.9 per cent)

Prior to the development of 'Class against Class', Smith had intervened in the Labour Party's protracted and divisive debate on the provision of birth control information at publicly funded clinics. The Labour Party leadership was hostile to the incorporation of this demand into party policy but the Labour Women's Conference supported the proposal. During the miners' lockout Rose secured the support of the Miners' Federation secretary, A. J. Cook, for the women's campaign. His views on the issue appeared in the *Sunday Worker* and prompted an exchange of letters between Smith and Dora Russell, one of the Workers' Birth Control Group secretaries. Smith tended to focus on the economic question and blamed the capitalist system for the poverty that – in conjunction with frequent child bearing – resulted in the premature aging of women. She insisted that the dissemination of birth control information had to be accompanied by better wages, which would make safer contraceptives more affordable for miners' wives. At the 1926 Labour Party Conference the MFGB delegation backed the women's campaign, giving them a narrow but temporary victory over the leadership.

Smith also considered that housework fostered women's enslavement, along with their lack of equal rights and economic inequality. In the early 1930s tension rose in the Smith household, partly because of financial difficulties and disputes over the sharing of housework. Smith complained that her husband did not help her enough with the domestic chores, while Alfred might have felt that she was away from home too often on Communist Party business. He certainly appears to have been uncomfortable with the style of Communist propaganda. The couple separated but never divorced, and Smith raised her sons with the support of family members and political friends.

The deterioration of Smith's marriage was concurrent with her increased prominence in the Communist Party. In 1927 she became a party organiser, and from 1929 until the dissolution of the party's Women's Department in 1933 she acted as National Women's Organiser. She sat on the Central Committee (1930–38) and the Politburo (1931–38). She constantly criticised the local and national leaders for their lack of interest in women and their problems in the workplace and the home. She also tried to reform the stifling and formal style of party work that alienated new recruits. Amongst her targets was the widely held view that only women employed in industry could play a proper part in the class struggle. Her experience of coalfield communities, where very few women had paid jobs, had revealed the falseness of this prejudice. Within the Communist Party she felt that the allocation of tasks within branches was deeply gendered. Moreover male party organisers failed to redress this situation by recommending women activists for party training.

Essentially, however, Smith was a loyal party member. From 1927–33 she made several trips to the Soviet Union, including attendance at the Sixth Comintern Congress in 1928 and the Fifth Congress of the Red International of Labour Unions in 1930. Three years later she was involved in a series of commissions organised for all communist parties on women's issues. As well as her fidelity to Soviet orthodoxy, Smith was known as an accomplished and passionate public speaker and fund raiser who was much in demand and able to take to the platform at a moment's notice. In 1930, during the preparations for the National Unemployed Workers'

Movement's (NUWM) third hunger march, Smith assisted Maud Brown with the organisation of NUWM women's sections in Lancashire and Yorkshire. These two female activists led the first women's contingent on the 1930 hunger march from Bradford to London. Initially Smith had hoped to create a politically motivated movement amongst unemployed female workers, but failed because of the NUWM's male-oriented agenda.

Her most significant campaign during the 'Third Period' was in the Lancashire cotton-weaving industry especially in Burnley. The industry had a tradition of employing married women, who were heavily unionised and had achieved close to parity with their male colleagues in terms of wages and conditions. Employers reacted to the international recession and the long-term decline in the Lancashire textile industry's position by seeking longer working hours and more looms per operative. Smith attempted to realise the 'Class against Class' perspective of the Textile Minority Movement. There should be separate revolutionary strike committees which could expose the collusion of union officials and employers. She insisted that the 'more looms' policy was especially directed against women workers, who would be replaced by men in a smaller workforce. Her involvement led to a three-month gaol sentence in Manchester's Strangeways prison in 1931. Her experiences in Burnley and her awareness of the party's limited resources led to scepticism about the grandiose vision of 'Class against Class'. She also became concerned about the inflexibility and impracticality of the party's official trade union policy. When the party's central committee debated the termination of the Minority Movement in early 1932 she argued against the ending of the organisation.

The demise of the Minority Movement and the Central Women's Department in 1933 meant the termination of Smith's principal arenas of party work, She developed a new party career as a journalist. She had already made contributions to the *Sunday Worker*, *Workers' Life* and the *Daily Worker*, and in 1934 she was appointed to the *Daily Worker* as a special correspondent. She was also involved in the revision of the paper's style that marked the transition from 'Class against Class' to 'Popular Front'. Her long hours were initially spent under the tutelage of Allen Hutt, the paper's chief sub-editor. Her own pieces were terse, rather pedestrian, backed by statistics and bore punchy headlines. Much of her reporting was on industrial issues. She lobbied for the unionisation of women workers and investigated the impact that the Bedaux system of 'payment by results' was having on engineering workers. Smith argued that the impact had been particularly severe for women workers in this male-dominated trade.

Her overall perspective was now far removed from that of 'Class against Class'. She had become an investigative journalist in the context of Popular Front politics. For two periods she served as editor of a women's page – 'Our Forum for Women' (July 1937 to April 1938) – and 'Rose Smith Calling' (February to April 1940). In the 1930s she played an active part in the campaign against fascism. In late 1938, after the withdrawal of the International Brigade from Spain, she reported for three months on behalf of Aid Spain, from the Republican side, for the *Daily Worker*. Her reports focused on the welfare of Spanish working-class women and children. Following the outbreak of war in September 1939 she shifted from a staunchly antifascist and prowar position to support for the new antiwar Communist Party line. Her possible ambivalence about this shift was suggested by the content of her women's column. Readers' support for the party line was limited to complaints of a specific character; there were no references to the war as 'unjust' or 'imperialistic'. During the time in which the *Daily Worker* was banned – January 1941 to August 1942 – she worked as a party propagandist. After the resumption of publication she worked as a reporter of home news until her retirement in 1955.

In the late 1950s Smith became somewhat disillusioned with the Communist Party's style of work and achievements. She readily in 1962 seized the opportunity to work in Beijing. From 1962–66 she worked as an English-language sub-editor in the Foreign Languages Press and from 1967–69 in the Domestic News for Overseas Service at the Xinhua News Agency. During the most tumultuous period of the Cultural Revolution she returned to Chesterfield. Most of her former British comrades ostracised her because she had challenged the British Communist Party's position on the Sino-Soviet rift. At the invitation of the Chinese

Government she resettled in Beijing on 21 July 1971 and worked in the International Department at Xinhua until she retired in the early 1980s. She met the Chinese Premier Chou En-lai three times; at one of those meetings he apologised publicly to her and other foreigners for the 'unfriendly behaviour' inflicted on them during the Cultural Revolution. When Sino-Soviet relations began to be normalised in the late 1970s, Smith assisted in the re-establishment of friendly relations between the Chinese and British Communist Parties, and between the *Morning Star* (successor to the *Daily Worker*) and the Xinhua News Agency. Smith died of pneumonia and heart failure on 23 July 1985. At her state funeral the Chinese leaders paid tribute to her as a working-class internationalist. Her ashes were buried in the Revolutionary Martyrs Cemetery in Beijing.

Writings: Smith wrote various pieces for an array of newspapers and periodicals, including her regular column in the *Daily Worker*, 'Rose Smith Calling' (February–April 1940), and 'A day in a chocolate factory', *Working Woman*, January 1928. Articles on the miners' strikes in Yorkshire and Nottinghamshire can be found in the *Daily Worker*, 19–21, 25–6, 29 January 1937, 4–5 February 1937, 2 March 1937.

Sources: (1) MSS: R. Smith, 'How I became a journalist', speech to postgraduates of the Institute of Journalism, Beijing, 28 October 1978; Interview with Rose Smith, 1978 (tape), Communist Party Records, Labour Party Annual Reports, National Museum of Labour History, Manchester; Smith Interview, Tape 6, D19C/1/17/1; 1903 Minute Book of Education Committee, Derbyshire Record Office; MRC, University of Warwick, MSS 292/112/2, Trades Union Congress, *Bedaux: The TUC Examines the Bedaux System of Payment by Results*, 1933. **(2) Newspapers and periodicals:** *Justice*, 17 March 1906, 18 August 1906; *Highway*, 2, 16, 1910; *Sunday Worker*, 20, 27 June 1926; Workers' *Weekly*, 1925–26; *Workers' Life*, 26 April 1929; *The Mansfield, Sutton and Kirkby Chronicle*, 19 April 1929; for Smith's fines and imprisonment see *Mansfield and North Notts. Advertiser*, 5 June 1926, 2 July 1926, *Oldham Evening Chronicle and Standard*, 23 December 1929, 18 January 1930, *Burnley News*, 14 October 1931, and *Daily Worker*, 2 March 1931; *Searchlight*, September 1932; E. Bidien, 'So much love for so many', *Beijing Review*, 12 August 1985; C. Esterson, 'Unforgettable Rose of Beijing', *Daily Worker*, 19 August 1985. **(3) Other:** A. R. Griffin, *The Miners of Nottinghamshire* (1962); J. Klugmann, *History of the Communist Party of Great Britain* (1969); N. Branson, *History of the Communist Party of Great Britain, 1927–1941* (1985); S. Bruley, *Leninism, Stalinism and the Women's Movement in Britain, 1920–1939* (New York, 1986); P. Graves, *Labour Women: women in British working-class politics* (Cambridge, 1994); G. Chan Man Fong, 'The times and life of Rose Smith in Britain and China, 1891–1985: an interplay between community, class and gender' (PhD thesis, Concordia University, Montreal, 1998); extracts of letters read by Fred Westacott at the farewell dinner to Rose Smith, Chesterfield, 4 March 1960; interview with Ida Hackett, Mansfield, 13 November 1993.

GISELA CHAN MAN FONG

STEPHENSON, Tom (1895–1962)
CUMBERLAND MINERS' LEADER

Tom Stephenson was born on 27 April 1895 at Moresby Parks, Moresby, Whitehaven, the second child of the seven born to Joseph Stephenson and his wife Lizzie Stephenson, née Gallantry. Joseph Stephenson was a coal miner at the local Walkmill Colliery, which was owned by the Moresby Coal Company, a major player in the Cumberland coal industry. Both parents were Liberals, although in later years Joseph became a committed supporter of the Labour

Party. Tom attended Moresby elementary school and left at the age of 14, following his father into employment at Walkmill. He showed an early concern with the welfare of his fellow workers and was eventually elected as pit delegate in 1922. He then became the Moresby representative on the District Executive of the Cumberland Miners' Association (CMA). Cumberland was one of the most isolated coalfields in the British Isles, but it had a significant socialist presence. According to Roy Gregory, before the First World War ILP speakers would stop at Workington and Whitehaven to address meetings when journeying between the party's bases in Lancashire and Clydeside [Gregory (1968) 88]. Stephenson devoured socialist texts and was drawn towards Independent Labour Party (ILP) activists in his local village.

As one of the smallest coalfields in the British Isles, the industry in Cumberland was particularly hard hit by depressions in the coal trade. Consequently union membership often fluctuated, making it difficult for union activists to hold the line in price-list negotiations. Stephenson quickly became an established figure, both for his union work and for his involvement in the community. The industrial relations culture at Walkmill was very consensual and Stephenson did not have to deal with many strikes. However this consensual system became subject to increasing pressure. Stephenson sharpened his negotiating skills and became adept at creating welfare initiatives for local miners. Tom Cape, a pioneer of the trade union movement in the district and from 1918 Labour MP for Workington, had also worked at Walkmill. He became a role model for Stephenson and others in terms of the ability of the miner to pursue a route of self-improvement that would also benefit the working class.

The Cumberland coalfield witnessed many fatalities because the majority of coal-extraction operations took place under the Irish Sea in difficult seams. A disaster at the Wellington Pit in 1910 led to the death of 136 miners, and in 1922 39 miners were killed at the Haig Colliery. Such tragedies increased the tension between coal owners and miners both locally and nationally. Stephenson played an active part during the 1921 lockout, emerging as one of the most militant activists in the CMA and gaining a reputation as a rousing platform orator. In 1923 there was a serious disturbance in Whitehaven when the owners tried to introduce new working practices at a number of pits. The miners came out on strike and the dispute lasted 15 weeks. The conflict intensified when miners and their wives attacked a colliery manager's home. This was followed by the looting of shops in Whitehaven, with clashes taking place between groups of miners and the police [*Whitehaven News*, 5 July 1923]. The disturbance deepened the suspicion between the miners and the coal owners, and for a time the negotiations between some companies and the CMA broke down. In 1923 the Cumberland Coal Conciliation Board disbanded as the miners were reluctant to take their claims to the organisation and the owners eventually relinquished their membership [*Colliery Guardian*, 8 January 1926].

During the coal crisis of 1925–26 Stephenson wrote a number of articles for the local press, calling for nationalisation as the only remedy for the problems of the industry. During the 1926 lockout the Cumberland miners were 'solid' and held out longer than those in some of the other smaller coalfields. By the middle of June the CMA's funds were almost exhausted. Single miners suffered most as they were not eligible to receive assistance from the local Board of Guardians. Stephenson was involved in a subsequent protest march of over 400 miners and their families from the miners' offices to the Whitehaven workhouse. As the distress became more acute the miners began to take a more robust approach towards those who were beginning to return to work, and Stephenson himself appeared before Whitehaven magistrates in August 1926 charged with intimidation. The trouble had started when the manager of Walkmill had tried to arrange a shift of coal cutting for safety purposes. Stephenson had organised the picket on the day in question and had prevented deputies from entering the colliery yard. He was found guilty and ordered to pay a fine of five pounds or face a prison sentence of one month's hard labour. The union probably paid the fine because Stephenson was not imprisoned [*Whitehaven News*, 19 August 1926]. In the same month, along with Lancashire, south Wales, Yorkshire and the Forest of Dean, Cumberland voted against the bishops' proposals for a settlement

The effects of the lockout burned into the collective memory and fuelled the campaign for public ownership. At subsequent miners' conferences Stephenson littered his speeches with images of intransigent owners, industrial strife, poverty and hunger. In the aftermath of the lockout Stephenson and other local miners' delegates had to work hard to hold on to members. Walkmill closed for two years and many miners became unemployed. Cumberland was not troubled by the breakaway organisations that had appeared in other coalfields, but the industry faced rapid decline, reaching catastrophic proportions by the 1930s. In 1935 all the collieries owned by the main company in Whitehaven were closed and did not reopen until 1937.

Stephenson continued his work for the miners locally while becoming more active in the ILP, serving as a Whitehaven town councillor from 1923 and as secretary of the Moresby branch of the party. During the term of the second Labour Government relations between the Labour Party and the ILP nationally became acrimonious and an increasing number of ILP members began to argue for disaffiliation from the larger organisation. Some argued for a split on the basis of the fundamental difference between the ILP's alleged revolutionary outlook and the Labour Party's gradualist approach. Prominent amongst the supporters of this position were members of the procommunist Revolutionary Policy Committee (RPC). Others were less sure about the prospects for the ILP outside the Labour Party but were prepared to split unless the larger party gave ILP MPs full freedom to engage in socialist criticism of the Labour Party leadership even when in government.

The question of continued affiliation to the Labour Party was put to the nine ILP divisional conferences in early 1932. The north-east, which included Cumberland was one of five divisions to vote for continued affiliation to the Labour Party, regardless of the situation in Parliament. However the north-east divisional representative on the National Administrative Council (NAC), Fred Tait, took the opposite position to the divisional majority and believed that the ILP should disaffiliate even if a satisfactory resolution could be found between Labour and the ILP in Parliament. Stephenson supported the intermediate position of affiliation on condition that an accommodation could be found for the ILP in Parliament. He was elected to replace Tait as divisional representative on the NAC, and was subsequently chosen as chairman of the North-East Divisional Council of the party. Presumably his more moderate position on interparty relations played a part in his election, but the 'moderate' tag that subsequent commentators have given to his position in this context is seriously misleading, even in light of the increasingly 'revolutionary' politics of the ILP in the 1930s. As an NAC member Stephenson did criticise aspects of the new, self-consciously revolutionary politics of the ILP. He was particularly unhappy with the emphasis the party placed on workers' councils, describing them as schemes that would sound 'quite unreal' to the working class. Instead, as one of a very small number of union activists on the NAC, he argued that the ILP should focus on the existing unions, whilst pointing out their failed policies [ILP NAC Minutes, 24–5 June 1933].

Despite his reservations Stephenson was one of the nine on the 13-strong NAC who voted in favour of the new policy [ILP NAC Minutes, 5–7 August 1933]. He was a loyal ILP member, was opposed to unity with the Communist Party and was never associated with the procommunist RPC. Nevertheless the tenor of his political outlook during this period was revealed by his regular support for RPC proposals on the NAC. As late as 1935, when the RPC was planning its defection from the ILP to the Communist Party, Stephenson was the only NAC member not openly associated with the RPC to support the latter's interpretation of the party's position on Soviet foreign policy [Interview with Jack Gaster; ILP NAC minutes, 19 April 1935].

Stephenson complemented his work for the miners and the ILP with involvement in local government. He was now chairman of the parish council and a member of the County Health and Public Assistance Committees. He remained on cordial terms with members of the Labour Party, especially those associated with the CMA, such as Tom Cape. The ILP initially planned to fight 50 seats in the 1935 general election but then went through a careful selection process, placing great emphasis on choosing prominent local figures as candidates for specific seats. Stephenson's profile made him an obvious choice and he was one of the 17 ILPers selected to stand. He was well known in the Workington constituency, but this was Tom Cape's seat and to avoid opposing his old friend and fellow miners' leader Stephenson instead contested the adjacent Whitehaven seat.

In order to neutralise the ILP challenge the Labour candidate, Frank Anderson, was careful to solicit as much support as possible from a range of figures in the MFGB. At a public meeting the General Secretary, Ebby Edwards, said that no matter who the Labour Party candidate was he would have the miners' support [*Whitehaven News*, 10 October 1935]. Much of Stephenson's thunder was stolen by Anderson, who attacked the means test and government policy on distressed areas, pointing out that 2500 miners had been thrown out of work in Whitehaven. Anderson also called for nationalisation of the coal industry. Stephenson, campaigning as a local figure, pointed to his successful fight for free school meals for needy children. He was successful in obtaining the backing of public figures such as the Reverend G. W. Parkinson, a Carlisle Unitarian minister.

The contest was a three-way fight between Stephenson, Anderson and William Nunn of the Conservative Party. In 1931 the Labour Party had only lost by 2031 votes, making the seat an important marginal. Stephenson's campaign began with an analysis of the Abyssinian war and he defined himself as the 'Socialist and No More War Candidate'. He sought to define the differences between the ILP and the Labour Party in their competing proposals for the achievement of socialism. Stephenson argued that that it was the capitalist system that was the cause of war, and economic crisis was driving capitalism towards fascism. This, he suggested, could be seen in Britain in the Sedition Act and the Unemployment Insurance Act, which had the potential to suppress the working class. His specific solutions did not differ much from Anderson's argument for nationalisation of the mines, a national wage agreement and opposition to rearmament. However as an ILP candidate he was able to make definite promises to abolish the means test and to raise unemployment benefit and old age pensions. The ILP ran an active campaign and the decision to fight Whitehaven was based on the local popularity of Stephenson. Nevertheless the campaign came to nothing and long before polling day it became clear that the party would perform poorly. The final meetings of the Labour and Conservative candidates were packed whilst those of the ILP were sparsely attended throughout.

Whitehaven, Cumberland, 1935: electorate 34 646, turnout 87.3 per cent

F. Anderson (Labour)	14 794 (48.9 per cent)
W. Nunn (Conservative)	14 442 (47.8 per cent)
T. Stephenson (ILP)	1 004 (3.3 per cent)
Majority	352 (1.1 per cent)

Stephenson tried to put a brave face on the result, congratulating Anderson and indicating that this 'was only the start of the fight as far as the ILP was concerned' [*Whitehaven News*, 21 November 1935]. However Walter Padley, a fellow trade union activist within the ILP who knew Stephenson well, commented that the result caused him to rethink his political perspective. According to Padley, although Stephenson remained committed to the ILP, the election had demonstrated to him the futility of remaining in isolation from the rest of the labour movement and the Labour Party in particular [Padley to Littlejohns, 7 November 1979; DLB Files]. The assessment by the Labour candidate was perhaps a more accurate indication of the ILP's position:

Actually the ILP challenge proved a fiasco. Mr Stephenson won his spurs as a speaker who can grip and hold a crowd, but he had no organisation behind him, and the man in the street could not detect anything more attractive in the ILP brand of socialism than that which he usually supported [*Whitehaven News*, 21 November 1935].

As a result of the ILP's challenge to the Labour Party in Whitehaven, local relations between the two organisations deteriorated. In 1936 a Labour candidate competed with Stephenson for a seat on the Ennerdale Rural District Council, but Stephenson won easily. Throughout the campaign he made good use of his local standing and attacked the Labour Party for its moderation:

> When I sing the red flag I mean every word of it. I have no desire to hide my socialist convictions, whether it be when dealing with the question of monarchy, religion or the Spanish situation. To see members of the Labour Party watering down their socialism for fear of losing votes makes me sick [*Whitehaven News*, 14 January 1937].

Further tensions arose when Stephenson organised a march of the unemployed to protest against the means test. The Cumberland miners were in a particularly difficult situation at that time as many of the Whitehaven pits had been closed due to the depression in the coal trade. A number of socialists worked together in the Cumberland Unity Committee, but the Cleator Moor Labour Party distanced itself from the campaign, citing Stephenson's challenge in the 1935 general election as the reason. Surprisingly it was left-wing members of the Labour Party who were most opposed to working with Stephenson and the ILP. The march was a success, but the ILP was being seriously undermined by the increasing ability of the Labour Party to secure votes from the ILP's core constituency. In 1936 the ILP contested two seats in the Whitehaven municipal elections, but was defeated in both.

Stephenson continued to campaign for local miners and was elected as a full-time official of the CMA in 1935, replacing J. R. Barker as financial secretary and later becoming general secretary upon the retirement of Tom Cape. As a result the family moved to the living quarters attached to the CMA headquarters in Workington. A year earlier, as a delegate to the MFGB annual conference, Stephenson had made his mark on the national stage. He had moved a resolution from Cumberland calling for one miners' union: 'We do this because of the fact, that in Cumberland we believe that the Miners' Federation as an instrument in the struggle of the workers against the capitalist class, is an inefficient machine at present' [MFGB Annual Conference Report (1936) 221]. In 1939 he was elected to the National Executive Committee (NEC) of the MFGB, where he found himself wedged between a left wing that was largely represented by the Communist Party and a right wing represented by established moderates from the Labour Party. During the Second World, Stephenson was perhaps the most outspoken member of the NEC. He attacked mining members of the Communist Party for opposing strikes after June 1941 and remained fully committed to the ILP's antiwar position, although he did not share the pacifism of some members of the ILP. The party's antiwar stance was not explicitly pacifist.

In MFGB gatherings Stephenson called for immediate nationalisation as the war effort was continuing to provide profits for private individuals involved in the coal industry. The CMA argued that miners were unlikely to put maximum effort into an industry in which they felt they had no stake. Stephenson accused the government of using fascist tactics in introducing compulsory arbitration and the Essential Work Order. He felt that the unions should maintain their independence irrespective of whether or not the Labour and Communist Parties supported government initiatives. In an article in the ILP's newspaper, the *New Leader*, he argued that:

> all those acts and orders weaken the power of the workers in their struggle to maintain or improve their wages and conditions. Not one of them has a similar effect upon the determination of the owning class to maintain their power and privileges. These changes have been pressed on the workers by their so-called leaders on the plea that they give the workers a share in the management. This is all ballyhoo ... The Labour leaders tell the rank and file that they must fight to prevent Hitler from suppressing the unions, but many see in the present class collaboration between the unions and the bosses and Government a structure being built-up which is similar to the German Labour front [*New Leader*, 22 September 1941].

During the war Stephenson spoke at many ILP meetings across the north-east, usually accompanied by Bob Edwards (later ILP chairman and from 1955 Labour MP for Bilston) and Tom Taylor (later Lord Taylor of Gryfe, the youngest of the ILP councillors in Glasgow). Jimmy Maxton, Fenner Brockway, John McGovern and Jennie Lee were close friends and visited the Stephenson household on many occasions. The party led a campaign against the Coalition Government, calling for a 'socialist Britain now'. The first conference was held in Gateshead, where Stephenson shared the platform with Will Ballantine, an ILP activist from the National Union of Railwaymen (NUR). Both attacked the Communist Party for blackening the name of the ILP by associating it with fifth columnists and Trotskyists. A resolution at the conference called for equality, social ownership, the liberation of Europe, help for Russia and the ending of the war by a peace offensive. Within the MFGB there was disquiet over miners' involvement in the campaign. Arthur Horner was critical of the initiative, feeling that it would threaten national unity at a time when it was important to unite the country against fascism.

From 1942 onwards, rank and file miners increasingly ignored their district officials and withdrew their labour in a number of damaging strikes. In June 1942, 5000 miners came out in Cumberland over pay levels, and there were strikes in south Wales, Kent and Yorkshire. Stephenson was scathing about the call by Will Lawther (the MFGB president) for workers and bosses to unite in this time of crisis, and told the readers of the *New Leader* that a more substantial rallying call would be 'not of bosses and workers unite – but of workers unite' [*New Leader*, 1 August 1942]. He was one of the few miners' leaders who openly supported the rank and file initiatives. He produced a pamphlet – with Hugh Brannan, a Scottish miner – entitled *The Miners' Case* (n.d. 1942?), in which he argued for significant wage rises and public ownership. Brannan went on to produce a newspaper, the *Militant Scottish Miner*, as a forum for the views of the rank and file throughout the coalfields. A number of ILP members contributed to the paper, but the Communist Party attacked it, most notably Abe Moffatt in Scotland, who claimed that the coal owners were funding it. Brannan stood against Moffatt for the presidency of the Scottish miners in 1944, gaining a respectable 10 640 votes to Moffat's 33 935. The first edition of the *Militant Scottish Miner*, published in February 1943, included an article by Stephenson on 'The Role of Trade Unionism Today'. Throughout the article he attacked labour leaders for slavishly following the dictates of both the Labour Party and the Communist Party:

> Far too many of our comrades in the Trade Unions and Political Parties think that Democracy means the uncritical advocacy of the official policy or party line ... Trade unions if they are to perform any useful function in the present conditions must refuse to be purely defensive within the capitalist economy. Their primary slogan must be the complete unconditional independence of the trade unions in relation to the capitalist state. They must not allow themselves to become part of the capitalist machine instead of a potential menace to it [*Militant Scottish Miner*, February 1943].

During the war a small group in the MFGB retained a militant stance on wages and hours. Stephenson and Brannan, along with Lance Rogers in south Wales, continued to attack the communist left within the union for distancing themselves from the rank and file. Stephenson took his campaign against repressive trade union legislation to the floor of the 1943 MFGB's annual conference. The Cumberland resolution, opposing the Essential Work Order, was rejected on the basis that it would be seen as a justification for unofficial stoppages [MFGB Annual Report (1943) 217–19].

In 1944 the MFGB held a series of conferences on restructuring the union. The eventual outcome was a compromise in which the districts of the MFGB would retain their autonomy in the new organisation, the National Union of Mineworkers (NUM). Stephenson was in favour of the federated model as otherwise the larger unions, such as Yorkshire and South Wales, might engulf the smaller districts such as Cumberland, north Wales and Kent. Nonetheless his notion of 'one big union' was conditioned by his desire to see a more militant organisation in the postwar period. At the 1944 MFGB conference he attacked a resolution that would require a two-thirds majority in a national ballot to sanction any national strike. Stephenson unsuccessfully moved an amendment calling for a simple majority to decide such matters: 'I know that it would be better if there were a big crowd one way and a small crowd the other way, but if democracy is to function, then I believe it should be the majority who should rule' [MFGB Annual Report (1944) 579–80].

In tandem with representing the Cumberland miners and fighting his corner on the MFGB executive, Stephenson continued his campaigning role in the ILP. However it was clear that he was increasingly aware of the futility of the party's position. In 1942 he retired as north-east representative on the party's NAC, citing increased union activity as the reason. He was replaced by T. Dan Smith. In the early years of the Second World War he addressed many meetings and produced reports on the mining industry for the party's publications. When supporting the ILP's John McNair in the by-election for Bristol Central in 1943 he claimed that 'socialism is our goal – not the Kingdom of Bevin!' [New Leader, 30 January 1943]. At the fiftieth conference of the ILP in the same year he moved a controversial motion from the Cumberland branch calling for armed support for the Soviet Union. The motion was defeated and Stephenson was criticised by the pacifist wing of the party. At the 1945 conference on the future course of the party, Stephenson was the most vociferous proponent of reaffiliation to the Labour Party. He argued that since the MFGB had reorganised itself into a national union and the labour movement in general was likely to make postwar advances, then the ILP had to reassess its position [New Leader, 7 April 1945]. The vote for reaffiliation was carried by 89 to 72, but the party's overtures for unity were blocked by the Labour NEC.

Within the NUM, Stephenson tried to convince Labour politicians of the need for a closed shop throughout the coal industry. He was acutely aware of the difficulty of ensuring that all miners were union members, and in a remark directed at Manny Shinwell (the Minister of Fuel Power) at an NUM conference in 1945, he stressed that 'it isn't always the men, it's the mother-in-law and everyone else you have to get past' [NUM Report of Special Conference, 10 October 1945, 491]. In 1946 Stephenson was returned unopposed for the Lowca Division of Cumberland, a council seat he had held for the ILP since the 1920s. He probably left the ILP later that year, either as an individual or more probably, as happened in many other places, as a result of his branch disbanding. Nevertheless he retained his belief in the ethos of the party and remained critical of the limitations of Labour gradualism. He refused to pay subs to the Labour Party, and his wife resorted to paying them on his behalf to the local branch.

With the coal industry coming into public ownership through the establishment of the National Coal Board (NCB) in 1947, Stephenson began to play a critical role in advancing the claims of the miners. He unfurled the NCB flag at his old pit, Walkmill, and warned the miners that 'the success or failure of nationalisation depends on your efforts' [Whitehaven News, 9 January 1947]. He soon had to deal with the first major disaster of the nationalisation period: the death of 104 miners in an explosion at the William Pit. He led the rescue teams and spent many hours above and below ground. He also oversaw the complex negotiations on mechanisation of the mines in Cumberland. Mechanisation was of particular concern to the Cumberland miners as power loading equipment was linked to a number of fatalities, including the death of 15 miners at the Harrington No. 10 pit in 1946.

Stephenson was the driving force behind the distribution of relief funds after the William Pit disaster and established a link with Czechoslovakian miners, who provided over £40 000 for the dependants of those killed. Stephenson visited that country on a number of occasions, often accompanied by Arthur Horner. In 1947 he toured the mining areas of the Ruhr with Ted Jones of north Wales. Stephenson and Jones, who were awarded the rank of colonel when visiting Germany so that they could stay at Dusseldorf's Park Hotel, went on to become the longest serving members of the NUM NEC. A year later Stephenson was a fraternal delegate to the Italian mineworkers' annual conference. On that occasion he met Pope Pius XII, which he found a truly humbling experience, although he retained his aversion to any form of religion.

While Stephenson welcomed the new spirit of consensus in the coal industry he felt that nationalisation had not gone far enough. In 1949 he supported calls from other coalfields for an inquiry into the running of the NCB and remained impatient with the pace of reform. In his view there was still a long way to go. 'What has happened is that we have taken over the coal mining industry, we have taken over the coal owners' organisation, and we have added to it certain individuals with regard to safety or in connection with welfare or medical services' [NUM Annual Report (1949) 357]. He continued to cut a rather awkward figure on the NEC, refusing to be constrained by the pragmatic outlook of both left and right within the union. At the 1953 NUM annual conference in Hastings he moved a resolution from Cumberland attacking the limitations of the conciliation scheme developed by the NCB and NUM. Stephenson opposed the rule that a decision made at a tribunal was final and binding. He felt that the union should have the option to consider the result and decide whether or not to accept it. The resolution was defeated, with Horner – speaking against the move – asserting that 'stability in the industry must be the immediate goal'. Stephenson also called for opposition to the Conservatives' plans to interfere in the industry now that they were back in office. In characteristic style he proclaimed that the miners would respond like Churchill: 'we will fight them on the beaches ... we will fight them in the coalfields, we will fight them wherever they are' [NUM Annual Report (1953) 398–9, 438–9]. Towards the end of his union career his criticisms of the nationalised industry were intensified by the growth of disputes in his own coalfield. He penned a number of letters to the press attacking NCB managers, claiming that their actions were undermining the initial ethos of public ownership.

Many of us took part in the ceremonies performed at each of the collieries in placing the National Coal Board flag at the pithead and we visualised much better labour relations than had existed in the past under private enterprise. Has this been borne out? In Cumberland it has not, largely due to the pits being run by men whose ideas of public ownership far from coincide with the minds of those who legislated for this change ... those in charge of the Board's side are completely out of touch with [the] feelings of those they employ. Something must be done, and must be done quickly, to alter this spirit if we are to avoid a major breakdown. ... We have no intention of allowing the Board to treat workmen as if they were sheep [*Whitehaven News*, 6 November 1958].

Stephenson retired as NUM area secretary in 1960 and was presented with a wallet containing £1000. He was replaced by Maurice Rowe. From one perspective Stephenson was among the last of the old guard of area leaders who, after initial reservations about the scope of nationalisation, had enjoyed some prominence in the consensual industrial relations culture, that emerged in the 1950s. This culture would be threatened in the late 1960s by internal factionalism in the union and the rapid rate of pit closures, which weakened the ability of some of the smaller coalfields to hold the balance of power on the NEC. However Stephenson was also a forerunner of a rather independent spirit in the national union that would emerge in the 1970s to challenge the previous orthodoxies of left and right. This was no doubt due to his history in the ILP and his aversion both to moderate Labour and to the Communist Party. On industrial matters he was further to the left than Communist NEC members such as Arthur Horner and Will Paynter. Yet he was also greatly admired by moderate area leaders such as Joe Gormley and Ted Jones. His activities on the NEC paint a more complex picture of the politics of the union than that which is dominant in the literature, and he does not fit the portrait of the militant miner presented by Arnot (1953), Allen (1981) and others.

Along with other NUM area leaders, Stephenson was not tempted by a more prominent career in the labour movement. Like Sam Watson of Durham and Ted Jones of north Wales, he preferred to stay close to his own people and was reluctant to leave the Cumberland coalfield. He was a friend of Fred Peart, who had won Workington for Labour in the 1945 general election – Stephenson had introduced Peart to local miners and was the driving force behind his subsequent success. He had no enemies in the NUM and he brightened many a tense conference with his sense of humour and turn of phrase. Politics might have been his life, but he was a committed family man and always found time to spend with his children. In quieter moments he enjoyed opera, the odd drink and devouring the books on socialism that he had acquired over the years. He was noted for his friendliness, kindness and wit. Like many others in the mining community he was keen on pigeons. He even appeared as himself in a film made by the NCB at the advent of nationalisation, *The Cumberland Story*, which contains scenes of Stephenson in negotiations with management and addressing the men from the pit bank.

Soon after his retirement Stephenson suffered a series of strokes that seriously weakened him. He died on 3 December 1962 at the age of 67. The funeral service, which was held at St Mary's Church, Westfield, Workington, was attended by mourners from the NUM and the ILP. He left £1706 9s. Three daughters and a son survived him – his wife, Sarah Stephenson, née Wilkinson, had died in 1960.

Writings: Tom Stephenson and Hugh Brannan, *The Miners' Case* (n.d. 1942?). Stephenson was also an infrequent writer of short articles, mostly for the *New Leader*.

Sources: (1) MSS: Cumberland NUM Records, NCB Area No. 10 Records, Whitehaven Record Office; Cumberland Coal Owners Papers, Carlisle Record Office; MFGB/NUM National Reports, NEC Minutes and National Conference Reports, CRO Hawarden, North Wales; Records of the Independent Labour Party, London School of Economics; Mining material and ILP material, NMLH, Manchester; DLB files University of York. **(2) Newspapers:** *New Leader*, 1932–46; *Colliery Guardian*, 1921–62; *Whitehaven Miners' Gazette*, 2 December 1922; *Whitehaven News*, 1921–62; *Cumberland Evening Star and Mail*, 13 December 1962; *Workington Star and Harrington Guardian*, 1926; *Militant Scottish Miner*, February 1943. **(3) Other:** R. Page Arnot, *The Miners' Years of Struggle: A History of the MFGB from 1910 onwards* (1953); Roy Gregory, *The Miners and British Politics 1906–1914* (Oxford, 1968); Vic Allen, *The Militancy of British Miners* (Shipley, 1981); Oliver Wood, *West Cumberland Coal 1600–1982/3* (Kendall, 1988); Gidon Cohen, 'The Independent Labour Party 1932–1939', unpublished DPhil thesis (University of York, 2000); personal information from the Stephenson family, Whitehaven, Cumberland. **(4) Obituaries:** *Whitehaven News*, 6 December 1962; *West Cumberland News*, 8 December 1962.

Keith Gildart
Gidon Cohen

See also: †Tom Cape; †Will Lawther; †Alexander Sloan.

TANNER, Frederick John Shirley (Jack) (1889–1965)
ENGINEERS' LEADER

Jack Tanner was born on 28 April 1889 in Whistable, Kent. He was the second of the three sons of John Silvanus Tanner and Regina Tanner, née de la Porte. John Tanner's occupation is listed on Jack Tanner's birth certificate as 'Of independent means'. Regina Tanner was the daughter of a musician. Tanner later described her as very beautiful, and his nickname – 'handsome Jack' – indicates that he had inherited her good looks. The family soon moved to London, where his father was sports organiser at Alexandra Palace. Tanner attended board schools in Hampstead and Camberwell, and at the age of 14 was apprenticed as a fitter and turner in a small engineering shop in Southwark.

As a young man Tanner took every chance to see the wider world. After finishing his apprenticeship he went to sea for two and a half years as a deckboy. According to an interview he gave in 1952, he had been a Conservative but his brother had converted him to socialism. The two went to antisocialist meetings to heckle the speakers, joined the Marxist Social Democratic Federation, and encountered a Hammersmith tailor who had known William Morris and taught the two boys about his particular brand of anarchism/communism.

Tanner joined the Amalgamated Society of Engineers (ASE) in 1912. Like his older engineering colleague, Tom Mann, Tanner was drawn to syndicalism. For most British trade union activists during the years of increasing militancy before 1914, interest in and support for syndicalism was pragmatic and not exclusive. Tanner served on the Industrial Syndicalist Education League's Executive, at one point becoming its chairman. During that time he also helped to establish the National Federation of Women Workers, showing early evidence of an abiding sympathy with feminism. He chaired the first International Syndicalist Congress, held in London on 27 September 1913, and during the congress met the prominent syndicalist engineer Alfred Rosmer. In 1913 Tanner walked from Ostend through France to Barcelona in the company of a young Scottish journalist. Upon his return to England he married a young woman from Hammersmith, Grace Elizabeth, and they set up home in a working-class neighbourhood near the river. In 1915 he returned to France for 18 months. He joined the Confédération Générale du Travail (CGT) and worked with Alfred Rosmer's syndicalist group within the CGT.

When Tanner returned to London in 1916 he was immediately caught up in the ferment of industrial unrest in engineering works in West London, and was soon holding leading positions in the shop stewards' movement. At the beginning of 1918, engineering militants in West London formed an unofficial organisation, with its own paper, the *West London Metal Workers' Record*, edited by Tanner. The latter was prosecuted in January 1918 because the *Record* was being published without a license. Nineteen toolmakers from Vandervells, a vehicle component works in Acton Vale, attended the trial and were subsequently sacked. After a mass meeting a deputation was sent to the Ministry of Labour to complain about the sackings but were told to go through official channels. They refused and threatened a general strike in west London. The ministry then saw to it that the men were reinstated. Buttressed by this success, the West London Engineering Workers' Committee was constituted more formally, with Tanner as its chairman. Its new organ, *Solidarity*, which was edited by Tanner, stated that the committee's aim was to organise engineering workers 'on a class basis, irrespective of craft, grade or sex, for the purpose of taking over control of industry' [Hinton (1969) 390–4]. Tanner continued to edit *Solidarity* until 1921. At that time he had the highest 'revolutionary' profile of all engineering militants in London.

In 1917 the various industrial centres where shop steward organisation had been formalised on an extra-union, 'revolutionary' basis came together to form a permanent national organisation, the Shop Stewards' and Workers' Committee Movement (SSWCM). The Bolshevik revolution in 1917 and the subsequent formation of the Third Communist International were viewed by militant shop stewards as heralds of wider radical changes. After the 'Hands Off Russia Conference', held in London on 18 January 1919, Tanner was appointed to the committee of 15 to oversee the agitation and ensure that the resolution threatening a general strike if Britain intervened was implemented. In January 1920 Tanner proposed to a national conference of the shop stewards' movement that delegates should be despatched to the second Comintern Congress. Those chosen – J. T. Murphy, Willie Gallacher, Dave Ramsay and Tanner – were duly sent to Moscow 'for extensive conversations with the Russians on the future trade union international and on the situation in Britain'. Tanner and Ramsay returned to Britain in September to report back to the National Administrative Council (NAC) of the SSWCM [Martin (1969) 18].

Tanner was impressed by the Moscow meetings and they confirmed his belief that the SSWCM should join a new revolutionary trade union international. It seemed entirely appropriate that Tanner was chosen to chair the founding conference of the British Communist Party (CPGB), which was held in Leeds on 29–30 January 1921. At that point Tanner was seen as a leading revolutionary shop steward and was therefore expected to follow other leading shop stewards, such as Harry Pollitt and Willie Gallacher, from the British Socialist Party into the CPGB. Indeed, after the successful conclusion of the Leeds conference Tanner joined the party as a founding member.

Activists felt an urgent need to regularise the relationship between the SSWCM and the new party. In February Tanner, J. R. Campbell, and J. T. Murphy represented the NAC in consultations with the newly elected leaders of the CPGB. A joint resolution was unanimously adopted:

> It is the business of the Communist Party to secure that all key positions [in the SSWCM] are held by Communists, and for all Communists working within the industrial movement to endeavour to secure the conversion of the rank and file to Communism and the complete subordination of the industrial movement to the Communist Party of Great Britain [Martin (1969) 18–19].

Although Tanner later denied that he had ever been a Communist Party member, he gave a different answer in 1936 to the Executive Council of the Amalgamated Engineering Union (AEU). He acknowledged that he had been a member of the CPGB for eight months, leaving in late 1921 or early 1922 [AEU Executive Minutes, 6 July 1936, 35–6]. Tanner's initial enthusiasm for the Communist Party but swift exit on friendly terms was not unique. For example Arthur Cook followed the same course at the same time in south Wales [Davies (1987) 54, 56]. Tanner and Cook were also leading participants in the National Minority Movement (NMM), which emerged in January 1924. Replacing the moribund SSWCM, the NMM represented a fresh bid by the Communist Party to transmit revolutionary consciousness to organised British workers. In engineering, activists organised to win elections in the AEU as the earlier reform movement had done in the ASE. The London district had been a stronghold of the amalgamation committee/reform movement, and the Metalworkers' Minority Movement (MMM) inherited its position of strength. Tanner served on the London District Committee of the AEU from 1921, and later became chairman of its organising subcommittee.

As a leading MMM member, Tanner was elected to serve as one of the two delegates from his division to the AEU National Committee (its policy making body) from 1923–30. Early successes for the Minority Movement were followed by the defeats of 1926. The trade union Right blamed the NMM for much of this disaster. The NMM's position was made more difficult by the Red International of Labour Unions (RILU) swing to the left in 1928. The response of most of the union activists in the NMM leadership was to moderate the impact of the RILU's strictures. In this connection Tanner worked closely with Harry Pollitt and others to muddy the ideological waters at the fifth annual conference of the NMM in August 1928. His rhetoric in a crucial motion on strike strategy apparently coincided with the RILU's requirements, but coded caveats were designed to enable activists to work unimpeded inside 'reformist' unions. Pressure followed from the RILU in Moscow. Pollitt and Tanner stood firm, arguing that 'it was necessary to recognise the need for a flexible policy of strike strategy without falling into the error of overlooking national circumstances and traditions' [Martin (1969) 110–13]. The intensifying pressure on the NMM from the RILU was reinforced by the CPGB leadership. In the spring of 1929 the NMM finally accepted the new line [Martin (1969) 189]. However a pamphlet written by Tanner in September 1929, *The Engineers' Struggle*, did not advocate revolutionary unions. Tanner returned to the old, still serviceable aim of amalgamation and an all-in industrial union for engineering and shipbuilding.

The MMM could not remain entirely immune from the increasing sectarianism and dogmatic rejection of trade unions, and even in London there were some setbacks. Tanner had been elected to the AEU's TUC delegation from 1926–8, but in 1929 he was beaten by J. D. Lawrence, one of the proposers of the emergency anti-MMM motion at the 1929 AEU National Committee. But in 1929, when Tanner stood as the MMM candidate in the presidential election, he received a substantial vote. He was the best known of the MMM cohort and the natural choice to be their standard bearer. Evidently the sectarian behaviour of a few Communists and other principled 'Class Against Class' followers had not seriously dented support for a loyalist, constitutional, militant position.

In 1930 Tanner scored a stunning victory against the incumbent, D. W. Hubbard, in the contest for the post of organising divisional delegate (ODD) for the division, which covered London north of the river, Middlesex, Hertfordshire and south-east Essex. On the first ballot Tanner won 732 votes compared with Hubbard's 784. The three other candidates won a total of 438 votes, necessitating a second ballot. Tanner won it comfortably by 1121 to Hubbard's 953 [*AEU Journal*, November 1930, January 1931]. In his election address he declared that he was a member of the Minority Movement 'because it stands for organising the workers around a militant policy based upon the Class Struggle'.

The step from union activist to full-time official was not so great in the AEU as in other unions. However during his first year a confrontation between leading MMM members and the AEU Executive put Tanner into an extremely awkward position, from which it appeared he could not extricate himself without choosing between his beliefs and his job. The problem was caused by the Engineering Employers' Federation (EEF) imposing swingeing cuts in piece rates and overtime rates in June 1931. Whilst the AEU Executive Council strongly resisted the EEF's demand for the cuts it declined to carry this resistance through to a national ballot for strike action. There was widespread anger over the EEF's high-handed unilateral action. As part of the campaign to stiffen the Executive's will to resist, leading MMM members issued a call to action in the *Daily Worker* on 20 June 1931. However they did so as 'a number of leading and influential engineering workers', and not in the MMM's name. The 'Call to All Engineers' appealed 'to all those Trade Union branches and District Committees which have already passed resolutions [against the EEF cuts] to at once convene conferences of all workers in their areas, in order to organise the resistance of the rank and file' [*Daily Worker*, 26 June 1931].

Predictably the AEU Executive Council reacted by expelling the six signatories of the *Daily Worker* letter, all of whom were lay officials and incidentally members of the CPGB. The seventh signatory, Jack Tanner, was merely suspended from his full-time post. The members of the Executive Council were evidently disposed to come to terms with Tanner, and he responded by meeting them immediately. Afterwards he accepted that he had been wrong to sign the letter, but did not repudiate its contents. He accepted that 'my signing was not in conformity with my position as an official of or member of the AEU' [*AEU Journal*, August 1931]. The Executive Council lifted his suspension forthwith and he resumed his ODD post.

In the 1931 election for the AEU presidency (the highest office in the union), which was held before the vicissitudes of his suspension as ODD, Tanner stood again as the MMM standard bearer. His election address was unaffected by the vagaries of 'Class Against Class', as dictated by the NMM. He polled well, receiving the second highest number of votes and forcing the incumbent, W. H. Hutchinson, into a second ballot. Tanner's support probably reflected activists' disillusionment with the Executive's acceptance of the EEF's cuts. In the second ballot Tanner won 13 161 votes against Hutchinson's 37 717 [*AEU Journal*, July 1931].

Tanner's monthly reports in the *AEU Journal* show that the pattern of union activity in his division was in no way disrupted by the 1931 events. The London district had adopted an active campaigning style through its organising subcommittee, utilising the energy and spare time of union activists. But these voluntary efforts became much more effective when augmented and indeed directed by a keen full-time officer. During 1931 Tanner gave ample evidence of his commitment to these important tasks by his meticulous attention to recruiting union members at the newly opened Ford and Briggs factories in Dagenham. He also took the lead in establishing an all-in union organising committee so that scarce resources could be pooled.

In September 1933, when Tanner defended his ODD post in an election, no left-wing candidate stood against him. He won handsomely in the first ballot, receiving 1459 votes to his opponents' combined vote of 449 [*AEU Journal*, October 1933]. After the retirement of Alonso Swales in May 1935, Tanner was elected executive councillor for Executive Division 7, centred on London but covering a geographically extensive area. The AEU was comparatively unusual in having a small full-time Executive. This seven-man Executive was chaired by the President, who was very much *primus inter pares*. Tanner served as executive councillor for four years. The minutes of Executive meetings do not show him to have been outstandingly active or energetic, and he apparently took care to fit in with the prevailing culture of strong collegiality. There were clear political differences and also conflicting views on the best strategy to adopt in relation to the EEF, but during this period councillors normally tried to minimise their effects and routinely strove to arrive at a genuine consensus. A tally of the votes taken at the Executive Council meetings shows that there was no permanent left-wing caucus, with the combination depending on the issue at hand. Tanner was the one who routinely proposed Communist-influenced political initiatives, for example on aid for the Spanish Republican government.

Jack Little retired from the union presidency in the summer of 1939, and in June Tanner won a decisive victory in the second ballot to succeed him. His position at the pinnacle of the AEU hierarchy provided substantial opportunities to effect internal change, and the coincidence of his accession with the beginning of the Second World War greatly increased his room for manoeuvre. He made serious attempts in three areas: developing the AEU as an industrial union; reinforcing the union's position in its relations with the EEF; and claiming its place as a central player in the wider trade union movement. He succeeded to varying degrees. That his record was ultimately disappointing can be partially accounted for by two significant external factors: the challenge presented by the Transport and General Workers' Union (TGWU) to the AEU's hegemony in engineering; and the alteration in the approach of the Communist network from the autumn of 1948, when the polarised international situation exerted a decisive influence on the union's affairs.

In addition Tanner's personal capacity as president was questionable. Yvonne Kapp, the CPGB member whom Tanner hired as the union's first research officer in May 1941, later recalled that he was intellectually lazy. She found him a weak negotiator who could only repeat himself under pressure. Jim Mortimer, who observed Tanner in meetings of the TUC General Council during 1946–7, was surprised how little Tanner participated in the proceedings. Nevertheless he filled the office with staff who could work round his deficiencies. Kapp took care to write speeches to his strength. Her memories were of 'a show off, a lovely presence, very engaging with a sense of humour'. He had a 'very strong, rather beautiful Cockney voice, a very pleasant baritone'. Even though he 'hadn't the words', when they were provided by her and from 1947 by her veteran successor George Aitken, Tanner delivered them stunningly [interview with Yvonne Kapp, 30 June 1996; interview with Jim Mortimer, 4 December 1996].

There was an additional personal factor that may well have restricted the amount of emotional energy and commitment that Tanner could bring to his job. The Tanner family suffered personal upheaval and tragedy in the war, and it is likely that the after effects continued to preoccupy Tanner. The family home since 1926 – in Skelwith Road, Hammersmith – was bombed in the Blitz and the Tanners moved to a semi-detached house in East Dulwich, conveniently near the AEU headquarters at 110 Peckham Road. This uprooting from what was probably a closely knit working-class neighbourhood would have been disorienting under any circumstances. Then in 1942 the Tanner's only child, a daughter, died from gastric jaundice. Tanner's relationship with his wife was close. Kapp remembered Grace Tanner as 'nice, modest', and unlike many officials Tanner took her to meetings away from London and spent time with her in the evenings – he was not in the habit of socialising 'with the lads'. At that time Grace Tanner always wore black, perhaps in deep mourning for her daughter.

Tanner's long experience in the union's myriad democratic institutions rendered him adept at handling the complex personal chemistry that prevailed in the numerous meetings over which he presided. Kapp's conclusions that nobody could have disliked him and that he was not an aggressive person are relevant here. Even at the height of the Cold War, Tanner was invariably affable and friendly towards communist delegates to the National Committee [interview with Edmund Frow, 5 June 1996; interview with Geoffrey Goodman, 12 September 1995]. He probably had more difficulty in the Executive Council. The councillors were seldom fractious and did not require strong order to be kept, but Tanner's lack of forcefulness and aggression made it difficult for him to provide a strong lead. Furthermore he took care not to challenge the councillors' belief in their own self-importance. During the period when the Communist Party opposed the war (October 1939 to June 1941), the Executive Council pursued leading Communist activists in the newly revitalised shop stewards' movement, and Tanner accomplished the difficult tactical manoeuvre of agreeing with the councillors while exculpating the party activists. He cobbled together a compromise that enabled both sides to save face and left him blameless of breaking faith with either [Fishman (1995) 260–5].

The most formidable obstacle to the AEU's aim of becoming the sole industrial union for engineering was the apparently inexorable expansion of the TGWU. Tanner continued Jack Little's strategy of allowing the TGWU no quarter on what both men regarded as the AEU's turf. At the outset of the war the TGWU had gained a major tactical advantage over the AEU: the latter's lay activists had consistently rejected a rule change that would allow the union to admit women as members, so AEU stewards had found themselves recruiting into the TGWU women arrivals in engineering factories. The rule change was eventually achieved by postal ballot in May 1942, organised quite irregularly outside the rulebook by the Executive Councillors, who had been frustrated by the 1940 Rules Revision Conference's refusal to admit women. According to Kapp, Tanner was the driving force behind the change. Tanner asked Kapp to look after the first women delegates to AEU National Committee in 1943, and to make sure they felt welcome – he was well aware that the women were likely to feel as though they were in highly hostile territory. Kapp organised a reception for the women, and showed tact and sensitivity for the male delegates' feelings by advising the women to refer to themselves as 'dilutees' rather than as trained engineers.

In the wider trade union world Tanner's ability to influence was limited by the fact that he did not become a member of the TUC General Council until 1943. His speeches to the AEU National Committee show that he knew full well that there was a real chance to reclaim the syndicalist side of the old shop stewards' movement and to develop it in a non-revolutionary atmosphere of mutuality. Nevertheless the AEU did not succeed in exploiting the opportunity presented by Joint Production Committees (JPCs). Nor did the Executive Council engage with the accumulating evidence that the workplace collective bargaining machinery developed during the First World War was inadequate to deal with the changed production relations that existed in the Second World War.

The AEU Executive Council's lack of interest in developing collective bargaining machinery that would incorporate a commitment to mutuality continued into the post-war period. Tanner's strong belief in the need for the rank and file to be positively involved in production questions and his vague, though passionate 'productionism' are not in doubt. John Boyd later recalled that Tanner's wartime nickname, 'Tanner the Planner', persisted into the post-war years [interview with John Boyd by John Givens]. However he was now a man of middle age whose character had mellowed, rather than sharpening or deepening. The force and energy he had clearly had in his twenties and thirties had dissipated, leaving only his good humour, engaging manner and desire to be liked. These qualities prevented him from pursuing what would have been a highly heterodox course of action inside the AEU.

After the Soviet Union's entry into the war, the CPGB subordinated all domestic considerations to the imperative of assisting the socialist motherland and the party leadership efficiently diluted the radical concerns of some of its engineering members – the vague productionist rhetoric that the party leaders dispensed was congenial to Tanner. The defeat of Germany freed the CPGB to concentrate on British politics. It began to develop its rhetorical productionism into a sharper strategy, focusing on the serious domestic political conflicts that a codification of mutuality would inevitably involve. However the increasingly polarised international situation rendered it impossible for the CPGB to continue this strategy. The leadership merely reverted to its economic perspective of the late 1930s; Tanner found an uneasy resting place with the right wing of the General Council and its embrace of productionism as part of the Marshall Plan's emphasis on productivity and efficiency.

However, Tanner's newfound anti-Communism did not vitiate his commitment to rank and file democracy. Nevertheless, there was literally nowhere else for Tanner to go once he had distanced himself from the political line of the CPGB and acquiesced in the logical necessity of severing his connections with the Communist network inside the AEU.

Tanner took this course reluctantly and evidently had little stomach for breaking with the men who had been his close, even intimate associates for 30 years. There are a number of factors to explain why he struck out on his own from 1947–48. It is likely that the shrewd tacticians in the right-wing trade union leadership made a concerted and conscious effort to win him over as the Cold War developed in 1946–47. As President of the AEU and a known productionist, Tanner was an obvious choice to serve on the many tripartite committees thrown up during the war and continued into the peace, and he was duly made a member of the Economic Planning Board, the Ministry of Labour Joint Consultative Committee and the National Production Advisory Council on Industry. The other factor that served to push him away from the CPGB was accumulating evidence of the USSR's determination to make Eastern Europe its political fiefdom. Nonetheless relations between Tanner and the Communist network in the union had not polarised sufficiently in the second half of 1947 for the party to put a candidate against him in the January 1948 election for president. He faced only six other candidates and won decisively in the first ballot, just as he had done in the 1942 and 1945 elections.

Tanner's publicly stated position was that the Communist coup in Czechoslovakia in the spring of 1948 had been the personal breaking point at which he had rejected the Soviet road to socialism and wholeheartedly embraced the Labour government's strategy. But though he had made a clear political break with the CPGB's policies and the communist network within the union, he did not embark upon an anticommunist crusade. Rather he maintained friendly personal relations with the Communists who worked at the AEU head office.

Tanner confined his political utterances to the minimum necessary to combat resolutions proposed by Communist and left-wing activists on the National Committee. He preferred to deal with the bread and butter issues of trade unionism. The members of the AEU Executive Council were united in their determination to pursue large wage increases for engineers in view of the increasingly high profits that many engineering firms were reaping from the post-war boom and subsequently from rearmament. The left-wing councillors argued for official national industrial action to back up their case; the rest did not dismiss strike action out of hand, but preferred to try for negotiated settlements first.

After the war the AEU's principal focus of national activity in relation to the EEF was the Confederation of Shipbuilding and Engineering Unions (Confed). The AEU had left the Confed in the interwar period, making national negotiations on engineering wages and conditions a protracted, circuitous procedure. Despite mixed results at the local level, at the national level the Confed was the main arena for conflict with the EEF. In the early post-war years positions were adopted by both sides in national negotiations that determined the shape of economic conflict in engineering for the next generation. Tanner contributed little to this development. Though he was nominally in charge of the AEU's Confed input as chairman of its engineering group, it was executive councilmen Joe Scott and Bob Openshaw who, according to John Boyd, ran the Confed [interview with John Boyd by John Givens].

Whilst serving on the TUC General Council, Tanner established regular social and institutional contact with high-profile members of the right-wing trade union establishment, notably Tom O' Brien, Florence Hancock and John Brown (Lincoln Evans' successor in the Iron and Steel Trades Confederation). They were charmed by his personality and must have been keen to use his talents in their anticommunist crusades. However he did not cleave to their side with enthusiasm. Such features of Tanner's persona were clear to the US labour attaché, Glenn R. Atkinson, in 1951. When the US ambassador invited the seven principal members of the TUC

General Council to dinner, Atkinson provided thumbnail sketches. His description of Tanner tallies with the recollections of Kapp: 'Personable and pleasant but not a heavy weight. He is lacking in breadth of view and in force of character. … Within the union there is a serious Communist problem which has shown improvement recently largely because of the effectiveness of other officers rather than Tanner' [NRA 469, Subject Files of Glenn Atkinson, 1950–2, Box 2 File in General Atkinson's Correspondence and Memos].

The logic of the Cold War meant that the communists in the AEU could not allow Tanner to carry on until his retirement without meting out some revenge for his turncoat behaviour. There was also enthusiasm amongst many party AEU activists for targeting Tanner, especially those too young to have had a personal association with him. In October 1950 Tanner provided the Communist network with an opportunity to act. His speech to the Acton branch included an unscripted remark about the claim for a £1 a week pay rise that had just been referred by the Confed Executive to the National Arbitration Tribunal. He observed that engineers could not expect to obtain the full amount, and would probably receive four or five shillings. This view was fully in accord with the TUC General Council's current position, which was that wage inflation was a danger both to the economy and to the survival of the Labour Government, with its very small majority. But the Trades Union Congress of September 1950 had narrowly rejected cooperating with the Labour government in a 'wage freeze' (including the AEU delegation). The Communist network in the AEU hounded Tanner and the Union's branches and district committees, all the time calling for his resignation. His speech, they said, amounted to a repudiation of the union's negotiating position on the wage claim. In the normal course of events an ill-judged remark made at a branch meeting would have been ignored, but in the Cold War milieu Tanner's remark proved a valuable hostage to fortune.

The party vendetta did not have a lasting impact on the union, but it did influence the 1951 election for union president, the last that Tanner would fight before retirement. Claude Berridge stood against him and forced him into an embarrassing second ballot. The Communist network used the Acton incident to good effect. There were ten candidates, and in the first ballot in March 1951 Berridge won the second highest number of votes: 15 349 to Tanner's 31 778. In the second ballot, held in June, Berridge won an impressive 37 158 to Tanner's 44 384. For Tanner the experience was discomforting and probably deeply wounding. It is likely that he served his last two years without engaging much in the union's internal business. John Boyd remembered him as driving 'a Rover fast', and as 'worn down by cares of office at the end' [interview with John Boyd by John Givens]. He had bought a smallholding with a large acreage five miles from Heathfield in Sussex, where he grew Christmas trees.

Tanner's last term of office culminated in his election as President of the 1954 Trades Union Congress. By union rule he retired as AEU president on his sixty-fifth birthday at the end of April 1954. Consequently from May to September 1954 he presided over the TUC without having any formal connection with the AEU, except as a retired member. In June 1954 he was awarded the CBE. Since 1945 TUC presidents had customarily been bestowed with a suitable honour, but interestingly Tanner was not awarded the knighthood that Citrine, Tewson, Lawther and other doughty anticommunists received and that some might have expected to be Tanner's entitlement. His failure sufficiently to repent his past probably tipped the balance. In his presidential address to the TUC in September 1954 he spoke in a productionist vein, but was clear that 'higher productivity like full employment is a means to an end. … The end that trade unions have in sight in concerning themselves about increased industrial efficiency is all the time the material well-being of their members' [TUC Report (1954) 78].

Tanner's survey of the international situation was upbeat and Anglo-centric. 'To my mind there is already in existence a third world force and our organised Movement is a part of it. The British Commonwealth of Nations is a bloc of countries which we do not take sufficiently into consideration' [ibid., 80]. His one explicit reference to Communism was anti, but neither shrill nor dogmatic. The peroration was an unapologetic invocation of his radical past, but with the qualification of mature hindsight:

> this, in effect, is my swan song. I may have sounded some discords; some notes may have been out of harmony with the more popular tunes played on more brassy instruments. Yet I believe what I have said. Like all of you I suppose in joining this great Movement I held some idealistic views, and also accepted some ill-digested theories. But I have never wavered in my conviction that through our Movement's activities things would be made better than well for the working people of this land. ... I have learned by experience, and at the end of a long and hard road I know that the coining of slogans and the adoption of resolutions can only be the beginning of any new stage of progress [ibid., 83].

The delegate who seconded the vote of thanks reinforced the image Tanner had presented of himself: 'At one time he was known as the stormy petrel of the Trade Union Movement; but Jack Tanner today ... has developed into one of the Trade Union Movement's great statesmen' [ibid., 84].

It is hardly surprising that there was an abiding and genuine affection for Tanner. Despite his faded performance in the quotidian business of union officialdom, his public persona remained engaging. He still radiated good humour, and his oratorical powers were undiminished. After his retirement he served as a member of the Eastern Region Railways Board and also continued his membership of the board of the National Fuel Efficiency Services Limited, a company formed on the initiative of the Ministry of Fuel and Power at the end of 1953. His duties would not have been onerous, and the remuneration they provided must have been welcome.

At the beginning of 1956 the right-wing group of trade unionists who had been beavering away in their anticommunist crusade decided it was time to launch a fresh initiative. The result was the foundation of the Industrial Research and Information Services (IRIS), the formal genealogy of which originated in earlier anticommunist crusades. In 1952 many of them, including right-wing union officials, came together to form Common Cause. Cecil Hallett's arrival at Peckham Road as assistant general secretary and his close ties with Common Cause produced a strong synergy. The AEU right-wing group evidently decided to move outside the union to conduct complementary activities in which they need not be inhibited by the rules of the union and could therefore wage a more vigorous and effective propaganda campaign. The memorandum and articles of association for IRIS list three directors, all of AEU provenance: Jack Tanner, Charles Sonnex and William McLaine. Sonnex's occupation was listed as an industrial consultant for the BBC, and McLaine was AEU assistant general secretary in the social insurance department from 1938–48.

According to Les Ambrose, Tanner was a mere figurehead and it was John Boyd who was the creative force behind IRIS [interview with Les Ambrose]. Presumably Hallett provided the initial contacts with the murky world of Common Cause and anticommunism, whilst Boyd contributed his time, energy and creative flair. Boyd and Openshaw apparently found Tanner to be a willing participant in IRIS. He had evidently been profoundly affected by the events of 1956 and the shock had been sufficient to produce an irrevocable emotional distance between himself and his past. Tanner performed a crucial function as the IRIS front man for the right-wing group in the AEU. It certainly enabled right-wing Labour MPs, committed anticommunist newspapers, notably the *Daily Telegraph*, and probably also the US labour attaché to make a serious bid to destabilise the British trade union movement.

Tanner was IRIS's most prominent trade union supporter, this exposure meant a hardening in the AEU's leftwing's attitude towards him. Nevertheless his articles and statements in IRIS newsletters are striking for their lack of witch-hunting rhetoric. For him the answer still lay in revitalising the rank and file. He wanted to develop democratic impulses on the shop floor and revitalise the trade union movement from below. The problem was that the Communists were the only ones who were active at the grass roots level, so he wrote to encourage young Labour shop stewards and branch officials to emulate the Communists in their dedication to union work.

From the early 1960s Tanner ceased to figure prominently in IRIS productions. As the ballot-rigging scandal unfolded in the Electrical Trades Union (ETU), Les Cannon and his Catholic associates provided a genuine anticommunist/anticorruption crusade that included elements of a detective drama. The right-wing group in the AEU became more coherent and less in need of a venerable icon. The election of Bill Carron as AEU President, in succession to Bob Openshaw, also meant that the right wing could feel more secure.

Jack Tanner died on 3 March 1965 at Roundels Nursing Home near Heathfield. He was survived by his wife. Bill Carron wrote a glowing obituary in the *AEU Journal* that conjured up a vision of Tanner as an early rebel succeeded in maturity by a trade union elder statesmen. Tanner left an estate valued at £7667.

Writings: 'The Engineer's Struggle', National Minority Movement, September 1929; 'Shop Stewards Victory', *Solidarity*, 4: 7 (July 1920), 1.

Sources: (1) **MSS:** Jack Tanner Papers, Nuffield College, Oxford; TUC biography, TUC Library Collection, London Metropolitan University; General Atkinson's correspondence and memos, NRA 469, Washington D.C. (2) **Interviews:** Yvonne Kapp, 30 June 1996; Edmund Frow, 5 June 1996; Geoffrey Goodman, 12 September 1995; Les Ambrose, 5 June 1992; Jim Mortimer, 4 December 1996; interview with John Boyd by John Givens, notes in author's possession. (3) **Other:** *AEU Journal*, July 1931, August 1931, October 1933, May 1951, August 1951; TUC Congress Report (1954), James Hinton, 'Rank and File Militancy in the British Engineering Industry, 1914–1918', unpublished PhD (University of London, 1969); Martin Roderick, *Communism and the British Trade Unions 1924–1933* (Oxford, 1969); Paul Davies, *A. J. Cook* (Manchester, 1987); Nina Fishman, *The British Communist Party and the Trade Unions, 1933–45* (Aldershot, 1995). (4) **Obituaries:** *The Times*, 4 March 1965; *Daily Express*, 4 March 1965; *AEU Journal*, April 1965.

NINA FISHMAN

WADE, Arthur Savage (1787–1845)
TRADE UNIONIST AND CHARTIST

Arthur Savage Wade, radical clergyman, was born in September 1787, the second son of Susanna and Charles Gregory Wade, a leading Warwick Tory. Having completed his education at the town's grammar school, Wade served briefly as a naval midshipman before entering St John's College, Cambridge, in 1806 (his father's brother William had been a Fellow there from 1777–98). He graduated in 1810. In 1811 he was presented by the Corporation of Warwick to the living of St Nicholas in the town. This he held until his death. As a young man Wade was influenced by the so-called 'Whig Dr Johnson', Samuel Parr, minister of the nearby village of Hatton. Latitudinarian in his views, Wade told Warwick's Unitarian minister, 'I wish my pulpit to be a place for delivering exhortations, relative to the great principles of our common Christianity, and not for uttering harsh or angry animadversions on the tenets of those who may conscientiously dissent' [Field (1828) 143].

In politics Wade rejected his father's Toryism and supported the Independents, a radical-Whig commercial and industrial faction that campaigned in both the Warwick borough and county constituencies in the early nineteenth century. In December 1816 he made his entry into active politics in a speech to a borough meeting called to consider poor relief; he also defended the introduction of calls for parliamentary reform into the same debate. In 1821 he was one of a deputation from the borough who presented a loyal address to Queen Caroline (whose chaplains were headed by Parr). Wade, however, was far from embracing popular radicalism at this point in his career. In 1819 he warned: 'we have to guard against numerous and formidable evils from that restless spirit of enquiry, which has risen among the middle and lower classes of society'. Wade opined, however, that 'the auspicious influence of our national institutions, ecclesiastical and civil' would prevail [*Sermon*, 30, 22].

During the 1820s Wade and his circle met informally in a Civil and Religious Liberty Club. John Tomes, a banker and member of the club, stood at a parliamentary by-election in February 1826, with Wade as his nominee. Tomes' support for Catholic emancipation was exploited mercilessly by the Tories, but he carried the seat at both hustings and poll. Wade again nominated Tomes (with a speech pledging to support 'peace, economy and reform') at the general election the following June. This time the election was uncontested. At Westminster, Tomes supported the emancipation of dissenters and Roman Catholics, as well as parliamentary reform. Wade did the same in Warwickshire, in 1827 publishing his *Letter to the Right Hon. G. Canning*. This was developed from a speech he had made at the annual dinner of Stratford's Shakespeare Club a few months before: the Test and Corporation Acts should be repealed because they 'scandalously prostituted to the basest selfish and party purposes ... the Lord's Supper, the most holy institution of the Gospel' [ibid., 19]. Wade also held that Roman Catholics should be judged on their present rather than their past conduct. Emancipation would strengthen, not weaken, the established Church because it would remove a focus of organised grievance and improve social harmony. This argument he developed further in a pamphlet vindicating the Act of Emancipation passed by Wellington's administration in 1829.

In the general election of 1830 Tomes was returned unopposed, again on Wade's nomination. Both men were unequivocally committed to parliamentary reform, and to press the cause Wade convened a public meeting of the inhabitants of Warwick in January 1831. In April he convened a meeting of the county that marked an important stage in the evolution of the Birmingham Political Union (BPU). Wade seconded Thomas Attwood's resolution of censure on the House of Commons for its neglect and lack of sympathy towards the people. He was once again to the fore in Tomes' cause during a bad-tempered and occasionally riotous contested election in the spring of 1831. Tomes' re-election consolidated Wade's reputation as a political speaker and manager: shortly afterwards he was elected to the BPU Council.

Wade's initial view of parliamentary reform seems to have been that it should be limited to extending the enfranchisement of the propertied. When and exactly how he was converted to universal suffrage is hard to determine, but the reform crisis certainly impelled him towards a more extreme political position. His attacks on the House of Lords for its rejection of the Reform Bill in October 1831 were outspoken and, significantly, he widened his target to embrace tithe and episcopal incomes. By the end of 1831 he was articulating a classic view of old corruption:

> The industrious classes are not hostile to the higher classes; but, properly so, to the close system of sin, of sinecurists, pensioners, placemen, noble and ignoble paupers, those locusts that devour the fruit of industry, the system of the tyrants of the oligarchical faction, that lay burdens upon them too heavy to be bourne, and who will not move a finger to assist them. While the productive classes respect the person and property of every man, they abominate the system of the corruptionists [*Warwick and Warwickshire Advertiser*, 12 November 1831].

Such sentiments quickly won Wade the reputation of being the most extreme member of the BPU Council. Shortly after this speech he moved to London, a departure not exactly deplored by fellow Council members. In a letter to the prominent London radical George Grote, the Birmingham solicitor Joseph Parkes described Wade as 'a living Huntite' and 'a man of no private character'. He added a message for the capital's leading moderate reformer: 'Tell [Francis] Place God writes a legible hand writing on every man's face, and to look at Dr Wade's' [Parkes to Grote, 4 December 1831, Add Mss 35,149, f. 130]. This was one of many occasions on which Wade's appearance (his weight allegedly peaked at around twenty stones) was the subject of comment by political opponents.

Wade remained a member of the BPU and at Attwood's urging became a significant link between it and London radicalism. On his arrival in the capital Wade briefly flirted with the National Political Union, but it was to be the co-operative movement and Owenism that absorbed his initial energies. Within a fortnight Wade chaired the meeting that established, at the Royal Bazaar in Grays Inn Road, Robert Owen's Association for Removing the Causes of Ignorance and Poverty, otherwise known as the Institution of the Industrious Classes. He was frequently called upon to chair meetings there and was thus involved in the formative stage of a number of key metropolitan initiatives. These included campaigns to support both the Derby spinners' strike in 1833–34 and, the following spring, the Tolpuddle martyrs. Wade also chaired the launch of the first London labour exchange (he was a member of the committee that established this organisation). In his own words he 'was a radical reformer' and viewed Owenism as practical Christianity [*Crisis*, 29 September 1832]. From the chair of the Third Co-operative Congress he declared: 'partial remedies for the evils now desolating the industrious classes have been tried, and issued in failure; and it is evident, that nothing but united effort or co-operation, will succeed' [*Proceedings of the Third Co-operative Congress* (1832) 64].

It was through the cooperative movement that Wade met the young William Lovett, who introduced him to the National Union of the Working Classes (NUWC). Not that Wade needed an introduction: at the first meeting he attended, 'when it became known he was present the whole meeting rose, and with acclamations testified their high respect for that gentleman and the Birmingham Union, of whose Council he is a member' [*Poor Man's Guardian*, 26 May 1832]. In the NUWC Wade spoke on a variety of radical causes, including the abolition of military flogging, the New Poor Law, anti-emigration and Irish home rule. He publicly criticised the prohibition of Sunday performances of sacred music and, daringly for a clergyman, licensing restrictions on the London theatre. He was also a leading supporter of the *True Sun*, the spirited but financially volatile radical daily newspaper. In the spring of 1834 Wade headed a committee, with Henry Hunt to secure its fortunes, emphasising the need for a paper 'identified with the best interests of the Working Classes'. The strategic importance of the paper is evident in the almost unique coalition of radical leaders who supported Hunt and Wade: Bronterre O'Brien, Feargus O'Connor, Henry Hetherington, John Cleave, Daniel O'Connell, Lovett and Owen. Wade's rationale for a radical press was simple: '[f]rom the conduct pursued by those in power it would appear that they would rather that the people were kept in ignorance ... for by keeping them in ignorance they hope a little longer to domineer over them' [*Workingman's Friend*, 26 January 1833]. Wade took a close interest in the unstamped press and the fortunes of its two most pioneering proponents: Hetherington and Cleave. He visited both in prison, chaired meetings in their support and headed a deputation to the home secretary to protest against the cholera-ridden conditions in Cold Bath Fields Prison, where many unstamped vendors were being held. The profits from the sale of Wade's *A Voice from the Church* (1832) (originally a sermon preached during a rare appearance at his church in Warwick) – in which he welcomed the Reform Act but called for further measures of parliamentary reform – went to the Victims' Fund. Robert Dale Owen in the *Crisis* and O'Brien in the *Poor Man's Guardian* eulogised the preacher:

How different a man is Dr Wade from the generality of his brethren! In his sermon there is no studied vagueness through fear of offending – no servile deference to rank, with a view to promotion – and no inculcation of slavery, under the name of 'humility', to reconcile the oppressed to the oppressor ... While other parsons *prudently* overlook the authors of guilt, and direct their spiritual fulminations only at its victims, the writer of this noble sermon grapples at once with the lordly oppressor, and makes him feel that he is answerable, before God and Man, for the poor man's crimes as well as his own, so long as he *knowingly* keeps him in ignorance and *poverty* [*Poor Man's Guardian*, 29 Sep 1832].

Having moved to London, Wade never returned to Warwick, save for the most temporary of visits. 'Dr Wade might be more laudably occupied in the performance of *clerical* duties, for which he is paid, *in Warwick*, while he is busy devoting his time among the most violent political madmen of the metropolis', one local paper commented. It added, 'Dr Wade courts the censure of the Christian world' [*Warwick and Warwickshire Advertiser*, 8 December 1832]. Though Wade had been given permission by the Bishop of Worcester to reside in London on the ground of ill-health, he contemplated a return to Warwick but was blocked. Wade opposed the tithe and had never exempted the Anglican Church from his criticisms of state corruption; indeed he felt that it would be purer if disestablished. At one point he even spoke of joining an association 'for the extinction of Ecclesiastical abuses' [*Poor Man's Guardian*, 6 October 1832] and it is difficult to see how he could have settled back into a conventional clerical life. 'I felt it my duty to tell Dr Wade very decidedly', his curate wrote to his bishop, 'that it was the full determination of his parishioners to prevent his return by every means in their power' [quoted in Lloyd (1973) 70]. A further 'strong remonstrance ... to the Bishop of Lichfield and Coventry for suffering Dr. Wade to be a non-resident' was submitted by St Nicholas parishoners at the end of the following year [*Gauntlet*, 15 December 1833].

Meanwhile Wade's personal popularity among London radicals made him a natural figure to initiate links between London and the provinces. That the NUWC should send missionaries to the major provincial centres was a suggestion he made from the chair of its quarterly meeting on 1 October 1832. On 29 October Wade returned to the midlands to preside at the meeting at which an NUWC delegation initiated the Midland Union of the Working Classes. Although this lasted only four months, it was pivotal in moving local working-class radicalism out of the orbit of the BPU and thus laying much of the basis for the later Chartist movement in Birmingham. Its launch also caused something of a furore in radical circles nationally. Hetherington, Wade and Hunt were the main speakers. Their impact was such that the *Poor Man's Guardian* dubbed Hunt and Wade the 'Castor and Pollux of Radicalism'. The BPU responded with a committee of enquiry into Wade's conduct, which according to Attwood suggested, if not 'any criminal motive', that he was a tool '*of spies and bad men*' [*Poor Man's Guardian*, 10 November 1832].

In his speech at Birmingham Wade had dismissed the Reform Act as a sham and made a barely veiled criticism of the BPU as being opposed to real reform:

> As a clergyman, he should feel ashamed if he did not do his utmost to protect persons and property; and these, and particularly the latter, certainly could not be safe, so long as the working classes remained in their present wretched condition. The rich, as a class, whether Whig or Tory, seemed to be against the interests of the working classes. The Tories hated and despised them, the Whigs had deceived and abandoned. ... [T]he working classes were now uniting as one man to claim equal laws and rights for the poor as for the rich [*Poor Man's Guardian*, 3 November 1832].

Wade now replied to the BPU's committee of enquiry that he 'would feel proud to be ostracised'. He entered into a close account of how, during the political crisis of 1831–32, Attwood had not only calculatedly sought to increase pressure on the government by recruiting mass working-class support for reform, but had commissioned Wade himself 'to join the metropolitan Unions of the Working Classes' to help achieve this. Wade also argued the case for establishing a separate workers' parliamentary reform organisation. This centred on what he had come to see as irreconcilable differences of interest between property and labour: 'he who lives on the profits of trade has an interest in obtaining labour as cheap as possible, and selling it at the dearest rate'. Labouring men should not be represented in parliament by 'men of property' who, moreover, 'move in a sphere above the working classes' and 'identified with aristocracy' [*Poor Man's Guardian*, 17 November 1832).

Wade had moved beyond the familiar radical critique of establishment corruption to an analysis of society that very much reflected the position of the NUWC and, more specifically, the influence of Thomas Hodgskin's recent *Natural and Artificial Rights of Property Contrasted*. Wade's subsequent involvement in the Grand National Consolidated Trades' Union (GNCTU) was thus a natural development not only from his support for Owen's initiatives at that time, but also of his broader political convictions. The GNCTU, he wrote, was 'a righteous union; its object is to enable the working classes to legally protect and establish the rights of industry and humanity' [*The Times*, 26 April 1834]. He held the title of chaplain to the Council of the Union and in this capacity walked alongside Owen in the procession to and from the great demonstration at Copenhagen Fields on 21 April 1834 in support of the Tolpuddle labourers:

> Our good chaplain passed us by in the procession, following the car; and truly it appeared to augur good, and gave a purer spirit to our Union, to see a minister of peace lead on the friendly host. ... The worthy doctor looked extremely well, however, for he was dressed in full canonicals, and wore the red badge of a Doctor of Divinity, which corresponded with the Union badge, and gave a grace and comeliness to him and moral dignity to the procession [*Pioneer*, 26 April 1834].

This episode earned Wade the greatest disapprobation of any in his present and future career. *The Times* [24 April 1834] pronounced him 'half-witted'; in Warwickshire it caused a minor sensation and the following month Wade was formally forbidden by his bishop to preach. As should now be clear, his participation was no isolated idiosyncracy: earlier he had chaired the two earliest metropolitan public meetings in support of the Tolpuddle labourers (the first of these drew up the petition for the pardon that formed the central element of the Tolpuddle campaign). Wade subsequently headed the delegation that presented a memorial to the crown calling for clemency. Ironically Copenhagen Fields appears to have been the only occasion on which Wade wore ecclesiastical vestments when attending a radical gathering, although he had presided over Tolpuddle protest meetings at Owen's Charlotte Street Institution, which had had a marked religious character: speeches and resolutions alternated with instrumental and vocal music, the institution's choir and organ leading in the singing of 'an ode to liberty and a Union hymn ... the whole assembly joined in the chorus, each individual taking off his hat, and those who were seated standing up in the most reverential manner. The effect was most electrifying' [*Pioneer*, 12 April 1834]. In 1838 Wade said grace at the triumphant public dinner organised by the London Dorchester Committee at White Conduit House to welcome home the Dorset labourers from Van Dieman's Land.

Radicals responded to the attacks on Wade with concerted support for 'the only one of the beneficed servants of the Most High who has consistency and virtue sufficient to enlist himself in the cause of poverty and oppression'. Owen's weekly, the *Crisis*, pronounced that 'Dr Wade's is the true Christianity' [*Crisis*, 3 May 1834]. John Cleave issued a threepenny portrait – 'a good likeness we say, though not sufficiently expressive of his extreme good nature', wrote the radical weekly *Pioneer* [3 May 1834].

As the NUWC, like the GNCTU before it, declined, Wade directed his energy into the new radical associations that emerged in the mid 1830s. He was a founder member of the Great Marylebone Radical Association in September 1835, through which Feargus O'Connor launched his career in English politics. As O'Connor shortly afterwards commenced his tours of the northern manufacturing districts it was left to others, Wade being prominent among them, to initiate similar associations elsewhere in the capital. Wade took a particular interest in the Southwark Radical Association. This was formed in 1836, the same year in which he supported O'Connor's unsuccessful Universal Suffrage Club, which was imitative of the cultural politics of the London Working Men's Association (LWMA) but intended to be less exclusive.

From its inception that summer Wade was an honorary member of the LWMA (those who were not waged workers could only be admitted on this basis). Mindful perhaps of the failure of the Universal Suffrage Club, the following year Wade also supported the Central National Association, another attempt to unite London radicalism that foundered partly because of the hostility of the LWMA and partly because of suspicions of its driving force, the Tory-radical economist James Bernard. Before its demise it briefly brought together a broad spectrum of metropolitan radicals, including O'Brien, Hetherington, O'Connor, John Bell (editor of the *True Sun*), Henry Vincent, G. J. Harney, most of the surviving Spenceans and a neglected figure in London radicalism, Thomas Murphy. The last was a Roman Catholic coal merchant and a leading member of the St Pancras vestry, a radical body that worked closely with neighbouring Marylebone radicals, among whom Wade (though never a vestryman) was prominent. When in May 1838 the LWMA sent a delegation to a mass gathering on Glasgow Green 'to present to that meeting our pamphlet entitled the "People's Charter" ', it comprised Murphy and Wade [Add MSS 37,773, f. 107]. This event launched the Chartist National Petition in Scotland. Wade caught the mood of the moment with a declaration of what the movement's tactics should be: 'We have sufficient physical power, but that is not necessary, for we have sufficient moral power to gain all we ask' [Gammage (1894) 21].

Wade played a principal part at two other mass meetings in 1838. He was the natural choice to represent the LWMA at the Birmingham demonstration on 6 August, a pivotal moment in what Epstein has termed 'the coming together of Chartism' [Epstein (1982) 90]. Wade bridged the middle and working classes, Midlands and London, and the BPU and the LWMA. Moreover his reputation for hard-edged, class-based radicalism at a time when many Chartists – especially from the north – were suspicious of both organisations made him a useful ally in O'Connor's bid to unite the movement. This edge was evident when on 17 September Wade, like O'Connor, spoke from the platform at a mass meeting in Westminster Palace Yard, organised by the LWMA. For much of the interval between the Birmingham and London meetings Wade had been in France, at the behest of the LWMA, to discuss the People's Charter with Parisian radicals. His presentation of fraternal greetings from the workers of France, who 'wished to hold out the right hand of fellowship and fraternisation to the working men of England in the great struggle for democracy and independence' [*Warwick Advertiser*, 22 September 1838], was an early harbinger of Chartist internationalism.

Almost naturally, one feels, Arthur Wade was among the delegates to Chartism's National Convention the following February; but he did not figure in the London delegation (which was dominated by the more moderate members of the LWMA) and instead represented Nottingham, Mansfield and Sutton-in-Ashfield. Proceedings on the first day of the convention began with prayers conducted by Wade:

> Grant, O God of Nations, that the folly or perverseness of our rulers, may not longer deprive the poor of the comforts of life, nor deny to thy people any of the social or political rights … we beseech thy blessing upon all moral means for obtaining our political and social improvement, be evermore our ruler and guide, that we may so pass through things temporal that we lose not things eternal [*Operative*, 10 February 1839].

Despite his clear emphasis on moral means, four days later Home Secretary Lord Russell signed a warrant authorising the interception of all Wade's mail [HO 79/4, 8 February 1839, f. 233]. Wade was one of four delegates so treated (Hartwell, Richardson and Vincent were the others). The rationale for the decision is hard to discern, unless it was that all four were delegates of major provincial centres and therefore their correspondence might be of particular interest. In the event it was not [copies in HO 40/53, ff. 969, 973–77, 1047]. Wade proved to be among the Convention's most resolute opponents of physical force. He first spoke out on the issue as early as 18 February, and played a leading part in opposing (and disciplining) those delegates who presented for the Convention's endorsement a series of resolutions passed by the East London Democratic Association. According to the *Northern Star*, Wade 'was one of the moral-force men, who would never resort to physical force, and he was anxious that the higher classes should have no ground for supposing that, under any circumstances, an appeal to physical force was contemplated' [*Northern Star*, 9 March 1839]. Next he forced to the vote a resolution to remove the now-famous phrase 'peaceably if you may, forcibly if you must' from the draft of an address to Ireland. Wade narrowly avoided formal censure (moved by O'Connor) for condemning (in a letter to the *Morning Chronicle* on 19 March 1839) sentiments expressed by physical-force delegates at a meeting outside the convention. Finally, on 28 March Wade resigned:

> Dr Wade said, that as much discussion had taken place upon the subject of moral and physical force, he could not, in justice to himself and his constituency, continue a member of the Convention, without knowing from that constituency by an appeal, whether or not he was the real representative of their wishes on that subject in the Convention. He was an avowed and acknowledged moral-force man; but occupying the position of an individual of the middle classes, he was not placed in a similar position to the class whom he represented, who were oppressed by the most stringent necessity, and whose opinions might be favourable to the physical force doctrine which he repudiated. It was for that reason that he would apply to the constituency, and in the event of their re-electing him, he would be happy to re-join the Convention, for the members of which he entertained the highest respect and regard [*Operative*, 31 March 1839].

It is unclear how far Wade's opposition to the use of force in pursuit of Chartist objectives was a principled one, and how far it derived from the conviction that it was a strategy doomed to fail. Certainly he believed that 'the cry of arms, without antecedent moral opinion and union of the middle classes with you, would only cause misery, blood and ruin' [*Morning Chronicle*, 19 March 1839]. Nottinghamshire Chartists, however, were unequivocal; Wade was not re-elected but replaced by James Woodhouse, a framework knitter.

Wade's resignation from the National Convention inevitably diminished the part he could play in Chartism, but he never broke from the movement. In June 1839 he chaired a meeting at the Theobalds Road Institute in support of the Polish patriotic struggle: 30 minutes of fighting preceded the meeting between Wade's Chartist supporters and those of a rival candidate for the chair, the Polish émigré aristocrat Beniowski, whose antidemocratic views were anathema to Chartists and most of the London Poles. Wade was also one of the figureheads of the campaign to pardon the Newport prisoners, and in February 1840 presented 'seven voluminous petitions from various parts of the kingdom' to Queen Victoria at a royal levee [*Northern Star*, 29 February 1840]. He continued to take a close interest in trade unionism, for example at a meeting at the Mechanics' Institute in May 1840 he spoke in favour of the campaign to build a London trades hall. His empathy with both middle-class and popular radicalism led him naturally into Joseph Sturge's Complete Suffrage Union, and he attended its inaugural conference at Birmingham in April 1842. When delegated by Tower Hamlets to the second conference in December, however, Wade publicly broke with Sturge. He spoke in support of the motion that Lovett proposed (and O'Connor seconded) that the title of the Charter must be retained as a condition of the Chartists' support, rather than suppressed as Sturge's circle demanded: 'It was not the name of the Charter to which the middle classes, whom the Complete Suffrage party wished to conciliate, objected but the principles it contained', Wade told the assembly. 'He believed that if the advocates of the Charter consented to change the name of the document, that the very next day the members of the Association would contrive some other loophole out of which to escape' [*Northern Star*, 7 January 1843].

Wade also played some part in Lovett's National Association and a more active one in the Metropolitan Parliamentary Reform Association. The latter had a strongly Sturgeite tone and did not long survive the events of December 1842: Wade sat on the committee formed to oversee its dissolution in March 1843. Thereafter his participation in radical circles appears to have diminished. In June 1844 he was among the platform party (with Feargus O'Connor) at a Covent Garden meeting to oppose the government's Irish policy. His last recorded political commitment was in February 1845, when he acted as chairman of a dinner organised by the London trades in honour of Thomas Slingsby Duncombe. On 17 November that year, whilst visiting his Regent Street tailor, Wade was seized by an apoplectic fit and died from the effects of this later that day. His entire estate, valued for probate purposes at £1000, was bequeathed to Miss Mary Anne Crafer of East Dereham, Norfolk. (Their exact relationship is obscure but the Crafer and Wade families were linked by marriage.) He was accorded no obituary in the *Northern Star*, which simply lifted from another paper a report of the coroner's inquest into his death, merely noting that Wade was 'well known in the political world' [*Northern Star*, 22 November 1845].

According to the *Gentlemen's Magazine*, Wade 'was a short thick-set man, and walked rather lame' [*Gentlemen's Magazine*, February 1846]. This doubtless enhanced an appearance of corpulency, a feature historians have commented upon as frequently as they have the 'full canonicals' worn at Copenhagen Fields in 1834. The latter event sealed Wade's reputation among critics and admirers alike, and provided the enduring image of the radical parson. It has, however, rather diverted attention from Wade's broader radical political career, which extended from the Queen Caroline agitation to the middle phase of Chartism. Conventionally he has been regarded as an eccentric and marginal figure in the history of radical politics. This, however, overlooks the esteem in which he was held by London workers and the part he played in assisting a national movement to cohere in the precursor and early years of Chartism. It would be fallacious to claim that his prominence was achieved purely through ability: his status as a clergyman and doctor of divinity (conferred by Cambridge in 1825) secured places on the platforms of meetings he might otherwise have addressed from the floor. That same status, however, made his conversion to Hodgskinite economic thinking in the early 1830s all the more remarkable. In the final analysis Wade's politics, like his resignation from the Chartist Convention in March 1839, seems to have rested on a troubled conscience. As he told the Third Co-operative Congress: 'He was proud to be a link between the poorer and the richer classes of society; and if his poorer brethren were to fall, he would rather perish with them than flourish with the rich' [*Crisis*, 28 April 1832].

The TUC's centenary commemorations of the Tolpuddle trial resurrected the memory of Wade. In November 1934 Andrew Conley (retiring chairman of the TUC) unveiled a plaque inscribed to Wade's memory in the churchyard of St Nicholas, Warwick. The ceremony was preceded by a service of commemoration led by the Christian Socialist rector of Birmingham, Guy Weston.

Writings: *A Sermon [on Collossians iv 5] Preached at a Visitation Holden at Stratford-upon-Avon, 13th of May 1819* (1819); *To Καλο Κρειττο or, the conduct of the Duke of Wellington's administration ... relative to Catholic Question, proved to be consistent with justice, sound policy and individual good faith* (1820); *A Letter to the Right Hon. G. Canning Intended as an Humble Vindication of the Present Ministry* (1827); 'To Thomas Attwood Esq. On the Conduct of the Birmingham Political Council, respecting the formation of a Midland Union of the Working Classes', *Poor Man's Guardian*, 17 November 1832; *A Voice from the Church: or, a Sermon (with a Few Notes and Amplifications) on Church Reform, Pledges, Cheap Government – Cheap Justice – Cheap Food – Cheap Knowledge – and on a Cheap and Efficient Medium of Exchange; also, on the Duties which the Electors and Elected will owe to the Represented and Unrepresented People of Great Britain and Ireland, especially the Working Classes* (1832); letter to the editor, *The Times*, 26 April 1834; letter to the editor, *Morning Chronicle*, 19 March 1839.

Sources: (1) **MSS**: British Museum, Department of Manuscripts, Add MSS 27,796, f. 333, 27,810, ff. 39–42, 55–6, 27,820, f. 123, 216,27,821, f.44, 35,149, f. 130, 37,773, f. 8–11, 24–5, 107; PRO, HO 40/37, f. 77, HO 40/53, ff. 969, 973–77, 1047, HO 45/102, f. 3, HO 79/4, f. 233, PROB 11/2027. (2) **Newspapers:** *Warwick and Warwickshire Advertiser*, 21 December 1816, 4 March 1820, 11 February 1826, 10 June 1826, 28 April 1827; *Warwick and Warwickshire Advertiser*, 7 August 1830, 1 and 27 January 1831, 5 February 1831, 9 and 30 April 1831, 8 and

14 October 1831, 12 November 1831; *The Times*, 5 December 1831; *Poor Man's Guardian*, 24 December 1831, 26 January 1832; *Crisis*, 14 and 28 April 1832; *Poor Man's Guardian*, 26 May 1832, 30 June 1832, 7 and 14 July 1832; *Crisis*, 14 July 1832; *Warwick and Warwickshire Advertiser*, 20 July 1832; *Crisis*, 21 July 1832, 22 and 29 September 1832; *Poor Man's Guardian*, 29 September 1832, 6, 20 and 27 October 1832, 3, 10 and 17 November 1832; *Crisis*, 17 November 1832; *Warwick and Warwickshire Advertiser*, 8 December 1832; *Crisis*, 12 January 1833; *Workingman's Friend*, 26 January 1833; *Warwick and Warwickshire Advertiser*, 20 July 1833, 17 August 1833; *Gauntlet*, 15 December 1833; *Pioneer; or, Grand National Consolidated Trades' Union Magazine*, 28 December 1833; *Poor Man's Guardian*, 31 December 1833; *Crisis*, 1 February 1834; *Poor Man's Guardian*, 15 and 29 March 1834; *True Sun*, 25 March 1834; *Crisis*, 29 March 1834; *Pioneer*, 29 March 1834; *Crisis*, 5 April 1834; *Pioneer*, 12 April 1834; *The Times*, 22 and 24 April 1834; *Pioneer*, 26 April 1834; *Poor Man's Guardian*, 26 April 1834; *Crisis*, 3 May 1834; *Warwick and Warwickshire Advertiser*, 3 and 10 May 1834; *Pioneer*, 24 May 1834; *Poor Man's Guardian*, 24 May 1834; *Globe*, 17 March 1838; *Northern Star*, 11 August 1838; *Warwick and Warwickshire Advertiser*, 24 September 1838; *Northern Star*, 10 November 1838; *Operative*, 10 February 1839; *Northern Star*, 9 and 23 February 1839, 2, 9, 16 and 30 March 1839, 20 and 27 April 1839, 4 May 1839, 1 June 1839, 29 February 1840, 16 May 1840, 3 December 1842; *The Nonconformist*, 13 and 20 April 1842; *Northern Star*, 7 January 1843, 6 July 1844, 8 February 1845; *Northern Star*, 22 November 1845; William Field, *Memoirs of Samuel Parr*, vol. 2 (1828); *Proceedings of the Third Co-operative Congress* (1832); *Report of the Proceedings at the Public Meeting of the Working Classes and Others … to Support the People's Daily Press, The True Sun* (1832, copy in HO 64/18); *Birmingham Post*, 26 November 1934; *Midland Daily Telegraph*, 26 November 1934; *Birmingham Morning News*, 27 November 1934; *Leamington Courier*, 30 November 1934; *Warwick and Warwickshire Advertiser*, 30 November 1934, **(3) Other:** *Brief sketches of the Birmingham Conference, by a Member. Comprising the Following Delegates: Joseph Sturge, William Lovett, James Adam, Henry Vincent, Rev. T. Spencer, Rev. John Ritchie, John Collins, J. B. O'Brien, Edward Miall, C. H. Neesom, J. H. Parry, Rev. A. Wade, Rev. H. Solly, etc.* (1842); R. G. Gammage, *History of the Chartist Movement, 1837–54* (1894); The Trades Union Congress, *The Book of the Martyrs of Tolpuddle, 1834–1934* (1934); F. C. Mather, *Public Order in the Age of the Chartists* (1959); I. Prothero, 'Chartism in London', *Past & Present*, 44 (1969); J. H. Wiener, *The War of the Unstamped: The Movement to Repeal the British Newspaper Tax, 1830–1836* (1969); D. J. Rowe, *London Radicalism: A Selection from the Papers of Francis Place* (1970); A. Plummer, *Bronterre: A Political Biography of Bronterre O'Brien, 1804–1864* (1971); T. H. Lloyd, 'Dr Wade and the working class', *Midland History*, 2:2 (Autumn 1973); C. Flick, *The Birmingham Political Union and the Movement for Reform in Britain, 1830–1839* (1978); I. Prothero, *Artisans and Politics in Early Nineteenth-Century London* (1979); J. Epstein, *The Lion of Freedom: Feargus O'Connor and the Chartist Movement, 1837–42* (1982); J. Belchem, *'Orator Hunt': Henry Hunt and English Working-Class Radicalism* (1985); E. G. Lyon, *Politicians in the Pulpit: Christian Radicalism in Britain from the Fall of the Bastille to the Disintegration of Chartism* (2000). **(4) Obituaries:** *The Times*, 20 November 1845; *Leamington Courier*, 22 November 1845; *Gentleman's Magazine*, February 1846.

There are two surviving portraits of Wade: a sketch by Benjamin Robert Haydon (*circa* 1830), in the City of Birmingham Museums and Art Gallery, and an engraving by Henry Meyer (1834), issued to raise funds for unstamped press victim John Cleave (copy in Warwickshire CRO, CR 351/1049).

MALCOLM CHASE

See also: †Robert OWEN; †William LOVETT; †John CLEAVE; †Thomas HODGKIN; †George Julian HARNEY; †Henry VINCENT; †Henry HETHRINGTON.

WROE, James (1789–1844)
CHARTIST

James Wroe was born in Manchester in 1789. As is the case with many working-class activists of that era, little is known about his family background and early life apart from the fact that he had at least two brothers. In about 1810 he commenced business as a seller of old books and scrap iron from a stall in Port Street, Manchester. By 1818 he had established a bookshop in Great Ancoats Street and become involved with a group known as the 'Friends of Liberty of the Press', participating in meetings to support those detained under the suspension of habeas corpus. Early in 1819 he became printer and publisher of the *Manchester Observer* and was present at Peterloo in August. Five weeks after the massacre he was arrested for libelling the Prince of Wales in the *Manchester Observer*, and on numerous counts of selling illegal newspapers. He was subsequently heavily fined and sentenced to three years' imprisonment. His wife and two brothers were also gaoled later. Wroe must have been married for several years by the time of his brush with the law as by then he and his wife already had five children under the age of ten. After serving six months he was brought before the Lancashire Assizes on further charges, but was given no additional punishment on the understanding that he would 'not interfere in any more political matters' – an injunction he defied for the next 20 years until his death in 1844.

After the expiry of his sentence Wroe faced outstanding fines and his printing and publishing business fell into financial difficulty. In 1826 he was forced to enter King's Bench Prison as a debtor and was released some time during 1827. After his liberation he set about re-establishing a book- and music-selling business, and in 1831–32 he combined this with running a Co-operative Society store. He also recommenced his career in radical politics. During 1827–28 he became part of Richard Carlile's provincial network of supporters, and he continued to be active in politics during the 1830s. In 1838 he was prominent in the rejuvenation of the Manchester Political Union. He was also on the platform at the first Chartist demonstration on Kersal Moor in September, where he was elected as a delegate to the Chartist General Convention. A month later he was elected to the Council of the Manchester Political Union. He did not attend the convention in London and resigned as a delegate in May 1839.

Despite his resignation Wroe continued to be active in Chartist affairs during 1839–42, but his main interest was local government. His career in local government began in 1830, when he was elected to the Manchester Police Commission for 'Cleansing, Lighting and Watching', and was subsequently re-elected in 1833, 1836 and 1839. In the late 1830s he was a leading figure in the campaign against the granting of a Charter of Incorporation for Manchester. During 1838–39 he was secretary of the Radical Electors' Association, an organisation committed to the election of candidates opposed to Incorporation. Wroe's opposition to Incorporation was on the ground that the extension of the franchise to ratepayers provided for under the Municipal Corporations' Act did not go far enough. His stance led him to clash publicly with Richard Cobden, a leading advocate of Incorporation. Responding to Cobden's jibes about Tory radicalism, Wroe reminded the future leader of the Anti-Corn Law League that he had advocated democracy when Cobden 'was in petticoats'.

In November 1839 Wroe was unsuccessful in his bid for election to the new Manchester Council. Apart from the Police Commission, he was regularly involved in other forums of local government, including the Select Vestry, and in the election of churchwardens. He served on the Board of the Surveyor of Highways between 1838 and 1844, where his assiduousness was evident in the fact that he attended all but one or two of the meetings held every year. Carlile, who lodged with Wroe on northern tours, regarded his host as a 'real Lancashire Radical in politics, with a Christian Religion to suit his political views': 'The sound of radical reform is, with Mr. Wroe, a gospel sound' [*Lion*, 11 January 1828]. Samuel Bamford, the well-known weaver, poet and veteran radical, held a poor opinion of 'little skinny ignorant, and impudent Jimmy Wroe', but another prominent Manchester radical, Archibald Prentice, disagreed. According to

Prentice – who bitterly opposed Wroe on the issue of incorporation – there were not many who 'in so long a career, have been so generally right' [*Manchester Times*, 10 August 1844].

Wroe died on 4 August 1844 of chronic inflammation of the liver. When measuring his significance it is important to remember that he stood up for his principles at a time when it was difficult and dangerous to do so. As one who struggled in the 'trade of agitation' during an era when the leisured gentleman still provided the model for public life, Wroe was a pioneer in the development of the tradition of independent radicalism, free from middle-class influence and compromise, that reached its apogee in the years of early Chartism.

Sources: (1) Newspapers: *Manchester Observer*, 1818–20; *Republican*, January 1823; *Lion*, January 1828; *Lancashire and Yorkshire Co-Operator*, June 1831; *Northern Star*, 1838–44; *Manchester Times*, 1835–44; *Manchester and Salford Advertiser*, 1837–42; *Manchester Guardian*, 1830–44. **(2) Other:** R. W. Procter, *Memorials of Manchester Streets* (Manchester, 1874), 53–4; J. T. Slugg, *Reminiscences of Manchester Fifty Years Ago* (1881, repr. Shannon, 1971), 86–7; P. A. Pickering, *Chartism and the Chartists in Manchester and Salford* (Basingstoke, 1995); M. Hewitt and R. Poole (eds), *The Diaries of Samuel Bamford* (Stroud, 2000), 333. **(3) Obituary:** *Manchester Times*, 10 August 1844.

PAUL A. PICKERING

See also: James SCHOLEFIELD; Reginald John RICHARDSON.

Consolidated List of Names
Volumes I–XI

ABBOTTS, William (1873–1930) I
ABLETT, Noah (1883–1935) III
ABRAHAM, William (Mabon) (1842–1922) I
ACLAND, Alice Sophia (1849–1935) I
ACLAND, Sir Arthur Herbert Dyke
 (1847–1926) I
ADAIR, John (1872–1950) II
ADAMS, David (1871–1943) IV
ADAMS, Francis William Lauderdale
 (1862–93) V
ADAMS, John Jackson (1st Baron Adams of
 Ennerdale) (1890–1960) I
ADAMS, Mary Jane Bridges (1855–1939) VI
ADAMS, William Edwin (1832–1906) VII
ADAMS, William Thomas (1884–1949) I
ADAMSON, Janet (Jennie) Laurel
 (1882–1962) IV
ADAMSON, William (1863–1936) VII
ADAMSON, William (Billy) Murdoch
 (1881–1945) V
ADDERLEY, The Hon. James Granville
 (1861–1942) IX
AINLEY, Theodore (Ted) (1903–68) X
AITKEN, William (1814?–69) X
ALDEN, Sir Percy (1865–1944) III
ALDERSON, Lilian (1885–1976) V
ALEXANDER, Albert Victor (1st Earl
 Alexander ofHillsborough) (1885–1965) I
ALLAN, William (1813–74) I
ALLEN, Reginald Clifford (1st Baron Allen
 of Hurtwood) (1889–1939) II
ALLEN, Robert (1827–77) I
ALLEN, Sir Thomas William (1864–1943) I
ALLINSON, John (1812/13–72) II
ALLSOP, Thomas (1795–1880) VIII
AMMON, Charles (Charlie) George (1st
 Baron Ammon of Camberwell)
 (1873–1960) I
ANDERSON, Frank (1889–1959) I
ANDERSON,
 William Crawford (1877–1919) II
ANDREWS Elizabeth (1882–1960) XI
APPLEGARTH, Robert (1834–1924) II
ARCH, Joseph (1826–1919) I
ARMSTRONG, William John (1870–1950) V

ARNOLD, Alice (1881–1955) IV
ARNOLD, Thomas George (1866–1944) I
ARNOTT, John (1871–1942) X
ASHTON, Thomas (1841–1919) VII
ASHTON, Thomas (1844–1927) I
ASHTON, William (1806–77) III
ASHWORTH, Samuel (1825–71) I
ASKEW, Francis (1855–1940) III
ASPINWALL, Thomas (1846–1901) I
ATKINSON, Hinley (1891–1977) VI
AUCOTT, William (1830–1915) II
AYLES, Walter Henry (1879–1953) V

BACHARACH, Alfred Louis (1891–1966) IX
BAILEY, Sir John (Jack) (1898–1969) II
BAILEY, William (1851–96) II
BALFOUR, William Campbell (1919–73) V
BALLARD, William (1858–1928) I
BAMFORD, Samuel (1846–98) I
BARBER, Jonathan (1800–59) IV
BARBER, [Mark] Revis (1895–1965) V
BARBER, Walter (1864–1930) V
BARKER, George (1858–1936) I
BARKER, Henry Alfred (1858–1940) VI
BARMBY, Catherine Isabella (1817?–53) VI
BARMBY, John [Goodwin] Goodwyn
 (1820–81) VI
BARNES, George Nicoll (1859–1940) IV
BARNES, Leonard John (1895–1977) VIII
BARNETT, William (1840–1909) I
BARR, James (1862–1949) VIII
BARRETT, Rowland (1877–1950) IV
BARROW, Harrison (1868–1953) V
BARTLEY, James (1850–1926) III
BARTLEY, Patrick (1909–56) X
BARTON, Alfred (1868–1933) VI
BARTON, Eleanor (1872–1960) I
BASTON, Richard Charles (1880–1951) V
BATES, William (1833–1908) I
BATEY, John (1852–1925) I
BATEY, Joseph (1867–1949) II
BATTLEY, John Rose (1880–1952) IV
BAX, Ernest Belfort (1854–1926) X
BAYLEY, Thomas (1813–74) I
BEATON, Neil Scobie (1880–1960) I

BEAUCHAMP, Joan (1890–1964) **X**
BECKETT, Clement (Clem) Henry
(1906–36) **IX**
BECKETT, John (William) Warburton
(1894–1964) **VI**
BEER, Max (1864–1943) **VII**
BELL, George (1874–1930) **II**
BELL, Letitia (1890–1981) **VIII**
BELL, Richard (1859–1930) **II**
BENBOW, William (1784–?) **VI**
BENNISON, Thomas Mason (1882–1960) **V**
BENTHAM, Ethel (1861–1931) **IV**
BERKELEY, Frederick Charles (1880–1938)
VII
BESANT, Annie (1847–1933) **IV**
BING, Frederick George (1870–1948) **III**
BIRD, Thomas Richard (1877–1965) **I**
BLAIR, William Richard (1874–1932) **I**
BLAND, Hubert (1855–1914) **V**
BLAND, Thomas (1825–1908) **I**
BLANDFORD, Thomas (1861–99) **I**
BLATCHFORD, Montagu John (1848–1910)
IV
BLATCHFORD, Robert Peel Glanville
(1851–1943) **IV**
BLYTH, Alexander (1835–85) **IV**
BOND, Frederick (1865–1951) **I**
BONDFIELD, Margaret Grace (1873–1953)
II
BONNER, Arnold (1904–66) **I**
BOON, Martin James (1840–88) **IX**
BOSWELL, James Edward Buchanan
(1906–71) **III**
BOWER, Sir Percival (1880–1948) **VI**
BOWERMAN, Charles William (1851–1947)
V
BOWMAN, Alexander (1854–1924) **XI**
BOYES, Watson (1868–1929) **III**
BOYLE, Hugh (1850–1907) **I**
BOYNTON, Arthur John (1863–1922) **I**
BRACE, William (1865–1947) **I**
BRADBURN, George (1795–1862) **II**
BRADLAUGH, Charles (1833–91) **VII**
BRADLEY, Benjamin Francis (1898–1957) **X**
BRAILSFORD, Henry Noel (1873–1958) **II**
BRAMLEY, Frederick (Fred) (1874–1925)
IX
BRANSON, Clive Ali Chimmo (1907–44) **II**
BRAUNTHAL, Julius (1891–1972) **V**
BRAY, John Francis (1809–97) **III**
BRIDGEMAN, Reginald Francis Orlando
(1884–1968) **VII**

BRIERLEY, Benjamin (1825–96) **XI**
BRIGGS, William (Billy) Layton
(1876–1957) **VIII**
BROADHEAD, Samuel (1818–97) **IV**
BROADHURST, Henry (1840–1911) **II**
BROCKLEHURST, Frederick (1866–1926)
VI
BRODZKY, Vivian (1892–1968) **X**
BROOKE, Willie (1895/6?–1939) **IV**
BROWN, Alfred Barratt (1887–1947) **VIII**
BROWN, George (1906–37) **III**
BROWN, Herbert Runham (1879–1949) **II**
BROWN, Isabel (1894–1984) **IX**
BROWN, James (1862–1939) **I**
BROWN, William Henry (1867/8–1950) **I**
BROWN, William John (1894–1960) **X**
BRUFF, Frank Herbert (1869–1931) **II**
BUCHANAN, George (1890–1955) **VII**
BUGG, Frederick John (1830–1900) **I**
BURNETT, John (1842–1914) **II**
BURNS, Isaac (1869–1946) **IV**
BURNS, John Elliott (1858–1943) **V**
BURT, Thomas (1837–1922) **I**
BUTCHER, James Benjamin (1843–1933)
III
BUTCHER, John (1833–1921) **I**
BUTCHER, John (1847–1936) **I**
BUTLER, Herbert William (1892–1971) **IV**
BUXTON, Charles Roden (1875–1942) **V**
BUXTON, Noel Edward (1st Baron Noel-
Buxton of Aylsham) (1869–1948) **V**
BYRON, Anne Isabella Lady Noel
(1792–1860) **II**

CAIRNS, John (1859–1923) **II**
CAMERON, Alexander Gordon (1886–1944)
X
CAMPBELL, Alexander (1796–1870) **I**
CAMPBELL, George Lamb (1849–1906) **IV**
CANN, Thomas Henry (1858–1924) **I**
CANTWELL, Thomas Edward (1864–1906)
III
CAPE, Thomas (1868–1947) **III**
CAPPER, James (1829–95) **II**
CARLILE, Richard (1790–1843) **VI**
CARPENTER, Edward (1844–1929) **II**
CARTER, Joseph (1818–61) **II**
CARTER, William (1862–1932) **I**
CASASOLA, Rowland (Roland) William
(1893–1971) **IV**
CATCHPOLE, John (1843–1919) **I**
CHADWICK, Albert Paxton (1903–61) **IX**

CHADWICK, William Henry (1829–1908) VII

CHALLENGER, John Ernest Stopford (1875–1906) **V**

CHAMPION, Henry Hyde (1859–1928) **VIII**

CHANCE, John (1840–71) **VI**

CHANDLER, Francis (1849–1937) **X**

CHAPPELLSMITH, Margaret (1806–83) **X**

CHARLESWORTH, John James (1900–93) **X**

CHARLTON, William Browell (1855/7?–1932) **IV**

CHARTER, Walter Thomas (1871–1932) **I**

CHATER, Daniel (Dan) (1870–1959) **IV**

CHATTERTON, Daniel (1820–95) **VIII**

CHEETHAM, Thomas (1828–1901) **I**

CHELMSFORD, 3rd Baron and 1st Viscount Chelmsford. *See* THESIGNER, Frederick John Napier, **V**

CHEW, Ada Nield (1870–1945) **V**

CHICHESTER, Sophia Catherine (1795–1847) **X**

CHURCH, Archibald George (1886–1954) **XI**

CIAPPESSONI, Francis Antonio (1859–1912) **I**

CLARK, Fred (1878–1947) **I**

CLARK, Gavin Brown (1846–1930) **IV**

CLARK, James (1853–1924) **IV**

CLARK, Thomas (1821?–57) **VI**

CLARKE, Andrew Bathgate (1868–1940) **I**

CLARKE, (Charles) Allen (1863–1935) **V**

CLARKE, John Smith (1885–1959) **V**

CLARKE, William (1852–1901) **II**

CLAY, Joseph (1826–1901) **I**

CLEAVE, John (1795?–1850) **VI**

CLERY, William Edward (1861–1931) **VII**

CLIMIE, Robert (1868–1929) **VI**

CLUSE, William Sampson (1875–1955) **III**

COATES, Alice Schofield (1881–1975) **IX**

COCHRANE, William (1872–1924) **I**

COHEN, Jack (1905–82) **IX**

COHEN, Max (1911–67) **IX**

COHEN Rose (1894–1937) **XI**

COLMAN, Grace Mary (1892–1971) **III**

COMBE, Abram (1785?–1827) **II**

COMSTIVE, William (1792–1834) **VIII**

CONDY, George (1790–1841) **X**

CONNELL, Jim (1852–1929) **X**

COOK, Arthur James (1883–1931) **III**

COOK, Cecily Mary (1887/90?–1962) **II**

COOK, Samuel (1786–1861) **VI**

COOK, Samuel Quartus (1822–90) **VI**

COOMBES, Bert Lewis (Louis) (1893–1974) **IV**

COOPER, George (1824–95) **II**

COOPER, Robert (1819–68) **II**

COOPER, Thomas (1805–92) **IX**

COOPER, William (1822–68) **I**

COPPOCK, Sir Richard (1885–1971) **III**

CORMACK, William Sloan (1898–1973) **III**

COULTHARD, Samuel (1853–1931) **II**

COURT, Sir Josiah (1841–1938) **I**

COWEN, Joseph (1829–1900) **I**

COWEN, Edward (Ned) (1839–1903) **I**

CRABTREE, James (1831–1917) **I**

CRAIG, Edward Thomas (1804–94) **I**

CRANE, Walter (1845–1915) **VI**

CRAWFORD, William (1833–90) **I**

CREMER, Sir William Randal (1828–1908) **V**

CROOKS, William (1852–1921) **II**

CRUMP, James (1873–1960) **V**

CUFFAY, William (1788–1870) **VI**

CULLEN, Alice (1891–1969) **VII**

CUMMINGS, David Charles (1861–1942) **VI**

CUNNINGHAME GRAHAM, Robert Bontine (1852–1936) **VI**

CURRAN, Peter (Pete) Francis (1860–1910) **IV**

DAGGAR, George (1879–1950) **III**

DALLAS, George (1878–1961) **IV**

DALLAWAY, William (1857–1939) **I**

DALY, James (?–1849) **I**

DARCH, Charles Thomas (1876–1934) **I**

DARLING, George (Baron Darling of Hillsborough) (1905–1985) **IX**

DASH, Jack O'Brien (1907–89) **IX**

DAVENPORT, Allen (1775–1846) **VIII**

DAVIES, Florence Rose (1882–1958) **XI**

DAVIES, Margaret Llewelyn (1861–1944) **I**

DAVIES, Stephen Owen (1886–1972) **VIII**

DAVIS, William John (1848–1934) **VI**

DAVISON, John (1846–1930) **I**

DEAKIN, Arthur (1890–1955) **II**

DEAKIN, Charles (1864–1941) **III**

DEAKIN, Jane (1869–1942) **III**

DEAKIN, Joseph Thomas (1858–1937) **III**

DEAN, Benjamin (1839–1910) **I**

DEAN, Frederick James (1868–1941) **II**

DEANS, James (1843/4?–1935) **I**

DEANS, Robert (1904–59) **I**

DENMAN, Sir Richard Douglas (1876–1957) **XI**

DENT, John James (1856–1936) **I**
DIAMOND, Charles (1858–1934) **VIII**
DICKENSON, Sarah (1868–1954) **VI**
DILKE, Emily (Emilia) Francis Strong, Lady (1840–1904) **III**
DIXON, George Henry (1902–72) **VII**
DIXON, John (1828–76) **I**
DIXON, John (1850–1914) **IV**
DOBB, Maurice Herbert (1900–76) **IX**
DOCKER, Abraham (1788/91?–1857) **II**
DODDS, Ruth (1890–1976) **VII**
DOUSE, William John (1842?–1927) **VII**
DRAKE, Henry John (1878–1934) **I**
DREW, William Henry (Harry) (1854–1933) **IV**
DUDLEY, Sir William Edward (1868–1938) **I**
DUNCAN, Andrew (1898–1965) **II**
DUNCAN, Charles (1865–1933) **II**
DUNN, Edward (1880–1945) **III**
DUNNING, Thomas Joseph (1799–1873) **II**
DYE, Sidney (1900–58) **I**
DYSON, James (1822/3–1902) **I**
DYSON, William Henry (1880–1938) **IX**

EADES, Arthur (1863–1933) **II**
EATON, Daniel Isaac (c.1753–1814) **X**
EDWARDS, Alfred (1888–1958) **IV**
EDWARDS, Allen Clement (1869–1938) **III**
EDWARDS, Ebenezer (Ebby) (1884–1961) **V**
EDWARDS, Enoch (1852–1912) **I**
EDWARDS, Huw Thomas (1892–1970) **XI**
EDWARDS, John (1861–1922) **VII**
EDWARDS, John Charles (1833–81) **I**
EDWARDS, Wyndham Ivor (1878–1938) **I**
ELVIN, Herbert Henry (1874–1949) **VI**
ENFIELD, Alice Honora (1882–1935) **I**
ETHERIDGE, Richard (Dick) Albert (1909–85) **IX**
EVANS, George (1842–93) **VI**
EVANS, Isaac (1847?–97) **I**
EVANS, Jonah (1826–1907) **I**
EVANS, Sir Lincoln (1889–1970) **IX**
EVANS, Thomas (1763–182?) **VIII**
EWART, Richard (1904–53) **IV**

FAIRBOTHAM, Harold (1883–1968) **VI**
FALLOWS, John Arthur (1864–1935) **II**
FARMERY, George Edward (1883–1942) **V**
FARRIMOND, Thomas (1766–1828?) **VIII**
FENWICK, Charles (1850–1918) **I**
FINCH, John (1784–1857) **I**

FINLEY, Lawrence (Larry) (1909–74) **IV**
FINNEY, Samuel (1857–1935) **I**
FISHWICK, Jonathan (1832–1908) **I**
FLANAGAN, James Aloysius (1876–1953) **III**
FLANAGAN, James Desmond (1912–69) **IV**
FLEMING, Robert (1869–1939) **I**
FLETCHER, George Henry (1879–1958) **IX**
FLYNN, Charles Richard (1882–1957) **III**
FORD, Isabella Ormston (1855–1924) **VIII**
FORGAN, Robert (1891–1976) **VI**
FORMAN, John (1822/3–1900) **I**
FORMAN, Robert (1887–1947) **I**
FOSTER, William (1887–1947) **I**
FOULGER, Sydney (1863–1919) **I**
FOWE, Thomas (1832/3?–94) **I**
FOX, James Challinor (1837–77) **I**
FOX, Thomas (Tom) (1860–1934) **II**
FOX, Thomas (Tom) Samuel (1905–56) **V**
FOX, William (1890–1968) **V**
FREEMAN, Arnold James (1886–1972) **IX**
FRITH, John (1837–1904) **I**

GALBRAITH, Samuel (1853–1936) **I**
GALLAGHER, Patrick (Paddy the Cope) (1871–1966) **I**
GAMMAGE, Robert George (1820/1–88) **VI**
GANLEY, Caroline Selina (1879–1966) **I**
GARSIDE, George (1843–1907) **VII**
GEE, Allen (1852–1939) **III**
GEORGE, John (1766/7–1842) **X**
GIBB, Margaret Hunter (1892–1984) **VIII**
GIBBS Charles (1843–1909) **II**
GIBSON, Arthur Lummis (1899–1959) **III**
GILL, Alfred Henry (1856–1914) **II**
GILLIANS, John Moffett (1873–1935) **IX·**
GILLILAND, James (1866–1952) **IV**
GILLIS, William (1859–1929) **III**
GLOVER, Thomas (1852–1913) **I**
GLYDE, Charles Augustus (1869–1923) **VI**
GOLDSTONE, Sir Frank Walter (1870–1955) **V**
GOLIGHTLY, Alfred William (1857–1948) **I**
GOODALL, William Kenneth (1877–1963) **V**
GOODY, Joseph (1816/7–91) **I**
GOSLING, Harry (1861–1930) **IV**
GOSSIP, Alexander (Alex) (1862–1952) **VII**
GOSSLING, Archibald (Archie) George (1878–1950) **V**
GOULD, Barbara Bodichon Ayrton (1886–1950) **VII**
GOULD, Gerald (1885–1936) **VII**

GRAHAM, Duncan MacGregor (1867–1942) **I**
GRAHAM, Robert Bontine Cunninghame.
  See CUNNINGHAME GRAHAM, **VI**
GRAHAM, William (Willie) (1887–1932) **XI**
GRAND, Cyril David (1892–1980) **VII**
GRAY, Alexander Stewart (1862–1937) **X**
GRAY, Jesse Clement (1854–1912) **I**
GRAY, John (1799–1883) **VI**
GREEN, Beatrice (1895–1927) **XI**
GREEN, George (1904–38) **X**
GREENHALL, Thomas (1857–1937) **I**
GREENING, Edward Owen (1836–1923) **I**
GREENWOOD, Abraham (1824–1911) **I**
GREENWOOD, Alfred (1837–1923) **IX**
GREENWOOD, Arthur (1880–1945) **XI**
GREENWOOD, Joseph (1833–1924) **I**
GRENFELL, Harold (1870–1948) **IX**
GRIBBLE, James (1868–1934) **VII**
GRIFFITHS, George Arthur (1878–1945) **III**
GROSER, St. John Beverley (John)
  (1890–1966) **VI**
GROVES, Thomas Edward (1882–1958) **V**
GROVES, William Henry (1876–1933) **II**
GRUNDY, Thomas Walter (1864–1942) **III**
GUEST, John (1867–1931) **III**
GUEST, Leslie Haden (1st Baron Haden-
  Guest of Saling) (1877–1960) **VIII**
GURNEY, Joseph (1814–93) **V**

HACKETT, Thomas (1869–1950) **II**
HADDOW, William Martin (1865–1945) **VII**
HADEN-GUEST, 1st Baron Haden-Guest of
  Saling) *See* Guest, Leslie Haden, **VIII**
HADFIELD, Charles (1821–84) **II**
HALL, Frank (1861–1927) **I**
HALL, Fred (1855–1933) **II**
HALL, Fred (1878–1938) **I**
HALL, George Henry (1st Viscount Hall of
  Cynon Valley) (1881–1965) **II**
HALL, Joseph Arthur (Joe) (1887–1964) **II**
HALL, Thomas George (1858–1938) **II**
HALLAM, William (1856–1902) **I**
HALLAS, Eldred (1870–1926) **I**
HALLS, Walter (1871–1953) **XI**
HALLIDAY, Thomas (Tom) (1835–1919) **III**
HALSTEAD, Robert (1858–1930) **II**
HAMILTON, Mary Agnes (1882–1966) **V**
HAMPSON, Walter ('Casey') (1866?–1932)
  VI
HAMSON, Harry Tom (1868–1951) **V**
HANCOCK, Dame Florence May
  (1893–1974) **IX**

HANCOCK, John George (1857–1940) **II**
HANCOCK, Thomas (1832–1903) **VIII**
HANDS, Thomas (1858–1938) **II**
HANNINGTON, Walter (1896–1966) **X**
HARDERN, Francis (Frank) (1846–1913) **I**
HARDIE, David (1870–1939) **VII**
HARDY, George (1884–1966) **XI**
HARES, Edward Charles (1897–1966) **I**
HARFORD, Edward (1837/8–98) **V**
HARKER, John (1864–1908) **VII**
HARKNESS, Margaret Elise (1854–1923)
  VIII
HARNEY, George Julian (1817–97) **X**
HARRIS, Samuel (1855–1915) **III**
HARRISON, Frederic (1831–1923) **II**
HARRISON, James (1899–1959) **II**
HARTLEY, Edward Robertshaw
  (1855–1918) **III**
HARTSHORN, Vernon (1872–1931) **I**
HARVEY, William Edwin (1852–1914) **I**
HASLAM, James (1842–1913) **I**
HASLAM, James (1869–1937) **I**
HASTINGS, Sir Patrick Gardner
  (1880–1952) **XI**
HAWKINS, George (1844–1908) **I**
HAYHURST, George (1862–1936) **I**
HAYWARD, Sir Fred (1876–1944) **I**
HEAD, Albert (Bert) Edward (1892–1978)
  VII
HEADLAM, Stewart Duckworth
  (1847–1924) **II**
HEATH, David William (1827/8?–80) **V**
HEMM, William Peck (1820–89) **VI**
HEMMERDE, Edward George (1871–1948)
  IX
HENDERSON, Arthur (1863–1935) **I**
HENSHALL, Henry (Harry) (1865–1946) **VI**
HENSON, John (Jack) (1879–1969) **V**
HEPBURN, Thomas (1796–1864) **III**
HERRIOTTS, John (1874–1935) **III**
HESLOP, Harold (1898–1983) **X**
HERRINGTON, Henry (1792–1849) **I**
HEYWOOD, Abel (1810–93) **VI**
HIBBERT, Charles (1828–1902) **I**
HICKEN, Henry (1882–1964) **I**
HICKS, Amelia (Amie) Jane
  (1839/40?–1917) **IV**
HIGDON, Annie Catharine (1864–1946) **VII**
HIGDON, Thomas George (1869–1939) **VII**
HILL, Howard (1913–80) **VII**
HILL, John (1862–1945) **III**
HILLIARD, Robert (1835–1904) **VII**

HILTON, James (1814–90) **I**
HINDEN, Rita (1909–71) **II**
HINES, George Lelly (1839–1914) **I**
HIRST, George Henry (1868–1933) **III**
HOBSON, Charles (1845–1923) **VII**
HOBSON, John Atkinson (1858–1940) **I**
HOBSON, Joshua (1810–76) **VIII**
HODGE, John (1855–1937) **III**
HODGKINSON, George Edward
    (1893–1986) **X**
HODGKIN, Thomas (1787–1869) **IX**
HODGSON, Sir Mark (1880–1967) **VII**
HOFFMAN, Philip Christopher
    (1878–1959) **IX**
HOGAN, Luke (1885–1954) **VII**
HOLBERRY, Samuel (1814–42) **IV**
HOLE, James (1820–95) **II**
HOLLIDAY, Jessie (1884–1915) **III**
HOLMES, James Headgoose (1861–1934)
    XI
HOLWELL, Walter Charles (1885–1965) **V**
HOLYOAKE, Austin (1826–74) **I**
HOLYOAKE, George Jacob (1817–1906) **I**
HOOSON, Edward (1825–69) **I**
HOPKIN, Daniel (1886–1951) **IV**
HORNER, Arthur Lewis (1894–1968) **V**
HORRABIN, Winifred (1887–1971) **XI**
HORROCKS, William (1844?–1918) **IX**
HOSKIN, John (1862–1935) **IV**
HOUGH, Edward (1879–1952) **III**
HOUSE, William (1854–1917) **II**
HOWARTH, Charles (1814–68) **I**
HOWELL, George (1833–1910) **II**
HUCKER, Henry (1871–1954) **II**
HUDSON, Walter (1852–1935) **II**
HUGHES, Agnes Paterson (Nan Hardie)
    (1885–1947) **VII**
HUGHES, Edward (1856–1925) **II**
HUGHES, Hugh (1878–1932) **I**
HUGHES, Will (1873–1938) **V**
HUMPHREYS, George Hubert (1878–1967)
    VI
HUTCHINGS, Harry (1864–1930) **II**
HYND, John Burns (1902–71) **X**
HYNDMAN, Henry Mayers (1842–1921) **X**

IRONSIDE, Isaac (1808–70) **II**
IRVING, David Daniel (Dan) (1854–1924)
    VIII

JACKSON, Henry (1840–1920) **I**
JACKSON, Thomas Alfred (1879–1955) **IV**

JARVIS, Henry (1839–1907) **I**
JENKINS, Arthur (1882–1946) **VIII**
JENKINS, Hubert (1866–1943) **I**
JENKINS, John Hogan (1852–1936) **IV**
JEWSON, Dorothea (Dorothy) (1884–1964)
    V
JOHN, William (1878–1955) **I**
JOHNS, John Ernest (1855/6–1928) **II**
JOHNSON, Henry (1869–1939) **II**
JOHNSON, John (1850–1910) **I**
JOHNSON, William (1849–1919) **II**
JOHNSTON, James (1846–1928) **V**
JONES, Benjamin (1847–1942) **I**
JONES, Ernest Charles (1819–69) **XI**
JONES, Joseph (Joe) (1891–1948) **V**
JONES, Morgan (1885–1939) **IX**
JONES, Patrick Lloyd (1811–86) **I**
JONES, Thomas (Tom) (1908–90) **XI**
JOWETT, Frederick William (1864–1944)
    IX
JOWITT, William Allen (1st Earl Jowitt of
    Stevenage) (1885–1957) **VII**
JOYNES, James Leigh (1853–93) **VIII**
JUGGINS, Richard (1843–95) **I**
JUPP, Arthur Edward (1906–73) **IV**

KANE, John (1819–76) **III**
KEAN, Charles (1874–1944) **X**
KEELING, Frederic Hillersdon (1886–1916)
    VII
KELLEY, George Davy (1848–1911) **II**
KENDALL, George (1811–86) **VI**
KENYON, Barnet (1850–1930) **I**
KERR, Anne Patricia (1925–73) **X**
KESSACK, James O' Connor (1879–1916)
    VI
KILLON, Thomas (1853–1931) **I**
KING, William (1786–1865) **I**
KLINGENDER, Francis Donald (1907–55)
    IX
KNEE, Fred (1868–1914) **V**
KNIGHT, Albert (1903–79) **VII**
KNIGHT, George Wilfred Holford
    (1877–1936) **XI**
KNIGHT, John (1762–1838) **IX**
KNIGHT, Robert (1833–1911) **VI**
KUMARAMANGALAM, Surendra Mohan
    (1916–73) **V**

LACEY, James Philip Durnford (1881–1974)
    III
LANNG, James (1870–1966) **I**

LANSBURY, George (1859–1940) II
LAST, Robert (1829–?) III
LATHAN, George (1875–1942) IX
LAW, Harriet Teresa (1831–97) V
LAWRENCE, Arabella Susan (1871–1947) III
LAWSON, Hugh McDowall (1912–97) XI
LAWSON, John James (1st Baron Lawson of Beamish)
LAWTHER, Sir William (Will) (1889–1976) VII
LEACH, James (1804?–69) IX
LEE, Frank (1867–1941) I
LEE, Peter (1864–1935) II
LENO, John Bedford (1826–94) XI
LEES, James (1806–91) I
LEES-SMITH, Hastings Bertrand (1878–1941) IX
LEICESTER, Joseph Lynn (1825–1903) III
LEON, Deborah Vaughan (1959–92) X
LEONARD, William (1887–1969) VII
LEVY, Hyman (Hymie) (1889–1975) IX
LEWIN, Julius (1907–84) IX
LEWINGTON, William James (1863–1933) VI
LEWIS, Richard James (1900–66) I
LEWIS, Thomas (Tommy) (1873–1962) I
LEWIS, Walter Samuel (1894–1962) III
LEYS, Norman Maclean (1875–1944) VIII
LIDDLE, Thomas (1863–1954) I
LINDGREN, George Samuel (Baron Lindgren of Welwyn Garden City) (1900–71) II
LINNEY, Joseph (1808–87) VI
LISTER, David Cook (1888–1961) VI
LITTLEWOOD, France (1863–1941) VII
LLOYD, Charles Mostyn (1878–1946) VII
LOCKEY, Walter Dalglish (1891–1956) V
LOCKWOOD, Arthur (1883–1966) II
LONGDEN, Fred (1886–1952) II
LONGDEN, John Miles (1921–91) X
LOUGHLIN, Anne (Dame) (1894–1979) X
LOVETT, Levi (1854–1929) II
LOVETT, William (1800–77) VI
LOW, Sir David (Alexander Cecil) (1891–1963) IX
LOWERY, Matthew Hedley (1858–1918) I
LOWERY, Robert (1809–63) IV
LUCRAFT, Benjamin (1809–97) VII
LUDLOW, John Malcolm Forbes (1821–1911) II
LUNN, William (Willie) (1872–1942) II

MABEN, William (1849–1901) VI
McADAM John (1806–83) V
MACARTHUR, Mary (1880–1921) II
McBAIN, John McKenzie (1882–1941) V
MACDONALD, Alexander (1821–81) I
MACDONALD, Gordon (Lord MacDonald of Gwaenysgor) (1888–1966) X
MACDONALD, James (1857–1938) VIII
MacDONALD, James Ramsay (1866–1937) I
MacDONALD Margaret Ethel Gladstone (1870–1911) VI
MACDONALD, Roderick (1840–94) IV
MACKAY, Ronald William Gordon (Kim) (1902–60) XI
McELWEE, Andrew (1882–1968) V
McENTEE, Valentine de la Touche (1871–1953) X
McGHEE, Henry George (1898–1959) I
McGHEE, Richard (1851–1930) VII
McGREE, Leo Joseph (1900–67) IX
McGURK, John (1874–1944) V
McHUGH, Edward (1853–1915) VII
McKEE, George William (1865–1949) V
MACPHERSON, John Thomas (1872–1921) V
McSHANE, Annie (1888–1962) IV
McSHEEDY, James Joseph (1852–1923) VIII
MADDISON, Fred (1856–1937) IV
MALLESON, John Graeme (1899–1956) X
MALLESON, William Miles (1888–1969) IX
MALONE, Cecil John L'Estrange (1890–1965) VII
MANN, Amos (1855–1939) I
MANN, James (1784?–1832) VIII
MANN Jean (1889–1964) VII
MANNING, (Elizabeth) Leah (1886–1977) VII
MARCROFT, William (1822–94) I
MARLOW, Arnold (1891–1939) I
MARSDEN, Richard (1802/3–58) VIII
MARSON, Charles Latimer (1859–1914) IX
MARTIN, Emma (1812–51) VI
MARTIN, James (1850–1933) I
MARTYN, Caroline Eliza Derecourt (1867–96) VI
MATHER, Joseph (1737–1804) VIII
MATHERS, George (1st Baron Mathers of Newton St Boswells) (1886–1965) VII
MATTHEWS, Sir James (Henry John) (1887–1981) VII

MATTHIAS, Thomas Davies (1823–1904) VII

MAW, James (1807–75) X

MAXWELL, Sir William (1841–1929) I

MAY, Henry John (1867–1939) I

MEEK, George Edward (1868–1921) X

MELL, Robert (1872–1941) V

MELLOR, William (1888–1942) IV

MELVILLE, Sir James Benjamin (1885–1931) IX

MERCER, Thomas William (1884–1947) I

MERCHANT, Emmanuel (1854–1924) VII

MERSON, Allan Leslie (1916–95) X

MESSER, Sir Frederick (Fred) (1886–1971) II

MIDDLETON, Dora Miriam (1897–1972) IV

MIDDLETON, George Edward (1886–1931) II

MIDDLETON, Lucy Annie (1894–1983) XI

MILLER, William Thomas (1880–1963) IX

MILLERCHIP, William (1863–1939) I

MILLIGAN, George Jardine (1868–1925) V

MILLINGTON, Joseph (1866–1952) II

MILLINGTON, William Greenwood (1850–1906) III

MITCHELL, John Thomas Whitehead (1828–95) I

MITCHISON, Gilbert Richard (Baron Mitchison of Carradale) (1890–1970) II

MOLE, Harriet Fisher (Jeannie) (1841–1912) IX

MOLESWORTH, William Nassau (1816–90) I

MOLL, William Edmund (1856–1932) VIII

MOLYNEUX, Sir John (Harry) (1882–1968) VII

MOORHOUSE, Thomas Edwin (1854–1922) I

MORGAN, David (Dai o'r Nant) (1840–1900) I

MORGAN, David Watts (1867–1933) I

MORGAN, Hyacinth Bernard Wenceslaus (1885–1956) IX

MORGAN, John Minter (1782–1854) I

MORLEY, Iris Vivienne (1910–53) IV

MORLEY, Ralph (1882–1955) VIII

MORLEY, Robert (1863–1931) IX

MOSLEY, Cynthia Blanche Lady (1898–1933) V

MOTT, William Henry (1812–82) VI

MUDIE, George (1788?–?) I

MUGGERIDGE, Henry Thomas Benjamin (1864–1942) V

MUIR, John William (1879–1931) VII

MUNRO, William John (Jack) (1873–1948) VII

MURDOCH, Mary Charlotte (1864–1916) V

MURNIN, Hugh (1861–1932) II

MURRAY, Robert (1869–1951) I

MURRAY, Sean (1898–1961) XI

MYCOCK, William Salter (1872–1950) III

NAHUM, Ram (Ephraim) Albert (1918–42) X

NEALE, Edward Vansittart (1810–92) I

NEESOM, Charles Hodgson (1785–1861) VIII

NEWBOLD, John Turner Walton (1888–1943) X

NEWCOMB, William Alfred (1849–1901) III

NEWTON, William (1822–76) II

NICHOL, Robert (1890–1925) VII

NICHOLLS, George (1864–1943) V

NOEL, Conrad le Despenser Roden (1869–1942) II

NOEL-BUXTON, 1st Baron Noel-Buxton of Aylsham. See BUXTON, Noel Edward, V

NOEL-BUXTON, Lucy Edith Pelham Lady (1880–1960) V

NOONAN, Robert (1870–1911) X

NORMANSELL, John (1830–75) I

NUTTALL, William (1835–1905) I

OAKEY, Thomas (1887–1953) IV

O'GRADY, Sir James (1866–1934) II

OLIVER, John (1861–1942) I

OLIVIER, Sydney Haldane (1st Baron Olivier of Ramsden) (1859–1943) VIII

O'NEILL, Arthur George (1819–96) VI

ONIONS, Alfred (1858–1921) I

ORAGE, [James] Alfred Richard (1873–1934) VI

OUTHWAITE, Robert Leonard (1868–1930) VIII

OWEN, Robert (1771–1858) VI

OWEN, William (1844–1912) IX

PALFREMAN, Robert William (Bill) (1904–54) IX

PALFREMAN, Stanley (Stan) (1919–80) IX

PALIN, John Henry (1870–1934) IV

PALING, Wilfrid (1883–1971) X

PARE, William (1805–73) I

PARKER, James (1863–1948) **II**
PARKINSON, John Allen (1870–1941) **II**
PARKINSON, Joseph (1854–1929) **X**
PARKINSON, Tom Bamford (1865–1939) **I**
PARROTT, William (1843–1905) **II**
PASSFIELD, 1st Baron Passfield of
  Passfield Corner. *See* WEBB, Sidney
  James, **II**
PATERSON, Emma Anne (1848–86) **I**
PATTERSON, William Hammond (1847–96)
  I
PATTISON, Lewis (1873–1956) **I**
PEASE, Edward Reynolds (1857–1955) **II**
PEASE, Mary Gammell (Marjory)
  (1861–1950) **II**
PEET, George (1883–1967) **V**
PENNY, John (1870–1938) **I**
PERKINS, George Leydon (1885–1961) **I**
PETCH, Arthur William (1886–1935) **IV**
PETRIE, George (1791–1836) **X**
PHILLIPS, Marion (1881–1932) **V**
PHIPPEN, William George (1889–1968) **V**
PICKARD, Benjamin (1842–1904) **I**
PICKARD, William (1821–87) **I**
PICTON-TURBERVILL, Edith (1872–1960)
  IV
PIGGOTT, Thomas (1836–87) **II**
PILLING, Richard (1799–1874) **VI**
PITMAN, Henry (1826–1909) **I**
PLUNKETT, Sir Horace Curzon
  (1854–1932) **V**
POINTER, Joseph (1875–1914) **II**
POLLARD, William (1832/3?–1909) **I**
POLLITT, James (1857–1935) **III**
PONSONBY, Arthur Augustus William
  Harry (1st Baron Ponsonby of Shulbrede)
  (1871–1946) **VII**
POOLE, Stephen George (1862–1924) **IV**
POSTGATE, Daisy (1892–1971) **II**
POSTGATE, Raymond William (1896–1971)
  II
POTTER, George (1832–93) **VI**
POTTS, John Samuel (1861–1938) **II**
PRATT, Hodgson (1824–1907) **I**
PRESTON, Thomas (1774–1850) **VIII**
PRICE, Gabriel (1879–1934) **III**
PRICE, Thomas William (1876–1945) **V**
PRINGLE, William Joseph Sommerville
  (1916–62) **II**
PRIOR, John Damrel (1840–1923) **VI**
PROTHERO, Cliff (1898–1990) **X**
PRYDE, David Johnstone (1890–1959) **II**

PURCELL, Albert Arthur (1872–1935) **I**

QUELCH, Henry (Harry) (1858–1913) **VIII**

RACKHAM, Clara Dorothea (1875–1966)
  IX
RACKSTRAW, Marjorie (1888–1981) **VIII**
RAE, William Robert (1858–1936) **II**
RAMSAY, Thomas (Tommy) (1810/1–73) **I**
RAWLINGS, Joseph (1894–1978) **VIII**
READE, Arthur Essex Edgeworth (1902–71)
  XI
READE, Henry Musgrave (1860–?) **III**
RECKITT, Eva Collet (1890–1976) **IX**
REDFERN, Percy (1875–1958) **I**
REED, Richard Bagnall (1831–1908) **IV**
REEVES, Samuel (1862–1930) **I**
REEVES, William Pember (1857–1932) **II**
RENTON, Donald (1912–77) **IX**
REYNOLDS, George William MacArthur
  (1814–79) **III**
REYNOLDS, Jack (1915–88) **X**
RICHARDS, Thomas (1859–1931) **I**
RICHARDS, Thomas Frederick (Freddy)
  (1863–1942) **III**
RICHARDSON, Reginald John (1808–61)
  XI
RICHARDSON, Robert (1862–1943) **II**
RICHARDSON, Thomas (Tom) (1868–1928)
  IV
RICHARDSON, William Pallister
  (1873–1930) **III**
RITSON, Joshua (Josh) (1874–1955) **II**
ROBERTS, George Henry (1868–1928) **IV**
ROBERTS, John (Jack) (1899–1979) **VII**
ROBINSON, Annot Erskine (1874–1925)
  VIII
ROBINSON, Charles Leonard (1845–1911)
  III
ROBINSON, Richard (1879–1937) **I**
ROBSON, James (1860–1934) **II**
ROBSON, John (1862–1929) **II**
ROEBUCK, Samuel (1871–1924) **IV**
ROGERS, Frederick (1846–1915) **I**
ROGERSON, William Matts (1873–1941)
  III
ROTHSTEIN, Theodore (1871–1953) **VII**
ROWLANDS, James (1851–1920) **VI**
ROWLINSON, Ernest George (1882–1941)
  VI
ROWLINSON, George Henry (1852–1937) **I**
ROWSON, Guy (1883–1937) **II**

ROYCE, William Stapleton (1858–1924) **XI**
RUDLAND, Frederick William (1866–1941)
VII
RUST, Henry (1831–1902) **II**
RUTHERFORD, John Hunter (1826–90) **I**

SAKLATVALA, Shapurji Dorabji
(1874–1936) **VI**
SANDHAM, Elijah (1875–1944) **XI**
SAMUELSON, James (1829–1918) **II**
SARA, Henry Thomas William (1886–1953)
XI
SAUNDERS, William (1823–95) **VIII**
SAWYER, George Francis (1871–1960) **VIII**
SCHOFIELD, Thomas (1825–79) **II**
SCHOLEFIELD, James (1790–1855) **XI**
SCHOLES, Benjamin (1779?–1823) **VIII**
SCOTTON, Amos (1833–1904) **VII**
SCOTT-BATEY, Rowland William John
(1913–80) **IX**
SCRYMGEOUR, Edwin (1866–1947) **VII**
SCURR, John (1876–1932) **IV**
SEDDON, James Andrew (1868–1939) **II**
SEWELL, William (1852–1948) **I**
SEXTON, Sir James (1856–1938) **IX**
SHACKLETON, Sir David James
(1863–1938) **II**
SHAFTOE, Samuel (1841–1911) **III**
SHALLARD, George (1877–1958) **I**
SHANN, George (1876–1919) **II**
SHARP, Andrew (1841–1919) **I**
SHARP, Clifford Dyce (1883–1935) **VII**
SHAW, Benjamin Howard (1865–1942) **VIII**
SHAW, Clarice Marion McNab (1883–1946)
VIII
SHAW, Fred (1881–1951) **IV**
SHEPPARD, Frank (1861–1956) **III**
SHIELD, George William (1876–1935) **III**
SHIELS, Sir Thomas Drummond
(1881–1953) **VIII**
SHILLITO, John (1832–1915) **I**
SHORROCKS, Peter (1834–86) **VI**
SHORT, Alfred (1882–1938) **IX**
SHURMER, Percy Lionel Edward
(1888–1959) **II**
SILKIN, John Ernest (1923–87) **X**
SILKIN, Lewis (Baron Silkin of Dulwich)
(1889–1972) **X**
SIMPSON, Henry (1866–1937) **III**
SIMPSON, James (1826–95) **I**
SIMPSON, William Shaw (1829–83) **II**
SITCH, Charles Henry (1887–1960) **II**

SITCH, Thomas (1852–1923) **I**
SKEFFINGTON, Arthur Massey (1908–71)
V
SKEVINGTON, John (1801–51) **I**
SKINNER, (James) Allen (1890–1974) **V**
SLATER, Harriet (1903–76) **VII**
SLESSER, Sir Henry Herman (1883–1979)
IX
SLOAN, Alexander (Sandy) (1879–1945) **II**
SMILLIE, Robert (1857–1940) **III**
SMITH, Albert (1867–1942) **III**
SMITH, Alfred (1877–1969) **III**
SMITH, Ellis (1896–1969) **IX**
SMITH, Francis Samuel (Frank)
(1854–1940) **IX**
SMITH, Henry Norman (1890–1962) **XI**
SMITH, Herbert (1862–1938) **II**
SMITH, Rosina (Rose) (1891–1985) **XI**
SMITHIES, James (1819–69) **I**
SOUTHALL, Joseph Edward (1861–1944) **V**
SPARKES, Malcolm (1881–1933) **II**
SPENCE, Thomas (1750–1814) **III**
SPENCER, George Alfred (1873–1957) **I**
SPENCER, John Samuel (1868–1943) **I**
STANLEY, Albert (1862–1915) **I**
STANTON, Charles Butt (1873–1946) **I**
STARR, Mark (1894–1985) **IX**
STEAD, Francis Herbert (1857–1928) **IV**
STEADMAN, William (Will) Charles
(1851–1911) **V**
STEPHEN, Campbell (1884–1947) **VII**
STEPHENSON, Tom (1895–1962) **XI**
STEVENS, John Valentine (1852–1925) **II**
STEWART, Aaron (1845–1910) **I**
STEWART, James (1863–1931) **VII**
STOKES, Richard Rapier (1897–1957) **VIII**
STOKES, William (Billy) Henry
(1894–1977) **X**
STOTT, Benjamin (1813–50) **IV**
STRACHEY, John St Loe (1901–63) **X**
STRAKER, William (1855–1941) **II**
STRINGER, Sidney (1889–1969) **V**
SULLIVAN, Joseph (1866–1935) **II**
SUMMERBELL, Thomas (1861–1910) **IV**
SUTHERLAND, Mary Elizabeth
(1895–1972) **VI**
SUTHERS, Robert Bentley (1870–1950) **IV**
SUTTON, John (Jack) Edward (1862–1945)
III
SWAN, John Edmund (1877–1956) **III**
SWANWICK, Helena Maria Lucy
(1864–1939) **IV**

SWEET, James (1804/5?–79) **IV**
SWIFT, Fred (1874–1959) **II**
SWINGLER, Stephen Thomas (1915–69) **III**
SYLVESTER, George Oscar (1898–1961) **III**

TANNER, Frederick John (Jack) Shirley (1889–1965) **XI**
TAYLOR, John Wilkinson (1855–1934) **I**
TAYLOR, Robert Arthur (1866–1934) **IV**
TAYLOR, John Thomas (1863–1958) **X**
TEER, John (1809?–83?) **IV**
THESIGER, Frederic John Napier 3rd Baron and 1st Viscount Chelmsford (1868–1933) **V**
THICKETT, Joseph (1865–1938) **II**
THOMPSON, William Henry (1885–1947) **X**
THORNE, William James (1857–1946) **I**
THORPE, George (1854–1945) **I**
THRING, Lillian Mary (1887–1964) **VIII**
TILLETT, Benjamin (Ben) (1860–1943) **IV**
TOFAHRN, Paul (1901–79) **X**
TOOLE, Joseph (Joe) (1887–1945) **VII**
TOOTILL, Robert (1850–1934) **II**
TOPHAM, Edward (1894–1966) **I**
TORKINGTON, James (1811–67) **II**
TOYN, Joseph (1838–1924) **II**
TRAVIS, Henry (1807–84) **I**
TRESSELL/TRESSALL. *See* NOONAN, Robert, **X**
TREVOR, John (1855–1930) **VI**
TROTTER, Thomas Ernest Newlands (1871–1932) **III**
TROW, Edward (1833–99) **III**
TUCKWELL, Gertrude Mary (1861–1951) **VI**
TURNER, Sir Ben (1863–1912) **VIII**
TWEDDELL, Thomas (1839–1916) **I**
TWIGG, Herbert James Thomas (1900–57) **I**
TWIST, Henry (Harry) (1871–1934) **II**
TYLECOTE, Mabel (1896–1987) **X**

VALLANCE, John (1794–1882) **IX**
VARLEY, Frank Bradley (1885–1929) **II**
VARLEY, Julia (1871–1952) **V**
VEITCH, Marian (1913–73) **III**
VERINDER, Frederick (1858–1948) **VIII**
VINCENT, Henry (1813–78) **I**
VIVIAN, Henry Harvey (1868–1931) **I**

WADE, Arthur Savage (1787–1845) **XI**
WADSWORTH, John (1851–1921) **I**

WALKDEN, Alexander George (1st Baron Walkden of Great Bookham) (1873–1951) **V**
WALKER, Benjamin (1803/4?–83) **I**
WALLAS, Graham (1858–1932) **V**
WALLHEAD, Richard [Christopher] Collingham (1869–1934) **III**
WALLWORK, Daniel (1824–1909) **VI**
WALSH, Stephen (1859–1929) **IV**
WALSHAM, Cornelius (1880–1958) **I**
WALTON, Alfred Armstrong (1816–83) **X**
WARD, George Herbert Bridges (1876–1957) **VII**
WARD, John (1866–1934) **IV**
WARDLE, George James (1865–1947) **II**
WARNE, George Henry (1881–1928) **IV**
WARWICK, Frances Evelyn (Daisy) Countess of (1861–1938) **V**
WATKINS, William Henry (1862–1924) **I**
WATSON, William (1849–1901) **III**
WATSON, William Foster (1881–1943) **VI**
WATTS, John (1818–87) **I**
WEBB, Beatrice (1858–1943) **II**
WEBB, Catherine (1859–1947) **II**
WEBB, Sidney James (1st Baron Passfield of Passfield Corner) (1859–1947) **II**
WEBB, Simeon (1864–1929) **I**
WEBB, Thomas Edward (1829–96) **I**
WEDDERBURN, Robert (1762–c.1835) **VIII**
WEIR, John (1851–1908) **I**
WEIR, William (1868–1926) **II**
WELLOCK, Wilfred (1879–1972) **V**
WELSH, James Carmichael (1880–1954) **II**
WEST, John (1812–87) **VII**
WESTWOOD, Joseph (1884–1948) **II**
WHEATLEY, John (1869–1930) **VII**
WHEELER, Thomas Marlin (1811–62) **VI**
WHITE, Arthur Daniel (1881–1961) **III**
WHITE, Charles Frederick (1891–1956) **V**
WHITEFIELD, William (1850–1926) **II**
WHITEHEAD, Alfred (1862–1945) **I**
WHITEHOUSE, Samuel Henry (1849–1919) **IV**
WHITELEY, William (1881–1955) **III**
WHITTAKER, James (1865–1940) **VIII**
WIGNALL, James (1856–1925) **III**
WILKIE, Alexander (1850–1928) **III**
WILLIAMS, Aneurin (1859–1924) **I**
WILLIAMS, David James (1897–1972) **IV**
WILLIAMS, Sir Edward (Ted) John (1890–1963) **III**
WILLIAMS, John (1861–1922) **I**

WILLIAMS, John (Jack) Edward
(1854?–1917) **VI**
WILLIAMS, Joseph (Joe) Bevir (1871–1929)
IX
WILLIAMS, Ronald Watkins (1907–58) **II**
WILLIAMS, Thomas (Tom) (Baron
Williams of Barnburgh) (1888–1967) **II**
WILLIAMS, Thomas Edward (1st Baron
Williams of Ynyshir) (1892–1966) **III**
WILLIS, Frederick Ebenezer (1869–1953) **II**
WILSON, Cecil Henry (1862–1945) **VI**
WILSON, John (1837–1915) **I**
WILSON, John (1856–1918) **II**
WILSON, Joseph Havelock (1858–1929) **IV**
WILSON, William Tyson (1855–1921) **III**
WINSTONE, James (1863–1921) **I**
WINTERBOTTOM, Richard Emanuel
(1899–1968) **IX**

WINTRINGHAM, Thomas (Tom) Henry
(1898–1949) **VII**
WINWOOD, Benjamin (1844–1913) **II**
WOODS, Samuel (1846–1915) **I**
WOOLF, Leonard Sidney (1880–1969) **V**
WOOTTON, Barbara Frances (Baroness
Wootton of Abinger, CH) (1897–1988) **X**
WORLEY, Joseph James (1876–1944) **I**
WRIGHT, Oliver Walter (1886–1938) **I**
WROE, James (1789–1844) **XI**
WYLD, Albert (1888–1961) **II**

YATES, Jeremiah (1808–52) **IX**

ZEITLIN, Morris (1873–1936) **VII**
ZILLIACUS, Konni (1894–1967) **X**

General Index

Board of Trade 25
  coal dispute (1931) 71
Boer War *see* South African War
Bondfield, Margaret 86, 196–7, 227
Book of the Labour Party, The (1925) 71
Boothby, Lord 194
Border Standard (newspaper) 66
Bottomley, Horatio 167
Bowen, Dai 58
Bowman, Alexander 11–16
Bowman, Guy 240
Bowman, Terence 11
Bowyer, George 28
boxing 58, 80
Boyd, John 279, 281, 282
Boyne, Leslie 239
Braddock, Tom 192
Bramley, Fred 85
Brannan, Hugh 271
Breene, Richard 125
Bresler, Fenton 128
Bretton Woods agreement 259
Brierley, Benjamin 17–24
Bristol North Forward (newspaper) 199
British Broadcasting Corporation 71
British Road to Socialism, The (CPGB
  publication) 108
British Science Guild 28, 29
British Socialist Party 263, 276
British Statesman (journal, 1842) 213
British Steel, Shotton 165
British Union of Fascists 190, 258
British Union Quarterly (fascist journal, 1938)
  210
British Workers' Sports Federation 107
Broadcasting Committee 71
Brockway, Fenner 178, 193, 227, 228, 246,
  248, 271
Browder, Earl 104
Brown, George 63–4
Brown, John (Iron and Steel Confederation)
  280
Brown, Maud 265
Brüning, Heinrich 27, 28, 29
Buchan, John 47
Buchanan, George 112, 227
Budden, Olive 34
Bukharin, Nikolai 244–5
Buxton, Noel 221
Buxton, Sydney 47

Caird, Edward 47

Cairo 'parliament' (1943) 174
Callaghan, James 199
Campbell, J. R. 35, 38, 70, 112–13, 248, 276
Campbell-Bannerman, Sir Henry 51
Canada, Socialist Party of 99
Cannon, Les 283
Cape, Tom 267, 268–9, 270
capital levy 67, 69, 70, 96, 110, 168, 218
capitalism
  collapse of 239
  European federalism and 192–3
  evolutionary change towards socialism
    165
  independence from American 259
  'Labour Parliament' and 151, 152, 158
  socialist distaste for 84, 86
  transition to socialism, by assent 233–4
  war, and fascism 269
Carlile, Richard 240, 292
Carlton, H. C. C. 119, 120, 121–2
Carlyle, Thomas 140
Carmichael, James 232
Caroline, Queen 251, 283
Carpenter, Edward 206
Carpenters' and Joiners' Union 212
Carre, Arthur Collings 47
Carron, Bill 283
Cartwright, John 212
Castle, Barbara 199
Cat and Mouse Act *see* Prisoners
  (Temporary Discharge for Ill-Health)
  Act (1913)
Catholic emancipation (1820s) 284
Caudle, Sam 49
Central Labour College (1909) 141, 142, 263
Central National Association (1837) 287–8
Central Tribunal 241
centralism, democratic (ILP, 1934) 233
Chamberlain, Sir Austen 72
Chamberlain, Neville 43, 56, 89
Charles H. Kerr & Co. (US publisher) 99
Charters of Incorporation (1830s) 252, 292
Chartist Land Company 252
Chartist movement 18, 146–8, 182–3,
  212–13, 252–3
  in Birmingham 286
  Kersal Moor rally (1838) 212, 252, 292
  late Chartism (post-1848) 150
  National Convention (1839) 288
  physical force question 288–9
Chartist National Conventions 157
Chartist National Executive 147

Oxonian Looks Back, An (Farnell, 1934)
    209–10

pacifism   142, 143, 237
    vs fascist threat   161
Padley, Walter   269
Paget, Cecil   92
Pan-Pacific Trade Union Secretariat (China)
    104, 105
Panama Canal   191
Pankhurst, Adela   140
Pankhurst, Sylvia   32, 40, 241, 242
    ejection from CPGB (1921)   243
Parkes, Joseph   284
Parkhurst Military Prison, Isle of Wight   241
Parlby, Cyril Everard   121, 122–3, 129
Parliament, relevance to working class   227
parliamentary action, and anarchist agitation
    239
Parliamentary and Financial Reform
    Association   252
Parliamentary Labour Party   53, 67, 90, 170
    Commonwealth Group   219
    Europe Group   192
    Executive Committee   70
    and Independent Labour Party   228–9
    leadership contest (1935)   88
parliamentary reform (1830s)   284
Parnell, Charles Stewart   12
Parr, Samuel   283
Parsons, Olive   32
Paton, John   110, 229
'payment by results'   265
Payment of Wages in Public Houses
    Prevention Bill (1881)   12
Paynter, Will   273
Peace Councils   161
peace movement(s)   6, 44, 196, 197
Peart, Fred   273
Peel, A. G. V.   217
Pennefather, John de Fonblanque   226
pensions
    Civil List   21
    war   67
    widows   9
People's Budget (1909)   48
People's Charter (1838)   288
People's League (1848)   213
People's Paper   147, 151, 152, 153, 155, 182
People's Vigilance Committees   9
Permanent Court of International Justice
    169

Peterloo Massacre (1819)   212, 251, 292
Pethick-Lawrence, F. W.   72, 73, 255
Petrovsky, Max   34, 35, 36, 244
Phillips, Jenny   40, 41
Phillips, Marion   4, 5, 7, 8, 45, 79, 80, 82,
    199
Phippen, George   248
physical force, and Chartists   288–9
Picken, Wilfred   234
Pickstone, Cornelius   95, 96
Picture Post   173
Pigou, A. C.   68, 84
Pilsudski, Józef   29, 143
Pius XII, Pope   272
Place, Francis   284
Plaid Cymru   58, 61, 62, 63, 64, 164
Plebs (journal)   141, 142, 143, 208, 243,
    247
Plebs League   141
Plug Plot riots (1842)   252
Poetic Magazine, The (Truelove, 1863)   183
Poland   56, 89
police
    and Savidge case   115
    procedures, reform of   116
    surveillance of Green Shirts   258
Polish patriotic struggle (1839)   289
Polish Socialist Party   91
Political Quarterly   83
Politics of Plenty, The (Smith, 1944)   258
Pollitt, Harry   34, 36, 37, 38, 102, 104–5,
    106, 142, 160, 207, 245, 246
Ponder, Walter   239
Ponsonby, Arthur   51, 206
Ponsonby, Harry   234
Poor Man's Guardian (newspaper, 1830s)
    285, 286
poor relief   79, 252
    for strikers' families   263
Popular Front politics   265
Portrait of the Labour Party (Wertheimer,
    1929)   71
Post Office   47, 49
Postgate, Daisy   37
Postgate, Margaret   32, 33
    see also Cole, Margaret
Postgate, Raymond   37, 208, 243
Potsdam conference (1945)   120
Potter, Charles   19
Potter, George   183
poverty   6, 53
    in East Africa   26

326

and women   7, 141, 142, 263, 265
see also individual district miners' unions
Trades Councils   48, 78, 93, 132, 159, 201,
    212, 263
Trades Union Congress   12, 54, 58, 131
    General Council   67, 73, 84, 170, 279
    Parliamentary Committee   136
    Regional Advisory Committee, and trades
        councils (1960s)   165
    rejection of wage freeze (1950)   281
    Welsh (1974)   165
Transport and General Workers' Record   164
Transport and General Workers' Union
    (TGWU)   59, 60–1, 62–3, 105, 160, 165
    challenge to AEU hegemony   278
    expansion (1940s)   279
    in north Wales (1950s)   163, 164
Trevelyan, Charles Philip (Sir)   51, 71
Tribune   143, 144
Trotsky, Leon   207–8, 244, 245
    Committee for the Defence of (1936–37)
        210, 247
Trotsky Memorial Meeting (1940)   248
Trotskyism   237, 246, 247
    critique of Stalinism   248
    'political deviation' (1925)   208
Troward, Eric   175, 190
True Sun (radical daily)   285
Truelove, Edward   183
Tryweryn Valley, flooding of   65
tuberculosis   5–6, 46
Tupper, 'Captain'   110
Turner, Ben   71

unemployment
    benefit cuts proposed (1931)   53, 73, 74, 86
    benefit revised (1929)   227
    in coal industry   8, 79
    cyclical, and state planning   87
    foreign labour and   164
    labour exchanges   50
    married women   97
    public works to reduce   70
Unemployment Insurance Act abused by
    'spongers'   170
Unemployment Insurance Bill (1929)   53
Union of Democratic Control   50, 94
Unionist Party   13
United Mineworkers of America   63
United Nations   191
United States, progressive politics *vs*
    anticommunism   128

United Workers' Organisation   14
Unity (Irish communist journal, 1942–6)
    204
Unity Campaign (1937)   230, 236
Unity Group (of ILP)   229, 230, 232–3, 234
Universal League for the Material Elevation
    of the Industrious Classes   184
universal suffrage   212, 284
university constituencies   28
University Socialist Federation   33, 206
Unser Kampf (Acland, 1940)   173
unstamped press (1832)   285
Uthwatt, Augustus Andrewes, report on land
    use   90
Utley, Freda   35, 36, 37
*Uxbridge Spirit of Freedom and Working
    Man's Vindicator* (Chartist journal)
    182

Valtin (Comintern agent)   106
Varga, Eugen   206
Venizelos, Eleutherios (Greek prime
    minister)   209
Versailles, Treaty of   51
Vincent, Henry   288
Voice from the Church, A (Wade, 1832)   285

Wade, Arthur Savage   283–91
wage freeze (1950)   281
Wage Labour and Capital   239
Wages Boards, and agricultural workers
    (1920s)   219
Wages of Labour, The (Graham, 1921)   68
Wake, Egerton   221
Wakefield Gaol   241
Wales
    industrial closures (1960s)   165
    Labour Movement   1–2, 5, 62, 76, 77, 164,
        165
    rural areas and underinvestment   164
Wales, Council of   62, 63, 64
Wales, University of   64, 165
Walker, James   178
Wall Street crash (1929)   255
Walmsley, Harry   18
Walsh, Stephen   59
Walters, Albert   106
War Agricultural Committee   216
War and Democracy, The (Greenwood et al.,
    1914)   84
War Crimes Commission   211
War on Want   198